Chicagoland

Project Management Software Survey

Project Management Software Survey

PROJECT MANAGEMENT INSTITUTE

NOTICE AND DISCLAIMER STATEMENT

The information contained in this publication was provided directly by the individual software vendors identified. The Project Management Institute, Inc. (PMI®) has not reviewed or evaluated any of the products listed herein, nor has any attempt been made to verify or authenticate any of the statements or claims made by any product vendors. PMIis providing the information contained in this publication on an "as is" basis, and makes no representations or warranties of any kind with respect to the information contained in this publication.

Additionally, The Project Management Institute, Inc. disclaims all representations or warranties with respect to the content or performance of the software products identified herein, including any implied warranties of merchantability or fitness for a particular purpose, or any warranties that such products are Year 2000 compliant. All questions regarding the content, performance, and/or appropriateness of any product should be addressed only to the product vendor or distributor.

Published by: Project Management Institute, Inc.
Four Campus Boulevard
Newtown Square, Pennsylvania 19073-3299 USA

Phone: 610-356-4600 or Visit our website: www.pmi.org

ISBN: 1-880410-52-4

10 9 8 7 6 5 4 3 2 1

Project Management Software Survey

PROJECT MANAGEMENT INSTITUTE

NOTICE AND DISCLAIMER STATEMENT

The information contained in this publication was provided directly by the individual software vendors identified. The Project Management Institute, Inc. (PMI®) has not reviewed or evaluated any of the products listed herein, nor has any attempt been made to verify or authenticate any of the statements or claims made by any product vendors. PMIis providing the information contained in this publication on an "as is" basis, and makes no representations or warranties of any kind with respect to the information contained in this publication.

Additionally, The Project Management Institute, Inc. disclaims all representations or warranties with respect to the content or performance of the software products identified herein, including any implied warranties of merchantability or fitness for a particular purpose, or any warranties that such products are Year 2000 compliant. All questions regarding the content, performance, and/or appropriateness of any product should be addressed only to the product vendor or distributor.

Published by: Project Management Institute, Inc.
Four Campus Boulevard
Newtown Square, Pennsylvania 19073-3299 USA

Phone: 610-356-4600 or Visit our website: www.pmi.org

ISBN: 1-880410-52-4

PMI® books are available at special quantity discounts to use as premiums and sales promotions, or for use in corporate training programs. For more information, please write to the Business Manager, PMI Publishing Division, Forty Colonial Square, Sylva, NC 28779 USA, or contact your local bookstore.

The paper used in this book complies with the Permanent Paper Standard issued by the National Information Standards Organization (Z39.48—1984).

10   9   8   7   6   5   4   3   2   1

Contents

Note: Not all products that are covered in the survey matrix supplied answers on the Narrative Questions portion of the questionnaire. If you don't see a product listed here, check the spreadsheet portion of the relevant chapter.

In addition, many vendors repeated the same Narrative Response from category to category. If you don't find your vendor's narrative in one chapter, check other chapters in the Table of Contents below. Due to space considerations, in some cases we have not repeated identical narratives. In Chapter Six, we have in most cases refrained from repeating identical narratives in each subcategory.

Foreword

At last! A Project Management Software Survey that we can all use.

I'm undecided ... should I praise Linda Williams and the *Project Management Software Survey* team, for the monumental contribution that they have made or should I display anger at the team for putting my career in danger? After many years of requests from the project management community for a comprehensive project management software survey, PMI® has responded with an impressive work, all that one could ask for from a group of volunteers. Praise is due without restraint.

While the core of the *Project Management Software Survey* is the vendor responses to the matrix, there are several other components of this publication that make it all work. The expanded set of definitions is very helpful, as it explains many of the functions of a project management system, while clarifying the criteria items, first for the vendors to understand, and then for the readers to use.

The narrative chapters, one for each segment, provide an introduction to the segment and a discourse on what to expect. This is followed by the responses from each vendor to the narrative questions in the survey. In many ways, this is more important than the spreadsheet sections. I do not recommend that you try to choose the best software for your needs by counting the "Y" responses. A "Yes" may say that the criteria item is supported. It doesn't say anything about how *well* the item is supported. The answer is that both the narrative and spreadsheet portions must be reviewed. Furthermore, once you have narrowed down your choices, it is imperative to get a vendor demonstration. This must be comprehensive. You don't want the quickie dog-and-pony show. The demo should address your needs and situation, and the vendor should be able to expand on items in the survey, to your requests.

One of my prior complaints about earlier software surveys was that there was basically one set of criteria. Yet the industry has changed from its monolithic past to one of great variety. Someone once remarked that the market offered several varieties of vanilla. Not so today. Therefore, the team responded by providing several sets of criteria for vendors to use. However, the move to segment the tools into different categories, with a specific set of criteria for each category, was not without obstacles, as many vendors were faced with difficult decisions as to where to position their products. My advice is to look in more than one section for vendor responses.

Getting back to my strange opening sentence, should I be concerned that this publication will endanger my project management consulting business? Actually, I think not. This product will help to make my clients more knowledgeable, both about what to expect from project management tools and what is available. There is nothing that frustrates a consultant more than a client who has no idea of what to expect from the consultant. So often, the project is slowed by having to bring the client up to speed on the subject before actually engaging in tool selection. I would love to have my clients to have access to this publication as part of the project.

The early phase of any tool selection project calls for a needs analysis and information gathering. In most cases, the serious client will still wish to bring a consultant in to educate and to guide this process. The PMI *Project Management Software Survey* will be a welcome aid to both the client and the consultant. In such cases where there is a consultant involved, the cost of this publication will be equivalent to pocket change. Yet, having this information available should easily reduce the effort on both the part of the consultant and the client. This will result in a better solution at an overall lower cost and a shorter time period. What more can we ask for?

We should also note that this project could not have been completed without the cooperation of the project management software vendors. I appreciate their contribution—not only to the *Project Management Software Survey*, but also to the advancement of modern project management via their tools and their support services. It is this partnership, between enlightened users and dedicated vendors, that has moved project management out of the shadows. A reviewer of my 1986 book (*Project Management Using Computers*), in the *New York Times*, referred to project management as "arcane." The growth of PMI and of the project management tools market has challenged that appraisal. The increase in tools knowledge, brought about by this publication, will serve as a basis for continued dialog and enhancement.

—Harvey A. Levine, Principal
The Project Knowledge Group, Saratoga Springs, N.Y.
and author of the *PMNetwork* Software Forum column
March, 1999

Preface

Tom Peters has written that we should "turn everything into a project" (*Circle of Innovation* 1997), and the world seems to be taking his advice. The market for project management software has exploded—Microsoft Project alone is well into its second million in sales—and dozens of new tools are being released each year.

The extraordinary growth in recent years of the project management profession has prompted the development of more, better, faster, and sleeker project-scheduling tools, time-management products, and cost-analysis software—all geared to help project managers complete their projects on time and within budget. Consequently, the selection process for finding the best project management software has become a project itself, and can pose quite a challenge even to the most experienced of project managers.

For project managers charged with choosing and evaluating software tools, it is sensory overload. The task of selecting software tools to track changes, make schedules, level resources, and perform the many other tasks that comprise project management has become almost overwhelming. And choosing the right tool, especially when, as for many companies, the project management culture is new or in startup mode, can be the difference between success and failure.

No one knows this better than the Project Management Institute (PMI®). That's why, with the help of an extraordinary team of volunteer subject-matter experts, we have created the *Project Management Software Survey*.

If you have been charged with selection of a project management software tool—perhaps one of the most important decisions your company will ever make—you can breathe a sigh of relief as you open this book. The pages that follow capture, as completely as a nine-month data collection project possibly could, the state of the project management software market. For each of the over two hundred products covered, a detailed, drill-down list of questions concerning features and functionality is designed to help you quickly narrow the field.

The 1998 *Project Management Software Survey* is the largest, most comprehensive, and up-to-date collection of information about project management software in the world. In fact, no other resource currently available offers you as much information about existing and forthcoming project management software tools. By comparison, PMI's previous software surveys, published in *PM Network* magazine (1995, 1996), were rudimentary in nature, consisting of approximately fifty questions and limited in scope primarily to cost and schedule-tracking products.

Designed *by* project managers *for* project managers, this software selection resource includes:
■ Information presented in an easy-to-understand matrix, with definitions and narrative enhancements
■ Industry-specific needs assessments
■ In-depth answers to hundreds of frequently asked questions.

By comparing and contrasting the capabilities of a wide variety of project management tools, this book provides users with a better understanding of individual vendors, thereby assisting customers in establishing all-important relationships with vendors. The survey provides a place for users and vendors to meet and match requirements and possibilities. It is PMI's hope that this interface of user wishes and vendor offerings will prompt vendors to become even more responsive to market and customer needs.

In addition, a special section in the introduction (see "How to Use this Book") prompts users to create a methodology for software tool selection within their own companies. After all, as labor-intensive as a software selection project is, it is only good for about three to five years, and then it must be done all over again. Putting in place a methodology for tool selection and evaluation now will save time and money over the long run.

As part of its process in designing the survey instrument, the team of volunteers who carried out the research behind this book explored the requirements of project managers across a wide variety of industries and application areas, as represented by PMI's specific interest groups (SIGs). An overview of the findings, which were developed through the use of the quality function deployment process, is also included in "How to Use this Book."

The book covers six basic categories of project management software: scheduling, cost management, risk management, human resource (HR) management, communications management, and process management. Each category is covered in a separate chapter. Within that chapter, the reader will find a category definition, a discussion of the business issues that the category addresses, and an overview of what functionality is important in this category. Following this discussion is a matrix-format grid answering a set of questions designed to drill deep for details of the products' features and capabilities, as well as a set of more qualitative dialogue questions. The dialogue questions are geared toward getting a better understanding of the vendor, because the relationship with the vendor is becoming more important.

The six categories of software are closely aligned with the knowledge areas (time management, cost management, HR management, risk management, communications management, etc.) described by PMI's standards document, *A Guide to the Project Management Body of Knowledge (PMBOK™ Guide)*—another new feature of the survey. Breaking down the products into *PMBOK™ Guide*-linked categories contributes to ease of use for the reader.

Still, the team acknowledges that the list of vendors and application areas is far from complete. Some examples: HR software products, procurement products, communications tools such as groupware, and quality management tools. Enterprise resource planning (ERP) software is one example of an emerging project management-related category that was not included in this book, but which the survey team recognizes is rapidly becoming a very significant player in the software market. Several ERP vendors were invited to participate in this survey but declined.

Thanks to the Team. The PMI members who responded to the call for volunteers in the December 1997 issue of *PM Network* might have been handpicked for their diversity. But, in fact, the team makeup was a lucky accident, providing viewpoints from a project management software-implementation consultant, a vendor, and expert users from four widely disparate application areas in locations from San Francisco to Brussels.

PMI, the project management software marketplace, and the profession all owe a debt of gratitude to the volunteers who comprised the survey team. Core volunteers (those who analyzed the data and provided written analyses of it for the textual portions of this book) are:

■ Linda Williams, technical leader for EDS' Project Management Consulting division. Linda has twelve years of experience using and evaluating project management software. A PMI member since 1995, she served as team leader for the volunteer project team that helped create the *Project Management Software Survey*.

Linda Williams was assisted by Jodi Bara, EDS research assistant, and by Steve Roberts, EDS research intern.

■ Bob Anello is director of project management for Fortis Information Technology in Milwaukee, Wisconsin. Anello is responsible for the implementation of project and resource management systems and methods, and assists in the development and rollout of systems development methods and processes for Fortis operations in the Midwest. He also develops and delivers project management education to technology and business units within Fortis.

■ Ketty Brown, PMP, is department head of Business Information Systems for Eli Lilly and Company. She has eighteen years of experience in the areas of manufacturing, financial, and information technology. She has written for *PM Network*, and is a trainer in communications management for the Central Indiana Chapter of PMI, and a speaker at the PMI Seminars & Symposium and ProjectWorld conferences.

■ Richard Wagner is author of *Project Control Project Management Framework* and an experienced teacher and presenter on project management technical and software skills since 1985, at PMI's conferences, ProjectWorld and other venues. A veteran project manager, a Microsoft Project guru and an expert on Internet project management and Project Office development, Wagner is a former PMI chapter president, and a member of the exclusive Top 20 Microsoft Project Solution Partner program. He is president and "technical evangelist" of Project Control in Annapolis, Maryland.

■ Linda Gillman, office administrator at PMI Publishing Division and a Certified Association Executive, served as customer project manager on behalf of PMI Publishing.

In addition, the following volunteers participated in scoping the project and developing the survey instrument:

■ John E. Martin, PMP, IBM-Belgium, manages the delivery of IBM Project Management Education at their International Education Center in Brussels, Belgium.

■ George Sukumar, general partner of Sukumar Consulting Co., Long Beach, California, a specialist in major capital construction projects.

Watching these folks at work in the development of this project was an inspiration and an object lesson in project management.

—Jeannette Cabanis, Acting Editor-in-Chief
PMI Publishing Division

Introduction

How to Use This Book

Part I: A Suggested Approach

Project Management Software Survey comprises a wealth of vendor and industry data. Those who mine it wisely will come away with not only valuable information regarding specific vendors, but also may save themselves considerable research time. (See the Conclusion of this Introduction for an estimate of time and cost savings from using this book for software selection.) On the other hand, it is possible to get lost in all the data. To avoid that possibility, we have included this suggested usage of the book.

It is not required that you use this approach, but please understand that in a paper-based document, the authors generally assemble the materials based on how we envision people will use it. If you understand how we viewed the material, it may help navigate this valuable data much more profitably.

The book is designed to bring to the reader information regarding a tentative fit of one or more vendors to a specific project management processing need. There are three sides to this concept of *fit*. First, in which area do you need processing assistance? You may not know what you need, so in each chapter on a particular category of processing type, there is a description of what that category entails. For example, while Resource Scheduling and Resource Management both address resources, they do so in quite different ways and knowing the difference will help keep you on target. This category description is addressed in the introduction to each of the category chapters.

As a further aid to understanding what you may really need from software, the categories in the book have been linked to the knowledge areas in the Project Management Institute's standards document, *A Guide to the Project Management Body of Knowledge* (*PMBOK™ Guide*, 1996). Whether you know these knowledge areas by heart or will need to refer to a copy of the *PMBOK™ Guide,* this guide indicates which project management processes are served by which categories of software (see Figure 1).

"Yes, but our industry is different from the others!" Is it really? If so, in what ways is it different? Find out in Part III of this Introduction, Quality Function Deployment. Here, we use the segmenting of our industries according to how the specific interest groups (SIGs) of PMI determine what is important to a particular industry. Briefly, quality function deployment (QFD) is a technique to prioritize different functions that are common across all the industries we serve, based on the importance of a particular function relative to all of the other functions. This profile may not match your organization exactly, but it should give you an idea of what things are of greater relative importance to your industry. For example, how important is equipment management in your industry compared to construction? If it is similar, you may want to look for vendors that cater more to construction.

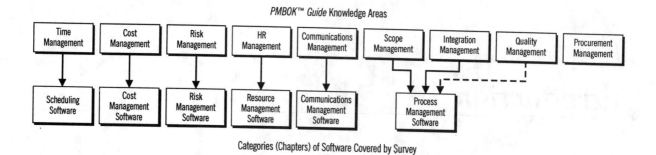

Figure 1   Mapping Software Categories to *PMBOK™ Guide* Knowledge Areas

The bulk of the data in this book is in the vendors' assessments of themselves; this is the area where it is easiest to get lost. For each vendor, there are "yes/no" and "how many" answers, and there are also narrative responses. The nonnarrative answers are presented in matrices located in each category, and in each category there are also compilations of the narrative responses. To save you the potential effort of reading through every response if you do not need to, we have included both our assessment of what are the significant trends in this software category and the vendors' responses to narrative questions that we included to highlight those trends.

The significant-trends discussion addresses three key areas. First, what functionality do we see the bulk of the vendors in this category providing? If there is a function listed here that a vendor you are interested in does not provide, that could be the basis of a discussion regarding their future directions. Second, do we see any new trends showing up in new functions offered by some of the vendors? Maybe the reason a vendor does not have that function is because the vendor has replaced it with a function that it perceives to be the *future of the business*. Third, are there any functions offered in the vendors' descriptions that really make us stand up and take notice? We are not presenting this book to promote any particular vendor's approach—indeed, in this section we will leave it up to you to locate the vendor with the *Aha!* function—nor can we guarantee that the function is as great as we think it to be by the vendor's description. Yet, we are presenting this function because, vaporware or not, we think that the function as it was described would be a great thing to have in the software of this category.

We brought together what we think are the two or three key questions for that category and present the responses of all the vendors in that category. What we hope is that this collection of responses, along with the responses compiled in the matrix, will help you to focus on a set of vendors that may suit your needs. You may then go to the vendor listing and peruse the information by vendor.

A word of caution when matching vendors to categories: While the authors attempted to pre-categorize the vendors, we did allow the vendors some choice influencing the categories in which they would appear. You may find a reference to some particular component of a vendor's total offering in the category you are researching. If that vendor is of assistance to you, it would be beneficial to look that vendor up in the appendix and see what other products the vendor is listing in other categories. It may give you a more complete picture of that vendor's total offering.

So there is the suggested process: Look at the software category descriptions to see if that category will address your needs. Reference the QFD table to sample an assessment of the relative importance of categories to your industry. Read the overall assessment of the survey results in the categories in which you are interested to get a preliminary view of what the authors discovered. Use the matrices and the narrative responses to certain, significant questions to perform a preliminary assessment of which vendors might satisfy your needs. Finally, with all that background information, view the vendor information in detail, including cross-referenced vendor information in other categories.

The authors believe that this approach will give you the maximum benefit in using this book. You do not have to use it, but, if you find yourself getting lost in the data, it is possible that turning to this approach will help you make sense of all of the data and get you to the information you envisioned when you bought this book.

Part II: Defining Our Terms

Software Category Definitions

The 1998 PMI Software Survey is organized into categories of software in order to comprehend the unique, specialized software designed for the project management marketplace.

The definitions listed in this section are designed to generalize about the kinds of features available in each category, and to point out how the categories align with the *PMBOK™ Guide*. Because not all areas of the *PMBOK™ Guide* have a one-to-one relationship to specialized software, not all are included.

Some software packages fall into subcategories, because they provide functionality that is a subset of an overall category.

The categories of software included in the 1998 PMI Software Survey were chosen by the team, then validated through a QFD effort. PMI SIG group chairpersons were used as the *customers* for the QFD.

The category definitions should allow readers of the finished survey to quickly narrow their focus to the kinds of products best suited to solve their company's business issues.

The categories are:

Software Category	**PMBOK™ *Guide* Knowledge Area(s)**
Schedule Management	Time Management
Resource Management	HR Management
Risk Management and Assessment	Risk Management
Process Management	Integration Management
Scope Management	
Communications Management	Communications Management
Subcategories:	
Graphics Add-ons	
Timesheets	
Web Publishers/Organizers	
Cost Management	Cost Management
Suites	

Each software category is described in detail at the beginning of the chapter covering those products.

Survey Question Definitions

Throughout the survey, you will find terms with an asterisk (*) following them. Below are definitions for asterisked terms in the order that they occur in the survey.

All Products

Drill-down/Rollup: Product has a built-in ability, based on a user-defined coding scheme, to summarize data upward and assist with navigation down through data. Capability must be based on fields designed to support drill-down/rollup.

Automatic E-mail notification: Events automatically generate E-mail messages to predefined recipients; does not mean files can be saved and attached to manually generated messages.

Macro recorder/batch-capable: Keystrokes the user would enter can be automated and then executed without human intervention.

Web access to product knowledge base: Vendor website has a database that users can access to see known problems, tricks, tips, etc.

Enhancement requests: Company has a published policy for comprehending customer requests in the product-enhancement process.

Modify source code, support through upgrades: Will vendor change the product's functionality for one customer, and then support the changes through future product upgrades?

Audit software quality-assurance process: Would the vendor allow a potential customer to audit the company's software quality-assurance process?

Configurable access privileges: Can access rights be configured by both groups of people and kinds of data accessed?

Schedule Management

Full critical path: Forward, backward, free float, and total float calculations.

Resource leveling: End date is pushed, and resources are not overallocated.

Resource smoothing: End date is not pushed but resource peaks are lowered by delaying tasks not on the critical path.

Team/crew scheduling: Permits defining teams composed of two or more types of resources.

Perishable resources: Resources expire after a specified date.

Consumable resources: Resource is depleted after task starts or is complete.

Assign role (skill): Software replaces with name at specific point in process. Converts homogeneous resources to heterogeneous; makes recommendations for which specific resource to assign or assigns names automatically.

Heterogeneous resources: Specifically recognizes individuals as unique resources.

Homogeneous resources: Recognizes resources as pools of one or more units of the same type of resource.

Hierarchical resources: Supports resource breakdown or related structure.

Dependency trace view: Graphically navigates user from a starting point in the network logic through predecessor or successor activities. Must be in a graphic view.

Resource Management

Resource leveling: Pushes the project-end date waiting for resources.

Resource smoothing: Tasks are delayed, waiting for resources, but the project end date is not moved.

Team/crew scheduling: Permits definition of teams of two or more types of resources.

Perishable resources: Resources expire and are no longer available after a set date.

Consumable resources: Resources can be depleted.

Assign role (skill): Software assigns individual later. User assigns a generic resource type, and allows the software to assign a specific individual at a date the user defines. User can override.

Hierarchical resources: Resources roll up through a resource breakdown structure.

Heterogeneous resources: Individuals are recognized as unique resources.

Homogeneous resources: Recognizes resources as pools of one or more units of the same type of resource.

Project templates: New project templates reside in the system, and do not have to be detailed in another software package before high-level resource requirements can be analyzed.

Process Management

Tasks in schedule linked to methodology guidelines: If tool outputs work breakdown structure (WBS) for import into scheduling tool, can tasks be linked back to the methodology for reference?

Communications Management

Workflow management: Tasks from the schedule are automatically sent to the person responsible. When a task can begin (predecessors are complete), the task and associated deliverables are automatically routed to the owning resources.

Risk Management

Suggest and document mitigation strategies based on knowledge database: Some software may have a built-in knowledge database or may permit adding on to an existing knowledge database.

Web Publishing

Generates website from Windows subdirectory structure: Software can be *pointed* at an existing directory, and it and its contents and subdirectories will be automatically converted into a website. The site's hierarchy is defined by the subdirectory structure.

Part III: Quality Function Deployment

What is quality function deployment (QFD)? It is a technique that captures the *voice of the customer*. It ensures that quality is designed into the product or service, because it translates customer requirements into technical characteristics as a way to influence the design of a product. It establishes a link between customer expectations and product characteristics.

The tool to deploy quality is portrayed as a matrix, also called the *house of quality*. It is a matrix that correlates customer needs and expectations versus product characteristics. Once you have defined needs and characteristics, you determine the strength of the correlation. When the relationship matrix is complete, you identify those technical characteristics that scored the highest.

Why did the team use the QFD approach?

QFD provides a sense of value. Instead of the traditional attempt to develop a survey based on all possible characteristics, this approach was geared to focus on what was important to our customers and, as such, proactively incorporate their expectations into the survey.

The QFD process helped identify early in the survey development if the categories we selected were important or relevant to the customer, or if we missed anything that merited inclusion.

QFD can be viewed as *closing the loop* because it helps a process start, by understanding customer requirements, and finish, by meeting these requirements.

How the QFD matrix came about.

As the team was brainstorming to determine which project management software characteristics ought to be included in the survey, they thought it would be valuable to ask PMI's SIGs for their input.

The QFD matrix correlates requirements and technical features. The matrix includes twenty requirements selected by the team, which have been included in the software survey:

1. Time management.
2. Resource management.
3. Cost management.
4. Risk management and assessment.
5. Ease of use.
6. Multiproject capability.
7. Year-2000 compliant.
8. Reporting.
9. Ease of learning.
10. Ease of installation.
11. Security.
12. Interface to other business systems.
13. Communication management.
14. Process management.
15. Suites.
16. Training.
17. *PMBOK™ Guide* alignment.
18. Timesheets.
19. System architecture.
20. Vendor information (reputation).

Requirement	Ranking Summary	Ranking for Aerospace and Defense	Ranking for Automotive	Ranking for Education	Ranking for Government	Ranking for Information Systems	Ranking for Manufacturing	Ranking for Oil and Gas and Petrochemical	Ranking for Pharmaceutical	Ranking for Risk Management
Time Management	1	7	1	4	1	3	2	2	12	2
Resource Management	2	3	4	7	4	1	1	6	3	11
Cost Management	3	5	n.a.	8	2	4	8	5	1	9
Risk Management and Assessment	4	4	n.a.	6	11	5	11	7	2	1
Ease of Use	5	12	5	1	5	13	4	4	15	6
Multiprojects Capability	6	8	3	5	13	6	5	14	5	3
Year-2000 Compliant	7	2	n.a.	n.a.	n.a.	2	n.a.	18	7	7
Reporting	8	10	2	n.a.	8	8	6	1	9	4
Ease of Learning	9	13	10	2	10	19	14	10	16	10
Ease of Installation	10	14	9	3	6	17	15	16	14	5
Security	11	1	n.a.	n.a.	15	18	12	3	6	17
Interface to Other Business Systems	12	6	7	11	9	11	7	9	10	12
Communication Management	13	9	11	10	16	12	3	15	8	19
Process Management	14	11	n.a.	12	3	14	10	11	4	13
Suites	15	n.a.	n.a.	n.a.	7	7	n.a.	17	19	20
Training	16	15	8	n.a.	n.a.	15	16	8	20	14
PMBOK™ Guide Alignment	17	16	n.a.	n.a.	n.a.	9	n.a.	19	11	18
Timesheets	18	n.a.	n.a.	9	17	10	13	12	17	8
System Architecture	19	n.a.	6	n.a.	14	16	9	13	13	15
Vendor Information (reputation)	20	17	n.a.	n.a.	12	20	n.a.	n.a.	18	16

n.a. — indicates that the requirement did not correlate with any of the technical features

Figure 2   Summary of the Results of the QFD Process

The technical features included in the matrix are:
- Earned value calculations
- Resource loading
- Charting Gantt, PERT
- Import/export
- Baseline versus actual
- What-if scenarios
- Project consolidation
- WBS numbering
- Reports (bar chart, network, spreadsheets)
- Scheduling based on resource skills
- Full critical path
- Duration in months, weeks, days, hours
- Support labor and nonlabor resources
- Resource smoothing
- Project prioritization
- Track actual resource usage
- Automated process methodology
- Auditable timesheets
- Online help and tutorial
- E-mail notifications
- Quick install
- Technical support (7x24), via phone and E-mail
- Windows 95 compatible
- Multilanguage
- Manipulate data at database level
- Object-oriented C/S design

- Support password security at file level
- Forecasting
- Variance analysis
- Track and report committed costs
- Compare cost and time tradeoff scenarios.

Who were called to participate?

Because the intent of the survey is to capture what is of interest to project managers depending on their industries, all PMI SIGs that represent specific industries were invited to participate. Other SIGs (such as Women in Project Management) were omitted because the interest group crossed industry boundaries, and what the team wanted to capture was what the specific industry would be looking for in a project management software.

The team got responses from the following SIGs:

- Aerospace & Defense
- Automotive
- Education
- Government
- Information Systems
- Manufacturing
- Oil, Gas, & Petrochemical
- Pharmaceutical
- Risk Management.

Some observations based on this data:

Time, resource, cost, and risk management are still the most important features in a project management software.

Though many software companies offer timesheet capability, it looks as if the usefulness or the benefits of timesheets are not yet valued.

With the growth of software vendors, project managers seem to look more at the technical features rather than at the reputation of the vendor. In other words, as long as the software performs as required and meets customer requirements, the vendor's reputation is of minimal impact on their choices. This is good news for the many startup and fledgling project management software companies featured.

The Government and Oil, Gas, & Petrochemical SIGs were the only ones that marked security as one of the first three highest choices.

Part IV: Developing an Evaluation Process

Simply picking a software product out of the hundreds listed in this book is not going to land you in project management heaven. In a way, saying "I'm evaluating a software tool" is misleading, because what must be evaluated are not only the product but also the setting in which it is to be used. Thus, a successful project management software-tool evaluation will include a hard look at your organization and your processes.

Software is a tool that makes the job of project management easier, but project management software can also be a nightmare for you, the project manager. Implementing software without a sound process and a plan, or implementing the wrong package(s), can be disastrous. You will spend lots of time and money with no improvements to show for it, and you will turn many people off to project management.

A well-planned approach to selecting project management software is just like any project plan—it is absolutely necessary to the success of the project. Here are some issues to think through when developing your evaluation approach.

No Silver Bullet

There is no one best project management software product on the market. Technology has enabled new functionality that may or may not help you meet business goals and manage projects better. Increased sophistication does not guarantee success. The product that offers the most features is also the most difficult to implement, learn, and support.

How do you select a software product to improve your project management processes?

That should *not* be an easy question for you to answer. Investment in new scheduling software is significant, especially when you consider the cost of training users, management, and systems administrators. You also have to budget for hardware upgrades, parallel system execution, and the cost of the software itself. Process reengineering is appropriate during a new project management systems deployment, adding to the cost. While the project of software selection and implementation is complex, like any other project, it begins with some simple steps. These steps, and some key areas to which you will want to pay attention, are covered in this chapter.

What Kind of Tool?

There are many different types of project management software that will help to improve the success of projects.

Historically, project management software meant traditional scheduling tools—those that calculate the critical path, level resources, and produce the project schedule. These tools were used by a small number of specialists to develop the project plan. Today, vendors have recognized that effective project management requires much more than a detailed Gantt chart.

The *Project Management Software Survey* takes into account a broad variety of tools, many of them new to the project management software marketplace. Highly specialized risk and cost tools dramatically differ from group communications or portfolio management tools. Thus, narrowing your search to the categories of software best suited to your business needs will save time. Many packages fall into multiple categories. Some vendors offer a single tool with features that cross over multiple categories. Other vendors offer many tools, often integrating them into a well-orchestrated suite of tools.

Prices range dramatically within and across categories, and your budget for software could have significant impact on your choice. *High-end* tools that offer functionality for multiple categories are typically used by a subset of specialists on the project team. These vendors often offer a complementary tool for desktop users that is less expensive. Other vendors offer solutions that require software purchased for every team member. These packages can be less expensive than the traditional high-end tools, but quantities purchased are higher.

An overall plan for the kind of environment that will enable project success will help you narrow the kinds of software packages that will be appropriate for your needs. Narrow the types of tools by creating a list of business problems to be solved. Group similar problems, then try to make a general statement about what is in that group. Identify the category of products marketed as designed to solve those kinds of issues. You may find that more than one approach seems appealing. There is a lot of overlap in the kinds of business problems that the different kinds of tools solve. Your organizational history and the maturation level of your current processes may be a deciding factor. Consider budget and the state of technology, and you should begin to see a preference toward one kind of tool.

Focus your product search there.

New Kinds of Tools

The PMI Software Survey team recognized many new vendors offering different software approaches to improving the project management process. These include group communications, portfolio management, Web publishers, graphics add-ons, and suites. Each type of product offers different information to assist the process. Team communications tools ensure that everyone on the team is involved and aware. Team tools track issues, action items, and status and delegate tasks to team members. These tools are used by every team member daily, drawing them into the process.

Project management tool suites address many issues beyond the schedule. Vendors offering suites of tools have designed them to complement one another, offering an integrated approach to solving a broad spectrum of project management problems. Some suites address all of the major problems faced by a specific industry, type of project, or project management process. These suites offer specialized modules developed to address very specific industry- or process-related problems. Other suites attempt to cover most or all of the *PMBOK™ Guide* areas, offering modules to address each. Suite vendors offer pre-integrated tools, so you do not have to spend any effort doing the integration in-house; this saves time and money.

The Process

Here is a quick process for evaluating project management software:
- State the business problem.
- State improvement objectives.
- Document or reengineer the project management process.
- Map the project management process to the appropriate category of software.
- Generate a requirements list.
- Select the short list.
- Test it yourself.
- Decide.

State the Business Problem

Why are you looking at new software? What is wrong with what you have? There are two typical reasons for looking at new software. The first is technology related—the infrastructure needs an upgrade, budget funds are available, or your needs exceed the capacity of the current system. The second is process related—project performance is below expectations. If you fall into the first category, you are somewhat less at risk when choosing new software. If projects are not performing up to expectations, be careful before assuming that new software will solve that problem. Take a deep dive into the reasons behind project performance. If the process is broken, new software will not fix it.

Assuming you fall into the first category, document the business problems associated with the current project management system. Your documentation should include specifics on what data is not available, how it will be used when it is available, and how that information will help meet your strategic objectives. Simply stating that "the current system does not produce the reports we need" is not adequate. You need to define the information required in detail in order to generate requirements to help direct you to the right package.

State Improvement Objectives

Your new system should meet improvement objectives for the project management process. If you can state the improvement objectives in detail in the early phase of the software-evaluation process, you can define requirements in terms of the features you will actually use. This process helps you identify which product differentiators will most benefit you. Without clear improvement objectives, companies tend to develop a laundry list of requirements compiled from product literature and published evaluation data. After implementation, you try to implement your project management process, only to find that the software does not have the one critical feature that you really need.

Stating the improvement objectives in detail means documenting the current state of things, quantifying the improvements, and, finally, defining the information required to support the improvements. Document what information is not available from your current system; do not refer to product literature for this exercise. Instead, look to industry publications explaining process improvements appropriate for your organization. Treat this as a visioning exercise, using subject-matter experts or consultants, as appropriate.

Document or Reengineer the Project Management Process

Analyze whether your current project management process is appropriate for solving the business problem, meeting the improvement objectives, and meeting the goals of the project management environment. If significant changes are required, spend the time to document the new process before continuing the evaluation process.

The documented process should be detailed enough that a person knowledgeable in project management, but not knowledgeable in your specific process, could describe the data required to support the process. This is the most important phase of the process of evaluating project management software.

Map the Process to the System

After the project management process has been refined, identify the software functionality required to support the project management environment. This step should be the most labor intensive. You are not trying to identify a package at this stage.

Schedule a series of detailed sessions to walk through each step in the process. Make detailed notes describing the inputs, outputs, and processing required to support the process. Involve subject matter experts who represent or have knowledge of your project management process, management, current system, information technology staff, and customer(s), if appropriate.

Produce a detailed document that explains how the system will support the project management process. Capture the data elements required. Identify reporting issues such as format, delivery mechanism, and cycles. Document update cycles, roles and responsibilities, security requirements, number of locations, number of users, projects and schedules, and all other relevant data required.

If these sessions are effective, a pattern will naturally emerge. You will focus on the nontraditional features required to make the new software successful. Your subject-matter experts will identify requirements that will be more difficult to meet with off-the-shelf software. These unique elements will help you identify the best product.

Be careful in this phase to not define exactly how the software must perform, or you may be disappointed. There are often many ways to achieve an information objective. The point of this exercise is to simply identify what is required—not how the software should make it happen.

Generate a Requirements List

This is the time in the evaluation process to research products, contact vendors, and reference all evaluation materials available, including the *Project Management Software Survey*. Add a column to the matrix created when you mapped the process to a system. In each cell, describe how software could meet that requirement, in terms of features.

It is not important to go to the *nth* degree with the requirements list; focus instead on the unique needs of your process. Many packages in a given category do many of the same things. You need to identify what makes your situation unique; then look for the package best suited to support those needs. Most critical requirements will be uncovered during the mapping process. Articulate these, and your short list will identify the best possible matches for your requirements.

Select the Short List

The short list is easily generated: just tabulate the results from your requirements list. Contact the vendors and invite them to introduce you to their software. A short list of three products is ideal. A list with more products shows that your requirements do not force a differentiating feature, so almost any product will do. A detailed set of requirements based on a sound process should always result in identification of a need that can only be met by one or two vendors.

Test It Yourself—The Hands-On Phase

Products on the short list will satisfy most of the functionality requirements documented during the mapping exercise. Testing them will validate which products handle the requirements closest to the way you expect. Testing the software, using data representing the business problem, is absolutely critical. None of the packages on your short list will calculate exactly as you would on paper. None will handle all of your requirements exactly as you imagined they would when you documented the requirements. A test drive against your data will uncover any showstoppers quickly.

Here's a testing example related to scheduling software:

When run against the same data, three products' time-analysis algorithms will produce three different sets of results. Complicate the equation with resource leveling, and differences become more obvious. Run a one-year schedule through three scheduling packages, and resource-leveled results will differ significantly—as much as four to eight weeks. Larger quantities of data exaggerate the difference, so it is important to have enough data available to clearly dramatize the differences.

Create a significant amount of test data, and bring the short list of packages in for a test drive. Use experienced people to evaluate the results. They have an understanding of what results are expected, can articulate the pros and cons of the differences between how the packages perform, and can comprehend the potential benefits of differentiators between products.

Here are a couple of key user-interface issues that can help identify which product feels best for your environment.

Rollup/Drill-down. Many products include fields designed to hold data elements created specifically for locating, filtering, summarizing, and otherwise manipulating data across multiple projects. These fields differ from the user-defined fields attached to each task or resource record. Rollup/drill-down features rely on structured coding, cascading the structure down through the data elements. Most products support rollup and drill-down of data, but each handles it differently. The differences are dramatic and could be a deciding feature. Here are some rollup/drill-down features to look for:

■ Ease of definition and population
■ Validation—users can/cannot add new values
■ Flexibility/templates—create once, use many times quickly and easily (share one scheme across multiple projects)
■ Space—holds enough data elements to comprehend everyone's requirements.

Multisite, Multiproject. Again, most tools support multiple users at geographically dispersed sites. But how they handle it can add an administrative burden and possibly dictate the project update cycle. The software has to know where projects are if they are not all on the same server. The administrative task of maintaining the pointers to project locations can be significant if new projects are created regularly, or if projects are moved. Some products require an exclusive lock on data before calculations. A large amount of data could require that updates be complete by 5 P.M. Friday for weekend processing, with no one allowed to access data until Monday when the schedules have been updated.

Vendor Support. Each vendor's ability to support you will become evident during this process. Every vendor provides curb service during the first phase of the sales cycle. During the hands-on phase of your evaluation, use the vendor's technical support staff. Try to go through the same help desk you will be using after the sale. Resist the temptation to lean exclusively on one contact, designated specifically for you during the sales pursuit, or you will not get a clear picture of what you can expect after the sale.

Take notes on all aspects of vendor support during the hands-on phase. How long does it take for calls to be returned? How long does technical support take to resolve issues? Remember that during major sales pursuits, the vendors' staffs are prepared for your calls. Is everyone prepared, or are you being directed to the senior staff? What happens when they are focused on the next large pursuit, and you are just a regular customer?

Decide

There are many more details to consider when investing in project management software. I have performed software evaluation efforts in as few as two days, and as long as four months. There is no one best product on the market today. But careful attention to the project management process and the information required to improve it can direct a project management software evaluation to a conclusion that meets the improvement objectives of your significant investment.

Conclusion

As a measure of the value of the data collected and processed here, PMI asked Survey Team Leader Linda Williams of Electronic Data Systems' Project Management Consulting division to estimate how much time and cost might be saved by using this selection tool, as opposed to selecting software from the marketplace without it. Her assessment was striking:

I've participated in software evaluation efforts ranging in duration from two to six months. As much as half of that time is spent researching which products are viable candidates. The data in the software survey allows the reader to achieve the viable short list of vendors in days, not months.

Creating the survey content, researching who the current vendor players are, identifying candidate products, contacting the vendors, waiting for responses, then compiling the responses takes a minimum of eight to twelve weeks. The cost of elapsed time and the effort of qualified people on the project runs at least $12,000–$15,000, and can be much more (see Table 1). The *Software Survey* accelerates the software selection process directly into the hands-on evaluation phase, dramatically accelerating the selection process.

The life cycle of an investment in a high-end project management system is about five years. At the end of that cycle, organizations with mature project management processes are ready to execute the evaluation cycle again.

The PMI Software Survey is a comprehensive list of project management-related products, categorized by application to the *PMBOK* knowledge areas. I am unaware of another source for the authoritative list of known and emerging software vendors in this industry. There are a substantial number of new entrants in this arena, with viable products. This single source of input to the software selection process is unprecedented, and profoundly valuable to an organization ready to invest in software.

She offered the following facts, gleaned from her experience with EDS as backup for her assessment:

Software evaluation efforts usually involve four to six people. The typical profile of this team includes:

■ One high-level manager (project management software project sponsor). This person has the budget to buy the tool, and has personal responsibility for the success of the new system.

■ Three functional managers. Mid-level management types, they represent their departmental needs for the new system.

■ Two end users (schedulers). These people are subject matter experts in the current system.

These people typically form a team that meets on a cyclic basis. They have a kickoff meeting, discuss things, and slowly create a matrix of requirements for the software selection process. After four or five meetings, they begin to draft a list of questions. They'll look at magazines and the Web to generate a list of visible vendors. They'll review and debate the vendor list for a few meetings, realizing that any vendor they include will want meeting opportunities to market their product. These meetings will take up more time, costing the total project in terms of effort.

Based on this scenario, Williams arrived at the $12,000–$15,000 figure as shown in Table 1.

It isn't every day that you can save your firm over $11,000 just by buying a book; but the *Project Management Software Survey* offers more than an opportunity to make your work easier and save some cash. It offers the users of the book the opportunity to become involved in the continuing evolution of PMI's research into the project management software market. As you use this book or CD-ROM, please note ways in which you feel the structure, content, or presentation could be enhanced. Your input is welcomed for future editions and may be addressed to the editor, Jeannette Cabanis, at pubprojects@pmi.org.

—Introduction contributed by Bob Anello (Part I);
Ketty Brown (Part III);
and Linda Williams (Part IV and Conclusion).

Based on a team of six people making an average of $40 per hour (low in this industry).

Prepare Questions

6 meetings, 3 hours long each = 90 hours.   90 hours @ $40.00 = 3,600.00

Compile Vendor List

1 person, 10 hours   10 hours @ $40.00 =   400.00

Develop Vendor List

2 meetings, 3 hours long each = 30 hours.   30 hours @ $40.00 = 1,200.00

Contact Vendors

1 person, 10 hours   10 hours @ $40.00 =   400.00

Table 1   Cost of a Typical Software Selection Project

Chapter 1

Suites

Project management software suites are groups of tools designed to work concurrently to bring together all information required to manage the project. Thus, suites are most closely aligned with the Integration Management knowledge area of *A Guide to the Project Management Body of Knowledge* (PMI® 1996).

The suite category is the most diverse covered in this survey, because most of the products evolved from a specific industry, although they are applicable to many.

Suite products can often be disassembled into their modules and evaluated separately, but their strength lies in the ability of the modules to work together. Modules in the suite are interfaced, and designed to support each other.

These products are mainly designed for and target large organizations in a wide range of industries and processes, and support simple through complex projects. Engineering, research and development, government, software, medical, electronics, aerospace, larger professional services and consulting companies, large-scale IT departments, telecommunications: all can benefit from the implementation of a project management suite. Some suite products target specific kinds of business users.

What to Expect

Software suites provides features like:
- Functionality for all phases of the project management process
- Summarization capability for all projects in the enterprise
- Strategic decision support
- Executive Information System (EIS) type interface.

What the Data Reveals

Most of the suite products had similar and expected features in the areas of reporting, cost, repository, and timesheets. As the scope of functionalities expanded into other areas of project management, such as process, risk, communications and document management, the breadth of many of the offerings trailed off. The majority of the products focused on integration with Microsoft Project as the sole desktop tool. It was also surprising that many of the suites either only had Web browser-based timesheets or did not provide Web browser interfaces. The products also have varying degrees of depth in the resource management area in terms of employee skills inventory and high-level resource capacity planning. Selection will depend on the project management maturity, how distributed the organization is, and the size and scope of the enterprise's project-based activities. If you haven't looked at Suites products in one or two years, it is time to take another look.

What the Majority of Vendors Offer

The majority have timesheets and multiple project reporting.

Almost all have the ability to easily tailor reports to the users' needs.

Most are built on open-architecture databases; over two-thirds of vendors responding offer a three-tier client/server design.

Support, training, consulting, and product enhancements at the customer's request are standard offerings.

What a Minority of Vendors Offer

Most vendors are not yet making multilingual product and technical support available.

Only about half have client interfaces that run on a Web browser.

Most don't integrate with multiple desktop project management tools.

Unique Features That Surfaced in Vendor Responses to the Narrative Questions

Grouping of projects and rollup to an enterprise portfolio.

Grouping of resources and rollup of OBS to enterprise level.

Some vendors extend the functionalities to include earned value, and accounting system integration for cost/schedule reporting.

What's New and Exciting

The number of recent entries into this category shows that enterprise project management is the current wave in project management trends. Among the vendors responding, while there are varying degrees of breadth of functionality, overall there is both breadth and depth that far exceeds what was available two years ago.

A reminder: The data in the matrix and in the narrative responses were supplied by the vendors and have not been independently verified.

Suites

Integrated components	ABT Results Management Suite 5.0	ADEPT Production Module	AMS REALTIME	Artemis Views	AutoPLAN Enterprise	Cascade PgM	Changepoint	DecisionTools Suite	Dekker TRAKKER Activity Based Cost Management and Performance System
Timesheets	Y	Y	Y	Y	Y	Y	Y	N	Y
Methodology/process	Y	N	Y	N	Y	Y	Y	N	Y
Cost	Y	Y	Y	Y	Y	Y	Y	Y	Y
Estimating	Y	N	Y	Y	Y	Y	Y	Y	Y
Repository	Y	Y	Y	Y	N	Y	Y	N	Y
Reporting module	Y	Y	Y	Y	Y	Y	Y	Y	Y
Configuration management	N	Y	Y	N	Y	Y	N	N	Y
Requirements management	N	Y	Y	Y	N	Y	N	N	Y
Risk management	Y	Y	N	Y	Y	Y	Y	Y	Y
Issues management	Y	Y	Y	Y	Y	Y	Y	Y	Y
Action items	Y	N	Y	Y	Y	Y	Y	N	Y
Communications management	Y	N	Y	Y	Y	Y	N	N	N
Document management	N	N	Y	N	N	N	N	N	N
Additional components (list them):	Scheduling, metrics, function point analysis	Simulation engine		OLAP executive reporting	None	Cost/schedule planning	Revenue and cost mgt., strategic mgt., client mgt., software development mgt.		Generic accounting interface, technical performance measurement system, integrated links to MS Project, OLE integration to MS Office, and OLE Interface to PS7

Repository (enterprise database)	ABT Results Management Suite 5.0	ADEPT Production Module	AMS REALTIME	Artemis Views	AutoPLAN Enterprise	Cascade PgM	Changepoint	DecisionTools Suite	Dekker TRAKKER
Multiproject Gantt charts	Y	Y	Y	Y	Y	Y	Y	N	Y
Multiproject resource utilization	Y	Y	Y	Y	Y	Y	Y	N	Y
Multiproject resource work graphs	Y	Y	Y	Y	Y	Y	Y	N	Y
Time period analysis	Y	Y	Y	Y	Y	Y	Y	Y	Y
Trending analysis	Y	Y	Y	Y	N	Y	Y	Y	Y
Variance analysis	Y	N	Y	Y	Y	Y	Y	Y	Y
Earned Value reporting	Y	N	Y	Y	Y	Y	Y	Y	Y
Ad-hoc query for reporting	Y	Y	Y	Y	Y	Y	N	N	Y
New project estimating	Y	Y	Y	Y	N	Y	Y	Y	Y
New project definition	Y	Y	Y	Y	Y	Y	Y	N	Y
Number of projects	Unlim.	1,000,000	Unlim.	Unlim.	Unlim.	Unlim.	Limited only by 3rd party planning tool		Unlim.

Resource management	ABT Results Management Suite 5.0	ADEPT Production Module	AMS REALTIME	Artemis Views	AutoPLAN Enterprise	Cascade PgM	Changepoint	DecisionTools Suite	Dekker TRAKKER
Capacity analysis	Y	Y	Y	Y	Y	Y	Y		Y
Demand analysis	Y	Y	Y	N	Y	Y	N		Y
Unused availability analysis	Y	Y	Y	Y	Y	Y	Y		Y

Feature	Product 1	Product 2	Product 3	Product 4	Product 5	Product 6	Product 7
Maps employees to resource type	Y	N	Y	N	Y	Y	Y
Skills and proficiency levels	Y	N	Y	N	Y	Y	Y
Standard role definitions as supported by the organization's methodology	Y	N	Y	N	Y	Y	Y
Document management							
Version control	N	N	N	N	N	Y	N
Document collaboration	N	N	N	N	N	Y	N
Methodology integration							
Product comes with methodologies (list)	ABC/Project Process Flow	N/A			N	N	ABT Results Management Method, SI Methods from Andersen Consulting, Oracle, CSC, etc.
Can input corporate methodologies	Y	N/A	Y	N	Y	N	Y
Suggests routes through methodologies	N	N/A	N	Y	N	N	N
Captures and re-uses best practices (re-use successful project plans as new models)	Y	N/A	Y	Y	Y	Y	Y
Attach guidelines	Y	N/A	Y	Y	Y	N	Y
Attach reference documents, templates	Y	N/A	Y	Y	Y	N	Y
Customized, context-sensitive guidelines (help for corporate methodologies)	Y	N/A	N	N	N	N	N
Reporting							
Report writer	Y	Y	Y	N	Y	Y	Y
Report wizard	Y	N	N	Y	N	N	Y
Publishes as HTML	Y	N	Y	Y	Y	Y	N
Number of user-defined fields	Unlim.	0	Varies	Unlim.	Unlim.	100	0
Drill-down/Roll-up *	Y	N	N	Y	Y	Y	Y
Import/export	Y	Y	Y	Y	Y	Y	Y
Automatic E-mail notification *	Y	N	Y	Y	Y	N	N
Macro recorder/batch capable *	Y	Y	N	Y	Y	Y	N
Can "canned" reports be modified?	Y	N	Y	N	Y	Y	Y
Sort, filter	Y	Y	Y	Y	Y	Y	Y
Architecture							
Databases supported	Oracle, MS SQL Server, Informix, MS Access, FoxPro	ODBC compliant	Lotus Notes, and MS SQL Server as of Jan. 99	Oracle	Oracle, MS SQL Server, Sybase, SQL Base	Oracle, ODBC compliant, Proprietary	Oracle, MS SQL Server, Sybase, Informix
Supports distributed databases	Y	Y	Y	Y	Y	N	Y

19

Suites

	ABT Results Management Suite 5.0	ADEPT Production Module	AMS REALTIME	Artemis Views	AutoPLAN Enterprise	Cascade PgM	Changepoint	DecisionTools Suite	Dekker TRAKKER Activity Based Cost Management and Performance System
Three-tier client/server	Y	N	Y	Y	Y	Y	Y	N	Y
Client operating systems	Win 95/98/NT		Win 95/NT, Unix, Mac, Power PC	Win 95/NT	Win 95/NT/3.x, Solaris, HP-UX, AIX	Win 95/98/NT	Win 95/NT/3.x	N/A	Win 95/98/NT
Server operating systems	Win NT		Win 95/NT, Unix, Mac, Power PC	Win NT, HP-UX, Solaris	Win NT, Solaris, HP-UX, AIX	Unix, Win NT	REMIND Suite requires one Domino server on Win NT	N/A	Win NT, Novell, Unix
Network operating systems	TCP/IP compatible		TCP/IP, IPX, NetBios, NetBEUI	IPX, Novell, Win NT	Win NT, Novell, Unix	TCP/IP	OS/2, Unix, Novell platform	N/A	Win NT, Novell, Unix
Minimum client configuration	Pentium 133		8 MB RAM, 486 or better	48 MB RAM, Pentium 166	P5 32 MB	PC 486/66 processor or above. Win 95 or Win NT V4. 16 MB RAM	REMIND desktop apps require Lotus Client 4.51 or greater	N/A	16 MB RAM, 1 GB HD, SVGA
Minimum server configuration	Pentium 266		16 MB RAM, 486 or better	Depends on hardware used (e.g., for Win NT same as the client configuration)	P5 32 MB, Unix machine with 64 MB	Any server supporting Oracle 7 or above	Refer to Lotus Notes Client and Lotus Domino server specification requirements from Lotus Development Corporation	N/A	128 MB RAM, 10 GB HD
Client runs under Web browser	Y	N	Y	Y	Y	N	Y	N	
Open architecture									
Supports OLE	Y	Y	N	Y	Y	Y	N	Y	Y
Documented Object Model	Y	Y	Y	Y	Y	Y	N	N	Y
Documented Application Programming Interface (API)	Y	N	Y	Y.	Y	Y	N	N	Y
Simultaneous edit of data file	Y	N	Y	Y	N	Y	Y	N	Y
Does product have a programming language?	N	N	Y	N	Y	Y	Y	N	Y
Are years stored as four-digit numbers?	Y	Y	N	Y	Y	Y	Y	Y	Y

Online Help								
Right mouse click	Y	Y	N	Y	N	N	Y	Y
Hover buttons	Y	Y	Y	Y	Y	Y	Y	Y
Interactive help	Y	Y	Y	Y	Y	Y	Y	Y
Help search feature	Y	Y	Y	Y	Y	Y	Y	Y
Web access to product knowledge base *	N	Y	Y	Y	N	N	Y	N
Vendor information								
Training								
Computer-based training	Y	N	Y	N	Y	N	N	Y
Training materials available	Y	Y	Y	Y	Y	Y	Y	Y
Customized training materials	Y	Y	Y	Y	Y	Y	Y	Y
Online tutorial	Y	Y	Y	N	N	N	Y	Y
Consulting available from vendor	Y	Y	Y	Y	Y	Y	Y	Y
Site license discounts	Y	Y	Y	Y	Y	Y	Y	Y
Enhancement requests *	Y	Y	Y	Y	Y	Y	N	Y
Modify source code, support through upgrades *	Y	Y	Y	Y	Y	N	N	Y
Global Presence								
Global offices	Y	N	Y	Y	Y	N	N	Y
Multilingual technical support	Y	N	Y	Y	Y	N	N	Y
Language versions (list):	Eng, Fre, Ger, Jpn	Eng	Chin, Dutch, Eng, Fre, Ger, Jpn, Kor, Pol, Rus	Eng, Fre, Ger, Ital	Eng, Fre	Eng, Fre	Eng	Fre, Ger, Span
Audit Software Quality Assurance process? *	Y	Y	Y	Y	Y	Y	N	Y
Security								
Configurable access privileges *	Y	N	Y	Y	Y	Y	N	Y
Passwords expire (forced update)	N	N	N	Y	Y	Y	N	Y
Electronic approvals	Y	N	Y	Y	Y	Y	N	Y
Password protect files	Y	N	Y	Y	Y	Y	N	Y

21

Suites

Integrated components

	Enterprise Controller	Enterprise Project	ER Project 1000	Global Project Management System	GroupProject	How's it going?	Innate Multi-Project & Timesheets	Intelligent Planner	Mesa/Vista
Timesheets	Y	Y	Y	Y	Y	Y	Y	Y	N
Methodology/process	N	Y	Y	Y	Y	Y	Y	N	Y
Cost	Y	Y	Y	Y	Y	Y	Y	Y	N
Estimating	Y	Y	Y	Y	Y	N	Y	Y	N
Repository	Y	Y	Y	Y	Y	Y	Y	Y	Y
Reporting module	Y	Y	Y	Y	Y	Y	Y	Y	Y
Configuration management	Y	Y	N	Y	Y	Y	Y	N	Y
Requirements management	Y	N	N	Y	Y	N	Y	Y	Y
Risk management	N	Y	Y	Y	Y	N	N	Y	Y
Issues management	N	Y	Y	Y	Y	Y	Y	N	Y
Action items	Y	Y	N	Y	Y	Y	Y	N	Y
Communications management	N	N	Y	Y	Y	Y	Y	N	Y
Document management	N	N	Y	Y	Y	Y	Y	N	Y
Additional components (list them):	Purchasing, billing, maintenance planning	Scheduling	Project architect, project expenses, management by threshold	Address mgt., document archive, customer care, workflow mgt., ARIS toolset interface, contract mgt.	Workflow	Project review meeting mgt., stakeholder information mgt., project charter documentation, bulletin board			Glossaries, meetings

Repository (enterprise database)

	Enterprise Controller	Enterprise Project	ER Project 1000	Global Project Management System	GroupProject	How's it going?	Innate Multi-Project & Timesheets	Intelligent Planner	Mesa/Vista
Multiproject Gantt charts	Y	Y	Y	Y	Y	N	Y	Y	Y
Multiproject resource utilization	N	Y	Y	Y	Y	Y	Y	Y	Y
Multiproject resource work graphs	N	Y	Y	Y	Y	N	Y	Y	N
Time period analysis	Y	Y	Y	Y	Y	Y	Y	Y	N
Trending analysis	Y	Y	Y	Y	N	N	Y	Y	N
Variance analysis	Y	Y	Y	Y	Y	Y	Y	Y	N
Earned Value reporting	Y	Y	Y	Y	Y	N	Y	Y	N
Ad-hoc query for reporting	Y	Y	Y	Y	N	Y	Y	Y	N
New project estimating	Y	Y	Y	Y	Y	N	Y	Y	N
New project definition	Y	Y	Y	Y	Y	Y	Y	Y	Y
Number of projects	Unlim.	Unlim.	16,000	1,000,000	Unlim.	Unlim.	2,000	Unlim.	Unlim.

Resource management

	Enterprise Controller	Enterprise Project	ER Project 1000	Global Project Management System	GroupProject	How's it going?	Innate Multi-Project & Timesheets	Intelligent Planner	Mesa/Vista
Capacity analysis	Y	Y	Y		Y	N	Y	Y	N
Demand analysis	Y	Y	Y		Y	N	Y	Y	N
Unused availability analysis	Y	Y	Y		Y	Y	Y	Y	N

Maps employees to resource type	Y	Y	Y	Y	Y	Y	Y	Y	N
Skills and proficiency levels	Y	Y	Y	Y	N	N	Y	Y	N
Standard role definitions as supported by the organization's methodology	Y	N	Y	Y	Y	Y	Y	Y	N
Document management									
Version control	N	N	N	Y	N	N	Y	N	Y
Document collaboration	N	N	Y	Y	Y	Y	N	N	Y
Methodology integration									
Product comes with methodologies (list)	N/A		MIL-STD-498 Software Development, IEEE 12207 Software Development, PMI Project Management	All MS Project features	N	N	N	N	N
Can input corporate methodologies	Y	N	Y	Y	Y	Y	Y	N	Y
Suggests routes through methodologies	Y	N	N	Y	N	N	Y	N	N
Captures and re-uses best practices (re-use successful project plans as new models)	Y	N	Y	Y	Y	Y	Y	Y	Y
Attach guidelines	N	N	Y	Y	Y	Y	Y	Y	Y
Attach reference documents, templates	N	N	Y	Y	Y	Y	Y	Y	Y
Customized, context-sensitive guidelines (help for corporate methodologies)	N	N	Y	Y	Y	Y	Y	N	Y
Reporting									
Report writer	Y	Y	Y	Y	N	N	Y	Y	Y
Report wizard	N	Y	Y	Y	N	N	Y	N	N
Publishes as HTML	Y	Y	Y	Y	Y	N	Y	Y	Y
Number of user-defined fields	Varies	0	100	Varies	10	8	Unlim.	100	25
Drill-down/Roll-up *	Y	Y	Y	Y	Y	Y	Y	Y	Y
Import/export	Y	Y	Y	Y	Y	Y	Y	Y	Y
Automatic E-mail notification *	N	N	N	Y	N	Y	Y	Y	Y
Macro recorder/batch capable *	N	N	N	Y	N	N	Y	N	N
Can "canned" reports be modified?	Y	Y	Y	Y	Y	Y	Y	Y	Y
Sort, filter	Y	Y	Y	Y	Y	Y	Y	Y	Y
Architecture									
Databases supported	Oracle	Oracle, Sybase, Informix, MS SQL Server, MS Access	Oracle, MS SQL Server, Interbase	MS SQL Server/Oracle	Lotus Notes	MS Access 97	MS Access, MS SQL Server, Oracle	Oracle, Sybase, MS SQL Server, Informix, Centura	MS SQL Server
Supports distributed databases	Y	Y	Y	Y	Y	Y	N	Y	N

Suites

	Enterprise Controller	Enterprise Project	ER Project 1000	Global Project Management System	GroupProject	How's it going?	Innate Multi-Project & Timesheets	Intelligent Planner	Mesa/Vista
Three-tier client/server	Y	Y	Y	Y	Y	Y	N	Y	N
Client operating systems	Win 95/NT/3.x	Win 95/98/NT	Win 95/98/NT 3.51/NT 4.0 (ER Project Satellite also Java and Win 3.x)	Win 95/NT, others via multiuser-multiclient (CITRIX/HYDRA) solutions	Win 95/NT/3.x, OS/2	Win 95	Win	Win 95/NT	N
Server operating systems	Unix, Win NT	Unix, Win NT	Win NT, Unix	Win NT Server	Win NT, Unix, AS400	Win 95	Any that support Win	Win NT	Y
Network operating systems	Novell, Win NT	Novell, Win NT, others	Win, NetBEUI/NetBios, TCP/IP, Novell	Win NT, others via TCP/IP and IPX	Win NT, Novell, Unix	Any	Any that support Win	TCP/IP, NetBios	Y
Minimum client configuration	16 MB RAM	486, 16 MB memory	Pentium, 16 MB memory (ER Project Satellite 8 MB)	thin client/Pentium 32 MB	Pentium PC, 16 MB RAM	10 MB for application	Pentium	Pentium 120, 16 MB RAM, 1 GB disk	Y
Minimum server configuration	64 MB RAM		Pentium, 32 MB memory	Pentium 128 MB RAM	Pentium PC, 128 MB RAM, 4 GB HD	5-100+ MB for shared databases	Capacity consideration only	Pentium 233, 128 MB RAM, 1 Gb disk	
Client runs under Web browser	N	Y	Y	Y	Y	N	Y	Y	Y
Open architecture									
Supports OLE	Y	Y	N	Y	Y	Y	Y	N	N
Documented Object Model	Y	Y	Y	Y	Y	N	Y	N	Y
Documented Application Programming Interface (API)	Y	Y	N	Y	Y	N	Y	Y	Y
Simultaneous edit of data file	Y	Y	Y	N	Y	Y	Y	Y	Y
Does product have a programming language?	Y	Y	N	Y	Y	Y	Y	Y	N
Are years stored as four-digit numbers?	Y	Y	Y	Y	Y	Y	Y	Y	Y

Online Help								
Right mouse click	Y	N	Y	Y	N	Y	Y	N
Hover buttons	Y	N	Y	Y	Y	Y	Y	N
Interactive help	N	Y	Y	Y	Y	Y	Y	Y
Help search feature	Y	Y	Y	Y	Y	Y	Y	Y
Web access to product knowledge base *	Y	N	Y	Y	Y	Y	Y	N
Vendor information								
Training								
Computer-based training	N	Y	N	Y	N	Y	N	N
Training materials available	Y	Y	Y	Y	N	Y	Y	Y
Customized training materials	Y	Y	Y	Y	Y	Y	Y	Y
Online tutorial	N	N	Y	Y	Y	Y	Y	Y
Consulting available from vendor	Y	Y	Y	Y	Y	Y	Y	Y
Site license discounts	Y	Y	Y	Y	Y	Y	Y	Y
Enhancement requests *	Y	Y	Y	Y	Y	Y	Y	N
Modify source code, support through upgrades *	Y	Y	Y	Y	Y	Y	Y	Y
Global Presence								
Global offices	Y	N	N	N	Y	N	Y	N
Multilingual technical support	N	Y	Y	Y	N	N	Y	N
Language versions (list):	Eng	Eng, Span	Eng	Eng, Ger	Eng, Ger, Dan	Eng	Eng, Fre, Ger	Eng, Fre, Ger, Dutch
Audit Software Quality Assurance process? *	Y	Y	Y	Y	Y	Y/N	Y	Y
Security								
Configurable access privileges *	Y	Y	Y	Y	Y	Y	Y	Y
Passwords expire (forced update)	Y	Y	N	Y	N	Y	Y	N
Electronic approvals	Y	Y	Y	Y	N	Y	Y	Y
Password protect files	Y	Y	Y	Y	Y	Y	Y	N

Suites

Integrated components

	MicroFusion Millennium	Microsoft Project 98	Open Plan/ Cobra/Spider	OPX2 Suite (OPX2 Pro, OPX2 TimeCard, OPX2 Server, OPX2 Intranet Server)	Panorama	PLANTRAC-OUTLOOK Level 4	PPS Corporate 4.0	Primavera Prospective	Project Control Software 6.0
Timesheets	N	Y	Y	Y	Y	Y	Y	Y	Y
Methodology/process	N	N	Y	N	Y	Y	Y	N	Y
Cost	Y	Y	Y	Y	Y	Y	Y	N	Y
Estimating	Y	Y	Y	N		Y	Y	N	Y
Repository	Y	Y	Y	Y	Y	Y	Y	Y	Y
Reporting module	Y	Y	Y	Y	Y	Y	Y	Y	Y
Configuration management	N	N	N	N		Y	Y	N	Y
Requirements management	N	N	N	N		Y	Y	N	Y
Risk management	N	N	Y	N		Y	N	N	N
Issues management	N	N	Y	N	Y	Y	Y	N	Y
Action items	N	Y	Y	N	Y	Y	Y	Y	Y
Communications management	N	Y	Y	N	Y	N	Y	Y	Y
Document management	N	N	N	N	Y	Y	N	N	Y
Additional components (list them):			Project management director, Web publisher	OPX2 Server = Consolidator for MS Project, Scitor Project Scheduler; OPX2 Intranet Server = Web publisher	Procurement	Time chainage charts	Quality Management		Accounting integration, earned value manager, online knowledge base
Number of projects		1,000	Unlim.	Unlim.	Unlim.	9,999	Unlim.	Unlim.	

Repository (enterprise database)

	MicroFusion Millennium	Microsoft Project 98	Open Plan/ Cobra/Spider	OPX2 Suite	Panorama	PLANTRAC-OUTLOOK Level 4	PPS Corporate 4.0	Primavera Prospective	Project Control Software 6.0
Multiproject Gantt charts	Y	Y	Y	Y	Y	Y	Y	Y	Y
Multiproject resource utilization	Y	Y	Y	Y	Y	Y	Y	Y	Y
Multiproject resource work graphs	N	Y	Y	Y	Y	Y	Y	Y	Y
Time period analysis	Y	Y	Y	Y	Y	Y	Y	Y	Y
Trending analysis	Y	N	Y	Y	Y	Y	Y	Y	Y
Variance analysis	Y	Y	Y	Y	Y	Y	Y	Y	Y
Earned Value reporting	Y	Y	Y	Y	Y	Y	Y	Y	Y
Ad-hoc query for reporting	Y	Y	Y	Y	Y	Y	N	Y	Y
New project estimating	Y	Y	Y	Y	Y	Y	Y	N	Y
New project definition	Y	Y	Y	Y	Y	Y	Y	Y	Y

Resource management

	MicroFusion Millennium	Microsoft Project 98	Open Plan/ Cobra/Spider	OPX2 Suite	Panorama	PLANTRAC-OUTLOOK Level 4	PPS Corporate 4.0	Primavera Prospective	Project Control Software 6.0
Capacity analysis		Y	Y	Y	Y	Y	Y	Y	Y
Demand analysis		Y	Y	Y	Y	Y	Y	Y	Y
Unused availability analysis		Y	Y	Y	Y	Y	Y	Y	Y

The following comparison table lists product features across eight products (column headers not visible on this page).

Feature	P1	P2	P3	P4	P5	P6	P7	P8
Maps employees to resource type	Y	Y	N	Y	N	Y	Y	N
Skills and proficiency levels	Y	Y	N	N	N	N	Y	N
Standard role definitions as supported by the organization's methodology	Y	Y	N	Y	N	N	Y	Y
Document management								
Version control	Y	N	N	Y	Y	Y	N	Y
Document collaboration	N	N	N	Y	N	Y	N	N
Methodology integration								
Product comes with methodologies (list)	Best Practices focusing on IT, engineering, enterprise initiatives, and pharmaceutical		PPS Methodology	PRINCE	N		Guidance from PMBOK™ included; other methodologies can be input	
Can input corporate methodologies	Y	Y	N	Y	Y	Y	Y	N
Suggests routes through methodologies	Y	N	N	Y	N	Y	Y	N
Captures and re-uses best practices (re-use successful project plans as new models)	Y	Y	Y	Y	Y	Y	Y	Y
Attach guidelines	Y	N	Y	Y	Y	Y	Y	Y
Attach reference documents, templates	Y	Y	Y	Y	Y	Y	Y	Y
Customized, context-sensitive guidelines (help for corporate methodologies)	Y	N	N	Y	Y	Y	Y	N
Reporting								
Report writer	Y	Y	Y	Y	Y	Y	Y	Y
Report wizard	N	Y	N	Y	N	N	Y	N
Publishes as HTML	Y	N	Y	N	Y	Y	Y	N
Number of user-defined fields	60	Unlim.	0	20	20	Unlim.	360	50
Drill-down/Roll-up *	Y	Y	Y	Y	Y	Y	N	Y
Import/export	Y	N	Y	Y	Y	Y	Y	Y
Automatic E-mail notification *	N	N	Y	Y	N	N	N	N
Macro recorder/batch capable *	Y	N	N	Y	Y	Y	Y	N
Can "canned" reports be modified?	Y	Y	Y	Y	Y	Y	Y	Y
Sort, filter	Y	Y	Y	Y	Y	Y	Y	Y
Architecture								
Databases supported	Oracle, MS Access, MS SQL Server, Sybase	Oracle	MS Access, MS SQL Server, DB2, Sybase, Oracle	ODBC	Oracle	Oracle, MS SQL Server, Informix, Sybase, Ingres	Oracle, Sybase, MS SQL Server, MS Access, FoxPro	MS SQL Server, Oracle
Supports distributed databases	Y	Y	Y	N	Y	Y	Y	Y

Suites

	MicroFusion Millennium	Microsoft Project 98	Open Plan/ Cobra/Spider	OPX2 Suite (OPX2 Pro, OPX2 TimeCard, OPX2 Server, OPX2 Intranet Server)	Panorama	PLANTRAC-OUTLOOK Level 4	PPS Corporate 4.0	Primavera Prospective	Project Control Software 6.0
Three-tier client/server	Y	N	N	Y	Y	Y	Y	Y	Y
Client operating systems	Win 95/98/NT	Win 95/98/NT 3.51 with Service Pack 5 or later/NT 4.0 with Service Pack 2 or later	Win 95 or later version	Win 95/98/NT/3.x, Mac, Unix	Win 95/NT	Win 95/98/NT	Win 95/NT, all other	Win 95/NT	Win 95/98/NT
Server operating systems	Win NT	Win 95/98/NT 3.51 with Service Pack 5 or later/NT 4.0 with Service Pack 2 or later	Specified by database vendor	Win NT, Unix	Any that support Oracle	Win 95/98/NT	Win NT	Database: Win NT, Unix; Application: Win NT	Unix, Win NT, HP, Sybase, others
Network operating systems		Any Win-supported network	Any that support Win	TCP/IP (Ethernet, Token Ring, WAN)	TCP/IP	Win 95/98/NT	TCP/IP	Win NT	Novell, IPX, XPX, Banyan, MS Network, TCP/IP
Minimum client configuration	Pentium 266, with 64 MB RAM	486 or higher processor with 12 MB memory for Win 95 or 16 MB for Win 98 or NT	Pentium or compatible, Win 95 or later: 16 MB RAM, Rec. 32 MB	486 + 16 MB RAM (light client), P100 + 32 MB RAM (fat client)	Pentium 133 MHz, 32 MB memory, 500 MB disk	8 MB	Pentium 100 MHz	166 MHz or better, 32 MB RAM, Win 95/NT	PC 486/66 processor or above. Win 95 or Win NT V4. 16 MB RAM
Minimum server configuration	Pentium 266, with 256 MB RAM	Run from server is available; configuration depends on number of users connecting to the server	Server optional	P2xx + 128 MB RAM	Depends on number of users	8 MB	NT 4 sp3	Win NT Server, 266 MHz or better, 128 to 512 MB RAM	Any Server supporting Oracle 7 or above
Client runs under Web browser	N	Y	Y	N	N	N	Y	Y	Y
Open architecture									
Supports OLE	Y	Y	Y	Y	Y	N	Y	Y	Y
Documented Object Model	Y	Y	Y	Y	Y	N	Y	Y	N
Documented Application Programming Interface (API)	N	N	N	N	Y	N	Y	Y	N
Simultaneous edit of data file	Y	N	Y	Y	Y	Y	Y	Y	Y
Does product have a programming language?	Y	Y	N	Y	Y	N	Y	N	N
Are years stored as four-digit numbers?	Y	Y	Y	Y	Y	Y	Y	Y	Y

28

Online Help							
Right mouse click	N	Y	Y	N	Y	Y	Y
Hover buttons	Y	Y	N	N	Y	Y	N
Interactive help	N	Y	N	Y	Y	Y	Y
Help search feature	Y	Y	Y	Y	Y	Y	Y
Web access to product knowledge base *	Y	N		N	N	Y	N
Vendor information							
Training							
Computer-based training	Y	N	Y	N	N	Y	N
Training materials available	Y	Y	Y	Y	Y	Y	Y
Customized training materials	Y	Y	Y	Y	Y	Y	N
Online tutorial	Y	Y	N	N	Y	Y	N
Consulting available from vendor	Y	Y	Y	Y	Y	Y	Y
Site license discounts	Y	Y	Y	Y	Y	Y	Y
Enhancement requests *	Y	Y	Y	Y	Y	Y	Y
Modify source code, support through upgrades *	Y	N	Y	Y	Y	Y	Y
Global Presence							
Global offices	Y	Y	Y	N	Y	Y	N
Multilingual technical support	N	Y	N	N	Y	Y	N
Language versions (list):	Eng	Eng, Ger, Fre, Ital, Span, Port, Dutch, Swed	Eng	Eng	Eng, Fre	Open Plan/Spider - Fre, Ger, Ital, Mand, Rus, Hangul; Cobra - Eng only	Ger, Fre, Swed, Ital, Span, Dan, Nor, Jpn, Traditional Chin, Simplified Chin, Kor, Heb, Brzl Port
Audit Software Quality Assurance process? *	Y	N	Y	Y	Y	N	Y
Security							
Configurable access privileges *	Y	Y	Y	Y	Y	Y	N
Passwords expire (forced update)	N	N	N	Y	N	N	N
Electronic approvals	Y	Y	Y	Y	Y	N	Y
Password protect files	Y	Y	Y	Y	Y	Y	Y

Suites

Integrated components

	ProjectExchange	Project Integrator 2.0 Enterprise Edition	Proj-Net	QEI Exec	QuickGantt for Windows	WebProject
Timesheets	Y	Y	N	N	N	Y
Methodology/process	Y	Y	Y	N	N	Y
Cost	Y	Y	Y	Y	Y	Y
Estimating	Y	Y	Y	Y	Y	Y
Repository	Y	Y	Y	Y	N	Y
Reporting module	Y	Y	Y	N	Y	Y
Configuration management	Y	N	N	N	N	Y
Requirements management	Y	Y	N	N	N	Y
Risk management	N	N	Y	N	N	Y
Issues management	Y	Y	Y	N	N	Y
Action items	Y	Y	Y	N	Y	Y
Communications management	Y	Y	Y	N	Y	Y
Document management	N	Y	Y	N	N	Y
Additional components (list them):	Information validation	Resource maintenance/availability, client maintenance, communication	Self-generating Web site, metric analysis, program reviews, collaboration tool	Schedule mgt., resource mgt.	Calendar, Gantt chart	Project issue boards, ERP integration, PM integration

Repository (enterprise database)

	ProjectExchange	Project Integrator 2.0 Enterprise Edition	Proj-Net	QEI Exec	QuickGantt for Windows	WebProject
Multiproject Gantt charts	Y	Y		Y	Y	Y
Multiproject resource utilization	Y	Y		Y	N	Y
Multiproject resource work graphs	Y	Y		Y	N	Y
Time period analysis	Y	Y		Y	Y	Y
Trending analysis	Y	Y	Y	Y	N	N
Variance analysis	Y	Y	Y	Y	Y	Y
Earned Value reporting	Y	N	Y	Y	N	Y
Ad-hoc query for reporting	Y	Y	Y	Y	N	Y
New project estimating	Y	Y	Y	Y	Y	Y
New project definition	Y	Y	Y	N	Y	Y
Number of projects	Unlim.	Unlim.	Unlim.	Unlim.	Unlim.	Unlim.

Resource management

	ProjectExchange	Project Integrator 2.0 Enterprise Edition	Proj-Net	QEI Exec	QuickGantt for Windows	WebProject
Capacity analysis	Y	N	Y	Y	N	Y
Demand analysis	Y	N	Y	Y	N	Y
Unused availability analysis	Y	Y	Y	Y	N	Y

Maps employees to resource type	Y	Y	Y	N	N	Y
Skills and proficiency levels	Y	Y	Y	N	N	Y
Standard role definitions as supported by the organization's methodology	Y	Y	Y	N	N	Y
Document management						
Version control	N	Y	N	N	N	Y
Document collaboration	N	Y	Y	N	N	Y
Methodology integration						
Product comes with methodologies (list)	N	Implementation Roadmap		N	N	Significant announcements shortly
Can input corporate methodologies	Y	Y	Y	N	N	Y
Suggests routes through methodologies	Y	Y	Y	N	N	N
Captures and re-uses best practices (re-use successful project plans as new models)	Y	Y	Y	N	N	Y
Attach guidelines	Y	Y	Y	Y	N	Y
Attach reference documents, templates	Y	Y	Y	Y	N	Y
Customized, context-sensitive guidelines (help for corporate methodologies)	Y	N	Y	N	N	Y
Reporting						
Report writer	Y	Y	Y	N	Y	N
Report wizard	Y	Y	Y	N	N	Y
Publishes as HTML	Y	Y	Java	N	N	Y
Number of user-defined fields	Unlim.	Unlim.	Unlim.	Unlim.	0	Varies
Drill-down/Roll-up *	Y	Y	Y	Y	Y	Y
Import/export	Y	Y	Y	Y	Y	Y
Automatic E-mail notification *	N	Y	Y	N	N	Y
Macro recorder/batch capable *	Y	Y	Y	N	N	N
Can "canned" reports be modified?	Y	Y	Y	Y	Y	Y
Sort, filter	Y	Y	Y	Y	Y	Y
Architecture						
Databases supported	Oracle, MS SQL Server, Sybase	MS SQL Server, Oracle, Sybase, SQL Anywhere	Oracle 7.3, 8	N/A	MS Access	Oracle, MS SQL Server, Informix, Sybase, any JDBC-compliant database
Supports distributed databases	Y	N	Y	N	Y	Y

Suites

	ProjectExchange	Project Integrator 2.0 Enterprise Edition	Proj-Net	QEI Exec	QuickGantt for Windows	WebProject
Three-tier client/server	Y	Y	Y	N	N	Y
Client operating systems	Win 32, Browser	Win 95/NT	Any browser environment with Netscape 4.0 and IE 4.0 and Oracle back end	Win 95/NT/3.x with Win32s, Solaris	Win 95/NT/3.x	Win 95/NT, Unix, Linux, other Java-enabled OS
Server operating systems	Unix, Win NT	Win NT	Any supported by Oracle	N/A	Win 95/NT/3.x	Win 95/NT, Unix, Linux, other Java-enabled OS
Network operating systems	Multiple	Novell, Win NT, Banyan	Net based	LAN Manager, TCP/IP, Novell	Win, Lantastic, Novell	Win 95/NT, Unix, Linux, other Java-enabled OS
Minimum client configuration	Role dependent	P166 MHz, 16 MB RAM, 30 MB HD	15	486, 16 MB RAM, mouse, XGA graphics	486, 12 MB RAM, 12 MB HD, VGA monitor, MS-compatible mouse	Java-enabled browser
Minimum server configuration	Pentium w/128 MB	P166 MHz, 16 MB RAM, 30 MB HD	Depends on Oracle and Web site	N/A	486 66 MHz, 12 MB RAM, 12 MB HD, VGA monitor, MS-compatible mouse	Win 95/NT, Unix, Linux, other Java-enabled OS
Client runs under Web browser	Y	Y	Y	N	N	Y
Open architecture						
Supports OLE	Y	Y	Y	N	N	N
Documented Object Model	Y	N	Y	Y	N	N
Documented Application Programming Interface (API)	N	N	Y	Y	N	N
Simultaneous edit of data file	Y	Y	Y	N	N	Y
Does product have a programming language?	N	N	Y	Y	N	N
Are years stored as four-digit numbers?	Y	Y	Y	Y	N	Y

Online Help						
Right mouse click	Y	Y	N	N	Y	N
Hover buttons	Y	Y	Y	Y	N	Y
Interactive help	N	N	Y	Y	Y	Y
Help search feature	Y	Y		Y	Y	Y
Web access to product knowledge base *	N	Y	Y	N	N	Y
Vendor information						
Training						
Computer-based training	N	N	N	N	N	Y
Training materials available	Y	Y	Y	Y	Y	Y
Customized training materials	Y	Y	Y	Y	Y	Y
Online tutorial	N	N	Y	N	Y	Y
Consulting available from vendor	Y	Y	Y	Y	Y	Y
Site license discounts	N	N	Y	Y	Y	Y
Enhancement requests *	Y	Y	Y	Y	Y	Y
Modify source code, support through upgrades *	Y	Y	Y	Y	N	Y
Global Presence						
Global offices	N	N	Y	N	N	Y
Multilingual technical support	N	N	N	N	N	Y
Language versions (list):	Eng	Eng	Eng	Eng	Eng	Eng, Ger
Audit Software Quality Assurance process? *	Y	Y	N	Y	N	Y
Security						
Configurable access privileges *	Y	Y	Y	Y	Y	Y
Passwords expire (forced update)	N	Y	N	Y	N	Y
Electronic approvals	Y	Y	N	Y	N	Y
Password protect files	Y	Y	Y	Y	Y	Y

33

VENDOR RESPONSES TO NARRATIVE QUESTIONS

ABT Results Management Suite 5.0 (ABT Corporation)

Describe what the product is designed to do.

The ABT Results Management 5.0 Suite is an integrated enterprise project management (EPM) system that provides program, project, process, and resource management capabilities. Centered on an EPM knowledge base, the ABT Repository, are a number of components that provide functionality targeted at specific constituents. ABT Planner provides methods authoring, project planning, and estimating. ABT Workbench provides program and project scheduling and analysis. ABT Resource provides resource pool demand and capacity management. ABT Team provides tracking and methods delivery. ABT Connect provides Web-based tracking and methods delivery. ABT Publisher provides Web-based reporting and stakeholder communication. Metrics Manager provides metrics collection, analysis, and reporting. Function Point Manager provides FP counting support.

The RM 5.0 Suite also provides MSP98 support, a powerful, programmable API to build custom system interfaces, and prepackaged toolkit interfaces to Oracle Projects and SAP.

Top three product differentiators; describe what makes your product unique.

1. Robust project management repository.
2. Highly integrated tool set.
3. Broad range of functionality to address all stakeholders.

To what business processes can this tool be applied?

Program and project management processes.
Resource management processes.
Process management processes.

Describe the ideal end-user environment for the current version of your product (size of organization, level of project management sophistication, effort and commitment required).

The RM Suite can benefit organizations of fifty to fifty thousand project-related resources, whatever the level of project management maturity.

Future strategies for this product.

Extend functionality and enhance scalability.

Product's target market.

Enterprise project management.

What are your product's three main benefits? (How does using the product add value to the customer?)

1. Improved executive decision-making.
2. Integrated project stakeholder information base.
3. More effective resource utilization.

Describe your quality management process. List any relevant certifications.

ABT's test-engineering organization provides extensive in-house product quality testing using a series of proprietary testing methodologies, supplemented by external resources to perform activities such as high volume benchmarking. ABT's test group has also been instrumental in contributing to the definition of IEEE Year 2000 testing standards.

Discuss your product pricing structure. Include volume discount levels, concurrent user options, site licenses, cost of implementation, and other issues.

Pricing is on a named-user basis. List prices: Repository seat—$250, Resource Manager—$125, ABT Connect/Team Workbench—$100, ABT Publisher—$75, ABT Planner—$300, ABT Workbench—$300. Volume discounts apply. Stand-alone product pricing: Project Workbench PMW—$1,275, Metrics Manager—$15,000, Function Point Manager—$1,500.

Rapid Implementation: Six-week process enablement around Resource Manager tool set—$75,000. Additional services include Project Management Maturity Evaluation, tool training, project management concepts training, process customization and implementation, and systems integration/custom programming work.

Annual maintenance (client support program): 15 percent of purchase price.

ADEPT

Describe what the product is designed to do.

ADEPT is a suite of software tools designed by DDTI to simulate the performance of complex projects and programs, especially those projects dealing with the development and support of complex products. ADEPT was initially created to help the Department of Defense manage the design, production, and support of major military systems and vehicles. ADEPT includes the following modules: Design & Engineering, Production, Operations & Support, Supply Chain, and Resources.

The ADEPT Production module is designed to simulate the performance of complex projects over time. This includes the dynamic allocation of resources (e.g., labor, material, and work stations) to tasks, dependencies among tasks, management functions (e.g., responses to schedule pressure such as adding overtime or adding labor), productivity losses (e.g., from fatigue or working out of sequence), and rework (e.g., from working out of sequence).

Top three product differentiators; describe what makes your product unique.

1. System dynamics modeling and simulation techniques used. These techniques provide true cause-and-effect linkages among project elements, rather than static spreadsheet "matching" of resources to tasks, giving realistic predictions of project performance. For instance, the work accomplished for a task is based on the labor applied to the task and the current productivity of that labor, where productivity varies over the course of a task in response to changing situations in the project (e.g., high fatigue from working long overtime hours).

2. Management functions allow the user to describe how management will respond to changes in project performance. For instance, management can assign overtime hours or additional labor to a task based on how late that task appears that it will be, or management can allow the task to begin working out of sequence.

3. User can define multiple "what-if" scenarios with changes in parameters, management functions and work plans. These multiple scenarios can then be compared for best course of action.

To what business processes can this tool be applied?

Production, manufacturing, software development, design, engineering, and services.

Describe the ideal end-user environment for the current version of your product (size of organization, level of project management sophistication, effort and commitment required).

ADEPT Production module is designed for medium to large organization or projects with a normal level of project management sophistication. Projects should be medium- to long-term to gain the benefits of simulation and predicting performance over time.

Future strategies for this product.

Integrate the ADEPT Production module with the other ADEPT modules, such as the Supply Chain module and the dynamic Resources module.

Client/server architecture.

Product's target market.

Medium to large organizations in all industries that have production, engineering, or software development processes.

What are your product's three main benefits? (How does using the product add value to the customer?)

1. Realistically simulates project performance over the life of the project using system dynamics modeling and simulation techniques.

2. Allows the user to compare different project scenarios with "What-if" analysis.

3. Flexibility that allows the simulation of multiple projects using multiple facilities and multiple resource pools. Also, it has flexibility that allows multiple levels of analysis from high-level analysis across multiple projects to low-level analysis of a subset of important tasks on one project.

Describe your quality management process. List any relevant certifications.

Behavioral analysis of underlying system dynamics models.

Software QA of interface.

Discuss your product pricing structure. Include volume discount levels, concurrent user options, site licenses, cost of implementation, and other issues.

Sliding-scale pricing structure based on size of organization and number of licenses sold. Volume discounts and site licenses available. 10 to 20 percent annual maintenance fee based on total licenses.

Cost of implementation includes license fees plus annual maintenance fees. Online tutorial available, and additional customized on-site training is available with price depending on organization and licenses. Technical support is provided at no additional cost.

AMS REALTIME Projects (Advanced Management Systems)

Describe what the product is designed to do.

AMS REALTIME Projects provides powerful project and resource management in an easy-to-use graphic software tool. Plan project tasks, network constraints, resource, and manpower utilizations by manipulating graphic images with your mouse, or import data from external sources. Costs and earned value are visible in real time as the project evolves. Employee actuals and estimates-to-complete automatically feed status back to project schedules, providing accurate status calculations from the lowest levels.

Distributed projects and subprojects offer unlimited project capacity, while merge-link, attached documents, shared calendars, shared resources, and command links to other systems provide the capability to build a complete enterprisewide project management system. Users may store project data in proprietary stand-alone files stored on a common file server, or store data on a database (ODBC-compliant database, AMS proprietary database, or Oracle) using an AMS REALTIME Projects server.

Resource managers get a clear picture of how employees are utilized across all projects, including unplanned and nonproject work. Generic skill assignments can be exchanged for resources that meet both skill and availability requirements. Organization hierarchy and access controls provide a security layer to ensure data integrity and protection. Resource modifications are updated back to each effected project.

Top three product differentiators; describe what makes your product unique.

1. Project and resource management modules interact in a way that mirrors real workflow processes, giving real-time visibility of accurate status information. Fully integrated schedule, resource, and cost give you an accurate look at one or more projects from any perspective.

2. AMS REALTIME Projects is fully equipped with powerful features: attached documents, command links, WBS tools, sorting and matching with stored views, calculated fields, cost breakdowns (labor, materials, ODC), rate tables, multiple revisions, and much more. AMS REALTIME Resources has a fast and powerful database that is both efficient and fully extendable, allowing unprecedented customization. ODBC drivers allow external access to the data, including calculated reports.

3. All software runs native on Windows (95, NT, 3.x), Macintosh, Sun, Solaris, HP, and RS with identical look and feel and direct data access from any platform.

To what business processes can this tool be applied?

AMS REALTIME is so flexible that it can be applied to virtually any business process, including proposals, maintenance operations, new development, manufacturing, and performance improvement processes.

AMS REALTIME is designed to allow automated project statusing that automatically feeds earned value performance measurements. Cost management is empowered. Costs can be tracked from a project summary level all the way down to the activity level, providing accurate information to pinpoint the source of cost overruns.

Describe the ideal end-user environment for the current version of your product (size of organization, level of project management sophistication, effort and commitment required).

AMS REALTIME is used by global companies in very large enterprise environments, all the way down to small companies with just a few people. While AMS REALTIME is used to support extremely sophisticated project management processes, it can still be used to benefit users with little or no project management background. Users can grow into the software as their project management expertise evolves. To make any project management implementation successful, senior management must be committed to supporting the process, and other participants must make the effort to be trained to use the tools and follow through. Working with a consultant to help adapt the software to your business practices and needs and to document these processes is the best way to ensure success.

Future strategies for this product.

Future development strategies include more active Web enablements, a more complex three-tiered server design to facilitate global replication, and more resource tools. AMS has always been on the cutting edge of technology, and we are dedicated to bringing our customers the best of this ever-changing world.

Product's target market.

Products are used across a wide variety of client bases. AMS does not target any particular market but is widely used in manufacturing, oil and gas, nuclear power, automotive, pharmaceutical, aerospace, software development, construction, research and development, and many other industries.

What are your product's three main benefits? (How does using the product add value to the customer?)

1. Accurate, up-to-date project schedule and cost problems can be identified immediately, allowing maximum time for proactive measures to eliminate problems.

2. All work assignments are instantly communicated to employees, who also have a medium to effectively communicate work performed, status, and other issues.

3. Selective automation allows managers to eliminate drudgery and inaccuracy, while still maintaining control over critical project and resource decisions.

Describe your quality management process. List any relevant certifications.

Advanced Management Solutions is fully committed to providing the highest quality software and services to all of our clients. We have implemented many internal standards and processes in order to ensure that we can track and manage our software development process to the highest standard of quality possible. Concurrent versions system has been implemented to help manage multiple programmers at multiple development sites. Peer review of source code and design strategy meetings with high-level program development leaders continue to ensure that our software remains on the leading edge of our evolving technology.

A dedicated testing department manages the initial alpha testing, which encompasses new functionality, system process testing, and full regression testing. Beta testing is initially performed internally. After a stable point has been reached, beta testing is extended to select client users. Client beta testing not only provides clients with an edge in using new software features, but also greatly expands the test environment scope relating to different hardware environments. As AMS REALTIME is one of the most flexible and highly configurable management products on the market today, client testing adds an exceptional dimension to our testing process.

Discuss your product pricing structure. Include volume discount levels, concurrent user options, site licenses, cost of implementation, and other issues.

Product price is different for clients based on their requirements for software and implementation. Volume discounts and site licenses are available. Please request a quote from an AMS sales representative for your specific requirements.

Annual maintenance is based on 20 percent of the current product cost, and includes all software upgrades (while support is active) and telephone hotline technical support. Training cost is based upon topics, requirements, training equipment and site, and days requested. Please request a quote from an AMS sales representative for your specific requirements.

Artemis Views

Describe what the product is designed to do.

Artemis Views is designed to help businesses plan and manage all aspects of their multiproject environment, including schedules, resources and costs, and project interdependencies. Views uses a modular, role-based design.

Views is used by organizations in a variety of industries to plan and control a diverse array of projects, including product introductions and time-to-market, software development and maintenance, resource allocation and tracking, and program management.

Artemis Views provides users across an organization with a centralized tool for coordinating, collaborating and communicating project-based information. This helps businesses improve decision making, minimize project durations, and improve resource efficiency.

Top three product differentiators; describe what makes your product unique.

1. Role-based approach to design and implementation.
2. Integrated, centralized repository.
3. Enterprise multiproject architecture.

To what business processes can this tool be applied?

Artemis Views can be used by businesses across all vertical markets to improve project predictability, control and performance. Views also helps to implement and maintain consistent business rules and project methodologies across all projects.

Describe the ideal end-user environment for the current version of your product (size of organization, level of project management sophistication, effort and commitment required).

No answer given.

Future strategies for this product.

Artemis is committed to continually enhancing our products' functionality and applicability to consistently meet or exceed the demands of project management professionals.

Future development plans include the expanded use of Web technology, increased integration with complementary application providers, and extension of the traditional scope of "project management."

Product's target market.

Artemis products are used in over twenty-five industry sectors from Banking and Finance to Aerospace and Defense. Any organization that wants to improve its results using a project-centric management technique can benefit from using the Views suite of products.

What are your product's three main benefits? (How does using the product add value to the customer?)

1. The Views modular suite of applications can be purchased and deployed as a fully integrated set or as stand-alone applications.
2. Unique role-based approach provides sophisticated set of applications tailored to the needs of different users across the enterprise.
3. Extensibility to integrate with existing systems including ERP applications, Line-of-business applications, and Microsoft Project.

Describe your quality management process. List any relevant certifications.

Internal software audits and reporting procedures. Formal Year 2000 testing and compliance process.

Discuss your product pricing structure. Include volume discount levels, concurrent user options, site licenses, cost of implementation, and other issues.

Artemis Views can be purchased and deployed as a fully integrated suite or as a series of independent applications.

Available as registered user and concurrent pricing. Volume discounts and site licenses are available. Implementation cost varies.

AutoPLAN Enterprise (Digital Tools)

Describe what the product is designed to do.

AutoPLAN Enterprise Release 4 is a Web-based software and process solution to help high-tech, engineering, and telecommunications companies predict, control, and improve cycle time of critical program development and deployment. The solution set provides deep functionality across the entire spectrum of product life-cycle elements including pipeline management, project management, resource alignment, process effectiveness, document support, and team collaboration. AutoPLAN Enterprise integrates realistic planning, resource-centric management, status and forecast tracking, team collaboration, process support, escalation management, and program execution across globally distributed organizations.

Organizations are evolving from functional teams to matrix or program teams, and this is creating cross-functional or multidisciplinary project teams. AutoPLAN Enterprise recognizes three different organizational patterns that coexist: dynamic peer-to-peer, functional, and program management. AutoPLAN Enterprise offers these organizations both project-centric and resource-centric management. AutoPLAN Enterprise addresses everyone involved in product development and deployment including executives; program, product, resource, and project managers; and team leaders and team members, as well as teams from marketing, operations, service, and quality.

As a result of extensive process and product consulting with clients engaged in new product development and deployment, DTI (Digital Tools, Inc.) has distilled four key reasons why products are late and descoped.

1. Product development pipeline and deployment structures that are not aligned with the company's time-to-market goals.

2. Unrealistic plans, overcommitted resources, and unmanaged cross-functional dependencies.

3. Status and forecast decisions that are based on hearsay, rather than facts or experience.

4. A lack of consistent processes that fit the company culture and practice, which is further exacerbated by distributed cross-functional teams.

Avoiding late and descoped products requires an overall view of product and project status, the involvement of cross-functional teams, and decision-evaluation tools. Increasingly accelerated product development cycles and shorter product life cycles require organizations to disseminate information quickly to remain competitive. To support today's geographically dispersed product-development environments, organizations require a common platform that enables effective cross-functional collaboration and communication on product development issues. It is also imperative that the introduction of new product information can be easily accessible by each stakeholder. Common platforms and accessible information by each stakeholder will result in accelerated organizational learning and decision-making within the organization.

DTI has created a cycle time management (CTM) framework comprising both application and process support. This framework emphasizes the critical components involved in introducing and deploying the right products and services to the market at the right time. Introducing and deploying these products and services requires companies to institute well-defined new product planning and execution processes, complemented with customer management and performance measurement processes. The new planning processes should consist of product portfolio, technology portfolio, product planning, and resource planning. The execution processes must consist of advanced technology development, platform development, product development, and market introduction and deployment.

CTM enables companies to strike a balance between flexibility and discipline that is tailored to their organization and culture. The CTM framework supports a flexible *shrink-to-fit* process, which is adaptable to an organization's process maturity. This process will provide a road map for decision-making and progress tracking within a new product introduction and deployment pipeline.

CTM consists of six fundamental elements: 1) processes, 2) projects, 3) resources, 4) documents, 5) deliverables, and 6) analysis. These six elements form the foundation objectives that drive AutoPLAN Enterprise. Organizations require a well-defined and structured process to accomplish their goals. Projects make up the mechanisms through which detailed plans and schedules are generated, executed, and tracked. Every organization faces resource constraints; thus, resource management is a critical component of CTM. All projects have deliverables associated with them either in the form of documents or the product itself. And all projects must be managed to ensure quality deliverables. Analysis tools enable various levels of stakeholders to evaluate and ensure proper support of all elements necessary to meet CTM objectives.

Top three product differentiators; describe what makes your product unique.

1. AutoPLAN Enterprise enables organizations to manage their pipeline of resources across programs and across the phase gates of each project. It assures an escalation process for critical issues, such as overallocations, by monitoring boundary conditions and alerting appropriate

people to the issues. Project managers are interested in the completion of tasks or milestones, while resource managers need to know all of the work planned for their resources. Both project and resource managers must collaborate to create realistic plans for meeting project objectives, as well as to juggle those resources and plans on a day-to-day basis, as changes occur. The nature of this work requires a resource-centric view of the plan, not just an activity-centric view. A resource-centric view will allow resource managers to view and allocate activities to their scarce resources rather than allocating resources to their activities. AutoPLAN Enterprise enables resource management by providing a resource-centric Gantt bar that displays overallocated resources. Managing overallocations can be as easy as reassigning activities to another resource.

Program management is a collaborative effort. Success depends upon identifying and communicating critical issues. Such identification and communication must be inherent to the system. AutoPLAN Enterprise is designed with a communications backbone. A mechanism of triggers identifies critical issues (e.g., when milestone or cost exceeds a threshold boundary) and automatically alerts and draws attention to these critical issues. Project bulletin boards within AutoPLAN Enterprise also enhance communication by providing a context-sensitive vehicle for communicating information across the project team. In addition, AutoPLAN Enterprise supports electronic mail systems, enabling triggers and bulletin board messages to be communicated to the various levels of stakeholders.

2. AutoPLAN Enterprise supports the distributed nature of project teams by matching real-world strategy with key scalable technologies. Enterprise customers need distributed project management capabilities that cater to multisite resource management, work distribution, progress tracking, global scheduling, consolidation, reporting, integration, and collaboration. DTI has met this challenge by investing over one hundred man-years in an enterprise-level, three-tier, distributed client/server architecture that leverages both Java and Internet technologies. AutoPLAN Enterprise provides full support for multiple internal operating divisions and external suppliers. AutoPLAN Enterprise leverages many platforms—Internet, Windows, NT, and Unix—providing reliable access across the organization. Additionally, AutoPLAN Enterprise enables common project data to be shared by different projects at different locations while being maintained in a central data center that is managed by pool-server software. Project data is maintained at each geographic location on either individual or multiple servers, depending on the number of internal operating divisions and projects. A divisional pool server can also be implemented to share the project data within divisional projects. AutoPLAN Enterprise application servers are capable of scalable distributed processing, and only the server needs the capacity for large multiproject operations. AutoPLAN Enterprise has multiserver cross-project dependency links. For example, the owner of a schedule that depends on the completion of activities in another project can create cross-project links that automatically update his schedule when changes occur in the other project, even if that project resides on a different server.

3. AutoPLAN Enterprise leverages client/server/Web technologies. The promise of Java, which AutoPLAN Enterprise supports, is that enterprise deployments, including organizations with heterogeneous environments, can be cost-effectively supported. DTI Web products are easier to use than Microsoft Project and are cheaper to deploy. The rapid spread of Internet protocols and Web servers into corporate infrastructure make the Internet an ideal vehicle to support both enterprise computing and mobile employees. In addition, systems administration is simplified since no maintenance is required on the client side.

A very practical use of AutoPLAN Enterprise Web clients is that they can run in a disconnected mode on the Internet. With AutoPLAN Enterprise, the user can simply log on and save activities and other information to a local file. She can then continue to work while disconnected. At any time, the connection can be reestablished, either remotely or locally, and the data is resynchronized. This may be useful for dial-up connections when working remotely. The Web server handles all communications with the Web clients, whether they are communicating via the Internet, dial-up, LAN, or WAN. The AutoPLAN Enterprise Web clients can be run from any browser that supports Java 1.1, and the Web server will dynamically download the Java code to run the application on the client. DTI's Web strategy supports *thin* client computing. In this case, database-oriented servers are serving lightweight clients through Web servers and standard protocols. The AutoPLAN Enterprise Web clients are ideally suited for running on a Java-based network computer.

To what business processes can this tool be applied?

From business analysis and redesign to system implementation and training, DTI has established its own process to support the customer through all phases of CTM system implementation. However, as to applying AutoPLAN Enterprise to the customer's business processes, DTI takes a very pragmatic approach. DTI has established processes to help customers with the following seven business pains:

1. Managing the development and deployment pipeline in detail.

2. Top-down and bottom-up planning that enables managers to use team members' knowledge during up-front planning.

3. Juggling resources realistically, so that resources are not overcommitted and parochial allocations are not made, but rather a mechanism for cooperation on resource tradeoffs is created.

4. Creating an organizational memory that captures organizational experience for reuse the next time.

5. Obtaining weekly integrated tracking information on how programs are progressing against their plans—this can be achieved by capturing: actual time spent, estimates-to-complete, percent complete, and actual start and finish.

6. Problem identification, escalation, and collaboration that allows management and the team to receive adequate notice of impending issues.

7. Interactive decision evaluation to understand the domino effect of a problem in one project and its possible cross-program impact, and obtain a swift resolution between participants.

Any combination of these processes will help organizations better understand and make use of critical path methodology, work breakdown structures, resource management, cost and earned value techniques, multiproject resource scheduling, resource allocation, status tracking, report generation, matrix management solutions, integration with other systems, middleware design, project management process design, project rollups, report generation, database design, customized product training courses, generic project management training, and more.

Describe the ideal end-user environment for the current version of your product (size of organization, level of project management sophistication, effort and commitment required).

AutoPLAN Enterprise is ideal for high-tech, engineering, and telecommunications organizations engaged in distributed product development and deployments. Its usage also extends to these organizations' distributors and partners. The role-based nature of AutoPLAN Enterprise spans all people involved, from executive management to the entire cross-functional product team. This includes experienced project and program managers, resource and development managers, and the team members creating or deploying the product. The AutoPLAN Enterprise Web client is specifically designed for those team leaders who are not full-time, experienced project managers. In fact, DTI has designed the AutoPLAN Enterprise Web client to be easier to use and more functional than Microsoft Project.

Organizations can start at either the program level right away and manage the overall pipeline of projects and resources at the business unit level, or at the individual project level. The AutoPLAN Enterprise Web client is not only easier to use than Microsoft Project, but also capable of managing cross-functional dependencies and resources and offering enterprise scalability when the organization is ready to expand.

Coordinating distributed projects is a difficult task. It involves resources not only from multiple projects, but also from multiple functions within those projects. The program manager responsible must understand all of the interactions and milestones required to complete the project, but he cannot and should not develop and manage the entire plan himself. Instead, he should rely on the distributed functional leaders who are responsible for their pieces of the project to plan and execute those pieces. As a program manager, he needs to be able to integrate the individual team plans into a single comprehensive project plan. In many organizations, this integration of people and data is difficult; AutoPLAN Enterprise is designed to help with it. Having processes in place, underpinned by enterprise software, is key to predicting, controlling, and improving product/project cycle times.

Future strategies for this product.

AutoPLAN Enterprise has been designed with an integrated product management platform for all information related to meeting CTM objectives. DTI will continue to support features needed for CTM, including pipeline and portfolio management. Future strategies will enhance the ability of customers to make informed decisions based on a comprehensive presentation of relevant data with powerful drill-down capabilities, further collaborative features that utilize the intranet and Internet, and continuing support for the free-flowing nature of the engineering culture. Application wizards will help first-time users, accelerate deployment, and reduce training cost. Process support is key to productivity improvements and to adhering to organizationwide standards. Existing process-support capabilities will be enhanced using the capabilities of Web technology and with more exchange of information across subsystems. Large organizations are geographically distributed to take advantage of global efficiencies. Local and global workgroups must collaborate and respond quickly to changing environment and work content. Both executive management and frontline team members must have access anytime, anywhere, and in any manner to enterprisewide product/project information located on geographically distributed servers. Existing multiserver capabilities of AutoPLAN Enterprise are being enhanced using Oracle.

AutoPLAN Enterprise will support key technologies including Oracle, NT 5.0, middleware, and Java. Distributed objects capability using industry-standard specifications such as CORBA will be incorporated. In addition, the AutoPLAN Enterprise application-programming interface will provide CORBA-compliant objects for seamless integration with other applications. The collaboration capabilities of AutoPLAN Enterprise will be enhanced by incorporating a workflow server. This workflow server will be based on industry-standard specifications and will incorporate process modeling and messaging components to enable customers to configure the collaboration features based upon their business needs. The security system will have additional features to address the security risks associated with the Internet. Directory servers conforming to LDAP standards will be incorporated for seamless integration with the underlying operating environment. This in turn will provide responsive security, configurability, and flexibility features.

Product's target market.

AutoPLAN Enterprise is specifically designed to support high-tech, engineering, and telecommunications organizations in predicting, controlling, and improving cycle time of critical program development and deployment.

What are your product's three main benefits? (How does using the product add value to the customer?)

1. AutoPLAN Enterprise provides at least a 10 percent improvement in enterprise time-to-market of product development and deployment. Viewing the value of CTM from an annual R&D cost perspective: consider a product development group of one thousand people, with an annual R&D expenditure of $100M. A modest 10 percent improvement would represent a cost savings value of $10M, with a revenue enhancement value of three to five times this.

2. AutoPLAN Enterprise facilitates an organization's transformation from functional project teams to matrix, or program-organized high-performance project teams. It also supports distributed teams resulting from acquisitions. It does both of these by providing built-in communication and rollup features from distributed multiserver projects. This support enables teamwide problem identification, escalation, collaboration, and resolution. AutoPLAN Enterprise recognizes that three different organizational patterns coexist: 1) dynamic peer-to-peer, 2) functional, and 3) program management. AutoPLAN Enterprise offers these organizations both project-centric and resource-centric management.

3. AutoPLAN Enterprise accommodates joint ventures, subcontracting, mergers and acquisitions, and reorganizations by leveraging the Web to minimize deployment and support costs. The creation of plans, assignment of work, and integration of activities across multiple functions and distributed work teams is critically important. However, that is only part of the story. With the Internet, AutoPLAN Enterprise can also efficiently equip thousands of personnel involved in the product development process with the information they need to do the best possible job. Demand

for skilled workers has been great, and turnover has risen as employees move from one company or job to another. The best practices in the world are of no value to a company if those who know those practices move on without first passing along the knowledge. Best practices developed at one site need to be shared with other sites, and a process for doing that is required. AutoPLAN Enterprise solves these problems through URL references and retrieval capability. With URL features, AutoPLAN Enterprise can help preserve best practices and other information and disseminate them geographically and functionally to team members currently doing the job. AutoPLAN Enterprise can also have associated URL references that point to mission-critical information/documentation that will enable product/project teams to achieve the activity. These references can also be attached to the top-level program schedule for project leader use or at specific functional schedules (e.g., to provide sourcing with specific third-party vendor requirements). URLs can enable:

- Sharing best practice information from one team to another
- Referencing documentation with checklists
- Sharing of engineering notes on installation processes.

Also, with the speed of organizational changes, a mix of project scheduling system usage is expected. As most people are educated on Microsoft Project, AutoPLAN Enterprise can coexist with its projects and data. AutoPLAN Enterprise's graphical user interfaces (GUIs) are not only familiar to Microsoft Project users, the Web version is easier and thus leverages simplicity and ease of use with enterprise functionality.

Describe your quality management process. List any relevant certifications.

DTI achieves excellence in product quality and customer satisfaction through its quality management process. DTI's quality objective is to build quality into its products and services at all stages of product life cycle, from requirement collection to customer usage. DTI's dedication to quality is reflected in its quality mission: "Doing things right the first time."

DTI's quality management group performs the functions of the software engineering process group, as defined by the industry-standard capability maturity model (CMM). The quality management group plans and implements DTI's quality system, which consists of processes and guidelines. The processes detail *what* is required for converting a set of inputs to outputs in the form of activities and tasks, primary and cooperative responsibilities, deliverables, and entry and exit criteria. The guidelines detail *how* to carry out the identified activities to ensure quality and consistency. The involvement of DTI personnel at all levels is fundamental to the implementation of the quality process. DTI personnel are drawn from various groups in the organization to author processes and guidelines, and all undergo training programs on the quality system.

DTI follows processes within Level 2 and Level 3 of the CMM. Some of the key processes within these levels include market requirement analysis, functional specification, high- and low-level design, coding, testing, release management, customer support, training, and maintenance. In addition, in-depth reviews are built into each of these processes.

DTI recognizes that enterprise growth and profitability are significantly impacted by time-to-market of new products in globally competitive high-tech markets. With this in mind, DTI's product development and quality processes are focused on meeting customers' needs and requirements. Therefore, DTI collaborates with its customers both in product definition and in assuring that the product functions are implemented as intended. To facilitate the fast-track delivery of innovative products and services, DTI has created process initiatives for increased test automation, usage of tools that will enable teams to better assess the quality of their work products, management of development tools, reuse of objects across products, and tightly controlled configuration management.

DTI's quality management process focuses on periodic reviews and feedback, offering means of monitoring the adherence of organizational activities to the process. Corrective and preventive actions play an important role in continuous improvement of the quality system and thereby the organizational activities.

DTI has a well-qualified team for quality management. DTI's teams, besides having the appropriate educational qualifications, have quality management-related certifications; some are certified quality analysts, and some hold certificates related to the CMM and its use. Many also have extensive internal audit experience.

The quality management group interacts periodically with key personnel of different functions within the organization and identifies new processes, guidelines, and improvements within the existing framework. The general approach to new process/guideline introduction is to discuss with representative users, define the process, pilot the process after review, evaluate the pilot implementation, revise the process based on feedback, plan organizationwide implementation, implement, measure, and maintain.

DTI is planning to get CMM certification at the appropriate level. The approach that would be followed for securing the certification includes mapping key process areas of the CMM to existing processes, identifying the *gaps*, preparing the implementation plan that describes how these gaps will be addressed, and executing the plan.

Discuss your product pricing structure. Include volume discount levels, concurrent user options, site licenses, cost of implementation, and other issues.

DTI's objective is to offer an integrated solution with a pricing structure that is based on enterprise requirements reflecting enterprise needs and individual needs. AutoPLAN Enterprise supports a floating license configuration, which allows any user to log into the system and consume one license. When the user has finished with the application, that license will be released for other users. Each floating license provides one concurrent use of the product. AutoPLAN Enterprise also supports a personal license configuration. Typical installations will use both personal and concurrent licensing.

Annual product maintenance is 15 percent of the list cost. Product maintenance entitles customers to engineering patches, updates and upgrades, and phone, fax, and E-mail response to issues. Professional services are separate from DTI product maintenance. As part of the business relationship with customers, DTI takes part in joint planning to identify the customer's business needs and services sought from DTI. Professional services are charged separately on an as-needed basis. These services are performed either at the customer site, online, or at DTI's headquarters in Cupertino, California. Professional services typically fall into two categories: 1) product consulting/implementation design review and 2) implementation support. Product consulting/implementation design review discusses areas such as, "How do I apply the software with a suitable process to solve a business need" and, "Which processes will we implement, how, and when to meet organizational objectives?" Implementation support consists of product training, project office services, upgrade migration services, systems administration services, and integration services.

Cascade PgM (Mantix)

Describe what the product is designed to do.

Cascade PgM from Mantix is a client/server program management product for use with Microsoft Project; aimed specifically at the facilities required by senior management and program managers. With a standard MS Windows user interface, it presents a multiuser, enterprisewide cost, schedule, and resource management system with powerful management-reporting facilities. Cascade PgM uses the proven, structured data model of work, responsibility, and cost breakdown to provide a complete view of the business. The benefits to the business associated with each project can also be modeled.

Cascade is integrated on existing user sites with Oracle Financials, SAP, Peoplesoft, Glovia, Baan Triton, and many other systems. This integration with the enterprise resource planning (ERP) systems provides the whole picture of all the activities in the business: where the cost is going, what the people are doing, and what results will be delivered, by when.

The combination of Cascade PgM and Microsoft Project provides a powerful corporate project-planning system. Cascade PgM provides the top-down information used to provide guidelines for managers working at a more detailed level. Working within these guidelines, users can go on to develop detailed schedules and cost and resource plans. Cascade PgM supports the concept of resource ownership and the delegation of resources down through the project, with complete visibility and tracking of where they are being used. In many cases, this includes use of the Web-based Cascade time recording functionality.

Top three product differentiators; describe what makes your product unique.

Cascade PgM is unique in its functionality for business control of the project-orientated organization through top-down delegation of targets and bottom-up measurement of performance. It offers a clear functional advantage in terms of:

1. Turns decisions into action, by enabling the creation of outline plans with budget, staff, and time scales to be delegated for detailed planning.

2. The structured data model is built interactively as graphical tree structures, rather than with the conventional alphanumeric coding, making the operation intuitive and changes to the plan simple and quick.

3. The program manager establishes the overall structure of the program, typically based on business drivers or internal/customer reporting. Links to the program from projects may be easily created or deleted allowing fast *what-if* analysis.

To what business processes can this tool be applied?

For lean organizations in fast-moving markets, good management is increasingly about setting goals and assembling the team to deliver them. Cascade PgM provides the tool to define a portfolio of projects to deliver strategic goals and then monitor the performance against these objectives. Cascade PgM backs up the implementation of effective management processes with the timely, consistent, and accurate provision of program and project information.

Describe the ideal end-user environment for the current version of your product (size of organization, level of project management sophistication, effort and commitment required).

The concepts behind Cascade PgM and the software architecture are completely scaleable. An organization of any size with a multiproject environment would benefit from Cascade PgM, irrespective of the level of project management sophistication.

The effort and commitment required to implement Cascade PgM depends on the customer's requirements for the system and the existing business processes. Typically, Cascade PgM is quick to implement, due in part to its use of MS Project, which is already present in most organizations. MS Project is transformed to become a key element of a business control system.

Future strategies for this product.

Mantix Systems will continue to develop Cascade PgM to ensure it remains a world-leading program management solution.

Product's target market.

As a leading program management solutions provider, Mantix Systems has a proven track record with some of the world's leading organizations in fifteen countries. This is in markets that include telecommunications, IT, utilities, government, pharmaceuticals, aerospace, and defense.

What are your product's three main benefits? (How does using the product add value to the customer?)

Cascade PgM brings structure, visibility, and control to the management of both individual projects and multiproject programs. This allows a customer to focus investment and staff time on the business activities that will add most value, and manage them to deliver increased revenue, profit and return on investment.

Describe your quality management process. List any relevant certifications.

The quality management process within Mantix Systems is accredited by, and conforms to ISO 9000.

Discuss your product pricing structure. Include volume discount levels, concurrent user options, site licenses, cost of implementation, and other issues.

The price of Cascade PgM depends on the type of functionality required and the number of users. Please contact Mantix Systems for details that are specific to your requirements.

Changepoint (Changepoint Corporation)

Describe what the product is designed to do.

Changepoint is the world's only supplier of integrated enterprise management for IT organizations. Changepoint solutions allow IT consulting firms, IT departments, and software companies to refine and control the business of delivering services to clients.

Top three product differentiators; describe what makes your product unique.

1. Business management capabilities with billing modules and ties to accounting systems.
2. Tools with which to manage the IT enterprise with integration to strategic plans, project management tools, and metrics capture.
3. Increased flexibility for resources with Web-based time and status tracking, and the 3Com PalmPilot.

To what business processes can this tool be applied?

Revenue and cost management, resource management, project and workflow management.

Describe the ideal end-user environment for the current version of your product (size of organization, level of project management sophistication, effort and commitment required).

Current end-user environment is one of the following:
1. An IT consulting organization that needs to collect its time, status, and expenses to properly manage its projects, bill its time, and manage its clients. Size, one hundred plus employees, with moderate project management experience.
2. Internal IT department: Department of twenty-five plus; this tool is powerful for IT managers and CIOs to manage their resources, projects, and IT costs. This includes cross-charging capabilities, IT initiative tracking, and help desk support.
3. Independent software vendors (ISV): Tracking development projects, time spent, and billing customers are all key aspects of the ISV user environment. A company of one hundred plus employees would find this tool to be an excellent business management tool.

Future strategies for this product.

Future strategies include extension to the SQL backend, integration with sales force automation tools and corporate methodologies.

Product's target market.

IT consulting firms and system integrators; independent software vendors; IT departments.

What are your product's three main benefits? (How does using the product add value to the customer?)

1. Revenue and cost management: track all billable costs and charge to appropriate customers.
2. Strategic management: Tie projects to high-level strategic plans for tracking initiatives within the company.
3. Project management: Integration to industry-standard planning tools with support for distributed teams.

Describe your quality management process. List any relevant certifications.

Changepoint has an extensive quality assurance department that tests all software before release. White papers on our testing environment are available.

Discuss your product pricing structure. Include volume discount levels, concurrent user options, site licenses, cost of implementation, and other issues.

Our tool is priced per seat (guideline is $1,000/seat). There is not a concurrent license structure. Implementation is quoted on an individual basis depending on needs of organization. Site licenses are quoted after one thousand seats.

Annual maintenance is 15 percent of full software price. Implementation ranges from $1,000–$1,500 per day, depending on needs of client. Please contact Changepoint for further details.

DecisionTools Suite (Palisade Corporation)

Describe what the product is designed to do.

Integrated suite of risk and decision analysis programs, working in Excel.
Includes @RISK, BestFit, PrecisionTree, RISKview, and TopRank.

Top three product differentiators; describe what makes your product unique.

1. Products are designed to work together.
2. They provide rigorous analysis unavailable in any other product.
3. There is a common interface among components.

To what business processes can this tool be applied?

Any.

Describe the ideal end-user environment for the current version of your product (size of organization, level of project management sophistication, effort and commitment required).

Any size; users need to be familiar with Excel and have a knowledge of risk and decision analysis. It can take weeks to become fully familiar with features if users have no previous experience.

Future strategies for this product.

Addition of features, tighter integration, faster performance.

Product's target market.

Decision-makers; spreadsheet analysts.

What are your product's three main benefits? (How does using the product add value to the customer?)

1. Make better decisions and account for risks in your projects.
2. Identify high-risk areas.
3. Save money on ventures.

Describe your quality management process. List any relevant certifications.

Extensive in-house testing and closed beta testing.

Discuss your product pricing structure. Include volume discount levels, concurrent user options, site licenses, cost of implementation, and other issues.

DecisionTools Suite: $995.

DecisionTools Professional Suite: $1,295.
Volume and site licensing available.
Free, unlimited tech support.
Maintenance contracts available.

Dekker TRAKKER Activity Based Cost Management and Performance System (DTMI)

Describe what the product is designed to do.

Activity-based costing (ABC) enables business environments to fully implement project accounting techniques to track project cost and revenue. ABC provides a disciplined approach to planning and seamlessly integrates contemporary project control to the finance system. TRAKKER combines the Dekker trademark of cost, schedule, and earned value integration with a sophisticated cost rate management system and accounting interface. Burden rates on direct costs can be implemented regardless of the detail required. By providing professional project managers with a tool that electronically interfaces actuals and revenue to the project management system, the accounting interface manages the most labor-intensive aspect of project costing.

Top three product differentiators; describe what makes your product unique.

1. Complete integration of cost, schedule, technical, and risk data within a cohesive user interface.
2. Accounting interface capable of generically integrating with both COTS and enterprise-developed accounting systems.
3. Scalable solution—TRAKKER is scalable from a single-user implementation to a complete three-tier client-server architecture incorporating MS SQL, Oracle, or Informix as the warehouse for the enterprise data.

To what business processes can this tool be applied?

The system can be applied to ABC, estimating, proposal development, project execution, project change control, EV reporting, revenue tracking, resource capacity planning, account reconciliation, material management (tracks commitments). Basis of estimate development, ETC/IEAC development, risk management, and enterprise support for each of the preceding categories.

Describe the ideal end-user environment for the current version of your product (size of organization, level of project management sophistication, effort and commitment required).

One of the key attributes of the TRAKKER system is scalability. TRAKKER has been designed to integrate into your business environment by establishing an organization's business rules within the system. This architecture enables TRAKKER to fit the needs and sophistication of any implementation. This flexibility enables TRAKKER to support a variety of implementation approaches. TRAKKER installations typically provide access to a range of users including cost account managers, cost/schedule analysts, and financial managers to meet the unique requirements of each for information and output.

Typical TRAKKER clients range from companies of one thousand employees to Fortune 500 corporations.

Future strategies for this product.

Dekker, Ltd. will continue to enhance the integration of TRAKKER with MS Office and MS Back Office suite of tools. The design of the TRAKKER architecture will continue to focus on making data more visual and accessible to the complete range of system users.

Product's target market.

R&D, government, software, medical, electronics, and aerospace.

What are your product's three main benefits? (How does using the product add value to the customer?)

1. Fully integrates cost/schedule, earned value, technical performance, and risk management to accounting. TRAKKER's integration eliminates the effort involved in reconciling differences between cost and schedule, plus eliminates errors associated with import/export, and provides the user more time to analyze the effects of change rather than managing the database.

2. User friendly—as a Windows application, TRAKKER makes interacting with the data simple and visual.

3. TRAKKER integrates with MS Office and MS Back Office Product Suite to simplify the dissemination and publishing of information.

Describe your quality management process. List any relevant certifications.

DTMI has modeled our development process from the Microsoft model while incorporating the quality guidelines established in ISO 9000.

Discuss your product pricing structure. Include volume discount levels, concurrent user options, site licenses, cost of implementation, and other issues.

DTMI offers both single and concurrent user licenses of TRAKKER. Our flexible pricing enables both small and large organizations to cost effectively implement ABC/ABM. TRAKKER pricing includes a progressive discount for volume purchases with reasonable thresholds for single- and multisite licenses. Further, DTMI offers both public and private training courses for both new and advanced users. DTMI also offers consulting services to support the enterprise implementation of TRAKKER.

DTMI provides training for the application of both ABC/AMB and TRAKKER. These workshops include Basic Project Management, TRAKKER Application Workshop, TRAKKER Intermediate Workshop, TRAKKER Report Writer Workshop, and TRAKKER MIS Integrator's Workshop. Through these courses, an enterprise can completely implement the TRAKKER system. In addition to our classroom training, DTMI offers consulting services to guide users though a structured approach to implementing TRAKKER.

Enterprise Contoller

Describe what the product is designed to do.

The Enterprise Controller suite of modules can operate stand-alone or, for maximum benefits can combine to form an Integrated Work Management System. The solution incorporates standard technologies such as Oracle, Windows NT or Unix, Windows Graphical Us.

Top three product differentiators; describe what makes your product unique.

1. The integration of project tasks with commercial processes.

2. Hierarchical project structures to provide visibility of information at all levels from the boardroom to work foreman.

3. Excellent product support including proactive User Group and Web-based customer online discussion forum.

To what business processes can this tool be applied?

Corporate planning and budgeting; project planning, resourcing, scheduling and costing; purchasing; billing; time writing; maintenance planning.

Describe the ideal end-user environment for the current version of your product (size of organization, level of project management sophistication, effort and commitment required).

Medium to large project based organizations looking to control their business and projects by integrating this process with existing applications and processes. The breadth of scope and nature of the implementation is such that a degree of change management is usually required.

Future strategies for this product.

Next release to include additional report generation facilities, easier E-mail facility for reports, additional Web functionality and an integrated Risk Management module. Currently evaluating Microsoft's Sequel Server as a database option.

Product's target market.

Oil & Gas, Defense, Rail Transport, Civil Engineering, Utilities and Ship Building.

What are your product's three main benefits? (How does using the product add value to the customer?)

1. Integration of project tasks to other business processes.
2. Hierarchical view of projects as they progress.
3. Excellent graphical and text reporting.

Describe your quality management process. List any relevant certifications.

We have internal auditable quality procedures in place which are equivalent to ISO 9000 standards. Accredited Investors in People.

Discuss your product pricing structure. Include volume discount levels, concurrent user options, site licenses, cost of implementation, and other issues.

System is priced per number of concurrent users for each module. Discounts are available for volume and multisite implementations. Full pricing is available on application.

Annual maintenance is 15 percent of license costs. Cost of professional services available on request.

Enterprise Project (jeTECH DATA SYSTEMS, INC.)

Describe what the product is designed to do.

Enterprise Project is a powerful new client/server software application that offers project-based organizations a simple way to define and staff projects, and record project labor and expenses throughout their enterprises. Essentially a suite of robust, user-friendly applications integrated into a single desktop, this comprehensive project management system enables team members to accurately plan and track labor resources across all projects. Perfect either as a *stand-alone* solution or as the ideal complement to the jeTECH labor-management system—Enterprise Labor—it is particularly well suited for multiuser, enterprisewide installations. Together, Enterprise Labor and Enterprise Project are the only systems currently on the market with extensive capabilities and integrated products for both the salaried professional (engineers and computer programmers, for instance) and the hourly employee (from factory workers to registered nurses).

Users access all functions via a single desktop with a Microsoft Office 98 *look and feel*. The system integrates completely with Enterprise Labor and Microsoft Project, as well as most popular accounting and human resource (HR) systems. In today's competitive environment, effective and efficient use of labor resources is key to completing mission-critical projects on time, on budget. Enterprise Project gives project leaders a comprehensive, potent tool with which to manage scarce technical resources.

With Enterprise Project, managers can budget and schedule projects based on staff skills and availability. Project team members can manage their own tasks, report actual labor and travel expenses, and provide status reports on these tasks. The system calculates actual project costs by automatically incorporating labor costs, material costs, and travel expenses.

Project managers can define and manage both contract and noncontract-based projects, and control work authorizations that will keep each project under control and on budget. As a project manager, you simply create activities for your projects, assign appropriate resources to these activities and define how labor will be charged to a contract. And by allowing employees to only charge preassigned tasks, Enterprise Project prevents performance of unauthorized work.

Enterprise Project enables all users to report labor charges right from their PC or workstation. Project managers need no longer compile project team information manually. Users can now report project time as well as other time, and the system automatically processes and transmits it to an interfaced time-and-attendance system for payroll use.

Enterprise Project includes a contract maintenance module. Companies with hourly employees contracted with outside firms—for instance, security guards or programmers—would benefit from using this module without the rest of the project management system. This module is primarily designed, however, to accommodate projects being managed for clients. This module allows contract managers to define contract information including budgets and rates per hour, as well as all products and services purchased by the customer. They can then use this information to evaluate projects based on user-defined deliverables. Contract maintenance is by no means static. So jeTECH has designed Enterprise Project to handle change orders, R&D projects, and discounts. A variety of unique reporting features enables contract managers to view cost overruns, variances, and milestone completions.

Top three product differentiators; describe what makes your product unique.

1. Resource scheduling from a common resource pool in a multiproject environment.
2. Integrated time collection and status reporting.
3. Sensitivity analysis (what-if scenarios).

To what business processes can this tool be applied?

Project planning/management, enterprise resource scheduling/management, time collection, performance measurement, time and expense reporting, budgeting and estimating, and project accounting.

Describe the ideal end-user environment for the current version of your product (size of organization, level of project management sophistication, effort and commitment required).

Any resource-constrained enterprise (IT, high-tech R&D, engineering) with multiple projects and multiple sites. Requires a low level of project management sophistication.

Future strategies for this product.

Maintenance and repair operations, incorporation of process ware/templates, enterprise-level project and resource integration, and full Internet capabilities.

Product's target market.

Companies with *task-oriented* professionals such as engineers, architects, IS professionals, researchers, advertising/marketing professionals, etc. See also the previous response to "ideal end-user environment."

What are your product's three main benefits? (How does using the product add value to the customer?)

1. Improved resource utilization and efficiencies.
2. Reduction in time to complete projects.
3. Cost control.

Describe your quality management process. List any relevant certifications.

Our current quality management process includes in-house testing, which incorporates both automated and manual processes and procedures.

Discuss your product pricing structure. Include volume discount levels, concurrent user options, site licenses, cost of implementation, and other issues.

Pricing is structured on a named-user basis. Pricing will also be dependent on a number of variables including the size of the enterprise, number of project managers, number of facilities, etc. Consequently, pricing is provided to each customer when we have been able to familiarize ourselves on their operations and their anticipated use of the system.

Several options are available for training, tech support, annual maintenance, etc. Costs are provided to each customer when they have been able to select the options deemed best for their operations.

ER Project 1000 (Eagle Ray Software Systems)

Describe what the product is designed to do.

The ER Project 1000 is an integrated suite of project management tools, which provide an enterprisewide project management solution. ER Project 1000 includes schedule/time management, centralized resource management, methodology/process management, project-workgroup communications, timesheets, risk/issue management, and enterprisewide cross-project tracking. Based on a client/server architecture with a centralized relational database, the ER Project 1000 provides networked access, multiproject capability, and true multiuser concurrency. It scales easily from handling small workgroup projects to large programs at the enterprise level.

Top three product differentiators; describe what makes your product unique.

1. Addresses the total project management life-cycle solution for the enterprise: Unlike most project management tools, the ER Project 1000 provides a completely integrated and centralized project management platform to support the entire life cycle of project management. Based on a client/server relational database (Oracle/SQL Server) architecture, ER Project 1000 fully supports today's multiproject/multiuser project environment. The product suite integrates full methodology/process management capabilities, project workgroup communications, and enterprisewide project tracking capabilities.

2. Provides a completely integrated suite of project management tools: The ER Project 1000 tool suite integrates industrial-strength project management functions with rich process improvement functionality and proactive management features. ER Project 1000 provides all the necessary industrial-strength core project management functions. Key features include support for WBS/OBS/RBS structures, cost, schedule, earned value analysis, built-in report writer, timesheet approvals, and centralized resource management. ER Project 1000 takes advantage of the Web by providing Java timesheets and extensive project website publishing capability. Best practices/process improvement is easily accomplished with the Methodology Manager and support for organizational standards, work products, and estimation. ER Project 1000 delivers an impressive array of proactive management features. These features include risk management, issue management, management by threshold, and full project tracking.

3. Is easy to use and implement: ER Project 1000 was designed with a simple, intuitive interface. Extensive wizards assist users for complex operations. ER Project 1000 can easily be configured to your organization by using our centralized administration functions and component architecture.

To what business processes can this tool be applied?

ER Project 1000 is a wrap-around solution for organizations that need to implement mature project management practices, proactively manage their projects, improve business processes, implement standards and documentation, and communicate at multiple levels. Eagle Ray's advanced suite of tools provides project managers with an integrated platform for project planning, time tracking, resource management, and executive oversight. With features such as risk management, issue tracking, and management by threshold, the ER Project 1000 gives project managers the ability to proactively manage complex projects and stay focused on the key issues.

Organizations that engage in process improvement/best practices will find that the ER Project 1000 Methodology Manager is the ideal platform for developing and delivering best practices to each new project plan. Project managers will be able to easily document and reuse lessons learned in new projects. Project team members and stakeholders will find that the integrated communications features of the ER Project 1000 suite facilitate a real-time dialogue between all members and ensure that no issues slip though the cracks.

Describe the ideal end-user environment for the current version of your product (size of organization, level of project management sophistication, effort and commitment required).

Size of organization: The ER Project 1000 product suite is ideal for managing projects with team sizes of ten to one thousand people per project in organizations where multiple projects are being performed at the same time. Project teams may be centralized or dispersed using client/server and Web-based communications technologies.

Level of sophistication: The tool suite is best suited for organizations that are moving beyond basic project management to a medium level of project management maturity or higher. These organizations are typically implementing tracking, costing, project management standards, risk/issue management, time tracking, centralized resource management, and possibly earned value. ER Project 1000 also supports organizations implementing a project office, best practices, process improvement, and reusable project templates. These features make ER Project 1000 an ideal platform for organizations implementing CMM level two or higher maturity levels.

Effort and commitment required: Successful implementation of the ER Project 1000 tool suite centers on an organization's commitment to realizing repeatable project management results from enterprisewide standardization of business processes and practices. Because of its integrated design and simple interface, ER Project 1000 delivers numerous advantages over standard project management tool sets with less staff effort.

Future strategies for this product.

Eagle Ray's future strategies include building new modules, expanding current modules, interfacing with corporate business systems, and preparing the product suite for the global marketplace. Major planned enhancements include significant modifications to the estimation module, costing module, methodology/process management module, and the Internet/intranet/Web capabilities. In addition, we will be constructing a problem/defect-tracking module.

We will be expanding the interfaces that integrate the ER Project 1000 system with additional enterprise business systems. Such systems include costing/accounting systems, HR systems, and additional commercial products. We also plan to complete our internationalization/localization efforts to prepare the ER Project 1000 for global distribution.

Product's target market.

ER Project 1000 is suitable for commercial and government organizations, which are managing projects that range from small workgroup-level projects to projects that span the entire enterprise. Essentially, the tool suite will support any project environment where the project team has access to or is working with computers.

What are your product's three main benefits? (How does using the product add value to the customer?)

1. Total integrated project management solution: The ER Project 1000 is an integrated, total project management solution providing complete support for the entire project management life cycle. The integrated tool suite does not require multiple add-on tools from different vendors,

resulting in fewer hidden costs and less frustration. Project managers will find it easy to manage projects with a higher level of maturity by using the various features of the too—for example, risk management, issue tracking, management by threshold, and multiproject capabilities.

2. Best practices/process improvement platform: The ER Project 1000 integrated process/methodology management platform provides a sophisticated, yet easy-to-use platform for implementing best practices, estimation metrics, organizational standards, documentation templates, and process improvement. Organizations can capture, integrate, and reuse their project knowledge and project plan templates from an enterprisewide integrated platform.

3. Enterprisewide tracking and communications: The ER Project 1000 facilitates communications between all project stakeholders. Program managers and executives can perform cross-project rollups, dynamic drill-down, and cost, schedule, and earned-value analysis for up-to-date information on all enterprise projects. The project team members can access all project information on the project website, and receive activity assignments and report status using Java timesheets. Automatic issue notification alerts project managers about possible deviations in cost and schedule. The built-in report writer lets you extract and summarize any data in the enterprisewide project database using customized formats.

Describe your quality management process. List any relevant certifications.

The Eagle Ray Quality Assurance Program is a comprehensive system that employs a series of product walkthroughs, builds, quality gates, configuration management, defect tracking, and comprehensive testing. The development staff members are constantly conducting requirements, design, and code walkthroughs in coordination with weekly product builds and passing mandatory quality gates. The Quality Assurance Program is integrated with our beta-testing program to ensure that all product releases undergo rigorous real-world testing prior to release.

Comprehensive testing scenarios include unit testing, integration testing, platform testing, stress testing, concurrency testing, environment testing, security testing, usability testing, vertical testing, upgrade testing, business scenario testing, and independent qualification testing.

During the design and construction of the ER Project 1000 product, Eagle Ray brought in several project management industry experts to assist in the design of the software functionality and usability. This process will be continued to ensure that our future enhancements meet the real-world needs of project management organizations. Additionally, Eagle Ray continues to invest heavily in the training of team members in technical and project management areas.

Discuss your product pricing structure. Include volume discount levels, concurrent user options, site licenses, cost of implementation, and other issues.

Call for latest prices.

Global Project Management System (2S Smart Solutions GmbH)

Describe what the product is designed to do.

The Global Project Management System (GPMS) is designed for efficient planning and control function and will organize the management of projects.

This productive, extremely flexible, and fast easy-to-use system is the right tool to cover the requirements of a central project management system regarding document management, groupware aspects, database management, messaging, workflow, and project planning tools.

GPMS offers a high degree of multifunctional features, which will optimize the interactions of several project teams regarding communication and cooperation. All relevant information and documents concerning the project will be provided by the GPMS to the access of authorized team members. GPMS offers all major advantages of modern document management, workflow management, and groupware systems in the intranet and Internet.

GPMS will increase your profitability, due to more efficient project work and communication. It will increase the experience of the project members (internal and external) and allow them to concentrate their efforts on core competence business.

All the relevant results could be easily identified by functions like index search, complete text search, etc.

GPMS is not only the right software for successful project management and communication; it also enables the controlling department to access and overview received services and invoices regarding relevant projects. The team leader is able to check out with the GPMS the qualifications and special skills of each team member for the selection of required team members.

The special concept of access control provides information and documents only to entitled persons and groups dedicated to work with them (e.g., contract documents can be only read, changed, and deleted by top management). External project members and customers could have a special secure access to their project information, for example via the Internet, which permits them to have an active impact on the path forward of the project.

The feature *office automation* will give great support in easily doing the day-to-day correspondence. This includes the automatic assumption of contact names or address files for the automatic transfer into faxes, letters, or any other communication forms.

The feature *contact manager* will organize all project-relevant business contacts when no established scheduling system exists. All required time-related information, milestones, appointments, or events could be scheduled and double-checked.

The *time management* feature will give an overview or update documentation regarding the project history at any time. The *trigger* function handles all required reminders about milestones, contract expiration date, birthdays, etc.

GPMS will provide an outstanding complete collection of project-relevant data without any additional special effort or separate input of the project members. It will file and handle information into a dedicated company *intelligent brain-form*. This complex *knowledge management system* will create a great advantage that helps to process projects in a faster and more effective way and to generate more business in the market.

Top three product differentiators; describe what makes your product unique.

1. Project management and communication system for global integration of project members using functionality of standard database, document management, groupware, messaging, workflow, and project planning tools.
2. Knowledge management system for reuse of project results.
3. Productive, extremely flexible, easy-to-use system.

To what business processes can this tool be applied?

Top management, controlling, marketing, sales, human resources, and any other business units.

Describe the ideal end-user environment for the current version of your product (size of organization, level of project management sophistication, effort and commitment required).

The company should use Microsoft client and server software. Groups and organizational units from five to one thousand members, as GPMS can *only* be the document management system for the project team. For example, the project plan can be used as *only a document* (as it often is today). On the other hand, GPMS is the knowledge management system that provides *all* information about project-related topics.

Future strategies for this product.

Complete integration of all project-related data in the MS SQL server database, especially all data created by Microsoft Project 98.

Product's target market.

Consulting companies and any kinds of companies that do project-related business (internal and external).

What are your product's three main benefits? (How does using the product add value to the customer?)

1. Opportunity for highly efficient and structural project work and communication.
2. Access to a company-dedicated knowledge management system with no extra input requirements (knowledge/results are created throughout the daily working process).
3. Offering wide support in easily doing the day-to-day work.

Describe your quality management process. List any relevant certifications.

ISO 9001 ff/Microsoft Solution Provider certification/Fabasoft Partner certification.

Discuss your product pricing structure. Include volume discount levels, concurrent user options, site licenses, cost of implementation, and other issues.

GPMS is based on the Fabasoft Components. The Components Base and CIS are needed to run GPMS. Base and CIS have a retail price of DM 900 per used computer. No additional costs for servers.

GPMS is shipped at a price of DM 300, conforming to the Fabasoft Components license scheme.

The cost of implementation varies depending on the size of the installation and the company size. GPMS can be used *out of the box* with an implementation effort of about three days for user and template management.

One-day training suits most of the users because of the generic integration of standard office and project management products. Administrators should be trained three to five days.

Maintenance for an average installation is about two days per month (depending on the amount of new users and new projects).

GroupProject

Describe what the product is designed to do.

GroupProject is the enterprisewide program management solution that harnesses the power of Lotus Notes and Microsoft Project or CA SuperProject. GroupProject enables better project definition, control, information sharing, management of project documentation.

Top three product differentiators; describe what makes your product unique.

1. Complete application for all aspects of program management.
2. Full support of workflow management.
3. Allows true EIS reporting using traffic lighting and key performance indicators.

To what business processes can this tool be applied?

No answer given.

Describe the ideal end-user environment for the current version of your product (size of organization, level of project management sophistication, effort and commitment required).

GroupProject is applicable to all companies of any size and level of sophistication. The product can be run out of the box with little effort required, or customized to suit a company's individual requirements.

Future strategies for this product.

No answer given.

Product's target market.

Any company determined to improve its project management performance.

What are your product's three main benefits? (How does using the product add value to the customer?)

1. Full program management control.
2. Automated distribution of work and collection of progress.
3. Full support of distributed work environment.

Describe your quality management process. List any relevant certifications.

GroupProject passes through a rigorous quality assurance program with full alpha and beta testing.

Discuss your product pricing structure. Include volume discount levels, concurrent user options, site licenses, cost of implementation, and other issues.

Pricing is dependent upon the numbers of users of each of the product's modules; full product pricing can be supplied on request. For implementation costs, please contact vendor.

How's it going?

Describe what the product is designed to do.

The product is designed to help project managers and project office staff document, track, and control one or more projects, manage issues and budgets, conduct project review meetings, and report status. It organizes information about multiple projects and makes it available to executives and authorized users in easy-to-understand online or report format. Its project archive and retrieval capabilities organize and store information about past projects and make it readily available when planning new ones. Its project office capabilities support the implementation of project standards, common terminology, and multiple ways to group and report on projects and programs.

Top three product differentiators; describe what makes your product unique.

1. It is simple to learn, use, and understand; executives can get the status information they need quickly. Many other project management systems are complex, require significant training, and would not be used by executives.
2. It has multiproject management and control features that will appeal to project office staff, as well as project managers and executives. Many *project office* systems would be viewed as *overhead* or extra work by project managers.
3. It has excellent, easy-to-use issue management and status-reporting capabilities. Many systems are primarily scheduling tools, which do not have comprehensive issue and status reporting capabilities.

To what business processes can this tool be applied?

Any business processes that need to be documented, monitored, and controlled.

Describe the ideal end-user environment for the current version of your product (size of organization, level of project management sophistication, effort and commitment required).

This product is geared primarily for small to medium-sized organizations, or individual users, although it will work in departments of large organizations. It is has a built-in project manager's guide and excellent help for unsophisticated users. Due to its low cost and quick setup, it requires minimal commitment of dollars or time. If used by project office, some thought should be given to how projects are to be grouped for rollup reporting. Customization and consulting help are available at low cost to make the product fit in and interface with existing practices.

Future strategies for this product.

Future releases will contain new features as requested by users, or as the market appears to warrant.

We are investigating use of other database products in addition to MSAccess97.

Product's target market.

Project office departments in small, medium, or large companies; project managers; and company executives who want a quick way to keep on top of project progress.

What are your product's three main benefits? (How does using the product add value to the customer?)

1. It saves time for project managers, project office staff, and executives by making status of one or more projects easy to document and readily available to authorized users.

2. It saves money with its low purchase cost, minimal training, and support requirements.

3. It will help customers make their projects more successful by giving them the information they need to find out about issues and take corrective action.

Describe your quality management process. List any relevant certifications.

The product is now in first release after final beta test. Quality management processes are currently being documented. Future releases will be subjected to rigorous testing procedures as per quality standards.

Discuss your product pricing structure. Include volume discount levels, concurrent user options, site licenses, cost of implementation, and other issues.

Individual version intended for use by a single person, includes up to one-half hour of free telephone support—$120. Requires Microsoft Access97. Run-time version for individual users without MSAccess97: $150.

Corporate version for use on a shared network, up to fifty workstations within a single site, and up to one-hour telephone support—$495. Requires MSAccess97. Run-time version without MSAccess97: $390.

$90 for each additional fifty workstations.

Implementation cost is internal to user. Technical support above initial free support time and enhancements available, if required, at a negotiated hourly rate. No annual maintenance fee required. Solutions to severe errors in noncustomized code (if any) will be E-mailed or provided at website.

Innate Multi-Project & Timesheets (Innate)

Describe what the product is designed to do.

Extends the use of Microsoft Project into organizationwide program management. Provides managers with personal browser-based report navigation facilities.

Top three product differentiators; describe what makes your product unique.

1. Full utilization of Microsoft Project 98.
2. Supports each role step by step through the business process.
3. Simple to implement and use.

To what business processes can this tool be applied?

The multiproject management process, supporting the project office and project leaders step by step through the process, from initial registration of projects to postimplementation review.

Describe the ideal end-user environment for the current version of your product (size of organization, level of project management sophistication, effort and commitment required).

IT development organization, up to 750 staff, 500 projects, 100 project leaders, Microsoft Project already in use.

Future strategies for this product.

Extend the project-related records and documentation-management capabilities.

Product's target market.

Organizations with multiple projects where resource constraints make changes to workload difficult to manage.

What are your product's three main benefits? (How does using the product add value to the customer?)

1. Consistent project plans through standards management.
2. Resource capacity check before committing to new projects.
3. Effective process support generates high-quality management information.

Describe your quality management process. List any relevant certifications.

Best practice software product development, based on twenty years industry experience.

Discuss your product pricing structure. Include volume discount levels, concurrent user options, site licenses, cost of implementation, and other issues.

Based on named users for each role, i.e., number in the project office, numbers of project leaders. Volume discounts apply.

Simple software modules support evolutionary change. Costs of implementation well below industry average; for example, project office—one-day training, project leaders—half-day training.

Intelligent Planner (Augeo Software)

Describe what the product is designed to do.

Optimize the allocation of resources across multiple projects, determine costs, and provide metrics for continuous process improvement.

Top three product differentiators; describe what makes your product unique.

1. Global repository for data and business rules.
2. Closed-loop system, from project proposal to time/expenses tracking.
3. Simulation and opimization based on skills and availability of resources.

To what business processes can this tool be applied?

Business processes involving the allocation of human resources, such as professional services and information services.

Describe the ideal end-user environment for the current version of your product (size of organization, level of project management sophistication, effort and commitment required).

Mid-sized to large-scale professional-services organizations sharing pool of scarce resources. Large IT departments managing budgets and resources on strategic projects. Consulting companies managing portfolio of intellectual activities.

Future strategies for this product.

One hundred percent Web-based management of project portfolio. Knowledge management integration. Advanced data mining features.

Product's target market.

Professional services organization; large-scale IT departments with cost-controlled project management; consulting companies.

What are your product's three main benefits? (How does using the product add value to the customer?)

1. Optimize scarce resource predictability.
2. Increase speed, throughput, and responsiveness.
3. Executive visibility.

Describe your quality management process. List any relevant certifications.

Source control. Usability verification process. Worldwide beta program.

Discuss your product pricing structure. Include volume discount levels, concurrent user options, site licenses, cost of implementation, and other issues.

Concurrent user pricing for client-server modules, named user pricing for Web modules. Volume discount, site license.
Implementation requires ten to twenty days of consulting.
Training: Project managers (two days), administrator (three days), Web users (half day).
Annual maintenance (includes new releases and online assistance): 15 percent license fee.

Mesa/Vista (Mesa/Vista Systems Guild)

Describe what the product is designed to do.

Mesa/Vista helps project teams manage, monitor, and comply with quality and government regulations by providing process management capabilities and access to all legacy and current project data through a Web browser. Mesa/Vista provides process management capabilities and integrates a development team's existing product environment, including tools like Rational Rose, TD Technologies' SLATE, Cayenne Teamwork, or any tool with an MPX interface, such as Microsoft Project.

Mesa/Vista links information between stand-alone products and exposes project data to authorized project team members, empowering them to anticipate and solve problems at early stages in the project life cycle.

Mesa/Vista automates the documentation process. This shaves time from a project that must comply with government or other regulatory standards because the documentation is available as soon as the project is complete.

Top three product differentiators; describe what makes your product unique.

1. Patent-pending technology intuitively links graphical objects such as those found in developer's modeling tools, not only within the stand-alone tool but also between tools.

2. Provides support of any business process through dynamic exchange of information.

3. Connects legacy and current data between development team's business and engineering tools.

To what business processes can this tool be applied?

SEI Capability Maturity Model Levels 1–5, ISO-compliant regulations, FDA requirements management.

Describe the ideal end-user environment for the current version of your product (size of organization, level of project management sophistication, effort and commitment required).

The ideal end-user environment for Mesa/Vista is a distributed, process-conscious product development group needing visibility and access to legacy and current project data across multiple platforms.

An organization trying to achieve or improve upon an SEI capability maturity model level, achieve an ISO 9000 quality standard, or comply with FDA requirements will greatly benefit from the Mesa/Vista environment.

Commitment: All project-related communications would go through the Mesa/Vista environment; it provides complete, automated project status information.

Future strategies for this product.

Future strategies for Mesa/Vista include integrating all engineering and business data together to be shared and accessed by the entire product development team, no matter where the data resides.

Plug-ins will include more scheduling tools, databases, business tools, document-editing tools, and modeling tools—all the tools the entire team would use within a product development environment.

Mesa/Vista will create an environment of collaboration, and expose information to help all members of the team work together without restraint of hardware or system requirements.

Product's target market.

Mesa/Vista is ideal for process-conscious project managers of distributed product development teams in the telecommunication, automotive, aerospace, medical, and software industries.

What are your product's three main benefits? (How does using the product add value to the customer?)

1. Provides accessibility to data from places other than the data's native machine, minimizing the number of copies of each software product that needs to be purchased.

2. Saves time by providing online access to all project data, rather than printing and faxing information in order to share it.

3. Automatic documentation mechanism for ease of tracking government regulations or quality standards control.

Describe your quality management process. List any relevant certifications.

Mesa/Vista is used to manage the development of Mesa/Vista. Also, extensive internal and external testing is done of the Mesa/Vista product line. Mesa has provided the software to Young America's design team (the New York Yacht Club's challenger in the America's Cup 2000) in exchange for feedback on Mesa/Vista and suggestions for improvements based on their real-life use of the product line.

Discuss your product pricing structure. Include volume discount levels, concurrent user options, site licenses, cost of implementation, and other issues.

Contact vendor.

Microsoft Project 98 (Microsoft)

Describe what the product is designed to do.

Microsoft Project 98 is an ideal tool for planning and tracking projects of all sizes. Because it is easy to use, it is an ideal tool for all levels of project management experience from the newcomer to the experienced project manager. Microsoft Project 98 focuses on three areas:

1. Control—gives users more control over their project plans.
2. Communication—improves project communication so everyone stays informed and involved.
3. Compatibility—provides programmability features so it can serve as a stand-alone product or as part of a broader company solution.

Top three product differentiators; describe what makes your product unique.

1. Ease of use: Microsoft Project 98 requires little or no training to begin using it to manage projects, so the *startup* costs required of new customers are much lower when compared to other project management software tools. The navigation map also helps inexperienced project managers and new Microsoft Project 98 customers to map their functional responsibilities to Microsoft Project 98's features.

2. Extensibility: Microsoft Project 98 is a pioneer in extensibility. It can store data in an open database format and supports VBA. Customers can easily integrate project management data with their existing corporate business systems, which enables Microsoft Project 98 to accommodate ever-increasing complexity as customers' project management needs change and grow throughout the organization.

3. Integration with other Microsoft applications: Microsoft Project 98 incorporates the best of Microsoft Office to make a tool that is easy to learn and use.

To what business processes can this tool be applied?

Microsoft Project 98 can be applied to any process for which the customer can identify specific tasks and their respective durations and dependencies. Customers can use Microsoft Project 98 to easily compare cost and profitability by project, balance resource requirements across projects, and track dependencies across multiple projects to assess a project's impact on the bottom line. Microsoft Project 98 can also be used to integrate project metrics with corporate accounting, human resources, timesheets, or manufacturing systems and organize project documentation so it is readily available to everyone involved in a project.

Describe the ideal end-user environment for the current version of your product (size of organization, level of project management sophistication, effort and commitment required).

Microsoft Project 98 is used in end-user environments of all sizes—from individuals planning single-resource projects to large corporations with thousands of employees. Customers with widely varying project management backgrounds can also use it. Even newcomers to project management principles can learn to use Microsoft Project 98 quickly and easily with the product's built-in help and other easy-to-use features. Microsoft Project 98 even contains features to extend a project team's communication capability over the Web or any MAPI-compliant E-mail system. And, customers won't *outgrow* Microsoft Project 98 since its programmability features allow them to tailor the program to their organization's unique and changing needs.

Future strategies for this product.

Microsoft will continue to focus on improved collaboration, performance, and ease of use in future versions of Microsoft Project. Microsoft Project has always focused on bringing project management techniques to a wider audience via improved ease of use and expanded communication capabilities for project teams and will continue to do so in the future.

Product's target market.

Anyone who deals with budgets, assignments, and deadlines can take advantage of the benefits offered by Microsoft Project 98. If you have thousands of details to manage, or even a few dozen, you're a potential Microsoft Project 98 customer.

What are your product's three main benefits? (How does using the product add value to the customer?)

1. Easy to learn and can grow with customers' projects and organization.
2. Ability to plan and track multiple projects in a consolidated manner.
3. Helps customers track and manage costs that affect the bottom line.

Describe your quality management process. List any relevant certifications.

Microsoft Project's quality management process begins with developing a product vision based on input from customers, internal and external developers, the product support team, and usability engineers. This ensures that the development process focuses on the right objectives, and that decisions regarding product quality reflect all of these perspectives.

Microsoft maintains a high developer to test ratio throughout the software development process to ensure that potential *bugs* are identified and resolved as early in the development cycle as possible. The testing process is based on five core attributes: 1) source code version control; 2) making the code testable; 3) use of automation for broader scenario testing; 4) beta testing—both internal and external; and 5) detailed bug tracking and reporting (throughout all Microsoft product groups in order to share learnings).

Finally, a new product is released only when the managers from development, testing, program management, and product support agree as a team that the product is ready. No product will be released until this agreement is reached.

Discuss your product pricing structure. Include volume discount levels, concurrent user options, site licenses, cost of implementation, and other issues.

The estimated retail price of Microsoft Project 98 is $499. Microsoft also offers several multiple-license pricing agreements. Detailed information on these agreements is available at www.microsoft.com/licensing.

The cost of implementation varies based on previous experience with project management principles, experience with other project management software tools, and the size and complexity of a customer's projects. Little or no training is needed for Microsoft Project 98 due to the extensive built-in help and other user-assistance features included in the product. Many additional low-cost books, self-help tools, and other training materials for Microsoft Project 98 are widely available. Microsoft Project 98's built-in VBA programmability features also help limit the cost of additional customization.

Open Plan (Welcom)

Describe what the product is designed to do.

Welcom's Open Plan is an enterprisewide project management system that substantially improves a company's ability to manage and complete multiple projects on time and within budget with a limited workforce. Unlike less sophisticated products, Open Plan is a highly integrated, comprehensive software system that can be customized to fit specific corporate requirements. It is the most technically advanced client/server project management system on the market, using the latest in Microsoft Windows development technology. The three versions of Open Plan are:

1. Open Plan Professional. Easy to use and powerful enough to manage even the largest projects, Open Plan Professional gives professional project managers such vital tools as advanced resource management, multiproject support, support for client/server databases, and the flexibility to customize the interface to support organization and industry-specific procedures.

2. Open Plan Desktop: Designed for occasional access to projects and ideal for executive users and tactical team members, Open Plan Desktop has extensive ease-of-use features and an affordable price point for companywide deployment. The system is well suited for users who usually work on individual components of a larger project. Users can roll their individual projects up to Open Plan Professional for a broader view of the overall project.

3. Open Plan Enterprise: Very similar to Open Plan Professional, integrates with popular ERP applications such as Baan and SAP. The resulting component-based suite automatically disseminates project data throughout an organization, giving users better control over enterprisewide multiproject planning, management, and implementation.

Top three product differentiators; describe what makes your product unique.

1. Multiproject.
2. Advanced resource modeling.
3. Open architecture.

To what business processes can this tool be applied?

Enterprise resource modeling, business process reengineering, project management, earned value analysis, risk assessment, and process modeling.

Describe the ideal end-user environment for the current version of your product (size of organization, level of project management sophistication, effort and commitment required).

Medium to large organizations for which project management is a serious business requirement. Meets the needs of users whose level of expertise varies from novice/occasional to advanced.

Future strategies for this product.

Our vision for the future is to provide a suite of component-based products that work together to provide advanced project management functionality using the very latest technology.

Welcom's development plans include extending the products' multiproject and enterprise resource-modeling capabilities while moving to a distributed-applications architecture with Web technology being a significant component. Plans also include leveraging existing integrations with Baan and SAP, and expanding integrations to include other ERP vendors.

Product's target market.

Fortune 1000 companies, government and multinational organizations implementing enterprisewide project management.

What are your product's three main benefits? (How does using the product add value to the customer?)

1. Increase quality of project communications.
2. Reduce cycle time through effective resource management.
3. Increase integration of project management with business systems.

Describe your quality management process. List any relevant certifications.

Adhere to standard industry processes in release and version strategies, including automated regression testing. ISO 9000 certified in the United Kingdom.

Discuss your product pricing structure. Include volume discount levels, concurrent user options, site licenses, cost of implementation, and other issues.

Please call for pricing on products and cost of implementation: (training, tech support, annual maintenance, etc.), training courses and consulting.

Tech support is available at no charge with current maintenance.

First year of maintenance is free with software purchase and can be renewed annually.

OPX2 Suite (OPX2 Pro + OPX2 Timecard + OPX2 Server + OPX2 Intranet Server from Planisware)

Describe what the product is designed to do.

OPX2 suite includes OPX2 Pro (schedule, cost, and resource management); OPX2 Timecard (Web-based timesheet); OPX2 Intranet Server (Web publisher for project data); and OPX2 Server (consolidator for Microsoft Project and Scitor Project Scheduler).

Top three product differentiators; describe what makes your product unique.

1. Management of multiple currencies.
2. Ability to handle project cash flow and profit at any level of structure.
3. Others: See OPX2 Pro (Schedule Management).

To what business processes can this tool be applied?

Project management: R&D project management (new product development, portfolio management), matrix organizations, IS departments, and software houses.

Scheduling of small serial manufacturing, engineering projects, heavy maintenance, and integration activities.

Cost management for public contract management, defense and aerospace programs, in-house product development, and subcontracting.

Describe the ideal end-user environment for the current version of your product (size of organization, level of project management sophistication, effort and commitment required).

Organization: From one hundred to twenty thousand resources managed.

Level of project management sophistication: Previous experience of other project management software implementation is profitable for implementing OPX2.

To be implemented using a methodology suited for enterprisewide consolidation: activity coding, resource identification, and ERP interfaces.

Future strategies for this product.

Development of partnerships with ERP providers.
International development (multilingual support and distributors).
Focus on decision-support functions.

Product's target market.

Manufacturing: Defense and aerospace, car/truck, drug/cosmetics development.
ICT: IS departments (enterprises and administrations), software house, telecommunications, and electronics.
Engineering: construction, energy, space, etc.

What are your product's three main benefits? (How does using the product add value to the customer?)

1. For the organization: Standardization of concepts and reporting process for project management in all departments; breaking of barriers between cost and schedule.
2. For the users: Less time spent to collect and enter data, more time available to analyze data.
3. For the management: Real visibility on activity progress for top management, and long-term historization of project data at multiproject scale.

Describe your quality management process. List any relevant certifications.

TEMPO (Thomson-CSF software development methodology), which is compliant with ISO 9001 standards.

No specific certification for Planisware.

Discuss your product pricing structure. Include volume discount levels, concurrent user options, site licenses, cost of implementation, and other issues.

OPX2 Pro (Scheduling + Cost Management + Report builder): From $12,000 (server plus first concurrent user license).

Typical user configurations: $17,000 to $1,000,000. Concurrent user licenses: yes. Site licenses: yes.

Cost of implementation: Twenty-five percent to 80 percent of license cost (consulting, training).

Annual maintenance: Fifteen percent of license cost (including tech support and upgrade of new releases).

Training: Contact OPX2 distributors in each country.

Panorama Program Manager

Describe what the product is designed to do.

Panorama Program Manager comprises five modules, which together form a fully integrated application but which can, if required, be used independently or can be integrated with preferred third party applications. Interfaces can also be provided to other applications.

Financial Control & Performance Measurement: Consolidates financial and performance information for any number of projects and provides multilevel views of all data. Departmental managers and team leaders can be provided with short-term tactical perspective.

Time Recording: This module is the collection point for all time expended by project staff. Timesheets may be entered by individual members of staff, or as a batch process. Extensive online validation ensures that mispostings are kept to a minimum.

Top three product differentiators; describe what makes your product unique.

1. *Scope:* Addresses in a single integrated application the major application areas required for comprehensive program management.
2. *Flexibility:* Inherent flexibility means that the system can be implemented to suit most companies' requirements without the need for bespoke development.
3. *Customization:* Ability to incorporate bespoke features to client's specification and willingness to provide support to customized elements.

To what business processes can this tool be applied?

Estimation, bid management, and project control.

Describe the ideal end-user environment for the current version of your product (size of organization, level of project management sophistication, effort and commitment required).

Typical users will have in excess of two hundred employees and be managing either large, complex projects or a large number (>150) of small/medium-size projects.

They will usually have experience of project management and already be users of project management tools.

A typical implementation will be six to twelve months and require the involvement of an implementation team that at any one time might include five to ten client staff.

Future strategies for this product.

Web-based operation; Integration of work flow management and document storage and retrieval.

Product's target market.

Cross-industry.

What are your product's three main benefits? (How does using the product add value to the customer?)

1. Consolidation of all project data to provide a corporate view of performance.
2. Standardization of project control methodology through use of a single corporatewide system.
3. Easy access at all levels in the organization of all aspects of project performance.

Describe your quality management process. List any relevant certifications.

In-house change control and configuration management software and control systems.

Discuss your product pricing structure. Include volume discount levels, concurrent user options, site licenses, cost of implementation, and other issues.

On application.

PLANTRAC-OUTLOOK Level 4 (Computerline Ltd)

Describe what the product is designed to do.

From conception to completion is what Level 4 offers projects. From setting up the project board and defining role responsibilities, you go on to designing the project in a breakdown structure. Each module can then be planned and scheduled knowing the estimates and costs. Advanced progress reporting allows the project to be rescheduled efficiently. Risk analysis and management backs up management decisions. Exceptional reporting gives management and clients clear views of the project.

Top three product differentiators; describe what makes your product unique.

1. All modules written and supported by one company.
2. Fully integrated.
3. Inexpensive.

To what business processes can this tool be applied?

Construction, manufacturing, and research and development.

Describe the ideal end-user environment for the current version of your product (size of organization, level of project management sophistication, effort and commitment required).

Both small and large organizations benefit. It can be used as a casual planner, by a professional project manager and for corporate planning and control.

Future strategies for this product.

PLANTRAC-OUTLOOK is very much user driven. It will keep up to date with both project management and technological trends.

Product's target market.

Broad market but specializing in construction, defense, and pharmaceutical.

What are your product's three main benefits? (How does using the product add value to the customer?)

1. Time saved in project creation and progressing/updating.
2. Realistic schedules assist project profitability.
3. Reporting flexibility, better project communications, and obtains client confidence.

Describe your quality management process. List any relevant certifications.

Quality management is based on a mix of PRINCE and ISO 9000 methodology.

Discuss your product pricing structure. Include volume discount levels, concurrent user options, site licenses, cost of implementation, and other issues.

Single user is $1,975. Network versions are available in modules of four users; $3,950 per module. Site licenses are $10,000–$70,000.

Implementation and training is $960 per day. Technical support is provided by telephone, fax, and E-mail and is free for first six months. Thereafter, it costs 17.5 percent of purchase price (including upgrades and enhancements).

PPS Corporate 4.0

Describe what the product is designed to do.

PPS is designed to allow the project manager to plan his project and then in an easy fashion to compare what is happening with the plan. If there is a deviation the project manager should be able to simulate different solutions and see the consequences of those.

The system supports communication within the project group and between the group and other interested parties in the company with reports that provide the information needed at each level. The CEO gets summaries with the possibility to bore down when needed. The member gets information about the projects in which he participates. On top of normal cost accounting it also supports activity-based costing, as this gives far more information about how the money is being spent.

Top three product differentiators; describe what makes your product unique.

1. PPS is more concerned with "what will happen if" rather than "what has happened."
2. PPS is prepared with export and import links to other business systems. Through a unique way of getting information from business systems, PPS keeps track of each cost even when more than one company is involved.
3. PPS is prepared to work in a global environment where resources can come from and cost can be caused and carried by different companies.

To what business processes can this tool be applied?

Consulting and R&D projects, sales and marketing projects, contract projects, service and process projects.

Describe the ideal end-user environment for the current version of your product (size of organization, level of project management sophistication, effort and commitment required).

For companies with 100 employees and up. The system supports with forecasts, resource management economy management and quality management a project management that is result-oriented.

Future strategies for this product.

Communication through alternative intelligent methods like mobile phones and TV.

Product's target market.

To be integrated with all major business systems.

What are your product's three main benefits? (How does using the product add value to the customer?)

1. Through a system of templates, PPS allows the user to divide its unique project in repeatable parts. This allows for faster planning, the possibility to compare the result, not only against plan but also against the expected performance.

2. By all the time showing where the project is going, the project manager can be proactive instead of reactive. The earlier a correction is taken the cheaper the correction.

3. A critical point in most systems is the will of the members to keep the system updated. With a mixture of whip and carrot, the participation of the members is simplified. A to-do list of all delayed time reports constitutes the whip; access to important information the carrot.

Describe your quality management process. List any relevant certifications.

We follow ISO 9001 and 10006.

Discuss your product pricing structure. Include volume discount levels, concurrent user options, site licenses, cost of implementation, and other issues.

For 1 PM the price starts at 1150 US$ and decreases with increasing numbers. For members it is a flat 190 US$ per member.

Training and implementation support maintenance and service agreement; includes service pack and new versions for 15 percent of license price.

Primavera Prospective

Describe what the product is designed to do.

Primavera Prospective is an integrated suite of Web-enabled, client/server, and desktop software solutions that provides user- and role-specific tools to satisfy each user's needs, responsibilities, and skills. It provides comprehensive information on all the projects in the enterprise, from executive-level summaries to detailed plans by project. Primavera Prospective gives executives an easy way to maintain the sweeping vision of projects they need to make strategic business decisions. At the same time, it enables project managers to control the minute detail that is necessary to finish projects. Primavera Prospective includes the following role-specific tools:

Primavera Project Planner (P3e): P3e is multiuser, multiproject management software for the professional project manager, with best-of-class scheduling and resource control capabilities. P3e supports multitiered project hierarchies; durations and scheduling down to the minute; powerful resource scheduling and leveling using resources, roles, and skills; recording of past-period data; customizable Gantt, PERT, and resource views; and user-definable data elements and calculations. P3e sets the standard for enterprisewide project management performance and analysis capability.

ESP: ESP is a Web-based executive information system integrated with Primavera Prospective. ESP provides up-to-the-minute, summary information about an enterprise's projects and project portfolios. ESP summarizes and graphically displays project scope, status, budgets, and cost and schedule variances to support long-range planning and critical decision-making. Executives are able to easily measure the "health" and performance of those projects as well as detect trends early so that they can strategically respond to the dynamics of the projects underway in their business.

Primavera Progress Reporter: Progress Reporter is a Web-based interproject communication and timekeeping system that is an integral part of Primavera Prospective. Progress Reporter is a jargon-free tool that helps team members focus on the work at hand with a simple cross-project to-do list of their current and upcoming assignments. It also provides views for manager approval of project changes and timesheets. Since team members use Progress Reporter to enter up-to-the-minute updates to their assignments and record time against their work load, project leaders can make crucial project decisions with the confidence that they have the most recent information possible.

Primavera Personal P3: Personal P3 is a single-user project management tool for managing stand-alone projects and for mobile use of projects checked out from the Primavera Prospective enterprisewide project database. Personal P3 is perfect for team leaders that manage projects as part of their overall responsibilities—whether at the office or on the road.

Primavera Prospective unites the various perspectives on project information required by not only the program and project managers, but also by project sponsors and executive management, as well as by the project participants doing the work. And it does so without requiring that everyone use the same tool in order to get at the information they need.

Top three product differentiators; describe what makes your product unique.

No answer given.

To what business processes can this tool be applied?

Primavera Prospective is Project Portfolio Management software specifically designed to help innovative companies speed new products to market. Using proven scheduling techniques, classical performance measurement, and resource optimization options, Primavera Prospective helps companies prioritize and manage projects so they can achieve faster times to market despite strapped resources and constant change. It ensures alignment of strategic planning with the more tactical project planning and execution.

Describe the ideal end-user environment for the current version of your product (size of organization, level of project management sophistication, effort and commitment required).

Primavera Prospective works for organizations of all sizes, but is specifically designed for enterprises with hundreds of projects, thousands of resources, multiple sites, and a commitment to improving new product development and times to market through project management techniques.

Future strategies for this product.

No answer given.

Product's target market.

Primavera Prospective targets businesses with a high degree of turnover in products, rapid technology improvements, and changing market requirements. They may have a few major projects or they may have several hundred smaller projects in consideration at any time. These projects are complex enough to warrant sophisticated project management techniques and tools; the resources required to complete the projects come from a variety of functional areas and must be coordinated because they are in high demand and tend to be knowledge workers; product launch timing is critical because of finite sales windows. The candidate industries include: high technology, telecommunications, pharmaceuticals, consumer electronics, automotive, information technology, and some consumer-packaged goods.

What are your product's three main benefits? (How does using the product add value to the customer?)

Primavera Prospective provides a consistent way to prioritize, budget, and plan projects with the greatest ROI potential, and to successfully move those projects to an on-time and on-budget completion. Primavera Prospective allows all of a firm's projects to be planned, analyzed, and controlled within a single framework, or project hierarchy, from prefunding to completion. It provides for both top-down as well as bottom-up planning—and compare the two perspectives to ensure that tactical plans are in line with the higher-level project objectives.

Primavera Prospective brings together the disciplines of project management and strategic planning because it helps firms choose projects with the highest market potential. It is a framework that provides the clarity of vision to unite overall strategic project objectives with the tactical plans to successfully implement them.

Primavera Prospective provide top executives and project managers with timely feedback about projects and project portfolios in real time. If something is going to take longer than planned, management gets that information immediately. Primavera Prospective provides project and line-of-business managers with insight into the strategic vision for the business—as set forth by the senior executives or strategic planners—so they also have a sense of ownership of the goals of the organization. Primavera Prospective brings front-line workers into the communication process. The workers are immediately informed about changes in priority so they are always working on the most important tasks. Primavera Prospective closes the communication loop by providing a real-time feedback mechanism whereby they can acknowledge what has been completed, but more importantly what remains to be done.

Describe your quality management process. List any relevant certifications.

No answer given.

Discuss your product pricing structure. Include volume discount levels, concurrent user options, site licenses, cost of implementation, and other issues.

Contact Primavera for details. 800/423-0245.

Project Control Software

Describe what the product is designed to do.

The Project Control Software suite supports project management across the entire organization. The system delivers information to all levels of the organization, from employees to project management, functional management, enterprise management, and global management. It focuses on analysis, drill-down reporting, portfolio management and business system integration to deliver the time, cost and resource information necessary to make good decisions.

Project Control Software extends desktop project management software into an enterprisewide management and reporting solution, by consolidating volumes of project files from leading project management software systems such as Microsoft Project, Primavera, and others. Project Control Software supports multiple operating systems (Windows, Macintosh, Unix), and databases (Oracle, Access, Microsoft SQL, Sybase). The entire Project Control Software suite runs on a Web browser or LAN. The enterprise rollup design supports the matrix organization's need to roll up projects to program or initiative, as well as the resource perspective by business unit and organizational structure.

Top three product differentiators; describe what makes your product unique.

1. No technology limits: Project Control Software supports all operating systems (Windows, Macintosh, Unix), consolidates files from multiple project management software systems (Microsoft Project, Primavera, and more) using your choice of databases (Oracle, Access, Microsoft SQL, Sybase) in a LAN or Internet solution. It is designed to integrate easily with existing business systems (such as accounting software) so an organization can leverage existing systems and immediately see productivity increases without changing everything.

2. The project office: The design and integration of Project Control Software modules supports the project office across all phases of the project management life cycle, from standard estimating and budgeting though timesheets and status tracking and accounting integration for actual costs and earned value analysis. The process manager and communications manager modules enable a corporate intranet.

3. Enterprise project management: Project Control Software offers a suite of integrated modules that can be used to deliver the big picture of project management across a distributed organization, as well as tracking the details. The enterprise rollup design supports the matrix organization's need to roll up projects to program or initiative, as well as the need to view data from a resource perspective by business unit and organizational structure. The entire Project Control Software suite (not just the time tracking) runs on a Web browser or LAN.

To what business processes can this tool be applied?

Project Control Software's enterprise rollup design supports the matrix organization's need to roll up projects to program or initiative, as well as the need to view data from a resource perspective by business unit and organizational structure.

The system supports project management, ERP, project office development, ISO registration, strategic planning, process management, methodology implementation, cost/schedule management, CMM, compliance, global information technology deployment, SAP, Peoplesoft, etc., implementations.

Describe the ideal end-user environment for the current version of your product (size of organization, level of project management sophistication, effort and commitment required).

Any organization operating in a competitive environment that manages multiple projects and resources to meet business goals and to increase profitability and productivity.

For example, a geographically distributed matrix organization with medium to high volume of project-based activities being managed in a standard desktop scheduling software. The system delivers information to all levels of the organization from employees to project management, functional management, enterprise management, and global management.

Future strategies for this product.

Project Control, the publisher of Project Control Software, was founded in 1989, developed the first Internet project management product in 1996, and is committed to its position as a technology leader in Internet project management software. Future plans include expanding functionality to better support the project office and to continually update Project Control Software features, based on ongoing client input.

Product's target market.

Organizations using Project Control Software represent companies in a wide variety of industries, including finance, services, pharmaceutical, federal government, defense, manufacturing, automotive, software publishing, etc. The disciplines typically involved in implementation include enterprise management, information technology, new product development, the project office, and engineering.

What are your product's three main benefits? (How does using the product add value to the customer?)

Client organizations can greatly improve productivity and lower costs when Project Control system is in place.

1. Ability to view all projects in a central repository.
2. Ability to do efficient enterprise resource and cost planning.
3. Ability to fully support the needs of the project office across all phases and areas of the project management process.

Describe your quality management process. List any relevant certifications.

Project Control, publishers of Project Control Software, follows standard and accepted practices for design, development, testing, and support for computer software. Project Control has set corporate objectives to achieve Level 2 and Level 3 CMM compliance using the capability maturity model from the Software Engineering Institute.

Discuss your product pricing structure. Include volume discount levels, concurrent user options, site licenses, cost of implementation, and other issues.

Project Control Software is priced by the module, with scalable client seat pricing based on number of users. Price quotations are available and are based on the current Project Control Software product and pricing schedule.

Price quotations are available and include costs of product, implementation, training, tech support, annual maintenance, etc. Quotations are based on the current Project Control Software product and pricing schedule, which is available to qualified organizations.

ProjectExchange (Information Management Services, Inc.)

Describe what the product is designed to do.

The ProjectExchange family of products provides a flexible solution for event-driven organizations that wish to maximize resource productivity, achieve project deliverables, and ensure projects are on time and within budget. Integrated solutions can easily be created to surround the existing capabilities of any of the ProjectExchange products to satisfy specific organizational objectives.

ProjectExplorer is utilized by project, program, and resource managers to navigate among the projects stored in the enterprise information repository that they have access rights to view and/or edit. A Windows-based explorer view provides project, task, resource, and assignment information across multiple projects in a single easy-to-use view. Depending upon the unique process flow of the organization, different project stakeholders may view a project at different stages in its development. Finance may initiate a project and share it with program management, followed by program management sharing the information with resource management.

The process flow is completely user configurable with capabilities only limited by the imagination of the management team. ProjectExplorer provides an easy-to-use method of finding, retrieving, and saving Microsoft Projects to the enterprise repository. This facilitates communication between project managers, team managers, and their team members.

WebTime is a browser-based interactive timesheet, providing the flexibility to report actual progress against Microsoft Project assignments and nonscheduled activities in a single timesheet interface at any time via the World Wide Web. ProjectExplorer provides communication of assignments from Microsoft Project. Assignments are added to WebTime, and actual progress committed by team members automatically updates the manager of the project. Team members utilize the WebTime to record project and nonproject actual progress, and to provide schedule feedback. This Web-based timesheet works independent of ProjectExplorer, giving the users a choice of either interface to manage activities from various managers, all in a consistent manner.

Top three product differentiators; describe what makes your product unique.

1. User-configurable information validation and process-flow execution.
2. Seamless integration with Microsoft Project and the ProjectExchange family of products provides a single repository spanning the entire enterprise.
3. Three-tier client/server-based architecture provides a system scalable across the entire enterprise.

To what business processes can this tool be applied?

Our tools are utilized across multiple business processes.

Describe the ideal end-user environment for the current version of your product (size of organization, level of project management sophistication, effort and commitment required).

Our primary market consists of Global 5000 organizations with objectives to increase their returns on people, time, and financial investments. We initially assist event-driven divisions within these organizations, with the ultimate goal of benefiting every user in the organization.

Future strategies for this product.

Corporate downsizing and business process reengineering have influenced many companies to investigate the concept of *managing by project* (MBP). Moving to MBP typically requires significant changes in business processes. After existing for over twenty-five years, project management is finally becoming recognized as a professional discipline that can contribute significant competitive advantages to any business. Project management is at last beginning to be understood as something more than just a process for controlling a project's cost and timing. Most industries outside of the aerospace, construction, and engineering sectors have only in recent years become more aware of the effectiveness of MBP processes and the extent of the body of knowledge pertaining to MBP.

The process of enabling the organization to use MBP techniques is gaining, and will continue to gain, momentum and be a driving trend in the industry.

Complementing the trend toward MBP is a trend to hold individuals accountable and to measure progress against responsibilities. We have witnessed this trend firsthand by deploying Enterprise Work Management solutions worldwide and will continue to be a market leader.

Product's target market.

Based on our experience, clients who benefit most from our products and services include information systems, professional services, product development, engineering, and other event-driven organizations. Among these groups, each has further defined a set of unique objectives critical to increasing their competitiveness. IMS provides the ProjectExchange Enterprise Toolkit to achieve these objectives from the departmental level to the entire enterprise.

What are your product's three main benefits? (How does using the product add value to the customer?)

1. A functionally complete suite of products provided by a single source lowers implementation risks.
2. An integrated tool set provides a lower cost of ownership.
3. Easily configurable to organization specific business requirements and therefore is more likely to be used in achieving corporate objectives.

Describe your quality management process. List any relevant certifications.

We have continually improved our system development methodology since 1991. Over time, our SDLC has incorporated the best practices learned while deploying ProjectExchange in world-class organizations across the globe. Our Research & Development division utilizes ProjectExchange, and quality measures are persistent throughout our methods and processes.

Discuss your product pricing structure. Include volume discount levels, concurrent user options, site licenses, cost of implementation, and other issues.

Please consult IMS for current pricing. Implementation costs vary and depend upon a particular organization's business requirements and level and availability of in-house expertise. We offer the following services to help achieve organizational objectives:

■ Installation
■ Process, methods, and integration consulting
■ Project office support
■ ProjectExchange add-on solution development
■ Implementation management
■ Microsoft Project and ProjectExchange two-day course
■ ProjectExchange for Project Managers one-day course
■ ProjectExchange for Team Members half-day course
■ MS Project Introduction one-day course
■ MS Project Basic two-day course
■ Project Planning & Management Fundamentals three-day course
■ Executive briefing on project management.

Annual maintenance is offered at 15 percent of the license costs. Maintenance includes telephone support and product upgrades.

Project Integrator

Describe what the product is designed to do.

SSL Project Integrator (PI) is a team-oriented project and process management tool that enables you to graphically define, track, report, and communicate projects, processes, tasks, and deliverables. Additionally, PI manages and maintains resources and clients, both locally and remotely.

Top three product differentiators; describe what makes your product unique.

1. All project processes (external, internal, and administrative) are managed via PI's graphic and interactive RoadMap. High-level steps graphically depict process flow. Each step can be drilled-down to display task lists, task details, resource delegation, deliverables, and quality checklists.

2. Teams can be defined at the project level, and are pulled from the database resource pool. Assigned tasks and open issues are sent to a team member's reminder window for immediate delegation and communication. Resources drag and drop tasks to a timecard for immediate project updating, and open issues remain on the reminder window until they are closed.

3. A wide range of reports are available. Each report can be filtered, and pull data from the database for macro or micro analysis and reporting. Users can also define their own reports, and any level of information can be exported from the database.

To what business processes can this tool be applied?

Any external, internal, or administrative business process, regardless of simplicity or complexity.

Describe the ideal end-user environment for the current version of your product (size of organization, level of project management sophistication, effort and commitment required).

Project-based organizations of any size (PI allows definition of teams, departments, and business units). Organizations do not need to be well-versed in project management practices and techniques. Implementation and training is simple when compared to sophisticated PM tools. A commitment to Distributed Project/Process Management (DPM) is required (the delegation of tasks and deliverables to distributed teams and team members, and distribution of the project management process).

Future strategies for this product.

Tailor versions of PI to specific industries by leveraging subject matter experts from same.

Full integration to other cost accounting applications (currently, PI is integrated with SBT Executive Series, although data can be exported to virtually any application).

Product's target market.

Project Integrator was created for project-oriented organizations (engineering, marketing, advertising, accounting, consulting, design firms, etc.) that have a need to enforce consistent quality in their project process and delivery, and minimize nonproductive hours.

What are your product's three main benefits? (How does using the product add value to the customer?)

1. Distribution of the project process (tasks, issues, deliverables, etc.) to local and remote team members via LAN, DBMS, and Internet tools.

2. Immediate feedback of status of all projects and tasks, allowing macro and micro views of the entire organization's performance at any given time.

3. All aspects of a business (external, internal, and administrative activity, including deliverables) are managed in a central DBMS and repository. Communications, projects, tasks, deliverables, issues, costs, clients resources, etc., are all managed via one tool in one database.

Describe your quality management process. List any relevant certifications.

Our documented QA process includes the use of test script software. We are currently implementing ISO 9001 and expect registry by early 1999.

Discuss your product pricing structure. Include volume discount levels, concurrent user options, site licenses, cost of implementation, and other issues.

PI's price is based on the number of users, and volume discounts are available.

Implementation lead time and required training is minimal when compared to high-end, sophisticated PM tools and suites.

Proj-Net

Describe what the product is designed to do.

Proj-Net is a set of project management tools that provides platform independence, distributed management tools, complete project repository, ad hoc query/reporting, and automated Web access.

Web Master automatically creates websites that serve as a project's center for collaboration. Schedule Master accepts input from existing scheduling software. Cost Master imports information on budget, actual, earned value, and man-hours.

Metric Master is a technical measurement tool that maintains a user-defined dictionary of metrics. Task Master is an action item reporting mechanism that incorporates action item work flow and E-mail notification. The Risk Master maintains a database of risk criteria.

Top three product differentiators; describe what makes your product unique.

1. Technology is 100 percent Web-based (Java and Oracle).
2. Integrates technical performance measures with cost and schedule.
3. Designed for program management and project control.

To what business processes can this tool be applied?

Software development process, cost management, schedule management and any other metric-based process.

Describe the ideal end-user environment for the current version of your product (size of organization, level of project management sophistication, effort and commitment required).

Medium maturity or *above* for program management capability. High technology environment or an environment that requires metrics for management. Must be committed to project management and seeking a competitive advantage.

Future strategies for this product.

Tighter integration with ERP systems, mature intranet model, support of Sql-Server.

Product's target market.

High technology companies or companies for whom integration of project data is required. Companies whose core business is projects.

What are your product's three main benefits? (How does using the product add value to the customer?)

1. Provides integration of technical performance measures and cost and schedule through a metric-based approach to project management.
2. Facilitates collaboration on the Web.
3. Supports distributed project environment with disparate desktop tools.

Describe your quality management process. List any relevant certifications.

Standard repeatable development that includes unit testing and integration testing in multiple platforms.

Discuss your product pricing structure. Include volume discount levels, concurrent user options, site licenses, cost of implementation, and other issues.

Proj-Net is priced on a per-project basis. We include volume discounts and site licenses. Implementation support is available.

Consulting and training is $1200 per day. Tech support is free with current maintenance. Annual maintenance is 20 percent of retail price per year and includes upgrades.

QEI Exec (PCF Limited)

Describe what the product is designed to do.

QEI Exec is best thought of as a toolkit for managing activity-based problems built around a high performance database engine. Data stored within the database can be presented and manipulated via any number of views, which can be graphical or tabular. The entire user interface to the delivered product is written in the product's own programming language, allowing complete customization to meet individual requirements.

It provides the following key areas of functionality:

- Graphical and tabular interface to data
- Scheduling
- Resource management
- Cost and performance management
- Flexible interfacing to other systems
- High degree of customization.

Top three product differentiators; describe what makes your product unique.

1. Highly graphical *CAD-like* approach to project construction gives total freedom of data layout.

2. Dynamic rollup of all schedule and resource data through an unlimited number of structures, yielding high performance even when dealing with tens of thousands of tasks.

3. Macro-based front end allows complete customization of user interface and generation of interactive specialist charts (e.g., time chainage diagrams).

To what business processes can this tool be applied?

It has a wide range of possible applications, including:

- *Traditional* project planning with earned value analysis
- Project-based MIS/EIS
- Program treasury management
- Maintenance and manufacturing forecasting
- Capacity planning
- MRP master schedule generation.

Describe the ideal end-user environment for the current version of your product (size of organization, level of project management sophistication, effort and commitment required).

Large organizations (to > $100M) with considerable experience of *rigorous* project management wishing to consolidate diverse sets of data (e.g., from multiple planning systems, manufacturing/ERP, and cost collection) into a single source of high-quality management information.

If customers wish to fully exploit the potential for tightly integrating the product with other systems or to introduce significant customizations, they will require suitable internal IT resources.

Future strategies for this product.

Extended database connectivity via ODBC.
Extended reporting and intranet functionality.

Product's target market.

Principal market: Aerospace and defense.
Product is also successfully used in make-to-order/contract manufacturing, transportation, and utilities.

What are your product's three main benefits? (How does using the product add value to the customer?)

1. Extremely high-quality interactive graphical views of data.
2. High performance consolidation/rollup permits rapid what-if scenario analysis.
3. Complete control over layout and presentation of data.

Describe your quality management process. List any relevant certifications.

We have started (but not yet completed) ISO 9001 certification.

Discuss your product pricing structure. Include volume discount levels, concurrent user options, site licenses, cost of implementation, and other issues.

The product is sold as a right-to-use license plus a number of user licenses. A small (three-user) system would cost about £15,000 while a larger (ten-user) system would cost about £30,000. The per-user price drops with increasing numbers of users. Site/multisite/corporate licenses are available.

It is strongly recommended that customers take training from us. List price for training is £500/day per course for up to six attendees. Various standard training courses are available, or custom courses can be developed on request. Annual maintenance is 15 percent of the list price of the software. This includes all upgrades and new releases and unlimited telephone support.

QuickGantt for Windows (Ballantine & Company, Inc.)

Describe what the product is designed to do.

QuickGantt lets you create professional schedules, cost estimates, and status reports in minutes. You enter project data easily with a familiar spreadsheet-like interface. A handy pop-up calendar makes entering dates a snap. You can drag and drop the task bars in Gantt View to adjust dates, or shift activity dates with a button click. Print reports and schedules for any timeframe, project, phase, or individual. Choose the version that's right for you: BASIC—great for planning; STANDARD—for more flexible editing, Gantt chart printing, exporting, and formatting; PLUS—for additional project management features like file importing, task-linking, plan-version comparison, and more. Unlimited toll-free support, thirty-day money-back guarantee.

Top three product differentiators; describe what makes your product unique.

1. Ease of use.
2. Low price.
3. Speed of generating Gantt charts and reports.

To what business processes can this tool be applied?

Project planning, project management, scheduling, estimating, proposal development, project tracking, etc.

Describe the ideal end-user environment for the current version of your product (size of organization, level of project management sophistication, effort and commitment required).

QuickGantt is designed for anyone who needs to plan projects, from members of a global organization to sole proprietors. It is used by a variety of professionals including engineers, architects, builders, contractors, professors, consultants, and business managers for internal and client projects. It is easy and flexible enough for anyone who works with projects.

Future strategies for this product.

Continued enhancement based on customer feedback.

Product's target market.

Architects, builders, contractors, engineers, consultants, planners and managers, marketers, and event managers—anyone who needs to plan projects or events.

What are your product's three main benefits? (How does using the product add value to the customer?)

1. You don't need to be a computer or project management guru to use QuickGantt. If you're familiar with PCs and Windows-based programs, you can be up and running within fifteen minutes. If not, make it about thirty minutes. Either way, you'll be able to generate professional Gantt charts and reports in minutes, not hours. Then you'll have more time to concentrate on your work instead of spending all your time learning complex software.
2. It saves money—with both its low price and in the time you save when you use it.
3. You get clean, professional-looking Gantt charts and reports.

Describe your quality management process. List any relevant certifications.

End-user testing for ease of use. Extensive QA testing.

Discuss your product pricing structure. Include volume discount levels, concurrent user options, site licenses, cost of implementation, and other issues.

BASIC ($99.95), STANDARD ($199), PLUS ($249).

Multiuser prices start at BASIC ($199), STANDARD ($299), PLUS ($349).

Volume discounts start at 20 percent for five users; educational discounts available. Call 800/536-6677 for more detailed pricing information.

We offer a thirty-day money-back guarantee and unlimited, free technical support. On-site project management training and consulting is available on a fee basis.

WebProject

Describe what the product is designed to do.

WebProject is designed for geographically dispersed project teams. WebProject is a Java-based project management tool with powerful collaboration and communications features. WebProject incorporates unique knowledge management/best practices capability.

Top three product differentiators; describe what makes your product unique.

1. WebProject is the first (only) pure Java project management suite that can utilize an open architecture database backend. WebProject allows corporations to utilize Oracle, SQL Server, Informix, Sybase, or other databases in their enterprise project management.

2. WebProject has introduced the first knowledge management/best practices capability within a project management software suite.

3. WebProject enables global project communication, including project issues boards, threaded task discussions, virtual project status meetings, and remote project statusing and updates.

To what business processes can this tool be applied?

Geographically dispersed project teams, projects that need to have access from remote locations, or integrating WebProject's proprietary information exchange with MS Project, Primavera, or other desktop systems.

WebProject allows the extraction of *knowledge* from the enterprise, such as resource capabilities or company *best practices*.

Describe the ideal end user environment for the current version of your product (size of organization, level of project management sophistication, effort and commitment required).

WebProject is an easy-to-use Java project management tool, which will enable teams to communicate and collaborate from remote locations. WebProject is designed for the enterprise and will work well with project teams as well.

Future strategies for this product.

WebProject has established many *firsts* in the project management industry. We will continue to move the industry forward with our new technologies on the Web and with JAVA.

Product's target market.

Geographically dispersed project teams, enterprise project management systems, integration with Primavera, MS Project, and other project management systems.

What are your product's three main benefits? (How does using the product add value to the customer?)

1. Enterprise project communication.
2. Project collaboration.
3. Geographically dispersed updates and communication.

Describe your quality management process. List any relevant certifications.

WebProject adheres to strict standards and processes for quality, both in development and customer service.

Discuss your product pricing structure. Include volume discount levels, concurrent user options, site licenses, cost of implementation, and other issues.

WebProject is priced at $790 for starter package, including the WebProject server. WebProject does provide enterprise and site licensing.

Chapter 2

Process Management Software

Projects are made up of processes. Project management involves integrating these processes in a way that allows project objectives to be realized. Thus, this category of software is linked to *A Guide to the Project Management Body of Knowledge (PMBOK™ Guide)* integration management and scope management knowledge areas (Chapters 4 and 5).

Process tools integrate the project management process with the work processes of the business units or functional areas involved (product development process, systems life cycle).

Process tools provide guidance in:
1. Initiating the project
2. Planning the execution
3. Executing the project
4. Controlling the project
5. Closing the project.

Process management tools make the corporate methodologies and supporting processes available electronically. The project manager can determine appropriate processes for the project, and the project team can access definitions or descriptions of them during execution.

Software development is targeted directly by many process management vendors. But most of these products allow input of the corporate methodology, and are appropriate for any industry that offers computer access to the methodology. New product development and reduction of cycle time are two topics frequently mentioned in vendors' marketing literature.

What to Expect

Process management software provides features like:
- Process flowcharting
- Ability to launch supporting software and reference materials
- Help customized to guide the user through the corporate methodology
- Interfaces to project management software.

Process management comprises documenting the corporate project management methodology, and often includes supporting methodologies, like a product development process or a software development process. Process management support can include simply documenting the methodology and related reference material, or can be as comprehensive as including risk assessment, business opportunities justification, return on investment analysis, issues logging, communications, estimating, and continuous improvement to the methodology.

What the Data Reveals

As a generalization, many process management tools are designed to accept data from the scheduling tool offered by that vendor. Many tools also support Microsoft Project. One tool, Project Kickstart, supports multiple project management software packages.

Process management support often means documenting the corporate project management methodology, as well as related methodologies. The survey asked vendors if their process management tool comes with a methodology that a user can implement if no corporate methodology exists. Vendors responded with:

- Results Management Methodology (ABT Corporation)
- MIL-STD-498 Software Development
- IEEE 12207 Software Development
- PMI® Project Management, *PMBOK™ Guide*-based
- PRINCE
- Simple methodology for brainstorming and planning projects
- Project Management.

What the Majority of Vendors Offer

Most vendors offer strong support for input of custom corporate methodologies. The majority of vendors in this category suggest routes through methodologies, helping to eliminate unnecessary work by identifying which parts of a methodology are appropriate to a specific project. Significant upfront work is necessary to define the parameters under which methodology routing is governed, but the work is worth it. Routing saves new users a lot of time navigating often complex methodologies, and eliminates focus on parts of the methodology that do not apply.

Reporting functionality is robust, offering report writers, publishing as HTML, and supporting industry-standard databases for further customization. Report wizards, E-mail notification, and macro capability were less common.

These tools are fairly sophisticated, with most vendors reporting use of industry-standard databases and true three-tier client/server design.

Most products reported customization capability, through a programming language, support of OLE, or by exposing an application programming interface.

These products range dramatically in price, usually based on the additional components of the suite that are purchased. They start at $199, topping out at over $4,000.

What a Minority of Vendors Offer

The miscellaneous category of the Process Management matrix, few products handled all of the project management-related tasks we asked about. We noticed that vendors concentrated on a few of the following list of features:

- Navigate methods via hyperlinks
- Complexity factor adjustments
- What-if analysis
- Cost-benefit analysis
- Issues management
- Action items
- Change management
- Requirements management
- Risk management.

A handful of vendors cover all of these areas. Most vendors cover some, so look carefully at this part of the matrix when deciding what are differentiating requirements for your software evaluation process.

Some downsides: Among process management vendors, there appears to be very limited support for the Macintosh platform.

Also, few products are fully Web enabled. Those that did respond with a positive answer often qualified that response, by limiting it to a specific function, like time tracking.

Only about half of the vendors responding in this category have offices globally, and only about half offer non-English language support.

Unique Features That Surfaced in Vendor Responses to the Narrative Questions

Some of these tools are marketed as designed, to be integrated with the organization's financial systems.

What's New and Exciting

Most vendors who offer process management have functionality tightly integrated with supporting modules, like cost tracking, estimating, and scheduling. The full benefit of these suites is realized by exposing the corporate methodology throughout the organization, and by capturing data one time for use throughout the system.

Many vendors noted that their product supports an organization with a low level of project management sophistication, and the products are easy to learn and use.

A reminder: The data in the matrix and in the narrative responses were supplied by the vendors and have not been independently verified.

Process Management

	ABT Planner	AMS REALTIME Projects	AutoPLAN Enterprise	Dekker TRAKKER Activity Based Cost Management and Performance System	Enterprise Project	ER Project 1000	Mesa/Vista	Milestones, Etc.	Open Plan
Document management									
Version control	N	Y	N	Y	Y	N	Y	N	N
Document collaboration	N	Y	Y	Y	Y	Y	Y	Y	Y
Estimating									
Top-down	Y	Y	N	Y	Y	Y	N	N	Y
Bottom-up	Y	Y	N	Y	Y	Y	N	N	Y
Generates WBS for use in scheduling tool									
List scheduling tools:	ABT Workbench and MS Project	AMS REALTIME Projects		Y	Y	ER Project Manager, all tools importing MPX		Milestones, Etc.	N/A
Role/resource assignment	Y	Y	Y	Y	Y	Y	N	N	N
Work effort estimates by resource	Y	Y	Y	Y	Y	Y	N	N	N
Methodologies									
Product comes with methodologies (list)	Results Management Methodology			TRAKKER provides for the ability to define an organization's process methodologies.		MIL-STD-498 Software Development, IEEE 12207 Software Development, PMI Project Management		N	PMBOK™-based
Can input corporate methodologies	Y	Y	N	Y	Y	Y	Y	N	Y
Suggests routes through methodologies	Y	N	Y	Y	Y	N	N	N	Y
Reference	Y	Y	Y	Y	Y	Y	Y	N	N
Attach guidelines	Y	Y	Y	Y	Y	Y	Y	N	Y
Attach reference documents, templates	Y	Y	Y	Y	N	Y	Y	N	Y
Customized, context sensitive guidelines (help)	Y	Y	Y	Y	Y	Y	Y	N	Y
Tasks in schedule linked to methodology guidelines	Y	Y	Y	Y	Y	Y	Y	N	N
Misc.									
Navigate methods via hyperlinks	Y	Y	N	Y	N	N	Y	Y	Y
Complexity factor adjustments	Y	N	N	Y	Y	Y	N	N	Y
What-if analysis	Y	Y	Y	Y	Y	Y	N	N	Y
Cost benefit analysis	Y	Y	N	Y	Y	Y	N	N	Y
Issues management	N	Y	Y	Y	Y	N	N	N	Y
Action items	N	Y	Y	Y	Y	Y	Y	N	Y
Change management	N	N	N	Y	Y	N	Y	N	Y
Requirements management	N	Y	Y	Y	Y	N	Y	N	Y
Risk management	Y	N	Y	Y	Y	N	Y	N	Y

Reporting

	P1	P2	P3	P4	P5	P6	P7	P8
Report writer	Y	Y	Y	Y	Y	Y	Y	Y
Report wizard	N	Y	N	Y	Y	Y	N	N
Publishes as HTML	Y	Y	Y	Y	Y	Y	Y	Y
Number of user-defined fields	Unlim.	200	20	100	Unlim.	25	100	100
Drill-down/roll-up *	Y	Y	Y	Y	Y	Y	Y	Y
Import/export	Y	Y	Y	Y	Y	Y	Y	Y
Automatic E-mail notification *	Y	Y	Y	N	Y	Y	N	N
Macro recorder/batch capable *	N	Y	N	N	Y	Y	Y	N
Can "canned" reports be modified?	Y	Y	Y	Y	Y	Y	Y	Y
Sort, filter	Y	Y	Y	Y	Y	Y	Y	Y

Architecture

	P1	P2	P3	P4	P5	P6	P7	P8
Databases Supported (list):	Oracle, MS SQL Server, Sybase, MS Access, FoxPro	MS SQL Server	Oracle, MS SQL Server, Interbase	Oracle, Sybase, Informix, MS SQL Server, MS Access	Y	Oracle	Oracle, any ODBC-compliant DB	Oracle, MS SQL Server, Sybase, Informix
Supports distributed databases	Y		N	Y	Y	Y	Y	Y
Three-tier client/server	Y		N	Y	Y	Y	Y	Y
Client operating systems	Win 95 or later	Win	Win 95/98/NT 3.51/NT 4.0 (ER Project Satellite also Java and Win 3.x)	Win 95/98/NT	Win 95/98/NT	Win 95/NT/3.x, Solaris, HP-UX, AIX	Win 95/NT/3.x, Solaris, HP, RS, Mac	Win 95/98/NT
Server operating systems	Specified by database vendor	Win	Win NT, Unix	Unix, Win NT	Win NT, Novell, Unix	Win NT, Solaris, HP-UX, AIX	Win 95/NT/3.x, Solaris, HP, RS, Mac	Win NT
Network operating systems	Any that support Win	Any	Win, NetBEUI/ NetBios, TCP/IP, Novell	Novell, Win NT, others	Win NT, Novell, Unix	Win NT, Novell, Unix	TCP/IP compatible	TCP/IP, Banyan, Novell, IPX
Minimum client configuration	Pentium or compatible, Win 95 or later: 16 MB RAM, Rec. 32 MB	N	Pentium, 16 MB memory (ER Project Satellite 8 MB)	486, 16 MB memory	16 MB RAM, 1 GB HD, SVGA	P5 32 MB	8 MB RAM, 20 MB disk, 486 or better	Pentium 132
Minimum server configuration	Server optional	N	Pentium, 32 MB memory	Pentium 200 CPU, 128 MB, 1 GB	128 MB RAM, 10 GB HD	P5 32 MB, Unix machine with 64 MB	32 MB RAM, 100 MB disk, Pentium or better	Pentium 266
Client runs under Web browser	N	N	Y	Y	N	Y	Y	Y

Open architecture

	P1	P2	P3	P4	P5	P6	P7	P8
Supports OLE	Y	Y	N	N	Y	N	N	Y
Documented Object Model	Y	Y	Y	Y	Y	Y	Y	Y

Process Management

	ABT Planner	AMS REALTIME Projects	AutoPLAN Enterprise	Dekker TRAKKER Activity Based Cost Management and Performance System	Enterprise Project	ER Project 1000	Mesa/Vista	Milestones, Etc.	Open Plan
Documented Application Programming Interface (API)	Y	Y	Y	Y	Y	N	Y	Y	N
Simultaneous edit of data file	Y	Y	N	Y	Y	Y	Y	Y	Y
Does product have a programming language?	N	Y	Y	Y	Y	N	N	Y	N
Are years stored as four-digit numbers?	Y	N	Y	Y	Y	Y	Y	Y	Y
Online help									
Right mouse click	Y	N	N	Y	N	Y	N	Y	Y
Hover buttons	Y	Y	Y	Y	N	Y	N	Y	Y
Interactive help	Y	Y	Y	Y	Y	Y	Y	Y	Y
Help search feature	Y	Y	Y	Y	Y	Y	Y	Y	Y
Web access to product knowledge base *	Y	Y	Y	N	N	Y	N	Y	Y
Vendor information									
Training									
Computer-based training	Y	Y	Y	Y	Y	N	N	Y	Y
Training materials available	Y	Y	Y	Y	Y	Y	Y	Y	Y
Customized training materials	Y	Y	Y	Y	Y	Y	Y	Y	Y
Online tutorial	Y	Y	N	Y	N	Y	Y	Y	Y
Consulting available from vendor	Y	Y	Y	Y	Y	Y	Y	Y	Y
Site license discounts	Y	Y	Y	Y	Y	Y	Y	Y	Y
Enhancement requests *	Y	Y	Y	Y	Y	Y	N	Y	Y
Modify source code, support through upgrades *	Y	Y	Y	Y	Y	Y	Y	Y	Y
Global Presence									
Global offices	Y	Y	Y	Y	N	N	N	N	Y
Multi-lingual technical support	Y	Y	Y	Y	Y	N	N	N	Y
Language versions (list):	Eng, Fr, Ger, Jpn	Chin, Dutch, Eng, Fr, Ger, Jpn, Kor, Pol, Rus	Eng, Fr	Eng	Eng, Span	Eng	Eng	Eng	Eng, Ital, Fr, Ger, Mand, Rus, Hangul
Audit software quality assurance process? *	Y	Y	Y	Y	Y	Y	Y	N	N
Security									
Configurable access privileges *	Y	Y	Y	Y	Y	Y	Y	N	Y
Passwords expire (forced update)	N	N	Y	Y	Y	N	Y	N	N
Electronic approvals	Y	Y	Y	Y	Y	Y	Y	N	N
Password protect files	Y	Y	Y	Y	Y	Y	N	N	Y

Process Management

	PLANTRAC-APROPOS	PlanView Software	Project Control 6.0 - Process Manager	ProjectExchange Portfolio Wizard, TaskClass, DocCheck	Project Integrator 2.0 Enterprise Edition	Project KickStart	TeamWork	WebProject
Document management								
Version control	Y	N	Y	N	Y	N	Y	Y
Document collaboration	Y	N	Y	N	Y	Y	Y	Y
Estimating								
Top-down	Y	Y	Y	Y	Y	Y	N	N
Bottom-up	Y	Y	Y	Y	Y	Y	N	Y
Generates WBS for use in scheduling tool								
List scheduling tools:	PLANTRAC-OUTLOOK	Planner	Y	MS Project	MS Project 98	MS Project, SureTrak, Project Scheduler, SuperProject, Milestones, Etc.	MS Project 98	Y
Role/resource assignment	Y	Y	Y	Y	Y	Y	Y	Y
Work effort estimates by resource	Y	Y	Y	Y	Y	N	Y	Y
Methodologies								
Product comes with methodologies (list)	PRINCE	User defined	Y	N		Simple methodology for brainstorming and planning projects	Project mgt.	Major announcements forthcoming
Can input corporate methodologies	Y	Y	Y	Y	Y	Y	Y	Y
Suggests routes through methodologies	Y	N	Y	Y	Y	Y	Y	Y
Reference	Y	N	Y	Y	Y	Y	Y	Y
Attach guidelines	Y	Y	Y	Y	Y	Y	Y	Y
Attach reference documents, templates	Y	Y	Y	Y	Y	N	Y	Y
Customized, context sensitive guidelines (help)	Y	N	Y	N	N	Y	Y	Y
Tasks in schedule linked to methodology guidelines	Y	Y	Y	Y	Y	N	Y	Y
Misc.								
Navigate methods via hyperlinks	N	N	Y	Y	Y	Y	Y	Y
Complexity factor adjustments	N	N	N	N	N	N	N	N
What-if analysis	Y	Y	Y	Y	N	N	N	Y
Cost benefit analysis	Y	Y	N	Y	Y	N	N	Y
Issues management	Y	Y	N	Y	Y	Y	N	Y
Action items	Y	Y	Y	Y	Y	Y	Y	Y
Change management	Y	Y	Y	Y	N	Y	Y	Y
Requirements management	Y	Y	Y	Y	Y	Y	Y	Y
Risk management	Y	Y	N	N	N	Y	Y	Y

Process Management

	PLANTRAC-APROPOS	PlanView Software	Project Control 6.0 - Process Manager	ProjectExchange Portfolio Wizard, TaskClass, DocCheck	Project Integrator 2.0 Enterprise Edition	Project KickStart	TeamWork	WebProject
Reporting								
Report writer	Y	Y	Y	Y	Y	Y	N	N
Report wizard	Y	Y	N	Y	Y	N	N	Y
Publishes as HTML	N	Y	Y	Y	Y	Y	N	Y
Number of user-defined fields	5	Unlim.	60	Unlim.	Unlim.	0	0	Varies
Drill-down/roll-up *	Y	Y	Y	Y	Y	Y	N	Y
Import/export	Y	Y	Y	Y	Y	Y	Y	Y
Automatic E-mail notification *	N	Y	N	N	Y	N	Y	Y
Macro recorder/batch capable *	N	N	Y	Y	Y	N	Y	Y
Can "canned" reports be modified?	Y	Y	Y	Y	Y	Y	N	Y
Sort, filter	Y	Y	Y	Y	Y	Y	Y	Y
Architecture								
Databases Supported (list):	ODBC	Oracle, Sybase, MS SQL Server, etc.	Oracle, MS Access, MS SQL Server, Sybase	Oracle, MS SQL Server, Sybase	MS SQL Server, Oracle, Sybase, SQL Anywhere	N/A	ODBC	Oracle, MS SQL Server, Informix, Sybase, any JDBC-compliant database
Supports distributed databases	N	N	Y	Y	N	N/A	Y	Y
Three-tier client/server	Y	Y	Y	Y	Y	N/A	Y	Y
Client operating systems	Y	Win 95/98/NT	Win 95/98/NT	Win 32, MS Project, MS Excel	Win 95/NT	Win 95/98/NT/3.x	Win NT, Novell	Win 95/NT, Unix, Linux, any Java-enabled OS
Server operating systems	Y	Win NT, Unix, Novell, IIS, Netscape	Unix, Win NT, HP, Sybase, others	Unix, Win NT	Win NT	N/A	Win NT, Novell	Win 95/NT, Unix, Linux, any Java-enabled OS
Network operating systems	Y	Win NT, Unix, Novell, IIS, Netscape	Novell, IPX, XPX, Banyan, MS Network, TCP/IP	Multiple	Novell, Win NT, Banyan	N/A	Win NT, Novell	Win 95/NT, Unix, Linux, any Java-enabled OS
Minimum client configuration	Y	486/66, 8 MB RAM, Win 3.1 +	PC 486/66 processor or above. Win 95 or Win NT V4. 16 MB RAM	Pentium w/32 MB	P166 MHz, 16 MB RAM, 30 MB HD	4 MB RAM, 2.2 MB HD	486/12 MB	Any Java-enabled browser
Minimum server configuration	Y	486/66, 32 MB RAM, Novell	Any server supporting Oracle 7 or above	Pentium w/128 MB	P166 MHz, 16 MB RAM, 30 MB HD	N/A	486/12 MB	
Client runs under Web browser	N	Y	Y	N	Y	N/A	Y	Y
Open architecture								
Supports OLE	N	Y	Y	Y	Y	N/A	N	N
Documented Object Model	N	Y	N	Y	N	N/A	N	N
Documented Application Programming Interface (API)	N	Y	N	N	N	N/A	N	N
Simultaneous edit of data file	Y	N	Y	Y	Y	N/A	Y	Y
Does product have a programming language?	N	Y	N	N	N	N	N	N

	1	2	3	4	5	6	7
Are years stored as four-digit numbers?	Y	Y	Y	Y	Y	Y	Y
Online help							
Right mouse click	Y	N	N	N	N	Y	N
Hover buttons	Y	Y	Y	Y	Y	Y	Y
Interactive help	Y	N	N	N	Y	Y	Y
Help search feature	Y	Y	Y	Y	Y	Y	Y
Web access to product knowledge base *	N	Y	N	Y	Y	Y	Y
Vendor information							
Training							
Computer-based training	Y	Y	N	N	Y	Y	Y
Training materials available	Y	Y	Y	Y	Y	Y	Y
Customized training materials	Y	Y	Y	Y	Y	Y	Y
Online tutorial	Y	N	N	N	Y	N	Y
Consulting available from vendor	Y	Y	Y	Y	Y	Y	Y
Site license discounts	Y	Y	N	Y	Y	Y	Y
Enhancement requests *	Y	Y	Y	Y	Y	Y	Y
Modify source code, support through upgrades *	Y	Y	Y	Y	N/A	Y	Y
Global Presence							
Global offices	N	Y	N	N	N	Y	Y
Multi-lingual technical support	N	N	N	Eng	N	Eng	Eng, Ger
Language versions (list):	Eng, Fr, Ger	Eng	Eng	Y	Eng, Fr	Y	Y
Audit software quality assurance process? *	Y	Y	Y		Y		
Security							
Configurable access privileges *	N	Y	Y	Y	N	Y	Y
Passwords expire (forced update)	N	Y	N	Y	N	N	Y
Electronic approvals	N	Y	Y	Y	N	N	N
Password protect files	N	Y	Y	DBMS	N	Y	Y

91

VENDOR RESPONSES TO NARRATIVE QUESTIONS

ABT Planner (ABT Corporation)

Describe what the product is designed to do.

ABT Planner is a flexible planning, estimating, and methodology delivery tool designed to work with a company's best practices to produce complete and reliable project plans and estimates.

Top three product differentiators; describe what makes your product unique.

1. Robust project management repository.
2. Works with any methodology.
3. Quick generation of plans and estimates.

To what business processes can this tool be applied?

Scope management.
Estimating and planning.
Knowledge management.

Describe the ideal end-user environment for the current version of your product (size of organization, level of project management sophistication, effort and commitment required).

Any size organization with an interest in improving its project management practices.

Future strategies for this product.

Browser-based interface.
Knowledge management.

Product's target market.

Enterprise project management.

What are your product's three main benefits? (How does using the product add value to the customer?)

1. Improves efficiency in estimating and planning.
2. Reengineering best practices.
3. Powerful customizing facilities.

Describe your quality management process. List any relevant certifications.

ABT's Test Engineering organization provides extensive in-house product quality testing using a series of proprietary testing methodologies, supplemented by external resources to perform activities such as high-volume benchmarking. ABT's test group has also been instrumental in contributing to the definition of IEEE Year 2000 testing standards.

Discuss your product pricing structure. Include volume discount levels, concurrent user options, site licenses, cost of implementation, and other issues.

Pricing is on a named-user basis. List price: ABT Planner—$300. Volume discounts apply.

Implementation programs vary according to suite installations or stand-alone product installations. Additional services include project management maturity evaluation, tool training, project management concepts training, process customization and implementation, and systems integration/custom programming work.

AMS REALTIME Projects (Advanced Management Systems)

Describe what the product is designed to do.

AMS REALTIME Projects provides powerful project management in an easy-to-use graphic software tool. Plan project tasks, network constraints, resource and manpower utilizations by manipulating graphic images with your mouse, or import data from external sources. Costs and earned value are visible in real time as the project evolves.

Distributed projects and subprojects offer unlimited project capacity, while merge-link, attached documents, shared calendars, shared resources, and command links to other systems provide the capability to build a complete enterprisewide project management system. Store project data in proprietary stand-alone files stored on a common file server, or store data on a database (ODBC-compliant database, AMS proprietary database, or Oracle) using an AMS REALTIME Projects server.

Customized help files that contain user-defined processes can be integrated into the projects software menu. Documents can be attached to activities that detail processes, controls, or other information. Command links can be created to provide information about processes specific to the overall project.

Top three product differentiators; describe what makes your product unique.

Fully integrated schedule, resource, and cost give you an accurate look at one or more projects from any perspective. User-defined process documentation can be integrated. AMS REALTIME Projects is fully equipped with powerful features: attached documents, command links, WBS tools, sorting and matching with stored views, calculated fields, cost breakdowns (labor, materials, ODC), rate tables, multiple revisions, much more.

All software runs native on Windows (95, NT, 3.x), Macintosh, Sun, Solaris, HP, RS with identical look and feel and direct data access from any platform.

To what business processes can this tool be applied?

AMS REALTIME is so flexible that it can be applied to virtually any business process, including proposals, maintenance operations, new development, manufacturing, and performance improvement processes.

AMS REALTIME is designed to allow automated project statusing that automatically feeds earned value performance measurements. Cost management is empowered when costs can be tracked from a project summary level all the way down to the activity level; providing accurate information to pinpoint the source of cost overruns.

Describe the ideal end-user environment for the current version of your product (size of organization, level of project management sophistication, effort and commitment required).

AMS REALTIME is used by global companies in very large enterprise environments all the way down to small companies with just a few people. While AMS REALTIME is used to support extremely sophisticated project management processes, it can still be used to benefit users with little or no project management background. Users can grow into the software as their project management expertise evolves. To make any project management implementation successful, senior management must be committed to supporting the process, and other participants must make the effort to be trained to use the tools and follow through. Working with a consultant to help adapt the software to your business practices and needs and to document these processes is the best way to ensure success.

Future strategies for this product.

Future development strategies include more active Web enablements, a more complex three-tiered server design to facilitate global replication, and more resource tools. AMS has always been on the cutting edge of technology, and we are dedicated to bringing our customers the best of this ever-changing world.

Product's target market.

Products are used across a wide variety of client bases. AMS does not target any particular market, but is widely used in manufacturing, oil and gas, nuclear power, automotive, pharmaceutical, aerospace, software development, construction, research and development, and many other industries. AMS REALTIME software allows for a flexible implementation that integrates with customer business processes.

What are your product's three main benefits? (How does using the product add value to the customer?)

1. Schedule, resources, and costs are fully integrated so that an accurate project and/or resource status can be obtained in real time. This provides accurate visibility that enables proactive decisions to keep the project on track.

2. Software runs on all major platforms, allowing companies to use their existing hardware investment while sharing the same data. Data can be stored in local or shared proprietary files, or stored on Oracle using client/server technology and integrated with other Oracle applications.

3. AMS REALTIME gives program managers, project managers, resource managers, and employees the tools to work within their functional areas. Each piece is a part of the solution that supports the whole enterprisewide management process.

Describe your quality management process. List any relevant certifications.

Advanced Management Solutions is fully committed to providing the highest-quality software and services to all our clients. We have implemented many internal standards and processes in order to ensure that we can track and manage our software development process to the highest standard of quality possible. Concurrent versions system has been implemented to help manage multiple programmers at multiple development sites. Peer review of source code and design strategy meetings with high-level program development leaders continue to ensure that our software remains on the leading edge of our evolving technology.

A dedicated testing department manages the initial alpha testing, which encompasses new functionality, system process testing, and full regression testing. Beta testing is initially performed internally. After a stable point has been reached, beta testing is extended to select client users. Client beta testing not only provides clients with an edge in using new software features, but also greatly expands the test environment scope relating to different hardware environments. As AMS REALTIME is one of the most flexible and highly configurable management products on the market today, client testing adds an exceptional dimension to our testing process.

Discuss your product pricing structure. Include volume discount levels, concurrent user options, site licenses, cost of implementation, and other issues.

Product price is different for clients, based on their requirements for software and implementation. Volume discounts and site licenses are available. Please request a quote from an AMS sales representative for your specific requirements.

Annual maintenance is based on 20 percent of the current product cost, and includes all software upgrades (while support is active) and telephone hotline technical support. Training cost is based upon topics, requirements, training equipment and site, and days requested. Please request a quote from an AMS sales representative for your specific requirements.

AutoPLAN Enterprise (Digital Tools)

Describe what the product is designed to do.

AutoPLAN Enterprise Release 4 is a Web-based software and process solution to help high-tech, engineering, and telecommunications companies predict, control, and improve cycle time of critical program development and deployment. The solution set provides deep functionality across the entire spectrum of product life-cycle elements including pipeline management, project management, resource alignment, process effectiveness, document support, and team collaboration. AutoPLAN Enterprise integrates realistic planning, resource-centric management, status and forecast tracking, team collaboration, process support, escalation management, and program execution across globally distributed organizations.

Organizations are evolving from functional teams to matrix or program teams, and this is creating cross-functional or multidisciplinary project teams. AutoPLAN Enterprise recognizes three different organizational patterns that coexist: 1) dynamic peer-to-peer; 2) functional; and 3) program management. AutoPLAN Enterprise offers these organizations both project-centric and resource-centric management. AutoPLAN Enterprise addresses everyone involved in product development and deployment including executives; program, product, resource, and project managers; and team leaders and team members, as well as teams from marketing, operations, service, and quality.

As a result of extensive process and product consulting with clients engaged in new product development and deployment, Digital Tools, Inc. (DTI) has distilled four key reasons why products are late and descoped:

1. Product development pipeline and deployment structures that are not aligned with the company's time-to-market goals.

2. Unrealistic plans, overcommitted resources, and unmanaged cross-functional dependencies.

3. Status and forecast decisions that are based on hearsay, rather than on facts or experience.

4. A lack of consistent processes that fit the company culture and practice, which is further exacerbated by distributed cross-functional teams.

Avoiding late and descoped products requires an overall view of product and project status, the involvement of cross-functional teams, and decision evaluation tools. Increasingly accelerated product development cycles and shorter product life cycles require organizations to disseminate information quickly to remain competitive. To support today's geographically dispersed product development environments, organizations require a common platform that enables effective cross-functional collaboration and communication on product development issues. It is also imperative that the introduction of new product information can be easily accessible by each stakeholder. Common platforms and accessible information by each stakeholder will result in accelerated organizational learning and decision-making within the organization.

DTI has created a cycle time management (CTM) framework comprised of both application and process support. This framework emphasizes the critical components involved in introducing and deploying the right products and services to the market at the right time. Introducing and deploying these products and services requires companies to institute well-defined new product planning and execution processes, complemented with customer management and performance measurement processes. The new planning processes should consist of product portfolio, technology portfolio, product planning, and resource planning. The execution processes must consist of advanced technology development, platform development, product development, and market introduction and deployment.

CTM enables companies to strike a balance between flexibility and discipline that is tailored to their organization and culture. The CTM framework supports a flexible *shrink-to-fit* process, which is adaptable to an organization's process maturity. This process will provide a road map for decision-making and progress tracking within a new product introduction and deployment pipeline.

CTM comprises six fundamental elements: 1) processes, 2) projects, 3) resources, 4) documents, 5) deliverables, and 6) analysis. These six elements form the foundation objectives that drive AutoPLAN Enterprise. Organizations require a well-defined and structured process to accomplish their goals. Projects make up the mechanisms through which detailed plans and schedules are generated, executed, and tracked. Every organization faces resource constraints; thus, resource management is a critical component of CTM. All projects have deliverables associated with them either in the form of documents or the product itself. And, all projects must be managed to ensure quality deliverables. Analysis tools enable various levels of stakeholders to evaluate and ensure proper support of all elements necessary to meet CTM objectives.

Top three product differentiators; describe what makes your product unique.

1. AutoPLAN Enterprise enables organizations to manage their pipeline of resources across programs and across the phase gates of each project. It assures an escalation process for critical issues, such as overallocations, by monitoring boundary conditions and alerting appropriate people to the issues. Project managers are interested in the completion of tasks or milestones, while resource managers need to know all of the work planned for their resources. Both project and resource managers must collaborate to create realistic plans for meeting project objectives, as well as juggle those resources and plans on a day-to-day basis, as changes occur. The nature of this work requires a resource-centric view of the plan, not just an activity-centric view. A resource-centric view will allow resource managers to view and allocate activities to their scarce resources rather than allocating resources to their activities. AutoPLAN Enterprise enables resource management by providing a resource-centric Gantt bar that displays overallocated resources. Managing overallocations can be as easy as reassigning activities to another resource.

Program management is a collaborative effort. Success depends upon identifying and communicating critical issues. Such identification and communication must be inherent in the system. AutoPLAN Enterprise is designed with a communications backbone. A mechanism of triggers identifies critical issues (e.g., when milestone or cost exceeds a threshold boundary) and automatically alerts and draws attention to these critical issues. Project bulletin boards within AutoPLAN Enterprise also enhance communication by providing a context-sensitive vehicle for communicating information across the project team. In addition, AutoPLAN Enterprise supports electronic mail systems enabling triggers and bulletin board messages to be communicated to the various levels of stakeholders.

2. AutoPLAN Enterprise supports the distributed nature of project teams by matching real-world strategy with key scalable technologies. Enterprise customers need distributed project management capabilities that cater to multisite resource management, work distribution, progress tracking, global scheduling, consolidation, reporting, integration, and collaboration. DTI has met this challenge by investing over one hundred man-years in an enterprise-level, three-tier, distributed client/server architecture that leverages both Java and Internet technologies. AutoPLAN Enterprise provides full support for multiple internal operating divisions and external suppliers. AutoPLAN Enterprise leverages many platforms—Internet, Windows, NT, and Unix—providing reliable access across the organization. Additionally, AutoPLAN Enterprise enables common project data to be shared by different projects at different locations while being maintained in a central data center that is managed by pool-server software. Project data is maintained at each geographic location on either individual or multiple servers, depending on the number of internal operating divisions and projects. A divisional pool server can also be implemented to share the project data within divisional projects. AutoPLAN Enterprise application servers are capable of scalable distributed processing, and only the server needs the capacity for large multiproject operations. AutoPLAN Enterprise has multiserver cross-project dependency links. For example, the owner of a schedule that depends on the completion of activities in another project can create cross-project links that automatically update his schedule when changes occur in the other project, even if that project resides on a different server.

3. AutoPLAN Enterprise leverages client/server/Web technologies. The promise of Java, which AutoPLAN Enterprise supports, is that enterprise deployments, including organizations with heterogeneous environments, can be cost-effectively supported. DTI Web products are easier to use than Microsoft Project and are cheaper to deploy. The rapid spread of Internet protocols and Web servers into corporate infrastructure makes the Internet an ideal vehicle to support both enterprise computing and mobile employees. In addition, systems administration is simplified since no maintenance is required on the client side.

A very practical use of AutoPLAN Enterprise Web clients is that they can run in a disconnected mode on the Internet. With AutoPLAN Enterprise, the user can simply log on and save activities and other information to a local file. She can then continue to work while disconnected. At any time, the connection can be reestablished, either remotely or locally, and the data is resynchronized. This may be useful for dial-up connections when working remotely. The Web server handles all communications with the Web clients, whether they are communicating via the Internet, dial-up, LAN, or

WAN. The AutoPLAN Enterprise Web clients can be run from any browser that supports Java 1.1, and the Web server will dynamically download the Java code to run the application on the client. DTI's Web strategy supports *thin* client computing. In this case, database-oriented servers are serving lightweight clients through Web servers and standard protocols. The AutoPLAN Enterprise Web clients are ideally suited for running on a Java-based network computer.

To what business processes can this tool be applied?

From business analysis and redesign to system implementation and training, DTI has established its own process to support the customer through all phases of CTM system implementation. However, as to applying AutoPLAN Enterprise to the customer's business processes, DTI takes a very pragmatic approach. DTI has established processes to help customers with the following seven business pains:

1. Managing the development and deployment pipeline in detail.
2. Top-down and bottom-up planning that enables managers to use team members' knowledge during up-front planning.
3. Juggling resources realistically, so that resources are not overcommitted and parochial allocations are not made, but rather a mechanism for cooperation on resource tradeoffs is created.
4. Creating an organizational memory that captures organizational experience for reuse the next time.
5. Obtaining weekly integrated tracking information on how programs are progressing against their plans. This can be achieved by capturing actual time spent, estimates to complete, percent complete, and actual start and finish.
6. Problem identification, escalation, and collaboration that allows management and the team to receive adequate notice of impending issues.
7. Interactive decision evaluation to understand the domino effect of a problem in one project and its possible cross-program impact, and obtain a swift resolution between participants.

Any combination of these processes will help organizations better understand and make use of critical path methodology, work breakdown structures, resource management, cost and earned value techniques, multiproject resource scheduling, resource allocation, status tracking, report generation, matrix management solutions, integration with other systems, middleware design, project management process design, project rollups, report generation, database design, customized product training courses, generic project management training, and more.

Describe the ideal end-user environment for the current version of your product (size of organization, level of project management sophistication, effort and commitment required).

AutoPLAN Enterprise is ideal for high-tech, engineering, and telecommunications organizations engaged in distributed product development and deployments. Its usage also extends to these organizations' distributors and partners. The role-based nature of AutoPLAN Enterprise spans all people involved, from executive management to the entire cross-functional product team. This includes experienced project and program managers, resource and development managers, and the team members creating or deploying the product. The AutoPLAN Enterprise Web client is specifically designed for those team leaders who are not full-time, experienced project managers. In fact, DTI has designed the AutoPLAN Enterprise Web client to be easier to use and more functional than Microsoft Project.

Organizations can start at either the program level right away and manage the overall pipeline of projects and resources at the business-unit level, or at the individual project level. The AutoPLAN Enterprise Web client is not only easier to use than Microsoft Project, but also is capable of managing cross-functional dependencies and resources and offering enterprise scalability when the organization is ready to expand.

Coordinating distributed projects is a difficult task. It involves resources not only from multiple projects, but also from multiple functions within those projects. The program manager responsible must understand all of the interactions and milestones required to complete the project, but he cannot and should not develop and manage the entire plan himself. Instead, he should rely on the distributed functional leaders who are responsible for their piece of the project to plan and execute that piece. As a program manager, he needs to be able to integrate the individual team plans into a single comprehensive project plan. In many organizations, this integration of people and data is difficult; AutoPLAN Enterprise is designed to help with this. Having processes in place, underpinned by enterprise software, is key to predicting, controlling, and improving product/project cycle times.

Future strategies for this product.

AutoPLAN Enterprise has been designed with an integrated product management platform for all information related to meeting CTM objectives. DTI will continue to support features needed for CTM, including pipeline and portfolio management. Future strategies will enhance the ability of customers to make informed decisions based on a comprehensive presentation of relevant data with powerful drill-down capabilities, further collaborative features that utilize the intranet and Internet, and continuing support for the free-flowing nature of the engineering culture. Application wizards will help first-time users, accelerate deployment, and reduce training cost. Process support is key to productivity improvements and to adhering to organizationwide standards. Existing process-support capabilities will be enhanced using the capabilities of Web technology and with more exchange of information across subsystems. Large organizations are geographically distributed to take advantage of global efficiencies. Local and global workgroups must collaborate and respond quickly to changing environment and work content. Both executive management and frontline team members must have access anytime, anywhere, and in any manner to enterprisewide product/project information located on geographically distributed servers. Existing multiserver capabilities of AutoPLAN Enterprise are being enhanced using Oracle.

AutoPLAN Enterprise will support key technologies including Oracle, NT 5.0, middleware, and Java. Distributed-objects capability using industry-standard specifications such as CORBA will be incorporated. In addition, the AutoPLAN Enterprise application-programming interface will provide CORBA-compliant objects for seamless integration with other applications. The collaboration capabilities of AutoPLAN Enterprise will be enhanced by incorporating a workflow server. This workflow server will be based on industry-standard specifications and will incorporate process modeling and messaging components to enable customers to configure the collaboration features based upon their business needs. The security system will have additional features to address the security risks associated with the Internet. Directory servers conforming to LDAP standards will be incorporated for seamless integration with the underlying operating environment. This in turn will provide responsive security, configurability, and flexibility features.

Product's target market.

AutoPLAN Enterprise is specifically designed to support high-tech, engineering, and telecommunications organizations in predicting, controlling, and improving cycle time of critical program development and deployment.

What are your product's three main benefits? (How does using the product add value to the customer?)

1. AutoPLAN Enterprise provides at least a 10 percent improvement in enterprise time-to-market of product development and deployment. Viewing the value of CTM from an annual R&D cost perspective: consider a product development group of one thousand people, with an annual R&D expenditure of $100M. A modest 10 percent improvement would represent a cost savings value of $10M, with a revenue enhancement value of three-to-five times this.

2. AutoPLAN Enterprise facilitates an organization's transformation from functional project teams to matrix, or program-organized high-performance project teams. It also supports distributed teams resulting from acquisitions. It does both of these by providing built-in communication and rollup features from distributed multiserver projects. This support enables teamwide problem identification, escalation, collaboration, and resolution. AutoPLAN Enterprise recognizes that three different organizational patterns coexist: 1) dynamic peer-to-peer, 2) functional, and 3) program management. AutoPLAN Enterprise offers these organizations both project-centric and resource-centric management.

3. AutoPLAN Enterprise accommodates joint ventures, subcontracting, mergers and acquisitions, and reorganizations by leveraging the Web to minimize deployment and support costs. The creation of plans, assignment of work, and integration of activities across multiple functions and distributed work teams is critically important. However, that is only part of the story. With the Internet, AutoPLAN Enterprise can also efficiently equip thousands of personnel involved in the product development process with the information they need to do the best possible job. Demand for skilled workers has been great, and turnover has risen as employees move from one company or job to another. The best practices in the world are of no value to a company if those who know those practices move on without first passing along the knowledge. Best practices developed at one site need to be shared with other sites, and a process for doing that is required. AutoPLAN Enterprise solves these problems through URL references and retrieval capability. With URL features, AutoPLAN Enterprise can help preserve best practices and other information and disseminate them geographically and functionally to team members currently doing the job. AutoPLAN Enterprise can also have associated URL references that point to mission-critical information/documentation that will enable product/project teams to achieve the activity. These references can also be attached to the top-level program schedule for project leader use or at specific functional schedules (e.g., to provide sourcing with specific third-party vendor requirements). URLs can enable:

- Sharing best practice information from one team to another
- Referencing documentation with checklists
- Sharing of engineering notes on installation processes.

Also, with the speed of organizational changes, a mix of project scheduling system usage is expected. As most people are educated on Microsoft Project, AutoPLAN Enterprise can coexist with its projects and data. AutoPLAN Enterprise's graphical user interfaces (GUIs) are not only familiar to Microsoft Project users; the Web version is easier and thus leverages simplicity and ease of use with enterprise functionality.

Describe your quality management process. List any relevant certifications.

DTI achieves excellence in product quality and customer satisfaction through its quality management process. DTI's quality objective is to build quality into its products and services at all stages of product life cycle, from requirement collection to customer usage. DTI's dedication to quality is reflected in its quality mission: "Doing things right the first time."

DTI's quality management group performs the functions of the software engineering process group as defined by the industry-standard capability maturity model (CMM). The quality management group plans and implements DTI's quality system, which consists of processes and guidelines. The processes detail out *what* is required for converting a set of inputs to outputs in the form of activities and tasks, primary and cooperative responsibilities, deliverables, and entry and exit criteria. The guidelines detail *how* to carry out the identified activities to ensure quality and consistency. The involvement of DTI personnel at all levels is fundamental to the implementation of the quality process. DTI personnel are drawn from various groups in the organization to author processes and guidelines, and all undergo training programs on the quality system.

DTI follows processes within Level 2 and Level 3 of the CMM. Some of the key processes within these levels include market requirement analysis, functional specification, high- and low-level design, coding, testing, release management, customer support, training, and maintenance. In addition, in-depth reviews are built into each of these processes.

DTI recognizes that enterprise growth and profitability are significantly impacted by time-to-market of new products in globally competitive high-tech markets. With this in mind, DTI's product development and quality processes are focused on meeting customer needs and requirements. Therefore, DTI collaborates with its customers both in product definition and in assuring that the product functions are implemented as intended. To facilitate the fast-track delivery of innovative products and services, DTI has created process initiatives for increased test automation, usage of tools that will enable teams to better assess the quality of their work products, management of development tools, reuse of objects across products, and tightly controlled configuration management.

DTI's quality management process focuses on periodic reviews and feedback, which are a means of monitoring the adherence of organizational activities to the process. Corrective and preventive actions play an important role in continuous improvement of the quality system and thereby the organizational activities.

DTI has a well-qualified team for quality management. DTI's teams, besides having the appropriate educational qualifications, have quality management-related certifications; some are certified quality analysts, and some hold certificates related to the CMM and its use. Many also have extensive internal audit experience.

The quality management group interacts periodically with key personnel of different functions within the organization and identifies new processes, guidelines, and improvements within the existing framework. The general approach to new process/guideline introduction is to discuss with representative users, define the process, pilot the process after review, evaluate the pilot implementation, revise the process based on feedback, plan organizationwide implementation, implement, measure, and maintain.

DTI is planning to get CMM certification at the appropriate level. The approach that would be followed for securing the certification includes mapping key process areas of the CMM to existing processes, identifying the *gaps*, preparing the implementation plan that describes how these gaps will be addressed, and executing the plan.

Discuss your product pricing structure. Include volume discount levels, concurrent user options, site licenses, cost of implementation, and other issues.

DTI's objective is to offer an integrated solution with a pricing structure that is based on enterprise requirements reflecting enterprise needs and individual needs. AutoPLAN Enterprise supports a floating license configuration, which allows any user to log into the system and consume one license. When the user has finished with the application, that license will be released for other users. Each floating license provides one concurrent use of the product. AutoPLAN Enterprise also supports a personal license configuration. Typical installations will use both personal and concurrent licensing.

Annual product maintenance is 15 percent of the list cost. Product maintenance entitles customers to engineering patches, updates and upgrades, and phone, fax, and E-mail response to issues. Professional services are separate from DTI product maintenance. As part of the business relationship with customers, DTI takes part in joint planning to identify the customer's business needs and services sought from DTI. Professional services are charged separately on an as-needed basis. These services are performed either at the customer site, online, or at DTI's headquarters in Cupertino, California. Professional services typically fall into two categories: 1) product consulting/implementation design review and 2) implementation support. Product consulting/implementation design review discusses areas such as, "How do I apply the software with a suitable process to solve a business need?" and, "Which processes will we implement, how, and when to meet organizational objectives?" Implementation support consists of product training, project office services, upgrade migration services, systems administration services, and integration services.

Dekker TRAKKER Activity Based Cost Management and Performance System (DTMI)

Describe what the product is designed to do.

Provide the user with the capability to model the process of a department, organization, or enterprise to determine the inputs and outputs of the activities of the organizational element. This system feature integrates with the other modules of TRAKKER to provide a complete ABC/ABM system.

Top three product differentiators; describe what makes your product unique.

1. Integration with the resource, cost, risk, and technical performance modules of the system.
2. Enterprise planning and tracking capability.
3. Flexible process modeling capability.

To what business processes can this tool be applied?

Scheduling, process flow, resource planning, and trend analysis.

Describe the ideal end-user environment for the current version of your product (size of organization, level of project management sophistication, effort and commitment required).

One of the key attributes of the TRAKKER system is scalability. TRAKKER has been designed to integrate into a business environment by establishing an organization's business rules within the system. This architecture enables TRAKKER to fit the needs and sophistication of any implementation. This flexibility enables TRAKKER to support a variety of implementation approaches. TRAKKER installations typically provide access to a range of users including cost account managers, cost/schedule analysts, and financial managers to meet the unique requirements of each for information and output. Typical TRAKKER clients range from companies of one thousand employees to Fortune 500 corporations.

Future strategies for this product.

Dekker, Ltd. will continue to enhance the integration of TRAKKER with MS Office and MS Back Office suite of tools. The design of the TRAKKER architecture will continue to focus on making data more visual and accessible to the complete range of system users.

Product's target market.

R&D, government, software, medical, electronics, and aerospace.

What are your product's three main benefits? (How does using the product add value to the customer?)

1. Integration with the resource, cost, risk, and technical performance modules of the system.
2. Enterprise planning and tracking capability.
3. Flexible process modeling capability.

Describe your quality management process. List any relevant certifications.

DTMI has modeled our development process from the Microsoft model while incorporating the quality guidelines established in ISO 9000.

Discuss your product pricing structure. Include volume discount levels, concurrent user options, site licenses, cost of implementation, and other issues.

DTMI offers both single and concurrent user licenses of TRAKKER. Our flexible pricing enables both small and large organizations to cost effectively implement costing and earned value management systems. TRAKKER pricing includes a progressive discount for volume purchases with reasonable thresholds for single and multisite licenses. Further, DTMI offers both public and private training courses for both new and advanced users. DTMI also offers consulting services to support the enterprise implementation of TRAKKER.

DTMI provides training for the discipline of both scheduling and attributes of TRAKKER. These workshops include Basic Project Management, TRAKKER Application Workshop, TRAKKER Intermediate Workshop, TRAKKER Report Writer Workshop, and TRAKKER MIS Integrator's Workshop. Through these courses, an enterprise can completely implement the TRAKKER system. In addition to our classroom training, DTMI offers consulting services to guide users though a structured approach to implementing TRAKKER.

Enterprise Project (jeTECH DATA SYSTEMS, INC.)

Describe what the product is designed to do.

Enterprise Project is a completely integrated solution (all applications share a common database and operate on the same hardware platform). Consequently, our response to the narrative questions here repeats what we supplied for the Suites category, as those responses apply to all of our applications.

Enterprise Project is a powerful new client/server software application that offers project-based organizations a simple way to define and staff projects, and record project labor and expenses throughout the enterprise. Essentially a suite of robust, user-friendly applications integrated into a single desktop, this comprehensive project management system enables team members to accurately plan and track labor resources across all projects. Perfect either as a *stand-alone* solution or as the ideal complement to the jeTECH labor-management system—Enterprise Labor—it is particularly well suited for multiuser, enterprisewide installations. Together, Enterprise Labor and Enterprise Project are the only systems currently on the market with extensive capabilities and integrated products for both the salaried professional (engineers and computer programmers, for instance) and the hourly employee (from factory workers to registered nurses).

Users access all functions via a single desktop with a Microsoft Office 98 *look and feel*. The system integrates completely with Enterprise Labor and Microsoft Project, as well as with most popular accounting and human resource (HR) systems. In today's competitive environment, effective and efficient use of labor resources is key to completing mission-critical projects on time, on budget. Enterprise Project gives project leaders a comprehensive, potent tool with which to manage scarce technical resources.

With Enterprise Project, managers can budget and schedule projects based on staff skills and availability. Project team members can manage their own tasks, report actual labor and travel expenses, and provide status reports on these tasks. The system calculates actual project costs by automatically incorporating labor costs, material costs, and travel expenses.

Project managers can define and manage both contract and noncontract-based projects, and control work authorizations that will keep each project under control and on budget. As a project manager, you simply create activities for your projects, assign appropriate resources to these activities, and define how labor will be charged to a contract. And by allowing employees to only charge preassigned tasks, Enterprise Project prevents performance of unauthorized work.

Enterprise Project enables all users to report labor charges right from their PC or workstations. Project managers need no longer compile project team information manually. Users can now report project time, as well as other time, and the system automatically processes and transmits it to an interfaced time and attendance system for payroll use.

Enterprise Project includes a contract maintenance module. Companies with hourly employees contracted with outside firms—for instance, security guards or programmers—would benefit from using this module without the rest of the project management system. This module is primarily designed, however, to accommodate projects being managed for clients. This module allows contract managers to define contract information including budgets and rates per hour, as well as all products and services purchased by the customer. They can then use this information to evaluate projects based on user-defined deliverables. Contract maintenance is by no means static. So jeTECH has designed Enterprise Project to handle change orders, R&D projects, and discounts. A variety of unique reporting features enables contract managers to view cost overruns, variances, and milestone completions.

Top three product differentiators; describe what makes your product unique.

1. Resource scheduling from a common resource pool in a multiproject environment.
2. Integrated time collection and status reporting.
3. Sensitivity analysis (what-if scenarios).

To what business processes can this tool be applied?

Project planning/management, enterprise resource scheduling/management, time collection, performance measurement, time and expense reporting, budgeting and estimating, and project accounting.

Describe the ideal end-user environment for the current version of your product (size of organization, level of project management sophistication, effort and commitment required).

Any resource-constrained enterprise (IT, high-tech R&D, engineering) with multiple projects and multiple sites. Requires a low level of project management sophistication.

Future strategies for this product.

Maintenance and repair operations, incorporation of process ware/templates, enterprise-level project and resource integration, and full Internet capabilities.

Product's target market.

Companies with *task-oriented* professionals such as engineers, architects, IS professionals, researchers, advertising/marketing professionals, etc. See also the previous response to "ideal end-user environment."

What are your product's three main benefits? (How does using the product add value to the customer?)

1. Improved resource utilization and efficiencies.
2. Reduction in time to complete projects.
3. Cost control.

Describe your quality management process. List any relevant certifications.

Our current quality management process includes in-house testing, which incorporates both automated and manual processes and procedures.

Discuss your product pricing structure. Include volume discount levels, concurrent user options, site licenses, cost of implementation, and other issues.

Pricing is structured on a named-user basis. Pricing will also be dependent on a number of variables including the size of the enterprise, number of project managers, number of facilities, etc. Consequently, pricing is provided to each customer when we have been able to familiarize ourselves on their operations and their anticipated use of the system.

Several options are available for training, tech support, annual maintenance, etc. Costs are provided to each customer when they have been able to select the options deemed best for their operations.

ER Project 1000 (Eagle Ray Software Systems)

Describe what the product is designed to do.

The ER Project 1000 is an integrated suite of project management tools, which provide an enterprisewide project management solution. ER Project 1000 includes schedule/time management, centralized resource management, methodology/process management, project-workgroup communications, timesheets, risk/issue management, and enterprisewide cross-project tracking. Based on a client/server architecture with a centralized relational database, the ER Project 1000 provides networked access, multiproject capability, and true multiuser concurrency. It scales easily from handling small workgroup projects to large programs at the enterprise level.

Top three product differentiators; describe what makes your product unique.

1. Addresses the total project management life-cycle solution for the enterprise: Unlike most project management tools, the ER Project 1000 provides a completely integrated and centralized project management platform to support the entire life cycle of project management. Based on a client/server relational database (Oracle/SQL Server) architecture, ER Project 1000 fully supports today's multiproject/multiuser project environment. The product suite integrates full methodology/process management capabilities, project workgroup communications, and enterprisewide project tracking capabilities.

2. Provides a completely integrated suite of project management tools: The ER Project 1000 tool suite integrates industrial-strength project management functions with rich process improvement functionality and proactive management features. ER Project 1000 provides all the necessary industrial-strength core project management functions. Key features include support for WBS/organizational breakdown structure/RBS structures, cost, schedule, earned value analysis, built-in report writer, timesheet approvals, and centralized resource management. ER Project 1000 takes advantage of the Web by providing Java timesheets and extensive project website publishing capability. Best practices/process improvement is easily accomplished with the methodology manager and support for organizational standards, work products, and estimation. ER Project 1000 delivers an impressive array of proactive management features. These features include risk management, issue management, management by threshold, and full project tracking.

3. Is easy to use and implement: ER Project 1000 was designed with a simple, intuitive interface. Extensive wizards assist users for complex operations. ER Project 1000 can easily be configured to your organization by using our centralized administration functions and component architecture.

To what business processes can this tool be applied?

ER Project 1000 is a wrap-around solution for organizations that need to implement mature project management practices, proactively manage their projects, improve business processes, implement standards and documentation, and communicate at multiple levels. Eagle Ray's advanced suite of tools provides project managers with an integrated platform for project planning, time tracking, resource management, and executive oversight. With features such as risk management, issue tracking, and management by threshold, the ER Project 1000 gives project managers the ability to proactively manage complex projects and stay focused on the key issues.

Organizations that engage in process improvement/best practices will find that the ER Project 1000 methodology manager is the ideal platform for developing and delivering best practices to each new project plan. Project managers will be able to easily document and reuse lessons learned in new projects. Project team members and stakeholders will find that the integrated communications features of the ER Project 1000 suite facilitate a real-time dialogue between all members, and ensure no issues slip though the cracks.

Describe the ideal end-user environment for the current version of your product (size of organization, level of project management sophistication, effort and commitment required).

Size of organization: The ER Project 1000 product suite is ideal for managing projects with team sizes of ten to one thousand people per project, in organizations where multiple projects are being performed at the same time. Project teams may be centralized or dispersed using client/server and Web-based communications technologies.

Level of sophistication: The tool suite is best suited for organizations that are moving beyond basic project management to a medium level of project management maturity or higher. These organizations are typically implementing tracking, costing, project management standards, risk/issue management, time tracking, centralized resource management, and possibly earned value. ER Project 1000 also supports organizations implementing a project office, best practices, process improvement, and reusable project templates. These features make ER Project 1000 an ideal platform for organizations implementing CMM level two or higher maturity levels.

Effort and commitment required: Successful implementation of the ER Project 1000 tool suite centers on an organization's commitment to realizing repeatable project management results from enterprisewide standardization of business processes and practices. Because of it's integrated design and simple interface, ER Project 1000 delivers numerous advantages over standard project management tool sets with less staff effort.

Future strategies for this product.

Eagle Ray's future strategies include building new modules, expanding current modules, interfacing with corporate business systems, and preparing the product suite for the global marketplace. Major planned enhancements include significant modifications to the estimation module, costing module, methodology/process management module, and the Internet/intranet/Web capabilities. In addition, we will be constructing a problem/defect-tracking module.

We will be expanding the interfaces that integrate the ER Project 1000 system with additional enterprise business systems. Such systems include costing/accounting systems, HR systems, and additional commercial products. We also plan to complete our internationalization/localization efforts to prepare the ER Project 1000 for global distribution.

Product's target market.

ER Project 1000 is suitable for commercial and government organizations, which are managing projects that range from small workgroup-level projects to projects that span the entire enterprise. Essentially, the tool suite will support any project environment where the project team has access to or is working with computers.

What are your product's three main benefits? (How does using the product add value to the customer?)

1. Total integrated project management solution: The ER Project 1000 is an integrated, total project management solution providing complete support for the entire project management life cycle. The integrated tool suite does not require multiple add-on tools from different vendors, resulting in fewer hidden costs and less frustration. Project managers will find it easy to manage projects with a higher level of maturity by using the various features of the tool—for example, risk management, issue tracking, management by threshold, and multiproject capabilities.

2. Best practices/process improvement platform: The ER Project 1000 integrated process/methodology management platform provides a sophisticated, yet easy-to-use platform for implementing best practices, estimation metrics, organizational standards, documentation templates, and process improvement. Organizations can capture, integrate, and reuse their project knowledge and project plan templates from an enterprisewide integrated platform.

3. Enterprisewide tracking and communications: The ER Project 1000 facilitates communications between all project stakeholders. Program managers and executives can perform cross-project rollups; dynamic drill-down; and cost, schedule and earned-value analysis for up-to-date information on all enterprise projects. The project team members can access all project information on the project website, and receive activity assignments and report status using Java timesheets. Automatic issue notification alerts project managers about possible deviations in cost and schedule. The built-in report writer lets you extract and summarize any data in the enterprisewide project database using customized formats.

Describe your quality management process. List any relevant certifications.

The Eagle Ray quality assurance program is a comprehensive system that employs a series of product walkthroughs, builds, quality gates, configuration management, defect tracking, and comprehensive testing. The development staff members are constantly conducting requirements, design, and code walkthroughs in coordination with weekly product builds and passing mandatory quality gates. The quality assurance program is integrated with our beta testing program to ensure that all product releases undergo rigorous real-world testing prior to release.

Comprehensive testing scenarios include unit testing, integration testing, platform testing, stress testing, concurrency testing, environment testing, security testing, usability testing, vertical testing, upgrade testing, business scenario testing, and independent qualification testing.

During the design and construction of the ER Project 1000 product, Eagle Ray brought in several project management industry experts to assist in the design of the software functionality and usability. This process will be continued to ensure that our future enhancements meet the real-world needs of project management organizations. Additionally, Eagle Ray continues to invest heavily in the training of team members in technical and project management areas.

Discuss your product pricing structure. Include volume discount levels, concurrent user options, site licenses, cost of implementation, and other issues.

Call for latest prices.

Mesa/Vista (Mesa Systems Guild, Inc.)

Describe what the product is designed to do.

Mesa/Vista helps project teams manage, monitor, and comply with quality and government regulations by providing process management capabilities and access to all legacy and current project data through a Web browser. Mesa/Vista provides process management capabilities and integrates a development team's existing product environment, including tools like Rational Rose, TD Technologies' SLATE, Cayenne Teamwork, or any tool with an MPX interface, such as Microsoft Project.

Mesa/Vista links information between stand-alone products and exposes project data to authorized project team members, empowering them to anticipate and solve problems at early stages in the project life cycle.

Mesa/Vista automates the documentation process. This shaves time from a project that must comply with government or other regulatory standards because the documentation is available as soon as the project is complete.

Top three product differentiators; describe what makes your product unique.

1. Patent-pending technology intuitively links graphical objects such as those found in developer's modeling tools, not only within the stand-alone tool but also between tools.
2. Provides support of any business process through dynamic exchange of information.
3. Connects legacy and current data between development team's business and engineering tools.

To what business processes can this tool be applied?

SEI capability maturity model levels 1–5.
ISO-compliant regulations.
FDA requirements management.

Describe the ideal end-user environment for the current version of your product (size of organization, level of project management sophistication, effort and commitment required).

The ideal end-user environment for Mesa/Vista is a distributed, process-conscious product development group needing visibility and access to legacy and current project data across multiple platforms.

An organization trying to achieve or improve upon an SEI capability maturity model level, achieve an ISO 9000 quality standard, or comply with FDA requirements will greatly benefit from the Mesa/Vista environment.

Commitment: All project-related communications would go through the Mesa/Vista environment; it provides complete, automated project status information.

Future strategies for this product.

Future strategies for Mesa/Vista include integrating all engineering and business data together to be shared and accessed by the entire product development team, no matter where the data resides.

Plug-ins will include more scheduling tools, databases, business tools, document editing tools, and modeling tools—all the tools that the entire team would use within a product development environment.

Mesa/Vista will create an environment of collaboration, and expose information to help all members of the team work together without restraint of hardware or system requirements.

Product's target market.

Mesa/Vista is ideal for process-conscious project managers of distributed product development teams in the telecommunication, automotive, aerospace, medical, and software industries.

What are your product's three main benefits? (How does using the product add value to the customer?)

1. Provides accessibility to data from places other than the data's native machine, minimizing the number of copies of each software product that needs to be purchased.

2. Saves time by providing online access to all project data, rather than printing and faxing information in order to share it.

3. Automatic documentation mechanism for ease of tracking government regulations or quality standards control.

Describe your quality management process. List any relevant certifications.

Mesa/Vista is used to manage the development of Mesa/Vista. Also, extensive internal and external testing is done of the Mesa/Vista product line. Mesa has provided the software to Young America's design team (NYYC's challenger in the America's Cup 2K) in exchange for feedback on Mesa/Vista and suggestions for improvements based on their real-life use of the product line.

Discuss your product pricing structure. Include volume discount levels, concurrent user options, site licenses, cost of implementation, and other issues.

Contact vendor.

Milestones, Etc. (Kidasa)

Describe what the product is designed to do.

Milestones, Etc. is designed to provide an easy-to-use product to produce high-quality schedules in a Gantt format.

Top three product differentiators; describe what makes your product unique.

1. Easy to learn.
2. Easy to use.
3. Easy-to-update schedules.

To what business processes can this tool be applied?

Scheduling of projects.

Describe the ideal end-user environment for the current version of your product (size of organization, level of project management sophistication, effort and commitment required).

Desktop Windows environment.

Future strategies for this product.

Continue to add user-requested features to make product do more, but still maintain ease of use.

Product's target market.

People who need to quickly produce schedules.

What are your product's three main benefits? (How does using the product add value to the customer?)

1. Enables customer to easily produce high-quality Gantt charts.
2. Enables customer to spend less time creating Gantt charts.
3. Enables customer to spend less time updating Gantt charts.

Describe your quality management process. List any relevant certifications.

Follow standard commercial software-development guidelines.

Discuss your product pricing structure. Include volume discount levels, concurrent user options, site licenses, cost of implementation, and other issues.

Single-user licenses are $199. Workgroup pricing is also available.

Cost implementation: Just the amount of time it takes to go over the supplied tutorials, usually no more than a few hours.

Open Plan (Welcom)

Describe what the product is designed to do.

Welcom's Open Plan is an enterprisewide project management system that substantially improves a company's ability to manage and complete multiple projects on time and within budget with a limited workforce. Unlike less sophisticated products, Open Plan is a highly integrated, comprehensive software system that can be customized to fit specific corporate requirements. It is the most technically advanced client/server project management system on the market, using the latest in Microsoft Windows development technology. The three versions of Open Plan are Open Plan Professional, Open Plan Desktop, and Open Plan Enterprise.

Open Plan Professional is easy to use and powerful enough to manage even the largest projects. It gives professional project managers such vital tools as advanced resource management, multiproject support, support for client/server databases, and the flexibility to customize the interface to support organization and industry-specific procedures.

Open Plan Desktop is designed for occasional access to projects and ideal for executive users and tactical team members. It has extensive ease-of-use features and an affordable price point for companywide deployment. The system is well-suited for users who usually work on individual components of a larger project. Users can roll their individual projects up to Open Plan Professional for a broader view of the overall project.

Open Plan Enterprise is very similar to Open Plan Professional. It integrates with popular ERP (enterprise resource planning) applications such as Baan and SAP. The resulting component-based suite automatically disseminates project data throughout an organization, giving users better control over enterprisewide multiproject planning, management, and implementation.

Top three product differentiators; describe what makes your product unique.

1. Multiproject.
2. Advanced resource modeling.
3. Open architecture.

To what business processes can this tool be applied?

Enterprise resource modeling, business process reengineering, project management, earned value analysis, risk assessment, and process modeling.

Describe the ideal end-user environment for the current version of your product (size of organization, level of project management sophistication, effort and commitment required).

Medium to large organizations for which project management is a serious business requirement. Meets the needs of users whose level of expertise varies from novice/occasional to advanced.

Future strategies for this product.

Our vision for the future is to provide a suite of component-based products that work together to provide advanced project management functionality using the very latest technology.

Welcom's development plans include extending the products' multiproject and enterprise resource-modeling capabilities while moving to a distributed applications architecture with Web technology being a significant component. Plans also include leveraging existing integrations with Baan and SAP, and expanding integrations to include other ERP vendors.

Product's target market.

Fortune 1000 companies, government and multinational organizations implementing enterprisewide project management.

What are your product's three main benefits? (How does using the product add value to the customer?)

1. Increase quality of project communications.
2. Reduce cycle time through effective resource management.
3. Increase integration of project management with business systems.

Describe your quality management process. List any relevant certifications.

Adhere to standard industry processes in release and version strategies, including automated regression testing. ISO 9000 certified in the United Kingdom.

Discuss your product pricing structure. Include volume discount levels, concurrent user options, site licenses, cost of implementation, and other issues.

Please call for pricing.
Training courses and consulting: Please call for pricing.
Tech support: No charge with current maintenance.
Maintenance: First year is free with software purchase. Renewed annually.

PLANTRAC-APROPOS (Computerline Ltd)

Describe what the product is designed to do.

PLANTRAC-APROPOS provides all the methodology required for projects from conception to realization.

It is based on a method known as PRINCE (PRojects In Controlled Environments).

It takes users (even if they are not familiar with project methods) step by step down the administrative road from setting up a project to monitoring and controlling it. It provides the standards and quality safeguards required for projects.

Top three product differentiators; describe what makes your product unique.

1. Proven methodology used.
2. Simple step-by-step use.
3. Product breakdown structure.

To what business processes can this tool be applied?

Construction; manufacturing; research and development; software development.

Describe the ideal end-user environment for the current version of your product (size of organization, level of project management sophistication, effort and commitment required).

Both small and large organizations benefit. It can be used as a casual planner, by a professional project manager, and for corporate planning and control.

Future strategies for this product.

PLANTRAC-APROPOS is very much user driven. It will keep up to date with both project management and technological trends.

Product's target market.

Broad market but specializing in construction, defense, and pharmaceutical.

What are your product's three main benefits? (How does using the product add value to the customer?)

1. Introduces a methodology.
2. Standardizes methodology.
3. Disciplines planning, monitoring, and control.

Describe your quality management process. List any relevant certifications.

Quality management is based on a mix of PRINCE and ISO 9000 methodology.

Discuss your product pricing structure. Include volume discount levels, concurrent user options, site licenses, cost of implementation, and other issues.

Single user is $575. Network versions are available in modules of four users, $1,050 per module. Site licenses are $2,500–$25,000.

Implementation and training is $960 per day. Technical support is provided by telephone, fax, and E-mail. Free for first six months. Thereafter, 17.5 percent of purchase price (includes upgrades and enhancements).

PlanView Software (PlanView, Inc.)

Describe what the product is designed to do.

PlanView Software has modules that let the user request project and nonproject work, scope, schedule, search the resource repository, create multiple what-ifs, etc., progress projects from time reported, and create metrics.

Top three product differentiators; describe what makes your product unique.

1. Customized according to your WBS.
2. Integrates with most popular process methodology systems (LBMS, etc.).
3. Manages all workflow, from scoping through closing.

To what business processes can this tool be applied?

Multiproject management, service request management, resource management, workflow management, work and resource *portfolio* management, etc.

Describe the ideal end-user environment for the current version of your product (size of organization, level of project management sophistication, effort and commitment required).

An organization with one hundred to multiple thousands of employees (we have implementations of four thousand plus), managed by five or more managers with access to a central database; includes matrix-style organizations.

Future strategies for this product.

Further conversion to Web browser-based interfaces; even easier report generation and Web publishing; more project management and cost management features.

Product's target market.

The resource-centric approach to work management is typically most useful for organizations with a highly skilled workforce of limited availability; with twenty plus managers, and one hundred plus staff; using client/server.

What are your product's three main benefits? (How does using the product add value to the customer?)

1. Keep data/templates from process systems on the PlanView central repository.
2. Integrates with most popular process software systems.
3. Adds work and resource management to your process management system.

Describe your quality management process. List any relevant certifications.

PlanView follows the guidelines set out in the book *Best Practices of Rapid Development* by Steve McConnell.

Discuss your product pricing structure. Include volume discount levels, concurrent user options, site licenses, cost of implementation, and other issues.

It is different for each case, but basically the cost is $200–400 per seat, with volume discounts. The repository products are included.

Standard SQL database is extra. Implementation and training are extra.

We offer a range of implementation packages, from rapid to standard, which include training. Additional services billed at time and cost. Phone and online tech support are free. Maintenance packages offered.

Project Control Software

Describe what the product is designed to do.

The Project Control Software suite supports process management across the entire organization. The Process Manager module enables project management standards, processes and training management through its document management and issues tracking functionalities. The system manages and delivers information to all levels of the organization, from Employees, to Project Management, Functional Management, Enterprise Management, Global Management.

Project Control Software extends desktop project management software into an enterprisewide management and reporting solution, by consolidating volumes of project files from leading project management software systems such as Microsoft Project, Primavera, and others. Project Control Software supports multiple operating systems (Windows, Macintosh, Unix), and databases (Oracle, Access, Microsoft SQL, Sybase). The entire Project Control Software suite runs on a Web browser or LAN. The enterprise rollup design supports the matrix organization's need to roll up projects to program or initiative, as well as the resource perspective by business unit and organizational structure.

Top three product differentiators; describe what makes your product unique.

1. No technology limits: Project Control Software supports all operating systems (Windows, Macintosh, Unix), consolidates files from multiple project management software systems (Microsoft Project, Primavera, and more) using your choice of databases (Oracle, Access, Microsoft SQL, Sybase) in a LAN or Internet solution. It is designed to integrate easily with existing business systems (such as accounting software) so an organization can leverage existing systems and immediately see productivity increases without changing everything.

2. The project office: The design and integration of Project Control Software modules supports the project office across all phases of the project management life cycle, from standard estimating and budgeting though timesheets and status tracking and accounting integration for actual costs and earned value analysis. The process manager and communications manager modules enable a corporate intranet.

3. Enterprise project management: Project Control Software offers a suite of integrated modules that can be used to deliver the big picture of project management across a distributed organization, as well as tracking the details. The enterprise rollup design supports the matrix organization's need to roll up projects to program or initiative, as well as the need to view data from a resource perspective by business unit and organizational structure. The entire Project Control Software suite (not just the time tracking) runs on a Web browser or LAN.

To what business processes can this tool be applied?

Project Control Software's enterprise rollup design supports the matrix organization's need to roll up projects to program or initiative, as well as the need to view data from a resource perspective by business unit and organizational structure.

The system supports project management, ERP, project office development, ISO registration, strategic planning, process management, methodology implementation, cost/schedule management, CMM, compliance, global information technology deployment, SAP, Peoplesoft, etc., implementations.

Describe the ideal end-user environment for the current version of your product (size of organization, level of project management sophistication, effort and commitment required).

Any organization operating in a competitive environment that manages multiple projects and resources to meet business goals and to increase profitability and productivity.

For example, a geographically distributed matrix organization with medium to high volume of project-based activities being managed in a standard desktop scheduling software. The system delivers information to all levels of the organization from employees to project management, functional management, enterprise management, and global management.

Future strategies for this product.

Project Control, the publisher of Project Control Software, was founded in 1989, developed the first Internet project management product in 1996, and is committed to its position as a technology leader in Internet project management software. Future plans include expanding functionality to better support the project office and to continually update Project Control Software features, based on ongoing client input.

Product's target market.

Organizations using Project Control Software represent companies in a wide variety of industries, including finance, services, pharmaceutical, federal government, defense, manufacturing, automotive, software publishing, etc. The disciplines typically involved in implementation include enterprise management, information technology, new product development, the project office, and engineering.

What are your product's three main benefits? (How does using the product add value to the customer?)

Client organizations can greatly improve productivity and lower costs when Project Control system is in place.

1. Ability to view all projects in a central repository.
2. Ability to do efficient enterprise resource and cost planning.
3. Ability to fully support the needs of the project office across all phases and areas of the project management process.

Describe your quality management process. List any relevant certifications.

Project Control, publishers of Project Control Software, follows standard and accepted practices for design, development, testing, and support for computer software. Project Control has set corporate objectives to achieve Level 2 and Level 3 CMM compliance using the capability maturity model from the Software Engineering Institute.

Discuss your product pricing structure. Include volume discount levels, concurrent user options, site licenses, cost of implementation, and other issues.

Project Control Software is priced by the module, with scalable client seat pricing based on number of users. Price quotations are available and are based on the current Project Control Software product and pricing schedule.

Price quotations are available and include costs of product, implementation, training, tech support, annual maintenance, etc. Quotations are based on the current Project Control Software product and pricing schedule, which is available to qualified organizations.

ProjectExchange Portfolio Wizard, TaskClass, DocCheck (Information Management Services, Inc.)

Describe what the product is designed to do.

TaskClass and DocCheck are used by project, program, and resource managers to validate task and project secondary information across multiple project plans to ensure consistent information and adherence to defined organizational methods and processes. DocCheck is also utilized for advanced scheduling process-flow capabilities and integration with other business systems. Other organizational information relating to project information is easily linked to a particular project plan. Unlimited reports, analysis, and what-ifs are provided by the ProjectExchange Portfolio Wizard to provide the project office with information needed.

TaskClass provides organizations with the ability to define standards and ensure task-level information is consistent across all project and nonproject activities. Geographically dispersed teams can easily classify task-level information to provide rollup capability to organizationally defined levels. Each organization can establish unique classifications for use throughout its team, group, or division. Standards are easily established by team members directly in Microsoft Project, to ensure organizational activities contain appropriate classification information. A setup wizard guides an administrator through the process of defining the unique classification business rules of the organization, and a utility is provided to maintain look-up values.

TaskClass ensures tasks are classified for the particular Microsoft Project plan being saved to the enterprise repository. If additional classification is required, an easy-to-use spellchecker-type interface directly in Microsoft Project leads the user through validating the information. By using a pick list to populate task-level fields, enterprise users are assured that information is accurate and consistent. This information helps to measure if organizational processes and methods are being followed. When utilized by multiple team members across the enterprise, TaskClass ensures information is consistent, accurate, and usable by other team members. Task classification provides a mechanism for integration with other business systems by relating other business information to particular activities.

ResourceXchange (purchased separately) provides the capability to define attributes such as *skill* or *role*, which can also be defined by TaskClass, thus providing aggregate demand and supply analysis.

Top three product differentiators describe what makes your product unique.

1. User configurable information validation and process-flow execution.
2. Easy to use and seamless Microsoft Project integration.
3. Three-tier client/server-based architecture provides a system scalable across the entire enterprise.

To what business processes can this tool be applied?

Our tools are utilized across multiple business processes.

Describe the ideal end-user environment for the current version of your product (size of organization, level of project management sophistication, effort and commitment required).

Our primary market comprises Global 5000 organizations with objectives to increase returns on people, time, and financial investments. We initially assist event-driven divisions within these organizations, with the ultimate goal of benefiting every user in the organization.

Future strategies for this product.

Organizations prefer to prioritize their business process flow above that of a particular software solution. In the past, software solutions have been inflexible in adapting to the particular client's unique method of doing business. Historically, organizations were forced to change their business process flow to match that of the particular solution. This has proven to be ineffective, and has created an opportunity to deliver a work management solution that is both functionally complete and flexible. A solution that is flexible and easily adapted to adjust to an organization's unique business-process flow improves the usefulness of the solution and the organizations' competitiveness, in addition to increasing their baggage. They prefer a solution that contains the exact elements needed to accomplish their method of work management. We will continue to be a market leader in providing organizational configurable systems.

Product's target market.

No answer given.

What are your product's three main benefits? (How does using the product add value to the customer?)

1. Project and task secondary information validation helps enforce management controls and creates a consistent reporting environment.
2. Easily integrated with other business systems providing seamless business process execution.
3. Multiple-level Microsoft Project security eliminates information overload and minimizes risks.

Describe your quality management process. List any relevant certifications.

We have continually improved our system-development methodology since 1991. Over time, our SDLC has incorporated the best practices learned while deploying ProjectExchange in world-class organizations across the globe. Our Research & Development division utilizes ProjectExchange, and quality measures are persistent throughout our methods and processes.

Discuss your product pricing structure. Include volume discount levels, concurrent user options, site licenses, cost of implementation, and other issues.

Please consult IMS for current pricing.

Implementation costs vary and depend upon a particular organization's business requirements and level and availability of in-house expertise. We offer the following services to help achieve organizational objectives.

- Installation
- Process, methods, and integration consulting
- Project office support
- ProjectExchange add-on solution development
- Implementation management
- Microsoft Project and ProjectExchange two-day course
- ProjectExchange for Project Managers one-day course
- ProjectExchange for Team Members half-day course
- MS Project Introduction one-day course
- MS Project Basic two-day course
- Project Planning & Management Fundamentals three-day course
- Executive briefing on project management.

Annual maintenance is offered at 15 percent of the license costs. Maintenance includes telephone support and product upgrades.

Project Integrator

Describe what the product is designed to do.

SSL Project Integrator (PI) is a team-oriented project and process management tool that enables you to graphically define, track, report, and communicate projects, processes, tasks, and deliverables. Additionally, PI manages and maintains resources and clients, both locally and remotely.

Top three product differentiators; describe what makes your product unique.

1. All project processes (external, internal, and administrative) are managed via PI's graphic and interactive RoadMap. High-level steps graphically depict process flow. Each step can be drilled-down to display task lists, task details, resource delegation, deliverables, and quality checklists.

2. Teams can be defined at the project level, and are pulled from the database resource pool. Assigned tasks and open issues are sent to a team member's reminder window for immediate delegation and communication. Resources drag and drop tasks to a timecard for immediate project updating, and open issues remain on the reminder window until they are closed.

3. A wide range of reports are available. Each report can be filtered, and pull data from the database for macro or micro analysis and reporting. Users can also define their own reports, and any level of information can be exported from the database.

To what business processes can this tool be applied?

Any external, internal, or administrative business process, regardless of simplicity or complexity.

Describe the ideal end-user environment for the current version of your product (size of organization, level of project management sophistication, effort and commitment required).

Project-based organizations of any size (PI allows definition of teams, departments, and business units). Organizations do not need to be well-versed in project management practices and techniques. Implementation and training is simple when compared to sophisticated PM tools. A commitment to Distributed Project/Process Management (DPM) is required (the delegation of tasks and deliverables to distributed teams and team members, and distribution of the project management process).

Future strategies for this product.

Tailor versions of PI to specific industries by leveraging subject matter experts from same.

Full integration to other cost accounting applications (currently, PI is integrated with SBT Executive Series, although data can be exported to virtually any application).

Product's target market.

Project Integrator was created for project-oriented organizations (engineering, marketing, advertising, accounting, consulting, design firms, etc.) that have a need to enforce consistent quality in their project process and delivery, and minimize nonproductive hours.

What are your product's three main benefits? (How does using the product add value to the customer?)

1. Distribution of the project process (tasks, issues, deliverables, etc.) to local and remote team members via LAN, DBMS, and Internet tools.

2. Immediate feedback of status of all projects and tasks, allowing macro and micro views of the entire organization's performance at any given time.

3. All aspects of a business (external, internal, and administrative activity, including deliverables) are managed in a central DBMS and repository. Communications, projects, tasks, deliverables, issues, costs, clients resources, etc., are all managed via one tool in one database.

Describe your quality management process. List any relevant certifications.

Our documented QA process includes the use of test script software. We are currently implementing ISO 9001 and expect registry by early 1999.

Discuss your product pricing structure. Include volume discount levels, concurrent user options, site licenses, cost of implementation, and other issues.

PI's price is based on the number of users, and volume discounts are available.

Implementation lead time and required training is minimal when compared to high-end, sophisticated PM tools and suites.

Project Kickstart

Describe what the product is designed to do.

Project KickStart is an easy-to-use project planning software for managers, executives, consultants and incidental project planners. The software leads users through an eight-step process to create a work breakdown structure for projects. Project KickStart then allows the user to flesh out the task list by considering the goals and objectives of the project, identifying people involved in the effort and anticipating obstacles or risks to be encountered in performing the work. Team members can be assigned to each of the tasks. Project KickStart then produces a project summary, which is an overview of who is doing what. Reports can be generated for each of the individual project team members. Through the easy to use menu-based system, the project can be exported to project management software. Project KickStart includes a Gantt chart for quick scheduling and built-in "hot links" to Microsoft Project, SureTrak, Super Project, Project Scheduler 7, Time Line, Milestones Etc., Word and Excel.

Top three product differentiators; describe what makes your product unique.

1. Can be used by virtually all corporate departments for project planning: No training necessary.
2. Provides a framework for brainstorming, planning and scheduling projects.
3. Links with project management software, such as Microsoft Project, SureTrak, Project Scheduler, adding value to each program as a front-end planning wizard.

To what business processes can this tool be applied?

Large sales are often treated as projects. Project KickStart enables salespeople to begin fleshing out the details of the customer requirements and the deliverables right away.

It can be used in conjunction with a training session, where users can have a successful experience planning their actual projects.

Consultants can use Project KickStart with clients to guide them through the process of planning a project.

It can be used "on the fly" for fast plans, e.g., recovering from a toxic spill.

Describe the ideal end-user environment for the current version of your product (size of organization, level of project management sophistication, effort and commitment required).

Project KickStart works great with any size organization. It has been successfully deployed at Sodexo Marriott Services, Eli Lilly, Long's Drugs, as well as for many consultants, schools and non-profits.

Project KickStart lets nonproject managers follow a sound planning methodology without even knowing it.

Its ease of use make it ideal to get people to follow a project planning methodology.

Future strategies for this product.

Discuss your product pricing structure. Include volume discount levels, concurrent user options, site licenses, cost of implementation, and other issues.

Project KickStart is available as a stand-alone program and as a wizard in Primavera SureTrak 2. We view Project KickStart as a universal planner and look forward to it being incorporated into other programs.

We see the benefit of Web enabling Project KickStart and are looking into developing it.

Product's target market.

Users of project management software, e.g., Microsoft Project; organizations that have small to midsize projects and would benefit from an easy to use project planner; and SOHO and small office users.

What are your product's three main benefits? (How does using the product add value to the customer?)

1. Fast and easy project planning.
2. Improved involvement of project team.
3. Improved coordination of project approaches within an organization.

Describe your quality management process. List any relevant certifications.

In addition to internal testing, we have worked with professional testers to identify and eliminate bugs.

Our many users have also identified areas for improvement that we are addressing.

Discuss your product pricing structure. Include volume discount levels, concurrent user options, site licenses, cost of implementation, and other issues.

$99.95 for first copy, $59.95 per copy for additional copies. Site license of one hundred to three hundred users $6,000. For site licenses, six-month maintenance fee is 15 percent of site license fee.

TeamWork

Describe what the product is designed to do.

TeamWork is the "project-centric" process management application for Microsoft Project 98. TeamWork provides all of the benefits of process management while working directly within Microsoft Project. You start by building a customized work plan template in Microsoft Project. Incorporate and automate your organization's methodologies as you easily link tasks to all of the intellectual assets required to perform the task ... detailed methodology steps, Microsoft Word or other document templates, multimedia files such as PowerPoint presentations, hot links to Internet URLs, Excel spreadsheets, Access databases, faxes and E-mail communications ... the only limit is your imagination. TeamWork 98 consists of:

The TeamWork 98 Developer's Kit: Use the TeamWork 98 Developer's Kit to incorporate your organization's methodology into the TeamWork 98 database and to link tasks to all of the intellectual assets required to perform each task.

The Workplan Wizard: Use the Workplan Wizard to create a work plan in TeamWork 98 for a new project.

TeamWork 98 (main application): Use TeamWork 98 to execute tasks in a project plan and to quickly access intellectual assets needed to complete each task. The central application and database reside on a server that can be accessed by client workstations across the traditional LAN/WAN, through the corporate intranet, or the Internet. An advanced bi-directional approach to database replication delivers a robust solution for the sharing of methodologies, work plans, and other collaborative documents.

Top three product differentiators; describe what makes your product unique.

1. Intranet/Internet-based process distribution.
2. Microsoft product based platform: NT, SQL Server, Project 98, Internet Information Server.
3. Ease of Use: The application can be quickly deployed from existing Microsoft Project plans and other methodology procedures, forms and templates cab be easily attached to the tasks in the work plans.

To what business processes can this tool be applied?

Any process-based business model can be deployed using TeamWork.

Describe the ideal end-user environment for the current version of your product (size of organization, level of project management sophistication, effort and commitment required).

TeamWork can be used by any organization capable of supporting a server-based application. Due to the ease of loading existing work plans and supporting methodologies, TeamWork can be quickly assimilated into just about any collaborative team environment.

Future strategies for this product.

TeamWork will continue to mature as an intranet/Internet-based tool for developing and delivering processes, methodologies, and work plans. As a companion product for Microsoft Project, TeamWork will continue to parallel Project's release schedule.

Product's target market.

IT Organizations, Engineering and Manufacturing Management, other process-based business disciplines.

What are your product's three main benefits? (How does using the product add value to the customer?)

Ease of use: TeamWork makes it easy to take existing work plans and processes documentation and immediately begin to use and improve the best of breed from these intellectual assets.

Microsoft product-based: TeamWork uses SQL Server, NT, and Microsoft Project as its technology foundation.

Easily deployed to field: The replication features allow field-based consultants to run connected or stand-alone and uses the intranet or Internet as the information delivery vehicle.

Describe your quality management process. List any relevant certifications.

TeamWork is developed by Project Assistants, a project management software development company. Project Assistants has a documented alpha and beta testing program that ensures that all GA software is completely quality-assured prior to release.

All defects which are reported during the alpha and beta test period are corrected and the entire application is regression-tested to assure that the product has achieved a satisfactory quality rating and is approaching zero defect.

Discuss your product pricing structure. Include volume discount levels, concurrent user options, site licenses, cost of implementation, and other issues.

The server-based components sell for a list price of $10,000 plus $500 per seat up to 100 seats. After 100 seats, significant discounts are offered.

Open enrollment training is offered for $495 per person. On-site training is $1500 per day, plus expenses. Technical support packages are available, and are priced by user or by organization.

Annual maintenance packages start at $995.

WebProject

Describe what the product is designed to do.

WebProject is designed for geographically dispersed project teams. WebProject is a Java-based project management tool with powerful collaboration and communications features. WebProject incorporates unique knowledge management/best practices capability.

Top three product differentiators; describe what makes your product unique.

1. WebProject is the first (only) pure Java project management suite that can utilize an open architecture database backend. WebProject allows corporations to utilize Oracle, SQL Server, Informix, Sybase, or other databases in their enterprise project management.

2. WebProject has introduced the first knowledge management/best practices capability within a project management software suite.

3. WebProject enables global project communication, including project issues boards, threaded task discussions, virtual project status meetings, and remote project statusing and updates.

To what business processes can this tool be applied?

Geographically dispersed project teams, projects that need to have access from remote locations, or integrating WebProject's proprietary information exchange with MS Project, Primavera, or other desktop systems.

WebProject allows the extraction of *knowledge* from the enterprise, such as resource capabilities or company *best practices*.

Describe the ideal end user environment for the current version of your product (size of organization, level of project management sophistication, effort and commitment required).

WebProject is an easy-to-use Java project management tool, which will enable teams to communicate and collaborate from remote locations. WebProject is designed for the enterprise and will work well with project teams as well.

Future strategies for this product.

WebProject has established many *firsts* in the project management industry. We will continue to move the industry forward with our new technologies on the Web and with JAVA.

Product's target market.

Geographically dispersed project teams, enterprise project management systems, integration with Primavera, MS Project, and other project management systems.

What are your product's three main benefits? (How does using the product add value to the customer?)

1. Enterprise project communication.
2. Project collaboration.
3. Geographically dispersed updates and communication.

Describe your quality management process. List any relevant certifications.

WebProject adheres to strict standards and processes for quality, both in development and customer service.

Discuss your product pricing structure. Include volume discount levels, concurrent user options, site licenses, cost of implementation, and other issues.

WebProject is priced at $790 for starter package, including the WebProject server. WebProject does provide enterprise and site licensing.

Chapter 3

Schedule Management Software

By definition, projects consume resources—the most important of which is time. Because the expression of time is effort, the project schedule is impacted by both time and the availability of resources.

Within *A Guide to the Project Management Body of Knowledge (PMBOK™ Guide)*, the management of time is covered in Chapter 6, Project Time Management. In line with its definition, scheduling tools provide functionalities, including putting boundaries on a specific activity and setting expectations for how much effort a resource will consume.

What to Expect

Scheduling software provides features like:

- Define and sequence activities
- Critical path calculation
- Time analysis
- Resource leveling
- Schedule status
- Reports, including Gantt charts and network logic diagrams.

Schedule management software provides features for program or project planning, as well as for either individual or enterprise project control. For many people, exposure to a scheduler product is synonymous with *project management*. For the vendors also in many cases, the scheduler product is the entry point into their products and services.

Scheduling is a requirement for all projects, across all application areas and industries, so this category of products is both widely used and almost universally applicable to most business and/or project processes.

What the Data Reveals

In past years, a technological gulf existed between the *big boys* and the *small fries*, with the large project and enterprise project tools on the mainframe and the PC workstation-based products being used for scheduling and controlling individual projects. With client/server environments, the gulf was filled. A scheduler may now operate on a single project or a group of related products while at the same time providing the user interface to a repository of projects. Keep in mind that many of the full-service functions that are necessary for a scheduler to be effective in a single project environment, such as a rudimentary time-collection capability, may not be a necessary function if the intent of the scheduler is to work in an enterprise environment.

Schedulers bring together the tangible descriptions of resource assignments to a task, the relationship of the task to other tasks, and some schedule of limitations for those resources and from these variables, then generates a project plan: a schedule of anticipated events and milestones. Once the project plan is confirmed, the scheduler is used to adjust the initial plan based on situations that are experienced in the execution of the plan: updates, changes, and reestimations of effort. For budgetary comparisons and for estimating process improvement, some type of variance reporting is usually supported by the scheduler tool.

Depending upon the nature of the project or the business setting, the type of scheduler considered useful can range from single project, stand-alone tool, to a high-powered tool that can effectively schedule tens of thousands of hours of effort and hundreds of human or nonhuman resources.

What the Majority of Vendors Offer

Not surprisingly, the overwhelming majority of the respondents in this category describe the primary purpose of their products as generating project schedules. This is a very mature software category, and most of the vendors who compete in this category support the vast majority of the features surveyed. The only weak area is in using resources other than human and work equipment and in some of the more esoteric types of reporting formats.

What a Minority of Vendors Offer

Web enablement and integration with E-mail were the two standouts in terms of nonparticipation. Also, very few packages support password protection. Both of these situations are a carryover from the heritage of most products as stand-alone schedulers.

Unique Features That Surfaced in Vendor Responses to the Narrative Questions

Vendors responding to the question about their *product differentiators* note that all the features surveyed are integrated. This appears to be something that the vendors consider unique, although in practice, this has become almost standard.

In the matrix portion of the survey, we asked about multiproject scheduling, and many of the vendors responded with discussions of enterprisewide scheduling and scalability. We briefly touched on *online view*, and the vendors responded with discussions of the graphical user interfaces (GUIs) and similar *look and feel* across a multiplicity of platforms and operating systems.

Among the quality management processes mentioned by the vendors were proprietary development and quality assurance (QA) processes, including testing tools and formal beta testing, pursuit or attainment of ISO 9000 or ISO 9001 certification or capability maturity model (CMM) level attainment, attainment of a Y2K standards level or self-test for Y2K preparedness, and version control management.

Many different pricing strategies exist, including named licenses, concurrent licensing, and site licensing. Many vendors offer volume discounts. Most vendors did not quote prices, but, where they did, the list price for a single copy ranged from $50–$1,275 for a stand-alone version. Annual support was 15–20 percent of the purchase price.

Support services offered range from installation to training to project management process engineering and project office implementation. Customization is allowed for some larger products. Support services are sold in addition to software license fees.

What's New and Exciting

Most of the former stand-alone scheduler vendors have either developed a repository-based version or have aligned themselves with one or more business partners who have. This feature has the potential to multiply the power and usefulness of a scheduling product by linking it to lessons learned in previous projects, as well as linking it in a more timely fashion to crucial current data that impact the project schedule. Since a schedule is only a piece of paper unless it is *live* and able to reflect changes and lessons learned, this is a big step toward project managers being able to trust what their core project management software tool—the scheduler product—tells them.

A reminder: The data in the matrix and in the narrative responses were supplied by the vendors and have not been independently verified.

Schedule Management

	ABT Workbench (repository-based) and Project Workbench PMW (standalone)	ActionPlan	AMS REALTIME Projects	Artemis ProjectView	AutoPLAN Enterprise	CA-SuperProject 4.0 & CA-SuperProject/ SuperProject/Net 1.0	Cascade PgM	Dekker TRAKKER Activity Based Cost Management and Performance System
Time analysis								
Full critical path	Y	N	Y	Y	Y	Y	Y	Y
Relationship types								
SS	Y	Y	Y	Y	Y	Y	Y	Y
FS	Y	Y	Y	Y	Y	Y	Y	Y
SF	Y	Y	Y	Y	N	Y	Y	Y
FF	Y	Y	Y	Y	Y	Y	Y	Y
Allow SS and FF on a set of tasks	Y	Y	Y	Y	Y	Y	Y	Y
Lags on relationships	Y	Y	Y	Y	Y	Y	Y	Y
Calendars on relationships	Y	N	Y	Y	Y	Y	Y	Y
Mixed durations (minutes, hours, days, weeks, months)	Y	Y	Y	Y	Y	Y	Y	Y
Time limited schedule calculation	Y	Y	Y	Y	Y	Y	Y	Y
Resource limited schedule calculation	Y	Y	Y	Y	Y	Y	Y	N
Query overallocations by:								
Skill	Y	Y	Y	Y	Y	Y	Y	Y
Resource type	Y	Y	Y	Y	Y	Y	Y	Y
Department	Y	Y	Y	Y	Y	Y	Y	Y
Other (user defined)	Y	Y	Y	Y	Y	Y	Y	Y
Resource calendars								
Individual resource calendars	Y	Y	Y	Y	Y	Y	Y	Y
Variable availability	Y	Y	Y	Y	Y	Y	Y	Y
Scheduling/leveling features								
Resource leveling	Y	Y	Y	Y	Y	Y	Y	Y
Resource smoothing	Y	Y	Y	Y	Y	Y	Y	Y
Leveling by date range	Y	N	Y	Y	Y	Y	Y	Y
"Do not level" flag (bypass project during leveling)	Y	N	Y	Y	Y	Y	Y	Y
User-defined resource profiles (spread curves)	Y	N	Y	Y	Y	N	Y	Y
Team/crew scheduling	Y	Y	N	Y	Y	Y	Y	Y
Skill scheduling	Y	Y	Y	Y	Y	N	Y	Y
Number of skills per resource	Unlim.		32 (more possible)	Unlim.	15	1	Unlim.	Unlim.
Alternate resource scheduling	Y	N	N	N	N	N	Y	Y
Rolling wave scheduling	Y	N	Y	Y	Y	N	Y	Y
Activity splitting	Y	Y	N	Y	Y	Y	Y	Y
Perishable resources	Y	N	Y	Y	N	N	Y	Y
Consumable resources	Y	N	Y	Y	N	Y	Y	Y
Assign role (skill), software replaces with name at specific point in process	Y	N	Y	N	Y	N	N	Y
Heterogeneous resources	Y	Y	Y	Y	Y	Y	Y	Y
Homogeneous resources	Y	N	Y	Y	Y	Y	Y	Y

Hierarchical resources	Y	N	Y	Y	Y	Y	Y	Y
Share resource pool across multiple projects	Y	Y	Y	Y	Y	Y	Y	Y
Number of resources to be included in resource scheduling	Unlim.	Unlim.	2,000	Unlim.	Unlim.	Unlim.	Unlim.	Unlim.
Resource costs								
Rate escalation	Y	N	Y	Y	Y	Y	Y	Y
Overtime	Y	N	Y	Y	Y	Y	Y	Y
Top-down budgeting	Y	N	Y	Y	Y	Y	Y	Y
Performance analysis/cost reporting								
Calculates BCWS	Y	N	Y	Y	Y	Y	Y	Y
Calculates BCWP	Y	N	Y	Y	Y	Y	Y	Y
Calculates ACWP	Y	N	Y	Y	Y	Y	Y	Y
Physical % complete (in addition to schedule %complete)	Y	N	Y	Y	Y	Y	Y	Y
Reports								
30-60-90 day and user-defined report windows	Y	N	Y	Y	Y	Y	Y	Y
Predecessor/successor report	Y	N	Y	Y	Y	Y	Y	Y
Updates out-of-sequence report	Y	N	N	Y	Y	Y	Y	Y
To-do list (turn-around report)	Y	Y	Y	Y	Y	Y	Y	Y
Number of structures per project								
WBS	Y	N	Y	Y	Y	Y	Y	Unlim.
OBS	Y	N	Y	Y	Y	Y	Y	Unlim.
RBS	Y	N	Y	Y	Y	Y	Y	Unlim.
User defined	Y	N	Y	Y	Y	Y	Y	Y
Maximum number of structures supported	User defined	Unlim.	up to 100	Unlim.	Unlim.	4	Unlim.	Unlim.
Features								
Outline view	Y	Y	N	Y	Y	Y	Y	Y
Number of tasks	Unlim.	Unlim.	25,000 per project	Unlim.	Unlim.	16,000	Unlim.	Unlim.
Number of resources	Unlim.	2,000+	2,000 per project	Unlim.	Unlim.	Unlim.	Unlim.	Unlim.
Multiproject								
Number of projects scheduled simultaneously	Unlim.	Unlim.	Depends on project size and detail level	Unlim.	Unlim.	Unlim.	Unlim.	Unlim.
Prioritize projects for scheduling	Y	N	Y	Y	Y	Y	Y	Y
Dependency trace view *	Y	Y	Y	Y	Y	Y	Y	Y
Charting								
Early start vs. resource leveled start Gantt chart	Y	N	Y	Y	Y	Y	Y	Y
Highlight critical path in charts	Y	N	Y	Y	Y	Y	Y	Y

Schedule Management

	ABT Workbench (repository-based) and Project Workbench PMW (standalone)	ActionPlan	AMS REALTIME Projects	Artemis ProjectView	AutoPLAN Enterprise	CA-SuperProject 4.0 & CA-SuperProject/Net 1.0	Cascade PgM	Dekker TRAKKER Activity Based Cost Management and Performance System
Variable timescale Gantt charts	Y	N	Y	Y	Y	Y	Y	Y
Variable timescale network logic diagrams (timephased network logic)	Y	N	Y	Y	Y	N	N	Y
Zoned network diagrams	Y	N	Y	Y	Y	N	N	Y
Structure drawings	Y	N	N	Y	Y	Y	Y	Y
PERT chart	Y	N	Y	Y	Y	Y	Y	Y
Maximums								
Number of tasks per project	Unlim.	Unlim.	25,000	Unlim.	Unlim.	16,000	Unlim.	Unlim.
Number of projects per Multiproject	Unlim.	Unlim.	Max. tasks 25,000	Unlim.	Unlim.	Unlim.	Unlim.	Unlim.
Number of layers of projects in program	Unlim.	1	Unlim.	Unlim.	128	Unlim.	Unlim.	Unlim.
Number of resources per task	Unlim.	Unlim.	2,000	Unlim.	Unlim.	Unlim.	Unlim.	Unlim.
Number of defined resources	Unlim.	Unlim.	2,000	Unlim.	Unlim.	Unlim.	Unlim.	Unlim.
Number of calendars per project	Unlim.	Unlim.	250	99	Unlim.	Unlim.	Unlim.	10
Reporting								
Report writer	Y	N	Y	Y	Y	Y	Y	Y
Report wizard	Y	N	N	Y	Y	Y	N	Y
Publishes as HTML	Y	N	N	Y	Y	Y	Y	Y
Number of user-defined fields		0	100	Unlim.	22	90	Unlim.	Unlim.
Drill-down/roll-up *	Y	Y	Y	Y	Y	Y	Y	Y
Import/export	Y	Y	Y	Y	Y	Y	Y	Y
Automatic E-mail notification *	Y	Y	N	Y	Y	N	Y	Y
Macro recorder/batch capable *	Y	N	Y	Y	Y	Y	Y	Y
Can "canned" reports be modified?	Y	Y	Y	Y	Y	Y	Y	Y
Sort, filter	Y	Y	Y	Y	Y	Y	Y	Y
Architecture								
Databases supported (list):	Oracle, MS SQL Server, Sybase, Informix	N/A	Oracle, any ODBC compliant DB	Oracle, MS SQL Server, Sybase, SQL Base	Oracle	CSV, WK1, dBaseII, SYLK, Fixed ASCII, Excel, MPX, ODBC	Oracle	Oracle, MS SQL Server, Informix, MS Access, FoxPro

Supports distributed databases	Y	Y	Y	Y	Y	Y	N	Y
Three-tier client/server	Y	Y	Y	Y	Y	Y	Y	Y
Client operating systems	Win 95/98/NT	Win 95/98/NT	DOS, Win, OS/2	Win 95/NT/3.x, Solaris, HP-UX, AIX	Win 95/98/NT	Win 95/NT/3.x, Solaris, HP, RS, Mac	Win 95/NT, Mac, Solaris	Win 95/98/NT
Server operating systems	Win NT, Novell, Unix	Unix, Win NT	Win NT	Win NT, Solaris, HP-UX, AIX	Win NT, HP-UX, Unix, Solaris, VMS	Win 95/NT/3.x, Solaris, HP, RS, Mac	Win NT, Solaris	Win NT
Network operating systems	Win NT, Novell, Unix	TCP/IP	All	Win NT, Novell, Unix	Novell, Win NT, IPX	TCP/IP, Banyan, Novell, IPX	TCP/IP	TCP/IP Compatible
Minimum client configuration	16 MB RAM, 1 GB HD, SVGA	PC 486/66 processor or above. Win 95 or Win NT V4. 16 MB RAM	386 processor w/25 MHz, 4 MB RAM, Mouse MS Win 3.x, MS-DOS V. 3.1	P5, 32 MB RAM	32 MB RAM, 64 MB RAM recommended	8 MB RAM, 20 MB disk, 486 or better	Mac: Power PC; System 8.x; Mac Runtime for Java (MRJ) 2.1; Quicktime 3; 5 MB for ActionPlan client, 5 MB for HotSheet client, 15 MB for MRJ (unless already installed). Win95 or NT	Pentium 133

Schedule Management

	ABT Workbench (repository-based) and Project Workbench PMW (standalone)	ActionPlan	AMS REALTIME Projects	Artemis ProjectView	AutoPLAN Enterprise	CA-SuperProject 4.0 & CA-SuperProject/Net 1.0	Cascade PgM	Dekker TRAKKER Activity Based Cost Management and Performance System
Minimum server configuration	Pentium 266	Win NT or Solaris, 64 MB RAM, 30 MB disk space, Webserver software	32 MB RAM, 100 MB disk, Pentium or better	user dependent	P5 32 MB, Unix machine with 64 MB	Win NT 3.51, 486 PC, 32 MB memory, 20 MB HD space, NT Internet Service Manager, Internet browser that supports HTML 3.0	Any server supporting Oracle 7 or above	128 MB RAM, 10 GB HD
Client runs under Web browser	N	Y	Y	Y	Y	Y	N	N
Open architecture								
Supports OLE	Y	N	N	Y	Y	Y	Y	Y
Documented Object Model	Y	N	Y	Y	Y	Y	Y	Y
Documented Application Programming Interface (API)	Y	N	Y	Y	Y	Y	Y	Y
Simultaneous edit of data file	Y	N	Y	Y	N	Y	Y	Y
Does product have a programming language?	N	N	Y	Y	Y	Y	Y	Y
Are years stored as four-digit numbers?	Y	N	N	Y	Y	Y	Y	Y
Online Help								
Right mouse click	Y	N	N	Y	N	Y	N	Y
Hover buttons	Y	N	Y	Y	Y	Y	~	Y
Interactive help	Y	Y	Y	Y	Y	Y	Y	Y
Help search feature	Y	Y	Y	Y	Y	Y	Y	Y
Web access to product knowledge base *	Y	N	Y	Y	Y	N	N	N
Vendor Information								
Training								
Computer-based training	Y	N	Y	Y	Y	N	Y	Y
Training materials available	Y	Y	Y	Y	Y	N	Y	Y
Customized training materials	Y	N	Y	Y	Y	Y	Y	Y
Online tutorial	Y	Y	Y	Y	N	Y	N	Y
Consulting available from vendor	Y	Y	Y	Y	Y	Y	Y	Y
Site license discounts	Y	Y	Y	Y	Y	Y	Y	Y

Enhancement requests *	Y	Y	Y	Y	Y	Y	Y	Y
Modify source code, support through upgrades *	Y	N	Y	Y	Y	Y	Y	Y
Global presence								
Global offices	Y	N	Y	Y	Y	Y	Y	Y
Multilingual technical support	Y	N	Y	Y	Y	Y	Y	Y
Language versions (list):	Eng, Fr, Ger, Jpn	N/A	Chin, Dutch, Eng, Fr, Ger, Jpn, Kor, Pol, Rus	Eng, Fr, Ger, Ital	Eng, Fr	Eng, Fr, Nor, Ital, Span, Ger	Eng, Fr	Eng, Span, Dutch, Fr
Audit Software Quality Assurance process? *	Y	N	Y	Y	Y	N	Y	Y
Security								
Configurable access privileges *	Y	Y	Y	Y	Y	Y	Y	Y
Passwords expire (forced update)	N	N	N	Y	Y	N	N	Y
Electronic approvals	Y	N	Y	Y	Y	N	Y	Y
Password protect files	Y	Y	Y	Y	Y	N	Y	Y

Schedule Management

	Enterprise Project	ER Project 1000	eRoom	FastTrack Schedule 5.02	Innate Multi-Project (with MS Project (MSP))	Intelligent Planner	Micro Planner X-Pert	Microsoft Project 98	Milestones, Etc.
Time analysis									
Full critical path	Y	Y	N	N	Y	Y	Y	Y	N
Relationship types									
SS	Y	Y	N	Y	Y	Y	Y	Y	Y
FS	Y	Y	N	Y	Y	Y	Y	Y	Y
SF	Y	Y	N	N	Y	N	Y	Y	Y
FF	Y	Y	N	Y	Y	Y	Y	Y	Y
Allow SS and FF on a set of tasks	Y	Y	N	Y	Y	Y	Y	N	Y
Lags on relationships	Y	Y	N	N	Y	Y	Y	Y	N
Calendars on relationships	Y	N	N	N	As MSP	Y	Y	N	N
Mixed durations (minutes, hours, days, weeks, months)	Y	Y	N	Y	Y	Y	Y	Y	Y
Time limited schedule calculation	Y	Y	N	N	Y	Y	Y	Y	N
Resource limited schedule calculation	Y	Y	N	N	Y	Y	Y	Y	N
Query overallocations by:									
Skill	Y	N	N	N	Y	Y	Y	N	N
Resource type	Y	Y	N	N	Y	Y	Y	N	N
Department	Y	Y	N	N	Y	Y	Y	N	N
Other (user defined)	Y	Y	N	N	Y	Y	Y	N	N
Resource calendars									
Individual resource calendars	Y	Y	N	N	Y	Y	Y	Y	N
Variable availability	Y	Y	N	N	Y	Y	Y	Y	N
Scheduling/leveling features									
Resource leveling	Y	Y	N	N	Y	Y	Y	Y	N
Resource smoothing	Y	Y	N	N	Y	Y	Y	Y	N
Leveling by date range	Y	N	N	N	Y	Y	Y	Y	N
"Do not level" flag (bypass project during leveling)	Y	N	N	N	Y	Y	Y	Y	N
User-defined resource profiles (spread curves)	Y	N	N	N	Y	Y	Y	Y	N
Team/crew scheduling	Y	N	N	N	As MSP	Y	Y	N	N
Skill scheduling	Y	N	N	N	Y	Y	Y	N	N
Number of skills per resource	Unlim.	1,000	N	N/A	Unlim.	Unlim.	20	N/A	N
Alternate resource scheduling	Y	N	N	N	Y	Y	N	Y	N
Rolling wave scheduling	Y	Y	N	N	Y	Y	Y	N	N
Activity splitting	Y	N	N	N	Y	Y	Y	Y	Y
Perishable resources	Y	N	N	N	Y	Y	Y	Y	Y
Consumable resources	Y	Y	N	N	Y	N	Y	N	N
Assign role (skill), software replaces with name at specific point in process	Y	Y	N	N	Y	Y	N	N	N
Heterogeneous resources	Y	Y	N	N	Y	Y	Y	Y	N
Homogeneous resources	Y	Y	N	N	Y	Y	Y	Y	N

Hierarchical resources								
Hierarchical resources	N	N	Y	Y	Y	N	Y	Y
Share resource pool across multiple projects	N	Y	Y	Y	Y	N	Y	Y
Number of resources to be included in resource scheduling	0	Limited by available memory	200	N/A	MSP limit	Unlim.	16,000	Unlim.
Resource costs								
Rate escalation	N	Y	Y	N	Y	Y	Y	Y
Overtime	N	Y	Y	N	Y	Y	Y	Y
Top-down budgeting	N	Y	Y	N	Y	Y	Y	Y
Performance analysis/cost reporting								
Calculates BCWS	N	Y	Y	N	Y	Y	Y	Y
Calculates BCWP	N	Y	Y	N	Y	Y	Y	Y
Calculates ACWP	N	Y	Y	N	Y	Y	Y	Y
Physical % complete (in addition to schedule %complete)	N	N	Y	N	Y	Y	Y	Y
Reports								
30-60-90 day and user-defined report windows	N	Y	Y	Y	Y	Y	Y	Y
Predecessor/successor report	N	Y	Y	N	Y	Y	Y	Y
Updates out-of-sequence report	N	N	Y	N	Y	Y	N	Y
To-do list (turn-around report)	N	Y	Y	N	Y	Y	N	Y
Number of structures per project								
WBS	Y	Y	Y	N	Y	Y	Y	Y
OBS	N	N	N	N	Y	Y	N	Y
RBS	N	N	Y	N	Y	Y	N	Y
User defined	Y	Y	Y	N	Y	Y	Y	N
Maximum number of structures supported	1	1	999	0	3	Unlim.	100+	Unlim.
Features								
Outline view	Y	Y	Y	N	Y	Y	Y	Y
Number of tasks	8,000	10,000	Unlim.	65,000	MSP Limit	Unlim.	32,000	Unlim.
Number of resources	0	Limited by available memory	200	65,000	MSP Limit	Unlim.	16,000	Limited by available memory
Multiproject								
Number of projects scheduled simultaneously	1	1,000	50	65,000	Unlim.	Unlim.	1,000	Unlim.
Prioritize projects for scheduling	N	N	Y	Y	Y	N	Y	N
Dependency trace view *	N	Y	Y	Y	Y	N	Y	Y
Charting								
Early start vs. resource leveled start Gantt chart	N	Y	Y	N	Y	N	Y	Y
Highlight critical path in charts	N	Y	Y	N	N	N	Y	Y

Schedule Management

	Enterprise Project	ER Project 1000	eRoom	FastTrack Schedule 5.02	Innate Multi-Project (with MS Project (MSP))	Intelligent Planner	Micro Planner X-Pert	Microsoft Project 98	Milestones, Etc.
Variable timescale Gantt charts	Y	Y	N	N	N	Y	Y	Y	Y
Variable timescale network logic diagrams (timephased network logic)	Y	N	N	N	N	N	N	N	N
Zoned network diagrams	Y	Y	N	N	N	N	Y	N	N
Structure drawings	Y	Y	N	N	N	Y	Y	N	N
PERT chart	Y	Y	N	N	Y	Y	Y	Y	N
Maximums									
Number of tasks per project	Unlim.	32,000	N	65,000	MSP Limit	Unlim.	10,000	Limited by available memory	8,000
Number of projects per Multiproject	Unlim.	1,000	N	65,000	MSP Limit	Unlim.	50	1,000	1
Number of layers of projects in program	Unlim.	2	N	65,000	MSP Limit	Unlim.	10	Unlim.	0
Number of resources per task	Unlim.	1,000	N	65,000	MSP Limit	Unlim.	20	Unlim.	0
Number of defined resources	Unlim.	16,000	N	65,000	MSP Limit	Unlim.	200	Limited by available memory	0
Number of calendars per project	Unlim.	16,000	N	1	MSP Limit	Unlim.	Unlim.	Limited by available memory	1
Reporting									
Report writer	Y	Y	Y	Y	Y	Y	Y	Y	Y
Report wizard	Y	Y	Y	Y	Y	N	N	N	Y
Publishes as HTML	Y	Y	N	Y	Y	Y	N	Y	Y
Number of user-defined fields	0	100	N	65,000	Unlim.	100	12	360	200
Drill-down/roll-up *	Y	Y	N	Y	Y	Y	Y	N	Y
Import/export	Y	Y	Y	Y	Y	Y	Y	Y	Y
Automatic E-mail notification *	N	Y	N	Y	Y	Y	N	Y	Y
Macro recorder/batch capable *	N	N	N	N	Y	Y	N	N	Y
Can "canned" reports be modified?	Y	Y	Y	Y	Y	Y	Y	Y	Y
Sort, filter	Y	Y	Y	Y	Y	Y	Y	Y	Y
Architecture									
Databases supported (list):	Oracle, Sybase, Informix, MS SQL Server, MS Access	Oracle, MS SQL Server, Interbase	SQL Anywhere		MS Access, MS SQL Server, Oracle	Oracle, Sybase, MS SQL Server, Informix, Centura		MS Access, MS SQL Server, or Oracle	

Supports distributed databases	Y	N	N	Y	Y/N	N	N	Y	Y
Three-tier client/server	N	N	N	Y	Y/N	N	N	Y	Y
Client operating systems	Win	Win 95/98/NT 3.51 with Service Pack 5 or later/Win NT 4.0 with Service Pack 2 or later	Win, Mac	Win 95/NT	Win	Win 95/98/NT 4.0/NT 5.0/3.x, Mac	Win 95/98/NT	Win 95/98/NT 3.51/4.0 (ER Project Satellite also Java and Win 3.x)	Win 95/98/NT
Server operating systems		Win 95/98/NT 3.51 with Service Pack 5 or later/NT 4.0 with Service Pack 2 or later	Win, Mac	Win NT	Win		NT	Win NT, Unix	Unix, Win NT
Network operating systems	Any	Any Win-supported network	Win, Mac	TCP/IP, NetBios	Any that support Win	Win NT, Novell, Banyan, AppleTalk	NT	Win, NetBEUI/NetBios, TCP/IP, Novell	Novell, Win NT, Others
Minimum client configuration		486 or higher processor with 12 MB memory for Win 95 or 16 MB for Win 98 or NT		Pentium 120, 16 MB RAM, 1 GB disk	Pentium	Win: 386DX or higher, Win 3.x or higher, 4 MB RAM, 10 MB HD. Mac: Mac Plus or higher, System 7.0 or higher, 4 MB RAM, 10 MB HD	16MB, Pentium 133	Pentium, 16 MB RAM (ER Project Satellite 8 MB)	486 with 16 MB RAM

Schedule Management

	Enterprise Project	ER Project 1000	eRoom	FastTrack Schedule 5.02	Innate Multi-Project (with MS Project (MSP))	Intelligent Planner	Micro Planner X-Pert	Microsoft Project 98	Milestones, Etc.
Minimum server configuration	Pentium 200 CPU, 128 MB, 1 GB	Pentium, 32 MB memory	NT-64 MB, Pentium 166	Same as minimum NOS requirements; see Client Operating System requirements.	Capacity only	Pentium 233, 128 MB RAM, 1 GB disk		Run from server is available; configuration depends on number of users connecting to the server	
Client runs under Web browser	Y	Y	Y	N	Y	Y	N	Y	N
Open architecture									
Supports OLE	Y	N	Y	Y	Y	N	N	Y	Y
Documented Object Model	Y	Y	N	N	Y	N	N	Y	Y
Documented Application Programming Interface (API)	Y	N	Y	N	Y	Y	N	N	Y
Simultaneous edit of data file	Y	Y	Y	N	As MSP	Y	N	N	Y
Does product have a programming language?	Y	N	N	N	Y	Y	N	Y	Y
Are years stored as four-digit numbers?	Y	Y	Y	Y	Y	Y	Y	Y	Y
Online Help									
Right mouse click	N	Y	Y	Y	Y	N	Y	Y	Y
Hover buttons	N	Y	Y	Y	Y	N	Y	Y	Y
Interactive help	Y	Y	Y	Y	Y	Y	Y	Y	Y
Help search feature	Y	Y	Y	Y	Y	Y	Y	Y	Y
Web access to product knowledge base *	N	Y	Y	Y	Y	Y	Y	Y	Y
Vendor Information									
Training									
Computer-based training	Y	N	N	N	Y	N	Y	N	Y
Training materials available	Y	Y	Y	Y	Y	Y	Y	Y	Y
Customized training materials	Y	Y	N	Y	Y	Y	Y	N	Y
Online tutorial	N	Y	Y	Y	Y	Y	Y	Y	Y
Consulting available from vendor	Y	Y	Y	Y	Y	Y	Y	Y	Y
Site license discounts	Y	Y	Y	Y	Y	Y	Y	Y	Y

Feature	Product 1	Product 2	Product 3	Product 4	Product 5	Product 6	Product 7
Enhancement requests *	Y	Y	Y	Y	Y	Y	Y
Modify source code, support through upgrades *	Y	N	Y	Y	Y	N	Y
Global presence							
Global offices	N	Y	Y	Y	Y	N	N
Multilingual technical support	N	Y	N	Y	Y	N	Y
Language versions (list):	Eng	Ger, Fr, Swed, Ital, Span, Dan, Nor, Jpn, Traditional Chin, Simplified Chin, Kor, Heb, Brzl. Port	Eng	Eng, Fr, Ger, Dutch	Eng, Fr, Ger	Eng, Ger, Swed	Eng, Span
Audit Software Quality Assurance process? *	N	N	Y	Y	Y	Y	Y
Security							
Configurable access privileges *	N	N	N	Y	Y	Y	Y
Passwords expire (forced update)	N	N	N	N	Y	N	Y
Electronic approvals	N	Y	N	Y	Y	N	Y
Password protect files	N	Y	Y	Y	Y	Y	Y

135

Schedule Management

	MinuteMan Project Management Software	Open Plan	OPX2 Pro	Panorama	Planning Controller	PLANTRAC-OUTLOOK	PlanView Software	Primavera Project Planner (P3) 2.0	ProChain	Project Commander
Time analysis										
Full critical path	Y	Y	Y	Y	Y	Y	Y	Y	Y	Y
Relationship types										
SS	N	Y	Y	Y	Y	Y	Y	Y	Y	Y
FS	Y	Y	Y	Y	Y	Y	Y	Y	Y	Y
SF	N	Y	Y	Y	Y	N	Y	Y	Y	Y
FF	N	Y	Y	Y	Y	Y	Y	Y	Y	Y
Allow SS and FF on a set of tasks	N	Y	Y	Y	Y	Y	Y	Y	Y	Y
Lags on relationships	N	Y	Y	Y	Y	Y	Y	Y	Y	Y
Calendars on relationships	N	Y	Y	Y	Y	Y	Y	N		N
Mixed durations (minutes, hours, days, weeks, months)	Y	Y	Y	Y	Y	Y	Y	Y	Y	N
Time limited schedule calculation	N	Y	Y	Y	Y	Y	Y	N	N	N
Resource limited schedule calculation	N	Y	Y	Y	Y	Y	Y	N	Y	Y
Query overallocations by:										
Skill	N	Y	Y	Y	Y	Y	Y	Y	N	N
Resource type	N	Y	Y	Y	Y	Y	Y	Y	N	Y
Department	N	Y	Y	Y	Y	Y	Y	Y	N	Y
Other (user defined)	N	Y	Y	Y	Y	Y	Y	Y	N	N
Resource calendars										
Individual resource calendars	N	Y	Y	Y	Y	Y	Y	Y	Y	Y
Variable availability	N	Y	Y	Y	Y	Y	Y	Y	Y	Y
Scheduling/leveling features										
Resource leveling	N	Y	Y	Y	Y	Y	Y	Y	Y	Y
Resource smoothing	N	Y	Y	Y	Y	Y		Y	N	Y
Leveling by date range	N	Y	Y	Y	Y	Y	Y	Y	N	Y
"Do not level" flag (bypass project during leveling)	N	Y	Y	N	N	Y	Y	N	Y	Y
User-defined resource profiles (spread curves)	N	Y	Y	Y	Y	Y	Y	Y	N	Y
Team/crew scheduling	N	Y	Y	N	Y	Y	Y	Y	Y	N
Skill scheduling	N	Y	Y	N	Y	N	Y	N	N	N
Number of skills per resource	N	Unlim.	Unlim.	N	Unlim.		Unlim.		1	0
Alternate resource scheduling	N	Y	Y	Y	N	Y	Y	N	Y	Y
Rolling wave scheduling	N	Cobra only	N	Y	N	Y	Y	N	N	N
Activity splitting	N	Y	Y	Y	N	Y	Y	Y	N	Y
Perishable resources	N	Y	N	N	N	N	N	Y	N	Y
Consumable resources	N	Y	Y	N	Y	Y	N	Y	N	Y
Assign role (skill), software replaces with name at specific point in process	N	Y	Y	N	N	Y	Y	N	N	Y
Heterogeneous resources	N	Y	Y	Y	Y	Y	Y	N	N	Y
Homogeneous resources	N	Y	Y	Y	Y	Y	Y	N	Y	Y

Hierarchical resources	N	N	Y	Y	Y	N	Y	N
Share resource pool across multiple projects	Y	Y	Y	Y	Y	Y	Y	N
Number of resources to be included in resource scheduling	Unlim.	Unlim.	Unlim.	400	Unlim.	Unlim.	Unlim.	0
Resource costs								
Rate escalation	Y	N	Y	Y	Y	Y	Y	N
Overtime	Y	Y	Y	N	Y	Y	Y	N
Top-down budgeting	N	N	Y	Y	Y	Y	Y	N
Performance analysis/cost reporting								
Calculates BCWS	Y	Y	Y	Y	Y	Y	Y	N
Calculates BCWP	Y	Y	Y	Y	Y	Y	Y	N
Calculates ACWP	Y	Y	Y	Y	Y	Y	Y	N
Physical % complete (in addition to schedule %complete)	N	Y	Y	Y	Y	Y	Y	Y
Reports								
30-60-90 day and user-defined report windows	Y	Y	Y	Y	Y	Y	Y	N
Predecessor/successor report	Y	Y	Y	Y	Y	Y	Y	Y
Updates out-of-sequence report	N	N	Y	Y	Y	Y	Y	N
To-do list (turn-around report)	Y	Y	Y	Y	Y	Y	Y	N
Number of structures per project								
WBS	Y	Y	Y	Y	Y	Y	Y	Y
OBS	N	N	Y	Y	Y	Y	Y	N
RBS	N	N	Y	Y	Y	Y	Y	N
User defined	Y	Y	Y	Y	Y	Y	Y	N
Maximum number of structures supported	Unlim.	Unlim.	Unlim.	20	Unlim.	10	90	5
Features								
Outline view	Y	N	Y	Y	Y	Y	Y	Y
Number of tasks	Limited by hardware's memory	100,000	Unlim.	5,000	Unlim.	Unlim.	Unlim.	1,000
Number of resources	Limited by hardware's memory	Unlim.	Unlim.	200	Unlim.	Unlim.	Unlim.	200
Multiproject								
Number of projects scheduled simultaneously	1,000	Unlim.	Unlim.	200	1	Unlim.	Unlim.	5
Prioritize projects for scheduling	Y	Y	Y	Y	N	Y	Y	N
Dependency trace view *	Y	Y	Y	Y	Y	Y	Y	N
Charting								
Early start vs. resource leveled start Gantt chart	Y	Y	Y	Y	Y	Y	Y	N
Highlight critical path in charts	Y	Y	Y	Y	Y	Y	Y	Y

Schedule Management

	MinuteMan Project Management Software	Open Plan	OPX2 Pro	Panorama	Planning Controller	PLANTRAC-OUTLOOK	PlanView Software	Primavera Project Planner (P3) 2.0	ProChain	Project Commander
Variable timescale Gantt charts	Y	Y	Y	Y	Y	Y	Y	N	Y	Y
Variable timescale network logic diagrams (timephased network logic)	N	Y	Y	N	Y	Y	N	N		N
Zoned network diagrams	N	Y	Y	N	Y	Y	N	N		N
Structure drawings	N	Y	Y	Y	N	Y	N	N		N
PERT chart	Y	Y	Y	Y	Y	Y	N	Y	Y	Y
Maximums										
Number of tasks per project	200	Unlim.	Unlim.	Unlim.	Unlim.	500,000	Unlim.	100,000	Limited by hardware memory	Unlim.
Number of projects per Multiproject	5	Unlim.	Unlim.	Unlim.	Unlim.	200	Unlim.	Unlim.	1,000	1,000
Number of layers of projects in program	1	Unlim.	Unlim.	Unlim.	2	5	Unlim.	Unlim.	1	Unlim.
Number of resources per task	100	Unlim.	Unlim.	Unlim.	Unlim.	16	Unlim.	Unlim.		Unlim.
Number of defined resources	200	Unlim.	Unlim.	Unlim.	Unlim.	200	Unlim.	Unlim.	Limited by hardware memory	Unlim.
Number of calendars per project	1	Unlim.	Unlim.	Unlim.	Unlim.	9,999	Unlim.	Unlim.	Limited by hardware memory	Unlim.
Reporting										
Report writer	Y	Y	Y	Y	Y	Y	Y	Y	Y	N
Report wizard	N	N	N	N	N	Y	Y	Y	N	Y
Publishes as HTML	N	Y	Y	Y	Y	N	Y	Y	Y	Y
Number of user-defined fields	0	Unlim.	Unlim.	20	Multiple	20	Unlim.	Unlim.		120
Drill-down/roll-up *	N	Y	Y	Y	Y	Y	Y	Y	N	Y
Import/export	N	Y	Y	Y	Y	Y	Y	Y	Y	Y
Automatic E-mail notification *	N	N	Y	N	N	N	Y	N	N	N
Macro recorder/batch capable *	N	Y	Y	N	Y	Y	N	Y	Y	N
Can "canned" reports be modified?	Y	Y	Y	Y	Y	Y	Y	Y	Y	N
Sort, filter	N	Y	Y	Y	Y	Y	Y	Y	Y	Y
Architecture										
Databases supported (list):		Oracle, MS SQL Server, Sybase, MS Access, Foxpro	Oracle, MS SQL Server, Informix, Sybase, Ingres	Oracle	Oracle	ODBC	Oracle, Sybase, MS SQL Server, etc.	Btrieve	MS Access	ODBC

Supports distributed databases	N	Y	Y	Y	Y	Y	N	Y	N	N
Three-tier client/server	N	N	Y	Y	Y	Y	Y	N	N	N
Client operating systems		Win 95 or later	Win 95/98/NT/3.x, Mac, Unix	Win 95/NT	Win 95/NT/3.x	Win 95/98/NT	Win 95/98/NT	Win 95/3.x, OS/2	Win 95/NT	Win 95/98/NT
Server operating systems		Specified by database vendor	Win NT, Unix	Any that support Oracle	Unix, Win NT	Win 95/98/NT	Win NT, Unix, Novell, IIS, Netscape	Win NT 3.5 or later		Win NT, Novell
Network operating systems		Any that support Win	TCP/IP (Ethernet, Token Ring, WAN)	TCP/IP	Novell, Win NT	Novell compatible	Win NT, Unix, Novell, IIS, Netscape			Win NT, Novell
Minimum client configuration		Pentium or compatible, Win 95 or later, 16 MB RAM, rec. 32 MB	486 + 16 MB RAM (light client), P100 + 32 MB RAM (fat client)	Pentium 133 MHz, 32 MB RAM, 500 MB disk	16 MB RAM	8 MB	486/66, 8 MB RAM, Win 3.x+	486/50 8 MB RAM	Same as MS Project	486 processor/12 MB

139

Schedule Management

	MinuteMan Project Management Software	Open Plan	OPX2 Pro	Panorama	Planning Controller	PLANTRAC-OUTLOOK	PlanView Software	Primavera Project Planner (P3) 2.0	ProChain	Project Commander
Minimum server configuration		Server optional	P2xx+128 MB RAM	Depends on number of users	64 MB RAM	8 MB	486/66, 32 MB RAM, Novell			
Client runs under Web browser	N	N	N	N	N	N	Y	N	N	N
Open architecture										
Supports OLE	N	Y	Y	Y	Y	N	Y	Y	Y	N
Documented Object Model	N	Y	Y	Y	Y	N	Y	Y	Y	N
Documented Application Programming Interface (API)	N	N	N	Y	Y	N	Y	Y	Y	N
Simultaneous edit of data file	N	Y	Y	Y	Y	Y	N	Y	N	N
Does product have a programming language?	N	N	Y	Y	Y	N	Y	Y	Y	N
Are years stored as four-digit numbers?	Y	Y	Y	Y	Y	Y	Y	Y	N	Y
Online Help										
Right mouse click	N	Y	Y	N	Y	Y	Y	Y	Y	Y
Hover buttons	Y	Y	Y	N	Y	Y	Y	Y	Y	Y
Interactive help	Y	Y	Y	Y	N	Y	Y	N	Y	Y
Help search feature	N	Y	Y	Y	Y	Y	Y	Y	Y	Y
Web access to product knowledge base *	N	Y	N	N	Y	N	Y	Y	Y	Y
Vendor Information										
Training										
Computer-based training	N	Y	N	N	N	Y	Y	Y	N	Y
Training materials available	Y	Y	Y	Y	Y	Y	Y	Y	Y	Y
Customized training materials	N	Y	Y	Y	Y	Y	Y	Y	N	Y
Online tutorial	Y	Y	N	N	N	Y	N	Y	N	Y
Consulting available from vendor	Y	Y	Y	Y	Y	Y	Y	Y	Y	Y
Site license discounts	Y	Y	Y	Y	Y	Y	Y	Y	Y	Y

Enhancement requests *	Y	Y	Y	Y	Y	Y	Y	Y	Y
Modify source code, support through upgrades *	Y	Y	Y	Y	Y	Y	Y	Y	Y
Global presence									
Global offices	N	Y	Y	N	Y	N	Y	Y	Y
Multilingual technical support	N	Y	Y	N	N	N	Y	Y	N
Language versions (list):	Eng	Eng, Ital, Fr, Ger, Mand, Rus, Hangul	Eng, Fr		Eng	Eng	Eng, Fr, Ger	Eng, Ger, Fr	Eng
Audit Software Quality Assurance process? *	N	N	Y	Y	Y	Y	Y	N	Y
Security									
Configurable access privileges *	N	Y	Y	Y	Y	Y	Y	N	N
Passwords expire (forced update)	N	N	N	Y	N	Y	Y	N	N
Electronic approvals	N	N	Y	Y	N	Y	Y	N	N
Password protect files	N	Y	Y	Y	N	N	Y	Y	Y

Schedule Management

	Project Control 6.0	ProjectExplorer for MS Project	Project Scheduler 7.6	QEI Exec	SAS Software	Schedule Insight	Spreadsheet Scheduler	SureTrak Project Management	TurboProject Professional 3.0	WebProject
Time analysis										
Full critical path	Y	Y	Y	Y	Y	Y	Y	Y	Y	Y
Relationship types										
SS	Y	Y	Y	Y	Y	Y	Y	Y	Y	Y
FS	Y	Y	Y	Y	Y	Y	Y	Y	Y	Y
SF	Y	Y	N	Y	Y	Y	Y	Y	N	Y
FF	Y	Y	Y	Y	Y	Y	Y	Y	Y	Y
Allow SS and FF on a set of tasks	Y	Y	Y	Y	N	Y	Y	Y	Y	Y
Lags on relationships	Y	Y	Y	Y	Y	Y	Y	Y	Y	Y
Calendars on relationships	Y	N	Y	Y	Y	N	Y	N	N	N
Mixed durations (minutes, hours, days, weeks, months)	Y	Y	Y	Y	N	Y	Y	Y	N	Y
Time limited schedule calculation	Y	Y	Y	Y	Y	Y	Y	Y	Y	N
Resource limited schedule calculation	Y	Y	Y	N	Y	Y	Y	Y	Y	N
Query overallocations by:										
Skill	Y	Y	Y	Y	Y	N	Y	N	Y	Y
Resource type	Y	Y	Y	Y	Y	Y	Y	Y	Y	Y
Department	Y	Y	Y	Y	Y	Y	N	Y	Y	Y
Other (user defined)	Y	Y	Y	Y	Y	Y	Y	Y	Y	Y
Resource calendars										
Individual resource calendars	Y	Y	Y	Y	Y	Y	Y	Y	Y	Y
Variable availability	Y	Y	Y	Y	Y	Y	Y	Y	Y	Y
Scheduling/leveling features										
Resource leveling	N	Y	Y	Y	Y	Y	Y	Y	Y	N
Resource smoothing	N	Y	N	N	N		Y	N	Y	N
Leveling by date range	N	Y	Y	N	Y		Y	N	Y	N
"Do not level" flag (bypass project during leveling)	N	Y	Y	N	N		N	Y	N	N
User-defined resource profiles (spread curves)	N	Y	N	N	N		N	N	Y	Y
Team/crew scheduling	N	Y	Y	N	N		Y	N	N	N
Skill scheduling	Y	Y	Y	N	Y		N	N	N	N
Number of skills per resource	Unlim.	Unlim.	Unlim.	Unlim.	Unlim.		Y	1	N/A	N
Alternate resource scheduling	Y	Y	Y	N	Y		N	N	Y	Y
Rolling wave scheduling	Y	Y	N	N	N		N	N	Y	N
Activity splitting	Y	Y	Y	N	Y		N	N	Y	Y
Perishable resources	N	Y	Y	N	Y		N	Y	N	N
Consumable resources	N	Y	N	N	Y		N	N	N	N
Assign role (skill), software replaces with name at specific point in process	Y	Y	Y	Y	N		N	N	N	N
Heterogeneous resources	Y	Y	Y	Y	Y	N	N	N	N	N
Homogeneous resources	Y	Y	Y	N	Y	N	N	N	N	Y

Hierarchical resources	Y	Y	N	Y	N	N	N	Y	Y
Share resource pool across multiple projects	Y	Y	Y	Y	Y	Y	Y	Y	Y
Number of resources to be included in resource scheduling	Unlim.	MSP limits	99,999	N/A	Unlim.		Unlim.	32,000	N
Resource costs									
Rate escalation	Y	Y	Y	Y	N	N	N	N	N
Overtime	Y	Y	Y	N	Y	Y	N	N	N
Top-down budgeting	Y	Y	Y	Y	Y	Y	Y	N	N
Performance analysis/cost reporting									
Calculates BCWS	Y	Y	Y	Y	Y	N	Y	Y	Y
Calculates BCWP	Y	Y	Y	Y	Y	N	Y	Y	Y
Calculates ACWP	Y	Y	Y	Y	Y	N	Y	Y	Y
Physical % complete (in addition to schedule %complete)	Y	Y	Y	Y	Y	N	Y	Y	Y
Reports									
30-60-90 day and user-defined report windows	Y	Y	Y	Y	Y	Y	Y	Y	Y
Predecessor/successor report	Y	Y	Y	Y	Y	Y	Y	Y	Y
Updates out-of-sequence report	Y	Y	Y	Y	N	N	N	Y	N
To-do list (turn-around report)	Y	Y	Y	Y	Y	Y	Y	Y	Y
Number of structures per project									
WBS	Y	Y	Y	Y	Y	Y	Y	Y	Y
OBS	Y	Y	Y	Y	N	Y	N	Y	N
RBS	N	Y	Y	Y	N	N	Y	Y	Y
User defined	N	N	Y	Y	Y	Y	Y	Y	Y
Maximum number of structures supported	Unlim.	MSP limits	10	Unlim.	Unlim.	10	2	Unlim.	Unlim.
Features									
Outline view	Y	Y	Y	Y	Y	Y	Y	Y	Y
Number of tasks	Unlim.	Unlim.	99,999	Unlim.	Unlim.	Unlim.	10,000	32,000	Unlim.
Number of resources	Unlim.	MSP limits	99,999	Unlim.	Unlim.	Unlim.	Unlim.	32,000	Unlim.
Multiproject									
Number of projects scheduled simultaneously	Unlim.	MSP limits	Limited by memory	1	Unlim.	1,000	936	1,000+	Unlim.
Prioritize projects for scheduling	Y	Y	Y	N/A	Y	N	N	Y	Y
Dependency trace view *	Y	Y	Y	N	Y	N	Y	Y	Y
Charting									
Early start vs. resource leveled start Gantt chart	N	Y	Y	Y	Y	N	Y	Y	N
Highlight critical path in charts	Y	Y	Y	Y	Y	Y	Y	Y	Y

Schedule Management

	Project Control 6.0	ProjectExplorer for MS Project	Project Scheduler 7.6	QEI Exec	SAS Software	Schedule Insight	Spreadsheet Scheduler	SureTrak Project Management	TurboProject Professional 3.0	WebProject
Variable timescale Gantt charts	Y	Y	Y	Y	Y	Y	Y	Y	Y	Y
Variable timescale network logic diagrams (timephased network logic)	Y	Y	N	Y	Y	N	N	Y	Y	N
Zoned network diagrams	N	Y	N	Y	Y	N	N	N	Y	N
Structure drawings	N	Y	Y	Y	Y	N	N	N	Y	Y
PERT chart	N	Y	Y	Y	Y	N	N	Y	N	N
Maximums										
Number of tasks per project	Unlim.	MSP limits	99,999	Unlim.	Unlim.	16,000	100	10,000	32,000	Unlim.
Number of projects per Multiproject	Unlim.	MSP limits	Unlim.	N/A	Unlim.	16,000	100	936	32,000	Unlim.
Number of layers of projects in program	Unlim.	MSP limits	Unlim.	N/A	Unlim.	16,000	100	2	100+	Unlim.
Number of resources per task	Unlim.	MSP limits	99,999	Unlim.	Unlim.	16,000	1	Unlim.	1,000+	Unlim.
Number of defined resources	Unlim.	MSP limits	99,999	Unlim.	Unlim.	16,000	100	Unlim.	32,000	Unlim.
Number of calendars per project	Unlim.	MSP limits	Unlim.	2	Unlim.	16,000	100	Unlim.	32,000	Unlim.
Reporting										
Report writer	Y	Y	Y	N	Y	Y	Y	N	N	N
Report wizard	N	Y	Y	N	N	N	N	Y	N	Y
Publishes as HTML	Y	Y	Y	N	Y	N	Y	Y	Y	Y
Number of user-defined fields	60	MSP limits	Unlim.	Unlim.	Unlim.	20	Y	20	20+	Variable
Drill-down/roll-up *	Y	Y	Y	Y	Y	Y	Y	Y	Y	Y
Import/export	Y	Y	Y	Y	Y	Y	Y	Y	Y	Y
Automatic E-mail notification *	N	N	N	N	N	N	N	Y	Y	Y
Macro recorder/batch capable *	Y	Y	Y	N	Y	N	Y	N	N/Y	Y
Can "canned" reports be modified?	Y	Y	Y	Y	Y	Y	Y	Y	N	Y
Sort, filter	Y	Y	Y	Y	Y	Y	Y	Y	Y	Y
Architecture										
Databases supported (list):	Oracle, MS Access, MS SQL Server, Sybase	Oracle, MS SQL Server, Sybase	Via ODBC: Oracle, Sybase, MS SQL Server, MS Access, et al.	N/A	Most major databases	N/A	Excel	Btrieve	ODBC-enabled databases	Oracle, MS SQL Server, Sybase, Informix, any JDBC- or ODBC compliant database

144

Supports distributed databases	Y	N	N	N	N	Y	N	Y	Y	Y
Three-tier client/server	Y	N	N	N	N	Y	N	N	Y	Y
Client operating systems	Web Project is 100 percent Java, Win 95/NT, Unix, Linux, any Java compliant OS	Win 95/98/NT 4.0/3.x, OS/2 if it includes Win OS/Support	Win 95/98/NT/3.x	Excel	Win 3.1 or higher	MVS, CMS, VSE; OpenVMS for VAX and AXP; Solaris, HP-UX, AIX, Digital Unix, MIPS ABI, Intel ABI; Win 95/NT, Mac, OS/2	Win 95/NT/3.x with Win 32s, Solaris	Win 95/98/NT4	Win 32, MS Project	Win 95/98/NT
Server operating systems	WebProject is 100 percent Java, Win 95/NT, Unix, Linux, any Java compliant OS	Win 95/98/NT 4.0/3.x if it includes Win OS/Support		Excel	Win NT 3.5 or higher	MVS, CMS, VSE; OpenVMS for VAX and AXP; Solaris, HP-UX, AIX, Digital Unix, MIPS ABI; Win95/NT, Mac, OS/2	N/A	N/A	Unix, Win NT	Unix, Win NT, HP, Sybase, others
Network operating systems	Web Project is 100 percent Java, Win 95/NT, Unix, Linux, any Java compliant OS	Most including Novell, Win NT	Novell, Win NT, Pathworks, Banyon, LAN Manager, Btrieve	Excel	Any	All major networks, including LAN Server, TCP/IP, Warp Server, Novell	LAN Manager, TCP/IP, Novell	Novell, Win NT	Multiple	Novell, IPX, XPX, Banyan, MS Network, TCP/IP
Minimum client configuration	thin client architecture—requires only Java-enabled browser (e.g., Netscape Navigator, Internet Explorer)	386 or greater, 16 MB RAM, 30 MB HD space, CD-ROM, VGA or higher	486, 8 MB RAM, 14-38 MB disk space, VGA	Excel	12 MB RAM, 12 MB disk	Varies by platform	486, 16 MB RAM, mouse, XGA graphics	486 or better, 16 MB RAM, 15 MB HD	Pentium w/32 MB RAM	PC 486/66 processor or above. Win 95 or Win NT V4. 16 MB RAM

Schedule Management

	Project Control 6.0	ProjectExplorer for MS Project	Project Scheduler 7.6	QEI Exec	SAS Software	Schedule Insight	Spreadsheet Scheduler	SureTrak Project Management	TurboProject Professional 3.0	WebProject
Minimum server configuration	Any server supporting Oracle 7 or above	Pentium w/128 MB	N/A	N/A	Varies by platform	32 MB memory, 20 MB disk	Excel		386 or greater, 16 MB memory, 30 MB HD space, CD-ROM, VGA or higher	Web Project is 100 percent Java, Win 95/NT, Unix, Linux, any Java compliant OS
Client runs under Web browser	Y	N	N	Y	Y	Y	Y	Y	Y	Y
Open architecture										
Supports OLE	Y	Y	Y	N	Y	N	Excel	N	N/A	Y
Documented Object Model	N	Y	Y							
Documented Application Programming Interface (API)	N	N	Y	N	N	N	Y	Y	N	N
Simultaneous edit of data file	Y	Y	Y	Y	N	N	Y	N	N	N
Does product have a programming language?	N	N	N	Y	N	N	Y	Y	N	N
Are years stored as four-digit numbers?	Y	Y	Y	N	Y	N	Y	Y	N	Y
Online Help										
Right mouse click	N	Y	Y	N	Y		N	Y	Y	Y
Hover buttons	Y	Y	N	Y	Y	Y	N	Y	Y	Y
Interactive help	N	N	Y	Y	Y	Y	Y	Y	Y	Y
Help search feature	Y	Y	Y	Y	Y	Y	Y	Y	Y	Y
Web access to product knowledge base *	Y	N	N	N	N	N	Y	N	Y	Y
Vendor Information										
Training										
Computer-based training	Y	N	N	N	N	N	Y	N	Y	Y
Training materials available	Y	Y	Y	Y	Y	N	Y	Y	Y	Y
Customized training materials	Y	Y	Y	Y	Y	N	N	Y	Y	Y
Online tutorial	Y	N	Y	Y	N	Y	Y	Y	Y	Y
Consulting available from vendor	Y	Y	Y	Y	Y	Y	Y	Y	Y	Y
Site license discounts	Y	N	Y	Y	Y	Y	Y	Y	Y	Y

Enhancement requests *	Y	Y	Y	Y	Y	Y	Y	Y	Y
Modify source code, support through upgrades *	Y	Y	Y	N	Y	Y	N	Y	Y
Global presence									
Global offices	Y	Y	N	Y	N	N	Y	N	Y
Multilingual technical support	N	N	Y	Y	N	N	Y	Y	Y
Language versions (list):	Eng	Eng	Eng, Fr, Chin, and 28 set languages	Jpn	Eng	Same as EXCEL	Eng, Fr, Ger, Jpn	Eng	Eng, Ger
Audit Software Quality Assurance process? *	Y	Y	N	Y	Y	Y	N	Y	Y
Security									
Configurable access privileges *	Y	N	N	Y	N	N	Y	N	Y
Passwords expire (forced update)	N	N	N	N	N	N	N	N	Y
Electronic approvals	Y	N	Y	N	N	N	Y	N	Y
Password protect files	Y	N	N	Y	N	N	Y	N	Y

VENDOR RESPONSES TO NARRATIVE QUESTIONS

ABT Workbench (repository-based) and Project Workbench PMW (stand-alone) (ABT Corporation)

Describe what the product is designed to do.

Project Workbench PMW is the leading project management tool for scheduling and controlling projects. Its strengths include managing resources; scheduling; tracking at a project, task, and/or resource level; and management of multiple projects and programs.

Top three product differentiators; describe what makes your product unique.

1. Integration with ABT Repository extends functionality.
2. Broad range of functionality addresses multiple stakeholders.
3. Comprehensive multiple project/program capabilities.

To what business processes can this tool be applied?

Program and project management processes, resource management processes, and process management processes.

Describe the ideal end-user environment for the current version of your product (size of organization, level of project management sophistication, effort and commitment required).

ABT Corporation's Project Workbench PMW can benefit organizations of fifty to fifty thousand project-related resources, whatever the level of project management maturity.

Future strategies for this product.

Extend functionality; enhance scalability.

Product's target market.

Enterprise project management.

What are your product's three main benefits? (How does using the product add value to the customer?)

Robust project scheduling and controlling capabilities; improved portfolio, program, and project management; and improved team communication.

Describe your quality management process. List any relevant certifications.

ABT's test engineering organization provides extensive in-house product quality testing using a series of proprietary testing methodologies, supplemented by external resources to perform activities such as high-volume benchmarking. ABT's test group has also been instrumental in contributing to the definition of IEEE Year 2000 testing standards.

Discuss your product pricing structure. Include volume discount levels, concurrent user options, site licenses, cost of implementation, and other issues.

Pricing is on a named-user basis. List price: Repository-based ABT Workbench—$300. Stand-alone Project Workbench PMW—$1,275. Volume discounts apply.

Implementation programs vary according to suite installations or stand-alone product installations. Additional services include project management maturity evaluation, tool training, project management concepts training, process customization and implementation, and systems integration/custom programming work.

Annual maintenance (client support program)=15 percent of purchase price.

ActionPlan

Describe what the product is designed to do.

ActionPlan is an enterprise-strength project management system that facilitates team collaboration on projects over organizational and geographical boundaries.

Top three product differentiators; describe what makes your product unique.

1. Automated project and task distribution. All project and task information is automatically delivered to each team member via an intranet.

2. Real-time project updates. ActionPlan gives team members the ability to update the status of the project through their HotSheet (to do list). As a team member completes a task displayed in their HotSheet, they simply check off the task.

3. Cross-project management. ActionPlan allows you to share both project information and resource usage across multiple projects. For instance, you can easily see how a resource(s) is distributed across multiple projects before and after you assign that per resource.

To what business processes can this tool be applied?

ActionPlan is currently being used for many diverse projects including product development and deployment within IT organizations, service task tracking within professional services organizations, and programs within marketing organizations.

Describe the ideal end-user environment for the current version of your product (size of organization, level of project management sophistication, effort and commitment required).

The following is the ideal end-user environment for ActionPlan: fifty or more team members that are geographically dispersed working on multiple related and/or nonrelated projects, very little to medium familiarity with project management.

Future strategies for this product.

Better integration of time/cost tracking capability.

Product's target market.

Large IT organizations with geographically dispersed teams.

What are your product's three main benefits? (How does using the product add value to the customer?)

1. Current status is visible and available to everyone.

2. Time saved by the project manager through real-time updates of project schedules directly from team members.

3. Product is widely used and adopted because of its ease of use and ease of deployment.

Describe your quality management process. List any relevant certifications.

Products go through extensive internal quality testing as well as external beta testing.

Discuss your product pricing structure. Include volume discount levels, concurrent user options, site licenses, cost of implementation, and other issues.

$995 for five nonconcurrent users, $1,895 for ten users, $4,495 for twenty-five users, $8,999 for fifty users, $16,995 for 100 users. Site licenses are available.

Subscription and maintenance pricing: $398 for five-user license, $758 for ten-user license, $1,798 for twenty-five-user license, $3,598 for fifty-user license, $6,798 for 100-user license.

AMS REALTIME Projects (Advanced Management Systems)

Describe what the product is designed to do.

AMS REALTIME Projects provides powerful project management in an easy-to-use graphic software tool. Plan project tasks, network constraints, resource and manpower utilizations by manipulating graphic images with your mouse, or import data from external sources. Costs and earned value are visible in real time as the project evolves.

Distributed projects and subprojects offer unlimited project capacity, while merge-link, attached documents, shared calendars, shared resources, and command links to other systems provide the capability to build a complete enterprisewide project management system. Store project data in proprietary stand-alone files stored on a common file server, or store data on a database (ODBC-compliant database, AMS proprietary database, or Oracle) using an AMS REALTIME projects server.

Vision lets you communicate your project plan with dazzling graphic or tabular reports. Use or modify any of our standard reports, or design your own using our cross-platform built-in drawing tools. Add custom graphics and logos, annotations, different first and last pages. Print paper reports or PDF output for Internet publishing.

Top three product differentiators; describe what makes your product unique.

1. Fully integrated schedule, resource, and cost give you an accurate look at one or more projects from any perspective.

2. AMS REALTIME Projects is fully equipped with powerful features: attached documents, command links, WBS tools, sorting and matching with stored views, calculated fields, cost breakdowns (labor, materials, ODC), rate tables, multiple revisions, and much more.

3. All software runs native on Windows (95, NT, 3.x), Macintosh, Sun, Solaris, HP, RS with identical look and feel and direct data access from any platform.

To what business processes can this tool be applied?

AMS REALTIME is so flexible that it can be applied to virtually any business process, including proposals, maintenance operations, new development, manufacturing, and performance improvement processes.

AMS REALTIME is designed to allow automated project statusing that automatically feeds earned-value performance measurements. Cost management is empowered when costs can be tracked from a project summary level all the way down to the activity level; providing accurate information to pinpoint the source of cost overruns.

Describe the ideal end-user environment for the current version of your product (size of organization, level of project management sophistication, effort and commitment required).

AMS REALTIME is used by global companies in very large enterprise environments, all the way down to small companies with just a few people. While AMS REALTIME is used to support extremely sophisticated project management processes, it can still be used to benefit users with little or no project management background. Users can grow into the software as their project management expertise evolves.

To make any project management implementation successful, senior management must be committed to supporting the process, and other participants must make the effort to be trained to use the tools and follow through. Working with a consultant to help adapt the software to your business practices and needs and to document these processes is the best way to ensure success.

Future strategies for this product.

Future development strategies include more active Web enablements, a more complex three-tiered server design to facilitate global replication, and more resource tools. AMS has always been on the cutting edge of technology, and we are dedicated to bringing our customers the best of this ever-changing world.

Product's target market.

Products are used across a wide variety of client bases. AMS does not target any particular market, but is widely used in manufacturing, oil and gas, nuclear power, automotive, pharmaceutical, aerospace, software development, construction, research and development, and many other industries. AMS REALTIME software allows for a flexible implementation that integrates with customer business processes.

What are your product's three main benefits? (How does using the product add value to the customer?)

1. Schedule, resources, and costs are fully integrated so that an accurate project and/or resource status can be obtained in real time. This provides accurate visibility that enables proactive decisions to keep the project on track.

2. Software runs on all major platforms, allowing companies to use their existing hardware investment while sharing the same data. Data can be stored in local or shared proprietary files, or stored on Oracle using client/server technology and integrated with other Oracle applications.

3. AMS REALTIME gives program managers, project managers, resource managers, and employees the tools to work within their functional areas. Each piece is a part of the solution that supports the whole enterprisewide management process.

Describe your quality management process. List any relevant certifications.

Advanced Management Solutions is fully committed to providing the highest quality software and services to all our clients. We have implemented many internal standards and processes in order to ensure that we can track and manage our software development process to the highest standard of quality possible.

Concurrent versions system has been implemented to help manage multiple programmers at multiple development sites. Peer review of source code and design strategy meetings with high-level program development leaders continue to ensure that our software remains on the leading edge of our evolving technology. A dedicated testing department manages the initial alpha testing, which encompasses new functionality, system process testing, and full regression testing. Beta testing is initially performed internally. After a stable point has been reached, beta testing is extended to select client users. Client beta testing not only provides clients with an edge in using new software features, but also greatly expands the test environment scope relating to different hardware environments. As AMS REALTIME is one of the most flexible and highly configurable management products on the market today, client testing adds an exceptional dimension to our testing process.

Discuss your product pricing structure. Include volume discount levels, concurrent user options, site licenses, cost of implementation, and other issues.

Product price is different for clients, based on their requirements for software and implementation. Volume discounts and site licenses are available. Please request a quote from an AMS sales representative for your specific requirements.

Annual maintenance is based on 20 percent of the current product cost, and includes all software upgrades (while support is active) and telephone hotline technical support. Training cost is based upon topics, requirements, training equipment and site, and days requested. Please request a quote from an AMS sales representative for your specific requirements.

Artemis ProjectView (Artemis)

Describe what the product is designed to do.

Views is a completely integrated enterprise-level project and program management system designed to improve the efficiency and productivity of project-based businesses. The Views suite of estimation, schedule, cost, time tracking, resource, and quality management applications apply proven methodologies and practices to project planning and management.

Top three product differentiators; describe what makes your product unique.

1. Scalability: Views can handle virtually an unlimited number of concurrent users and projects in a distributed environment, meaning you can use Views as a standard project management tool for the entire company.

2. Enterprise multiproject: Allows cross-functional and matrix-driven organizations to schedule, assign, and track resources and projects across the entire enterprise.

3. Microsoft Project integration: Allows existing MSP-based organizations to leverage existing investments, while adding consistency, multiproject planning, resource scheduling/tracking, and reporting to their environment.

To what business processes can this tool be applied?

Project management, proposal management, budget/forecast management, performance measurement, and resource management.

Describe the ideal end-user environment for the current version of your product (size of organization, level of project management sophistication, effort and commitment required).

Views is a scalable solution that lets you define unique roles for each user, letting you deploy the product's features within your organization in a virtually unlimited way.

For large organizations, Views provides project templates, standardized resource pools and rates, and centralized security to streamline project planning and control.

Future strategies for this product.

Artemis is committed to continually enhancing our product's functionality and applicability to consistently meet or exceed the demands of project management professionals.

Product's target market.

Artemis products are used in over twenty-five industry sectors from banking and finance to aerospace and defense. Any organization that wants to improve its results using a project-centric management technique can benefit from using the Views suite of products.

What are your product's three main benefits? (How does using the product add value to the customer?)

1. Improves project results, yielding better business performance.
2. Minimize project durations.
3. Assign resources to activities across multiple projects.

Describe your quality management process. List any relevant certifications.

Internal software audits and reporting procedures. Formal Year 2000 testing and compliance process.

Discuss your product pricing structure. Include volume discount levels, concurrent user options, site licenses, cost of implementation, and other issues.

Artemis Views can be purchased and deployed as a fully integrated suite or as a series of independent applications.

Available as registered user and concurrent pricing. Volume discounts and site licenses are available.

Cost of implementation varies.

AutoPLAN Enterprise (Digital Tools)

Describe what the product is designed to do.

AutoPLAN Enterprise Release 4 is a Web-based software and process solution to help high-tech, engineering, and telecommunications companies predict, control, and improve cycle time of critical program development and deployment. The solution set provides deep functionality across the entire spectrum of product life-cycle elements including pipeline management, project management, resource alignment, process effectiveness, and document support and team collaboration. AutoPLAN Enterprise integrates realistic planning, resource-centric management, status and forecast tracking, team collaboration, process support, escalation management, and program execution across globally distributed organizations.

Organizations are evolving from functional teams to matrix or program teams, and this is creating cross-functional or multidisciplinary project teams. AutoPLAN Enterprise recognizes three different organizational patterns that coexist: dynamic peer-to-peer, functional, and program management. AutoPLAN Enterprise offers these organizations both project-centric and resource-centric management. AutoPLAN Enterprise addresses everyone involved in product development and deployment including executives; program, product, resource, and project managers; and team leaders and team members, as well as teams from marketing, operations, service, and quality.

As a result of extensive process and product consulting with clients engaged in new product development and deployment, DTI has distilled four key reasons why products are late and descoped:

1. Product development pipeline and deployment structures that are not aligned with the company's time-to-market goals.

2. Unrealistic plans, overcommitted resources, and unmanaged cross-functional dependencies.

3. Status and forecast decisions that are based on hearsay, rather than on facts or experience.

4. A lack of consistent processes that fit the company culture and practice, which is further exacerbated by distributed cross-functional teams.

Avoiding late and descoped products requires an overall view of product and project status, the involvement of cross-functional teams, and decision evaluation tools. Increasingly accelerated product development cycles and shorter product life cycles require organizations to disseminate information quickly to remain competitive. To support today's geographically dispersed product development environments, organizations require a common platform that enables effective cross-functional collaboration and communication on product development issues. It is also imperative that the introduction of new product information can be easily accessible by each stakeholder. Common platforms and accessible information by each stakeholder will result in accelerated organizational learning and decision-making within the organization.

DTI has created a cycle time management (CTM) framework comprising both application and process support. This framework emphasizes the critical components involved in introducing and deploying the right products and services to the market at the right time. Introducing and deploying these products and services requires companies to institute well-defined new product planning and execution processes, complemented with customer management and performance measurement processes. The new planning processes should consist of product portfolio, tech-

153

nology portfolio, product planning, and resource planning. The execution processes must consist of advanced technology development, platform development, product development, market introduction and deployment.

CTM enables companies to strike a balance between flexibility and discipline that is tailored to their organization and culture. The CTM framework supports a flexible *shrink-to-fit* process, which is adaptable to an organization's process maturity. This process will provide a road map for decision-making and progress tracking within a new product introduction and deployment pipeline.

CTM consists of six fundamental elements: 1) processes, 2) projects, 3) resources, 4) documents, 5) deliverables, and 6) analysis. These six elements form the foundation objectives that drive AutoPLAN Enterprise. Organizations require a well-defined and structured process to accomplish their goals. Projects make up the mechanisms through which detailed plans and schedules are generated, executed, and tracked. Every organization faces resource constraints; thus, resource management is a critical component of CTM. All projects have deliverables associated with them either in the form of documents or the product itself. And, all projects must be managed to ensure quality deliverables. Analysis tools enable various levels of stakeholders to evaluate and ensure proper support of all elements necessary to meet CTM objectives.

Top three product differentiators; describe what makes your product unique.

1. AutoPLAN Enterprise enables organizations to manage their pipeline of resources across programs and across the phase gates of each project. It assures an escalation process for critical issues, such as overallocations, by monitoring boundary conditions and alerting appropriate people to the issues. Project managers are interested in the completion of tasks or milestones, while resource managers need to know all of the work planned for their resources. Both project and resource managers must collaborate to create realistic plans for meeting project objectives, as well as juggle those resources and plans on a day-to-day basis as changes occur. The nature of this work requires a resource-centric view of the plan, not just an activity-centric view. A resource-centric view will allow resource managers to view and allocate activities to their scarce resources, rather than allocating resources to their activities. AutoPLAN Enterprise enables resource management by providing a resource-centric Gantt bar that displays overallocated resources. Managing overallocations can be as easy as reassigning activities to another resource.

Program management is a collaborative effort. Success depends upon identifying and communicating critical issues. Such identification and communication must be inherent in the system. AutoPLAN Enterprise is designed with a communications backbone. A mechanism of triggers identifies critical issues (e.g., when milestone or cost exceeds a threshold boundary) and automatically alerts and draws attention to these critical issues. Project bulletin boards within AutoPLAN Enterprise also enhance communication by providing a context-sensitive vehicle for communicating information across the project team. In addition, AutoPLAN Enterprise supports electronic mail systems, enabling triggers and bulletin board messages to be communicated to the various levels of stakeholders.

2. AutoPLAN Enterprise supports the distributed nature of project teams by matching real-world strategy with key scalable technologies. Enterprise customers need distributed project management capabilities that cater to multisite resource management, work distribution, progress tracking, global scheduling, consolidation, reporting, integration, and collaboration. DTI has met this challenge by investing over one hundred man-years in an enterprise-level, three-tier, distributed client/server architecture that leverages both Java and Internet technologies. AutoPLAN Enterprise provides full support for multiple internal operating divisions and external suppliers. AutoPLAN Enterprise leverages many platforms—Internet, Windows, NT, and Unix—providing reliable access across the organization. Additionally, AutoPLAN Enterprise enables common project data to be shared by different projects at different locations while being maintained in a central data center that is managed by pool server software. Project data is maintained at each geographic location on either individual or multiple servers, depending on the number of internal operating divisions and projects. A divisional pool server can also be implemented to share the project data within divisional projects. AutoPLAN Enterprise application servers are capable of scalable distributed processing, and only the server needs the capacity for large multiproject oper-

ations. AutoPLAN Enterprise has multiserver cross-project dependency links. For example, the owner of a schedule that depends on the completion of activities in another project can create cross-project links that automatically update his schedule when changes occur in the other project, even if that project resides on a different server.

3. AutoPLAN Enterprise leverages client/server/Web technologies. The promise of Java, which AutoPLAN Enterprise supports, is that enterprise deployments, including organizations with heterogeneous environments, can be cost-effectively supported. DTI Web products are easier to use than Microsoft Project and are cheaper to deploy. The rapid spread of Internet protocols and Web servers into corporate infrastructure make the Internet an ideal vehicle to support both enterprise computing and mobile employees. In addition, systems administration is simplified since no maintenance is required on the client side.

A very practical use of AutoPLAN Enterprise Web clients is that they can run in a disconnected mode on the Internet. With AutoPLAN Enterprise, the user can simply log on and save activities and other information to a local file. She can then continue to work while disconnected. At any time, the connection can be reestablished, either remotely or locally, and the data is resynchronized. This may be useful for dial-up connections when working remotely. The Web server handles all communications with the Web clients, whether they are communicating via the Internet, dial-up, LAN, or WAN. The AutoPLAN Enterprise Web clients can be run from any browser that supports Java 1.1, and the Web server will dynamically download the Java code to run the application on the client. DTI's Web strategy supports *thin* client computing. In this case, database-oriented servers are serving lightweight clients through Web servers and standard protocols. The AutoPLAN Enterprise Web clients are ideally suited for running on a Java-based network computer.

To what business processes can this tool be applied?

From business analysis and redesign to system implementation and training, DTI has established its own process to support the customer through all phases of CTM system implementation. However, as to applying AutoPLAN Enterprise to the customer's business processes, DTI takes a very pragmatic approach. DTI has established processes to help customers with the following seven business pains:

1. Managing the development and deployment pipeline in detail.
2. Top-down and bottom-up planning that enables managers to use team members' knowledge during up-front planning.
3. Juggling resources realistically, so that resources are not overcommitted and parochial allocations are not made, but rather a mechanism for cooperation on resource tradeoffs is created.
4. Creating an organizational memory that captures organizational experience for reuse the next time.
5. Obtaining weekly integrated tracking information on how programs are progressing against their plans. This can be achieved by capturing actual time spent, estimates-to-complete, percent complete, and actual start and finish.
6. Problem identification, escalation, and collaboration that allows management and the team to receive adequate notice of impending issues.
7. Interactive decision evaluation to understand the domino effect of a problem in one project and its possible cross-program impact, and obtain a swift resolution between participants.

Any combination of these processes will help organizations better understand and make use of critical path methodology, work breakdown structures, resource management, cost and earned value techniques, multiproject resource scheduling, resource allocation, status tracking, report generation, matrix management solutions, integration with other systems, middleware design, project management process design, project rollups, report generation, database design, customized product training courses, generic project management training, and more.

Describe the ideal end-user environment for the current version of your product (size of organization, level of project management sophistication, effort and commitment required).

AutoPLAN Enterprise is ideal for high-tech, engineering, and telecommunications organizations engaged in distributed product development and deployments. Its usage also extends to these organizations' distributors and partners. The role-based nature of AutoPLAN Enterprise spans all people involved, from executive management to the entire cross-functional product team. This includes experienced project and program managers, resource and development managers, and the team members creating or deploying the product. The AutoPLAN Enterprise Web client is specifically designed for those team leaders who are not full-time, experienced project managers. In fact, DTI has designed the AutoPLAN Enterprise Web client to be easier to use and more functional than Microsoft Project.

Organizations can start at either the program level right away and manage the overall pipeline of projects and resources at the business unit level, or at the individual project level. The Auto-PLAN Enterprise Web client is not only easier to use than Microsoft Project, but is also capable of managing cross-functional dependencies and resources and offering enterprise scalability when the organization is ready to expand.

Coordinating distributed projects is a difficult task. It involves resources not only from multiple projects, but also from multiple functions within those projects. The program manager responsible must understand all of the interactions and milestones required to complete the project, but he cannot and should not develop and manage the entire plan himself. Instead, he should rely on the distributed functional leaders who are responsible for their piece of the project to plan and execute that piece. As a program manager, he needs to be able to integrate the individual team plans into a single comprehensive project plan. In many organizations, this integration of people and data is difficult; AutoPLAN Enterprise is designed to help with this. Having processes in place, underpinned by enterprise software, is key to predicting, controlling, and improving product/project cycle times.

Future strategies for this product.

AutoPLAN Enterprise has been designed with an integrated product management platform for all information related to meeting CTM objectives. DTI will continue to support features needed for CTM, including pipeline and portfolio management. Future strategies will enhance the ability of customers to make informed decisions based on a comprehensive presentation of relevant data with powerful drill-down capabilities, further collaborative features that utilize the intranet and Internet, and continuing support for the free-flowing nature of the engineering culture. Application wizards will help first-time users, accelerate deployment, and reduce training cost. Process support is key to productivity improvements and to adhering to organizationwide standards. Existing process-support capabilities will be enhanced using the capabilities of Web technology and with more exchange of information across subsystems. Large organizations are geographically distributed to take advantage of global efficiencies. Local and global workgroups must collaborate and respond quickly to changing environment and work content. Both executive management and front-line team members must have access anytime, anywhere, and in any manner to enterprisewide product/project information located on geographically distributed servers. Existing multiserver capabilities of AutoPLAN Enterprise are being enhanced using Oracle.

AutoPLAN Enterprise will support key technologies including Oracle, NT 5.0, middleware, and Java. Distributed objects capability using industry-standard specifications such as CORBA will be incorporated. In addition, the AutoPLAN Enterprise application-programming interface will provide CORBA-compliant objects for seamless integration with other applications. The collaboration capabilities of AutoPLAN Enterprise will be enhanced by incorporating a workflow server. This workflow server will be based on industry-standard specifications and will incorporate process modeling and messaging components to enable customers to configure the collaboration features based upon their business needs. The security system will have additional features to address the security risks associated with the Internet. Directory servers conforming to LDAP standards will be incorporated for seamless integration with the underlying operating environment. This in turn will provide responsive security, configurability, and flexibility features.

Product's target market.

AutoPLAN Enterprise is specifically designed to support high-tech, engineering, and telecommunications organizations in predicting, controlling, and improving cycle time of critical program development and deployment.

What are your product's three main benefits? (How does using the product add value to the customer?)

1. AutoPLAN Enterprise provides at least a 10 percent improvement in enterprise time-to-market of product development and deployment. Viewing the value of CTM from an annual R&D cost perspective: consider a product development group of one thousand people, with an annual R&D expenditure of $100M. A modest 10 percent improvement would represent a cost savings value of $10M, with a revenue enhancement value of three to five times this.

2. AutoPLAN Enterprise facilitates an organization's transformation from functional project teams to matrix, or program-organized high-performance project teams. It also supports distributed teams resulting from acquisitions. It does both of these by providing built-in communication and rollup features from distributed multiserver projects. This support enables teamwide problem identification, escalation, collaboration, and resolution. AutoPLAN Enterprise recognizes that three different organizational patterns coexist: 1) dynamic peer-to-peer, 2) functional, and 3) program management. AutoPLAN Enterprise offers these organizations both project-centric and resource-centric management.

3. AutoPLAN Enterprise accommodates joint ventures, subcontracting, mergers and acquisitions, and reorganizations by leveraging the Web to minimize deployment and support costs. The creation of plans, assignment of work, and integration of activities across multiple functions and distributed work teams is critically important. However, that is only part of the story. With the Internet, AutoPLAN Enterprise can also efficiently equip thousands of personnel involved in the product-development process with the information they need to do the best possible job. Demand for skilled workers has been great, and turnover has risen as employees move from one company or job to another. The best practices in the world are of no value to a company if those who know those practices move on without first passing along the knowledge. Best practices developed at one site need to be shared with other sites, and a process for doing that is required. AutoPLAN Enterprise solves these problems through URL references and retrieval capability. With URL features, AutoPLAN Enterprise can help preserve best practices and other information and disseminate them geographically and functionally to team members currently doing the job. AutoPLAN Enterprise can also have associated URL references that point to mission-critical information/documentation that will enable product/project teams to achieve the activity. These references can also be attached to the top-level program schedule for project leader use, or at specific functional schedules (e.g., to provide sourcing with specific third-party vendor requirements). URLs can enable:

- Sharing best practice information from one team to another
- Referencing documentation with checklists
- Sharing engineering notes on installation processes.

Also, with the speed of organizational changes, a mix of project-scheduling system usage is expected. As most people are educated on Microsoft Project, AutoPLAN Enterprise can coexist with its projects and data. AutoPLAN Enterprise's GUIs are not only familiar to Microsoft Project users, the Web version is easier and thus leverages simplicity and ease of use with enterprise functionality.

Describe your quality management process. List any relevant certifications.

DTI achieves excellence in product quality and customer satisfaction through its quality management process. DTI's quality objective is to build quality into its products and services at all stages of product life cycle from requirement collection to customer usage. DTI's dedication to quality is reflected in its quality mission: "Doing things right the first time."

DTI's quality management group performs the functions of the software engineering process group as defined by the industry-standard CMM. The quality management group plans and implements DTI's quality system, which consists of processes and guidelines. The processes detail out *what* is required for converting a set of inputs to outputs in the form of activities and tasks, primary and cooperative responsibilities, deliverables, and entry and exit criteria. The guidelines detail *how* to carry out the identified activities to ensure quality and consistency. The involvement of DTI personnel at all levels is fundamental to the implementation of the quality process. DTI personnel are drawn from various groups in the organization to author processes and guidelines, and all undergo training programs on the quality system.

DTI follows processes within Level 2 and Level 3 of the CMM. Some of the key processes within these levels include market requirement analysis, functional specification, high- and low-level design, coding, testing, release management, customer support, training, and maintenance. In addition, in-depth reviews are built into each of these processes.

DTI recognizes that enterprise growth and profitability are significantly impacted by time-to-market of new products in globally competitive high-tech markets. With this in mind, DTI's product development and quality processes are focused on meeting customer needs and requirements. Therefore, DTI collaborates with its customers both in product definition and in assuring that the product functions are implemented as intended. To facilitate the fast-track delivery of innovative products and services, DTI has created process initiatives for increased test automation, usage of tools that will enable teams to better assess the quality of their work products, management of development tools, reuse of objects across products, and tightly controlled configuration management.

DTI's quality management process focuses on periodic reviews and feedback, which are a means of monitoring the adherence of organizational activities to the process. Corrective and preventive actions play an important role in continuous improvement of the quality system and thereby the organizational activities.

DTI has a well-qualified team for quality management. DTI's teams, besides having the appropriate educational qualifications, have quality management-related certifications; some are certified quality analysts, and some hold certificates related to the CMM and its use. Many also have extensive internal audit experience.

The quality management group interacts periodically with key personnel of different functions within the organization and identifies new processes, guidelines, and improvements within the existing framework. The general approach to new process/guideline introduction is to discuss with representative users, define the process, pilot the process after review, evaluate the pilot implementation, revise the process based on feedback, plan organizationwide implementation, implement, measure, and maintain.

DTI is planning to get CMM certification at the appropriate level. The approach that would be followed for securing the certification includes mapping key process areas of the CMM to existing processes, identifying the *gaps*, preparing the implementation plan that describes how these gaps will be addressed, and executing the plan.

Discuss your product pricing structure. Include volume discount levels, concurrent user options, site licenses, cost of implementation, and other issues.

DTI's objective is to offer an integrated solution with a pricing structure that is based on enterprise requirements reflecting enterprise needs and individual needs. AutoPLAN Enterprise supports a floating license configuration, which allows any user to log into the system and consume one license. When the user has finished with the application, that license will be released for other users. Each floating license provides one concurrent use of the product. AutoPLAN Enterprise also supports a personal license configuration. Typical installations will use both personal and concurrent licensing.

Annual product maintenance is 15 percent of the list cost. Product maintenance entitles customers to engineering patches, updates, and upgrades, and phone, fax, and E-mail response to issues. Professional services are separate from DTI product maintenance. As part of the business relationship with customers, DTI takes part in joint planning to identify the customer's business needs and services sought from DTI. Professional services are charged separately on an as-needed basis. These services are performed either at the customer site, online, or at DTI's headquarters in Cupertino, California. Professional services typically fall into two categories: 1) product consulting/implementation design review and 2) implementation support. Product consulting/implementation design review discusses areas such as, "How do I apply the software with a suitable process to solve a business need?" and, "Which processes will we implement, how, and when to meet organizational objectives?" Implementation support consists of product training, project office services, upgrade migration services, systems administration services, and integration services.

CA-SuperProject 4.0 & CA-SuperProject/Net 1.0 (Computer Associates)

Describe what the product is designed to do.

CA-SuperProject is a powerful yet easy to use project management tool designed to manage the full range of enterprise projects from the simple to the very complex. With its four unique outlines and five informative graphical views, project information can be managed and communicated with relative ease. CA-SuperProject was designed to provide end-to-end solutions for all your project management needs.

CA-SuperProject/Net represents the next generation in project management tools, from project rollout to project completion; CA-SuperProject/Net automates the communication process. It is a Internet/intranet-enabled project management tool used to process and route project-related communication and return project status information in a series of simple but specific home pages for managers, executives, and other project team members. CA-SuperProject/Net completes the communication loop by providing end-to-end project management information on a real-time basis.

Top three product differentiators; describe what makes your product unique.

1. Flexible outline and chart views.
2. Flexiable yet powerful reporting capability.
3. Multiproject management capability.

To what business processes can this tool be applied?

Business processes that can be defined with a starting and ending point and that have at least one objective.

Describe the ideal end user environment for the current version of your product (size of organization, level of project management sophistication, effort and commitment required).

CA-SuperProject is designed to accommodate both the casual and professional user, where managing the simple or very complex is made easy with scalable functionality.

Future strategies for this product.

Further-refined functionality, navigation improvements, and project team communications.

Product's target market.

The enterprise project management community.

What are your product's three main benefits? (How does using the product add value to the customer?)

1. Easy to get started.
2. Has to power and functionally to stay with.
3. Real-time communication through distributive processing.

Describe your quality management process. List any relevant certifications.

No answer given.

Discuss your product pricing structure. Include volume discount levels, concurrent user options, site licenses, cost of implementation, and other issues.

Products: CA-SuperProject 4.0, $455; CA-SuperProject/Net, $1,750. Volume discounts available. Network and site licenses available.

Training: Basics, three day; advanced, two day.

Tech Support: 24/7 $100/year.

Cascade PgM (Mantix)

Describe what the product is designed to do.

Cascade PgM from Mantix is a client-server program management product for use with Microsoft Project, aimed specifically at the facilities required by senior management and program managers. With a standard MS Windows user interface, it presents a multiuser, enterprisewide cost, schedule, and resource management system, with powerful management reporting facilities. Cascade PgM uses the proven, structured data model of work, responsibility, and cost breakdown to provide a complete view of the business. The benefits to the business associated with each project can also be modeled.

Cascade is integrated on existing user sites with Oracle Financials, SAP, Peoplesoft, Glovia, Baan, Triton, and many other systems. This integration with the ERP (enterprise resource planning) systems provides the whole picture of all the activities in the business—where the cost is going, what the people are doing, and what results will be delivered, by when.

The combination of Cascade PgM and Microsoft Project provides a powerful corporate project planning system. Cascade PgM provides the top-down information used to provide guidelines for managers working at a more detailed level. Working within these guidelines, users can go on to develop detailed schedules, cost, and resource plans. Cascade PgM supports the concept of resource ownership and the delegation of resources down through the project, with complete visibility and tracking of where they are being used. In many cases, this includes use of the Web-based Cascade time-recording functionality.

Top three product differentiators; describe what makes your product unique.

Cascade PgM is unique in its functionality for business control of the projectoriented organization through top-down delegation of targets and bottom-up measurement of performance. It offers a clear functional advantage in terms of the following.

1. Turns decisions into action, by enabling the creation of outline plans with budget, staff, and time scales to be delegated for detailed planning.

2. The structured data model is built interactively as graphical tree structures, rather than with the conventional alpha numeric coding, making the operation intuitive and changes to the plan simple and quick.

3. The program manager establishes the overall structure of the program, typically based on business drivers or internal/customer reporting. Links to the program from projects may be easily created or deleted allowing fast *what-if* analysis.

To what business processes can this tool be applied?

For lean organizations in fast-moving markets, good management is increasingly about setting goals and assembling the team to deliver them. Cascade PgM provides the tool to define a portfolio of projects to deliver strategic goals, and then monitor the performance against these objectives. Cascade PgM backs up the implementation of effective management processes with the timely, consistent, and accurate provision of program and project information.

Describe the ideal end-user environment for the current version of your product (size of organization, level of project management sophistication, effort and commitment required).

The concepts behind Cascade PgM and the software architecture are completely scaleable. Any size organization with a multiproject environment would benefit from Cascade PgM, irrespective of the level of project management sophistication. The effort and commitment required to implement Cascade PgM depends on the customer's requirements for the system and the existing business processes. Typically, Cascade PgM is quick to implement; this is due in part to its use of MS Project, which is already present in most organizations. MS Project is transformed to become a key element of a business control system.

Future strategies for this product.

Mantix Systems will continue to develop Cascade PgM to ensure it remains a world leading program management solution.

Product's target market.

As a leading program management solution's provider, Mantix Systems has a proven track record with some of the world's leading organizations in fifteen countries. This is in markets that include telecommunications, IT, utilities, government, pharmaceuticals, aerospace, and defense.

What are your product's three main benefits? (How does using the product add value to the customer?)

Cascade PgM brings structure, visibility, and control to the management of both individual projects and multiproject programs. This allows a customer to focus investment and staff time on the business activities that will add most value, and manage them to deliver increased revenue, profit, and return on investment.

Describe your quality management process. List any relevant certifications.

The quality management process within Mantix Systems is accredited by and conforms to ISO 9000.

Discuss your product pricing structure. Include volume discount levels, concurrent user options, site licenses, cost of implementation, and other issues.

The price of Cascade PgM depends on the type of functionality required and the number of users. Please contact Mantix Systems for details that are specific to your requirements.

Dekker TRAKKER Activity Based Cost Management and Performance System (DTMI)

Describe what the product is designed to do.

With a full-featured CPM scheduling engine and graphical user interface, TRAKKER makes planning and tracking of simple or complex projects easy. By providing users with an enterprise-level system, TRAKKER can manage an unlimited number of tasks across an unlimited number of projects. The sophisticated baseline and what-if analysis capability provides for the concurrent comparison of up to five versions of a project, thus allowing the user to see and evaluate trends that occur over time. TRAKKER also supports a number of activity types to meet the expanding requirements of contemporary project plans. Included in the list of supported types are summary activities, logical milestones, interim milestones, Gantt activities, and hammocks. As an integrated component of the TRAKKER system, the data from this feature integrates directly with the resource planning to establish the time frames for the work to complete and enables capacity planning.

Top three product differentiators; describe what makes your product unique.

1. Integration with the resource, cost, risk, and technical performance modules of the system.
2. Enterprise planning and tracking capability.
3. Trend analysis.

To what business processes can this tool be applied?

Scheduling, process flow, resource planning, and trend analysis.

Describe the ideal end-user environment for the current version of your product (size of organization, level of project management sophistication, effort and commitment required).

One of the key attributes of the TRAKKER system is scalability. TRAKKER has been designed to integrate into a business environment by establishing an organization's business rules within the system. This architecture enables TRAKKER to fit the needs and sophistication of any implementation. This flexibility enables TRAKKER to support a variety of implementation approaches. TRAKKER installations typically provide access to a range of users including cost account managers, cost/schedule analysts, and financial managers to meet the unique requirements of each for information and output. Typical TRAKKER clients range from companies of one thousand employees to Fortune 500 corporations.

Future strategies for this product.

Dekker, Ltd. will continue to enhance the integration of TRAKKER with MS Office and MS Back Office suite of tools. The design of the TRAKKER architecture will continue to focus on making data more visual and accessible to the complete range of system users.

Product's target market.

R&D, government, software, medical, electronics, and aerospace.

What are your product's three main benefits? (How does using the product add value to the customer?)

1. Integration with the resource, cost, risk, and technical performance modules of the system.
2. Enterprise planning and tracking capability.
3. Trend analysis.

Describe your quality management process. List any relevant certifications.

DTMI has modeled our development process from the Microsoft model while incorporating the quality guidelines established in ISO 9000.

Discuss your product pricing structure. Include volume discount levels, concurrent user options, site licenses, cost of implementation, and other issues.

DTMI offers both single and concurrent user licenses of TRAKKER. Our flexible pricing enables both small and large organizations to cost-effectively implement costing and earned value. TRAKKER pricing includes a progressive discount for volume purchases with reasonable thresholds for single and multisite licenses. Further, DTMI offers both public and private training courses for both new and advanced users. DTMI also offers consulting services to support the enterprise implementation of TRAKKER.

DTMI provides training for both the discipline of scheduling and attributes of TRAKKER. These workshops include Basic Project Management, TRAKKER Application Workshop, TRAKKER Intermediate Workshop, TRAKKER Report Writer Workshop, and TRAKKER MIS Integrator's Workshop. Through these courses, an enterprise can completely implement the TRAKKER system. In addition to our classroom training, DTMI offers consulting services to guide users though a structured approach to implementing TRAKKER.

Enterprise Project (jeTECH DATA SYSTEMS, INC.)

Describe what the product is designed to do.

Enterprise Project is a completely integrated solution (all applications share a common database and operate on the same hardware platform). Consequently, our response to the narrative questions here repeats what we supplied for the Suites chapter, as those responses apply to all our applications.

Enterprise Project is a powerful new client/server software application that offers project-based organizations a simple way to define and staff projects, and record project labor and expenses throughout their enterprise. Essentially a suite of robust, user-friendly applications integrated into a single desktop, this comprehensive project management system enables team members to accurately plan and track labor resources across all projects. Perfect either as a *stand-alone* solution or as the ideal complement to the jeTECH labor-management system—Enterprise Labor—it is particularly well-suited for multiuser, enterprisewide installations. Together, Enterprise Labor and Enterprise Project are the only systems currently on the market with extensive capabilities and integrated products for both the salaried professional (engineers and computer programmers, for instance) and the hourly employee (from factory workers to registered nurses).

Users access all functions via a single desktop with a Microsoft Office 98 *look and feel*. The system integrates completely with Enterprise Labor and Microsoft Project, as well as with most popular accounting and human resource (HR) systems. In today's competitive environment, effective and efficient use of labor resources is key to completing mission-critical projects on time, on budget. Enterprise Project gives project leaders a comprehensive, potent tool with which to manage scarce technical resources.

With Enterprise Project, managers can budget and schedule projects based on staff skills and availability. Project team members can manage their own tasks, report actual labor and travel expenses, and provide status reports on these tasks. The system calculates actual project costs by automatically incorporating labor costs, material costs, and travel expenses.

Project managers can define and manage both contract and noncontract-based projects, and control work authorizations that will keep each project under control and on budget. As a project manager, you simply create activities for your projects, assign appropriate resources to these activities, and define how labor will be charged to a contract. And by allowing employees to only charge preassigned tasks, Enterprise Project prevents performance of unauthorized work.

Enterprise Project enables all users to report labor charges right from their PC or workstation. Project managers need no longer compile project team information manually. Users can now report project time, as well as other time, and the system automatically processes and transmits it to an interfaced time-and-attendance system for payroll use.

Enterprise Project includes a contract maintenance module. Companies with hourly employees contracted with outside firms—for instance, security guards or programmers—would benefit from using this module without the rest of the project management system. This module is primarily designed, however, to accommodate projects being managed for clients. This module allows contract managers to define contract information including budgets and rates per hour, as well as all products and services purchased by the customer. They can then use this information to evaluate projects based on user-defined deliverables. Contract maintenance is by no means static. So jeTECH has designed Enterprise Project to handle change orders, R&D projects, and discounts. A variety of unique reporting features enables contract managers to view cost overruns, variances, and milestone completions.

Top three product differentiators; describe what makes your product unique.

1. Resource scheduling from a common resource pool in a multiproject environment.
2. Integrated time collection and status reporting.
3. Sensitivity analysis (what-if scenarios).

To what business processes can this tool be applied?

Project planning/management, enterprise resource scheduling/management, time collection, performance measurement, time and expense reporting, budgeting and estimating, and project accounting.

Describe the ideal end-user environment for the current version of your product (size of organization, level of project management sophistication, effort and commitment required).

Any resource-constrained enterprise (IT, high-tech R&D, engineering) with multiple projects and multiple sites. Requires a low level of project management sophistication.

Future strategies for this product.

Maintenance and repair operations, incorporation of process ware/templates, enterprise-level project and resource integration, and full Internet capabilities.

Product's target market.

Companies with *task-oriented* professionals such as engineers, architects, IS professionals, researchers, advertising/marketing professionals, etc. See also the previous response to "ideal end-user environment."

What are your product's three main benefits? (How does using the product add value to the customer?)

1. Improved resource utilization and efficiencies.
2. Reduction in time to complete projects.
3. Cost control.

Describe your quality management process. List any relevant certifications.

Our current quality management process includes in-house testing, which incorporates both automated and manual processes and procedures.

Discuss your product pricing structure. Include volume discount levels, concurrent user options, site licenses, cost of implementation, and other issues.

Pricing is structured on a named-user basis. Pricing will also be dependent on a number of variables including the size of the enterprise, number of project managers, number of facilities, etc. Consequently, pricing is provided to each customer when we have been able to familiarize ourselves on their operations and their anticipated use of the system.

Several options are available for training, tech support, annual maintenance, etc. Costs are provided to each customer when they have been able to select the options deemed best for their operations.

ER Project 1000 (Eagle Ray Software Systems)

Describe what the product is designed to do.

The ER Project 1000 is an integrated suite of project management tools, which provide an enterprisewide project management solution. ER Project 1000 includes schedule/time management, centralized resource management, methodology/process management, project-workgroup communications, timesheets, risk/issue management, and enterprisewide cross-project tracking. Based on a client/server architecture with a centralized relational database, the ER Project 1000 provides networked access, multiproject capability, and true multiuser concurrency. It scales easily from handling small workgroup projects to large programs at the enterprise level.

Top three product differentiators; describe what makes your product unique.

1. Addresses the total project management life-cycle solution for the enterprise: Unlike most project management tools, the ER Project 1000 provides a completely integrated and centralized project management platform to support the entire life cycle of project management. Based on a client/server relational database (Oracle/SQL Server) architecture, ER Project 1000 fully supports

today's multiproject/multiuser project environment. The product suite integrates full methodology/process management capabilities, project workgroup communications, and enterprisewide project tracking capabilities.

2. Provides a completely integrated suite of project management tools: The ER Project 1000 tool suite integrates industrial-strength project management functions with rich-process improvement functionality and proactive management features. ER Project 1000 provides all the necessary industrial-strength core project management functions. Key features include support for WBS/organizational breakdown structure/RBS structures, cost, schedule, earned value analysis, built-in report writer, timesheet approvals, and centralized resource management. ER Project 1000 takes advantage of the Web by providing Java timesheets and extensive project website publishing capability. Best practices/process improvement is easily accomplished with the methodology manager and support for organizational standards, work products, and estimation. ER Project 1000 delivers an impressive array of proactive management features. These features include risk management, issue management, management by threshold, and full project tracking.

3. Is easy to use and implement: ER Project 1000 was designed with a simple, intuitive interface. Extensive wizards assist users for complex operations. ER Project 1000 can easily be configured to your organization by using our centralized administration functions and component architecture.

To what business processes can this tool be applied?

ER Project 1000 is a wrap-around solution for organizations that need to implement mature project management practices, proactively manage their projects, improve business processes, implement standards and documentation, and communicate at multiple levels. Eagle Ray's advanced suite of tools provides project managers with an integrated platform for project planning, time tracking, resource management, and executive oversight. With features such as risk management, issue tracking, and management by threshold, the ER Project 1000 gives project managers the ability to proactively manage complex projects and stay focused on the key issues.

Organizations that engage in process improvement/best practices will find that the ER Project 1000 methodology manager is the ideal platform for developing and delivering best practices to each new project plan. Project managers will be able to easily document and reuse lessons learned in new projects. Project team members and stakeholders will find that the integrated communications features of the ER Project 1000 suite facilitate a real-time dialogue between all members and ensure no issues slip though the cracks.

Describe the ideal end-user environment for the current version of your product (size of organization, level of project management sophistication, effort and commitment required).

Size of organization: The ER Project 1000 product suite is ideal for managing projects with team sizes of ten to one thousand people per project in organizations where multiple projects are being performed at the same time. Project teams may be centralized or dispersed using client/server and Web-based communications technologies.

Level of sophistication: The tool suite is best suited for organizations that are moving beyond basic project management to a medium level of project management maturity or higher. These organizations are typically implementing tracking, costing, project management standards, risk/issue management, time tracking, centralized resource management, and possibly earned value. ER Project 1000 also supports organizations implementing a project office, best practices, process improvement, and reusable project templates. These features make ER Project 1000 an ideal platform for organizations implementing CMM level 2 or higher maturity levels.

Effort and commitment required: Successful implementation of the ER Project 1000 tool suite centers on an organization's commitment to realizing repeatable project management results from enterprisewide standardization of business processes and practices. Because of its integrated design and simple interface, ER Project 1000 delivers numerous advantages over standard project management tool sets with less staff effort.

Future strategies for this product.

Eagle Ray's future strategies include building new modules, expanding current modules, interfacing with corporate business systems, and preparing the product suite for the global marketplace. Major planned enhancements include significant modifications to the estimation module, costing module, methodology/process management module, and the Internet/intranet/Web capabilities. In addition, we will be constructing a problem/defect-tracking module.

We will be expanding the interfaces that integrate the ER Project 1000 system with additional enterprise business systems. Such systems include costing/accounting systems, HR systems, and additional commercial products. We also plan to complete our internationalization/localization efforts to prepare the ER Project 1000 for global distribution.

Product's target market.

ER Project 1000 is suitable for commercial and government organizations, which are managing projects that range from small workgroup-level projects to projects that span the entire enterprise. Essentially, the tool suite will support any project environment where the project team has access to or is working with computers.

What are your product's three main benefits? (How does using the product add value to the customer?)

1. Total integrated project management solution: The ER Project 1000 is an integrated, total project management solution providing complete support for the entire project management life cycle. The integrated tool suite does not require multiple add-on tools from different vendors, resulting in fewer hidden costs and less frustration. Project managers will find it easy to manage projects with a higher level of maturity by using the various features of the tool—for example, risk management, issue tracking, management by threshold, and multiproject capabilities.

2. Best practices/process improvement platform: The ER Project 1000 integrated process/methodology management platform provides a sophisticated yet easy-to-use platform for implementing best practices, estimation metrics, organizational standards, documentation templates, and process improvement. Organizations can capture, integrate, and reuse their project knowledge and project plan templates from an enterprisewide integrated platform.

3. Enterprisewide tracking and communications: The ER Project 1000 facilitates communications between all project stakeholders. Program managers and executives can perform cross-project rollups, dynamic drill-down, and cost, schedule, and earned-value analysis for up-to-date information on all enterprise projects. The project team members can access all of project information on the project website, and receive activity assignments and report status using Java timesheets. Automatic issue notification alerts project managers about possible deviations in cost and schedule. The built-in report writer lets you extract and summarize any data in the enterprisewide project database using customized formats.

Describe your quality management process. List any relevant certifications.

The Eagle Ray quality assurance program is a comprehensive system that employs a series of product walkthroughs, builds, quality gates, configuration management, defect tracking, and comprehensive testing. The development staff members are constantly conducting requirements, design, and code walkthroughs in coordination with weekly product builds and passing mandatory quality gates. The quality assurance program is integrated with our beta testing program to ensure that all product releases undergo rigorous real-world testing prior to release.

Comprehensive testing scenarios include unit testing, integration testing, platform testing, stress testing, concurrency testing, environment testing, security testing, usability testing, vertical testing, upgrade testing, business scenario testing, and independent qualification testing.

During the design and construction of the ER Project 1000 product, Eagle Ray brought in several project management industry experts to assist in the design of the software functionality and usability. This process will be continued to ensure that our future enhancements meet the real-world needs of project management organizations. Additionally, Eagle Ray continues to invest heavily in the training of team members in technical and project management areas.

Discuss your product pricing structure. Include volume discount levels, concurrent user options, site licenses, cost of implementation, and other issues.

Call for latest prices.

eRoom

Describe what the product is designed to do.

eRoom is a Web-based project coordination tool. It provides a persistent project space on the Web, giving all of your team members access to the latest project information and status.

Team members can either create or drag in any Windows application file. They can review and revise project files, discuss issues, and take votes. eRoom notifies team members when project information arrives or changes, permitting immediate response and rapid progress.

eRooms are protected by full NT network security: only people you make eRoom members can access the project eRoom.

Top three product differentiators; describe what makes your product unique.

1. Easy to use. Familiar browser and Windows interface requires no adjustment or training. No HTML experience needed—uses your Windows applications and files.
2. Administered by end-users, not IT, so it works at the speed of the team.
3. Since an eRoom is on the Web, it works both within your organization and outside with partners, contractors, and customers.

To what business processes can this tool be applied?

Development projects, consulting projects, intercompany discussions and negotiations.

Describe the ideal end-user environment for the current version of your product (size of organization, level of project management sophistication, effort and commitment required).

Medium to large organizations; fast-cycle, distributed project teams; team members who need to reach and work on the project from anywhere at any time.

Future strategies for this product.

Support real-time interaction within the project team; allow members to be notified immediately when particular project information changes; and extend the API to allow even more integration and customization.

Product's target market.

Consulting companies, manufacturing/high technology companies, and professional services providers.

What are your product's three main benefits? (How does using the product add value to the customer?)

1. Project team can create and manage the project eRoom quickly without needing IT, using the desktop browser and applications they use today.
2. The project lives and grows in the eRoom so new team members can quickly come up to speed and project files can be "harvested" and re-used after the project is completed.
3. IT likes it because it complies with common standards and they can let users proceed without heavy support.

Describe your quality management process. List any relevant certifications.

No answer given.

Discuss your product pricing structure. Include volume discount levels, concurrent user options, site licenses, cost of implementation, and other issues.

eRoom server at $4,995 per server, clients start at $199 per user. Volume discount and site license pricing available on request.

Server maintenance contract—$750/year; client maintenance contract—$30/year per user. Consulting services and outsourcing available.

FastTrack Schedule 5.02

Describe what the product is designed to do.

FastTrack Schedule 5.02 makes it easy to organize tasks, meet deadlines and achieve project goals. Whether you need to schedule a day's worth of activities or plan a project into the 21st century, FastTrack Schedule creates presentation-quality timelines.

New Collaboration and Automation ProTools provide real-time scheduling across an intranet or the Internet, and customized macros through Visual Basic. Enhance your schedules with graphics, logos, floating text blocks and titles, then export them directly.

Top three product differentiators; describe what makes your product unique.

1. Easy to use and learn.
2. Highly customizable, presentation-quality project scheduling.
3. Outstanding price/performance ratio.

To what business processes can this tool be applied?

All processes benefiting from the application of project scheduling.

Describe the ideal end-user environment for the current version of your product (size of organization, level of project management sophistication, effort and commitment required).

FastTrack Schedule 5.02 is ideal for professionals and support staff who are not project managers by vocation and who seek a project scheduling application requiring little or no training.

Future strategies for this product.

Continued enhancements and new technology for professionals and support staff requiring easy-to-use, customizable, presentation-quality project scheduling applications.

Product's target market.

A/E/C (Architecture, Engineering, Contracting); aerospace, manufacturing and production; marketing, advertising and entertainment.

What are your product's three main benefits? (How does using the product add value to the customer?)

1. The easiest project scheduling application to learn and use.
2. Highly customizable, presentation-quality project scheduling.
3. Outstanding price/performance ratio.

Describe your quality management process. List any relevant certifications.

No answer given.

Discuss your product pricing structure. Include volume discount levels, concurrent user options, site licenses, cost of implementation, and other issues.

AEC Software offers single-user licenses, server version concurrent-usage licenses, and site licenses. Contact AEC Software at 703/450-1980 for price quotation.

Multivolume training tapes available, $49 each. Free and unlimited technical support for all registered users.

One- and three-year maintenance agreements available, call for quotation.

Innate Multi-Project (with Microsoft Project MSP)

Describe what the product is designed to do.

Extends the use of Microsoft Project into organizationwide program management.

Top three product differentiators; describe what makes your product unique.

1. Full utilization of Microsoft Project 98.
2. Supports each role step by step through the business process.
3. Simple to implement and use.

To what business processes can this tool be applied?

The multiproject management process, supporting the project office and project leaders step by step through the process, from initial registration of projects to postimplementation review.

Describe the ideal end-user environment for the current version of your product (size of organization, level of project management sophistication, effort and commitment required).

IT development organization, up to 750 staff, five hundred projects, one hundred project leaders, Microsoft Project already in use.

Future strategies for this product.

Project-related records and documentation management.

Product's target market.

Organizations with multiple projects where resource constraints make changes to workload difficult to manage.

What are your product's three main benefits? (How does using the product add value to the customer?)

1. Consistent project plans through standards management.
2. Resource capacity check before committing to new projects.
3. Effective process support generates high quality management information.

Describe your quality management process. List any relevant certifications.

Best practice software product development, based on twenty years industry experience.

Discuss your product pricing structure. Include volume discount levels, concurrent user options, site licenses, cost of implementation, and other issues.

Based on named users, for each role; i.e., number in the project office, numbers of project leaders.

Volume discounts apply.

Simple software modules support evolutionary change. Cost of implementation is therefore well below industry average. Fore example, project office—one-day training, project leaders—half-day training.

Intelligent Planner (Augeo Software)

Describe what the product is designed to do.

Optimize the allocation of resources across multiple projects, determine costs, and provide metrics for continuous process improvement.

Top three product differentiators; describe what makes your product unique.

1. Global repository for data and business rules.
2. Closed-loop system, from project proposal to time/expenses tracking.
3. Simulation and optimization based on skills and availability of resources.

To what business processes can this tool be applied?

Business processes involving the allocation of human resources, such as professional services and information services.

Describe the ideal end-user environment for the current version of your product (size of organization, level of project management sophistication, effort and commitment required).

Mid-sized to large-scale professional services organizations sharing pool of scarce resources; large IT departments managing budgets and resources on strategic projects; or consulting companies managing a portfolio of intellectual activities.

Future strategies for this product.

Knowledge management integration; 100 percent Web-based management of project portfolio; and advanced data-mining features.

Product's target market.

Professional services organizations.
Large scale IT departments with cost-controlled project management.
Consulting companies.

What are your product's three main benefits? (How does using the product add value to the customer?)

1. Optimize scarce resource predictability.
2. Increase speed, throughput, and responsiveness.
3. Executive visibility.

Describe your quality management process. List any relevant certifications.

Source control. Usability verification process. Worldwide beta program.

Discuss your product pricing structure. Include volume discount levels, concurrent user options, site licenses, cost of implementation, and other issues.

Concurrent user pricing for client-server modules, named-user pricing for Web modules. Volume discount, site license. Implementation requires ten to twenty days of consulting.
Training: Project managers (two days), administrator (three days), Web users (half-day).
Annual maintenance (includes new releases and online assistance): 15 percent of license fee.

Micro Planner X-Pert (Micro Planning International)

Describe what the product is designed to do.

X-Pert is a sophisticated full-featured project management system designed for the serious project manager. Ideal for large projects utilizing a finite number of resources across multiple projects.

Top three product differentiators; describe what makes your product unique.

1. Resource optimization.
2. Excellent report writer and graphics views/outputs.
3. Designed for the serious manager.

To what business processes can this tool be applied?

Software/hardware development, engineering/design, medical.

Describe the ideal end-user environment for the current version of your product (size of organization, level of project management sophistication, effort and commitment required).

Medium to large-sized companies with a thorough knowledge of project management, who are serious about getting their projects done on time and within budget.

Future strategies for this product.

Web interaction.
Shared project components.
Client/server.

Product's target market.

Aerospace/defense, high-tech, biotechnology.

What are your product's three main benefits? (How does using the product add value to the customer?)

1. Results oriented.
2. Maximizes resources.
3. Excellent management reporting capabilities for decision-making.

Describe your quality management process. List any relevant certifications.

No answer given.

Discuss your product pricing structure. Include volume discount levels, concurrent user options, site licenses, cost of implementation, and other issues.

Fixed licenses starting at $1,995. Floating licenses starting at $2,995. Discounts apply beginning at a quantity of two.

Training courses cost $2,200 for two-day course plus expenses (on-site). Support/annual maintenance plans start at $395/year for fixed license; includes free upgrades.

Microsoft Project 98 (Microsoft)

Describe what the product is designed to do.

Microsoft Project 98 is an ideal tool for planning and tracking projects of all sizes. Because it is easy to use, it is an ideal tool for all levels of project management experience from the newcomer to the experienced project manager. Microsoft Project 98 focuses on three areas:

1. Control—gives users more control over their project plans.
2. Communication—improves project communication so everyone stays informed and involved.
3. Compatibility—provides programmability features so it can serve as a stand-alone product or as part of a broader company solution.

Top three product differentiators; describe what makes your product unique.

1. Ease of use: Microsoft Project 98 requires little or no training to begin using it to manage projects, so the *startup* costs required of new customers are much lower when compared to other project management software tools. The navigation map also helps inexperienced project managers and new Microsoft Project 98 customers to map their functional responsibilities to Microsoft Project 98's features.

2. Extensibility: Microsoft Project 98 is a pioneer in extensibility. It can store data in an open database format and supports VBA. Customers can easily integrate project management data with their existing corporate business systems, which enables Microsoft Project 98 to accommodate ever-increasing complexity as customers' project management needs change and grow throughout the organization.

3. Integration with other Microsoft applications: Microsoft Project 98 incorporates the best of Microsoft Office to make a tool that is easy to learn and use.

To what business processes can this tool be applied?

Microsoft Project 98 can be applied to any process for which the customer can identify specific tasks and their respective durations and dependencies. Customers can use Microsoft Project 98 to easily compare cost and profitability by project, balance resource requirements across projects, and track dependencies across multiple projects to assess a project's impact on the bottom line. Microsoft Project 98 can also be used to integrate project metrics with corporate accounting, human resources, timesheets, or manufacturing systems and organize project documentation so it is readily available to everyone involved in a project.

Describe the ideal end-user environment for the current version of your product (size of organization, level of project management sophistication, effort and commitment required).

Microsoft Project 98 is used in end-user environments of all sizes—from individuals planning single-resource projects to large corporations with thousands of employees. Customers with widely varying project management backgrounds can also use it. Even newcomers to project management principles can learn to use Microsoft Project 98 quickly and easily with the product's built-in help and other easy-to-use features. Microsoft Project 98 even contains features to extend a project team's communication capability over the Web or any MAPI-compliant E-mail system. And, customers won't *outgrow* Microsoft Project 98 since its programmability features allow them to tailor the program to their organization's unique and changing needs.

Future strategies for this product.

Microsoft will continue to focus on improved collaboration, performance, and ease of use in future versions of Microsoft Project. Microsoft Project has always focused on bringing project management techniques to a wider audience via improved ease of use and expanded communication capabilities for project teams and will continue to do so in the future.

Product's target market.

Anyone who deals with budgets, assignments, and deadlines can take advantage of the benefits offered by Microsoft Project 98. If you have thousands of details to manage, or even a few dozen, you're a potential Microsoft Project 98 customer.

What are your product's three main benefits? (How does using the product add value to the customer?)

1. Easy to learn and can grow with customers' projects and organization.
2. Ability to plan and track multiple projects in a consolidated manner.
3. Helps customers track and manage costs that affect the bottom line.

Describe your quality management process. List any relevant certifications.

Microsoft Project's quality management process begins with developing a product vision based on input from customers, internal and external developers, the product support team, and usability engineers. This ensures that the development process focuses on the right objectives, and that decisions regarding product quality reflect all of these perspectives.

Microsoft maintains a high developer to test ratio throughout the software development process to ensure that potential *bugs* are identified and resolved as early in the development cycle as possible. The testing process is based on five core attributes: 1) source code version control; 2) making the code testable; 3) use of automation for broader scenario testing; 4) beta testing—both internal and external; and 5) detailed bug tracking and reporting (throughout all Microsoft product groups in order to share learning).

Finally, a new product is released only when the managers from development, testing, program management, and product support agree as a team that the product is ready. No product will be released until this agreement is reached.

Discuss your product pricing structure. Include volume discount levels, concurrent user options, site licenses, cost of implementation, and other issues.

The estimated retail price of Microsoft Project 98 is $499. Microsoft also offers several multiple-license pricing agreements. Detailed information on these agreements is available at www.microsoft.com/licensing.

The cost of implementation varies based on previous experience with project management principles, experience with other project management software tools, and the size and complexity of a customer's projects. Little or no training is needed for Microsoft Project 98 due to the extensive built-in help and other user-assistance features included in the product. Many additional low-cost books, self-help tools, and other training materials for Microsoft Project 98 are widely available. Microsoft Project 98's built-in VBA programmability features also help limit the cost of additional customization.

Milestones, Etc. (Kidasa)

Describe what the product is designed to do.

Milestones, Etc. is designed to provide an easy-to-use product to produce high-quality schedules in a Gantt format.

Top three product differentiators; describe what makes your product unique.

1. Easy to learn.
2. Easy to use.
3. Easy to update schedules.

To what business processes can this tool be applied?

Scheduling of projects.

Describe the ideal end-user environment for the current version of your product (size of organization, level of project management sophistication, effort and commitment required).

Desktop Windows environment.

Future strategies for this product.

Continue to add user-requested features to make product do more, but still maintain ease of use.

Product's target market.

People who need to quickly produce schedules.

What are your product's three main benefits? (How does using the product add value to the customer?)

1. Enables customer to easily produce high-quality Gantt charts.
2. Enables customer to spend less time creating Gantt charts.
3. Enables customer to spend less time updating Gantt charts.

Describe your quality management process. List any relevant certifications.

Follow standard commercial software development guidelines.

Discuss your product pricing structure. Include volume discount levels, concurrent user options, site licenses, cost of implementation, and other issues.

Single-user licenses are $199. Workgroup pricing is also available.

Cost of implementation: Just the amount of time it takes to go over the supplied tutorials, usually no more than a few hours.

MinuteMan Project Management Software (MinuteMan Systems)

Describe what the product is designed to do.

This program focuses on providing the basic functions needed to effectively manage projects. It provides outlining, critical-path scheduling, resource tracking, and a number of useful reports.

Top three product differentiators; describe what makes your product unique.

1. Low cost ($50); very easy to use.
2. PERT and Gantt charts can be distributed electronically.
3. Unique PERT/OUTLINE view.

To what business processes can this tool be applied?

Small businesses with limited budget for software or training.

Describe the ideal end-user environment for the current version of your product (size of organization, level of project management sophistication, effort and commitment required).

An organization of one-to-twenty persons with individual PCs. Novice users who cannot afford the unit cost or training time associated with larger programs.

Future strategies for this product.

Developing a major *front-end* wizard to simplify original project definition.

Product's target market.

Construction contractors, not-for-profit organizations.

What are your product's three main benefits? (How does using the product add value to the customer?)

Quickly provides time and cost estimates.

Describe your quality management process. List any relevant certifications.

Not ISO certified.

Discuss your product pricing structure. Include volume discount levels, concurrent user options, site licenses, cost of implementation, and other issues.

Usually single-unit purchases. Will provide volume pricing when requested.
Cost of implementation: next to nothing!

Open Plan (Welcom)

Describe what the product is designed to do.

Welcom's Open Plan is an enterprisewide project management system that substantially improves a company's ability to manage and complete multiple projects on time and within budget with a limited workforce. Unlike less-sophisticated products, Open Plan is a highly integrated, comprehensive software system that can be customized to fit specific corporate requirements. It is the most technically advanced client/server project management system on the market, using the latest in Microsoft Windows development technology.

The three versions of Open Plan are:

Open Plan Professional: Easy to use and powerful enough to manage even the largest projects. Open Plan Professional gives professional project managers such vital tools as advanced resource management, multiproject support, support for client/server databases, and the flexibility to customize the interface to support organization and industry-specific procedures.

Open Plan Desktop: Designed for occasional access to projects and ideal for executive users and tactical team members. Open Plan Desktop has extensive ease-of-use features and an affordable price point for companywide deployment. The system is well-suited for users who usually work on individual components of a larger project. Users can roll their individual projects up to Open Plan Professional for a broader view of the overall project.

Open Plan Enterprise: Very similar to Open Plan Professional, integrates with popular ERP applications such as Baan and SAP. The resulting component-based suite automatically disseminates project data throughout an organization, giving users better control over enterprisewide multiproject planning, management, and implementation.

Top three product differentiators; describe what makes your product unique.

1. Multiproject.
2. Advanced resource modeling.
3. Open architecture.

To what business processes can this tool be applied?

Enterprise resource modeling, business process reengineering, project management, earned value analysis, risk assessment, and process modeling.

Describe the ideal end-user environment for the current version of your product (size of organization, level of project management sophistication, effort and commitment required).

Medium to large organizations for which project management is a serious business requirement. Meets the needs of users whose level of expertise varies from novice/occasional to advanced.

Future strategies for this product.

Our vision for the future is to provide a suite of component-based products that work together to provide advanced project management functionality using the very latest technology.

Welcom's development plans include extending the products' multiproject and enterprise resource modeling capabilities while moving to a distributed applications architecture with Web technology being a significant component. Plans also include leveraging existing integrations with Baan and SAP, and expanding integrations to include other ERP vendors.

Product's target market.

Fortune 1000 companies, government and multinational organizations implementing enterprisewide project management.

What are your product's three main benefits? (How does using the product add value to the customer?)

1. Increase quality of project communications.
2. Reduce cycle time through effective resource management.
3. Increase integration of project management with business systems.

Describe your quality management process. List any relevant certifications.

Adhere to standard industry processes in release and version strategies, including automated regression testing. ISO 9000 certified in the United Kingdom.

Discuss your product pricing structure. Include volume discount levels, concurrent user options, site licenses, cost of implementation, and other issues.

Please call for pricing.
Training courses and consulting: Please call for pricing.
Tech support: No charge with current maintenance.
Maintenance: First year is free with software purchase. Renewed annually.

OPX2 Pro (Planisware)

Describe what the product is designed to do.

OPX2 is an integrated software package for cost, schedule, and resource management at enterprise scale.

Full support of state-of-the-art CPM, resource, and cost management techniques, with multiproject consolidation for medium or large sized organizations. Modern, highly customizable graphic user interface.

Top three product differentiators; describe what makes your product unique.

1. Full integration of cost, resource, and schedule management in the same user interface, with decision-support and simulation functions. Integration with third-party accounting software and ERP (such as SAP R/3, Oracle Applications).

2. Open, extendible model of project management objects, customizable without programming (alerts, business rules, report builder, chart wizards) to support management models.

3. Scalable for large-sized configurations: support of main market databases, smooth installation process, Web-based timesheet (OPX2 Timecard), and communication module (OPX2 Intranet Server).

To what business processes can this tool be applied?

Project management: R&D project management (new product development, portfolio management), matrix organizations, IS departments, and software houses.

Scheduling of small serial manufacturing, engineering projects, heavy maintenance, and integration activities.

Cost management for public contract management, defense and aerospace programs, in-house product development, and subcontracting.

Describe the ideal end-user environment for the current version of your product (size of organization, level of project management sophistication, effort and commitment required).

Organization: from one hundred to twenty thousand resources managed.

Level of project management sophistication: previous experience of other project management software implementation is profitable for implementing OPX2.

To be implemented using a methodology suited for enterprisewide consolidation: activity coding, resource identification, and ERP interfaces.

Future strategies for this product.

Development of partnerships with ERP providers.

International development (multilingual support and distributors).

Focus on decision-support functions.

Product's target market.

Manufacturing: defense and aerospace, car/truck, drug/cosmetics development.

ICT: IS departments (enterprises and administrations), software house, telecommunications, and electronics.

Engineering: construction, energy, and space.

What are your product's three main benefits? (How does using the product add value to the customer?)

1. For the organization: standardization of concepts and reporting process for project management in all departments; breaking of barriers between cost and schedule.

2. For the users: Less time spent to collect and enter data, more time available to analyze them.

3. For the management: Real visibility on activity progress for top management, and long-term historization of project data at multiproject scale.

Describe your quality management process. List any relevant certifications.

TEMPO (Thomson-CSF software development methodology). TEMPO is compliant with ISO 9001 standards.

No specific certification for Planisware.

Discuss your product pricing structure. Include volume discount levels, concurrent user options, site licenses, cost of implementation, and other issues.

OPX2 Pro (Scheduling + Cost Management + Report builder): from $12,000 (server + first concurrent user license).

Typical user configurations: $17,000 to $1,000,000. Concurrent user licenses: yes. Site licenses: yes.

Cost of implementation: Twenty-five to 80 percent of license cost for consulting and training.

Annual maintenance: Fifteen percent of license cost (including tech support and upgrade of new releases).

Training: contact OPX2 distributors in each country.

Panorama Program Manager

Describe what the product is designed to do.

Panorama Program Manager comprises five modules, which together form a fully integrated application but which can, if required, be used independently or can be integrated with preferred third party applications. Interfaces can also be provided to other applications.

Financial Control & Performance Measurement: Consolidates financial and performance information for any number of projects and provides multilevel views of all data. Departmental managers and team leaders can be provided with short-term tactical perspective.

Time Recording: This module is the collection point for all time expended by project staff. Timesheets may be entered by individual members of staff, or as a batch process. Extensive online validation ensures that mispostings are kept to a minimum.

Top three product differentiators; describe what makes your product unique.

1. *Scope:* Addresses in a single integrated application the major application areas required for comprehensive program management.

2. *Flexibility:* Inherent flexibility means that the system can be implemented to suit most companies' requirements without the need for bespoke development.

3. *Customization:* Ability to incorporate bespoke features to client's specification and willingness to provide support to customized elements.

To what business processes can this tool be applied?

Estimation, bid management, and project control.

Describe the ideal end-user environment for the current version of your product (size of organization, level of project management sophistication, effort and commitment required).

Typical users will have in excess of two hundred employees and be managing either large, complex projects or a large number (>150) of small/medium-size projects.

They will usually have experience of project management and already be users of project management tools.

A typical implementation will be six to twelve months and require the involvement of an implementation team that at any one time might include five to ten client staff.

Future strategies for this product.

Web-based operation; Integration of work flow management and document storage and retrieval.

Product's target market.

Cross-industry.

What are your product's three main benefits? (How does using the product add value to the customer?)

1. Consolidation of all project data to provide a corporate view of performance.
2. Standardization of project control methodology through use of a single corporatewide system.
3. Easy access at all levels in the organization of all aspects of project performance.

Describe your quality management process. List any relevant certifications.

In-house change control and configuration management software and control systems.

Discuss your product pricing structure. Include volume discount levels, concurrent user options, site licenses, cost of implementation, and other issues.

On application.

Planning Controller

Describe what the product is designed to do.

Planning Controller has been developed to provide effective enterprisewide project management and control in a client/server Oracle database environment. The product provides project planners with an intuitive Windows-based system.

Top three product differentiators; describe what makes your product unique.

1. Breadth of functionality offered by complementary modules to provide an Integrated Work Management System.
2. Powerful hierarchical work management structure and reporting.
3. Provides control over the business and project-specific planning.

To what business processes can this tool be applied?

Project planning, costing, scheduling, leveling and management. Additional modules for corporate planning, billing, purchasing, time writing and planned maintenance scheduling.

Describe the ideal end-user environment for the current version of your product (size of organization, level of project management sophistication, effort and commitment required).

Medium to large project-based organizations looking to control their business and projects by integrating this process with existing applications and processes. The nature of the implementation is such that a degree of change management is usually required.

Future strategies for this product.

Next release to include additional report generation facilities, easier E-mail facility for reports, additional Web functionality and an integrated Risk Management module. Currently evaluating Microsoft's Sequel Server as a database option.

Product's target market.

Oil & gas, defense, rail transport, civil engineering, utilities and shipbuilding.

What are your product's three main benefits? (How does using the product add value to the customer?)

1. Hierarchical view of project performance within the whole business.
2. Integration with other processes such as time writing, purchasing, billing and maintenance management.
3. Excellent graphical and text based reporting tools.

Describe your quality management process. List any relevant certifications.

We have internal auditable quality procedures in place which are equivalent to ISO 9000 standards. Accredited Investors in People.

Discuss your product pricing structure. Include volume discount levels, concurrent user options, site licenses, cost of implementation, and other issues.

System is priced per number of concurrent users for each module. Discounts available for volume and multisite implementations. Full pricing available on application.

Annual Maintenance 15 percent of license costs. Cost of Professional Services available on request.

PLANTRAC-OUTLOOK (Computerline Ltd)

Describe what the product is designed to do.

PLANTRAC-OUTLOOK provides total project management easily. Several methods of data input allow fast entry. The well-proven engine provides realistic schedules. With features such as out-of-sequence scheduling and multiple activities per line, together with a powerful report writer, communications improve dramatically. Project efficiency and profitability will improve.

Top three product differentiators; describe what makes your product unique.
1. Four compatible input methods for fast data entry.
2. Realistic time and resource scheduling.
3. Powerful report writer and report embellisher for effective communications.

To what business processes can this tool be applied?

Construction; manufacturing; marketing; research and development; software development.

Describe the ideal end-user environment for the current version of your product (size of organization, level of project management sophistication, effort and commitment required).

Both small and large organizations benefit. It can be used as a casual planner, by a professional project manager, and for corporate planning and control.

Future strategies for this product.

PLANTRAC-OUTLOOK is very much user driven. It will keep up to date with both project management and technological trends.

Product's target market.

Broad market but specializing in construction, defense, and pharmaceutical.

What are your product's three main benefits? (How does using the product add value to the customer?)
1. Time saved in project creation and progressing/updating.
2. Realistic schedules assist project profitability.
3. Reporting flexibility gives client confidence.

Describe your quality management process. List any relevant certifications.

Quality management is based on a mix of PRINCE and ISO 9000 methodology.

Discuss your product pricing structure. Include volume discount levels, concurrent user options, site licenses, cost of implementation, and other issues.

Single user is $975. Network versions are available in modules of four users—$1,950 per module. Site licenses are $5,000–$50,000.

Implementation and training is $960 per day. Technical support is provided by telephone, fax, and E-mail. Free for first six months. Thereafter, 17.5 percent of purchase price (includes upgrades and enhancements).

PlanView Software (PlanView, Inc.)

Describe what the product is designed to do.

PlanView Software has modules that let the user request project and nonproject work, scope, schedule, search the resource repository, create multiple what ifs, etc., progress projects from time reported, and create metrics.

Top three product differentiators; describe what makes your product unique.
1. Customized according to your WBS.
2. Integrates with most popular process methodology systems (LBMS, etc.).
3. Manages all workflow, from scoping through closing.

To what business processes can this tool be applied?

Multiproject management, service request management, resource management, workflow management, work and resource *portfolio* management, etc.

Describe the ideal end-user environment for the current version of your product (size of organization, level of project management sophistication, effort and commitment required).

An organization with one hundred to multiple thousands of employees (we have implementations of four thousand plus), managed by five or more managers with access to a central database; includes matrix-style organizations.

Future strategies for this product.

Further conversion to Web browser-based interfaces; even easier report generation and Web publishing; more CPM and cost management features.

Product's target market.

The resource-centric approach to work management is typically most useful for organizations with a highly skilled workforce of limited availability; with twenty plus managers, and one hundred plus staff; using client/server.

What are your product's three main benefits? (How does using the product add value to the customer?)
1. Keep data/templates from process systems on the PlanView central repository.
2. Integrates with most popular process software systems.
3. Adds work and resource management to your process management system.

Describe your quality management process. List any relevant certifications.

PlanView follows the guidelines set out in the book *Best Practices of Rapid Development* by Steve McConnell.

Discuss your product pricing structure. Include volume discount levels, concurrent user options, site licenses, cost of implementation, and other issues.

It is different for each case, but basically the cost is $200–400 per seat, with volume discounts. The repository products are included.

Standard SQL database is extra. Implementation and training are extra. We offer a range of implementation packages, from rapid to standard, which include training. Additional services billed at time and cost. Phone and online tech support are free. Maintenance packages offered.

Primavera Project Planner (P3) 2.0

Describe what the product is designed to do.

Primavera Project Planner (P3) is the premiere project management software for large projects. P3 offers multiuser and multiproject capabilities, resource management, E-mail support/Primavera Post Office, Web publishing, PERT, bar chart graphics, in-depth analysis, and cost control and system connectivity. It also includes Object Linking and Embedding as well as ReportSmith for Primavera.

No other answers given.

ProChain

Describe what the product is designed to do.

Allows the user to apply Critical Chain methodology.

Top three product differentiators; describe what makes your product unique.

1. Allows user to apply Critical Chain methodology.
2. Buffer Management Tools.
3. Central resource scheduling to stagger multiple projects.

To what business processes can this tool be applied?

Anything that includes the management of projects.

Describe the ideal end-user environment for the current version of your product (size of organization, level of project management sophistication, effort and commitment required).

Applicable across all sizes of organizations.

Future strategies for this product.

No answer given.

Product's target market.

No answer given.

What are your product's three main benefits? (How does using the product add value to the customer?)

1. Signifcantly higher probability of meeting scheduled due dates.
2. Focused decision support through Buffer Management.

Describe your quality management process. List any relevant certifications.

No answer given.

Discuss your product pricing structure. Include volume discount levels, concurrent user options, site licenses, cost of implementation, and other issues.

ProChain: $695/copy with discounts for multiple copies, site licenses available.

ProChain Plus: Prices vary according the capability to schedule a number of projects centrally.

ProjectCommander

Describe what the product is designed to do.

ProjectCommander is the latest release of this leading add-on companion product for Microsoft Project. Now available for Microsoft Project 98, ProjectCommander provides a menu-driven approach to project management. ProjectCommander contains a structured set of functions organized into a process flow that assists the project manager in both using the standard Microsoft Project functions and extending those functions through new features that add to the extensive capabilities of Project 98. ProjectCommander is seamlessly integrated within the familiar Microsoft Project desktop. The ProjectCommander menu choices provide a logical project management flow. Reduce the learning curve of Microsoft Project as ProjectCommander leads you through the process of project management with its intuitive planning, tracking, analyzing, and reporting menus. With the powerful new features of Project 98, the complexity of using the newer, more sophisticated functions can be overwhelming; the logical flow of ProjectCommander ensures that they are now easily tamed. With ProjectCommander, you can follow the intuitive menus and functions that lead you through the process of project management. There's no need to worry about where to double-click, secondary click, split the screen, or apply views, tables, and filters to get at your most critical project data. ProjectCommander takes you to the right information at the right time.

Top three product differentiators; describe what makes your product unique.

1. Enhances and extends the features of Microsoft Project 98.
2. Adds a logical flow to users of Microsoft Project 98.
3. Does not require external files (no import/export required).

To what business processes can this tool be applied?

Project management.

Describe the ideal end-user environment for the current version of your product (size of organization, level of project management sophistication, effort and commitment required).

New users of Microsoft Project 98 will find this tool useful to flatten the learning curve of Microsoft Project 98.

Future strategies for this product.

Project Commander will continue to be released on the same schedule as Microsoft Project.

Product's target market.

IT organizations.
Engineering and manufacturing management.
Other process-based business disciplines.

What are your product's three main benefits? (How does using the product add value to the customer?)

1. Makes using Microsoft Project 98 easier.
2. Adds function to Microsoft Project 98.
3. Provides process for managing projects.

Describe your quality management process. List any relevant certifications.

TeamWork is developed by Project Assistants, a project management software development company. Project Assistants has a documented alpha and beta testing program that ensures that all GA software is completely quality assured prior to release. All defects which are reported during the alpha and beta test period are corrected, and the entire application is regression-tested to assure that the product has achieved a satisfactory quality rating and is approaching zero defect.

Discuss your product pricing structure. Include volume discount levels, concurrent user options, site licenses, cost of implementation, and other issues.

Pricing structure is as follows: 1–9 copies: $199 per copy; 10–19 copies: $189 per copy; 20–29 copies: $179 per copy; 30–39 copies: $169 per copy; 40–49 copies: $159 per copy; 50–59 copies: $149 per copy; 60–69 copies: $139 per copy; 70–79 copies: $129 per copy; 80–89 copies: $119 per copy; 90–99 copies: $109 per copy; >100 copies: $99 per copy.

Cost of implementation: Open enrollment training is offered for $295 per person. On-site training is $1,500 per day, plus expenses. Technical support packages are available, and are priced by user or by organization. Annual maintenance packages start at $39.95.

ProjectExplorer for Microsoft Project (Information Management Services, Inc.)

Describe what the product is designed to do.

Project, program, and resource managers utilize ProjectExplorer to navigate among the projects stored in the enterprise information repository that they have access rights to view and/or edit. A Windows-based explorer view provides project, task, resource, and assignment information across multiple projects in a single easy-to-use view.

Depending upon the unique process flow of the organization, different project stakeholders may view a project at different stages in its development. Finance may initiate a project and share it with program management, followed by program management sharing the information with resource management. The process flow is completely user-configurable with capabilities only limited by the imagination of the management team. ProjectExplorer provides an easy-to-use method of finding, retrieving, and saving Microsoft Projects to the enterprise repository. This facilitates communication between project managers, team managers, and their team members.

Schedulers of any type utilize ProjectExplorer directly in Microsoft Project to communicate tasks to assigned resources. Assignments have different states to provide alternative assignment process flows. Tasks with a state of hold are not seen by team members to report actual progress outside of the defined schedule. Although a flexible assignment is not advised if you follow a strict critical path scheduling technique, the option is provided for other non-CPM-based activities occurring in the organization.

A task with an assign state allows the team member to view the assignment and to report time against the defined activity. A task's state can be set by default or via an easy-to-use dialogue directly in Microsoft Project.

ProjectExplorer provides communication of assignments from Microsoft Project. Assignments are added to the team member's ProjectExplorer timesheet view or WebTime, and actual progress committed by team members automatically updates the manager of the project. Team members utilize the ProjectExplorer timesheet module to record project and nonproject actual progress, and to provide schedule feedback. This Windows-based timesheet works independently of WebTime, giving the users a choice of either interface to manage activities from various managers, all in a consistent manner. The ProjectExplorer enterprise project module is utilized to establish non-scheduled projects and activities.

TaskClass (sold separately) and DocCheck (sold separately) work in conjunction with ProjectExplorer and are used by project, program, and resource managers to validate task and project secondary information across multiple project plans to ensure consistent information and adherence to defined organizational methods and processes. DocCheck is also utilized for advanced scheduling process-flow capabilities and integration with other business systems. Other organizational information relating to information is easily linked to a particular project plan. Unlimited reports, analysis, and what ifs are provided by the ProjectExchange Portfolio Wizard to provide the project office with information needed.

Utilizing TimeReview (sold separately) allows time to be verified against corporate business rules to ensure time-reporting compliance guidelines are met. WebTime (sold separately) provides Internet-based team members with the ability to view and status assignments initiated and managed in ProjectExplorer. Schedulers utilizing the ProjectExplorer apply actuals module directly in Microsoft Project to automatically update the status of the manager's project file, which improves efficiency as well as accuracy of information by updating the complete plan with one click of the mouse.

By closing the loop between project managers, team members, and other project stakeholders, managers are freed from the tedious task of disseminating information and gathering progress and estimates, while team members obtain task ownership and are provided a mechanism to provide schedule feedback. This ensures that all team members are tied into the planning process with minimum effort expended.

Top three product differentiators; describe what makes your product unique.

1. User configurable to organization-specific requirements.

2. Seamless integration with Microsoft Project provides a single project repository spanning the entire enterprise.

3. Three-tier client/server-based architecture provides a system scalable across the entire enterprise.

To what business processes can this tool be applied?

Our tools are utilized across multiple business processes.

Describe the ideal end-user environment for the current version of your product (size of organization, level of project management sophistication, effort and commitment required).

Our primary market includes Global 5000 organizations with objectives to increase their return on people, time, and financial investments. We initially assist event-driven divisions within these organizations, with the ultimate goal of benefiting every user in the organization.

Future strategies for this product.

Consolidating desktop scheduling information into a central resource-allocation repository is gaining, and will continue to gain, market momentum. By consolidating information generated by multiple project managers, organizations are able to balance across multiple project managers the demands placed on them with the supply of available people, time, and funds. Microsoft Project provides individual project managers with the tools necessary to plan a particular project with a particular set of resources. An opportunity exists to provide an enterprise work-management solution to provide this aggregated information to help organizations make informed business decisions. Without a central resource-allocation repository, organizations find themselves being managed by multiple islands of project managers, each not knowing what the other is doing. By consolidating resource-allocation information, organizations are better able to share resources among and depend on other parts of the organization. We will continue to be a leader in the program and project scheduling market.

Product's target market.

Based on our experience, clients who benefit most from our products and services include information systems, professional services, product development, engineering, and other event-driven organizations. Among these groups, each has further defined a set of unique objectives critical to increasing their competitiveness. IMS provides the ProjectExchange Enterprise Toolkit to achieve these objectives from the departmental level to the entire enterprise.

What are your product's three main benefits? (How does using the product add value to the customer?)

1. Secure access to organizational project improves team productivity and reduces operating costs.

2. A single project repository provides information used by multiple business systems, ensures information is consistent.

3. Aggregating assignments across all projects helps project managers schedule within available resource capacity.

Describe your quality management process. List any relevant certifications.

We have continually improved our system-development methodology since 1991. Over time, our SDLC has incorporated the best practices learned while deploying ProjectExchange in world-class organizations across the globe. Our Research & Development division utilizes ProjectExchange, and quality measures are persistent throughout our methods and processes.

Discuss your product pricing structure. Include volume discount levels, concurrent user options, site licenses, cost of implementation, and other issues.

Please consult IMS for current pricing.

Implementation costs vary and depend upon a particular organization's business requirements and level and availability of in-house expertise. We offer the following services to help achieve organizational objectives:

- Installation
- Process, methods, and integration consulting
- Project office support
- ProjectExchange add-on solution development
- Implementation management
- Microsoft Project and ProjectExchange two-day course
- ProjectExchange for Project Managers one-day course
- ProjectExchange for Team Members half-day course
- MS Project Introduction one-day course
- MS Project Basic two-day course
- Project Planning & Management Fundamentals three-day course
- Executive briefing on project management.

Annual maintenance is offered at 15 percent of the license costs. Maintenance includes telephone support and product upgrades.

Project Scheduler 7.6 (Scitor Corporation)

Describe what the product is designed to do.

PS7 is built from the ground up to take full advantage of today's technology. Whether you're performing basic task scheduling on your desktop or working on multiple megaprojects using our powerful SQL database repository, PS7 will meet your needs. Wizards, Guides, Tip-of-the-Day suggestions, and field level help provide an easy-to-navigate path to project management. You'll find PS7 provides extraordinary flexibility to organize, consolidate, and view project information.

For serious users, PS7 provides support for: subprojects, grouped projects, accounting periods, time-phased availability, inflation factors, multiple-cost tables, earned value, unlimited user fields/formulas, five baselines, custom reports, and much more.

The add-on package, Project Communicator (described in the Timesheets section), permits resources to view their task assignments, and report back actual work and estimated remaining work via a powerful two-tier client/server database system.

Top three product differentiators; describe what makes your product unique.

1. Approachable power: PS7 meets the needs of the most demanding project management professionals, without sacrificing the ease of use demanded in today's state-of-the-art applications.

2. Scalability: PS7 is designed and built from the ground up to scale from the single desktop user to the entire enterprise.

3. Customer support: PS7 isn't just another software product. In its seventh generation, PS7 continues to be designed and built by project management professionals for project management professionals.

To what business processes can this tool be applied?

Project planning and tracking.
Resource management and team communications.
Cost estimation and control.

Describe the ideal end-user environment for the current version of your product (size of organization, level of project management sophistication, effort and commitment required).

PS7 is designed to meet the needs of all sizes of organizations, including individuals, product teams, workgroups, and the enterprise. PS7 is the most configurable project management package available. It meets the needs of beginning project managers on up to serious project management professionals.

Future strategies for this product.

We will continue to provide leading-edge project management products and services by listening to and working with customers to predict the future needs of a changing management environment.

Product's target market.

General business and professional project management.
All major industries.

What are your product's three main benefits? (How does using the product add value to the customer?)

1. Plans and tracks project/resource costs and schedules.
2. Allows *early* detection and resolution of problems.
3. Facilitates communications between all stakeholders.

Describe your quality management process. List any relevant certifications.

Best commercial practices.

Discuss your product pricing structure. Include volume discount levels, concurrent user options, site licenses, cost of implementation, and other issues.

Single unit: $595, discounts at ten, twenty-five, and fifty plus.
$2,900 for five-pack concurrent licenses, discounts at two, five, and ten plus.
Site licenses available for five hundred licenses and up.
Regional and on-site training and consulting is available.
Telephone tech support is available at no charge.
Annual maintenance: not applicable.

QEI Exec (PCF Limited)

Describe what the product is designed to do.

QEI Exec is best thought of as a toolkit for managing activity-based problems built around a high performance database engine. Data stored within the database can be presented and manipulated via any number of views, which can be graphical or tabular. The entire user interface to the delivered product is written in the product's own programming language, allowing complete customization to meet individual requirements. It provides the following key areas of functionality:

- Graphical and tabular interface to data
- Scheduling
- Resource management
- Cost and performance management
- Flexible interfacing to other systems
- High degree of customization.

Top three product differentiators; describe what makes your product unique.

1. Highly graphical *CAD-like* approach to project construction gives total freedom of data layout.

2. Dynamic rollup of all schedule and resource data through an unlimited number of structures, yielding high performance even when dealing with tens of thousands of tasks.

3. Macro-based front end allows complete customization of user interface and generation of interactive specialist charts (such as time chainage diagrams).

To what business processes can this tool be applied?

It has a wide range of possible applications, including:
- *Traditional* project planning with earned value analysis
- Project-based MIS/EIS
- Program treasury management
- Maintenance and manufacturing forecasting
- Capacity planning
- MRP master schedule generation.

Describe the ideal end-user environment for the current version of your product (size of organization, level of project management sophistication, effort and commitment required).

Large organizations (to > $100M) with considerable experience of *rigorous* project management wishing to consolidate diverse sets of data (from multiple planning systems, manufacturing/ERP, and cost collection) into a single source of high-quality management information.

If customers wish to fully exploit the potential for tightly integrating the product with other systems or to introduce significant customizations, they will require suitable internal IT resources.

Future strategies for this product.

Extended database connectivity via ODBC.
Extended reporting and intranet functionality.

Product's target market.

Principal markets are aerospace and defense. Product is also successfully used in make-to-order/contract manufacturing, transportation, and utilities.

What are your product's three main benefits? (How does using the product add value to the customer?)

1. Extremely high-quality interactive graphical views of data.
2. High performance consolidation/rollup permits rapid what-if scenario analysis.
3. Complete control over layout and presentation of data.

Describe your quality management process. List any relevant certifications.

We have started (but not yet completed) ISO 9001 certification.

Discuss your product pricing structure. Include volume discount levels, concurrent user options, site licenses, cost of implementation, and other issues.

The product is sold as a right-to-use license, plus a number of user licenses. A small (three-user) system would cost about £15,000 while a larger (ten-user) system would cost about £30,000. The per-user price drops with increasing numbers of users. Site/multisite/corporate licenses are available.

It is strongly recommended that customers take training from us. List price for training is £500/day per course for up to six attendees. Various standard training courses are available, or custom courses can be developed on request. Annual maintenance is 15 percent of the list price of the software. This includes all upgrades and new releases and unlimited telephone support.

Schedule Insight

Describe what the product is designed to do.

Schedule Insight is a read-only browser of Microsoft Project schedules and is designed for executives, managers, and staff that need quick, no-nonsense access to Microsoft Project schedule information. It automatically rolls up multiple projects by company, project, department, resource, and task. A built-in report writer allows users to create their own reports.

Top three product differentiators; describe what makes your product unique.

1. Read-only browser of Microsoft Project schedules.
2. Familiar spreadsheet and folder architecture for ease of use.
3. All views and reports can be customized by the end user.

To what business processes can this tool be applied?

Dissemination of project information.

Describe the ideal end-user environment for the current version of your product (size of organization, level of project management sophistication, effort and commitment required).

Companies or departments using Microsoft Project where five or more people (who are not project managers) have an interest in viewing and printing project information for their own needs.

Future strategies for this product.

Database support with qualified updating.

Product's target market.

Users of Microsoft Project in groups of five or more covering all industry segments.

What are your product's three main benefits? (How does using the product add value to the customer?)

1. Improves schedule quality and timeliness through improved team awareness.
2. Reduces need for project meetings.
3. Empowers individuals to obtain their own project information.

Describe your quality management process. List any relevant certifications.

Internally documented.

Discuss your product pricing structure. Include volume discount levels, concurrent user options, site licenses, cost of implementation, and other issues.

Single user—$99. Network license—$995 (unlimited users).

The point-and-click interface with read-only capabilities allows users to quickly and safely learns on their own while project data always remains safe. In addition, the online tutorial and free E-mail support greatly minimize implementation costs.

SureTrak (Primavera)

Describe what the product is designed to do.

SureTrak offers the most comprehensive set of tracking, reporting, and analytical features in a highly graphical, easy-to-use environment. Version 2.0 features the Project KickStart wizard, an interactive PERT view, the Primavera Post Office, Web publishing and dozens of usability enhancements.

Top three product differentiators; describe what makes your product unique.

SureTrak offers the easiest way to get your project started, with its getting started wizard, Project KickStart. Project KickStart guides users through the initial stages of project planning with a proven framework for brainstorming and anticipating challenges. And, with Progress Spotlight, SureTrak enables users to view all activities within a specified time period within a graphical to do list, seeing which activities need updating and which may cause potential delays.

To what business processes can this tool be applied?

Any.

Describe the ideal end-user environment for the current version of your product (size of organization, level of project management sophistication, effort and commitment required).

SureTrak is designed specifically for controlling small to medium sized projects and can be utilized by experienced project managers, as well as, novice project schedulers.

Future strategies for this product.

No answer given.

Product's target market.

No answer given.

What are your product's three main benefits? (How does using the product add value to the customer?)

SureTrak from Primavera offers multiproject scheduling, simultaneous access to project within project groups, and critical path scheduling.

Describe your quality management process. List any relevant certifications.

No answer given.

Discuss your product pricing structure. Include volume discount levels, concurrent user options, site licenses, cost of implementation, and other issues.

No answer given.

TurboProject

Describe what the product is designed to do.

TurboProject is a powerful project management program that you can use to efficiently plan, manage, and communicate a project schedule and information. TurboProject is ideal for building a project, especially during the early stages of a project's definition. Using the methodology of top-down, Turbo Project thinks the way a project manager does. It permits you to start with what you know, allowing the project plan to be developed in a structured manner. Adhering to this top-down methodology allows you to build your project structure with what you know now, but with the advantage that you can fill in the details later. With unsurpassed control provided by the intuitive project Tree navigator, you can move through the hierarchy of a project by simply pointing and clicking with your mouse, collapse, expand, zoom, and view only the parts you need to. Why have power and capacity if getting to the core of your project is a constant struggle. TurboProject combines the best of traditional project management features with unique and useful capabilities such as loose layout, dynamic leveling, multilevel planning, hierarchical scheduling, and single-click support for *distribution and integration* of multiple subprojects. Combine all of this with features such as *auto-progress* and unlimited *undo redo*, and support for *smart* 32 Bit ODBC at a price that is way below any other product in this segment of the project management market. With three products to choose from—Express, Standard, and Professional—TurboProject offers scalability for all types and levels of individuals and corporations who are serious about being successful in managing and controlling projects.

Top three product differentiators; describe what makes your product unique.

1. Elegant and intuitive multiproject support.
2. Project navigation tree.
3. Top-down methodology.

To what business processes can this tool be applied?

TurboProject's comprehensive features set allows the product to be used in a variety of different ways and in many industries. If the requirement is to streamline your project management activities and to be even more competitive in your market segment, then TurboProject provides a feature set that suits these requirements. Industries include software development, telecommunications, financial services, service industries, automotive, mining, aerospace/defense, and construction.

Describe the ideal end-user environment for the current version of your product (size of organization, level of project management sophistication, effort and commitment required).

Whether the requirement is for a simple scheduler or a robust tracking and analysis tool, TurboProject offers something for all users and corporations who want to be more successful at planning, managing, and controlling projects. With three levels of product—TurboProject Express, TurboProject Standard, and TurboProject Professional—TurboProject, IMSI provides a scaleable solution that is ideally suited for use by individuals or even corporations requiring hundreds of users to be involved in the project management process. TurboProject has been used with great success by managers of all experience levels. All can easily find a level that supports their project planning and management requirements. Adherence to top-down methodology enables implementation to be carried out in a structured manner, and TurboProject integrates easily into organizations committed to the adoption of sound project management practices.

Future strategies for this product.

Client/server and save-to-database features, enhanced groupware capabilities, intelligent resource scheduling.

Product's target market.

TurboProject Professional: Organizations with requirements to manage multiple projects using shared resources.

TurboProject Standard: A practical solution for project managers requiring superior functionality, but not required to distribute and integrate subprojects.

TurboProject Express: Designed specifically for people who want scheduling solutions fast and easy. It targets users wanting to create professional plans for smaller projects, who demand presentation-quality output, at a reasonable price.

What are your product's three main benefits? (How does using the product add value to the customer?)

1. Top-down planning.
2. Product scalability.
3. Cost of ownership.

Describe your quality management process. List any relevant certifications.

Our quality management process can be described in three phases. We have a highly technical QA team that works directly with the engineers on a daily basis, and that is responsible for verifying the correct functionality and implementation of TurboProject.

Once development milestones are achieved, copies of TurboProject are sent to about thirty different companies participating in our beta test program. We feel these testers represent a good sampling of the product management industry and provide invaluable feedback concerning their individual working styles and needs.

Our final quality assurance cycle performs a battery of system tests to ensure that TurboProject will run smoothly on all the current hardware standards.

Discuss your product pricing structure. Include volume discount levels, concurrent user options, site licenses, cost of implementation, and other issues.

IMSI offers a site license pricing structure, with volume discounts. TurboProject Professional SRP is $295.95 per copy, and TurboProject Standard SRP is $99.95 per copy. Our site license pricing begins with a ten-user site, and then progresses to an eleven to forty-nine-user site, a fifty to ninety-nine-user site, a one hundred to 249-user site, and so on. At present, we do not offer a concurrent user license. For more information, please contact IMSI Corporate Sales at 888/467-4223.

IMSI offers a corporate support and training program that includes a local two-day course for $675 per person, and on-site training beginning at $1,500 a day. We also offer a premium support and maintenance program for corporate users. For more information visit the TurboProject homepage http://www.imsisoft.com/turboproject or E-mail corporate@imsisoft.com.

WebProject

Describe what the product is designed to do.

WebProject is designed for geographically dispersed project teams. WebProject is a Java-based project management tool with powerful collaboration and communications features. WebProject incorporates unique knowledge management/best practices capability.

Top three product differentiators; describe what makes your product unique.

WebProject is the first (only) pure Java project management suite that can utilize an open architecture database backend. WebProject allows corporations to utilize Oracle, SQL Server, Informix, Sybase, or other databases in their enterprise project management.

WebProject has introduced the first knowledge management/best practices capability within a project management software suite.

WebProject enables global project communication including project issues boards, threaded task discussions, virtual project status meetings, and remote project statusing and updates.

To what business processes can this tool be applied?

Geographically dispersed project teams, projects that need to have access from remote locations, or integrating WebProject's proprietary information exchange with MS Project, Primavera, or other desktop systems.

WebProject allows the extraction of knowledge from the enterprise, such as resource capabilities or company *best practices*.

Describe the ideal end-user environment for the current version of your product (size of organization, level of project management sophistication, effort and commitment required).

WebProject is an easy-to-use Java project management tool that will enable teams to communicate and collaborate from remote locations. WebProject is designed for the enterprise and will work well with project teams as well.

Future strategies for this product.

WebProject has established many *firsts* in the project management industry. We will continue to move the industry forward with our new technologies on the Web and with Java.

Product's target market.

Geographically dispersed project teams, enterprise project management systems, integration with Primavera, MS Project, and other project management systems.

What are your product's three main benefits? (How does using the product add value to the customer?)

1. Enterprise project communication.
2. Project collaboration.
3. Geographically dispersed updates and communication.

Describe your quality management process. List any relevant certifications.

WebProject adheres to strict standards and processes for quality, both in development and customer service.

Discuss your product pricing structure. Include volume discount levels, concurrent user options, site licenses, cost of implementation, and other issues.

WebProject is priced at $790 for starter package including the WebProject server. WebProject does provide enterprise and site licensing.

Chapter 4

Cost Management Software

Traditionally, the project management system creates the schedule, and the cost system prices the project. Cost management software features vary from relatively simple tools that enhance scheduling tools' cost-tracking capabilities to sophisticated tools that can detail and manage all cost components across the life cycle of the project—from estimates during project startup to the final summarization and analysis of the cost of the project at completion.

Proposal pricing can be hand entered, driven by historic performance on similar projects, or built through templates. Budget management helps identify cost overruns, underruns, and other potential issues.

Forecasting looks beyond past project-financial performance through the remainder of the project and often supports *what-if* analysis.

Performance measurement provides an objective measure of project performance, comparing the project's time-versus-cost status. Variance-analysis tools help direct the user to the source of cost differentials.

Different industries have different requirements for cost management. Construction cost management often links the contract deliverables and change requests to the costing system. Information technology costing systems often interface with the corporate human resources system for rate data. Government contractors require electronic audit trails and conformance to government-reporting specifications, like the United States cost/schedule control systems criteria.

Many businesses already have systems that perform proposal costing and require only the performance measurement functionality. Other sites want the complete package. The wide variety of cost management packages on the market provides options for most requirements.

Some of the business processes supported by this category of products include estimating, proposal development, project execution, change control, earned value reporting, and material management.

Most industries can benefit from cost management software. Some of the target markets listed by vendors covered in the survey include product development, construction, software development, pharmaceuticals, aerospace and defense, and manufacturing.

Cost management is covered in Chapter 7 of *A Guide to the Project Management Body of Knowledge (PMBOK™ Guide)*.

What to Expect:

Cost management software provides features like:
- Proposal pricing
- Budget management
- Forecasting, including rate escalation
- Performance measurement
- Variance analysis.

What the Data Reveals

Many vendors responded in this category with tools that were also entered in other categories. Most scheduling packages perform rudimentary cost calculations, including the rudimentary earned value elements, budgeted cost of work performed (BCWP), budgeted cost of work scheduled (BCWS), and actual cost of work performed (ACWP). Packages that are listed exclusively under the cost management category include Cobra, Artemis CostView, Corporate Controller, JobPROMS, P3 Connect, Project Connect for wInsight, Project Connect for OPP, PLANTRAC-CORoNET, Prolog Manager Version 5.0, Prolog Executive Version 1.0, and Dekker TRAKKER Advanced Cost.

The rest of the cost management packages in the survey perform other functions (scheduling, risk, etc.) in addition to cost. These are the vendor's cost modules in an integrated suite-of-tools approach. Integration eliminates the effort involved in reconciling differences between cost and schedule, if those are maintained in two different packages.

When evaluating cost management software, first decide if you are implementing or upgrading an entire project management system or just the cost capability.

Custom calculations are useful for organizations with mature budgeting processes. Control over the buildup of indirect costs is critical to government-reporting requirements.

Irregular reporting calendars and fiscal calendars are important for integration of project cost data with corporate financial systems.

Some tools support posting actual costs based on resource usage as reported through a time-tracking tool. Others also allow integration with corporate financial systems, for loading of cost data from external systems.

There are a number of comprehensive, flexible cost packages that cover the full spectrum of functionality in a single application, with integration of all project costs—budgets, forecasts, history, variances, commitments, changes, trends, expenditures, and more. The differentiating features include coding schemes; support of multiple breakdown structures, whether or not the package supports estimating and proposal development; integration with supporting software; industry-standard database support; and customization.

Each of the major headings on the selection matrix should be prioritized. There are many packages with functionality that address each heading, but not all of those features may be required for each customer. The more features that are supported, the more expensive and complex the product will be.

Cost management packages range from about $495 to $12,000 per license. This wide variance in cost has to do with exactly what the product will do. Less-expensive products will often capture only one cost entry (field) per task or resource. Lower-priced products will not support estimating or detailed performance measurement. The cost functionality in the lower-priced tools is generally designed to capture rudimentary earned value data and capture gross costs in a *quick-and-dirty* fashion.

Higher-priced products allow the user to fully configure elements of cost, budget, and estimates. Elaborate budget feature sets allow the cost management tool to detail costs to such a fine level of granularity that the data collected can be linked directly to corporate financial systems for billing and payroll. These features can also support government reporting requirements.

What the Majority of Vendors Offer

All products responding in the cost management category calculate the basic earned value fields BCWP, BCWS, and ACWP.

Under the performance measurement heading, vendors' support of the different calculation methods varies widely. Some products support all calculation methods, some are missing a few, and others support about half.

What a Minority of Vendors Offer

Coverage of multiple languages is spotty. Every product is available in English, but fewer than half the products come in English only. Microsoft Project offers the most non-English options: German, French, Swedish, Italian, Spanish, Danish, Norwegian, Japanese, Traditional Chinese,

Simplified Chinese, Korean, Hebrew, and Brazilian Portuguese. French and German are common. Some vendors responded that additional languages would be supported by request.

Some of the products are integrated with enterprise requirements planning (ERP) systems, but most are not. Some vendors referenced pursuing this integration in future releases.

Forecasting the budget impact through *what-if* scenarios is supported by some products. The ability to create and save multiple forecasts is supported by only a few vendors. Multiple budgets supported by different rates, then saved for options analysis, are not supported by many tools.

Unique Features That Surfaced in Vendor Responses to the Narrative Questions

Coding of the data is critical to the product's ability to summarize, slice and dice, and produce meaningful reports. Each product handles this differently. Some products support a small set of simple user-defined text or number fields that can be tagged with data for sorting and filtering. Some products support a hierarchical coding scheme, so various levels of a structure are automatically rolled up. A few products support multiple coding schemes. Some are simple, and some are fascinatingly complex and flexible. Some of the user-defined or code fields may be used to link one package to another, so be sure to consult with each vendor when integration is an issue to be sure you have all of the fields you need available for coding your data. The coding capability can be a differentiating feature, and should be tested in the hands-on portion of the evaluation process.

Some packages run on multiple platforms, summarizing data across them. Vendors that support multiple platforms note that the software has the same interface—look and feel—on any platform.

Some products are trying to simplify the process of developing budgets and estimates. Wizards and context-sensitive help reduce the learning curve for new users, and ensure consistency among all users.

What's New and Exciting

Some products support ten to twenty different foreign currencies. For some of the lower-priced products, support of a foreign currency means that the product will display the currency symbol. If support of multiple currencies is important, this feature should be tested during the hands-on portion of the evaluation process.

Future strategies for the product should be considered during the selection process. Few organizations find the tool that does everything they need; the final selection is usually the tool that has most of the required features. Vendors may be planning a feature that is not common to cost management software, but may be very significant to an organization's success. Some of the future strategies listed in the cost management category include 100 percent Web-based management of project portfolio, knowledge management integration, and advanced data-mining features.

A reminder: The data in the matrix and in the narrative responses were supplied by the vendors and have not been independently verified.

Cost Management

	AMS REALTIME Projects	Artemis CostView	AutoPLAN Enterprise	Cascade PgM	Cobra	Corporate Controller	CostLink Project Controller	Dekker TRAKKER Advanced Cost	Enterprise Project
Performance measurement calculation methods									
Weighted milestones	Y	Y	Y	Y	Y	Y	Y	Y	Y
Apportioned	Y	Y	Y	Y	Y	Y	Y	Y	Y
50-50	Y	Y	Y	Y	Y	N	Y	Y	Y
Level of Effort (LOE)	Y	Y	Y	Y	Y	Y	Y	Y	Y
Percent complete	Y	Y	Y	Y	Y	Y	Y	Y	Y
Units complete	Y	Y	Y	Y	Y	Y	Y	Y	Y
50-50	Y	Y	Y	Y	Y	N	Y	Y	Y
0-100	Y	Y	Y	Y	Y	N	Y	Y	Y
100-0	Y	Y	Y	?	Y	N	Y	Y	Y
User defined	N	Y	Y	N	N	Y	Y	Y	Y
Earned value calculations									
BCWP	Y	Y	Y	Y	Y	Y	Y	Y	Y
BCWS	Y	Y	Y	Y	Y	Y	Y	Y	Y
ACWP	Y	Y	Y	Y	Y	Y	Y	Y	Y
Proposal pricing									
Top-down budgeting	Y	Y	N	Y	Y	Y	Y	Y	Y
Forecasting									
Forecasting (what if budget increases by 10 %; statistical methods)	Y	Y	N	Y	Y	Y	Y	Y	Y
Saves simultaneous forecasts	N	Y	N	Y	Y	Y	Y	Y	Y
Budget management									
Rate build-up	Y	Y	N	Y	Y	N	N	Y	Y
Customize budget elements	Y	Y	N	Y	Y	Y	Y	Y	Y
Number of work packages in a cost account	7	Unlim.	Unlim.	Unlim.	Unlim.	Unlim.	Unlim.	Unlim.	Unlim.
Direct costs	Y	Y	N	Y	Y	Y	Y	Y	Y
Indirect costs	Y	Y	N	Y	Y	Y	Y	Y	Y
Burden templates for indirect costs	Y	Y	N	Y	Y	Y	Y	Y	Y
Custom calculations	Y	Y	N	Y	Y	Y	N	Y	Y
Multiple Estimate-to-Complete calculations	N	Y	N	Y	Y	Y	Y	Y	Y
Foreign currencies supported (list)	Any number can be supported through conversion rate tables	All currencies with a 3 char. ISO code		User defined, therefore any foreign currency	Unlim.	All currencies can be entered and converted to a base currency of choice	All	All supported by Win. System provides for currency conversions.	None
Reporting									
Aggregate costs over multiple projects	Y	Y	Y	Y	Y	Y	Y	Y	Y
Cumulative reporting	Y	Y	Y	Y	Y	Y	Y	Y	Y

Feature	Product 1	Product 2	Product 3	Product 4	Product 5	Product 6	Product 7	Product 8	Product 9
Fiscal calendars	Y	Y	N	Y	Y	Y	Y	Y	Y
Irregular reporting calendars	Y	Y	N	Y	Y	Y	Y	Y	Y
Cash flow									
Periodic cost profile (cost during a time period)	Y	Y	N	Y	Y	Y	Y	Y	Y
By resource (summarize costs incurred by use of a resource)	Y	Y	N	Y	Y	Y	Y	Y	Y
Cash flow reports	Y	Y	N	Y	Y	Y	Y	Y	Y
Report writer	N	N	Y	N	N	N	Y	Y	Y
Report wizard	Y	Y	Y	Y	Y	Y	Y	Y	Y
Publishes as HTML	Y	Y	Y	Y	Y	Y	Y	Y	Y
Number of user-defined fields	100	22	Unlim.	Unlim.	Unlim.	Multiple text, date, and numeric fields	Unlim.	Unlim.	0
Drill-down/roll-up *	Y	Y	Y	Y	Y	Y	Y	Y	Y
Import/export	Y	Y	Y	Y	Y	Y	Y	Y	Y
Automatic E-mail notification *	N	Y	Y	N	N	N	N	N	N
Macro recorder/batch capable *A67	Y	Y	Y	Y	Y	Y	N	N	N
Can "canned" reports be modified?	Y	Y	Y	Y	Y	Y	Y	Y	Y
Sort, filter	Y	Y	Y	Y	Y	Y	Y	Y	Y
Architecture									
Databases supported (list):	Oracle, ODBC compliant, proprietary	Oracle, MS SQL Server, Sybase, SQL Base	Oracle	Oracle	Oracle, MS SQL Server, FoxPro	Oracle	MS Access, Oracle, MS SQL Server	Oracle, MS SQL Server, Informix, MS Access, FoxPro	Oracle, Sybase, Informix, MS SQL Server, MS Access
Supports distributed databases	Y	Y	Y	Y	Y	Y	Y	Y	Y
Three-tier client/server	Y	Y	Y	Y	N	Y	Y	Y	Y
Client operating systems	Win 95/NT/3.x, Solaris, HP, RS, Mac	Win 95/NT	Win 95/NT/3.x, Solaris, HP-UX, AIX	Win 95/98/NT	Win 95 or later	Win 95/NT/3.x	Win 95/98/NT	Win 95/98/NT	Win 95/98/NT

Cost Management

	AMS REALTIME Projects	Artemis CostView	AutoPLAN Enterprise	Cascade PgM	Cobra	Corporate Controller	CostLink Project Controller	Dekker TRAKKER Advanced Cost	Enterprise Project
Server operating systems	Win 95/NT/3.x, Solaris, HP, RS, Mac	Win NT, Solaris, HP-UX	Win NT, Solaris, HP-UX, AIX	Unix, Win NT	Win 95/NT, Unix (Oracle)	Unix, Win NT	Win, Unix	Win NT, Novell, Unix	Unix, Win NT
Network operating systems	TCP/IP, Banyan, Novell, IPX	IPX, Novell, Win NT	Win NT, Novell, Unix	TCP/IP	IPX, TCPI	Novell, Win NT	Win, Novell	Win NT, Novell, Unix	Novell, Win NT, others
Minimum client configuration	8 MB RAM, 20 MB disk, 486 or better	48 MB RAM, Pentium 166	P5 32 MB	PC 486/66 processor or above. Win 95 or Win NT V4. 16 MB RAM	16 MB RAM	16 MB RAM	Pentium, 24 MB	16 MB RAM, 1 GB HD, SVGA	486, 16 MB memory
Minimum server configuration	32 MB RAM, 100 MB disk, Pentium or better	Depends on hardware used (e.g., for Win NT same as the client configuration)	P5 32 MB, Unix machine with 64 MB	Any server supporting Oracle 7 or above	Server optional	64 MB RAM	Pentium, 32 MB	128 MB RAM, 10 GB HD	Pentium 200 CPU, 128 MB, 1 GB
Client runs under Web browser	Y	N	Y	N	N	N	Y	N	Y
Open architecture									
Supports OLE	N	N	Y	Y	N	Y	Y	Y	Y
Documented Object Model	Y	Y	Y	Y	N	Y	N	Y	Y
Documented Application Programming Interface (API)	Y	Y	Y	Y	N	Y	N	Y	Y
Simultaneous edit of data file	Y	Y	N	Y	Y	Y	Y	Y	Y
Does product have a programming language?	Y	N	Y	Y	N	Y	N	Y	Y
Are years stored as four-digit numbers?	N	Y	Y	Y	Y	Y	Y	Y	Y
Online help									
Right mouse click	N	Y	N	N	Y	Y	Y	Y	N
Hover buttons	Y	Y	Y	Y	Y	Y	Y	Y	N
Interactive help	Y	Y	Y	Y	Y	N	Y	Y	Y

Feature	V1	V2	V3	V4	V5	V6	V7	V8	V9
Help search feature	Y	Y	Y	Y	Y	Y	Y	Y	Y
Web access to product knowledge base *	N	N	Y	Y	Y	N	Y	Y	Y
Vendor information									
Training									
Computer-based training	Y	Y	N	N	N	Y	Y	N	Y
Training materials available	Y	Y	Y	Y	Y	Y	Y	Y	Y
Customized training materials	Y	Y	Y	Y	Y	Y	Y	Y	Y
Online tutorial	N	Y	N	N	Y	N	N	N	Y
Consulting available from vendor	Y	Y	Y	Y	Y	Y	Y	Y	Y
Site license discounts	Y	Y	Y	Y	Y	Y	Y	Y	Y
Enhancement requests *	Y	Y	Y	Y	Y	Y	Y	Y	Y
Modify source code, support through upgrades *	Y	Y	Y	Y	Y	Y	Y	Y	Y
Global presence									
Global offices	N	Y	Y	Y	Y	Y	Y	Y	Y
Multilingual technical support	Y	Y	Y	N	N	Y	Y	Y	Y
Language versions (list):	Eng, Span	Eng	Eng, Fr, Ital	Eng	Eng	Eng, Fr	Eng, Fr	Eng, Fr, Ger, Ital	Chin, Dutch, Eng, Fr, Ger, Jpn, Kor, Pol, Rus
Audit Software Quality Assurance process? *	Y	Y	Y	Y	N	Y	Y	Y	Y
Security									
Configurable access privileges *	Y	Y	Y	Y	Y	Y	Y	Y	Y
Passwords expire (forced update)	Y	Y	Y	Y	N	N	Y	Y	N
Electronic approvals	Y	Y	Y	Y	N	Y	Y	Y	Y
Password protect files	Y	Y	Y	Y	Y	Y	Y	Y	Y

Cost Management

	ER Project 1000	Intelligent Planner	JobPROMS	MicroFusion Millennium	Micro Planner X-Pert	Microsoft Project 98	OPX2 Pro	P3Connect	Panorama
Performance measurement calculation methods									
Weighted milestones	N	Y	Y	Y	Y	N	Y	N	Y
Apportioned	N	Y	N	N	Y	Y	Y	N	Y
50-50	Y	Y	Y	Y	Y	Y	Y	N	Y
Level of Effort (LOE)	N	Y	Y	Y	Y	Y	Y	N	Y
Percent complete	Y	Y	Y	Y	Y	Y	Y	Y	Y
Units complete	Y	Y	Y	Y	Y	N	Y	Y	Y
50-50	Y	Y	Y	Y	Y	Y	Y	N	Y
0-100	Y	Y	Y	Y	Y	Y	Y	N	Y
100-0	Y	Y	Y	Y	Y	Y	Y	N	Y
User defined	Y	Y	Y	Y	Y	Y	Y	N	Y
Earned value calculations									
BCWP	Y	Y	Y	Y	Y	Y	Y	Y	Y
BCWS	Y	Y	Y	Y	Y	Y	Y	Y	Y
ACWP	Y	Y	Y	Y	Y	Y	Y	Y	Y
Proposal pricing									
Top-down budgeting	Y	Y	Y	N	Y	Y	Y	N	Y
Forecasting									
Forecasting (what if budget increases by 10 %; statistical methods)	Y	Y	Y	Y	Y	N	Y	Y	Y
Saves simultaneous forecasts	Y	Y	Y	Y	Y	N	Y	Y	Y
Budget management									
Rate build-up	Y	Y	Y	Y	Y	Y	Y	N	Y
Customize budget elements	Y	Y	Y	Y	Y	N	Y	N	Y
Number of work packages in a cost account	16,000	Unlim.	Unlim.	Unlim.		Unlim.	Unlim.	Unlim.	Unlim.
Direct costs	Y	Y	Y	Y	Y	Y	Y	Y	Y
Indirect costs	N	Y	Y	Y	Y	Y	Y	Y	Y
Burden templates for indirect costs	N	Y	Y	Y	N	N	N	N	Y
Custom calculations	N	Y	Y	Y	N	Y	N	Y	Y
Multiple Estimate-to-Complete calculations	Y	N	Y	Y	Y	N	Y	Y	N
Foreign currencies supported (list)	US	Unlim.	Unlim.			Any currency symbol is supported	Unlim.	N	Unlim.
Reporting									
Aggregate costs over multiple projects	Y	Y	Y	Y	Y	Y	Y	Y	Y
Cumulative reporting	Y	Y	Y	Y	Y	Y	Y	Y	Y

Fiscal calendars	Y	Y	Y	Y	Y	Y	N	Y
Irregular reporting calendars	N	Y	Y	Y	N	N	N	Y
Cash flow								
Periodic cost profile (cost during a time period)	Y	Y	Y	Y	Y	Y	Y	Y
By resource (summarize costs incurred by use of a resource)	Y	Y	Y	Y	Y	Y	N	Y
Cash flow reports	Y	Y	Y	Y	Y	Y	N	Y
Report writer	Y	Y	Y	N	Y	Y	N	Y
Report wizard	Y	N	N	N	N	N	N	N
Publishes as HTML	Y	Y	Y	N	Y	Y	Y	Y
Number of user-defined fields	100	100	Unlim.	12	360	Unlim.	Unlim.	20
Drill-down/roll-up *	Y	Y	Y	Y	N	Y	Y	Y
Import/export	Y	Y	Y	Y	Y	Y	Y	Y
Automatic E-mail notification *	Y	N	N	N	N	Y	N	N
Macro recorder/batch capable *A67	N	Y	N	N	Y	Y	Y	Y
Can "canned" reports be modified?	Y	Y	Y	Y	Y	Y	N	Y
Sort, filter	Y	Y	Y	Y	Y	Y	Y	Y
Architecture	Win, NetBEUI/NetBios, TCP/IP, Novell	TCP/IP, NetBios	Win 95/NT/3.x and Win-compatible file servers	Win, Mac	Any Win-supported network	TCP/IP (Ethernet, Token Ring, WAN)	Any that support Win client	TCP/IP
Databases supported (list):	Oracle, MS SQL Server, Interbase	Oracle, Sybase, MS SQL Server, Informix, Centura	MS Access, MS SQL Server; potentially Oracle	MS SQL Server, Oracle, Sybase, MS Access				
Supports distributed databases					MS Access, MS SQL Server, or Oracle	Oracle, MS SQL Server, Informix, Sybase, Ingres	MS Access, Oracle, MS SQL Server	Oracle
Three-tier client/server	Y	Y	Y	N	Y	Y	N	Y
Client operating systems	Y	Y	N	N	N	Y	N	Y

Cost Management

	ER Project 1000	Intelligent Planner	JobPROMS	MicroFusion Millennium	Micro Planner X-Pert	Microsoft Project 98	OPX2 Pro	P3Connect	Panorama
Server operating systems	Win 95/98/NT 3.51/NT 4.0 (ER Project Satellite also Java and Win 3.x)	Win 95/NT	Win 95/NT/3.x	Win 95/98/NT	Win, Mac	Win 95/98/NT 3.51 with Service Pack 5 or later/NT 4.0 with Service Pack 2 or later	Win 95/98/NT/3.x, Mac, Unix	Win 95/98/NT	Win 95/NT
Network operating systems	Win NT, Unix	Win NT	Win 95/NT/3.x and Win-compatible file servers	Win NT	Win, Mac	Win 95/98/NT 3.51 with Service Pack 5 or later/NT 4.0 with Service Pack 2 or later	Win NT, Unix	Any that support Win client	Any that support Oracle
Minimum client configuration	Pentium, 16 MB memory (ER Project Satellite 8 MB)	Pentium 120, 16 MB RAM, 1 GB disk	Pentium 120, 16 MB RAM, 30 MB disk space	Pentium 266, with 64 MB RAM		486 or higher processor with 12 MB memory for Win 95 or 16 MB for Win 98 or NT	486+16 MB RAM (light client), P100+32 MB RAM (fat client)	Pentium, 16 MB RAM	Pentium 133 MHz, 32 MB memory, 500 MB disk
Minimum server configuration	Pentium, 32 MB memory	Pentium 233, 128 MB RAM, 1 GB disk	Pentium 120, 16 MB RAM, 30 MB disk space or equivalent	Pentium 266, with 256 MB RAM		Run from server is available; configuration depends on number of users connecting to the server	P2xx+128 MB RAM	N/A	Depends on number of users
Client runs under Web browser	Y (ER Project Satellite)	Y	N	N	N	Y	N	N	N
Open architecture									
Supports OLE	N	N	Y	Y	N	Y	Y	Y	Y
Documented Object Model	Y	N	Y	Y	N	Y	Y	Y	Y
Documented Application Programming Interface (API)	N	Y	Y	Y	N	N	N	Y	Y
Simultaneous edit of data file	Y	Y	Y	Y	N	N	Y	Y	Y
Does product have a programming language?	N	Y	Y	N	N	Y	Y	N	Y
Are years stored as four-digit numbers?	Y	Y	Y	Y	Y	Y	Y	Y	Y
Online help									
Right mouse click	Y	N	Y	Y	Y	Y	Y	Y	N
Hover buttons	Y	N	N	Y	Y	Y	Y	Y	N
Interactive help	Y	Y	Y	N	Y	Y	Y	Y	Y

Help search feature	Y	Y	Y	Y	Y	Y	Y	Y
Web access to product knowledge base *	Y	Y	N	Y	Y	Y	N	N
Vendor information								
Training								
Computer-based training	N	N	N	Y	N	N	N	N
Training materials available	Y	Y	Y	Y	Y	Y	Y	Y
Customized training materials	Y	Y	Y	Y	N	N	Y	Y
Online tutorial	Y	Y	Y	N	Y	Y	Y	N
Consulting available from vendor	Y	Y	Y	Y	Y	Y	Y	Y
Site license discounts	Y	Y	Y	Y	Y	Y	Y	Y
Enhancement requests *	Y	Y	Y	Y	Y	Y	Y	Y
Modify source code, support through upgrades *	Y	Y	Y	Y	Y	N	Y	Y
Global presence								
Global offices	N	Y	Y	Y	N	Y	N	N
Multilingual technical support	N	Y	Y	N	N	Y	Y	N
Language versions (list):	Eng	Eng, Fr, Ger, Dutch	Eng, Ger, others available on request	Eng	Eng	Ger, Fr, Swed, Ital, Span, Dan, Nor, Jpn, Traditional Chin, Simplified Chin, Kor, Heb, Brzl. Port	Eng, Fr	Eng
Audit Software Quality Assurance process? *	Y	Y	Y	Y	Y	N	N	Y
Security								
Configurable access privileges *	Y	Y	Y	N	N	N	Y	Y
Passwords expire (forced update)	N	N	N	Y	N	N	N	Y
Electronic approvals	Y	Y	N	N	N	Y	Y	Y
Password protect files	Y	Y	Y	Y	Y	Y	Y	Y

Cost Management

	Plantrac-Coronet	Primavera Project Planner (P3) 2.0	Project Commander	Project Connect for OPP	Project Connect for wInsight	Project Control 6.0	Project Scheduler 7.6	Prolog Manager 5.0, Prolog Executive 1.0	QEI Exec	WebProject
Performance measurement calculation methods										
Weighted milestones	Y	N		N	Y	Y	Y	N	N	Y
Apportioned	Y	N	Y	N	Y	Y	Y	N	N	Y
50-50	Y	N		N	Y	Y	Y	Y	N	N
Level of Effort (LOE)	Y	N		N	Y	N	Y	N	N	Y
Percent complete	Y	Y	Y	Y	Y	Y	Y	Y	Y	Y
Units complete	Y	Y	Y	Y	Y	N	Y	Y	N	N
50-50	Y	N		N	Y	Y	Y	Y	N	N
0-100	Y	N		N	Y	Y	Y	Y	N	N
100-0	Y	N		N	Y	Y	Y	Y	N	N
User defined	Y	N		N	Y	N	Y	Y	N	Y
Earned value calculations										
BCWP	Y	Y	Y	Y	Y	Y	Y	Y	Y	Y
BCWS	Y	Y	Y	Y	Y	Y	Y	Y	Y	Y
ACWP	Y	Y	Y	Y	Y	Y	Y	Y	Y	Y
Proposal pricing										
Top-down budgeting	Y	Y		N	N	Y	Y	Y	Y	N
Forecasting										
Forecasting (what if budget increases by 10 %; statistical methods)	Y	N		Y	Y	Y	N	Y	Y	N
Saves simultaneous forecasts	Y	N		Y	Y	Y	Y	Y	N	N
Budget management										
Rate build-up	Y	Y	Y	N	N	Y	Y	Y	Y	N
Customize budget elements	Y	Y	Y	N	N	Y	Y	Y	Y	N
Number of work packages in a cost account	999	Unlim.		Unlim.	Unlim.	Unlim.	Unlim.	Y	Unlim.	
Direct costs	Y	Y	Y	Y	Y	Y	Y	Y	Y	Y
Indirect costs	Y	Y	Y	Y	Y	Y	Y	Y	Y	N
Burden templates for indirect costs	N	N	N	N	N	Y	Y	Y	N	Y
Custom calculations	Y	Y	Y	Y	Y	N	Y	Y	Y	Y
Multiple Estimate-to-Complete calculations	Y	Y	Y	Y	Y	Y	Y	Y	N	N
Foreign currencies supported (list)	N	N	All	N	N	Supports foreign currency per PM tool, but no inoperability	All	Unlim.	Y-define a resource type corresponding to costs in that currency	Complete list is available at www.wproj.com
Reporting										
Aggregate costs over multiple projects	Y	Y	Y	Y	Y	Y	Y	Y	Y	Y
Cumulative reporting	Y	Y	Y	Y	Y	N	Y	Y	Y	Y

Fiscal calendars	Y	Y	Y	N	N	Y	Y	N	N
Irregular reporting calendars	Y	N		N	N	N	Y	N	Y	Y
Cash flow										
Periodic cost profile (cost during a time period)	Y	Y		Y	Y	Y	Y	Y	Y	N
By resource (summarize costs incurred by use of a resource)	Y	Y		N	N	Y	Y	Y	Y	Y
Cash flow reports	Y	Y		N	N	N	N	Y	N	N
Report writer	Y	Y		N	N	Y	Y	N	N	N
Report wizard	Y	Y		N	N	N	Y	N	N	Y
Publishes as HTML	N	Y		Y	Y	Y	Y	N	N	Y
Number of user-defined fields	20	20		Unlim.	Unlim.	60	Unlim.	Unlim.	Unlim.	Variable
Drill-down/roll-up *	Y	Y		Y	Y	Y	Y	Y	Y	Y
Import/export	Y	Y		Y	Y	Y	Y	Y	Y	Y
Automatic E-mail notification *	N	Y		N	N	N	N	Y	N	Y
Macro recorder/batch capable *A67	Y	N		Y	Y	Y	Y	Y	macro language but no recorder	Y
Can "canned" reports be modified?	Y	Y		N	N	Y	Y	Y	Y	Y
Sort, filter	Y	Y		Y	Y	Y	Y	Y	Y	Y
Architecture										
Databases supported (list):	ODBC	Btrieve		MS Access, Oracle, MS SQL Server	MS Access, Oracle, MS SQL Server	Oracle, MS Access, MS SQL Server, Sybase	Via ODBC: Oracle, Sybase, MS SQL Server, MS Access, et al.	MS Jet, MS SQL Server	N/A	Oracle, MS SQL Server, Informix, Sybase, any JDBC-compliant database
Supports distributed databases	N	N		N	N	Y	Y	Y	N	Y
Three-tier client/server	Y	N		N	N	Y	Y	Y	N	Y
Client operating systems	Win 95/98/NT	Win 95/NT/3.x		Win 95/98/NT	Win 95/98/NT	Win 95/98/NT	Win 95/98/NT4	Win 95/98/NT	Win 95/NT/3.x with Win 32s, Solaris	Win 95/NT, Unix, Linux, any Java-enabled database

Cost Management

	Plantrac-Coronet	Primavera Project Planner (P3) 2.0	Project Commander	Project Connect for OPP	Project Connect for wInsight	Project Control 6.0	Project Scheduler 7.6	Prolog Manager 5.0, Prolog Executive 1.0	QEI Exec	WebProject
Server operating systems	Win 95/98/NT			Any that support Win client	Any that support Win client	Unix, Win NT, HP, Sybase, others	N/A	Win NT	N/A	Win 95/NT, Unix, Linux, any Java-enabled database
Network operating systems	Win 95/98/NT	Most popular operating systems (e.g., Novell)		Any that support Win client	Any that support Win client	Novell, IPX, XPX, Banyan, MS Network, TCP/IP	Novell, Win NT	Any that support Win NT	LAN Manager, TCP/IP, Novell	Win 95/NT, Unix, Linux, any Java-enabled database
Minimum client configuration	8 MB	486, 32 MB RAM		Pentium, 16 MB RAM	Pentium, 16 MB RAM	PC 486/66 processor or above. Win 95 or Win NT V4. 16 MB RAM	486 or better, 16 MB memory, 15 MB HD		486, 16 MB RAM, mouse, XGA graphics	Java-enabled browser
Minimum server configuration	8 MB	Not specified		N/A	N/A	Any server supporting Oracle 7 or above	N/A		N/A	Win 95/NT, Unix, Linux, any Java-enabled database
Client runs under Web browser	N	N		N	N	Y	N	N	N	Y
Open architecture										
Supports OLE	N	Y		Y	Y	Y	Y	Y	N	N
Documented Object Model	N	Y		Y	Y	N	Y	Y	Y	N
Documented Application Programming Interface (API)	N	Y		Y	Y	N	Y	N	Y	Y
Simultaneous edit of data file	Y	Y		Y	Y	Y	Y	Y	N	Y
Does product have a programming language?	N	N		N	N	N	N	N	Y	N
Are years stored as four-digit numbers?	Y	N		Y	Y	Y	Y	Y	Y	N
Online help										
Right mouse click	Y	Y	Y	Y	Y	N	Y	Y	N	N
Hover buttons	Y	Y	Y	Y	N	Y	N	N	Y	Y
Interactive help	Y	Y	Y	Y	Y	N	Y	Y	Y	Y

Help search feature	Y	Y	Y	Y	Y	Y	Y	Y
Web access to product knowledge base *	N	Y	N	N	N	N	N	N
Vendor information								
Training								
Computer-based training	Y	N	Y	N	N	N	Y	N
Training materials available	N	Y	Y	Y	Y	Y	Y	Y
Customized training materials	Y	Y	Y	Y	Y	Y	Y	Y
Online tutorial	Y	Y	Y	Y	Y	Y	Y	Y
Consulting available from vendor	Y	Y	Y	Y	Y	Y	Y	Y
Site license discounts	Y	Y	Y	Y	Y	Y	Y	Y
Enhancement requests *	Y	Y	Y	Y	Y	Y	Y	Y
Modify source code, support through upgrades *	Y	N	Y	Y	Y	Y	N	Y
Global presence								
Global offices	N	Y	N	Y	Y	Y	N	Y
Multilingual technical support	N	N	N	N	N	N	N	N
Language versions (list):	Eng	Eng	Eng	Eng	Eng, Fr, Ger, Jpn	User definable via dictionaries	Eng	Eng, Ger
Audit Software Quality Assurance process? *	Y	N	N	Y	N	Y	N	Y
Security								
Configurable access privileges *	N	Y	N	Y	Y	Y	Y	Y
Passwords expire (forced update)	N	N	N	N	N	Y	N	Y
Electronic approvals	N	N	N	Y	N	Y	N	Y
Password protect files	N	Y	N	Y	Y	Y	Y	Y

VENDOR RESPONSES TO NARRATIVE QUESTIONS

AMS REALTIME Projects (Advanced Management Systems)

Describe what the product is designed to do.

AMS REALTIME Projects fully integrates schedule, resource assignments, and costs. BCWS, BCWP, ACWP, and ETC are calculated and maintained, based on cost bins from an accounting calendar. Cost rules are strictly followed. Costs and earned value are visible in real time as resources enter actual hours and estimates onto their timesheets. Approved hours update the project and feed earned value calculations.

Cost can be calculated from resource usage (baselined, planned, and actual) or loaded from external systems. Elements of cost can be defined to breakdown-activity costs to different components, such as labor, material, or ODC. Rate tables, burden-rate formulas, and calculation overrides can customize cost results.

Actual burdened costs can be loaded at a summary level, while other costs can be calculated from resource usage and burdened within projects. Variance reporting and other cost fields can provide a direct visual assessment of real-time project costs.

Top three product differentiators; describe what makes your product unique.

1. Fully integrated schedule, resource, and cost provide an accurate look at one or more projects from any perspective in real time. Costs can be calculated from the baselined and current project, or can also be loaded from external systems.

2. Elements of cost provide user-defined cost breakdowns (labor, materials, ODC) using rate tables, burden formulas, calculation overrides, and resource categories. Cost centers can also be used to determine cost breakdowns, or a combination of cost center and resource category.

3. All software runs native on Windows (95, NT, 3.x), Macintosh, Sun, Solaris, HP, RS with identical look and feel, and direct data access from any platform.

To what business processes can this tool be applied?

AMS REALTIME is so flexible that it can be applied to virtually any business process, including proposals, estimates, operations, new development, manufacturing, and performance improvement processes.

AMS REALTIME is designed to allow automated project statusing that automatically feeds earned value performance measurements. Cost management is empowered when costs can be tracked from a project-summary level all the way down to the activity level; providing accurate information to pinpoint the source of cost overruns.

Describe the ideal end-user environment for the current version of your product (size of organization, level of project management sophistication, effort and commitment required).

AMS REALTIME is used by global companies in very large enterprise environments all the way down to small companies with just a few people. While AMS REALTIME is used to support extremely sophisticated project management processes, it can still be used to benefit users with little or no project management background. Users can grow into the software as their project management expertise evolves.

To make any project management implementation successful, senior management must be committed to supporting the process, and other participants must make the effort to be trained to use the tools and follow through. Working with a consultant to help adapt the software to your business practices and needs and to document these processes is the best way to ensure success.

Future strategies for this product.

Future development strategies include more active Web enablements, a more complex three-tiered server design to facilitate global replication, and more resource tools. AMS has always been on the cutting edge of technology, and we are dedicated to bringing our customers the best of this ever-changing world.

Product's target market.

Products are used across a wide variety of client bases. AMS does not target any particular market, but is widely used in manufacturing, banking, oil and gas, nuclear power, automotive, pharmaceutical, aerospace, software development, construction, research and development, and many other industries.

What are your product's three main benefits? (How does using the product add value to the customer?)

1. Accurate, up-to-date project schedule and cost problems can be identified immediately, allowing maximum time for proactive measures to eliminate problems.

2. All work assignments are instantly communicated to employees, who also have a medium to effectively communicate work performed, status, and other issues.

3. Selective automation allows managers to eliminate drudgery and inaccuracy, while still maintaining control over critical project and resource decisions.

Describe your quality management process. List any relevant certifications.

Advanced Management Solutions is fully committed to providing the highest-quality software and services to all our clients. We have implemented many internal standards and processes in order to ensure that we can track and manage our software development process to the highest standard of quality possible.

Concurrent versions system has been implemented to help manage multiple programmers at multiple development sites. Peer review of source code and design strategy meetings with high-level program development leaders continue to ensure that our software remains on the leading edge of our evolving technology.

A dedicated testing department manages the initial alpha testing, which encompasses new functionality, system process testing, and full regression testing. Beta testing is initially performed internally. After a stable point has been reached, beta testing is extended to select client users. Client beta testing not only provides clients with an edge in using new software features, but also greatly expands the test environment scope relating to different hardware environments. As AMS REALTIME is one of the most flexible and highly configurable management products on the market today, client testing adds an exceptional dimension to our testing process.

Discuss your product pricing structure. Include volume discount levels, concurrent user options, site licenses, cost of implementation, and other issues.

Product price is different for clients, based on their requirements for software and implementation. Volume discounts and site licenses are available. Please request a quote from an AMS sales representative for your specific requirements.

Cost of implementation: Annual maintenance is based on 20 percent of the current product cost, and includes all software upgrades (while support is active) and telephone hotline technical support. Training cost is based upon topics, requirements, training equipment and site, and days requested. Please request a quote from an AMS sales representative for your specific requirements.

Artemis CostView

Describe what the product is designed to do.

Artemis CostView is one part of a fully integrated set of project planning, cost control, activity tracking, and project analysis applications. Based on a scalable client/server design, Views offers a unique *role-based* approach to project management. Designed for program managers, financial managers, cost account managers, and cost controllers, CostView provides complete project, contract, or financial management, analysis, and reporting.

Top three product differentiators; describe what makes your product unique.

1. CostView was designed for enterprise-level application in an organization; as a result, all elements of the product's design are incorporated to support this notion including all processes, analysis, reporting, security, integration with ERP vendors.

2. Common data elements shared with Artemis' ProjectView provides a tightly integrated cost and schedule system for analyzing time, resource, and cost data at the task level up to the enterprise level.

3. CostView's easy-to-use tab-orientated user interface allows users to concentrate on areas of the system relevant to their roles in an organization. Coupled with the security system that allows for role definition, CostView provides a very flexible implementation program.

To what business processes can this tool be applied?

Project/multiproject cost analysis with easy-to-use color coding provides users of the system simple access to the budgets, actual costs, earned values, revenues, cost of sales, profits, etc., at detailed levels or summarized levels, enabling better overall cost management.

Cost plan approval cycles (e.g., budget approvals) through use of proposed cost plan versus approved cost plans. User can propose any number of cost plans, but, based on responsibility and ownership of data, the proposed plans stay in a proposed state until formally finalized.

Project/multiproject *what-if* modeling scenarios through use of CostView's extensive cost plan/rating processes allow a user to model several different scenarios priced accordingly and compare them to each other.

Describe the ideal end-user environment for the current version of your product (size of organization, level of project management sophistication, effort and commitment required).

Medium- to large-sized organizations that require multiple users with concurrent access to the database and application.

User should have some project management knowledge; however, with the role-based configuration of a user's desktop, the application supports the novice levels to the sophisticated levels of project management knowledge.

CostView helps an organization enforce data consistency and standardizes business rules within an organization requiring a level commitment to the application and the project management process by the user.

Future strategies for this product.

Artemis is committed to continually enhancing our product's functionality and applicability to meet or exceed the demands of project management professionals.

Product's target market.

Program managers, cost controllers, financial controllers, and project cost accountants in businesses across multiple vertical markets and lines of business.

What are your product's three main benefits? (How does using the product add value to the customer?)

1. Provides management with accurate cost information integrated with scheduling information in order to make informed decisions about the business today, as well as the future of the business.

2. Enterprise-level architecture and processing capabilities allow users to process data for the entire business in short periods of time.

3. Role-based philosophy of the application allows various users of the system from task managers to executive-level managers to obtain value from the application.

Describe your quality management process. List any relevant certifications.

Internal software audits and reporting procedures. Formal Year 2000 testing and compliance process.

Discuss your product pricing structure. Include volume discount levels, concurrent user options, site licenses, cost of implementation, and other issues.

Artemis Views can be purchased and deployed as a fully integrated suite or as a series of independent applications.

Available as registered user and concurrent pricing. Volume discounts and site licenses are available.

Cost of implementation (training, tech support, annual maintenance, etc.) varies.

AutoPLAN Enterprise (Digital Tools)

AutoPLAN Enterprise Release 4 is a Web-based software and process solution to help high-tech, engineering, and telecommunications companies predict, control, and improve cycle time of critical program development and deployment. The solution set provides deep functionality across the entire spectrum of product life-cycle elements including pipeline management, project management, resource alignment, process effectiveness, and document support and team collaboration. AutoPLAN Enterprise integrates realistic planning, resource-centric management, status and forecast tracking, team collaboration, process support, escalation management, and program execution across globally distributed organizations.

Organizations are evolving from functional teams to matrix or program teams, and this is creating cross-functional or multidisciplinary project teams. AutoPLAN Enterprise recognizes three different organizational patterns that coexist: dynamic peer-to-peer, functional, and program management. AutoPLAN Enterprise offers these organizations both project-centric and resource-centric management. AutoPLAN Enterprise addresses everyone involved in product development and deployment including executives; program, product, resource, and project managers; and team leaders and team members, as well as teams from marketing, operations, service, and quality.

As a result of extensive process and product consulting with clients engaged in new product development and deployment, DTI has distilled four key reasons why products are late and descoped:

1. Product development pipeline and deployment structures that are not aligned with the company's time-to-market goals.

2. Unrealistic plans, overcommitted resources, and unmanaged cross-functional dependencies.

3. Status and forecast decisions that are based on hearsay, rather than on facts or experience.

4. A lack of consistent processes that fit the company culture and practice, which is further exacerbated by distributed cross-functional teams.

Avoiding late and descoped products requires an overall view of product and project status, the involvement of cross-functional teams, and decision evaluation tools. Increasingly accelerated product development cycles and shorter product life cycles require organizations to disseminate information quickly to remain competitive. To support today's geographically dispersed product development environments, organizations require a common platform that enables effective cross-functional collaboration and communication on product development issues. It is also imperative that the introduction of new product information can be easily accessible by each stakeholder. Common platforms and accessible information by each stakeholder will result in accelerated organizational learning and decision-making within the organization.

DTI has created a cycle time management (CTM) framework comprising both application and process support. This framework emphasizes the critical components involved in introducing and deploying the right products and services to the market at the right time. Introducing and deploying these products and services requires companies to institute well-defined new product planning and execution processes, complemented with customer management and performance measurement processes. The new planning processes should consist of product portfolio, technology portfolio, product planning, and resource planning. The execution processes must consist of advanced technology development, platform development, product development, market introduction and deployment.

CTM enables companies to strike a balance between flexibility and discipline that is tailored to their organization and culture. The CTM framework supports a flexible *shrink-to-fit* process, which is adaptable to an organization's process maturity. This process will provide a road map for decision-making and progress tracking within a new product introduction and deployment pipeline.

CTM consists of six fundamental elements: 1) processes, 2) projects, 3) resources, 4) documents, 5) deliverables, and 6) analysis. These six elements form the foundation objectives that drive AutoPLAN Enterprise. Organizations require a well-defined and structured process to accomplish their goals. Projects make up the mechanisms through which detailed plans and schedules are generated, executed, and tracked. Every organization faces resource constraints; thus, resource management is a critical component of CTM. All projects have deliverables associated with them either in the form of documents or the product itself. And, all projects must be managed to ensure quality deliverables. Analysis tools enable various levels of stakeholders to evaluate and ensure proper support of all elements necessary to meet CTM objectives.

Top three product differentiators; describe what makes your product unique.

1. AutoPLAN Enterprise enables organizations to manage their pipeline of resources across programs and across the phase gates of each project. It assures an escalation process for critical issues, such as overallocations, by monitoring boundary conditions and alerting appropriate people to the issues. Project managers are interested in the completion of tasks or milestones, while resource managers need to know all of the work planned for their resources. Both project and resource managers must collaborate to create realistic plans for meeting project objectives, as well as juggle those resources and plans on a day-to-day basis as changes occur. The nature of this work requires a resource-centric view of the plan, not just an activity-centric view. A resource-centric view will allow resource managers to view and allocate activities to their scarce resources, rather than allocating resources to their activities. AutoPLAN Enterprise enables resource management by providing a resource-centric Gantt bar that displays overallocated resources. Managing overallocations can be as easy as reassigning activities to another resource.

Program management is a collaborative effort. Success depends upon identifying and communicating critical issues. Such identification and communication must be inherent in the system. AutoPLAN Enterprise is designed with a communications backbone. A mechanism of triggers identifies critical issues (e.g., when milestone or cost exceeds a threshold boundary) and automatically alerts and draws attention to these critical issues. Project bulletin boards within AutoPLAN Enterprise also enhance communication by providing a context-sensitive vehicle for communicating information across the project team. In addition, AutoPLAN Enterprise supports electronic mail systems, enabling triggers and bulletin board messages to be communicated to the various levels of stakeholders.

2. AutoPLAN Enterprise supports the distributed nature of project teams by matching real-world strategy with key scalable technologies. Enterprise customers need distributed project management capabilities that cater to multisite resource management, work distribution, progress tracking, global scheduling, consolidation, reporting, integration, and collaboration. DTI has met

this challenge by investing over one hundred man-years in an enterprise-level, three-tier, distributed client/server architecture that leverages both Java and Internet technologies. AutoPLAN Enterprise provides full support for multiple internal operating divisions and external suppliers. AutoPLAN Enterprise leverages many platforms—Internet, Windows, NT, and Unix—providing reliable access across the organization. Additionally, AutoPLAN Enterprise enables common project data to be shared by different projects at different locations while being maintained in a central data center that is managed by pool server software. Project data is maintained at each geographic location on either individual or multiple servers, depending on the number of internal operating divisions and projects. A divisional pool server can also be implemented to share the project data within divisional projects. AutoPLAN Enterprise application servers are capable of scalable distributed processing, and only the server needs the capacity for large multiproject operations. AutoPLAN Enterprise has multiserver cross-project dependency links. For example, the owner of a schedule that depends on the completion of activities in another project can create cross-project links that automatically update his schedule when changes occur in the other project, even if that project resides on a different server.

3. AutoPLAN Enterprise leverages client/server/Web technologies. The promise of Java, which AutoPLAN Enterprise supports, is that enterprise deployments, including organizations with heterogeneous environments, can be cost-effectively supported. DTI Web products are easier to use than Microsoft Project and are cheaper to deploy. The rapid spread of Internet protocols and Web servers into corporate infrastructure make the Internet an ideal vehicle to support both enterprise computing and mobile employees. In addition, systems administration is simplified since no maintenance is required on the client side.

A very practical use of AutoPLAN Enterprise Web clients is that they can run in a disconnected mode on the Internet. With AutoPLAN Enterprise, the user can simply log on and save activities and other information to a local file. She can then continue to work while disconnected. At any time, the connection can be reestablished, either remotely or locally, and the data is resynchronized. This may be useful for dial-up connections when working remotely. The Web server handles all communications with the Web clients, whether they are communicating via the Internet, dial-up, LAN, or WAN. The AutoPLAN Enterprise Web clients can be run from any browser that supports Java 1.1, and the Web server will dynamically download the Java code to run the application on the client. DTI's Web strategy supports *thin* client computing. In this case, database-oriented servers are serving lightweight clients through Web servers and standard protocols. The AutoPLAN Enterprise Web clients are ideally suited for running on a Java-based network computer.

To what business processes can this tool be applied?

From business analysis and redesign to system implementation and training, DTI has established its own process to support the customer through all phases of CTM system implementation. However, as to applying AutoPLAN Enterprise to the customer's business processes, DTI takes a very pragmatic approach. DTI has established processes to help customers with the following seven business pains:

1. Managing the development and deployment pipeline in detail.

2. Top-down and bottom-up planning that enables managers to use team members' knowledge during up-front planning.

3. Juggling resources realistically, so that resources are not overcommitted and parochial allocations are not made, but rather a mechanism for cooperation on resource tradeoffs is created.

4. Creating an organizational memory that captures organizational experience for reuse the next time.

5. Obtaining weekly integrated tracking information on how programs are progressing against their plans. This can be achieved by capturing actual time spent, estimates-to-complete, percent complete, and actual start and finish.

6. Problem identification, escalation, and collaboration that allows management and the team to receive adequate notice of impending issues.

7. Interactive decision evaluation to understand the domino effect of a problem in one project and its possible cross-program impact, and obtain a swift resolution between participants.

Any combination of these processes will help organizations better understand and make use of critical path methodology, work breakdown structures, resource management, cost and earned value techniques, multiproject resource scheduling, resource allocation, status tracking, report generation, matrix management solutions, integration with other systems, middleware design, project management process design, project rollups, report generation, database design, customized product training courses, generic project management training, and more.

Describe the ideal end-user environment for the current version of your product (size of organization, level of project management sophistication, effort and commitment required).

AutoPLAN Enterprise is ideal for high-tech, engineering, and telecommunications organizations engaged in distributed product development and deployments. Its usage also extends to these organizations' distributors and partners. The role-based nature of AutoPLAN Enterprise spans all people involved, from executive management to the entire cross-functional product team. This includes experienced project and program managers, resource and development managers, and the team members creating or deploying the product. The AutoPLAN Enterprise Web client is specifically designed for those team leaders who are not full-time, experienced project managers. In fact, DTI has designed the AutoPLAN Enterprise Web client to be easier to use and more functional than Microsoft Project.

Organizations can start at either the program level right away and manage the overall pipeline of projects and resources at the business unit level, or at the individual project level. The AutoPLAN Enterprise Web client is not only easier to use than Microsoft Project, but is also capable of managing cross-functional dependencies and resources and offering enterprise scalability when the organization is ready to expand.

Coordinating distributed projects is a difficult task. It involves resources not only from multiple projects, but also from multiple functions within those projects. The program manager responsible must understand all of the interactions and milestones required to complete the project, but he cannot and should not develop and manage the entire plan himself. Instead, he should rely on the distributed functional leaders who are responsible for their piece of the project to plan and execute that piece. As a program manager, he needs to be able to integrate the individual team plans into a single comprehensive project plan. In many organizations, this integration of people and data is difficult; AutoPLAN Enterprise is designed to help with this. Having processes in place, underpinned by enterprise software, is key to predicting, controlling, and improving product/project cycle times.

Future strategies for this product.

AutoPLAN Enterprise has been designed with an integrated product management platform for all information related to meeting CTM objectives. DTI will continue to support features needed for CTM, including pipeline and portfolio management. Future strategies will enhance the ability of customers to make informed decisions based on a comprehensive presentation of relevant data with powerful drill-down capabilities, further collaborative features that utilize the intranet and Internet, and continuing support for the free-flowing nature of the engineering culture. Application wizards will help first-time users, accelerate deployment, and reduce training cost. Process support is key to productivity improvements and to adhering to organizationwide standards. Existing process-support capabilities will be enhanced using the capabilities of Web technology and with more exchange of information across subsystems. Large organizations are geographically distributed to take advantage of global efficiencies. Local and global workgroups must collaborate and respond quickly to changing environment and work content. Both executive management and front-line team members must have access anytime, anywhere, and in any manner to enterprisewide product/project information located on geographically distributed servers. Existing multiserver capabilities of AutoPLAN Enterprise are being enhanced using Oracle.

AutoPLAN Enterprise will support key technologies including Oracle, NT 5.0, middleware, and Java. Distributed objects capability using industry-standard specifications such as CORBA will be incorporated. In addition, the AutoPLAN Enterprise application-programming interface will provide CORBA-compliant objects for seamless integration with other applications. The collaboration capabilities of AutoPLAN Enterprise will be enhanced by incorporating a workflow server. This workflow server will be based on industry-standard specifications and will incorporate process modeling and messaging components to enable customers to configure the collaboration features based upon their business needs. The security system will have additional features to address the security risks associated with the Internet. Directory servers conforming to LDAP standards will be incorporated for seamless integration with the underlying operating environment. This in turn will provide responsive security, configurability, and flexibility features.

Product's target market.

AutoPLAN Enterprise is specifically designed to support high-tech, engineering, and telecommunications organizations in predicting, controlling, and improving cycle time of critical program development and deployment.

What are your product's three main benefits? (How does using the product add value to the customer?)

1. AutoPLAN Enterprise provides at least a 10 percent improvement in enterprise time-to-market of product development and deployment. Viewing the value of CTM from an annual R&D cost perspective: consider a product development group of one thousand people, with an annual R&D expenditure of $100M. A modest ten percent improvement would represent a cost savings value of $10M, with a revenue enhancement value of three to five times this.

2. AutoPLAN Enterprise facilitates an organization's transformation from functional project teams to matrix, or program-organized high-performance project teams. It also supports distributed teams resulting from acquisitions. It does both of these by providing built-in communication and rollup features from distributed multiserver projects. This support enables teamwide problem identification, escalation, collaboration, and resolution. AutoPLAN Enterprise recognizes that three different organizational patterns coexist: 1) dynamic peer-to-peer, 2) functional, and 3) program management. AutoPLAN Enterprise offers these organizations both project-centric and resource-centric management.

3. AutoPLAN Enterprise accommodates joint ventures, subcontracting, mergers and acquisitions, and reorganizations by leveraging the Web to minimize deployment and support costs. The creation of plans, assignment of work, and integration of activities across multiple functions and distributed work teams is critically important. However, that is only part of the story. With the Internet, AutoPLAN Enterprise can also efficiently equip thousands of personnel involved in the product-development process with the information they need to do the best possible job. Demand for skilled workers has been great, and turnover has risen as employees move from one company or job to another. The best practices in the world are of no value to a company if those who know those practices move on without first passing along the knowledge. Best practices developed at one site need to be shared with other sites, and a process for doing that is required. AutoPLAN Enterprise solves these problems through URL references and retrieval capability. With URL features, AutoPLAN Enterprise can help preserve best practices and other information and disseminate them geographically and functionally to team members currently doing the job. AutoPLAN Enterprise can also have associated URL references that point to mission-critical information/documentation that will enable product/project teams to achieve the activity. These references can also be attached to the top-level program schedule for project leader use, or at specific functional schedules (e.g., to provide sourcing with specific third-party vendor requirements). URLs can enable:

- Sharing best practice information from one team to another
- Referencing documentation with checklists
- Sharing engineering notes on installation processes.

Also, with the speed of organizational changes, a mix of project-scheduling system usage is expected. As most people are educated on Microsoft Project, AutoPLAN Enterprise can coexist with its projects and data. AutoPLAN Enterprise's graphical user interfaces are not only familiar to Microsoft Project users, the Web version is easier and thus leverages simplicity and ease of use with enterprise functionality.

217

Describe your quality management process. List any relevant certifications.

DTI achieves excellence in product quality and customer satisfaction through its quality management process. DTI's quality objective is to build quality into its products and services at all stages of product life cycle from requirement collection to customer usage. DTI's dedication to quality is reflected in its quality mission: "Doing things right the first time."

DTI's quality management group performs the functions of the software engineering process group as defined by the industry-standard capability maturity model (CMM). The quality management group plans and implements DTI's quality system, which consists of processes and guidelines. The processes detail out *what* is required for converting a set of inputs to outputs in the form of activities and tasks, primary and cooperative responsibilities, deliverables, and entry and exit criteria. The guidelines detail *how* to carry out the identified activities to ensure quality and consistency. The involvement of DTI personnel at all levels is fundamental to the implementation of the quality process. DTI personnel are drawn from various groups in the organization to author processes and guidelines, and all undergo training programs on the quality system.

DTI follows processes within Level 2 and Level 3 of the CMM. Some of the key processes within these levels include market requirement analysis, functional specification, high- and low-level design, coding, testing, release management, customer support, training, and maintenance. In addition, in-depth reviews are built into each of these processes.

DTI recognizes that enterprise growth and profitability are significantly impacted by time-to-market of new products in globally competitive high-tech markets. With this in mind, DTI's product development and quality processes are focused on meeting customer needs and requirements. Therefore, DTI collaborates with its customers both in product definition and in assuring that the product functions are implemented as intended. To facilitate the fast-track delivery of innovative products and services, DTI has created process initiatives for increased test automation, usage of tools that will enable teams to better assess the quality of their work products, management of development tools, reuse of objects across products, and tightly controlled configuration management.

DTI's quality management process focuses on periodic reviews and feedback, which are a means of monitoring the adherence of organizational activities to the process. Corrective and preventive actions play an important role in continuous improvement of the quality system and thereby the organizational activities.

DTI has a well-qualified team for quality management. DTI's teams, besides having the appropriate educational qualifications, have quality management-related certifications; some are certified quality analysts, and some hold certificates related to the CMM and its use. Many also have extensive internal audit experience.

The quality management group interacts periodically with key personnel of different functions within the organization and identifies new processes, guidelines, and improvements within the existing framework. The general approach to new process/guideline introduction is to discuss with representative users, define the process, pilot the process after review, evaluate the pilot implementation, revise the process based on feedback, plan organizationwide implementation, implement, measure, and maintain.

DTI is planning to get CMM certification at the appropriate level. The approach that would be followed for securing the certification includes mapping key process areas of the CMM to existing processes, identifying the *gaps*, preparing the implementation plan that describes how these gaps will be addressed, and executing the plan.

Discuss your product pricing structure. Include volume discount levels, concurrent user options, site licenses, cost of implementation, and other issues.

DTI's objective is to offer an integrated solution with a pricing structure that is based on enterprise requirements reflecting enterprise needs and individual needs. AutoPLAN Enterprise supports a floating license configuration, which allows any user to log into the system and consume one license. When the user has finished with the application, that license will be released for other users. Each floating license provides one concurrent use of the product. AutoPLAN Enterprise also supports a personal license configuration. Typical installations will use both personal and concurrent licensing.

Annual product maintenance is 15 percent of the list cost. Product maintenance entitles customers to engineering patches, updates, and upgrades, and phone, fax, and E-mail response to issues. Professional services are separate from DTI product maintenance. As part of the business relationship with customers, DTI takes part in joint planning to identify the customer's business needs and services sought from DTI. Professional services are charged separately on an as-needed basis. These services are performed either at the customer site, online, or at DTI's headquarters in Cupertino, California. Professional services typically fall into two categories: 1) product consulting/implementation design review and 2) implementation support. Product consulting/implementation design review discusses areas such as, "How do I apply the software with a suitable process to solve a business need?" and, "Which processes will we implement, how, and when to meet organizational objectives?" Implementation support consists of product training, project office services, upgrade migration services, systems administration services, and integration services.

Cascade PgM (Mantix)

Describe what the product is designed to do.

Cascade PgM from Mantix is a client-server program management product for use with Microsoft Project, aimed specifically at the facilities required by senior management and program managers. With a standard MS Windows user interface it presents a multiuser, enterprisewide cost, schedule, and resource management system, with powerful management reporting facilities. Cascade PgM uses the proven, structured data model of work, responsibility, and cost breakdown to provide a complete view of the business. The benefits to the business associated with each project can also be modeled.

Cascade is integrated on existing user sites with Oracle Financials, SAP, Peoplesoft, Glovia, Baan, Triton, and many other systems. This integration with the ERP systems provides the whole picture of all the activities in the business: where the cost is going, what the people are doing, and what results will be delivered, by when.

The combination of Cascade PgM and Microsoft Project provides a powerful corporate project-planning system. Cascade PgM provides the top-down information used to provide guidelines for managers working at a more detailed level. Working within these guidelines, users can go on to develop detailed schedules, cost, and resource plans. Cascade PgM supports the concept of resource ownership and the delegation of resources down through the project, with complete visibility and tracking of where they are being used. In many cases, this includes use of the Web-based Cascade Time Recording functionality.

Top three product differentiators; describe what makes your product unique.

Cascade PgM is unique in its functionality for business control of the project-oriented organization through top-down delegation of targets and bottom-up measurement of performance. It offers a clear functional advantage in terms of:

1. Turns decisions into action, by enabling the creation of outline plans with budget, staff, and time scales to be delegated for detailed planning.

2. The structured data model is built interactively as graphical tree structures, rather than with the conventional alpha numeric coding, making the operation intuitive and changes to the plan simple and quick.

3. The program manager establishes the overall structure of the program, typically based on business drivers or internal/customer reporting. Links to the program from projects may be easily created or deleted allowing fast *what-if* analysis.

To what business processes can this tool be applied?

For lean organizations in fast-moving markets, good management is increasingly about setting goals and assembling the team to deliver them. Cascade PgM provides the tool to define a portfolio of projects to deliver strategic goals and then monitor the performance against these objectives. Cascade PgM backs up the implementation of effective management processes with the timely, consistent, and accurate provision of program and project information.

Describe the ideal end-user environment for the current version of your product (size of organization, level of project management sophistication, effort and commitment required).

The concepts behind Cascade PgM and the software architecture are completely scaleable. Any size of organization with a multiproject environment would benefit from Cascade PgM, irrespective of the level of project management sophistication. The effort and commitment required to implement Cascade PgM depends on the customer's requirements for the system and the existing business processes. Typically, Cascade PgM is quick to implement; this is due in part to its use of MS Project, which is already present in most organizations. MS Project is transformed to become a key element of a business control system.

Future strategies for this product.

Mantix Systems will continue to develop Cascade PgM to ensure that it remains a world-leading program management solution.

Product's target market.

As a leading program management solution's provider, Mantix Systems has a proven track record with some of the world's leading organizations in fifteen countries. This is in markets that include telecommunications, IT, utilities, government, pharmaceuticals, aerospace, and defense.

What are your product's three main benefits? (How does using the product add value to the customer?)

Cascade PgM brings structure, visibility, and control to the management of both individual projects and multiproject programs. This allows a customer to focus investment and staff time on the business activities that will add most value, and manage them to deliver increased revenue, profit, and return on investment.

Describe your quality management process. List any relevant certifications.

The quality management process within Mantix Systems is accredited by and conforms to ISO 9000.

Discuss your product pricing structure. Include volume discount levels, concurrent user options, site licenses, cost of implementation, and other issues.

The price of Cascade PgM depends on the type of functionality required and the number of users. Please contact Mantix Systems for details that are specific to your requirements.

Cobra

Describe what the product is designed to do.

Cobra is a powerful and comprehensive system designed to manage and analyze budget, earned value, actual, and forecasts. Cobra helps you meet the exacting standards of your organization, as well as the rigorous earned value management system (EVMS) required by the United States government. Cobra is flexible enough to be used effectively in any situation where the earned value approach to project management is to be implemented.

Top three product differentiators; describe what makes your product unique.

1. Cost and schedule integration: Combined with Open Plan or other scheduling tools, Cobra provides a truly integrated cost and schedule management solution at any phase of the project life cycle.

2. What-if scenarios: Create multiple budgets, each with different rates, for *what-if* analyses. Track actual, committed, and accrued expenses. Create an unlimited number of forecasts per project to estimate the final project cost with confidence.

3. Reporting: Cobra reporting is extremely powerful. It is designed to help you build custom reports using step-by-step reporting wizards. Report generation produces familiar Excel-style spreadsheets.

To what business processes can this tool be applied?

Cobra can be applied to project management, earned value management, cost management, proposal pricing, cash-flow management, strategic planning, budgeting, and cost estimating.

Describe the ideal end-user environment for the current version of your product (size of organization, level of project management sophistication, effort and commitment required).

Cobra is flexible enough to be used effectively in any situation where the earned value approach to project management is to be implemented. The earned value approach is typically used on large projects, projects with high risk, or projects involving subcontractors.

Future strategies for this product.

Our vision for the future is to provide a suite of component-based products that work together to provide advanced project management functionality using the very latest technology.

Continue to support and expand into the world of EVMS within organizations. Increase ERP integration. Continue expanding database capabilities.

Product's target market.

Cobra's target market is government contractors, prime contractors, companies who deal with large projects, and contractors who require multiple currencies.

What are your product's three main benefits? (How does using the product add value to the customer?)

The strength in Cobra lies in its ability to handle diverse cost management needs for commercial enterprises and government contractors—proposal pricing, cash flow management, strategic planning, and earned value management. Cobra combines unmatched flexibility, functionality, and usability to meet even the most exacting cost management challenges.

Describe your quality management process. List any relevant certifications.

Adhere to standard industry processes in release and version strategies, including automated regression testing.

ISO 9000 certified in the United Kingdom.

Discuss your product pricing structure. Include volume discount levels, concurrent user options, site licenses, cost of implementation, and other issues.

Please call for pricing information.

Tech support: No charge with current maintenance.

Maintenance: First year free with software purchase; renewed annually.

Corporate Controller

Describe what the product is designed to do.

The Corporate Controller module is the key foundation module of monitor's integrated work management system, Enterprise Controller. It provides integrated budget planning, project costing, reporting, and scheduling. As actual costs are applied to the individual projects through the entry of timesheet, procurement, and subcontractor information, the system monitors the performance of actual against planned.

Costs can be applied at any level of the projects, from job cards to corporate plans, and the hierarchical structure allows these costs to be rolled up and down to provide visibility at all levels.

Top three product differentiators; describe what makes your product unique.

1. Integration with business processes such as time writing, purchasing, and billing, which influence project costs.
2. Interface to corporate account systems to ensure single view of project and business cost information.
3. Flexible user-defined report options.

To what business processes can this tool be applied?

Project budgeting and costing, exception reporting, planned versus actual monitoring.

Describe the ideal end-user environment for the current version of your product (size of organization, level of project management sophistication, effort and commitment required).

Medium to large project-based organizations with a need for an integrated work-management system, which will control all aspects of the project, including budgeting, costing, planning, resourcing, and scheduling.

Future strategies for this product.

Enhanced functionality in the areas of report generation, E-mailing of reports, and Web processing. Currently evaluating Microsoft's Sequel Server as a database option.

Product's target market.

Oil and gas, defense, rail transport, civil engineering, utilities, and shipbuilding.

What are your product's three main benefits? (How does using the product add value to the customer?)

1. Integrates the project planning and costing processes.
2. Allows costs to be entered against all levels of the project, from job cards to corporate plans.
3. Rolls costs up and down through the project hierarchy to provide visibility of the costs at all levels.

Describe your quality management process. List any relevant certifications.

We have internal auditable quality procedures in place, which are equivalent to ISO 9000 standards. Accredited Investors in People.

Discuss your product pricing structure. Include volume discount levels, concurrent user options, site licenses, cost of implementation, and other issues.

System is priced per number of concurrent users for each module.
Discounts available for volume and multisite implementations.
Full pricing available on application.
Annual maintenance: Fifteen percent of license costs.
Cost of professional services available on request.

CostLink Project Controller

Describe what the product is designed to do.

CostLink is a comprehensive project cost management system. It provides decision support for all project phases. An advanced multiproject package, it is linked with P3, MS Project, Oracle Financials and other ERP systems to create a truly integrated project management environment.

CostLink supports budgeting, forecasting, escalation, contingency, progress payment certification, fiscal reporting, S-curve graphing, cash-flow projections, multiple currency handling, and full project accounting.

Top three product differentiators; describe what makes your product unique.

1. Based on a proven, documented project cost control methodology.
2. Supports bi-directional linkages with project scheduling and ERP software.
3. Supports international projects with multicurrency and multilingual features.

To what business processes can this tool be applied?

Project fiscal budgeting; project progress measurement and reforecasting; contract administration and project accounting.

Describe the ideal end-user environment for the current version of your product (size of organization, level of project management sophistication, effort and commitment required).

The user environment typically consists of owner organizations that manage their own projects. These organizations often have their own technical staff of engineers and designers. They usually have extensive project management expertise.

Future strategies for this product.

Application functionality: integrated workflow management.
Application functionality: support for evolving international project management standards.
System architecture: move toward DCOM model.

Product's target market.

The market targeted by CostLink is comprised primarily of medium to large public or private organizations that manage their own projects. Many are in the power generation and distribution business. Others are in the transportation, construction or related sectors.

What are your product's three main benefits? (How does using the product add value to the customer?)

1. Reduce omissions by applying a proven project cost management methodology.
2. Reduce dependency on disparate systems and improve reporting consistency due to a centralized data repository.
3. Eliminate duplicate data entry through direct integration with scheduling and ERP systems.

Describe your quality management process. List any relevant certifications.

Multiphased methodology based on Optiplan's 14-year software development experience. Software quality is monitored through a combination of automated tools and external usability testing. Optiplan participates in national and international software quality associations.

Discuss your product pricing structure. Include volume discount levels, concurrent user options, site licenses, cost of implementation, and other issues.

CostLink licensing is based on a concurrent usage model. Volume discounts and site licenses are available.

The cost of implementation includes on-site user training, support hotline and possible application enhancements.

Software subscription and support services range from 20 percent to 25 percent of the software license costs.

Dekker TRAKKER Advanced Costing

Describe what the product is designed to do.

Advanced Costing implements earned value techniques to monitor project progress in terms of cost, schedule, and resources. TRAKKER Advanced Costing's seamless integration allows full compatibility of data within all TRAKKER modules. Advanced Costing offers a powerful, user-friendly project-costing system, which operates in either a stand-alone mode or accompanies TRAKKER's Activity Based Costing, C/CSC, Time Card, and Report Writer components. Advanced Costing provides businesses with a cost-effective solution for a true project cost and pricing system.

Top three product differentiators; describe what makes your product unique.

1. Fully integrates cost/schedule, earned value, technical performance, and risk management. TRAKKER's integration eliminates the effort involved in reconciling differences between cost and schedule, plus, eliminates errors associated with import/export, and provides the user more time to analyze the effects of change rather than managing the database.

2. User friendly—as a Windows application, TRAKKER makes interacting with the data simple and visual.

3. TRAKKER integrates with MS Office and MS Back Office Product Suite to simplify the dissemination and publishing of information.

To what business processes can this tool be applied?

Business processes supported by TRAKKER include estimating, proposal development, project execution, change control, EV reporting, and material management (tracks commitments). Provides the basis of estimate development and ETC/IEAC development.

Describe the ideal end-user environment for the current version of your product (size of organization, level of project management sophistication, effort and commitment required).

One of the key attributes of the TRAKKER system is scalability. TRAKKER has been designed to integrate into a business environment by establishing an organization's business rules within the system.

This architecture enables TRAKKER to fit the needs and sophistication of any implementation.

This flexibility enables TRAKKER to support a variety of implementation approaches. TRAKKER installations typically provide access to a range of users including cost account managers, cost/schedule analysts, and financial managers to meet the unique requirements of each for information and output. Typical TRAKKER clients range from companies of one thousand employees to Fortune 500 corporations.

Future strategies for this product.

Dekker, Ltd. will continue to enhance the integration of TRAKKER with MS Office and MS Back Office suite of tools. The design of the TRAKKER architecture will continue to focus on making data more visual and accessible to the complete range of system user.

Product's target market.

R&D, government, software, medical, electronics, and aerospace.

What are your product's three main benefits? (How does using the product add value to the customer?)

1. Fully integrates cost/schedule, earned value. TRAKKER's integration eliminates the effort involved in reconciling differences between cost and schedule, plus, eliminates errors associated with import/export and provides the user more time to analyze the effects of change rather than managing the database.

2. User friendly—as a Windows application, TRAKKER makes interacting with the data simple and visual.

3. TRAKKER integrates with MS Office and MS Back Office Product Suite to simplify the dissemination and publishing of information.

Describe your quality management process. List any relevant certifications.

DTMI has modeled our development process from the Microsoft model while incorporating the quality guidelines established in ISO 9000.

Discuss your product pricing structure. Include volume discount levels, concurrent user options, site licenses, cost of implementation, and other issues.

DTMI offers both single and concurrent user licenses of TRAKKER. Our flexible pricing enables both small and large organizations to cost effectively implement costing and earned value.

TRAKKER pricing includes a progressive discount for volume purchases with reasonable thresholds for single and multisite licenses.

Further, DTMI offers both public and private training courses for both new and advanced users. DTMI also offers consulting services to support the enterprise implementation of TRAKKER.

DTMI provides training for both the discipline of scheduling and attributes of TRAKKER.

These workshops include Basic Project Management, TRAKKER Application Workshop, TRAKKER Intermediate Workshop, TRAKKER Report Writer Workshop, and TRAKKER MIS Integrator's Workshop.

Through these courses, an enterprise can completely implement the TRAKKER system.

In addition to our classroom training, DTMI offers consulting services to guide users through a structured approach to implementing TRAKKER.

Enterprise Project (jeTECH DATA SYSTEMS, INC.)

Describe what the product is designed to do.

Enterprise Project is a completely integrated solution (all applications share a common database and operate on the same hardware platform). Consequently, our response to the narrative questions here repeats what we supplied for the "Suites" chapter, as those responses apply to all of our applications.

Enterprise Project is a powerful new client/server software application that offers project-based organizations a simple way to define and staff projects, and record project labor and expenses throughout their enterprise. Essentially a suite of robust, user-friendly applications integrated into a single desktop, this comprehensive project management system enables team members to accurately plan and track labor resources across all projects. Perfect either as a *stand-alone* solution or as the ideal complement to the jeTECH labor-management system—Enterprise Labor—it is particularly well suited for multiuser, enterprisewide installations. Together, Enterprise Labor and Enterprise Project are the only systems currently on the market with extensive capabilities and integrated products for both the salaried professional (engineers and computer programmers, for instance) and the hourly employee (from factory workers to registered nurses).

Users access all functions via a single desktop with a Microsoft Office 98 *look and feel*. The system integrates completely with Enterprise Labor and Microsoft Project, as well as with most popular accounting and human resource (HR) systems. In today's competitive environment, effective and efficient use of labor resources is key to completing mission-critical projects on time, on budget. Enterprise Project gives project leaders a comprehensive, potent tool with which to manage scarce technical resources.

With Enterprise Project, managers can budget and schedule projects based on staff skills and availability. Project team members can manage their own tasks, report actual labor and travel expenses, and provide status reports on these tasks. The system calculates actual project costs by automatically incorporating labor costs, material costs, and travel expenses.

Project managers can define and manage both contract and noncontract-based projects, and control work authorizations that will keep each project under control and on budget. As a project manager, you simply create activities for your projects, assign appropriate resources to these activities, and define how labor will be charged to a contract. And by allowing employees to only charge pre-assigned tasks, Enterprise Project prevents performance of unauthorized work.

Enterprise Project enables all users to report labor charges right from their PC or workstation. Project managers need no longer compile project team information manually. Users can now report project time, as well as other time, and the system automatically processes and transmits it to an interfaced time-and-attendance system for payroll use.

Enterprise Project includes a contract maintenance module. Companies with hourly employees contracted with outside firms—for instance, security guards or programmers—would benefit from using this module without the rest of the project management system. This module is primarily designed, however, to accommodate projects being managed for clients. This module allows contract managers to define contract information including budgets and rates per hour, as well as all products and services purchased by the customer. They can then use this information to evaluate projects based on user-defined deliverables. Contract maintenance is by no means static. So jeTECH has designed Enterprise Project to handle change orders, R&D projects, and discounts. A variety of unique reporting features enables contract managers to view cost overruns, variances and milestone completions.

Top three product differentiators; describe what makes your product unique.

1. Resource scheduling from a common resource pool in a multiproject environment.
2. Integrated time collection and status reporting.
3. Sensitivity analysis (what-if scenarios).

To what business processes can this tool be applied?

Project planning/management, enterprise resource scheduling/management, time collection, performance measurement, time and expense reporting, budgeting and estimating, and project accounting.

Describe the ideal end-user environment for the current version of your product (size of organization, level of project management sophistication, effort and commitment required).

Any resource-constrained enterprise (IT, high-tech R&D, engineering) with multiple projects and multiple sites. Requires a low level of project management sophistication.

Future strategies for this product.

Maintenance and repair operations, incorporation of process ware/templates, enterprise-level project and resource integration, and full Internet capabilities.

Product's target market.

Companies with *task-oriented* professionals such as engineers, architects, IS professionals, researchers, advertising/marketing professionals, etc. See also the previous response to "ideal end-user environment."

What are your product's three main benefits? (How does using the product add value to the customer?)

1. Improved resource utilization and efficiencies.
2. Reduction in time to complete projects.
3. Cost control.

Describe your quality management process. List any relevant certifications.

Our current quality management process includes in-house testing, which incorporates both automated and manual processes and procedures.

Discuss your product pricing structure. Include volume discount levels, concurrent user options, site licenses, cost of implementation, and other issues.

Pricing is structured on a named-user basis. Pricing will also be dependent on a number of variables including the size of the enterprise, number of project managers, number of facilities, etc. Consequently, pricing is provided to each customer when we have been able to familiarize ourselves on their operations and their anticipated use of the system.

Several options are available for training, tech support, annual maintenance, etc. Costs are provided to each customer when they have been able to select the options deemed best for their operations.

ER Project 1000 (Eagle Ray Software Systems)

Describe what the product is designed to do.

The ER Project 1000 is an integrated suite of project management tools, which provides an enterprisewide project management solution. ER Project 1000 includes schedule/time management, centralized resource management, methodology/process management, project-workgroup communications, timesheets, risk/issue management, and enterprisewide cross-project tracking. Based on a client/server architecture with a centralized relational database, the ER Project 1000 provides networked access, multiproject capability, and true multiuser concurrency. It scales easily from handling small workgroup projects to large programs at the enterprise level.

Top three product differentiators; describe what makes your product unique.

1. Addresses the total project management life-cycle solution for the enterprise: Unlike most project management tools, the ER Project 1000 provides a completely integrated and centralized project management platform to support the entire life cycle of project management. Based on a client/server relational database (Oracle/SQL Server) architecture, ER Project 1000 fully supports today's multiproject/multiuser project environment. The product suite integrates full methodology/process management capabilities, project workgroup communications, and enterprisewide project tracking capabilities.

2. Provides a completely integrated suite of project management tools: The ER Project 1000 tool suite integrates industrial strength project management functions with rich process improvement functionality and proactive management features. ER Project 1000 provides all of the necessary industrial-strength core project management functions. Key features include support for WBS/organizational breakdown structure/RBS structures, cost, schedule, earned value analysis, built-in report writer, timesheet approvals, and centralized resource management. ER Project 1000 takes advantage of the Web by providing Java timesheets and extensive project website publishing capability. Best practices/process improvement is easily accomplished with the Methodology Manager, and support for organizational standards, work products, and estimation. ER Project 1000 delivers an impressive array of proactive management features. These features include risk management, issue management, management by threshold, and full project tracking.

3. Is easy to use and implement: ER Project 1000 was designed with a simple, intuitive interface. Extensive wizards assist users for complex operations. ER Project 1000 can easily be configured to your organization by using our centralized administration functions and component architecture.

To what business processes can this tool be applied?

ER Project 1000 is a wrap-around solution for organizations that need to implement mature project management practices, proactively manage their projects, improve business processes, implement standards and documentation, and communicate at multiple levels. Eagle Ray's advanced suite of tools provides project managers with an integrated platform for project planning, time tracking, resource management, and executive oversight. With features such as risk management, issue tracking, and management by threshold, the ER Project 1000 gives project managers the ability to proactively manage complex projects and stay focused on the key issues.

Organizations that engage in process improvement/best practices will find that the ER Project 1000 Methodology Manager is the ideal platform for developing and delivering best practices to each new project plan. Project managers will be able to easily document and reuse lessons learned in new projects. Project team members and stakeholders will find that the integrated communications features of the ER Project 1000 suite facilitate a real-time dialogue between all members and ensure that no issues slip though the cracks.

Describe the ideal end-user environment for the current version of your product (size of organization, level of project management sophistication, effort and commitment required).

Size of organization: The ER Project 1000 product suite is ideal for managing projects with team sizes of ten to one thousand people per project, in organizations where multiple projects are being performed at the same time. Project teams may be centralized or dispersed using client/server and Web-based communications technologies.

Level of sophistication: The tool suite is best suited for organizations that are moving beyond basic project management to a medium level of project management maturity, or higher. These organizations are typically implementing tracking, costing, project management standards, risk/issue management, time tracking, centralized resource management, and possibly earned value. ER Project 1000 also supports organizations implementing a project office, best practices, process improvement, and reusable project templates. These features make ER Project 1000 an ideal platform for organizations implementing CMM level 2 or higher maturity levels.

Effort and commitment required: Successful implementation of the ER Project 1000 tool suite centers on an organization's commitment to realizing repeatable project management results from enterprisewide standardization of business processes and practices. Because of its integrated design and simple interface, ER Project 1000 delivers numerous advantages over standard project management tool sets with less staff effort.

Future strategies for this product.

Eagle Ray's future strategies include building new modules, expanding current modules, interfacing with corporate business systems, and preparing the product suite for the global marketplace. Major planned enhancements include significant modifications to the estimation module, costing module, methodology/process management module, and the Internet/intranet/Web capabilities. In addition, we will be constructing a problem/defect-tracking module.

We will be expanding the interfaces that integrate the ER Project 1000 system with additional enterprise business systems. Such systems include costing/accounting systems, HR systems, and additional commercial products. We also plan to complete our internationalization/localization efforts to prepare the ER Project 1000 for global distribution.

Product's target market.

ER Project 1000 is suitable for commercial and government organizations, which are managing projects that range from small workgroup-level projects to projects that span the entire enterprise. Essentially, the tool suite will support any project environment where the project team has access to or is working with computers.

What are your product's three main benefits? (How does using the product add value to the customer?)

1. Total integrated project management solution: The ER Project 1000 is an integrated, total project management solution providing complete support for the entire project management life cycle. The integrated tool suite does not require multiple add-on tools from different vendors, resulting in fewer hidden costs and less frustration. Project managers will find it easy to manage projects with a higher level of maturity by using the various features of the tool—for example, risk management, issue tracking, management by threshold, and multiproject capabilities.

2. Best practices/process improvement platform: The ER Project 1000 integrated process/ methodology management platform provides a sophisticated, yet easy-to-use platform for implementing best practices, estimation metrics, organizational standards, documentation templates, and process improvement. Organizations can capture, integrate, and reuse their project knowledge and project plan templates from an enterprisewide integrated platform.

3. Enterprisewide tracking and communications: The ER Project 1000 facilitates communications between all project stakeholders. Program managers and executives can perform cross-project rollups, dynamic drill-down, and cost, schedule, and earned value analysis for up-to-date information on all enterprise projects. The project team members can access all project information on the project website, and receive activity assignments and report status using Java timesheets. Automatic issue notification alerts project managers about possible deviations in cost and schedule. The built-in report writer lets you extract and summarize any data in the enterprisewide project database using customized formats.

Describe your quality management process. List any relevant certifications.

The Eagle Ray quality assurance program is a comprehensive system that employs a series of product walkthroughs, builds, quality gates, configuration management, defect tracking, and comprehensive testing. The development staff members are constantly conducting requirements, design, and code walkthroughs in coordination with weekly product builds and passing mandatory quality gates. The quality assurance program is integrated with our beta testing program to ensure that all product releases undergo rigorous real-world testing prior to release.

Comprehensive testing scenarios include unit testing, integration testing, platform testing, stress testing, concurrency testing, environment testing, security testing, usability testing, vertical testing, upgrade testing, business scenario testing, and independent qualification testing.

During the design and construction of the ER Project 1000 product, Eagle Ray brought in several project management industry experts to assist in the design of the software functionality and usability. This process will be continued to ensure that our future enhancements meet the real-world needs of project management organizations. Additionally, Eagle Ray continues to invest heavily in the training of team members in technical and project management areas.

Discuss your product pricing structure. Include volume discount levels, concurrent user options, site licenses, cost of implementation, and other issues.

Call for latest prices.

Intelligent Planner (Augeo Software)

Describe what the product is designed to do.

Optimize the allocation of resources across multiple projects, determine costs, and provide metrics for continuous process improvement.

Top three product differentiators; describe what makes your product unique.

1. Global repository for data and business rules.
2. Closed-loop system, from project proposal to time/expenses tracking.
3. Simulation and optimization based on skills and availability of resources.

To what business processes can this tool be applied?

Business processes involving the allocation of human resources, such as professional services and information services.

Describe the ideal end-user environment for the current version of your product (size of organization, level of project management sophistication, effort and commitment required).

Mid-sized to large-scale professional services organizations sharing pool of scarce resources; large IT departments managing budgets and resources on strategic projects; or consulting companies managing a portfolio of intellectual activities.

Future strategies for this product.

Knowledge management integration; 100 percent Web-based management of project portfolio; advanced data-mining features.

Product's target market.

Professional services organizations.
Large-scale IT departments with cost-controlled project management.
Consulting companies.

What are your product's three main benefits? (How does using the product add value to the customer?)

1. Optimize scare resource predictability.
2. Increase speed, throughput, and responsiveness.
3. Executive visibility.

Describe your quality management process. List any relevant certifications.

Source control. Usability verification process. Worldwide beta program.

Discuss your product pricing structure. Include volume discount levels, concurrent user options, site licenses, cost of implementation, and other issues.

Concurrent user pricing for client-server modules, named-user pricing for Web modules. Volume discount, site license. Implementation requires ten to twenty days of consulting.
Training: Project managers (two days), administrator (three days), Web users (half-day).
Annual maintenance (includes new releases and online assistance): Fifteen percent of license fee.

JobPROMS

Describe what the product is designed to do.

JobPROMS—the benchmark in cost engineering—ensures that you're always in control. Kildrummy's cost-management system provides budget, forecast, commitment, and expenditure control for projects of any scale in any sector. Continuously monitoring project costs, highlighting any deviation from budget, JobPROMS helps you make informed decisions and predictions of project cost performance. JobPROMS complements your accounting system and encourages a consistent approach to cost management throughout your organization. Whether you're working on one project or many, JobPROMS brings the control and reporting straight to your desktop. Flexible project structures and user-defined reporting help you to change as the demands of the job change. JobPROMS is the international benchmark for cost-management systems.

Designed originally for the energy industry, JobPROMS brings project cost control to multinational corporations and small enterprises alike, in sectors as diverse as aerospace, construction, defense, engineering, nuclear, oil and gas, pharmaceuticals, and utilities. It plays a crucial role in day-to-day project management, tenaciously pursuing commitment and expenditure that might be running away with the budget.

JobPROMS empowers you. Its familiar Windows format and its flexible project and reporting structures get you operational quickly and easily. On-screen analysis through all levels of the project puts you in control from day one, eliminating the need to play catch-up with fleeing budgets. You can examine, predict, and manage trends, variances, and overruns from a single source. You are free to focus on the big picture, secure in the knowledge that the detail is under tight control. You are free to manage.

Top three product differentiators; describe what makes your product unique.

1. Powerful ability to structure your data according to project requirements. Ability to control against a variety of structures per project (i.e., work breakdowns) in as much or little detail as required.

2. Integration of all project costs, including full multicurrency capability, in a single application: budgets, forecasts, history, variances, man-hours, commitments, changes, trends, expenditures, and more. Designed to complement and interface with your existing accounting systems.

3. One hundred percent output flexibility. Easy-to-create cost statements including user-defined terminology, report columns, and formulas that allow you to design your reports to meet project/client requirements. You can print reports (or on-screen drill-down) to any level of your reporting structures, or export them into MS Office applications. User-defined reports and queries can be created in MS Access, and thereafter added to the standard JobPROMS menu providing 100 percent output flexibility.

To what business processes can this tool be applied?

1. Program management: The multiproject structures provide a view of project costs through the company by any combination of category, function, client, location, division, discipline, etc.

2. Project management provides the project with effective cost control.

3. Functional/organizational management: Cost breakdown/chart of accounts structures provide visibility of project costs throughout the organization by cost code/category.

Describe the ideal end-user environment for the current version of your product (size of organization, level of project management sophistication, effort and commitment required).

Typically, organizations with a turnover of GBP 50 million and over. Normally project management techniques are relatively sophisticated. However, a weakness often exists in controlling project costs, which for many is proving elusive. Depending on the number and complexity of projects, JobPROMS typically requires one to five users per site and can be successfully implemented in a week.

Future strategies for this product.

In the short term, we plan to enhance the product's position as the cost control tool of choice. To that end, we have recently incorporated in the United States and have established an office based in Houston, Texas.

We also propose to develop a simpler cost-management system that can be used effectively by smaller companies with smaller workloads, and which can be extended by ourselves and third-party developers to handle unusual or niche-market business problems.

Product's target market.

Typical end users (energy, engineering, construction) are those with major infrastructure projects with sizeable budgets and contracts that require effective cost management.

Outside this group, JobPROMS is used by smaller high-technology companies where project cost-management techniques have been adopted to control a multitude of engineering jobs.

What are your product's three main benefits? (How does using the product add value to the customer?)

1. Provides a consistent albeit flexible approach to project cost management throughout the organization, thereby saving time on developing, maintaining, and training in other systems.

2. Allows you effective control of your project from day one, keeping the engineers focussed on the *big picture* while at the same time providing drill-down visibility to all the necessary detail.

3. User-friendly product: Reports and control structures can be designed quickly to meet project and client requirements.

Describe your quality management process. List any relevant certifications.

Kildrummy has been engaged for the last year in a process leading to ISO 9001 certification, with a target completion date of Q2 1999. We gained Investors in People in March 1998 as part of this process.

The nature of our work has changed over this period, and we are currently redocumenting our technical methodology in light of the experience gained on more recent major software developments.

Discuss your product pricing structure. Include volume discount levels, concurrent user options, site licenses, cost of implementation, and other issues.

Prices from GBP 7,500/$12,000 (stand-alone). Network configurations and other license options, including discount schemes, are available on request.

Standard two-day JobPROMS training course for up to six users is from GBP 1,950/$3,200. Further details available on request.

Technical support and annual maintenance, including upgrades, is charged at 15 percent of the current software license price.

Further on-site implementation consultancy, specialist training, and development work is available by contacting our London, Houston, or Perth (Australia) offices.

MicroFusion Millennium

Describe what the product is designed to do.

MicroFusion Millennium is an enterprise-scale client/server project control and project management system that integrates with SQL Server, Oracle, Sybase, and MS Access databases. It is a very powerful yet extremely easy-to-use application.

Top three product differentiators; describe what makes your product unique.

1. The architecture of MicroFusion Millennium conforms to the classical three-tier client/server model. These three tiers or layers are the presentation layer, business logic layer, and database layer.

2. MicroFusion Millennium takes advantage of the latest technologies introduced by Microsoft, including VBA, multithreaded SMP, BackOffice, Internet Explorer 4.0, NT 4.0, ActiveX, and Remote OLE.

3. MicroFusion Millennium's Interface Wizard was developed to maximize the use of automation in the creation of budgets, reducing reentry errors. The explorer navigation and the extensive uses of context menus make getting to your data an easy task.

To what business processes can this tool be applied?

Any project-related activity. MicroFusion Millennium was designed to be a cross-industry product.

Describe the ideal end-user environment for the current version of your product (size of organization, level of project management sophistication, effort and commitment required).

MicroFusion Millennium is scaleable from a small organization (approximately five million dollars in revenue) to a large-scale multibillion-dollar operation.

Future strategies for this product.

IMC plans to introduce a Web-enabled version of our product, and intends to capitalize on the growing E-commerce (business to business) activity, using our core engine and Web-enabled applets.

Product's target market.

MicroFusion Millennium was designed as a project management tool to be utilized by companies or organizations that have complex rate structures.

What are your product's three main benefits? (How does using the product add value to the customer?)

1. Easy interface for entering complex data.
2. Rating/performance measurement algorithms produce meaningful management data.
3. Presentation of the data in a timely fashion allows in-depth analysis and decision-making.

Describe your quality management process. List any relevant certifications.

IMC has adopted a total quality management approach with team reviews of all internal processes and continual refinement of these processes.

Discuss your product pricing structure. Include volume discount levels, concurrent user options, site licenses, cost of implementation, and other issues.

IMC offers a tiered approach for the purchase of the product in the network environment. We also offer site/corporate licenses that are negotiated based on company size and geographic location.

IMC offers a competitive implementation program including on-site assistance and technical support. Our maintenance costs are in line with other like products. The basis product price is highly competitive and costs two to three times less then the competition.

Microsoft Project 98

Describe what the product is designed to do.

Microsoft Project 98 is an ideal tool for planning and tracking projects of all sizes. Because it is easy to use, it is an ideal tool for all levels of project management experience from the newcomer to the experienced project manager. Microsoft Project 98 focuses on three areas: 1) control—gives users more control over their project plans; 2) communication—improves project communication so everyone stays informed and involved; and 3) compatibility—provides programmability features so it can serve as a stand-alone product or as part of a broader company solution.

Top three product differentiators; describe what makes your product unique.

1. Ease of use: Microsoft Project 98 requires little or no training to begin using it to manage projects, so the *startup* costs required of new customers are much lower when compared to other project management software tools. The Navigation Map helps inexperienced project managers

and new Microsoft Project 98 customers to map their functional responsibilities to Microsoft Project 98's features.

2. Extensibility: Microsoft Project 98 is a pioneer in extensibility. It can store data in an open database format and supports VBA. Customers can easily integrate project management data with their existing corporate business systems, which enables Microsoft Project 98 to accommodate ever-increasing complexity as customers' project management needs change and grow throughout the organization.

3. Integration with other Microsoft applications: Microsoft Project 98 incorporates the best of Microsoft Office to make a tool that is easy to learn and use.

To what business processes can this tool be applied?

Microsoft Project 98 can be applied to any process for which the customer can identify specific tasks and their respective durations and dependencies. Customers can use Microsoft Project 98 to easily compare cost and profitability by project, balance resource requirements across projects, and track dependencies across multiple projects to assess a project's impact on the bottom line. Microsoft Project 98 can also be used to integrate project metrics with corporate accounting, human resources, timesheets, or manufacturing systems and organize project documentation so it is readily available to everyone involved in a project.

Describe the ideal end-user environment for the current version of your product (size of organization, level of project management sophistication, effort and commitment required).

Microsoft Project 98 is used in end-user environments of all sizes—from individuals planning single-resource projects to large corporations with thousands of employees. Customers with widely varying project management backgrounds can also use it. Even newcomers to project management principles can learn to use Microsoft Project 98 quickly and easily with the product's built-in help and other easy-to-use features. Microsoft Project 98 even contains features to extend a project team's communication capability over the Web or any MAPI-compliant E-mail system. And, customers won't *outgrow* Microsoft Project 98 since its programmability features allow them to tailor the program to their organizations' unique and changing needs.

Future strategies for this product.

Microsoft will continue to focus on improved collaboration, performance, and ease of use in future versions of Microsoft Project. Microsoft Project has always focused on bringing project management techniques to a wider audience via improved ease of use and expanded communication capabilities for project teams and will continue to do so in the future.

Product's target market.

Anyone who deals with budgets, assignments, and deadlines can take advantage of the benefits offered by Microsoft Project 98. If you have thousands of details to manage—or even a few dozen—you're a potential Microsoft Project 98 customer.

What are your product's three main benefits? (How does using the product add value to the customer?)

1. Easy to learn and can grow with customers' projects and organization.
2. Ability to plan and track multiple projects in a consolidated manner.
3. Helps customers track and manage costs that affect the bottom line.

Describe your quality management process. List any relevant certifications.

Microsoft Project's quality management process begins with developing a product vision based on input from customers, internal and external developers, the product support team, and usability engineers. This ensures that the development process focuses on the right objectives, and that decisions regarding product quality reflect all of these perspectives.

Microsoft maintains a high developer-to-tester ratio throughout the software development process to ensure that potential *bugs* are identified and resolved as early in the development cycle as possible. The testing process is based on five core attributes: 1) source code version control; 2) making the code testable; 3) use of automation for broader scenario testing; 4) beta testing, both internal and external; and 5) detailed bug tracking and reporting (throughout all Microsoft product groups in order to share learning).

Finally, a new product is released only when the managers from development, testing, program management, and product support agree as a team that the product is ready. No product will be released until this agreement is reached.

Discuss your product pricing structure. Include volume discount levels, concurrent user options, site licenses, cost of implementation, and other issues.

The estimated retail price of Microsoft Project 98 is $499. Microsoft also offers several multiple-license pricing agreements. Detailed information on these agreements is available at http://www.microsoft.com/licensing.

The cost of implementation varies, based on previous experience with project management principles, experience with other project management software tools, and the size and complexity of a customer's projects. Little or no training is needed for Microsoft Project 98 due to the extensive built-in help and other user-assistance features included in the product. Many additional low-cost books, self-help tools, and other training materials for Microsoft Project 98 are widely available. Microsoft Project 98's built-in VBA programmability features also help limit the cost of additional customization.

OPX2 Pro

Describe what the product is designed to do.

Program cost management is fully integrated with OPX2 Pro schedule management features. It includes multiproject cost consolidation, earned value, and performance analysis. User permissions can be defined according to the type and level of data in the project and/or organization structure.

Top three product differentiators; describe what makes your product unique.

1. Management of multiple currencies.
2. Ability to handle project cash flow and profit at any level of structure.

For others, see OPX2 Pro in the Schedule Management section.

To what business processes can this tool be applied?

Project management: R&D project management (new product development and portfolio management), matrix organizations, IS departments, and software houses.

Scheduling of small serial manufacturing, engineering projects, heavy maintenance, and integration activities.

Cost management for public contract management, defense and aerospace programs, in-house product development, and subcontracting.

Describe the ideal end-user environment for the current version of your product (size of organization, level of project management sophistication, effort and commitment required).

Organization: From one hundred to twenty thousand resources managed.

Level of project management sophistication: Previous experience of other project management software implementation is profitable for implementing OPX2.

To be implemented using a methodology suited for enterprisewide consolidation: activity coding, resource identification, ERP interfaces.

Future strategies for this product.

Development of partnerships with ERP providers.
International development (multilingual support and distributors).
Focus on decision-support functions.

Product's target market.

Manufacturing: Defense and aerospace, car/truck, drug/cosmetics development.
ICT: IS departments (enterprises and administrations), software house, and telecommunications, and electronics.
Engineering: Construction, energy, space.

What are your product's three main benefits? (How does using the product add value to the customer?)

1. For the organization: Standardization of concepts and reporting process for project management in all departments, breaking of barriers between cost and schedule.
2. For users: Less time spent to collect and enter data, more time available to analyze them.
3. For management: Real visibility on activity progress for top management and long-term historization of project data at multiproject scale.

Describe your quality management process. List any relevant certifications.

TEMPO (Thomson-CSF software development methodology). TEMPO is compliant with ISO 9001 standards.

Discuss your product pricing structure. Include volume discount levels, concurrent user options, site licenses, cost of implementation, and other issues.

OPX2 Pro (Scheduling + Cost management + Report builder): from $12,000 (server + first concurrent-user license).
Typical user configurations: $17,000 to $1,000,000. Concurrent user licenses: yes. Site licenses: yes.
Cost of implementation: Twenty-five to 80 percent of license cost for consulting and training.
Annual maintenance: Fifteen percent of license cost (including tech. support and upgrade of new releases).
Training: Contact OPX2 distributors in each country.

P3 Connect

Describe what the product is designed to do.

P3 Connect for wInsight integrates with Primavera's P3 to export the EV data to wInsight for analysis and sharing of earned value information.

wInsight is an earned-value analysis tool that provides state-of-the-art techniques to quickly find problem areas, review performance trends, and generate statistical estimates at complete.

wInsight is specifically designed to engage technical managers, integrated product development (IPD) team leaders, program managers, and cost/schedule professionals in proactive project management.

Top three product differentiators; describe what makes your product unique.

1. Collection of earned value data from Primavera's P3.
2. Management-by-exception tools.
3. Earned value analysis forecasts, graphics, and reports.

To what business processes can this tool be applied?

Project cost/schedule tracking, assessment, and forecasting.

Describe the ideal end-user environment for the current version of your product (size of organization, level of project management sophistication, effort and commitment required).

Organizations that currently build and maintain schedules on complex projects; cost account managers, program managers, and program control staff.

Future strategies for this product.

No answer given.

Product's target market.

P3 Connect for wInsight is targeted at schedule-savvy organizations that wish to use earned-value management techniques, but don't need the complexity of traditional earned value systems.

What are your product's three main benefits? (How does using the product add value to the customer?)

1. Quick visibility into project cost/schedule performance.
2. Management by exception.
3. Meets government EDI standards.

Describe your quality management process. List any relevant certifications.

No answer given.

Discuss your product pricing structure. Include volume discount levels, concurrent user options, site licenses, cost of implementation, and other issues.

Stand-alone, concurrent user, and site licenses.

Panorama Program Manager

Describe what the product is designed to do.

Panorama Program Manager comprises five modules, which together form a fully integrated application but which can, if required, be used independently or can be integrated with preferred third-party applications. Interfaces can also be provided to other applications.

Financial control and performance measurement: Consolidates financial and performance information for any number of projects and provides multilevel views of all data. Departmental managers and team leaders can be provided with short-term tactical perspectives.

Time Recording: This module is the collection point for all time expended by project staff. Timesheets may be entered by individual members of staff, or as a batch process. Extensive online validation ensures that mispostings are kept to a minimum.

Top three product differentiators; describe what makes your product unique.

1. Scope: Addresses in a single integrated application the major application areas required for comprehensive program management.
2. Flexibility: Inherent flexibility means that the system can be implemented to suit most companies' requirements without the need for bespoke development.
3. Customization: Ability to incorporate bespoke features to client's specification and willingness to provide support to customized elements.

To what business processes can this tool be applied?

Estimation, bid management, and project control.

Describe the ideal end-user environment for the current version of your product (size of organization, level of project management sophistication, effort and commitment required).

Typical users will have in excess of two hundred employees and be managing either large, complex projects or a large number (>150) of small/medium-sized projects.

They will usually have experience of project management and will already be users of project management tools.

A typical implementation will be six to twelve months and will require the involvement of an implementation team, which at any one time might include five to ten client staff.

Future strategies for this product.

Web-based operation.
Integration of workflow management and document storage and retrieval.

Product's target market.

Cross-industry.

What are your product's three main benefits? (How does using the product add value to the customer?)

1. Consolidation of all project data to provide a corporate view of performance.
2. Standardization of project control methodology through use of a single corporatewide system.
3. Easy access at all levels in the organization of all aspects of project performance.

Describe your quality management process. List any relevant certifications.

In-house change control and configuration management software and control systems.

Discuss your product pricing structure. Include volume discount levels, concurrent user options, site licenses, cost of implementation, and other issues.

On application.

PLANTRAC-CORoNET

Describe what the product is designed to do.

PLANTRAC-CORoNET provides cost estimates together with cost forecasts based on performance on the project. It allows project budgets to be set and actuals to be input.

From the progress on the schedule, realistic forecasts are made. Striking graphics provide management with the information it needs to make sound decisions early.

Top three product differentiators; describe what makes your product unique.

1. Schedule integration.
2. Time-scaled reports.
3. Flexible reporting.

To what business processes can this tool be applied?

Construction, manufacturing, and research and development.

Describe the ideal end-user environment for the current version of your product (size of organization, level of project management sophistication, effort and commitment required).

Both small and large organizations benefit. It can be used as a casual planner, by a professional project manager, and for corporate planning and control.

Future strategies for this product.

PLANTRAC-CORoNET is very much user driven. It will keep up to date with both project management and technological trends.

Product's target market.

Broad market but specializing in construction, defense, and pharmaceutical.

What are your product's three main benefits? (How does using the product add value to the customer?)

1. Sound early estimating.
2. Early predictions of profit/loss based on productivity.
3. Sound information for project control.

Describe your quality management process. List any relevant certifications.

Quality management is based on a mix of PRINCE and ISO 9000 methodology.

Discuss your product pricing structure. Include volume discount levels, concurrent user options, site licenses, cost of implementation, and other issues.

$450, single copy. $275 per user site license.

Implementation and training is $960 per day. Technical support is provided by telephone, fax, and E-mail. Free for first six months. Thereafter, 17.5 percent of purchase price (includes upgrades and enhancements).

Project Connect for wInsight (OPP)

Describe what the product is designed to do.

Project Connect for wInsight integrates with MS Project 98 to enhance its earned value calculations and provide export of the earned value data to wInsight for analysis and sharing of earned value information.

wInsight is an earned value analysis tool that provides state-of-the-art techniques to quickly find problem areas, review performance trends, and generate statistical estimates at complete.

wInsight is specifically designed to engage technical managers, integrated product development team leaders, program managers, and cost/schedule professionals in proactive project management.

Top three product differentiators; describe what makes your product unique.

1. Collection of earned value data from Primavera's P3.
2. Management-by-exception tools.
3. Earned value analysis forecasts, graphics, and reports.

To what business processes can this tool be applied?

Project cost/schedule tracking, assessment, and forecasting.

Describe the ideal end-user environment for the current version of your product (size of organization, level of project management sophistication, effort and commitment required).

Organizations that currently build and maintain schedules on complex projects; cost account managers, program managers, and program control staff.

Future strategies for this product.

No answer given.

Product's target market.

Project Connect for wInsight is targeted at schedule-savvy organizations that wish to use earned-value management techniques, but don't need the complexity of traditional earned value systems.

What are your product's three main benefits? (How does using the product add value to the customer?)

1. Quick visibility into project cost/schedule performance.
2. Management by exception.
3. Meets government EDI standards.

Describe your quality management process. List any relevant certifications.

No answer given.

Discuss your product pricing structure. Include volume discount levels, concurrent user options, site licenses, cost of implementation, and other issues.

Stand-alone, concurrent user, and site licenses.
Project cost/schedule tracking, assessment, and forecasting.

Project Control 6.0

Describe what the product is designed to do.

The Definition Manager, Accounting Integrator, and Earned Value Manager modules specifically address cost management. Definition Manager is an easy-to-use tool that uses best practices to define, create budgets, and plan new projects and exports to MS Project. The Accounting Integrator links project management to your accounting system, eliminating double entry. Integrate your project management schedules and accounting system actual costs to calculate real-time progress, costs, and earned value. With Earned Value Manager, you save time and money by integrating project schedules and actual costs calculating real-time progress, costs, and earned value. The system supports six types of earned value calculations, so you can choose the standard that suits your organization. The Definition Manager, Accounting Integrator, and Earned Value modules are part of the Project Control Software suite.

The Project Control Software suite supports the project office across all phases of the project management life cycle, from standard estimating and budgeting though timesheets and status tracking and integration with any accounting system for actual costs and earned value analysis. The Process Manager module enables project management standards, processes, and training management through its document management and issues-tracking functionalities.

Project Control Software extends desktop project management software into an enterprisewide management and reporting solution, by consolidating volumes of project files from leading project management software systems such as Microsoft Project, Primavera, and others. Project Control Software supports multiple operating systems (Windows, Macintosh, Unix), and databases (Oracle, Access, Microsoft SQL, Sybase). The entire Project Control Software suite runs on a Web browser or

LAN. The enterprise rollup design supports the matrix organization's need to roll up projects to program or initiative, as well as the resource perspective by business unit and organizational structure.

Top three product differentiators; describe what makes your product unique.

1. No technology limits: Project Control Software supports all operating systems (Windows, Macintosh, Unix), consolidates files from multiple project management software systems (Microsoft Project, Primavera, and more) using your choice of databases (Oracle, Access, Microsoft SQL, Sybase) in a LAN or Internet solution. It is designed to integrate easily with existing business systems (such as accounting software) so an organization can leverage existing systems and immediately see productivity increases without changing everything.

2. The project office: The design and integration of Project Control Software modules supports the project office across all phases of the project management life cycle, from standard estimating and budgeting though timesheets and status tracking and accounting integration for actual costs and earned value analysis.

3. Enterprise project management: Project Control Software offers a suite of integrated modules that can be used to deliver the big picture of project management across a distributed organization, as well as tracking the details. The enterprise rollup design supports the matrix organization's need to roll up projects to program or initiative, as well as the need to view data from a resource perspective by business unit and organizational structure. The entire Project Control Software suite (not just the time tracking) runs on a Web browser or LAN.

To what business processes can this tool be applied?

Project Control Software's enterprise rollup design supports the matrix organization's need to roll up projects to program or initiative, as well as the need to view data from a resource perspective by business unit and organizational structure.

The system supports project management, ERP, project office development, ISO registration, strategic planning, process management, methodology implementation, cost/schedule management, CMM, compliance, global information technology deployment, SAP, Peoplesoft, etc., implementations.

Describe the ideal end-user environment for the current version of your product (size of organization, level of project management sophistication, effort and commitment required).

Any organization operating in a competitive environment that manages multiple projects and resources to meet business goals and to increase profitability and productivity.

For example, a geographically distributed matrix organization with medium to high volume of project-based activities being managed in a standard desktop scheduling software. The system delivers information to all levels of the organization from employees to project management, functional management, enterprise management, and global management.

Future strategies for this product.

Project Control, the publisher of Project Control Software, was founded in 1989, developed the first Internet project management product in 1996, and is committed to its position as a technology leader in Internet project management software. Future plans include expanding functionality to better support the project office and to continually update Project Control Software features, based on ongoing client input.

Product's target market.

Organizations using Project Control Software represent companies in a wide variety of industries, including finance, services, pharmaceutical, federal government, defense, manufacturing, automotive, software publishing, etc. The disciplines typically involved in implementation include enterprise management, information technology, new product development, the project office, and engineering.

What are your product's three main benefits? (How does using the product add value to the customer?)

Client organizations can greatly improve productivity and lower costs when Project Control system is in place.

1. Ability to view all projects in a central repository.

2. Ability to do efficient enterprise resource and cost planning.

3. Ability to fully support the needs of the project office across all phases and areas of the project management process.

Describe your quality management process. List any relevant certifications.

Project Control, publishers of Project Control software, follows standard and accepted practices for design, development, testing, and support for computer software. Project Control has set corporate objectives to achieve Level 2 and Level 3 CMM compliance using the capability maturity model from the Software Engineering Institute.

Discuss your product pricing structure. Include volume discount levels, concurrent user options, site licenses, cost of implementation, and other issues.

Project Control Software is priced by the module, with scalable client seat pricing based on number of users. Price quotations are available and are based on the current Project Control software product and pricing schedule.

Price quotations are available and include costs of product, implementation, training, tech support, annual maintenance, etc. Quotations are based on the current Project Control software product and pricing schedule, which is available to qualified organizations.

Project Scheduler 7.6 (Scitor Corporation)

Describe what the product is designed to do.

PS7 is built from the ground up to take full advantage of today's technology. Whether you're performing basic task scheduling on your desktop or working on multiple megaprojects using our powerful SQL database repository, PS7 will meet your needs. Wizards, guides, tip-of-the-day suggestions, and field-level help provide an easy-to-navigate path to project management. You'll find PS7 provides extraordinary flexibility to organize, consolidate, and view project information.

For serious users, PS7 provides support for: subprojects, grouped projects, accounting periods, time-phased availability, inflation factors, multiple cost tables, earned value, unlimited user fields/formulas, five baselines, custom reports, and much more.

The add-on package, Project Communicator (described in Timesheets section), permits resources to view their task assignments and report back actual work and estimated remaining work via a powerful two-tier client/server database system.

Top three product differentiators; describe what makes your product unique.

1. Approachable power: PS7 meets the needs of the most demanding project management professionals, without sacrificing the ease of use demanded in today's state-of-the-art applications.

2. Scalability: PS7 is designed and built from the ground up to scale from the single desktop user to the entire enterprise.

3. Customer Support: PS7 isn't just another software product. In its seventh generation, PS7 continues to be designed and built by project management professionals for project management professionals.

To what business processes can this tool be applied?

Project planning and tracking; resource management and team communications; cost estimation and control.

Describe the ideal end-user environment for the current version of your product (size of organization, level of project management sophistication, effort and commitment required).

PS7 is designed to meet the needs of all sizes of organizations, including individuals, product teams, workgroups, and the enterprise. PS7 is the most configurable project management package available; it meets the needs of beginning project managers on up to serious project management professionals.

Future strategies for this product.

We will continue to provide leading-edge project management products and services by listening to and working with customers to predict the future needs of a changing management environment.

Product's target market.

General business and professional project management.
All major industries.

What are your product's three main benefits? (How does using the product add value to the customer?)

1. Plans and tracks project/resource costs and schedules.
2. Allows *early* detection and resolution of problems.
3. Facilitates communications between all stakeholders.

Describe your quality management process. List any relevant certifications.

Best commercial practices.

Discuss your product pricing structure. Include volume discount levels, concurrent user options, site licenses, cost of implementation, and other issues.

Single unit $595, discounts at ten, twenty-five, and fifty plus.
$2,900 for five-pack concurrent licenses, discounts at two, five, and ten plus.
Site licenses available for five hundred licenses and up.
Regional and on-site training and consulting is available.
Telephone tech support is available at no charge.
Annual maintenance: not applicable.

Prolog Manager 5.0, Prolog Executive 1.0

Describe what the product is designed to do.

Prolog Manager is the ultimate computer software program for complete project control. It is unique because it is easy to use and emulates the way construction professionals traditionally track and manage project information.

Top three product differentiators; describe what makes your product unique.

1. Ease of use.
2. Built-in word processor.
3. Central location for all project information.

To what business processes can this tool be applied?

Any business model that has as mission-critical the tracking of budgets and potential deviations from the budget. Relationships based upon heavy documentation. Comprehensive time-minded retrieval of documents pertaining to critical issues.

Describe the ideal end-user environment for the current version of your product (size of organization, level of project management sophistication, effort and commitment required).

Designed to meet the broad organizational size spectrum, from major government agencies to smaller organizations. Interface and software process aptitude is minimal; information storage and manipulation abilities of Prolog are vast.

Future strategies for this product.

Taking advantage of Internet technology and real-time data collaboration.

Product's target market.

A/E/C, public and private owners, and agencies.

What are your product's three main benefits? (How does using the product add value to the customer?)

1. Best Practices: Methods and means that make business sense to a company evolve into *best practices*. These standards are rooted in proven procedural guidelines that are forged over time.

2. Industry Requirements: Many owners and consultants are making proprietary in their specification the use of Prolog Manager. Top-down standardization requirements make the selection of a flexible software application mandatory.

Describe your quality management process. List any relevant certifications.

Extensive quality assurance testing, client-based Product Development Advisory Council.

Discuss your product pricing structure. Include volume discount levels, concurrent user options, site licenses, cost of implementation, and other issues.

Prolog Manager Version 5.0 sold based upon LAN/WAN concurrent use. Also sold as detachable stand-alone licenses. Discount structure based upon bulk procurement or anticipated procurement within definable time frame.

Implementation costs based upon level of Meridian Project Systems, Inc.'s involvement; group training, private training, full turnkey solutions. Hourly consultation available.

Annual maintenance is free for first twelve months, afterward is billed at 15 percent of the purchase price.

Training costs vary, based upon curriculum, number of attendees and location of training.

QEI Exec (PCF Limited)

Describe what the product is designed to do.

QEI Exec is best thought of as a toolkit for managing activity-based problems built around a high-performance database engine. Data stored within the database can be presented and manipulated via any number of views, which can be graphical or tabular. The entire user interface to the delivered product is written in the product's own programming language, allowing complete customization to meet individual requirements.

It provides the following key areas of functionality:

- Graphical and tabular interface to data
- Scheduling

- Resource management
- Cost and performance management
- Flexible interfacing to other systems
- High degree of customization.

Top three product differentiators; describe what makes your product unique.

1. Highly graphical *CAD-like* approach to project construction gives total freedom of data layout.

2. Dynamic rollup of all schedule and resource data through an unlimited number of structures, yielding high performance even when dealing with tens of thousands of tasks.

3. Macro-based front end allows complete customization of user interface and generation of interactive specialist charts (such as time chainage diagrams).

To what business processes can this tool be applied?

It has a wide range of possible applications, including:

- *Traditional* project planning with earned value analysis
- Project-based MIS/EIS
- Program treasury management
- Maintenance and manufacturing forecasting
- Capacity planning
- MRP master schedule generation.

Describe the ideal end-user environment for the current version of your product (size of organization, level of project management sophistication, effort and commitment required).

Large organizations (to >$100M) with considerable experience of *rigorous* project management wishing to consolidate diverse sets of data (from multiple planning systems, manufacturing/ERP, and cost collection) into a single source of high-quality management information.

If customers wish to fully exploit the potential for tightly integrating the product with other systems or to introduce significant customizations, they will require suitable internal IT resources.

Future strategies for this product.

Extended database connectivity via ODBC.
Extended reporting and intranet functionality.

Product's target market.

Principal markets are aerospace and defense. Product is also successfully used in make-to-order/contract manufacturing, transportation, and utilities.

What are your product's three main benefits? (How does using the product add value to the customer?)

1. Extremely high-quality interactive graphical views of data.
2. High performance consolidation/rollup permits rapid what-if scenario analysis.
3. Complete control over layout and presentation of data.

Describe your quality management process. List any relevant certifications.

We have started (but not yet completed) ISO 9001 certification.

Discuss your product pricing structure. Include volume discount levels, concurrent user options, site licenses, cost of implementation, and other issues.

The product is sold as a right-to-use license, plus a number of user licenses. A small (three-user) system would cost about £15,000 while a larger (ten-user) system would cost about £30,000. The per-user price drops with increasing numbers of users. Site/multisite/corporate licenses are available.

It is strongly recommended that customers take training from us. List price for training is £500/day per course for up to six attendees. Various standard training courses are available, or custom courses can be developed on request. Annual maintenance is 15 percent of the list price of the software. This includes all upgrades and new releases and unlimited telephone support.

WebProject

Describe what the product is designed to do.

WebProject is designed for geographically dispersed project teams. WebProject is a Java-based project management tool with powerful collaboration and communications features. WebProject incorporates unique knowledge management/best practices.

Top three product differentiators; describe what makes your product unique.

WebProject is the first (only) pure Java project management suite that can utilize an open architecture database backend. WebProject allows corporations to utilize Oracle, SQL Server, Informix, Sybase, or other databases in their enterprise project management.

WebProject has introduced the first knowledge management/best practices capability within a project management software suite.

WebProject enables global project communication including project issues boards, threaded task discussions, virtual project status meetings, and remote project statusing and updates.

To what business processes can this tool be applied?

Geographically dispersed project teams, projects that need to have access from remote locations, or integrating WebProject's proprietary information exchange with MS Project, Primavera, or other desktop systems.

WebProject allows the extraction of knowledge from the enterprise, such as resource capabilities or company *best practices*.

Describe the ideal end-user environment for the current version of your product (size of organization, level of project management sophistication, effort and commitment required).

WebProject is an easy-to-use Java project management tool that will enable teams to communicate and collaborate from remote locations. WebProject is designed for the enterprise and will work well with project teams as well.

Future strategies for this product.

WebProject has established many *firsts* in the project management industry. We will continue to move the industry forward with our new technologies on the Web and with Java.

Product's target market.

Geographically dispersed project teams, enterprise project management systems, integration with Primavera, MS Project, and other project management systems.

What are your product's three main benefits? (How does using the product add value to the customer?)

1. Enterprise project communication.
2. Project collaboration.
3. Geographically dispersed updates and communication.

Describe your quality management process. List any relevant certifications.

WebProject adheres to strict standards and processes for quality, both in development and customer service.

Discuss your product pricing structure. Include volume discount levels, concurrent user options, site licenses, cost of implementation, and other issues.

WebProject is priced at $790 for starter package including the WebProject server. WebProject does provide enterprise and site licensing.

Chapter 5

Resource Management Software

The key component of a resource management system is the ability to match available resources—usually human resources—to requests for resources, and to communicate to the performers and the requestors the schedule of anticipated events.

The most effective use of this classification is in a department that provides staffing for multiple projects, and in which resource needs are communicated via some request process.

A resource management system can be considered for nonhuman resources but if the nature of the requests indicates a process or job-shop environment, a materials-requirements planning system may be more appropriate. If the nature of the resource requests is of a high frequency with low duration, some type of trouble ticket system may be more appropriate.

Summarization and rollup capabilities generate an overall view of the organization's project status. The software must also be able to depict the organization's resources according to multiple views, such as by department or by skill.

There are several related resource management functions detailed in *A Guide to the Project Management Body of Knowledge (PMBOK™ Guide)* (Chapter 9): Organizational Planning; Staff Acquisition; and Team Development. These objectives are achieved through skills databases, staffing planning databases, training planning software, and others. These are necessary functions but have not in the past been the focus of software marketed to the project management industry. The vendors surveyed here indicate that their products can be applied to most of the core *PMBOK™ Guide* processes. Resource management, project (i.e., task) management, cost (i.e., time) management, and schedule management were mentioned, but in cases where a different description was offered by the vendor, program management improvement and more effective use of corporate resources were also mentioned.

One question that the survey team asked themselves was whether enterprise resource planning (ERP) software should be included under this category. After much deliberation, the answer was "No." ERP software is in a major expansion into project management, but these products would be more properly covered in a separate category, and will be in the next edition of this book. In an attempt to clarify for ourselves and the reader the differences in resource management and ERP products, we contacted John Seitz, principal of Enterprise Software Resources, a consulting firm specializing in ERP implementations. We asked him how the project manager's view of resource requirements and planning differs from that of the enterprise. Seitz replied that the project manager in the ERP model must remember the word *integration*. The project manager in an ERP system must worry about several projects all at the same time. Each project must finish at the same time or the system won't function. "You can no longer let teams get into a race to get done," he said. "Unless all teams finish at the same time the project will fail."

Seitz sees a bright future for the melding of project management and ERP:

> Project-based organizations must learn to plan several activities at the same time. The traditional IS project was more serial in nature. The project went from A to Z. The ERP project will start with A but may go to P before B and start XY and Z at the same time. Example: You will configure a new system, business process and technical environment all at the same time. In the past you matched the system to your existing business process, and technical environment.

For the 1999 software survey, resource management software is therefore concentrated in products that capture the organization's current resource pool, and assist with the assignment of available resources to project plans, and predict resource availability/overload based on new workload.

What to Expect:

Resource management software provides features like:

- Identifying the resource pool
- Organizing resources by skill, department, or other meaningful codes
- Requesting resources from functional or departmental managers
- Demand management based on current projects, future projects, strategic initiatives, and growth
- Summary views and reports across multiple projects.

For the most part, the technological gulf between the *big boys* and the *small fries* in what are usually referred to as *project management tools* (most of them being some type of resource-task schedule and control tool) was that the large project and enterprise project tools had the capability through their repository or database to provide a view of the resources as a whole. On the other hand, the stand-alone products were used for scheduling and controlling individual projects and *assumed* the availability of the resource. In many cases, a project manager with a project on a stand-alone product could not communicate to another project manager an anticipated change in the availability of a shared resource; nor could that manager find out that some other project manager had other plans for a resource.

With client/server environments, the gulf was filled. Most of the resource manager tools, regardless of their patrimony, now operate on a client-server basis, accessing a repository of projects. This has significantly opened the availability of resource management tools; but keep in mind that some products are not fully interactive resource management tools and may only be project plan *consolidators* with a few custom views or reports added for a departmental or enterprisewide view.

Resource management tools, in the full planning process, allow the project planner to develop a full project plan of tasks and assignments without considerations for the availability of actual resources. While this may seem to be unrealistic, it does allow the planner to develop his optimal view of the project before suboptimizing the plan to accommodate actual resource constraints. It also allows the planner to share information with other planners regarding changes to the anticipated use of a resource as adjustments to the plan are made by the planner, or occur as a result of forces out of the planner's control.

The key to this process is the ability to exchange roles or generic descriptions of skills and specialties necessary for a task with named resources, real human beings, or equipment to be used in execution of the task. Related to this process is the ability to *go shopping* for another named resource to exchange with the originally named resource. This may occur in the case of an unplanned unavailability or need for additional availability, and still have access to the skills and specialties that caused the planner to select the originally named resource in the beginning.

The result of this is that someone, associated with the resource but not directly with the projects, can work with the project managers to ensure effective utilization of all available resources and avoid resource bottlenecks on the projects for which resources are supplied.

What the Data Reveals

Resource management products provide many of the same features for program or project planning; however, the perspective for resource management software is a resource-centric view of the project task plan rather than a task-centric view of the project resource plan. If you are reading the listing of responding vendors in Resource Management after reading Schedule Management, you may feel that you stumbled back into that chapter. That is because there are only a half-dozen different vendors and, of the vendors that are the same, there are only two or three with different products or descriptions.

What a Majority of Vendors Offer

With so much overlap between this category and schedule management, most vendors describe the primary purpose of their product as generating project schedules. Most have the skills database search capabilities and project portfolio-resource matching capabilities that differentiates resource management from schedule management. The only weak area was in using crews rather than individual human and work equipment resources and in not being able to allocate or schedule perishable or consumable resources, which may be a capability more common to ERP, rather than project resource planning.

What a Minority of Vendors Offer

Integration with E-mail surprisingly stands out as something lacking in the majority of respondents in terms of nonparticipation, especially considering the importance of communication across multiple organizations to the success of resource planning.

Also, very few packages support password protection. This is bothersome because there are a lot of capabilities within resource management to which access should be limited and if the product does not either have its own security or allow the network security to operate at a level below simple product access, confidentiality may be compromised.

Unique Features That Surfaced in Vendor Responses to the Narrative Questions

Vendors reported a wide array of quality management processes being used in the development of their products, including proprietary development and quality assurance processes, including testing tools and formal beta testing, pursuit or attainment of ISO 9000 or ISO 9001 certification, or capability maturity module (CMM)-level attainment, attainment of a Y2K standards level or self-test for Y2K preparedness, and version control management.

Although many different pricing strategies exist including named licenses, concurrent licensing, and site licensing and volume discounts, very few vendors quoted prices that can be used for cost comparisons.

Services offered range from installation to training, project management process engineering, and project office implementation. Customization allowed in some larger products. Support services are sold in addition to software license fee.

What's New and Exciting

The level of sophistication in resource matching will be a real eye-opener to someone who has struggled with enterprise resource management issues while running a project on a stand-alone scheduler tool.

A reminder: The data in the matrix and in the narrative responses were supplied by the vendors and have not been independently verified.

Resource Management

	ABT Resource	ActionPlan	Allegro	AMS REALTIME Resources	AutoPLAN Enterprise	Cascade PgM	Dekker TRAKKER Activity Based Cost Management and Performance System	Enterprise Project	Innate Resource Manager
Scheduling/leveling features									
Resource leveling	Y	Y	N	Y	Y	Y	Y	Y	Y
Resource smoothing	Y	N	N	Y	Y	Y	Y	Y	Y
Leveling by date range	Y	Y	Y	Y	Y	Y	Y	Y	Y
"Do not level" flag (bypass project during leveling)	Y	N	Y	Y	Y	Y	Y	Y	Y
User-defined resource profiles (spread curves)	Y	N	N	N	Y	Y	Y	Y	Y
Team/crew scheduling	Y	Y	N	N	Y	Y	Y	Y	N
Skill scheduling	Y	Y	Y	Y	Y	Y	Y	Y	Y
Number of skills per resource	Unlim.	N	20	32 +	15	Unlim.	Unlim.	Y	Unlim.
Alternate resource scheduling	Y	N	N	Y	Y	Y	Y	Y	Manual
Rolling wave scheduling	Y	N	N	Y	Y	Y	Y	Y	Y
Activity splitting	Y	Y	N	N	Y	Y	Y	Y	Y
Variable availability	Y	Y	Y	Y	Y	Y	Y	Y	Y
Perishable resources	Y	N	N	Y	N	Y	Y	Y	N
Consumable resources	Y	N	N	Y	N	Y	Y	Y	N
Assign role (skill), software assigns individual later	Y	Y	N	Y	Y	N	Y	Y	Y
Hierarchical resources	Y	N	N	Y	Y	Y	Y	Y	Y
Heterogeneous resources	Y	N	Y	Y	Y	Y	Y	Y	Y
Homogeneous resources	Y	N	Y	Y	Y	Y	Y	Y	Y
Query overallocations by:									
Skill	Y	Y	Y	Y	Y	Y	Y	Y	Y
Resource type	Y	Y	Y	Y	Y	Y	Y	Y	Y
Department	Y	Y	Y	Y	Y	Y	Y	Y	Y
User defined	Y	Y	Y	Y	Y	Y	Y	Y	Y
Resource costs									
Rate escalation	Y	N	Y	Y	Y	Y	Y	Y	Y
Overtime	Y	N	N	Y	Y	Y	Y	Y	Y
Top-down budgeting	Y	N	Y	Y	Y	Y	Y	Y	Y
Bottom-up cost summarization	Y	N	Y	Y	Y	Y	Y	Y	Y
Calculate unit cost	Y	Y	Y	Y	Y	Y	Y	N	Y
Skills Database									
Resumes	Y	N	N	N	Y	N	Y	N	Y
Search by skill	Y	Y	N	Y	Y	Y	Y	Y	Y
Portfolio resource analysis									
What-if scenarios	Y	N	Y	Y	Y	Y	Y	Y	Y
Project templates	Y	Y	Y	Y	Y	Y	Y	Y	Y
Misc									
Individual resource calendars	Y	Y	Y	Y	Y	Y	Y	Y	Y
Share resource pool across multiple projects	Y	Y	Y	Y	Y	Y	Y	Y	Y

	A	B	C	D	E	F	G	H	I
Electronic resource requestor (send message to functional manager asking for his people)	Y	N	N	Y	Y	Y	Y	N	Y
Reporting									
Report writer	Y	N	Y	Y	Y	Y	Y	Y	Y
Report wizard	Y	N	N	N	Y	N	Y	Y	Y
Publishes as HTML	Y	N	Y	N	Y	Y	Y	Y	Y
Number of user-defined fields		N/A	30	100	25	Unlim.	Unlim.	0	Unlim.
Drill-down/roll-up	Y	Y	Y	Y	Y	Y	Y	Y	Y
Import/export	Y	N	Y	Y	Y	Y	Y	Y	Y
Automatic E-mail notification	Y	Y	N	N	Y	Y	Y	N	Y
Macro recorder/batch capable *	Y	N	N	Y	Y	Y	Y	Y	Y
Can "canned" reports be modified?	Y	N	Y	Y	Y	Y	Y	Y	Y
Sort, filter	Y	N	Y	Y	Y	Y	Y	Y	Y
Architecture									
Databases supported (list):	Oracle, MS SQL Server, Sybase, Informix	N/A	MS SQL Server, Oracle, Sybase, SQL Anywhere	ODBC Server to MS Access, Oracle, etc.	Oracle	Oracle	Oracle, MS SQL Server, Informix, MS Access, FoxPro	Oracle, Sybase, Informix, MS SQL Server, MS Access	MS Access, MS SQL Server, Oracle
Supports distributed databases	Y	Y	N	Y	Y	Y	Y	Y	N
Three-tier client/server	Y	Y	N	Y	Y	Y	Y	Y	N
Client operating systems	Win 95/98/NT	Mac, Win 95/NT, Solaris	Win 95/NT	Win 95/NT/3.x, Solaris, HP, RS, Mac	Win 95/NT/3.x, Solaris, HP-UX, AIX	Win 95/98/NT	Win 95/98/NT	Win 95/98/NT	Win
Server operating systems	Win NT	Win NT, Solaris	Win 95 (32-bit)/NT, TCP/IP	Win 95/NT/3.x, Solaris, HP, RS, Mac	Win NT, Solaris, HP-UX, AIX	Unix, Win NT	Win NT, Novell, Unix	Unix, Win NT	Any that support Win

Resource Management

	ABT Resource	ActionPlan	Allegro	AMS REALTIME Resources	AutoPLAN Enterprise	Cascade PgM	Dekker TRAKKER Activity Based Cost Management and Performance System	Enterprise Project	Innate Resource Manager
Network operating systems	TCP/IP compatible	TCP/IP	Novell, Win NT, Pathworks	TCP/IP, Banyan, Novell, IPX	Win NT, Novell, Unix	TCP/IP	Win NT, Novell, Unix	Novell, Win NT, others	Any that support Win
Minimum client configuration	Pentium 133		Pentium class machine, 32 MB RAM	8 MB RAM, 20 MB disk, 486 or better	P5 32 MB	PC 486/66 processor or above. Win 95 or Win NT V4. 16 MB RAM	16 MB RAM, 1 GB HD, SVGA	486, 16 MB memory	Pentium
Minimum server configuration	Pentium 266		High grade Pentium II, 20 MB available disk space	32 MB RAM, 100 MB disk, Pentium or better	P5 32 MB, Unix machine with 64 MB	Any server supporting Oracle 7 or above	128 MB RAM, 10 GB HD	Pentium 200 CPU, 128 MB, 1 GB	Capacity consideration only
Client runs under Web browser	N	Y	N	Y	Y	N	N	Y	Y
Open architecture									
Supports OLE	Y	N	N	N	Y	Y	Y	Y	Y
Documented Object Model	Y	N	N		Y	Y	Y	Y	Y
Documented Application Programming Interface (API)	Y	N	N		Y	Y	Y	Y	Y
Simultaneous edit of data file	Y	N	N		N	Y	Y	Y	Y
Does product have a programming language?	N	N	N		Y	Y	Y	Y	Y
Are years stored as four-digit numbers?	Y	N	Y		Y	Y	Y	Y	Y
Online help									
Right mouse click	Y	N	N	N	N	N	Y	N	Y
Hover buttons	Y	N	Y	Y	Y	Y	Y	N	Y
Interactive help	Y	Y	N	Y	Y	Y	Y	Y	Y
Help search feature	Y	Y	Y	Y	Y	Y	Y	Y	Y
Web access to product knowledge base *	Y	N	N	Y	Y	N	N	N	Y
Vendor information									
Training									
Computer-based training	Y	N	N	Y	Y	Y	Y	Y	Y
Training materials available	Y	Y	Y	Y	Y	Y	Y	Y	Y

254

Customized training materials	Y	Y	Y	Y	Y	Y	N
Online tutorial	Y	N	Y	N	N	Y	Y
Consulting available from vendor	Y	Y	Y	Y	Y	Y	Y
Site license discounts	Y	Y	Y	Y	Y	Y	Y
Enhancement requests *	Y	Y	Y	Y	Y	Y	Y
Modify source code, support through upgrades *	Y	Y	Y	Y	Y	N	N
Global presence							
Global offices	Y	N	Y	Y	Y	Y	N
Multilingual technical support	Y	Y	Y	Y	Y	N	N
Language versions (list):	Eng, Fr, Ger	Eng, Span	Eng	Eng, Fr	Eng, Fr	Eng	Eng, Fr, Ger, Jpn
Audit Software Quality Assurance process? *	Y	Y	Y	Y	Y	N	Y
Security							
Configurable access priviledges *	Y	Y	Y	Y	Y	Y	Y
Passwords expire (forced update)	Y	Y	Y	N	N	N	N
Electronic approvals	Y	Y	Y	Y	Y	N	Y
Password protect files	Y	Y	Y	Y	Y	Y	Y

Resource Management

	Intelligent Planner	Micro Planner X-Pert	Microsoft Project 98	Milestones, Etc.	Open Plan	Panorama	PLANTRAC-OUTLOOK	PlanView Software	Primavera Project Planner (P3) 2.0
Scheduling/leveling features									
Resource leveling	Y	Y	Y	N	Y	Y	Y	Y	Y
Resource smoothing	Y	Y	Y	N	Y	Y	Y	Y	Y
Leveling by date range	Y	Y	Y	N	Y	Y	Y	Y	Y
"Do not level" flag (bypass project during leveling)	Y	Y	Y	N	Y	Y	Y	Y	Y
User-defined resource profiles (spread curves)	Y	Y	Y	N	Y	Y	Y	Y	Y
Team/crew scheduling	Y	Y	N	N	N	N	Y	Y	Y
Skill scheduling	Y	Y	N	N	N	N	N	Y	N
Number of skills per resource	Unlim.	20	N/A	0	Unlim.	N	N	Unlim.	N
Alternate resource scheduling	Y	N	Y	N	Y	Y	Y	Y	N
Rolling wave scheduling		Y	N	N	Y	Y	N	Y	N
Activity splitting	Y	Y	Y	Y	Y	Y	Y	Y	Y
Variable availability	Y	Y	Y	N	Y	Y	Y	Y	Y
Perishable resources	Y	Y	Y	N	Y	N	N	N	Y
Consumable resources	Y	Y	N	N	Y	N	Y	N	Y
Assign role (skill), software assigns individual later	Y	N	N	N	Y	N	N	Y	N
Query overallocations by:									
Hierarchical resources	Y	Y	N	N	Y	N	Y	Y	Y
Heterogeneous resources	Y	Y	Y	N	Y	Y	Y	Y	Y
Homogeneous resources	Y	Y	Y	N	Y	Y	Y	Y	Y
Skill	Y	Y	N	N	Y	N	N	N	N
Resource type	Y	Y	N	N	Y	Y	Y	Y	Y
Department	Y	Y	N	N	Y	Y	Y	Y	Y
User defined	Y	Y	N	N	Y	Y	Y	Y	Y
Resource costs									
Rate escalation	Y	Y	Y	N	Y	Y	Y	Y	Y
Overtime	Y	Y	Y	N	Y	Y	N	Y	Y
Top-down budgeting	Y	Y	Y	N	Y	Y	Y	Y	Y
Bottom-up cost summarization	Y	Y	Y	N	Y	Y	Y	Y	Y
Calculate unit cost	Y	Y	N	N	Y	Y	Y	Y	Y
Skills Database									
Resumes	Y	N	N	N	N	N	N	N	N
Search by skill	Y	Y	N	N	Y	N	N	Y	N
Portfolio resource analysis									
What-if scenarios	Y	Y	Y	N	Y	Y	Y	Y	Y
Project templates	Y	Y	N	N	Y	Y	Y	Y	Y
Misc									
Individual resource calendars	Y	Y	Y	N	Y	Y	Y	Y	Y
Share resource pool across multiple projects	Y	Y	Y	N	Y	Y	Y	Y	Y

Electronic resource requestor (send message to functional manager asking for his people)	Y	N	Y	N	Y	N	N	Y	N
Reporting									
Report writer	Y	Y	Y	Y	Y	Y	Y	Y	Y
Report wizard	Y	N	N	Y	N	N	Y	Y	Y
Publishes as HTML	Y	N	Y	Y	Y	Y	N	Y	Y
Number of user-defined fields	100	12	360	200	Unlim.	20	20	Unlim.	20
Drill-down/roll-up	Y	Y	N	Y	Y	Y	Y	Y	Y
Import/export	Y	Y	Y	Y	Y	Y	Y	Y	Y
Automatic E-mail notification	Y	N	N	Y	N	N	N	N	N
Macro recorder/batch capable *	Y	N	Y	Y	Y	Y	Y	N	Y
Can "canned" reports be modified?	Y	Y	Y	Y	Y	Y	Y	Y	Y
Sort, filter	Y	Y	Y	Y	Y	Y	Y	Y	Y
Architecture									
Databases supported (list):	Oracle, Sybase, MS SQL Server, Informix, Centura		MS Access, MS SQL Server, or Oracle		Oracle, MS SQL Server, Sybase, MS Access, FoxPro	ORACLE	ODBC	Oracle, Sybase, MS SQL Server, etc.	Btrieve
Supports distributed databases	Y	N	Y		Y	Y	Y	N	N
Three-tier client/server	Y	N	N		N	Y	Y	Y	N
Client operating systems	Win 95/NT	Win, Mac	Win 95/98/NT 3.51 with Service Pack 5 or later/NT 4.0 with Service Pack 2 or later	Win	Win 95 or later	Win 95/NT	Win 95/98/NT	Win 95/98/NT	Win 95/NT/3.x
Server operating systems	Win NT	Win, Mac	Win 95/98/NT 3.51 with Service Pack 5 or later/NT 4.0 with Service Pack 2 or later	Win	Specified by database vendor	Any that support Oracle	Win 95/98/NT	Win NT, Unix, Novell, IIS, Netscape	Most popular operating systems (e.g., Novell)

Resource Management

	Intelligent Planner	Micro Planner X-Pert	Microsoft Project 98	Milestones, Etc.	Open Plan	Panorama	PLANTRAC-OUTLOOK	PlanView Software	Primavera Project Planner (P3) 2.0
Network operating systems	TCP/IP, NetBios	Win, Mac	Any Win-supported network	Any	Any that support Win	TCP/IP	Novell compatible	Win NT, Unix, Novell, IIS, Netscape	Most popular operating systems (e.g., Novell)
Minimum client configuration	Pentium 120, 16 MB RAM, 1 GB disk		486 or higher processor with 12 MB memory for Win 95 or 16 MB for Win 98 or NT	Win	Pentium or compatible, Win 95 or later: 16 MB RAM, Rec. 32 MB	Pentium 133 MHz, 32 MB RAM, 500 MB disk	8 MB	486/66, 8 MB RAM, Win 3.x+	486, 32 MB RAM
Minimum server configuration	Pentium 233, 128 MB RAM, 1 GB disk		Run from server is available; configuration depends on number of users connecting to the server	Win	Server optional	Depends on number of users	8 MB	486/66, 32 MB RAM, Novell	Not specified
Client runs under Web browser	Y	N	Y	N	N	N	N	Y	N
Open architecture									
Supports OLE	N	N	Y	Y	Y	Y	N	Y	Y
Documented Object Model	N	N	Y	Y	Y	Y	N	Y	Y
Documented Application Programming Interface (API)	Y	N	N	Y	N	Y	N	Y	Y
Simultaneous edit of data file	Y	N	N	Y	Y	Y	Y	N	Y
Does product have a programming language?	Y	N	Y	Y	N	Y	N	Y	N
Are years stored as four-digit numbers?	Y	Y	Y	Y	Y	Y	Y	Y	N
Online help									
Right mouse click	N	Y	Y	Y	Y	N	Y	Y	Y
Hover buttons	N	Y	Y	Y	Y	N	Y	Y	Y
Interactive help	Y	Y	Y	Y	Y	Y	Y	Y	Y
Help search feature	Y	Y	Y	Y	Y	Y	Y	Y	Y
Web access to product knowledge base *	Y	Y	Y	Y	Y	N	N	Y	N
Vendor information									
Training									
Computer-based training	N	Y	N	Y	Y	N	Y	Y	N
Training materials available	Y	Y	Y	Y	Y	Y	Y	Y	Y

	Col 1	Col 2	Col 3	Col 4	Col 5	Col 6	Col 7	Col 8
Customized training materials	Y	Y	N	Y	Y	Y	Y	Y
Online tutorial	Y	Y	Y	N	Y	N	Y	Y
Consulting available from vendor	Y	Y	Y	Y	Y	Y	Y	Y
Site license discounts	Y	Y	Y	Y	Y	Y	Y	Y
Enhancement requests *	Y	Y	Y	Y	Y	Y	Y	Y
Modify source code, support through upgrades *	Y	N	Y	Y	Y	Y	Y	N
Global presence								
Global offices	Y	Y	N	Y	N	N	Y	Y
Multilingual technical support	N	Y	N	N	N	N	Y	Y
Language versions (list):	Eng, Fr, Ger, Dutch	Eng	Ger, Fr, Swed, Ital, Span, Dan, Nor, Jpn, Traditional Chin, Simplified Chin, Kor, Heb, Brzl. Port	Eng, Ital, Fr, Ger, Mand, Rus, Hangul		Eng	Eng, Fr, Ger	Ger
Audit Software Quality Assurance process? *	Y	Y	N	N	Y	Y	Y	N
Security								
Configurable access priviledges *	Y	N	N	Y	Y	N	Y	Y
Passwords expire (forced update)	N	N	N	Y	Y	N	Y	N
Electronic approvals	Y	N	Y	N	Y	N	Y	N
Password protect files	Y	Y	Y	Y	Y	N	Y	Y

Resource Management

	ProChain	Project Control 6.0 - Resource Manager	Project Integrator 2.0 Enterprise Edition	Project Scheduler 7.6	QEI Exec	ResourceXchange for MS Project	SAS Software	TurboProject Professional 3.0	WebProject	WorkLink Resource Manager
Scheduling/leveling features										
Resource leveling	Y	N	Y	Y	Y	Y	Y	Y	N	Visual
Resource smoothing	N	N	Y	Y	N	Y	Y	Y	N	Visual
Leveling by date range	N	N	Y	N	N	Y	Y	Y	N	Visual
"Do not level" flag (bypass project during leveling)	Y	N	Y	Y	N	Y	N	Y	N	N
User-defined resource profiles (spread curves)	N	Y	Y	Y	N	Y	N	Y	N	Y
Team/crew scheduling	N	Y	Y	N	N	Y	N	N	N	N
Skill scheduling	N	Y	Y	Y	N	Y	Y	N	N	Y
Number of skills per resource		Unlim.	Unlim.	Unlim.	Unlim.	Unlim.	Unlim.	N/A	N	Unlim.
Alternate resource scheduling		Y	Y	Y	N	Y	N	Y	Y	N
Rolling wave scheduling	N	N	Y	N	N	Y	Y	Y	N	Y
Activity splitting	N	N	Y	Y	N	Y	Y	Y	Y	Y
Variable availability	Y	N	Y	Y	N	Y	Y	Y	N	N
Perishable resources	N	N	Y	Y	N	Y	Y	N	Y	N
Consumable resources	N	N	Y	N	N	Y	Y	N	N	N
Assign role (skill), software assigns individual later	N	Y	Y	N	N	Y	N	N	Y	N
Hierarchical resources	Y	Y	N	Y	Y	Y	N	Y	Y	Y
Heterogeneous resources	N	Y	Y	Y	Y	Y	Y	N	Y	Y
Homogeneous resources	Y	Y	N	N	N	Y	Y	Y	Y	N
Query overallocations by:										
Skill	N	Y	Y	Y	Y	Y	Y	Y	Y	Y
Resource type	N	Y	Y	Y	Y	Y	Y	Y	Y	Y
Department	N	Y	Y	Y	Y	Y	Y	Y	Y	Y
User defined	N	Y	Y	Y	Y	Y	Y	Y	Y	N
Resource costs										
Rate escalation	Y	Y	Y	Y	Y	Y	N	Y	N	Y
Overtime	Y	Y	Y	Y	N	Y	Y	N	Y	Y
Top-down budgeting	N	Y	Y	Y	Y	Y	Y	N	N	Y
Bottom-up cost summarization	Y	Y	Y	Y	Y	Y	Y	Y	N	Y
Calculate unit cost	Y	Y	Y	Y	N	Y	Y	Y	N	Y
Skills Database										
Resumes	N	N	Y	Y	N	Y	N	N	Y	N
Search by skill	N	Y	Y	Y	N	Y	Y	N	Y	Y
Portfolio resource analysis										
What-if scenarios	N	Y	N	Y	Y	Y	Y	Y	Y	Y
Project templates	Y	Y	Y	Y	Y	Y	Y	Y	Y	Y
Misc										
Individual resource calendars	Y	Y	Y	Y	Y	Y	Y	Y	Y	N
Share resource pool across multiple projects	Y	Y	Y	Y	Y	Y	Y	Y	Y	Y

Feature	1	2	3	4	5	6	7	8	9	10
Electronic resource requestor (send message to functional manager asking for his people)	N	Y	Y	N	Y	N	N	Y	N	N
Reporting										
Report writer	Y	N	N	Y	Y	N	Y	Y	Y	Y
Report wizard	N	Y	N	Y	Y	N	Y	Y	N	N
Publishes as HTML	Y	Y	Y	Y	Y	N	Y	Y	Y	Y
Number of user-defined fields	Unlim.	Variable	20+	Unlim.	MSP limits	Unlim.	Unlim.	Unlim.	60	250
Drill-down/roll-up	Y	Y	Y	Y	Y	Y	Y	Y	Y	N
Import/export	Y	Y	N	Y	N	N	N	Y	Y	Y
Automatic E-mail notification	N	N	N	N	N	N	Y	Y	N	N
Macro recorder/batch capable *	Y	Y	Y	Y	Y	Y/N	Y	Y	Y	Y
Can "canned" reports be modified?	Y	Y	Y	Y	Y	Y	Y	Y	Y	Y
Sort, filter	Y	Y	Y	Y	Y	Y	Y	Y	Y	Y
Architecture										
Databases supported (list):	MS Access, Oracle, MS SQL Server	Oracle, MS SQL Server, Informix, Sybase, any JDBC-compliant database	ODBC-enabled databases	Most major databases	Oracle, MS SQL Server, Sybase	N/A	Via ODBC: Oracle, Sybase, MS SQL Server, MS Access, et al.	MS SQL Server, Oracle, Sybase, SQL Anywhere	Oracle, MS Access, MS SQL Server, Sybase	MS Access
Supports distributed databases	Y	Y	N	Y	Y	N	Y	N	Y	N
Three-tier client/server	Y	Y	N	Y	Y	N	N	Y	Y	N
Client operating systems	Win 95/98/NT	Win 95/NT, Unix, Linux, any Java-enabled OS	Win 95/98/NT 4.0/3.x, OS/2 if it includes Win OS/Support	MVS, CMS, VSE; OpenVMS for VAX and AXP; Solaris, HP-UX, AIX, Digital Unix, Intel MIPS ABI; Win 95/NT, Mac, OS/2	Win 32, MS Project	Win 95/NT/3.x with Win 32s, Solaris	Win 95/98/NT4	Win 95/NT	Win 95/98/NT	Win 95/NT
Server operating systems	Win, Unix	Win 95/NT, Unix, Linux, any Java-enabled OS	Win 95/98/NT 4.0/3.x, OS/2 if it includes Win OS/Support	MVS, CMS, VSE; OpenVMS for VAX and AXP; Solaris, HP-UX, AIX, Digital Unix, Intel MIPS ABI; Win 95/NT, Mac, OS/2	Unix, Win NT	N/A	N/A	Win NT		Unix, Win NT, HP, Sybase, others

Resource Management

Feature	ProChain	Project Control 6.0 - Resource Manager	Project Integrator 2.0 Enterprise Edition	Project Scheduler 7.6	QEI Exec	ResourceXchange for MS Project	SAS Software	TurboProject Professional 3.0	WebProject	WorkLink Resource Manager
Network operating systems		Novell, IPX, XPX, Banyan, MS Network, TCP/IP	Novell, Win NT, Banyan	Novell, Win NT	LAN Manager, TCP/IP, Novell	Multiple	All major network environments, including LAN Server, TCP/IP, Warp Server, Novell	Most including Novell, Win NT	Win 95/NT, Unix, Linux, any Java-enabled OS	Win, Novell
Minimum client configuration	Same as MS Project	PC 486/66 processor or above. Win 95 or Win NT V4. 16 MB RAM	P166 MHz, 16 MB RAM, 30 MB HD	486 or better, 16 MB memory, 15 MB HD	486, 16 MB RAM, mouse, XGA graphics	Pentium w/32 MB	Varies by platform	386 or greater 16 MB memory, 30 MB HD space, CD-ROM, VGA or higher	Any Web-enabled browser	Pentium, 24 MB
Minimum server configuration	N	Any server supporting Oracle 7 or above	P166 MHz, 16 MB RAM, 30 MB HD	N/A	N/A	Pentium w/128 MB	Varies by platform	386 or greater 16 MB memory, 30 MB HD space, CD-ROM, VGA or higher	Win 95/NT, Unix, Linux, any Java-enabled OS	Pentium, 32 MB
Client runs under Web browser	N	Y	Y	N	N	N	Y	N/A	Y	N
Open architecture										
Supports OLE	Y	Y	Y	Y	N	Y	N	N	N	Y
Documented Object Model	Y	N	N	Y	Y	Y	N	N	N	N
Documented Application Programming Interface (API)	Y	N	N	Y	Y	N	N	N	N	N
Simultaneous edit of data file	N	Y	Y	Y	N	Y	Y	N	Y	Y
Does product have a programming language?	Y	N	N	N	Y	N	Y	N	N	N
Are years stored as four-digit numbers?	N	Y	Y	Y	Y	Y	Y	Y	Y	Y
Online help										
Right mouse click	Y	N	N	Y	N	Y	Y	Y	N	Y
Hover buttons	Y	Y	Y	N	Y	Y	Y	Y	Y	Y
Interactive help	Y	N	N	Y	Y	N	Y	Y	Y	Y
Help search feature	Y	Y	Y	Y	Y	Y	Y	Y	Y	Y
Web access to product knowledge base *	Y	Y	Y	N	N	N	N	Y	Y	Y
Vendor information										
Training										
Computer-based training	N	Y	N	N	N	N	N	Y	Y	N
Training materials available	Y	Y	Y	Y	Y	Y	Y	Y	Y	Y

Customized training materials	Y	Y	Y	Y	Y	Y	Y	Y	N
Online tutorial	N	Y	Y	N	N	Y	Y	N	N
Consulting available from vendor	Y	Y	Y	Y	Y	Y	Y	Y	Y
Site license discounts	Y	Y	Y	Y	N	Y	Y	Y	Y
Enhancement requests *	Y	Y	Y	Y	Y	Y	Y	Y	Y
Modify source code, support through upgrades *	Y	Y	Y	N	Y	Y	Y	Y	Y
Global presence									
Global offices	Y	Y	Y	N	N	N	Y	Y	Y
Multilingual technical support	Y	Y	Y	Y	N	N	N	N	N
Language versions (list):	Eng, Fr, Ital	Eng, Ger	Eng	Jpn	Eng	Eng	Eng, Fr, Ger, Jpn	Eng	Eng
Audit Software Quality Assurance process? *	Y	Y	Y	Y	Y	N	N	Y	N
Security									
Configurable access priviledges *	Y	Y	N	Y	Y	Y	Y	Y	N
Passwords expire (forced update)	Y	Y	N	N	N	N	N	Y	N
Electronic approvals	Y	Y	N	N	Y	N	N	Y	N
Password protect files	Y	Y	N	Y	Y	Y	Y	DBMS	N

VENDOR RESPONSES TO NARRATIVE QUESTIONS

ABT Resource (ABT Corporation)

Describe what the product is designed to do.

A powerful application supporting project and resource managers, ABT Resource aligns mission-critical people with an organization's mission-critical programs. ABT Resource assists you in identifying available resources by role and proficiency, requesting and allocating them to programs and projects, as well as planning for future requirements. Deploying sizable numbers of resources within your programs efficiently and with flexibility, providing improved communication and collaboration.

Top three product differentiators; describe what makes your product unique.

1. Integration with ABT Repository extends functionality.
2. Comprehensive functionality addresses broad range of stakeholders.
3. Granular views of skills and proficiency levels.

To what business processes can this tool be applied?

Resource management processes.
Program and project management processes.
Process management processes.

Describe the ideal end user environment for the current version of your product (size of organization, level of project management sophistication, effort and commitment required).

ABT Resource can benefit organizations of fifty to fifty thousand project-related resources, regardless of project management maturity level.

Future strategies for this product.

Extend functionality.
Enhance scalability.

Product's target market.

Enterprise project management, especially those organizations with three hundred plus resources.

What are your product's three main benefits? (How does using the product add value to the customer?)

1. Standardized roles ensure consistency, which improves resource planning.
2. Granular views that profile information the way you need to see it.
3. Promotes a common approach to tracking skills and proficiencies, which helps determine project time, cost, scope, and quality.

Describe your quality management process. List any relevant certifications.

ABT's test engineering organization provides extensive in-house product quality testing using a series of proprietary testing methodologies, supplemented by external resources to perform activities such as high-volume benchmarking. ABT's test group has also been instrumental in contributing to the definition of IEEE Year 2000 testing standards.

Discuss your product pricing structure. Include volume discount levels, concurrent user options, site licenses, cost of implementation, and other issues.

Pricing is on a named-user basis. List price: ABT Resource, $125. Volume discounts apply.

Implementation programs vary according to suite installations or stand-alone product installations. Additional services include project management maturity evaluation, tool training, project management concepts training, process customization and implementation, and systems integration/custom programming work.

Annual maintenance (client support program) = Fifteen percent of purchase price.

ActionPlan

Describe what the product is designed to do.

ActionPlan is an enterprise-strength project management system that facilitates team collaboration on projects over organizational and geographical boundaries.

Top three product differentiators; describe what makes your product unique.

1. Automated project and task distribution. All project and task information is automatically delivered to each team member via an intranet.

2. Real-time project updates. ActionPlan gives team members the ability to update the status of the project through their HotSheet (to do list). As a team member completes a task displayed in their HotSheet, they simply check off the task.

3. Cross-project management. ActionPlan allows you to share both project information and resource usage across multiple projects. For instance, you can easily see how a resource(s) is distributed across multiple projects before and after you assign that per resource.

To what business processes can this tool be applied?

ActionPlan is currently being used for many diverse projects including product development and deployment within IT organizations, service task tracking within professional services organizations, and programs within marketing organizations.

Describe the ideal end-user environment for the current version of your product (size of organization, level of project management sophistication, effort and commitment required).

The following is the ideal end-user environment for ActionPlan: fifty or more team members that are geographically dispersed working on multiple related and/or nonrelated projects, very little to medium familiarity with project management.

Future strategies for this product.

Better integration of time/cost tracking capability.

Product's target market.

Large IT organizations with geographically dispersed teams.

What are your product's three main benefits? (How does using the product add value to the customer?)

1. Current status is visible and available to everyone.

2. Time saved by the project manager through real-time updates of project schedules directly from team members.

3. Product is widely used and adopted because of its ease of use and ease of deployment.

Describe your quality management process. List any relevant certifications.

Products go through extensive internal quality testing as well as external beta testing.

Discuss your product pricing structure. Include volume discount levels, concurrent user options, site licenses, cost of implementation, and other issues.

$995 for five nonconcurrent users, $1,895 for ten users, $4,495 for twenty-five users, $8,999 for fifty users, $16,995 for 100 users. Site licenses are available.

Subscription and maintenance pricing: $398 for five-user license, $758 for ten-user license, $1,798 for twenty-five-user license, $3,598 for fifty-user license, $6,798 for 100-user license.

Allegro

Describe what the product is designed to do.

With a spreadsheet-style interface, Allegro gives project managers a powerful, easy-to-learn tool to manage project resources, develop project forecasts and schedule employees across multiple projects. Users can schedule hours by employee or labor category and see historical actuals side-by-side with their plans. Nonlabor costs can be estimated and historical actuals viewed as well.

Allegro performs all the calculations for labor costs, application of overhead rates, and revenue forecasting. Estimate-to-complete, estimate-to-completion, and original budget by employee, labor category, and cost account are all at the user's fingertips in the project spreadsheet. In the employee spreadsheet, an employee's previously charged projects are shown side-by-side with the upcoming schedule. Planning for vacation schedules and holidays is easily accommodated.

Allegro stores actual and planned project costs and revenue in a scalable, accessible, and open relational database. With Allegro's standard reports and ad-hoc reportwriting capabilities, managers can easily access important cost and revenue information. Allegro's reports and graphs provide the information to manage resource allocation and report project cost and revenue information at any level of the organization.

Top three product differentiators; describe what makes your product unique.

1. Increases communication across accounting, organizational, and project management functions to accomplish corporate goals.
2. Summarizes project plans at the organization level and requires no additional re-keying of data; relates project status by manager.
3. Creates contract budgets, spreads them over time, and compares actual to planned performance.

To what business processes can this tool be applied?

Allegro should be applied to resource management and project management. As well as labor tracking processes.

Describe the ideal end-user environment for the current version of your product (size of organization, level of project management sophistication, effort and commitment required).

Professional services firms.
It should be an integral part of any business where people are the main resource.

Future strategies for this product.

Increase the level at which it maintains and tracks budgets.

Product's target market.

Architecture, engineering, design, consulting, and other professional services firms.

What are your product's three main benefits? (How does using the product add value to the customer?)

1. Provides a clear picture of expected present and future performance; analyzes revenues and profits, including the impact of new projects on future business.

2. Increases communication across accounting, organizational, and project management functions to accomplish corporate goals, by combining cost accounting and general project management information and allowing the different departments to see the various effects on cash flow, revenues, etc. of a particular project in several stages.

3. Users experience fewer entry errors, time savings, and an accurate, complete forecast of revenue and direct labor.

Describe your quality management process. List any relevant certifications.

Allegro goes through an extensive QC process and is then tested in Deltek labs and pilot programs.

Discuss your product pricing structure. Include volume discount levels, concurrent user options, site licenses, cost of implementation, and other issues.

Minimum: $20,000 (four named or one concurrent user plus 60 hours of consulting). Volume discounts are available as user count increases.

AMS REALTIME Resources

Describe what the product is designed to do.

Resource managers get a high-level project plan from a project manager. Generic skill assignments can be exchanged for resources that meet both skill and availability requirements, or specific resources, which are underloaded or overloaded, can be adjusted or reassigned. Resource modifications are updated back to each effected project.

Resource managers see a clear picture of how employees are utilized across all projects, including unplanned and nonproject work. This provides more accurate work estimates that better reflect (and estimate) actual completion of work.

Organization hierarchy and access controls provide a security layer to ensure data integrity and protection. Management approval of actuals and estimates provide data verification.

Top three product differentiators; describe what makes your product unique.

Project and resource management modules interact in a way that mirrors real workflow processes, giving real-time visibility of accurate status information. Fully integrated schedule, resource, and cost gives you an accurate look at one or more projects from any perspective.

AMS REALTIME Resources has a fast and powerful database that is both efficient and fully extendable, allowing unprecedented customization. Linked tables allow for efficient and powerful data access and control. ODBC drivers allow external access to the data, including calculated reports.

All software runs native on Windows (95, NT, 3.x), Macintosh, Sun, Solaris, HP, and RS with identical look and feel and direct data access from any platform.

To what business processes can this tool be applied?

AMS REALTIME Resources is so flexible that it can be applied to virtually any business process, including proposals, maintenance operations, new development, manufacturing, and performance improvement processes.

AMS REALTIME Resources is designed to allow automated project statusing that automatically feeds earned value performance measurements. Cost management is empowered when costs can be tracked from a project summary level all the way down to the activity level; providing accurate information to pinpoint the source of cost overruns.

Describe the ideal end user environment for the current version of your product (size of organization, level of project management sophistication, effort and commitment required).

AMS REALTIME Resources is used by global companies in very large enterprise environments, all the way down to small companies with just a few people. While AMS REALTIME is used to support extremely sophisticated project management processes, it can still be used to benefit users with little or no project management background. Users can grow into the software as their project management expertise evolves. To make any project management implementation successful, senior management must be committed to supporting the process, and other participants must make the effort to be trained to use the tools and follow through. Working with a consultant to help adapt the software to your business practices and needs and to document these processes is the best way to ensure success.

Future strategies for this product.

Future development strategies include more active Web enablements, a more complex three-tiered server design to facilitate global replication, and more resource tools. AMS has always been on the cutting edge of technology, and we are dedicated to bringing our customers the best of this ever-changing world.

Product's target market.

Products are used across a wide variety of client bases. AMS does not target any particular market but is widely used in manufacturing, oil and gas, nuclear power, automotive, pharmaceutical, aerospace, software development, construction, research and development, and many other industries. AMS REALTIME software allows for a flexible implementation that integrates with customer business processes and organization structure.

What are your product's three main benefits? (How does using the product add value to the customer?)

1. Resources can be effectively utilized by providing managers with visibility and control over planned, unplanned, and nonproject work.

2. All work assignments are instantly communicated to employees, who also have a medium to effectively communicate work performed, status, and other issues. Organization hierarchy and access control protects data access and viability.

3. Selective automation allows managers to eliminate drudgery and inaccuracy, while still maintaining control over critical project and resource decisions.

Describe your quality management process. List any relevant certifications.

Advanced Management Solutions is fully committed to providing the highest quality software and services to all of our clients. We have implemented many internal standards and processes in order to ensure that we can track and manage our software development process to the highest standard of quality possible. Concurrent versions system has been implemented to help manage multiple programmers at multiple development sites. Peer review of source code and design strategy meetings with high-level program development leaders continue to ensure that our software remains on the leading edge of our evolving technology.

A dedicated testing department manages the initial alpha testing, which encompasses new functionality, system process testing, and full regression testing. Beta testing is initially performed internally. After a stable point has been reached, beta testing is extended to select client users. Client beta testing not only provides clients with an edge in using new software features but also greatly expands the test environment scope relating to different hardware environments. As AMS REALTIME Resources is one of the most flexible and highly configurable management products on the market today, client testing adds an exceptional dimension to our testing process.

Discuss your product pricing structure. Include volume discount levels, concurrent user options, site licenses, cost of implementation, and other issues.

Product price is different for clients, based on their requirements for software and implementation. Volume discounts and site licenses are available. Please request a quote from an AMS sales representative for your specific requirements.

Annual maintenance is based on of 20 percent of the current product cost, and includes all software upgrades (while support is active) and telephone hotline technical support. Training cost is based upon topics, requirements, training equipment and site, and days requested. Please request a quote from an AMS sales representative for your specific requirements.

AutoPLAN Enterprise (Digital Tools)

Describe what the product is designed to do.

AutoPLAN Enterprise Release 4 is a Web-based software and process solution to help high-tech, engineering, and telecommunications companies predict, control, and improve cycle time of critical program development and deployment. The solution set provides deep functionality across the entire spectrum of product life-cycle elements including pipeline management, project management, resource alignment, process effectiveness, document support, and team collaboration. AutoPLAN Enterprise integrates realistic planning, resource-centric management, status and forecast tracking, team collaboration, process support, escalation management, and program execution across globally distributed organizations.

Organizations are evolving from functional teams to matrix or program teams, and this is creating cross-functional or multidisciplinary project teams. AutoPLAN Enterprise recognizes three different organizational patterns that coexist: dynamic peer-to-peer, functional, and program management. AutoPLAN Enterprise offers these organizations both project-centric and resource-centric management. AutoPLAN Enterprise addresses everyone involved in product development and deployment including executives; program, product, resource, and project managers; and team leaders and team members, as well as teams from marketing, operations, service, and quality.

As a result of extensive process and product consulting with clients engaged in new product development and deployment, DTI has distilled four key reasons why products are late and descoped:

1. Product development pipeline and deployment structures that are not aligned with the company's time-to-market goals.

2. Unrealistic plans, overcommitted resources, and unmanaged cross-functional dependencies.

3. Status and forecast decisions that are based on hearsay, rather than on facts or experience.

4. A lack of consistent processes that fit the company culture and practice, which is further exacerbated by distributed cross-functional teams.

Avoiding late and descoped products requires an overall view of product and project status, the involvement of cross-functional teams, and decision evaluation tools. Increasingly accelerated product development cycles and shorter product life cycles require organizations to disseminate information quickly to remain competitive. To support today's geographically dispersed product development environments, organizations require a common platform that enables effective cross-functional collaboration and communication on product-development issues. It is also imperative that the introduction of new product information can be easily accessed by each stakeholder. Common platforms and accessible information by each stakeholder will result in accelerated organizational learning and decision-making within the organization.

DTI has created a cycle time management (CTM) framework comprised of both application and process support. This framework emphasizes the critical components involved in introducing and deploying the right products and services to the market at the right time. Introducing and deploying these products and services requires companies to institute well-defined new product planning and execution processes, complemented with customer management and performance measurement processes. The new planning processes should consist of product portfolio, technology portfolio, product planning, and resource planning. The execution processes must consist of advanced technology development, platform development, product development, and market introduction and deployment.

CTM enables companies to strike a balance between flexibility and discipline that is tailored to their organization and culture. The CTM framework supports a flexible *shrink-to-fit* process, which is adaptable to an organization's process maturity. This process will provide a road map for decision-making and progress tracking within a new product introduction and deployment pipeline.

CTM is comprised of six fundamental elements: 1) processes, 2) projects, 3) resources, 4) documents, 5) deliverables, and 6) analysis. These six elements form the foundation objectives that drive AutoPLAN Enterprise. Organizations require a well-defined and structured process to accomplish their goals. Projects make up the mechanisms through which detailed plans and schedules are generated, executed, and tracked. Every organization faces resource constraints; thus, resource management is a critical component of CTM. All projects have deliverables associated with them either in the form of documents or the product itself. And, all projects must be managed to ensure quality deliverables. Analysis tools enable various levels of stakeholders to evaluate and ensure proper support of all elements necessary to meet CTM objectives.

Top three product differentiators; describe what makes your product unique.

1. AutoPLAN Enterprise enables organizations to manage their pipeline of resources across programs and across the phase gates of each project. It assures an escalation process for critical issues, such as overallocations, by monitoring boundary conditions, and alerting appropriate people to the issues. Project managers are interested in the completion of tasks or milestones, while resource managers need to know all of the work planned for their resources. Both project and resource managers must collaborate to create realistic plans for meeting project objectives, as well as juggle those resources and plans on a day-to-day basis as changes occur. The nature of this work requires a resource-centric view of the plan, not just an activity-centric view. A resource-centric-view will allow resource managers to view and allocate activities to their scarce resources rather than allocating resources to their activities. AutoPLAN Enterprise enables resource management by providing a resource-centric Gantt bar that displays overallocated resources. Managing overallocations can be as easy as reassigning activities to another resource.

Program management is a collaborative effort. Success depends upon identifying and communicating critical issues. Such identification and communication must be inherent to the system. AutoPLAN Enterprise is designed with a communications backbone. A mechanism of triggers identifies critical issues (e.g., when milestone or cost exceeds a threshold boundary) and automatically alerts and draws attention to these critical issues. Project bulletin boards within AutoPLAN Enterprise also enhance communication by providing a context-sensitive vehicle for communicating information across the project team. In addition, AutoPLAN Enterprise supports electronic mail systems enabling triggers and bulletin board messages to be communicated to the various levels of stakeholders.

2. AutoPLAN Enterprise supports the distributed nature of project teams by matching real-world strategy with key scalable technologies. Enterprise customers need distributed project management capabilities that cater to multisite resource management, work distribution, progress tracking, global scheduling, consolidation, reporting, integration, and collaboration. DTI has met this challenge by investing over one hundred man-years in an enterprise-level, three-tier, distributed client/server architecture that leverages both Java and Internet technologies. AutoPLAN Enterprise provides full support for multiple internal operating divisions and external suppliers. AutoPLAN Enterprise leverages many platforms—Internet, Windows, NT, and Unix, providing reliable access across the organization. Additionally, AutoPLAN Enterprise enables common project data to be shared by different projects at different locations while being maintained in a central data center that is managed by pool-server software. Project data is maintained at each geographic location on either individual or multiple servers, depending on the number of internal operating divisions and projects. A divisional pool server can also be implemented to share the project data within divisional projects. AutoPLAN Enterprise application servers are capable of scalable distributed processing, and only the server needs the capacity for large multiproject operations. AutoPLAN Enterprise has multiserver cross-project dependency links. For example, the owner of a schedule that depends on the completion of activities in another project can create

cross-project links that automatically update her schedule when changes occur in the other project, even if that project resides on a different server.

3. AutoPLAN Enterprise leverages client/server/Web technologies. The promise of Java, which AutoPLAN Enterprise supports, is that enterprise deployments, including organizations with heterogeneous environments, can be cost effectively supported. DTI Web products are easier to use than Microsoft Project and are cheaper to deploy. The rapid spread of Internet protocols and Web servers into corporate infrastructure makes the Internet an ideal vehicle to support both enterprise computing and mobile employees. In addition, systems administration is simplified since no maintenance is required on the client side.

A very practical use of AutoPLAN Enterprise Web clients is that they can run in a disconnected mode on the Internet. With AutoPLAN Enterprise, the user can simply log on and save activities and other information to a local file. He can then continue to work while disconnected. At any time, the connection can be reestablished, either remotely or locally, and the data is resynchronized. This may be useful for dial-up connections when working remotely. The Web server handles all communications with the Web clients, whether they are communicating via the Internet, dial-up, LAN, or WAN. The AutoPLAN Enterprise Web clients can be run from any browser that supports Java 1.1, and the Web server will dynamically download the Java code to run the application on the client. DTI's Web strategy supports *thin* client computing. In this case, database-oriented servers are serving lightweight clients through Web servers and standard protocols. The AutoPLAN Enterprise Web clients are ideally suited for running on a Java-based network computer.

To what business processes can this tool be applied?

From business analysis and redesign to system implementation and training, DTI has established its own process to support the customer through all phases of CTM system implementation. However, as to applying AutoPLAN Enterprise to the customer's business processes, DTI takes a very pragmatic approach. DTI has established processes to help customers with the following seven business pains:

1. Managing the development and deployment pipeline in detail.

2. Top-down and bottom-up planning that enables managers to use team members' knowledge during up-front planning.

3. Juggle resources realistically so that resources are not overcommitted and parochial allocations are not made, but rather a mechanism for cooperation on resource tradeoffs is created.

4. Creating an organizational memory that captures organizational experience for reuse the next time.

5. Obtaining weekly integrated tracking information on how programs are progressing against their plans. This can be achieved by capturing actual time spent, estimates-to-complete, percent complete, and actual start and finish.

6. Problem identification, escalation, and collaboration that allows management and the team to receive adequate notice of impending issues.

7. Interactive decision evaluation to understand the domino effect of a problem in one project and its possible cross-program impact, and obtain a swift resolution between participants.

Any combination of these processes will help organizations better understand and make use of critical path methodology, work breakdown structures, resource management, cost and earned value techniques, multiproject resource scheduling, resource allocation, status tracking, report generation, matrix management solutions, integration with other systems, middleware design, project management process design, project rollups, report generation, database design, customized product training courses, generic project management training, and more.

Describe the ideal end user environment for the current version of your product (size of organization, level of project management sophistication, effort and commitment required).

AutoPLAN Enterprise is ideal for high-tech, engineering, and telecommunications organizations engaged in distributed product development and deployments. Its usage also extends to these organizations' distributors and partners. The role-based nature of AutoPLAN Enterprise spans all people involved, from executive management to the entire cross-functional product team. This includes experienced project and program managers, resource and development managers, and the team members creating or deploying the product. The AutoPLAN Enterprise Web client is specifically designed for those team leaders who are not full-time, experienced project managers. In fact, DTI has designed the AutoPLAN Enterprise Web client to be easier to use and more functional than Microsoft Project.

Organizations can start at either the program level right away and manage the overall pipeline of projects and resources at the business unit level, or at the individual project level. The AutoPLAN Enterprise Web client is not only easier to use than Microsoft Project, but is also capable of managing cross-functional dependencies and resources and offering enterprise scalability when the organization is ready to expand.

Coordinating distributed projects is a difficult task. It involves resources not only from multiple projects, but also from multiple functions within those projects as well. The program manager responsible must understand all of the interactions and milestones required to complete the project, but she cannot and should not develop and manage the entire plan herself. Instead, she should rely on the distributed functional leaders who are responsible for their piece of the project to plan and execute that piece. As a program manager, he needs to be able to integrate the individual team plans into a single comprehensive project plan. In many organizations, this integration of people and data is difficult. AutoPLAN Enterprise is designed to help with this. Having processes in place, underpinned by enterprise software, is key to predicting, controlling, and improving product/project cycle times.

Future strategies for this product.

AutoPLAN Enterprise has been designed with an integrated product management platform for all information related to meeting CTM objectives. DTI will continue to support features needed for CTM, including pipeline and portfolio management. Future strategies will enhance the ability of customers to make informed decisions based on a comprehensive presentation of relevant data with powerful drill-down capabilities, further collaborative features that utilize the intranet and Internet, and continuing support for the free-flowing nature of the engineering culture. Application wizards will help first-time users, accelerate deployment, and reduce training cost. Process support is key to productivity improvements and to adhering to organizationwide standards. Existing process support capabilities will be enhanced using the capabilities of Web technology and with more exchange of information across subsystems. Large organizations are geographically distributed to take advantage of global efficiencies. Local and global workgroups must collaborate together and respond quickly to changing environment and work content. Both executive management and front-line team members must have access anytime, anywhere, and in any manner to enterprisewide product/project information located on geographically distributed servers. Existing multiserver capabilities of AutoPLAN Enterprise are being enhanced using Oracle.

AutoPLAN Enterprise will support key technologies including Oracle, NT 5.0, middleware, and Java. Distributed objects capability using industry-standard specifications such as CORBA will be incorporated. In addition, the AutoPLAN Enterprise application-programming interface will provide CORBA-compliant objects for seamless integration with other applications. The collaboration capabilities of AutoPLAN Enterprise will be enhanced by incorporating a workflow server. This workflow server will be based on industry-standard specifications and will incorporate process modeling and messaging components to enable customers to configure the collaboration features based upon their business needs. The security system will have additional features to address the security risks associated with Internet. Directory servers conforming to LDAP standards will be incorporated for seamless integration with the underlying operating environment. This in turn will provide responsive security, configurability, and flexibility features.

Product's target market.

AutoPLAN Enterprise is specifically designed to support high-tech, engineering, and telecommunications organizations in predicting, controlling, and improving cycle time of critical program development and deployment.

What are your product's three main benefits? (How does using the product add value to the customer?)

1. AutoPLAN Enterprise provides at least a 10 percent improvement in enterprise time-to-market of product development and deployment. Viewing the value of CTM from an annual R&D cost perspective: consider a product development group of one thousand people, with an annual R&D expenditure of $100M. A modest 10 percent improvement would represent a cost savings value of $10M, with a revenue enhancement value of three to five times this.

2. AutoPLAN Enterprise facilitates an organization's transformation from functional project teams to matrix, or program-organized high-performance project teams. It also supports distributed teams resulting from acquisitions. It does both of these by providing built-in communication and rollup features from distributed multiserver projects. This support enables teamwide problem identification, escalation, collaboration, and resolution. AutoPLAN Enterprise recognizes that three different organizational patterns coexist: 1) dynamic peer-to-peer, 2) functional, and 3) program management. AutoPLAN Enterprise offers these organizations both project-centric and resource-centric management.

3. AutoPLAN Enterprise accommodates joint ventures, subcontracting, mergers and acquisitions, and reorganizations by leveraging the Web to minimize deployment and support costs. The creation of plans, assignment of work, and integration of activities across multiple functions and distributed work teams is critically important. However, that is only part of the story. With the Internet, AutoPLAN Enterprise can also efficiently equip thousands of personnel involved in the product development process with the information they need to do the best possible job. Demand for skilled workers has been great, and turnover has risen as employees move from one company or job to another. The best practices in the world are of no value to a company if those who know those practices move on without first passing along the knowledge. Best practices developed at one site need to be shared with other sites, and a process for doing that is required. AutoPLAN Enterprise solves these problems through URL references and retrieval capability. With URL features, AutoPLAN Enterprise can help preserve best practices and other information and disseminate them geographically and functionally to team members currently doing the job. AutoPLAN Enterprise can also have associated URL references that point to mission-critical information/documentation that will enable product/project teams to achieve the activity. These references can also be attached to the top-level program schedule for project leader use or at specific functional schedules (e.g,. to provide sourcing with specific third-party vendor requirements). URLs can enable:

- Sharing best practice information from one team to another
- Referencing documentation with checklists
- Sharing of engineering notes on installation processes.

Also, with the speed of organizational changes, a mix of project scheduling system usage is expected. As most people are educated on Microsoft Project, AutoPLAN Enterprise can coexist with its projects and data. AutoPLAN Enterprise's graphical user interfaces are not only familiar to Microsoft Project users, the Web version is easier and thus leverages simplicity and ease of use with enterprise functionality.

Describe your quality management process. List any relevant certifications.

DTI achieves excellence in product quality and customer satisfaction through its quality management process. DTI's quality objective is to build quality into its products and services at all stages of the product life cycle, from requirement collection to customer usage. DTI's dedication to quality is reflected in its quality mission: "Doing things right the first time."

DTI's quality management group performs the functions of the software engineering process group, as defined by the industry-standard CMM. The quality management group plans and implements DTI's quality system, which consists of processes and guidelines. The processes detail out *what* is required for converting a set of inputs to outputs in the form of activities and tasks, primary and cooperative responsibilities, deliverables, and entry and exit criteria. The guidelines detail *how* to carry out the identified activities to ensure quality and consistency. The involvement of DTI personnel at all levels is fundamental to the implementation of the quality process. DTI personnel are drawn from various groups in the organization to author processes and guidelines, and all undergo training programs on the quality system.

DTI follows processes within Level 2 and Level 3 of the CMM. Some of the key processes within these levels include market requirement analysis, functional specification, high- and low-level design, coding, testing, release management, customer support, training, and maintenance. In addition, in-depth reviews are built into each of these processes.

DTI recognizes that enterprise growth and profitability are significantly impacted by time-to-market of new products in globally competitive high-tech markets. With this in mind, DTI's product development and quality processes are focused on meeting customers' needs and requirements. Therefore, DTI collaborates with its customers both in product definition and in assuring that the product functions are implemented as intended. To facilitate the fast-track delivery of innovative products and services, DTI has created process initiatives for increased test automation, usage of tools that will enable teams to better assess the quality of their work products, management of development tools, reuse of objects across products, and tightly controlled configuration management.

DTI's quality management process focuses on periodic reviews and feedback, which are means of monitoring the adherence of organizational activities to the process. Corrective and preventive actions play an important role in continuous improvement of the quality system and thereby the organizational activities.

DTI has a well-qualified team for quality management. DTI's teams, besides having the appropriate educational qualifications, have quality management-related certifications; some are certified quality analysts, and some hold certificates related to the CMM and its use. Many also have extensive internal audit experience.

The quality management group interacts periodically with key personnel of different functions within the organization and identifies new processes, guidelines, and improvements within the existing framework. The general approach to new process/guideline introduction is to discuss with representative users, define the process, pilot the process after review, evaluate the pilot implementation, revise the process based on feedback, plan organizationwide implementation, implement, measure, and maintain.

DTI is planning to get CMM certification at the appropriate level. The approach that would be followed for securing the certification includes mapping key process areas of the CMM to existing processes, identifying the *gaps*, preparing the implementation plan that describes how these gaps will be addressed, and executing the plan.

Discuss your product pricing structure. Include volume discount levels, concurrent user options, site licenses, cost of implementation, and other issues.

DTI's objective is to offer an integrated solution with a pricing structure that is based on enterprise requirements reflecting enterprise needs and individual needs. AutoPLAN Enterprise supports a floating license configuration, which allows any user to log into the system and consume one license. When the user has finished with the application, that license will be released for other users. Each floating license provides one concurrent use of the product. AutoPLAN Enterprise also supports a personal license configuration. Typical installations will use both personal and concurrent licensing.

Annual product maintenance is 15 percent of the list cost. Product maintenance entitles customers to engineering patches, updates, and upgrades, and phone, fax, and E-mail response to issues. Professional services are separate from DTI product maintenance. As part of the business relationship with customers, DTI takes part in joint planning to identify the customer's business needs and services sought from DTI. Professional services are charged separately on an as-needed basis. These services are performed either at the customer site, online, or at DTI's headquarters in Cupertino, California. Professional services typically fall into two categories: product consulting/implementation design review and implementation support. Product consulting/implementation design review discusses areas such as "How do I apply the software with a suitable process to solve a business need?" and "Which processes will we implement, how, and when to meet organizational objectives?" Implementation support consists of product training, project office services, upgrade-migration services, systems administration services, and integration services.

Cascade PgM (Mantix)

Describe what the product is designed to do.

Cascade PgM from Mantix is a client-server program management product for use with Microsoft Project, aimed specifically at the facilities required by senior management and program managers. With a standard MS Windows user interface, it presents a multiuser, enterprisewide cost, schedule, and resource management system, with powerful management reporting facilities. Cascade PgM uses the proven, structured data model of work, responsibility, and cost breakdown to provide a complete view of the business. The benefits to the business associated with each project can also be modeled.

Cascade is integrated on existing user sites with Oracle Financials, SAP, Peoplesoft, Glovia, Baan, Triton, and many other systems. This integration with the ERP (enterprise resource planning) systems provides the whole picture of all the activities in the business—where the cost is going, what the people are doing, and what results will be delivered, by when.

The combination of Cascade PgM and Microsoft Project provides a powerful corporate project planning system. Cascade PgM provides the top-down information used to provide guidelines for managers working at a more detailed level. Working within these guidelines, users can go on to develop detailed schedules, cost, and resource plans. Cascade PgM supports the concept of resource ownership and the delegation of resources down through the project, with complete visibility and tracking of where they are being used. In many cases, this includes use of the Web-based Cascade time-recording functionality.

Top three product differentiators; describe what makes your product unique.

Cascade PgM is unique in its functionality for business control of the projectoriented organization through top-down delegation of targets and bottom-up measurement of performance. It offers a clear functional advantage in terms of the following.

1. Turns decisions into action, by enabling the creation of outline plans with budget, staff, and time scales to be delegated for detailed planning.

2. The structured data model is built interactively as graphical tree structures, rather than with the conventional alpha numeric coding, making the operation intuitive and changes to the plan simple and quick.

3. The program manager establishes the overall structure of the program, typically based on business drivers or internal/customer reporting. Links to the program from projects may be easily created or deleted allowing fast *what-if* analysis.

To what business processes can this tool be applied?

For lean organizations in fast-moving markets, good management is increasingly about setting goals and assembling the team to deliver them. Cascade PgM provides the tool to define a portfolio of projects to deliver strategic goals, and then monitor the performance against these objectives. Cascade PgM backs up the implementation of effective management processes with the timely, consistent, and accurate provision of program and project information.

Describe the ideal end-user environment for the current version of your product (size of organization, level of project management sophistication, effort and commitment required).

The concepts behind Cascade PgM and the software architecture are completely scaleable. Any size organization with a multiproject environment would benefit from Cascade PgM, irrespective of the level of project management sophistication. The effort and commitment required to implement Cascade PgM depends on the customer's requirements for the system and the existing business processes. Typically, Cascade PgM is quick to implement; this is due in part to its use of MS Project, which is already present in most organizations. MS Project is transformed to become a key element of a business control system.

Future strategies for this product.

Mantix Systems will continue to develop Cascade PgM to ensure it remains a world leading program management solution.

Product's target market.

As a leading program management solution's provider, Mantix Systems has a proven track record with some of the world's leading organizations in fifteen countries. This is in markets that include telecommunications, IT, utilities, government, pharmaceuticals, aerospace, and defense.

What are your product's three main benefits? (How does using the product add value to the customer?)

Cascade PgM brings structure, visibility, and control to the management of both individual projects and multiproject programs. This allows a customer to focus investment and staff time on the business activities that will add most value, and manage them to deliver increased revenue, profit, and return on investment.

Describe your quality management process. List any relevant certifications.

The quality management process within Mantix Systems is accredited by and conforms to ISO 9000.

Discuss your product pricing structure. Include volume discount levels, concurrent user options, site licenses, cost of implementation, and other issues.

The price of Cascade PgM depends on the type of functionality required and the number of users. Please contact Mantix Systems for details that are specific to your requirements.

Dekker TRAKKER Activity Based Cost Management and Performance System (DTMI)

Describe what the product is designed to do.

The resource management features of TRAKKER provide organizations with an integrated tool for planning resource requirements and managing the capacity of the enterprise. The resourcing capabilities in TRAKKER seamlessly integrate with the scheduling and costing modules to provide cost/schedule impacts on capacity planning and resource management. This system component provides technical managers with the information required to manage limited resources across multiple projects, and to implement the adjustments required to smooth schedules and minimize the cost impacts on projects as resource requirements change within the business base of the organization.

Top three product differentiators; describe what makes your product unique.

1. Escalated resource availability.
2. Exception reporting, providing quick view into the impact of schedule slips or limited capacity.
3. Enterprise database allows capacity planning across all projects within the organization.

To what business processes can this tool be applied?

Resource Planning in TRAKKER can be accomplished in hours, heads, or equivalencies. Each user can plan tasks and project, utilizing the approach to data that best fits their needs. Once planned, data can be displayed or reviewed in any format. With the time-phased availability and resource equivalency, the enterprise can manage the flow of resources through the organization and quickly identify how and when critical resources are available. Enterprise data management capabilities of TRAKKER enable the organization to manage resources across the enterprise, or allocate resources specifically to a project.

Describe the ideal end user environment for the current version of your product (size of organization, level of project management sophistication, effort and commitment required).

One of the key attributes of the TRAKKER system is scalability. TRAKKER has been designed to integrate into a business environment by establishing an organization's business rules within the system. This architecture enables TRAKKER to fit the needs and sophistication of any implementation. This flexibility enables TRAKKER to support a variety of implementation approaches. TRAKKER installations typically provide access to a range of users including cost account managers, cost/schedule analysts, and financial managers to meet the unique requirements of each for information and output. Typical TRAKKER clients range from companies of one thousand employees to Fortune 500 corporations.

Future strategies for this product.

Dekker, Ltd. will continue to enhance the integration of TRAKKER with MS Office and MS Back Office suite of tools. The design of the TRAKKER architecture will continue to focus on making data more visual and accessible to the complete range of system users.

Product's target market.

R&D, government, software, medical, electronics, and aerospace.

What are your product's three main benefits? (How does using the product add value to the customer?)

1. Integration with the scheduling and costing modules within TRAKKER.
2. Time-phased availability and equivalency by resource.
3. Enterprise database allows capacity management across all of the projects engaged by the organization.

Describe your quality management process. List any relevant certifications.

DMTI has modeled our development process from the Microsoft model while incorporating the quality guidelines established in ISO 9000.

Discuss your product pricing structure. Include volume discount levels, concurrent user options, site licenses, cost of implementation, and other issues.

DMTI offers both single and concurrent user licenses of TRAKKER. Our flexible pricing enables both small and large organizations to cost effectively implement costing and earned value. TRAKKER pricing includes a progressive discount for volume purchases with reasonable thresholds for single and multisite licenses. Further, DMTI offers both public and private training courses for both new and advanced users. DMTI also offers consulting services to support the enterprise implementation of TRAKKER.

DMTI provides training for both the discipline of scheduling and attributes of TRAKKER. These workshops include Basic Project Management, TRAKKER Application Workshop, TRAKKER Intermediate Workshop, TRAKKER Report Writer Workshop, and TRAKKER MIS Integrator's Workshop. Through these courses, an enterprise can completely implement the TRAKKER system. In addition to our classroom training, DMTI offers consulting services to guide users though a structured approach to implementing TRAKKER.

Enterprise Project (jeTECH DATA SYSTEMS, INC.)

Describe what the product is designed to do.

Enterprise Project is a completely integrated solution (all applications share a common database and operate on the same hardware platform). Consequently, our response to the narrative questions here repeats what we supplied for the Suites chapter, as those responses apply to all our applications.

Enterprise Project is a powerful new client/server software application that offers project-based organizations a simple way to define and staff projects, and record project labor and expenses throughout their enterprise. Essentially a suite of robust, user-friendly applications integrated into a single desktop, this comprehensive project management system enables team members to accurately plan and track labor resources across all projects. Perfect either as a *stand-alone* solution or as the ideal complement to the jeTECH labor-management system—Enterprise Labor—it is particularly well-suited for multiuser, enterprisewide installations. Together, Enterprise Labor and Enterprise Project are the only systems currently on the market with extensive capabilities and integrated products for both the salaried professional (engineers and computer programmers, for instance) and the hourly employee (from factory workers to registered nurses).

Users access all functions via a single desktop with a Microsoft Office 98 *look and feel*. The system integrates completely with Enterprise Labor and Microsoft Project, as well as with most popular accounting and human resource (HR) systems. In today's competitive environment, effective and efficient use of labor resources is key to completing mission-critical projects on time, on budget. Enterprise Project gives project leaders a comprehensive, potent tool with which to manage scarce technical resources.

With Enterprise Project, managers can budget and schedule projects based on staff skills and availability. Project team members can manage their own tasks, report actual labor and travel expenses, and provide status reports on these tasks. The system calculates actual project costs by automatically incorporating labor costs, material costs, and travel expenses.

Project managers can define and manage both contract and noncontract-based projects, and control work authorizations that will keep each project under control and on budget. As a project manager, you simply create activities for your projects, assign appropriate resources to these activities, and define how labor will be charged to a contract. And by allowing employees to only charge preassigned tasks, Enterprise Project prevents performance of unauthorized work.

Enterprise Project enables all users to report labor charges right from their PC or workstation. Project managers need no longer compile project team information manually. Users can now report project time, as well as other time, and the system automatically processes and transmits it to an interfaced time-and-attendance system for payroll use.

Enterprise Project includes a contract maintenance module. Companies with hourly employees contracted with outside firms—for instance, security guards or programmers—would benefit from using this module without the rest of the project management system. This module is primarily designed, however, to accommodate projects being managed for clients. This module allows contract managers to define contract information including budgets and rates per hour, as well as all products and services purchased by the customer. They can then use this information to evaluate projects based on user-defined deliverables. Contract maintenance is by no means static. So jeTECH has designed Enterprise Project to handle change orders, R&D projects, and discounts. A variety of unique reporting features enable contract managers to view cost overruns, variances, and milestone completions.

Top three product differentiators; describe what makes your product unique.

1. Resource scheduling from a common resource pool in a multiproject environment.
2. Integrated time collection and status reporting.
3. Sensitivity analysis (what-if scenarios).

To what business processes can this tool be applied?

Project planning/management, enterprise resource scheduling/management, time collection, performance measurement, time and expense reporting, budgeting and estimating, and project accounting.

Describe the ideal end-user environment for the current version of your product (size of organization, level of project management sophistication, effort and commitment required).

Any resource-constrained enterprise (IT, high-tech R&D, engineering) with multiple projects and multiple sites. Requires a low level of project management sophistication.

Future strategies for this product.

Maintenance and repair operations, incorporation of process ware/templates, enterprise-level project and resource integration, and full Internet capabilities.

Product's target market.

Companies with *task-oriented* professionals such as engineers, architects, IS professionals, researchers, advertising/marketing professionals, etc. See also the previous response to "ideal end-user environment."

What are your product's three main benefits? (How does using the product add value to the customer?)

1. Improved resource utilization and efficiencies.
2. Reduction in time to complete projects.
3. Cost control.

Describe your quality management process. List any relevant certifications.

Our current quality management process includes in-house testing, which incorporates both automated and manual processes and procedures.

Discuss your product pricing structure. Include volume discount levels, concurrent user options, site licenses, cost of implementation, and other issues.

Pricing is structured on a named-user basis. Pricing will also be dependent on a number of variables including the size of the enterprise, number of project managers, number of facilities, etc. Consequently, pricing is provided to each customer when we have been able to familiarize ourselves on their operations and their anticipated use of the system.

Several options are available for training, tech support, annual maintenance, etc. Costs are provided to each customer when they have been able to select the options deemed best for their operations.

Innate Resource Manager

Describe what the product is designed to do.

Forecast skills bottlenecks and match people to tasks.

Top three product differentiators; describe what makes your product unique.

1. Two-way interface with MSP and Project Workbench.
2. Accommodates nonproject tasks.
3. Excellent visual allocation screen.

To what business processes can this tool be applied?

Forecast skills bottlenecks to show capacity to take on new work.
Match people to tasks to maximize the utilization of staff.

Describe the ideal end user environment for the current version of your product (size of organization, level of project management sophistication, effort and commitment required).

Organization where team leaders or resource managers are responsible for matching people to individual tasks.

Future strategies for this product.

Accommodate different organization models, e.g., assign people across pools.

Product's target market.

Organization where high occupancy and staff utilization is a key goal. New projects and tasks can arrive unexpectedly.

What are your product's three main benefits? (How does using the product add value to the customer?)

1. Forecast skills bottlenecks to show capacity to take on new work.
2. Match people to tasks to maximize the utilization of staff.
3. Populate timesheet system with task lists.

Describe your quality management process. List any relevant certifications.

Best practice software product development, based on twenty years of industry experience.

Discuss your product pricing structure. Include volume discount levels, concurrent user options, site licenses, cost of implementation, and other issues.

Based on number of resource managers and people in the pool.
Volume discounts apply.
Simple software modules support evolutionary change. Costs of implementation well below industry average.

Intelligent Planner (Augeo Software)

Describe what the product is designed to do.

Optimize the allocation of resources across multiple projects, determine costs, and provide metrics for continuous process improvement.

Top three product differentiators; describe what makes your product unique.

1. Global repository for data and business rules.
2. Closed-loop system, from project proposal to time/expenses tracking.
3. Simulation and optimization based on skills and availability of resources.

To what business processes can this tool be applied?

Business processes involving the allocation of human resources, such as professional services and information services.

Describe the ideal end-user environment for the current version of your product (size of organization, level of project management sophistication, effort and commitment required).

Mid-sized to large-scale professional services organizations sharing pool of scarce resources; large IT departments managing budgets and resources on strategic projects; or consulting companies managing a portfolio of intellectual activities.

Future strategies for this product.

Knowledge management integration; 100 percent Web-based management of project portfolio; and advanced data-mining features.

Product's target market.

Professional services organizations.
Large scale IT departments with cost-controlled project management.
Consulting companies.

What are your product's three main benefits? (How does using the product add value to the customer?)

1. Optimize scarce resource predictability.
2. Increase speed, throughput, and responsiveness.
3. Executive visibility.

Describe your quality management process. List any relevant certifications.

Source control. Usability verification process. Worldwide beta program.

Discuss your product pricing structure. Include volume discount levels, concurrent user options, site licenses, cost of implementation, and other issues.

Concurrent user pricing for client-server modules, named-user pricing for Web modules. Volume discount, site license. Implementation requires ten to twenty days of consulting.
Training: Project managers (two days), administrator (three days), Web users (half-day).
Annual maintenance (includes new releases and online assistance): 15 percent of license fee.

Micro Planner X-Pert (Micro Planning International)

Describe what the product is designed to do.

X-Pert is a sophisticated full-featured project management system designed for the serious project manager. Ideal for large projects utilizing a finite number of resources across multiple projects.

Top three product differentiators; describe what makes your product unique.

1. Resource optimization.
2. Excellent report writer and graphics views/outputs.
3. Designed for the serious manager.

To what business processes can this tool be applied?

Software/hardware development, engineering/design, and medical.

Describe the ideal end-user environment for the current version of your product (size of organization, level of project management sophistication, effort and commitment required).

Medium to large-sized companies with a thorough knowledge of project management, who are serious about getting their projects done on time and within budget.

Future strategies for this product.

Web interaction.
Shared project components.
Client/server.

Product's target market.

Aerospace/defense, high-tech, and biotechnology.

What are your product's three main benefits? (How does using the product add value to the customer?)

1. Results oriented.
2. Maximizes resources.
3. Excellent management reporting capabilities for decision-making.

Describe your quality management process. List any relevant certifications.

No answer given.

Discuss your product pricing structure. Include volume discount levels, concurrent user options, site licenses, cost of implementation, and other issues.

Fixed licenses starting at $1,995. Floating licenses starting at $2,995. Discounts apply beginning at a quantity of two.

Training courses cost $2,200 for two-day course plus expenses (on-site). Support/annual maintenance plans start at $395/year for fixed license; includes free upgrades.

Microsoft Project 98 (Microsoft)

Describe what the product is designed to do.

Microsoft Project 98 is an ideal tool for planning and tracking projects of all sizes. Because it is easy to use, it is an ideal tool for all levels of project management experience from the newcomer to the experienced project manager. Microsoft Project 98 focuses on three areas:

1. Control—gives users more control over their project plans.
2. Communication—improves project communication so everyone stays informed and involved.
3. Compatibility—provides programmability features so it can serve as a stand-alone product or as part of a broader company solution.

Top three product differentiators; describe what makes your product unique.

1. Ease of use: Microsoft Project 98 requires little or no training to begin using it to manage projects, so the *startup* costs required of new customers are much lower when compared to other project management software tools. The navigation map also helps inexperienced project managers and new Microsoft Project 98 customers to map their functional responsibilities to Microsoft Project 98's features.

2. Extensibility: Microsoft Project 98 is a pioneer in extensibility. It can store data in an open database format and supports VBA. Customers can easily integrate project management data with their existing corporate business systems, which enables Microsoft Project 98 to accommodate ever-increasing complexity as customers' project management needs change and grow throughout the organization.

3. Integration with other Microsoft applications: Microsoft Project 98 incorporates the best of Microsoft Office to make a tool that is easy to learn and use.

To what business processes can this tool be applied?

Microsoft Project 98 can be applied to any process for which the customer can identify specific tasks and their respective durations and dependencies. Customers can use Microsoft Project 98 to easily compare cost and profitability by project, balance resource requirements across projects, and track dependencies across multiple projects to assess a project's impact on the bottom line. Microsoft Project 98 can also be used to integrate project metrics with corporate accounting, human resources, timesheets, or manufacturing systems and organize project documentation so it is readily available to everyone involved in a project.

Describe the ideal end-user environment for the current version of your product (size of organization, level of project management sophistication, effort and commitment required).

Microsoft Project 98 is used in end-user environments of all sizes—from individuals planning single-resource projects to large corporations with thousands of employees. Customers with widely varying project management backgrounds can also use it. Even newcomers to project management principles can learn to use Microsoft Project 98 quickly and easily with the product's built-in help and other easy-to-use features. Microsoft Project 98 even contains features to extend a project team's communication capability over the Web or any MAPI-compliant E-mail system. And, customers won't *outgrow* Microsoft Project 98 since its programmability features allow them to tailor the program to their organization's unique and changing needs.

Future strategies for this product.

Microsoft will continue to focus on improved collaboration, performance, and ease of use in future versions of Microsoft Project. Microsoft Project has always focused on bringing project management techniques to a wider audience via improved ease of use and expanded communication capabilities for project teams and will continue to do so in the future.

Product's target market.

Anyone who deals with budgets, assignments, and deadlines can take advantage of the benefits offered by Microsoft Project 98. If you have thousands of details to manage, or even a few dozen, you're a potential Microsoft Project 98 customer.

What are your product's three main benefits? (How does using the product add value to the customer?)

1. Easy to learn and can grow with customers' projects and organization.
2. Ability to plan and track multiple projects in a consolidated manner.
3. Helps customers track and manage costs that affect the bottom line.

Describe your quality management process. List any relevant certifications.

Microsoft Project's quality management process begins with developing a product vision based on input from customers, internal and external developers, the product support team, and usability engineers. This ensures that the development process focuses on the right objectives, and that decisions regarding product quality reflect all of these perspectives.

Microsoft maintains a high developer to test ratio throughout the software development process to ensure that potential *bugs* are identified and resolved as early in the development cycle as possible. The testing process is based on five core attributes: 1) source code version control; 2) making the code testable; 3) use of automation for broader scenario testing; 4) beta testing—both internal and external; and 5) detailed bug tracking and reporting (throughout all Microsoft product groups in order to share learnings).

Finally, a new product is released only when the managers from development, testing, program management, and product support agree as a team that the product is ready. No product will be released until this agreement is reached.

Discuss your product pricing structure. Include volume discount levels, concurrent user options, site licenses, cost of implementation, and other issues.

The estimated retail price of Microsoft Project 98 is $499. Microsoft also offers several multiple-license pricing agreements. Detailed information on these agreements is available at www.microsoft.com/licensing.

The cost of implementation varies based on previous experience with project management principles, experience with other project management software tools, and the size and complexity of a customer's projects. Little or no training is needed for Microsoft Project 98 due to the extensive built-in help and other user-assistance features included in the product. Many additional low-cost books, self-help tools, and other training materials for Microsoft Project 98 are widely available. Microsoft Project 98's built-in VBA programmability features also help limit the cost of additional customization.

Milestones, Etc. (Kidasa)

Describe what the product is designed to do.

Milestones, Etc. is designed to provide an easy-to-use product to produce high-quality schedules in a Gantt format.

Top three product differentiators; describe what makes your product unique.

1. Easy to learn.
2. Easy to use.
3. Easy to update schedules.

To what business processes can this tool be applied?

Scheduling of projects.

Describe the ideal end-user environment for the current version of your product (size of organization, level of project management sophistication, effort and commitment required).

Desktop Windows environment.

Future strategies for this product.

Continue to add user-requested features to make product do more, but still maintain ease of use.

Product's target market.

People who need to quickly produce schedules.

What are your product's three main benefits? (How does using the product add value to the customer?)

1. Enables customer to easily produce high-quality Gantt charts.
2. Enables customer to spend less time creating Gantt charts.
3. Enables customer to spend less time updating Gantt charts.

Describe your quality management process. List any relevant certifications.

Follow standard commercial software development guidelines.

Discuss your product pricing structure. Include volume discount levels, concurrent user options, site licenses, cost of implementation, and other issues.

Single-user licenses are $199. Workgroup pricing is also available.

Cost of implementation: Just the amount of time it takes to go over the supplied tutorials, usually no more than a few hours.

Open Plan (Welcom)

Describe what the product is designed to do.

Welcom's Open Plan is an enterprisewide project management system that substantially improves a company's ability to manage and complete multiple projects on time and within budget with a limited workforce. Unlike less-sophisticated products, Open Plan is a highly integrated, comprehensive software system that can be customized to fit specific corporate requirements. It is the most technically advanced client/server project management system on the market, using the latest in Microsoft Windows development technology.

The three versions of Open Plan are:

Open Plan Professional: Easy to use and powerful enough to manage even the largest projects. Open Plan Professional gives professional project managers such vital tools as advanced resource management, multiproject support, support for client/server databases, and the flexibility to customize the interface to support organization and industry-specific procedures.

Open Plan Desktop: Designed for occasional access to projects and ideal for executive users and tactical team members. Open Plan Desktop has extensive ease-of-use features and an affordable price point for companywide deployment. The system is well-suited for users who usually work on individual components of a larger project. Users can roll their individual projects up to Open Plan Professional for a broader view of the overall project.

Open Plan Enterprise: Very similar to Open Plan Professional, integrates with popular ERP applications such as Baan and SAP. The resulting component-based suite automatically disseminates project data throughout an organization, giving users better control over enterprisewide multiproject planning, management, and implementation.

Top three product differentiators; describe what makes your product unique.

1. Multiproject.
2. Advanced resource modeling.
3. Open architecture.

To what business processes can this tool be applied?

Enterprise resource modeling, business process reengineering, project management, earned value analysis, risk assessment, and process modeling.

Describe the ideal end-user environment for the current version of your product (size of organization, level of project management sophistication, effort and commitment required).

Medium to large organizations for which project management is a serious business requirement. Meets the needs of users whose level of expertise varies from novice/occasional to advanced.

Future strategies for this product.

Our vision for the future is to provide a suite of component-based products that work together to provide advanced project management functionality using the very latest technology.

Welcom's development plans include extending the products' multiproject and enterprise resource modeling capabilities while moving to a distributed applications architecture with Web technology being a significant component. Plans also include leveraging existing integrations with Baan and SAP, and expanding integrations to include other ERP vendors.

Product's target market.

Fortune 1000 companies, government and multinational organizations implementing enterprisewide project management.

What are your product's three main benefits? (How does using the product add value to the customer?)

1. Increase quality of project communications.
2. Reduce cycle time through effective resource management.
3. Increase integration of project management with business systems.

Describe your quality management process. List any relevant certifications.

Adhere to standard industry processes in release and version strategies, including automated regression testing. ISO 9000 certified in the United Kingdom.

Discuss your product pricing structure. Include volume discount levels, concurrent user options, site licenses, cost of implementation, and other issues.

Please call for pricing.
Training courses and consulting: Please call for pricing.
Tech support: No charge with current maintenance.
Maintenance: First year is free with software purchase. Renewed annually.

Panorama Program Manager

Describe what the product is designed to do.

Panorama Program Manager comprises five modules, which together form a fully integrated application but which can, if required, be used independently or can be integrated with preferred third party applications. Interfaces can also be provided to other applications.

Financial Control & Performance Measurement: Consolidates financial and performance information for any number of projects and provides multilevel views of all data. Departmental managers and team leaders can be provided with short-term tactical perspective.

Time Recording: This module is the collection point for all time expended by project staff. Timesheets may be entered by individual members of staff, or as a batch process. Extensive online validation ensures that mispostings are kept to a minimum.

Top three product differentiators; describe what makes your product unique.

1. *Scope:* Addresses in a single integrated application the major application areas required for comprehensive program management.
2. *Flexibility:* Inherent flexibility means that the system can be implemented to suit most companies' requirements without the need for bespoke development.
3. *Customization:* Ability to incorporate bespoke features to client's specification and willingness to provide support to customized elements.

To what business processes can this tool be applied?

Estimation, bid management and project control.

Describe the ideal end-user environment for the current version of your product (size of organization, level of project management sophistication, effort and commitment required).

Typical users will have in excess of two hundred employees and be managing either large, complex projects or a large number (>150) of small/medium-size projects.

They will usually have experience of project management and already be users of project management tools.

A typical implementation will be six to twelve months and require the involvement of an implementation team that at any one time might include five to ten client staff.

Future strategies for this product.

Web-based operation; Integration of work flow management and document storage and retrieval.

Product's target market.

Cross-industry.

What are your product's three main benefits? (How does using the product add value to the customer?)

1. Consolidation of all project data to provide a corporate view of performance.
2. Standardization of project control methodology through use of a single corporatewide system.
3. Easy access at all levels in the organization of all aspects of project performance.

Describe your quality management process. List any relevant certifications.

In-house change control and configuration management software and control systems.

Discuss your product pricing structure. Include volume discount levels, concurrent user options, site licenses, cost of implementation, and other issues.

On application.

PLANTRAC-OUTLOOK (Computerline Ltd)

Describe what the product is designed to do.

PLANTRAC-OUTLOOK provides total project management easily. Several methods of data input allow fast entry. The well-proven engine provides realistic schedules. With features such as out-of-sequence scheduling and multiple activities per line, together with a powerful report writer, communications improve dramatically. Project efficiency and profitability will improve.

Top three product differentiators; describe what makes your product unique.

1. Four compatible input methods for fast data entry.
2. Realistic time and resource scheduling.
3. Powerful report writer and report embellisher for effective communications.

To what business processes can this tool be applied?

Construction; manufacturing; marketing; research & development; software development.

Describe the ideal end-user environment for the current version of your product (size of organization, level of project management sophistication, effort and commitment required).

Both small and large organizations benefit. It can be used as a casual planner, by a professional project manager and for corporate planning and control.

Future strategies for this product.

PLANTRAC-OUTLOOK is very much user-driven. It will keep up to date with both project management and technological trends.

Product's target market.

Broad market but specializing in construction; defense and pharmaceutical.

What are your product's three main benefits? (How does using the product add value to the customer?)

1. Time saved in project creation and progressing/updating.
2. Realistic schedules assist project profitability
3. Reporting flexibility gives client confidence.

Describe your quality management process. List any relevant certifications.

Quality management is based on a mix of PRINCE and ISO 9000 methodology.

Discuss your product pricing structure. Include volume discount levels, concurrent user options, site licenses, cost of implementation, and other issues.

Single user is $975. Network versions are available in modules of four users at $1,950 per module. Site licenses are $5,000–$50,000. Implementation and training is $960 per day. Technical support is provided by telephone, fax and e-mail, free for the first six months. Thereafter technical support is 17.5% of purchase price (includes upgrades and enhancements).

PlanView Software (PlanView, Inc)

Describe what the product is designed to do.

PlanView Software has modules that let the user request project and nonproject work, scope, schedule, search the resource repository, create multiple what-ifs, etc., progress projects from time reported, and create metrics.

Top three product differentiators; describe what makes your product unique.

1. PlanView's resource-based approach looks at all work scheduled to your resources.
2. PlanView progresses projects from staff reporting their time.
3. PlanView is multi-tier and *infinitely* scalable.

To what business processes can this tool be applied?

Multiproject management, service request management, resource management, workflow management, work and resource *portfolio* management, etc.

Describe the ideal end-user environment for the current version of your product (size of organization, level of project management sophistication, effort and commitment required).

An organization with one hundred to multiple thousands of employees (we have implementations of four thousand plus), managed by five or more managers with access to a central database; includes matrix-style organizations.

Future strategies for this product.

Further conversion to Web browser-based interfaces; even easier report generation and Web publishing; more CPM and cost management features.

Product's target market.

The resource-centric approach to work management is typically most useful for organizations with a highly skilled workforce of limited availability; with twenty plus managers, and one hundred plus staff; using client/server.

What are your product's three main benefits? (How does using the product add value to the customer?)

1. All work—project, service request, and administrative—is tracked and managed.
2. The true capacity of the organization determines the project schedules and priorities.
3. Integrated time accounting means that projects are progressed by staff reporting their time.

Describe your quality management process. List any relevant certifications.

PlanView follows the guidelines set out in the book *Best Practices of Rapid Development* by Steve McConnell.

Discuss your product pricing structure. Include volume discount levels, concurrent user options, site licenses, cost of implementation, and other issues.

It is different for each case, but basically the cost is $200–400 per seat, with volume discounts. The repository products are included.

Standard SQL database is extra. Implementation and training are extra. We offer a range of implementation packages, from rapid to standard, which include training. Additional services billed at time and cost. Phone and online tech support are free. Maintenance packages offered.

Project Control Software Resource Manager

Describe what the product is designed to do.

The Project Control Software Resource Manager module provides resource workloads across all projects in the organization from a single database. Enables staffing projections, resource conflicts identification and resolution. Supports a skills inventory that enables finding the right type of resource as well as staffing and outsourcing projections. The Resource Manager module is part of the Project Control Software suite.

Project Control Software extends desktop project management software into an enterprisewide management and reporting solution, by consolidating volumes of project files from leading project management software systems such as Microsoft Project, Primavera, and others. Project Control Software supports multiple operating systems (Windows, Macintosh, Unix), and databases (Oracle, Access, Microsoft SQL, Sybase). The entire Project Control Software suite runs on a Web browser or LAN. The enterprise rollup design supports the matrix organization's need to roll up projects to program or initiative, as well as the resource perspective by business unit and organizational structure.

Top three product differentiators; describe what makes your product unique.

1. No technology limits: Project Control Software supports all operating systems (Windows, Macintosh, Unix), consolidates files from multiple project management software systems (Microsoft Project, Primavera, and more) using your choice of databases (Oracle, Access, Microsoft SQL, Sybase) in a LAN or Internet solution. It is designed to integrate easily with existing business systems (such as accounting software) so an organization can leverage existing systems and immediately see productivity increases without changing everything.

2. The project office: The design and integration of Project Control Software modules supports the project office across all phases of the project management life cycle, from standard estimating and budgeting though timesheets and status tracking and accounting integration for actual costs and earned value analysis. The process manager and communications manager modules enable a corporate intranet.

3. Enterprise project management: Project Control Software offers a suite of integrated modules that can be used to deliver the big picture of project management across a distributed organization, as well as tracking the details. The enterprise rollup design supports the matrix organization's need to roll up projects to program or initiative, as well as the need to view data from a resource perspective by business unit and organizational structure. The entire Project Control Software suite (not just the time tracking) runs on a Web browser or LAN.

To what business processes can this tool be applied?

Project Control Software's enterprise rollup design supports the matrix organization's need to roll up projects to program or initiative, as well as the need to view data from a resource perspective by business unit and organizational structure.

The system supports project management, ERP, project office development, ISO registration, strategic planning, process management, methodology implementation, cost/schedule management, CMM, compliance, global information technology deployment, SAP, Peoplesoft, etc., implementations.

Describe the ideal end-user environment for the current version of your product (size of organization, level of project management sophistication, effort and commitment required).

Any organization operating in a competitive environment that manages multiple projects and resources to meet business goals and to increase profitability and productivity.

For example, a geographically distributed matrix organization with medium to high volume of project-based activities being managed in a standard desktop scheduling software. The system delivers information to all levels of the organization from employees to project management, functional management, enterprise management, and global management.

Future strategies for this product.

Project Control, the publisher of Project Control Software, was founded in 1989, developed the first Internet project management product in 1996, and is committed to its position as a technology leader in Internet project management software. Future plans include expanding functionality to better support the project office and to continually update Project Control Software features, based on ongoing client input.

Product's target market.

Organizations using Project Control Software represent companies in a wide variety of industries, including finance, services, pharmaceutical, federal government, defense, manufacturing, automotive, software publishing, etc. The disciplines typically involved in implementation include enterprise management, information technology, new product development, the project office, and engineering.

What are your product's three main benefits? (How does using the product add value to the customer?)

Client organizations can greatly improve productivity and lower costs when Project Control system is in place.

1. Ability to view all projects in a central repository.
2. Ability to do efficient enterprise resource and cost planning.
3. Ability to fully support the needs of the project office across all phases and areas of the project management process.

Describe your quality management process. List any relevant certifications.

Project Control, publishers of Project Control Software, follows standard and accepted practices for design, development, testing, and support for computer software. Project Control has set corporate objectives to achieve Level 2 and Level 3 CMM compliance using the capability maturity model from the Software Engineering Institute.

Discuss your product pricing structure. Include volume discount levels, concurrent user options, site licenses, cost of implementation, and other issues.

Project Control Software is priced by the module, with scalable client seat pricing based on number of users. Price quotations are available and are based on the current Project Control Software product and pricing schedule.

Price quotations are available and include costs of product, implementation, training, tech support, annual maintenance, etc. Quotations are based on the current Project Control Software product and pricing schedule, which is available to qualified organizations.

Project Integrator

Describe what the product is designed to do.

SSL Project Integrator (PI) is a team-oriented project and process management tool that enables you to graphically define, track, report, and communicate projects, processes, tasks, and deliverables. Additionally, PI manages and maintains resources and clients, both locally and remotely.

Top three product differentiators; describe what makes your product unique.

1. All project processes (external, internal, and administrative) are managed via PI's graphic and interactive RoadMap. High-level steps graphically depict process flow. Each step can be drilled-down to display task lists, task details, resource delegation, deliverables, and quality checklists.

2. Teams can be defined at the project level, and are pulled from the database resource pool. Assigned tasks and open issues are sent to a team member's reminder window for immediate delegation and communication. Resources drag and drop tasks to a timecard for immediate project updating, and open issues remain on the reminder window until they are closed.

3. A wide range of reports are available. Each report can be filtered, and pull data from the database for macro or micro analysis and reporting. Users can also define their own reports, and any level of information can be exported from the database.

To what business processes can this tool be applied?

Any external, internal, or administrative business process, regardless of simplicity or complexity.

Describe the ideal end-user environment for the current version of your product (size of organization, level of project management sophistication, effort and commitment required).

Project-based organizations of any size (PI allows definition of teams, departments, and business units). Organizations do not need to be well-versed in project management practices and techniques. Implementation and training is simple when compared to sophisticated PM tools. A commitment to Distributed Project/Process Management (DPM) is required (the delegation of tasks and deliverables to distributed teams and team members, and distribution of the project management process).

Future strategies for this product.

Tailor versions of PI to specific industries by leveraging subject matter experts from same.

Full integration to other cost accounting applications (currently, PI is integrated with SBT Executive Series, although data can be exported to virtually any application).

Product's target market.

Project Integrator was created for project-oriented organizations (engineering, marketing, advertising, accounting, consulting, design firms, etc.) that have a need to enforce consistent quality in their project process and delivery, and minimize nonproductive hours.

What are your product's three main benefits? (How does using the product add value to the customer?)

1. Distribution of the project process (tasks, issues, deliverables, etc.) to local and remote team members via LAN, DBMS, and Internet tools.

2. Immediate feedback of status of all projects and tasks, allowing macro and micro views of the entire organization's performance at any given time.

3. All aspects of a business (external, internal, and administrative activity, including deliverables) are managed in a central DBMS and repository. Communications, projects, tasks, deliverables, issues, costs, clients' resources, etc., are all managed via one tool in one database.

Describe your quality management process. List any relevant certifications.

Our documented QA process includes the use of test script software. We are currently implementing ISO 9001 and expect registry by early 1999.

Discuss your product pricing structure. Include volume discount levels, concurrent user options, site licenses, cost of implementation, and other issues.

PI's price is based on the number of users, and volume discounts are available.

Implementation lead time and required training is minimal when compared to high-end, sophisticated PM tools and suites.

Project Scheduler 7.6 (Scitor Corporation)

Describe what the product is designed to do.

PS7 is built from the ground up to take full advantage of today's technology. Whether you're performing basic task scheduling on your desktop or working on multiple megaprojects using our powerful SQL database repository, PS7 will meet your needs. Wizards, Guides, Tip-of-the-Day suggestions, and field level help provide an easy-to-navigate path to project management. You'll find PS7 provides extraordinary flexibility to organize, consolidate, and view project information.

For serious users, PS7 provides support for: subprojects, grouped projects, accounting periods, time-phased availability, inflation factors, multiple cost tables, earned value, unlimited user fields/formulas, five baselines, custom reports, and much more.

The add-on package, Project Communicator (described in the Timesheets section) permits resources to view their task assignments, and report back actual work and estimated remaining work via a powerful two-tier client/server database system.

Top three product differentiators; describe what makes your product unique.

Approachable power: PS7 meets the needs of the most demanding project management professionals, without sacrificing the ease of use demanded in today's state-of-the-art applications.

Scalability: PS7 is designed and built from the ground up to scale from the single desktop user to the entire enterprise.

Customer support: PS7 isn't just another software product. In its seventh generation, PS7 continues to be designed and built by project management professionals for project management professionals.

To what business processes can this tool be applied?

Project planning and tracking.
Resource management and team communications.
Cost estimation and control.

Describe the ideal end-user environment for the current version of your product (size of organization, level of project management sophistication, effort and commitment required).

PS7 is designed to meet the needs of all sizes of organizations, including individuals, product teams, workgroups, and the enterprise. PS7 is the most configurable project management package available. It meets the needs of beginning project managers on up to serious project management professionals.

Future strategies for this product.

We will continue to provide leading-edge project management products and services by listening to and working with customers to predict the future needs of a changing management environment.

Product's target market.

General business and professional project management.
All major industries.

What are your product's three main benefits? (How does using the product add value to the customer?)

1. Plans and tracks project/resource costs and schedules.
2. Allows *early* detection and resolution of problems.
3. Facilitates communications between all stakeholders.

Describe your quality management process. List any relevant certifications.

Best commercial practices.

Discuss your product pricing structure. Include volume discount levels, concurrent user options, site licenses, cost of implementation, and other issues.

Single unit: $595, discounts at ten, twenty-five, and fifty plus.
$2,900 for five-pack concurrent licenses, discounts at two, five, and ten plus.
Site licenses available for five hundred licenses and up.
Regional and on-site training and consulting is available.
Telephone tech support is available at no charge.
Annual maintenance: not applicable.

QEI Exec (PCF Limited)

Describe what the product is designed to do.

QEI Exec is best thought of as a toolkit for managing activity-based problems built around a high-performance database engine. Data stored within the database can be presented and manipulated via any number of views, which can be graphical or tabular. The entire user interface to the delivered product is written in the product's own programming language, allowing complete customization to meet individual requirements. It provides the following key areas of functionality:

- Graphical and tabular interface to data
- Scheduling
- Resource management
- Cost and performance management
- Flexible interfacing to other systems
- High degree of customization.

Top three product differentiators; describe what makes your product unique.

1. Highly graphical *CAD-like* approach to project construction gives total freedom of data layout.
2. Dynamic rollup of all schedule and resource data through an unlimited number of structures, yielding high performance even when dealing with tens of thousands of tasks.
3. Macro-based front end allows complete customization of user interface and generation of interactive specialist charts (such as time chainage diagrams).

To what business processes can this tool be applied?

It has a wide range of possible applications, including:
- *Traditional* project planning with earned value analysis
- Project-based MIS/EIS
- Program treasury management

- Maintenance and manufacturing forecasting
- Capacity planning
- MRP master schedule generation.

Describe the ideal end-user environment for the current version of your product (size of organization, level of project management sophistication, effort and commitment required).

Large organizations (to > $100M) with considerable experience of *rigorous* project management wishing to consolidate diverse sets of data (from multiple planning systems, manufacturing/ERP, and cost collection) into a single source of high-quality management information.

If customers wish to fully exploit the potential for tightly integrating the product with other systems or to introduce significant customizations, they will require suitable internal IT resources.

Future strategies for this product.

Extended database connectivity via ODBC.
Extended reporting and intranet functionality.

Product's target market.

Principal markets are aerospace and defense. Product is also successfully used in make-to-order/contract manufacturing, transportation, and utilities.

What are your product's three main benefits? (How does using the product add value to the customer?)

1. Extremely high-quality interactive graphical views of data.
2. High performance consolidation/rollup permits rapid what-if scenario analysis.
3. Complete control over layout and presentation of data.

Describe your quality management process. List any relevant certifications.

We have started (but not yet completed) ISO 9001 certification.

Discuss your product pricing structure. Include volume discount levels, concurrent user options, site licenses, cost of implementation, and other issues.

The product is sold as a right-to-use license, plus a number of user licenses. A small (three-user) system would cost about £15,000 while a larger (ten-user) system would cost about £30,000. The per-user price drops with increasing numbers of users. Site/multisite/corporate licenses are available.

It is strongly recommended that customers take training from us. List price for training is £500/day per course for up to six attendees. Various standard training courses are available, or custom courses can be developed on request. Annual maintenance is 15 percent of the list price of the software. This includes all upgrades and new releases and unlimited telephone support.

ResourceXchange for Microsoft Project (Information Management Services, Inc.)

Describe what the product is designed to do.

ResourceXchange provides organizations with the ability to define security groups, resource attributes, and a unique OBS. Resource managers use this additional information to analyze supply and availability and to perform scheduling across multiple projects.

ResourceXchange helps resource managers define and maintain resource attributes. Attributes can include resource cost, skill, location, calendar, or other resource-related information. Resource attribute definitions are organizationally specific and are used by other members of the ProjectExchange family of products and by Microsoft Project. Geographically dispersed managers utilize information from ResourceXchange to ensure information is consistent across the entire organization. The flexibility to establish organization-specific resource-attribute information provides the ability to analyze supply and availability at several levels.

Project and portfolio security groups are established with ResourceXchange and used by Doc-Check and the ProjectExchange Portfolio Wizard. Advanced scheduling is empowered by the resource attributes and OBS information established in ResourceXchange. Team managers are able to extract their teams' assignments, among multiple projects based on any resource attribute, into a single Microsoft Project plan. This provides resource managers with the ability to staff across multiple projects. If a strong matrix management style is desired, ResourceXchange provides the ability for project managers to assign activities to a skill, role, or other resource attribute and for functional managers, the ability to replace skilled assignments with specific team members.

An outline view of the OBS is available to add, view, and modify an individual's organizational position. Utilized with TimeReview (purchased separately), the OBS provides information for advanced time approval and notification. After establishing organizational and team member information, ResourceXchange creates and maintains consistent and accurate resource information for Microsoft Project without requiring the use of a shared resource pool. Utilized with the ProjectExchange Portfolio Wizard (purchased separately), ResourceXchange provides analysis at any organizational level or for any resource attribute.

ResourceXchange working in conjunction with Microsoft Project provides organizations with a flexible, easy-to-use, and comprehensive resource management solution.

Top three product differentiators; describe what makes your product unique.

1. Unlimited resource attributes and attribute groups provide organizational-specific resourcing capabilities.

2. Seamless integration with Microsoft Project provides a single-resource repository spanning the entire enterprise, ensuring resource information is consistent across projects.

3. Three-tier client/server-based architecture provides a system scalable across the entire enterprise.

To what business processes can this tool be applied?

Our tools are utilized across multiple business processes.

Describe the ideal end user environment for the current version of your product (size of organization, level of project management sophistication, effort and commitment required).

Our primary market consists of Global 5000 organizations desiring to increase their return on people, time, and financial investments. We initially assist event-driven divisions within these organizations, with the ultimate goal of benefiting every user in the organization.

Future strategies for this product.

Many organizations today are moving to a strong matrix style of management. In a strong matrix, project managers rely on functional managers to provide resources needed to accomplish the project activities. Communication and signoff between the project manager and functional manager are essential and vital to the success of the strong matrix style. Because functional managers are responsible for activities across projects and from various project managers, a central resource-allocation repository and a flexible method of communication are essential to the organization's overall success. We will continue to be a market leader in helping matrix-managed organizations.

Product's target market.

Based on our experience, clients who benefit most from our products and services include information systems, professional services, product development, engineering, and other event-driven organizations. Among these groups, each has further defined a set of unique objectives critical to increasing their competitiveness. IMS provides the ProjectExchange Enterprise Toolkit to achieve these objectives from the departmental level to the entire enterprise.

What are your product's three main benefits? (How does using the product add value to the customer?)

1. Configurable team attributes and work-process flows provide an organization with a solution that matches their unique process of conducting business, thus increasing return on investment.

2. A single-resource repository unifies managers across the entire enterprise and ensures demands placed on the organization are achievable.

3. Aggregating resource assignments across all projects helps resource managers balance supply and demand.

Describe your quality management process. List any relevant certifications.

We have continually improved our system-development methodology since 1991. Over time, our SDLC has incorporated the best practices learned while deploying ProjectExchange in world-class organizations across the globe. Our Research & Development division utilizes ProjectExchange, and quality measures are persistent throughout our methods and processes.

Discuss your product pricing structure. Include volume discount levels, concurrent user options, site licenses, cost of implementation, and other issues.

Please consult IMS for current pricing.

Implementation costs vary and depend upon a particular organization's business requirements and level and availability of in-house expertise. We offer the following services to help achieve organizational objectives:

- Installation
- Process, methods, and integration consulting
- Project office support
- ProjectExchange add-on solution development
- Implementation management
- Microsoft Project and ProjectExchange two-day course
- ProjectExchange for Project Managers one-day course
- ProjectExchange for Team Members one-half-day course
- MS Project Introduction one-day course
- MS Project Basic two-day course
- Project Planning & Management Fundamentals three-day course
- Executive briefing on project management.

Annual maintenance is offered at 15 percent of the license costs. Maintenance includes telephone support and product upgrades.

SAS Software

Describe what the product is designed to do.

The project management capabilities of SAS software are designed to help you plan, manage, and track single or multiple projects. These projects can range from the small to the very large, from the simple to the complex. Next, SAS software gives you the tools to add information on the progress that has been made in completing the tasks scheduled.

Top three product differentiators; describe what makes your product unique.

1. The most obvious differentiator for the SAS software project management tools is their ability to run on virtually every major operating system—PC, Unix, mainframe, or Macintosh.

2. Another distinct feature of SAS software project management is its integration with an unparalleled suite of operations research and management science tools.

3. Finally, SAS Institute Inc., the world's largest privately held software vendor, has a record of steady growth and commitment to its customers. We've been in business since 1976 (providing project management software since 1983).

To what business processes can this tool be applied?

The project management tools in SAS software can be applied to any business process, but you will obtain the best results when you apply them to processes for which you have at least approximate starting dates or times.

Describe the ideal end-user environment for the current version of your product (size of organization, level of project management sophistication, effort and commitment required).

SAS software's project management tools can really be applied in any user environment, but some users will get more benefit from the tools' capabilities than others. In general, an ideal user of SAS software project management tools should be well acquainted with project management processes.

Owing to its flexibility, SAS software can easily accommodate users with widely varying levels of commitment. Users less committed to the SAS system may choose to store their project data in another database format.

SAS software can also accommodate users of varying technical expertise.

Future strategies for this product.

Continued multiplatform support and the addition of features designed to increase the software's usefulness and ease of use.

Product's target market.

The target market for SAS software project management is the user who is not satisfied with a "one size fits all" solution or a strictly "off the shelf" product. We aim for users who want to take direct control of their project models.

What are your product's three main benefits? (How does using the product add value to the customer?)

Using SAS software for project management has many advantages, but the most prominent benefits come from gaining direct, detailed control over your project models and the schedules that arise from them.

Describe your quality management process. List any relevant certifications.

In software development at SAS Institute, we recognize that quality is not simply added to the software product by testing at the end of development. Developing quality SAS software requires building quality into each step of the software development process.

Discuss your product pricing structure. Include volume discount levels, concurrent user options, site licenses, cost of implementation, and other issues.

Price varies. Technical support and maintenance are included in the annual license fee.

TurboProject Professional 3.0

Describe what the product is designed to do.

TurboProject is a powerful project management program that you can use to efficiently plan, manage, and communicate a project schedule and information. TurboProject is ideal for building a project, especially during the early stages of a project's definition. Using the methodology of top-down, Turbo Project thinks the way a project manager does. It permits you to start with what you know, allowing the project plan to be developed in a structured manner. Adhering to this top-down methodology allows you to build your project structure, with what you know now, but with the advantage that you can fill in the details later. With unsurpassed control provided by the intuitive project tree navigator, you can move through the hierarchy of a project by simply pointing and clicking with your mouse, collapse, expand, zoom, and view only the parts you need to. Why have power and capacity if getting to the core of your project is constant struggle. TurboProject combines the best of traditional project management features with unique and useful capabilities such as loose layout, dynamic leveling, multilevel planning, hierarchical scheduling, and single click support for *distribution and integration* of multiple subprojects. Combine all of this with features such as *auto-progress* and unlimited *undo redo*, and support for *smart* 32 Bit ODBC at a price that is way below any other product in this segment of the project management market. With three products to choose from—Express, Standard, and Professional—TurboProject offers scalability for all types and levels of individuals and corporations who are serious about being successful in managing and controlling projects.

Top three product differentiators; describe what makes your product unique.

1. Elegant and intuitive multiproject support.
2. Project navigation tree.
3. Top-down methodology.

To what business processes can this tool be applied?

TurboProject's comprehensive features set allows the product to be used in a variety of different ways and in many industries. If the requirement is to streamline your project management activities and to be even more competitive in your market segment, then TurboProject provides a feature set that suits these requirements. Industries include software development, telecommunications, financial services, service industries, automotive, mining, aerospace/defense, and construction.

Describe the ideal end-user environment for the current version of your product (size of organization, level of project management sophistication, effort and commitment required).

Whether the requirement is for a simple scheduler or a robust tracking and analysis tool, TurboProject offers something for all users and corporations who want to be more successful at planning, managing, and controlling projects. With three levels of product—TurboProject Express, TurboProject, and TurboProject Professional—TurboProject, IMSI provides a scaleable solution that is ideally suited for use by individuals or even corporations requiring hundreds of users to be involved in the project management process. TurboProject has been used with great success by managers of all experience levels. All can easily find a level that supports their project planning and management requirements. Adherence to top-down methodology enables implementation to be carried out in a structured manner, and TurboProject integrates easily into organizations committed to the adoption of sound project management practices.

Future strategies for this product.

Client/server and save-to-database features.
Enhanced groupware capabilities.
Intelligent resource scheduling.

Product's target market.

TurboProject Professional: Organizations with requirements to manage multiple projects using shared resources.

TurboProject: A practical solution for project managers requiring superior functionality, but not required to distribute and integrate subprojects.

TurboProject Express: Designed specifically for people who want scheduling solutions fast and easy. It targets users wanting to create professional plans for smaller projects, who demand presentation-quality output, at a reasonable price.

What are your product's three main benefits? (How does using the product add value to the customer?)

1. Top-down planning.
2. Product scalability.
3. Cost of ownership.

Describe your quality management process. List any relevant certifications.

Our quality management process can be described in three phases. We have a highly technical quality assurance team that works directly with the engineers on a daily basis, and that is responsible for verifying the correct functionality and implementation of TurboProject.

Once development milestones are achieved, copies of TurboProject are sent to about thirty different companies participating in our beta test program. We feel these testers represent a good sampling of the product management industry and provide invaluable feedback concerning their individual working styles and needs.

Our final quality assurance cycle performs a battery of system tests to ensure that TurboProject will run smoothly on all the current hardware standards.

Discuss your product pricing structure. Include volume discount levels, concurrent user options, site licenses, cost of implementation, and other issues.

IMSI offers a site license pricing structure, with volume discounts. TurboProject Professional SRP is $295.95 per copy, and TurboProject Standard SRP is $99.95 per copy. Our site license pricing begins with a ten-user site, and then progresses to an eleven to forty-nine-user site, a fifty to ninety-nine-user site, a one hundred to 249-user site, and so on. At present, we do not offer a concurrent user license. For more information, please contact IMSI Corporate Sales at 888/467-4223.

IMSI offers a corporate support and training program that includes a local two-day course for $675 per person, and on-site training beginning at $1,500 a day. We also offer a premium support and maintenance program for corporate users. For more information visit the TurboProject homepage http://www.imsisoft.com/turboproject or E-mail corporate@imsisoft.com.

WebProject

Describe what the product is designed to do.

WebProject is designed for geographically dispersed project teams. WebProject is a Java-based project management tool with powerful collaboration and communications features. WebProject incorporates unique knowledge management/best practices capability.

Top three product differentiators; describe what makes your product unique.

WebProject is the first (only) pure Java project management suite that can utilize an open architecture database backend. WebProject allows corporations to utilize Oracle, SQL Server, Informix, Sybase, or other databases in their enterprise project management.

WebProject has introduced the first knowledge management/best practices capability within a project management software suite.

WebProject enables global project communication including project issues boards, threaded task discussions, virtual project status meetings, and remote project statusing and updates.

To what business processes can this tool be applied?

Geographically dispersed project teams, projects that need to have access from remote locations, or integrating WebProject's proprietary information exchange with MS Project, Primavera, or other desktop systems.

WebProject allows the extraction of knowledge from the enterprise, such as resource capabilities or company *best practices*.

Describe the ideal end-user environment for the current version of your product (size of organization, level of project management sophistication, effort and commitment required).

WebProject is an easy-to-use Java project management tool that will enable teams to communicate and collaborate from remote locations. WebProject is designed for the enterprise and will work well with project teams as well.

Future strategies for this product.

WebProject has established many *firsts* in the project management industry. We will continue to move the industry forward with our new technologies on the Web and with Java.

Product's target market.

Geographically dispersed project teams, enterprise project management systems, integration with Primavera, MS Project, and other project management systems.

What are your product's three main benefits? (How does using the product add value to the customer?)

1. Enterprise project communication.
2. Project collaboration.
3. Geographically dispersed updates and communication.

Describe your quality management process. List any relevant certifications.

WebProject adheres to strict standards and processes for quality, both in development and customer service.

Discuss your product pricing structure. Include volume discount levels, concurrent user options, site licenses, cost of implementation, and other issues.

WebProject is priced at $790 for starter package including the WebProject server. WebProject does provide enterprise and site licensing.

WorkLink Resource Manager

Describe what the product is designed to do.

WorkLink supports the planning and control of work within engineering and design work groups. Key features include the planning, budgeting and reforecasting of workhours. WorkLink helps coordinate resources, work orders, payroll integration and project cost control.

Top three product differentiators; describe what makes your product unique.

Based on a proven, documented project cost control methodology.
Supports bi-directional linkages with project scheduling and ERP software.
Integrated management of both internal and external resources and costs.

To what business processes can this tool be applied?

Resource planning and forecasting.
Progress monitoring.

Describe the ideal end-user environment for the current version of your product (size of organization, level of project management sophistication, effort and commitment required).

The user environment typically consists of owner organizations that manage their own projects. These organizations often have their own technical staff of engineers and designers. Their projects usually involve a mix of external procurement and internal design costs. They usually have extensive project management expertise.

Future strategies for this product.

Application functionality: integrated workflow management.
Application functionality: support for evolving international project management standards.
System architecture: move toward DCOM model.

Product's target market.

WorkLink's target market is comprised primarily of medium to large owner organizations that manage their own projects. Typically these organizations have their own technical staff of engineers and designers.
Many WorkLink users are utilities or mass-transit organizations.

What are your product's three main benefits? (How does using the product add value to the customer?)

Reduce omissions by applying a proven project cost management methodology.
Reduce dependency on disparate systems and improve reporting consistency due to a centralized data repository.
Eliminate duplicate data entry through direct integration with scheduling and ERP systems.

Describe your quality management process. List any relevant certifications.

Multiphased methodology based on Optiplan's 14-year software development experience. Software quality is monitored through a combination of automated tools and external usability testing. Optiplan participates in national and international software quality associations.

Discuss your product pricing structure. Include volume discount levels, concurrent user options, site licenses, cost of implementation, and other issues.

WorkLink licensing is based on a concurrent usage model. Volume discounts and site licenses are available.
The cost of implementation includes on-site user training, support hotline and possible application enhancements.
Software subscription and support services range from 20 percent to 25 percent of the software license costs.

Chapter 6

Communications Management Software

Subcategories: Timesheets, Graphics Add-ons, Web Publishers

Communications is the heart of project management in any organization. In fact, project management starts with people communicating.

Team members talking to project managers ... project managers E-mailing functional managers ... functional managers reporting to enterprise or program managers.

Project-driven organizations, operating in a multisite, matrix structure are looking to information technology and, more recently, Internet, intranet, and extranet technologies to support and facilitate project-based communications and activities.

Accumulation, collaboration, and dissemination of project information should also be fully integrated into the business process model of the project-driven organization. These products are designed for and target small groups to large organizations in a wide range of industries and processes, and support simple through complex projects.

Communications management is covered in Chapter 10 of *A Guide to the Project Management Body of Knowledge (PMBOK™ Guide)*.

What to Expect:

Communications management software provides features like:
- Progress reporting
- Requirements documentation
- Management of project documents
- Team member communication
- Bulletin boards, message triggers, and other team notification devices.

Communications Management Subcategory: Timesheets

Time collection automates the schedule update process and forms the basis for improved estimating based on historic actuals. Basic timesheet tools allow project team members to electronically capture their actual work on tasks or activities as detailed.

More sophisticated products allow users to add tasks to assist in further defining the schedule.

Some businesses require an auditable timesheet, where any changes are electronically traceable. Approval trails are available for some tools, allowing supervisors to approve or reject timesheet data before importing it into the scheduling tool.

Timesheet tools that run under a Web browser allow access for remote users with no access to a LAN/WAN. Industry-standard databases integrate with corporate systems, like payroll.

There are many types of timesheet tools on the market, from simple data-entry spreadsheets designed for a small departmental project through enterprise caliber, distributed systems designed for integration with a mature project management environment.

What to Expect:

Timesheet software provides features like:
- Electronic to-do list for resources assigned to the project
- Audit trail for changes to timesheets
- Interfaces with popular project management software packages to automate updates to the project schedule
- Support for billable and nonbillable projects
- Interfaces with financial systems
- Customizable views for preparers and approvers.

This category of tools takes data generated in other software packages and presents it in customizable graphical formats.

Traditional project management graphics like Gantt charts, network logic diagrams, breakdown structures, and PERT charts are examples of project management graphical outputs.

Communications Management Subcategory: Graphics Add-ons

What to Expect:

Graphics add-ons provide features like:
- Extracting data from project management software and other data sources
- Filtering, sorting, and selecting capability
- Customizable project management graphics.

Communications Management Subcategory: Web Publishers and Organizers

Web organizers is a category of products that accepts a variety of project-related documents and assembles them into a website, complete with hyperlinks, creating an online project workbook.

What to Expect:

Web publishers and organizers provide features like:
- Publishing reports that are viewable using common Web browsers and supporting tools
- Organizing an electronic project workbook
- Publishing project documents and linking via hyperlinks for Web posting.

What the Data Reveals

Most of the suite products had similar and expected features in the areas of reporting, cost, repository, and timesheets. As the scope of functionalities expanded into other areas of project management—such as process, risk, communications, and document management—the breadth of many of the offerings trailed off. The majority of the products focused on integration with Microsoft Project as the sole desktop tool. It was also surprising that many of the suites either only had Web browser-based timesheets or did not provide Web-browser interfaces. The products also have varying degrees of depth in the resource management area in terms of employee-skills inventory and high-level resource capacity planning. Selection will depend on the organization's project management maturity, how distributed the organization is, and the size and scope of the enterprise's project-based activities.

There are only fourteen entries in communication management, over half of which are modules of suites products. These products are strong on team management but weak in newer communications technologies such as threaded discussions, newsgroups, and so forth.

Over two-thirds of the products have strong support for tracking and communicating action items, issues, agendas, and the like. All products appear to be strong in the reporting areas. While some offerings are cutting edge, overall this category is weaker in the areas of utilizing newer technology. Less than two-thirds are E-mail enabled, and fewer than 50 percent support management and version control of documents. Less than 40 percent of the products score strong on workflow management.

While there are varying degrees of breadth of functionality, overall there is both breadth and depth that far exceeds what was available two years ago. Some vendors are beginning to take advantage of the latest technologies in communications management. In the next few years, communications management will become one of the most important areas of doing business.

What the Majority of Vendors Offer

Almost all have reporting and the ability to easily tailor reports to the users' needs. They are also strong in the team, issue, and task management areas.

Most vendors offer support, training, consulting, and product enhancements at the customer's request.

What a Minority of Vendors Offer

Most vendors are not yet making multilingual product and technical support available.

Only about two-thirds are E-mail enabled, and fewer than half have client interfaces that run on a Web browser.

Fewer than 40 percent have functionality to deal with workflow management.

Unique Features that Surfaced in Vendor Responses to the Narrative Questions

Grouping of projects and rollup to enterprise portfolio.

Grouping of resources and rollup of organizational breakdown structure to enterprise level.

Some vendors extend the value in the communication management area because the communications management vehicle is part of an overall integrated suite of tools for project management across the organization. While this is not essential, it may be attractive to larger organizations or those interested in a more integrated approach.

A reminder: The data in the matrix and in the narrative responses were supplied by the vendors and have not been independently verified.

Communications Management

	ABT Repository	AutoPLAN Enterprise	ER Project 1000	eRoom	Global Project Management System	Mesa/Vista	Microsoft Project 98	Milestones, Etc.	PlanView Software
Communications features									
Team "push" communication channels	Y	Y	N	Y	Y	Y	Y	N	Y
Threaded discussion	Y	N	Y	Y	Y	Y	N	N	N
Bulletin board	Y	Y	N	Y	Y	N	N	N	Y
Newsgroups	Y	Y	N	N	Y	N	N	N	N
Team management									
Creates and delivers action items	Y	Y	N	Y	Y	Y	Y	N	Y
Creates and delivers task lists	Y	Y	Y	Y	Y	N	Y	N	Y
Delegates work requests to team	Y	Y	Y	N	Y	N	Y	N	Y
Electronic resource requestor (send message to functional manager asking for his people)	Y	N	N	N	Y	N	Y	N	Y
Document management									
Version control	N	N	N	Y	Y	Y	Y	N	N
Document collaboration	N	N	Y	Y	Y	Y	Y	Y	N
Online project management methodology	Y	N	Y	N	Y	N	Y	Y	N
Online deliverables templates	Y	Y	Y	Y	Y	Y	N	N	Y
Features									
Action items	Y	Y	N	Y	Y	Y	Y	Y	Y
Risk documentation	Y	N	Y	N	Y	Y	N	N	Y
Issues management	Y	Y	Y	Y	Y	Y	N	N	Y
Meeting minutes	Y	N	Y	Y	Y	Y	N	N	Y
Agendas	Y	N	Y	N	Y	Y	N	N	Y
Project templates	Y	Y	Y	Y	Y	Y	Y	N	Y
Integrates with scheduling tools									
Project templates	Y	Y	Y	N	Y	Y	Y	Y	Y
Task status updates	Y	Y	Y	Y	Y	Y	Y	Y	Y
E-mail enabled	Y	Y	Y	Y	Y	Y	Y	Y	Y
Workflow management *	N	Y	Y	Y	Y	N	N	N	Y
Reporting									
Report writer	Y	Y	Y	N	Y	Y	Y	N	Y
Report wizard	Y	Y	Y	N	Y	N	N	N	Y
Publishes as HTML	Y	Y	Y	N	Y	Y	Y	N	Y
Number of user-defined fields		25	100		Y	25	360	200	Unlim.
Drill-down/Roll-up *	Y	Y	Y		Y	Y	N	Y	Y
Import/export	Y	Y	Y	N	Y	Y	Y	Y	Y
Automatic E-mail notification *	Y	Y	Y	Y	Y	Y	N	Y	Y
Macro recorder/batch capable *A64	Y	Y	N	N	Y	N	Y	Y	N
Can "canned" reports be modified?	Y	Y	Y	Y	Y	Y	Y	Y	Y
Sort, filter	Y	Y	Y	Y	Y	Y	Y	Y	Y

Architecture

	Oracle, Sybase, MS SQL Server, Informix	Oracle	Oracle, MS SQL Server, Interbase	SQL Anywhere	MS SQL Server, Oracle	MS SQL Server	MS Access, MS SQL Server, or Oracle	Oracle, Sybase, MS SQL Server, etc.
Databases supported (list):	Oracle, Sybase, MS SQL Server, Informix	Oracle	Oracle, MS SQL Server, Interbase	SQL Anywhere	MS SQL Server, Oracle	MS SQL Server	MS Access, MS SQL Server, or Oracle	Oracle, Sybase, MS SQL Server, etc.
Supports distributed databases	Y	Y	Y	Y	Y	N	Y	N
Three-tier client/server	Y	Y	Y	N	Y	N	N	Y
Client operating systems	Win 95/98/NT	Win 95/NT/3.x, Solaris, HP-UX, AIX	Win 95/98/NT 3.51/NT 4.0 (ER Project Satellite also Java and Win 3.x)	Win 95/98/NT	Y	Y	Win 95/98/NT 3.51 with Service Pack 5 or later/NT 4.0 with Service Pack 2 or later	Win 95/98/NT
Server operating systems	Win NT	Win NT, Solaris, HP-UX, AIX	Win NT, Unix	Win NT	Y	Y	Win 95/98/NT 3.51 with Service Pack 5 or later/NT 4.0 with Service Pack 2 or later	Win NT, Unix, Novell, IIS, Netscape
Network operating systems	TCP/IP compatible	Win NT, Novell, Unix	Win, NetBEUI/NetBios, TCP/IP, Novell	Win NT	Y	Y	Any Win-supported network	Win NT, Unix, Novell, IIS, Netscape
Minimum client configuration	Pentium 133	P5 32 MB	Pentium, 16 MB memory (ER Project Satellite 8 MB)	16 MB Pentium	Y		486 or higher processor with 12 MB memory for Win 95 or 16 MB for Win 98 or NT	486/66, 8 MB RAM, Win 3.x
Minimum server configuration	Pentium 266	P5 32 MB, Unix machine with 64 MB	Pentium, 32 MB memory	64 MB Pentium	Y		Run from server is available; configuration depends on number of users connecting to server	486/66, 32 MB RAM, Novell
Client runs under Web browser	Y	Y	Y (ER Project Satellite)	Y	Y	Y	N	Y
Open architecture								
Supports OLE	Y	Y	N	Y	Y	N	Y	Y
Documented Object Model	Y	Y	Y	Y	Y	Y	Y	Y
Documented Application Programming Interface (API)	Y	Y	N	Y	Y	Y	N	Y

Communications Management

	ABT Repository	AutoPLAN Enterprise	ER Project 1000	eRoom	Global Project Management System	Mesa/Vista	MS Project 98	Milestones, Etc.	PlanView Software
Simultaneous edit of data file	Y	N	Y	N	Y	Y	N	Y	N
Does product have a programming language?	N	Y	N	N	Y	N	Y	Y	Y
Are years stored as four-digit numbers?	Y	Y	Y	Y	Y	Y	Y	Y	Y
Online help									
Right mouse click	Y	N	Y	Y	Y	N	Y	Y	Y
Hover buttons	Y	Y	Y	Y	Y	N	Y	Y	Y
Interactive help	Y	Y	Y	Y	Y	Y	Y	Y	Y
Help search feature	Y	Y	Y	Y	Y	Y	Y	Y	Y
Web access to product knowledge base *	Y	Y	Y	Y	Y	N	Y	Y	Y
Vendor information									
Training									
Computer-based training	Y	Y	N	Y	Y	N	N	Y	Y
Training materials available	Y	Y	Y	Y	Y	Y	Y	Y	Y
Customized training materials	Y	Y	Y	Y	Y	Y	N	Y	Y
Online tutorial	Y	N	Y	Y	Y	Y	Y	Y	N
Consulting available from vendor	Y	Y	Y	Y	Y	Y	Y	Y	Y
Site license discounts	Y	Y	Y	Y	Y	Y	Y	Y	Y
Enhancement requests *	Y	Y	Y	N	Y	N	Y	Y	Y
Modify source code, support through upgrades *	Y	Y	Y	Y	Y	Y	N	Y	Y
Global presence									
Global offices	Y	Y	N	N	Y	N	Y	N	Y
Multilingual technical support	Y	Y	N	N	Y	N	Y	N	Y
Language versions (list):	Eng, Fr, Ger, Jpn	Eng, Fr	Eng	Eng	Y	Eng	Ger, Fr, Swed, Ital, Span, Dan, Nor, Jpn, Traditional Chin, Simplified Chin, Kor, Heb, Brzl. Port	Eng	Eng, Fr, Ger
Audit Software Quality Assurance process? *	Y	Y	Y	N	Y	Y	N	N	Y
Security									
Configurable access priviledges *	Y	Y	Y	Y	Y	Y	N	N	Y
Passwords expire (forced update)	N	Y	N	N	Y	Y	N	N	Y
Electronic approvals	Y	Y	Y	Y	Y	Y	Y	N	Y
Password protect files	Y	Y	Y	Y	Y	N	Y	N	Y

Communications Management

Feature	Project Control 6.0	Project Integrator 2.0 Enterprise Edition	Project KickStart	ProjectExchange Hyperlink	ProjectSite for the Web	Schedule Insight	WebProject
Communications features							
Team "push" communication channels	Y	Y	N	Y	Y	N	Y
Threaded discussion	Y	Y	N	N	N	N	Y
Bulletin board	Y	Y	N	N	N	N	Y
Newsgroups	Y	N	N	N	N	N	Y
Team management							
Creates and delivers action items	Y	Y	Y	Y	N	N	Y
Creates and delivers task lists	Y	Y	Y	Y	N	N	Y
Delegates work requests to team	N	Y	Y	Y	N	N	Y
Electronic resource requestor (send message to functional manager asking for his people)	N	Y	N	N	N	N	Y
Document management							
Version control	Y	Y	N	N	N	N	Y
Document collaboration	Y	Y	N	Y	N	N	Y
Online project management methodology	Y	Y	Y	Y	N	N	N
Online deliverables templates	Y	Y	Y	Y	N	N	Y
Features							
Action items	Y	Y	Y	Y	N	N	Y
Risk documentation	Y	N	Y	Y	N	N	N
Issues management	Y	Y	Y	Y	N	N	Y
Meeting minutes	Y	Y	N	Y	N	N	Y
Agendas	Y	Y	N	Y	N	N	Y
Project templates	Y	Y	Y	Y	N	N	Y
Integrates with scheduling tools							
Project templates	Y	Y	Y	Y	N	N	Y
Task status updates	Y	Y	N	Y	Y	N	Y
E-mail enabled	Y	Y	N	N	Y	N	Y
Workflow management *	N	Y	N	N	N	N	Y
Reporting							
Report writer	Y	Y	Y	N	Y	Y	N
Report wizard	N	Y	Y	N	N	N	Y
Publishes as HTML	Y	Y	Y	N	Y	N	Y
Number of user-defined fields	60	Unlim.	0	N	80	N	Varies
Drill-down/Roll-up *	Y	Y	Y	N	Y	Y	Y
Import/export	Y	Y	Y	N	Y	Y	Y
Automatic E-mail notification *	N	Y	N	N	N	N	Y
Macro recorder/batch capable *A64	Y	Y	N	N	N	N	Y
Can "canned" reports be modified?	Y	Y	Y	Y	Y	Y	Y
Sort, filter	Y	Y	Y	N	Y	Y	Y

Communications Management

Architecture

	Project Control 6.0	Project Integrator 2.0 Enterprise Edition	Project KickStart	ProjectExchange Hyperlink	ProjectSite for the Web	Schedule Insight	WebProject
Databases supported (list):	Oracle, MS Access, MS SQL Server, Sybase	MS SQL Server, Oracle, Sybase, SQL Anywhere	N/A	Oracle, MS SQL Server, Sybase	MS SQL Server, MS Access, Oracle, ODBC	N	Oracle, SQL Server, Sybase, Informix, any JDBC-compliant database
Supports distributed databases	Y	N	N/A	Y	N	N	Y
Three-tier client/server	Y	Y	N/A	Y	Y	N	Y
Client operating systems	Win 95/98/NT	Win 95/NT	Win 95/98/NT/3.x	Win 32, MS Project	Web browser	Win 3.x or higher	Win 95/NT, Unix, Linux, any Java-enabled OS
Server operating systems	Unix, Win NT, HP, Sybase, others	Win NT	N/A	Unix, Win NT	Win NT 4.0 or higher	Win NT 3.5 or higher	Win 95/NT, Unix, Linux, any Java-enabled OS
Network operating systems	Novell, IPX, XPX, Banyan, MS Network, TCP/IP	Novell, Win NT, Banyan	N/A	Multiple	Web/http	Any	Win 95/NT, Unix, Linux, any Java-enabled OS
Minimum client configuration	PC 486/66 processor or above. Win 95 or Win NT V4. 16 MB RAM	P166 MHz, 16 MB RAM, 30 MB HD	4 MB RAM, 2.2 MB HD	Pentium w/32 MB	Web browser	12 MB memory, 12 MB disk	Web-enabled browser
Minimum server configuration	Any server supporting Oracle 7 or above	P166 MHz, 16 MB RAM, 30 MB HD	N/A	Pentium w/128 MB	64 MB memory, 200 MB disk	32 MB memory, 20 MB disk	Win 95/NT, Unix, Linux, any Java-enabled OS
Client runs under Web browser	Y	Y	N/A	N	Y	N	Y
Open architecture							
Supports OLE	Y	Y	N/A	Y	Y	N	N
Documented Object Model	N	N	N/A	Y	Y	N	N
Documented Application Programming Interface (API)	N	N	N/A	N	Y	N	N

Simultaneous edit of data file	Y	Y	N/A	Y	Y	Y	N	Y
Does product have a programming language?	N	N	N	N	N	N	N	N
Are years stored as four-digit numbers?	Y	Y	Y	Y	Y	Y	Y	Y
Online help								
Right mouse click	N	N	N	Y	Y	Y	Y	N
Hover buttons	Y	Y	Y	Y	Y	Y	Y	Y
Interactive help	N	N	Y	N	N	Y	Y	Y
Help search feature	Y	Y	Y	Y	Y	Y	Y	Y
Web access to product knowledge base *	Y	Y	Y	N	N	N	N	Y
Vendor information								
Training								
Computer-based training	Y	N	Y	N	N	N	N	Y
Training materials available	Y	Y	Y	Y	N	N	N	Y
Customized training materials	Y	Y	Y	Y	N	N	N	Y
Online tutorial	Y	N	Y	N	Y	Y	Y	Y
Consulting available from vendor	Y	Y	Y	Y	Y	Y	Y	Y
Site license discounts	Y	Y	Y	N	Y	Y	Y	Y
Enhancement requests *	Y	Y	Y	Y	Y	Y	Y	Y
Modify source code, support through upgrades *	Y	Y	N/A	Y	Y	Y	Y	Y
Global presence								
Global offices	Y	N	N	N	N	N	N	Y
Multilingual technical support	N	N	N	N	N	N	N	Y
Language versions (list):	Eng	Eng	Eng, Fr	Eng	Eng	Eng	Eng	Eng, Ger
Audit Software Quality Assurance process? *	Y	Y	Y	Y	Y	Y	Y	Y
Security								
Configurable access priviledges *	Y	Y	N	Y	Y	Y	N	Y
Passwords expire (forced update)	N	Y	N	N	N	N	N	Y
Electronic approvals	Y	Y	N	Y	N	Y	N	Y
Password protect files	Y	DBMS	N	Y	Y	Y	N	Y

VENDOR RESPONSES TO NARRATIVE QUESTIONS

Communications Management

ABT Repository (ABT Corporation)

Describe what the product is designed to do.

The ABT Results Management (RM) 5.0 Suite is an integrated enterprise project management (ERP) system that provides program, project, process, and resource management capabilities. Centered on an EPM knowledge base, the ABT Repository, are a number of components that provide functionality targeted at specific constituents. ABT Planner provides methods authoring, project planning, and estimating. ABT Workbench provides program and project scheduling and analysis. ABT Resource provides resource-pool demand and capacity management. ABT Team provides tracking and methods delivery. ABT Connect provides Web-based tracking and methods delivery. ABT Publisher provides Web-based reporting and stakeholder communication. Metrics Manager provides metrics collection, analysis and reporting. Function Point Manager provides FP counting support.

The RM 5.0 Suite also provides Microsoft Project 98 support, a powerful, programmable API to build custom system interfaces, and prepackaged toolkit interfaces to Oracle Projects and SAP.

Top three product differentiators; describe what makes your product unique.

1. Robust project management repository.
2. Highly integrated tool set.
3. Broad range of functionality to address all stakeholders.

To what business processes can this tool be applied?

Program and project management, resource management, and process management processes.

Describe the ideal end user environment for the current version of your product (size of organization, level of project management sophistication, effort and commitment required).

The RM Suite can benefit organizations of fifty to fifty thousand project-related resources, whatever the level of project management maturity.

Future strategies for this product.

Extend functionality.
Enhance scalability.

Product's target market.

Enterprise project management.

What are your product's three main benefits? (How does using the product add value to the customer?)

1. Improved executive decision-making.
2. Integrated project stakeholder information base.
3. More effective resource utilization.

Describe your quality management process. List any relevant certifications.

ABT's test enginering organization provides extensive in-house product quality testing using a series of proprietary testing methodologies, supplemented by external resources to perform activities such as high-volume benchmarking. ABT's test group has also been instrumental in contributing to the definition of IEEE Year 2000 testing standards.

Discuss your product pricing structure. Include volume discount levels, concurrent user options, site licenses, cost of implementation, and other issues.

Pricing is on a named-user basis. List prices: ABT Repository seat: $250. Volume discounts apply.

Cost of rapid implementation: Six-week process enablement around RM tool set = $75k. Additional services include project management maturity evaluation, tool training, project management concepts training, process customization and implementation, and systems integration/custom programming work.

Annual maintenance (client support program)=15 percent of purchase price.

AutoPLAN Enterprise (Digital Tools)

Describe what the product is designed to do.

AutoPLAN Enterprise Release 4 is a Web-based software and process solution to help high-tech, engineering, and telecommunications companies predict, control, and improve cycle time of critical program development and deployment. The solution set provides deep functionality across the entire spectrum of product life-cycle elements including pipeline management, project management, resource alignment, process effectiveness, and document support and team collaboration. AutoPLAN Enterprise integrates realistic planning, resource-centric management, status and forecast tracking, team collaboration, process support, escalation management, and program execution across globally distributed organizations.

Organizations are evolving from functional teams to matrix or program teams, and this is creating cross-functional or multidisciplinary project teams. AutoPLAN Enterprise recognizes three different organizational patterns that coexist: dynamic peer-to-peer, functional, and program management. AutoPLAN Enterprise offers these organizations both project-centric and resource-centric management. AutoPLAN Enterprise addresses everyone involved in product development and deployment including executives; program, product, resource, and project managers; and team leaders and team members, as well as teams from marketing, operations, service, and quality.

As a result of extensive process and product consulting with clients engaged in new product development and deployment, DTI has distilled four key reasons why products are late and descoped:

1. Product development pipeline and deployment structures that are not aligned with the company's time-to-market goals.

2. Unrealistic plans, overcommitted resources, and unmanaged cross-functional dependencies.

3. Status and forecast decisions that are based on hearsay, rather than on facts or experience.

4. A lack of consistent processes that fit the company culture and practice, which is further exacerbated by distributed cross-functional teams.

Avoiding late and descoped products requires an overall view of product and project status, the involvement of cross-functional teams, and decision evaluation tools. Increasingly accelerated product development cycles and shorter product life cycles require organizations to disseminate information quickly to remain competitive. To support today's geographically dispersed product development environments, organizations require a common platform that enables effective cross-functional collaboration and communication on product development issues. It is also imperative that the introduction of new product information can be easily accessible by each stakeholder. Common platforms and accessible information by each stakeholder will result in accelerated organizational learning and decision-making within the organization.

DTI has created a cycle time management (CTM) framework comprising both application and process support. This framework emphasizes the critical components involved in introducing and deploying the right products and services to the market at the right time. Introducing and deploying these products and services requires companies to institute well-defined new product planning and execution processes, complemented with customer management and performance measurement processes. The new planning processes should consist of product portfolio, technology portfolio, product planning, and resource planning. The execution processes must consist of advanced technology development, platform development, product development, market introduction and deployment.

CTM enables companies to strike a balance between flexibility and discipline that is tailored to their organization and culture. The CTM framework supports a flexible *shrink-to-fit* process, which is adaptable to an organization's process maturity. This process will provide a road map for decision-making and progress tracking within a new product introduction and deployment pipeline.

CTM consists of six fundamental elements: 1) processes, 2) projects, 3) resources, 4) documents, 5) deliverables, and 6) analysis. These six elements form the foundation objectives that drive AutoPLAN Enterprise. Organizations require a well-defined and structured process to accomplish their goals. Projects make up the mechanisms through which detailed plans and schedules are generated, executed, and tracked. Every organization faces resource constraints; thus, resource management is a critical component of CTM. All projects have deliverables associated with them either in the form of documents or the product itself. And, all projects must be managed to ensure quality deliverables. Analysis tools enable various levels of stakeholders to evaluate and ensure proper support of all elements necessary to meet CTM objectives.

Top three product differentiators; describe what makes your product unique.

1. AutoPLAN Enterprise enables organizations to manage their pipeline of resources across programs and across the phase gates of each project. It assures an escalation process for critical issues, such as overallocations, by monitoring boundary conditions and alerting appropriate people to the issues. Project managers are interested in the completion of tasks or milestones, while resource managers need to know all of the work planned for their resources. Both project and resource managers must collaborate to create realistic plans for meeting project objectives, as well as juggle those resources and plans on a day-to-day basis as changes occur. The nature of this work requires a resource-centric view of the plan, not just an activity-centric view. A resource-centric view will allow resource managers to view and allocate activities to their scarce resources, rather than allocating resources to their activities. AutoPLAN Enterprise enables resource management by providing a resource-centric Gantt bar that displays overallocated resources. Managing overallocations can be as easy as reassigning activities to another resource.

Program management is a collaborative effort. Success depends upon identifying and communicating critical issues. Such identification and communication must be inherent in the system. AutoPLAN Enterprise is designed with a communications backbone. A mechanism of triggers identifies critical issues (e.g., when milestone or cost exceeds a threshold boundary) and automatically alerts and draws attention to these critical issues. Project bulletin boards within AutoPLAN Enterprise also enhance communication by providing a context-sensitive vehicle for communicating information across the project team. In addition, AutoPLAN Enterprise supports electronic mail systems, enabling triggers and bulletin board messages to be communicated to the various levels of stakeholders.

2. AutoPLAN Enterprise supports the distributed nature of project teams by matching real-world strategy with key scalable technologies. Enterprise customers need distributed project management capabilities that cater to multisite resource management, work distribution, progress tracking, global scheduling, consolidation, reporting, integration, and collaboration. DTI has met this challenge by investing over one hundred man-years in an enterprise-level, three-tier, distributed client/server architecture that leverages both Java and Internet technologies. AutoPLAN Enterprise provides full support for multiple internal operating divisions and external suppliers. AutoPLAN Enterprise leverages many platforms—Internet, Windows, NT, and Unix—providing reliable access across the organization. Additionally, AutoPLAN Enterprise enables common project data to be shared by different projects at different locations while being maintained in a central data center that is managed by pool server software. Project data is maintained at each

geographic location on either individual or multiple servers, depending on the number of internal operating divisions and projects. A divisional pool server can also be implemented to share the project data within divisional projects. AutoPLAN Enterprise application servers are capable of scalable distributed processing, and only the server needs the capacity for large multiproject operations. AutoPLAN Enterprise has multiserver cross-project dependency links. For example, the owner of a schedule that depends on the completion of activities in another project can create cross-project links that automatically update his schedule when changes occur in the other project, even if that project resides on a different server.

3. AutoPLAN Enterprise leverages client/server/Web technologies. The promise of Java, which AutoPLAN Enterprise supports, is that enterprise deployments, including organizations with heterogeneous environments, can be cost-effectively supported. DTI Web products are easier to use than Microsoft Project and are cheaper to deploy. The rapid spread of Internet protocols and Web servers into corporate infrastructure make the Internet an ideal vehicle to support both enterprise computing and mobile employees. In addition, systems administration is simplified since no maintenance is required on the client side.

A very practical use of AutoPLAN Enterprise Web clients is that they can run in a disconnected mode on the Internet. With AutoPLAN Enterprise, the user can simply log on and save activities and other information to a local file. She can then continue to work while disconnected. At any time, the connection can be reestablished, either remotely or locally, and the data is resynchronized. This may be useful for dial-up connections when working remotely. The Web server handles all communications with the Web clients, whether they are communicating via the Internet, dial-up, LAN, or WAN. The AutoPLAN Enterprise Web clients can be run from any browser that supports Java 1.1, and the Web server will dynamically download the Java code to run the application on the client. DTI's Web strategy supports *thin* client computing. In this case, database-oriented servers are serving lightweight clients through Web servers and standard protocols. The AutoPLAN Enterprise Web clients are ideally suited for running on a Java-based network computer.

To what business processes can this tool be applied?

From business analysis and redesign to system implementation and training, DTI has established its own process to support the customer through all phases of CTM system implementation. However, as to applying AutoPLAN Enterprise to the customer's business processes, DTI takes a very pragmatic approach. DTI has established processes to help customers with the following seven business pains:

1. Managing the development and deployment pipeline in detail.

2. Top-down and bottom-up planning that enables managers to use team members' knowledge during up-front planning.

3. Juggling resources realistically, so that resources are not overcommitted and parochial allocations are not made, but rather a mechanism for cooperation on resource tradeoffs is created.

4. Creating an organizational memory that captures organizational experience for reuse the next time.

5. Obtaining weekly integrated tracking information on how programs are progressing against their plans. This can be achieved by capturing actual time spent, estimates-to-complete, percent complete, and actual start and finish.

6. Problem identification, escalation, and collaboration that allows management and the team to receive adequate notice of impending issues.

7. Interactive decision evaluation to understand the domino effect of a problem in one project and its possible cross-program impact, and obtain a swift resolution between participants.

Any combination of these processes will help organizations better understand and make use of critical path methodology, work breakdown structures, resource management, cost and earned value techniques, multiproject resource scheduling, resource allocation, status tracking, report generation, matrix management solutions, integration with other systems, middleware design, project management process design, project rollups, report generation, database design, customized product training courses, generic project management training, and more.

Describe the ideal end-user environment for the current version of your product (size of organization, level of project management sophistication, effort and commitment required).

AutoPLAN Enterprise is ideal for high-tech, engineering, and telecommunications organizations engaged in distributed product development and deployments. Its usage also extends to these organizations' distributors and partners. The role-based nature of AutoPLAN Enterprise spans all people involved, from executive management to the entire cross-functional product team. This includes experienced project and program managers, resource and development managers, and the team members creating or deploying the product. The AutoPLAN Enterprise Web client is specifically designed for those team leaders who are not full-time, experienced project managers. In fact, DTI has designed the AutoPLAN Enterprise Web client to be easier to use and more functional than Microsoft Project.

Organizations can start at either the program level right away and manage the overall pipeline of projects and resources at the business unit level, or at the individual project level. The Auto-PLAN Enterprise Web client is not only easier to use than Microsoft Project, but is also capable of managing cross-functional dependencies and resources and offering enterprise scalability when the organization is ready to expand.

Coordinating distributed projects is a difficult task. It involves resources not only from multiple projects, but also from multiple functions within those projects. The program manager responsible must understand all of the interactions and milestones required to complete the project, but he cannot and should not develop and manage the entire plan himself. Instead, he should rely on the distributed functional leaders who are responsible for their piece of the project to plan and execute that piece. As a program manager, he needs to be able to integrate the individual team plans into a single comprehensive project plan. In many organizations, this integration of people and data is difficult; AutoPLAN Enterprise is designed to help with this. Having processes in place, underpinned by enterprise software, is key to predicting, controlling, and improving product/project cycle times.

Future strategies for this product.

AutoPLAN Enterprise has been designed with an integrated product management platform for all information related to meeting CTM objectives. DTI will continue to support features needed for CTM, including pipeline and portfolio management. Future strategies will enhance the ability of customers to make informed decisions based on a comprehensive presentation of relevant data with powerful drill-down capabilities, further collaborative features that utilize the intranet and Internet, and continuing support for the free-flowing nature of the engineering culture. Application wizards will help first-time users, accelerate deployment, and reduce training cost. Process support is key to productivity improvements and to adhering to organizationwide standards. Existing process-support capabilities will be enhanced using the capabilities of Web technology and with more exchange of information across subsystems. Large organizations are geographically distributed to take advantage of global efficiencies. Local and global workgroups must collaborate and respond quickly to changing environment and work content. Both executive management and front-line team members must have access anytime, anywhere, and in any manner to enterprisewide product/project information located on geographically distributed servers. Existing multiserver capabilities of AutoPLAN Enterprise are being enhanced using Oracle.

AutoPLAN Enterprise will support key technologies including Oracle, NT 5.0, middleware, and Java. Distributed objects capability using industry-standard specifications such as CORBA will be incorporated. In addition, the AutoPLAN Enterprise application-programming interface will provide CORBA-compliant objects for seamless integration with other applications. The collaboration capabilities of AutoPLAN Enterprise will be enhanced by incorporating a workflow server. This workflow server will be based on industry-standard specifications and will incorporate process modeling and messaging components to enable customers to configure the collaboration features based upon their business needs. The security system will have additional features to address the security risks associated with the Internet. Directory servers conforming to LDAP standards will be incorporated for seamless integration with the underlying operating environment. This in turn will provide responsive security, configurability, and flexibility features.

Product's target market.

AutoPLAN Enterprise is specifically designed to support high-tech, engineering, and telecommunications organizations in predicting, controlling, and improving cycle time of critical program development and deployment.

What are your product's three main benefits? (How does using the product add value to the customer?)

1. AutoPLAN Enterprise provides at least a 10 percent improvement in enterprise time-to-market of product development and deployment. Viewing the value of CTM from an annual R&D cost perspective: consider a product development group of one thousand people, with an annual R&D expenditure of $100M. A modest 10 percent improvement would represent a cost savings value of $10M, with a revenue enhancement value of three to five times this.

2. AutoPLAN Enterprise facilitates an organization's transformation from functional project teams to matrix, or program-organized high-performance project teams. It also supports distributed teams resulting from acquisitions. It does both of these by providing built-in communication and rollup features from distributed multiserver projects. This support enables teamwide problem identification, escalation, collaboration, and resolution. AutoPLAN Enterprise recognizes that three different organizational patterns coexist: 1) dynamic peer-to-peer, 2) functional, and 3) program management. AutoPLAN Enterprise offers these organizations both project-centric and resource-centric management.

3. AutoPLAN Enterprise accommodates joint ventures, subcontracting, mergers and acquisitions, and reorganizations by leveraging the Web to minimize deployment and support costs. The creation of plans, assignment of work, and integration of activities across multiple functions and distributed work teams is critically important. However, that is only part of the story. With the Internet, AutoPLAN Enterprise can also efficiently equip thousands of personnel involved in the product-development process with the information they need to do the best possible job. Demand for skilled workers has been great, and turnover has risen as employees move from one company or job to another. The best practices in the world are of no value to a company if those who know those practices move on without first passing along the knowledge. Best practices developed at one site need to be shared with other sites, and a process for doing that is required. AutoPLAN Enterprise solves these problems through URL references and retrieval capability. With URL features, AutoPLAN Enterprise can help preserve best practices and other information and disseminate them geographically and functionally to team members currently doing the job. AutoPLAN Enterprise can also have associated URL references that point to mission-critical information/documentation that will enable product/project teams to achieve the activity. These references can also be attached to the top-level program schedule for project leader use, or at specific functional schedules (e.g., to provide sourcing with specific third-party vendor requirements). URLs can enable:

■ Sharing best practice information from one team to another
■ Referencing documentation with checklists
■ Sharing engineering notes on installation processes.

Also, with the speed of organizational changes, a mix of project-scheduling system usage is expected. As most people are educated on Microsoft Project, AutoPLAN Enterprise can coexist with its projects and data. AutoPLAN Enterprise's graphical user interfaces (GUIs) are not only familiar to Microsoft Project users, the Web version is easier and thus leverages simplicity and ease of use with enterprise functionality.

Describe your quality management process. List any relevant certifications.

DTI achieves excellence in product quality and customer satisfaction through its quality management process. DTI's quality objective is to build quality into its products and services at all stages of product life cycle from requirement collection to customer usage. DTI's dedication to quality is reflected in its quality mission: "Doing things right the first time."

DTI's quality management group performs the functions of the software engineering process group as defined by the industry-standard capability maturity model (CMM). The quality management group plans and implements DTI's quality system, which consists of processes and guidelines. The processes detail out *what* is required for converting a set of inputs to outputs in the form of activities and tasks, primary and cooperative responsibilities, deliverables, and entry and exit criteria. The guidelines detail *how* to carry out the identified activities to ensure quality and consistency. The involvement of DTI personnel at all levels is fundamental to the implementation of the quality process. DTI personnel are drawn from various groups in the organization to author processes and guidelines, and all undergo training programs on the quality system.

DTI follows processes within Level 2 and Level 3 of the CMM. Some of the key processes within these levels include market requirement analysis, functional specification, high- and low-level design, coding, testing, release management, customer support, training, and maintenance. In addition, in-depth reviews are built into each of these processes.

DTI recognizes that enterprise growth and profitability are significantly impacted by time-to-market of new products in globally competitive high-tech markets. With this in mind, DTI's product development and quality processes are focused on meeting customer needs and requirements. Therefore, DTI collaborates with its customers both in product definition and in assuring that the product functions are implemented as intended. To facilitate the fast-track delivery of innovative products and services, DTI has created process initiatives for increased test automation, usage of tools that will enable teams to better assess the quality of their work products, management of development tools, reuse of objects across products, and tightly controlled configuration management.

DTI's quality management process focuses on periodic reviews and feedback, which are a means of monitoring the adherence of organizational activities to the process. Corrective and preventive actions play an important role in continuous improvement of the quality system and thereby the organizational activities.

DTI has a well-qualified team for quality management. DTI's teams, besides having the appropriate educational qualifications, have quality management-related certifications; some are certified quality analysts, and some hold certificates related to the capability maturity model (CMM) and its use. Many also have extensive internal audit experience.

The quality management group interacts periodically with key personnel of different functions within the organization and identifies new processes, guidelines, and improvements within the existing framework. The general approach to new process/guideline introduction is to discuss with representative users, define the process, pilot the process after review, evaluate the pilot implementation, revise the process based on feedback, plan organizationwide implementation, implement, measure, and maintain.

DTI is planning to get CMM certification at the appropriate level. The approach that would be followed for securing the certification includes mapping key process areas of the CMM to existing processes, identifying the *gaps*, preparing the implementation plan that describes how these gaps will be addressed, and executing the plan.

Discuss your product pricing structure. Include volume discount levels, concurrent user options, site licenses, cost of implementation, and other issues.

DTI's objective is to offer an integrated solution with a pricing structure that is based on enterprise requirements reflecting enterprise needs and individual needs. AutoPLAN Enterprise supports a floating license configuration, which allows any user to log into the system and consume one license. When the user has finished with the application, that license will be released for other users. Each floating license provides one concurrent use of the product. AutoPLAN Enterprise also supports a personal license configuration. Typical installations will use both personal and concurrent licensing.

Annual product maintenance is 15 percent of the list cost. Product maintenance entitles customers to engineering patches, updates, and upgrades, and phone, fax, and E-mail response to issues. Professional services are separate from DTI product maintenance. As part of the business relationship with customers, DTI takes part in joint planning to identify the customer's business needs and services sought from DTI. Professional services are charged separately on an as-needed basis. These services are performed either at the customer site, online, or at DTI's headquarters in Cupertino, California. Professional services typically fall into two categories: 1) product consulting/implementation design review and 2) implementation support. Product consulting/implementation design review discusses areas such as, "How do I apply the software with a suitable process to solve a business need?" and, "Which processes will we implement, how, and when to meet organizational objectives?" Implementation support consists of product training, project office services, upgrade migration services, systems administration services, and integration services.

ER Project 1000 (Eagle Ray Software Systems)

Describe what the product is designed to do.

The ER Project 1000 is an integrated suite of project management tools, which provide an enterprisewide project management solution. ER Project 1000 includes schedule/time management, centralized resource management, methodology/process management, project-workgroup communications, timesheets, risk/issue management, and enterprisewide cross-project tracking. Based on a client/server architecture with a centralized relational database, the ER Project 1000 provides networked access, multiproject capability, and true multiuser concurrency. It scales easily from handling small workgroup projects to large programs at the enterprise level.

Top three product differentiators; describe what makes your product unique.

1. Addresses the total project management life-cycle solution for the enterprise: Unlike most project management tools, the ER Project 1000 provides a completely integrated and centralized project management platform to support the entire life cycle of project management. Based on a client/server relational database (Oracle/SQL Server) architecture, ER Project 1000 fully supports today's multiproject/multiuser project environment. The product suite integrates full methodology/process management capabilities, project workgroup communications, and enterprisewide project tracking capabilities.

2. Provides a completely integrated suite of project management tools: The ER Project 1000 tool suite integrates industrial-strength project management functions with rich-process improvement functionality and proactive management features. ER Project 1000 provides all the necessary industrial-strength core project management functions. Key features include support for WBS/OBS/RBS structures, cost, schedule, earned value analysis, built-in report writer, timesheet approvals, and centralized resource management. ER Project 1000 takes advantage of the Web by providing Java timesheets and extensive project website publishing capability. Best practices/process improvement is easily accomplished with the methodology manager and support for organizational standards, work products, and estimation. ER Project 1000 delivers an impressive array of proactive management features. These features include risk management, issue management, management by threshold, and full project tracking.

3. Is easy to use and implement: ER Project 1000 was designed with a simple, intuitive interface. Extensive wizards assist users for complex operations. ER Project 1000 can easily be configured to your organization by using our centralized administration functions and component architecture.

To what business processes can this tool be applied?

ER Project 1000 is a wrap-around solution for organizations that need to implement mature project management practices, proactively manage their projects, improve business processes, implement standards and documentation, and communicate at multiple levels. Eagle Ray's advanced suite of tools provides project managers with an integrated platform for project planning, time tracking, resource management, and executive oversight. With features such as risk management, issue tracking, and management by threshold, the ER Project 1000 gives project managers the ability to proactively manage complex projects and stay focused on the key issues.

Organizations that engage in process improvement/best practices will find that the ER Project 1000 methodology manager is the ideal platform for developing and delivering best practices to each new project plan. Project managers will be able to easily document and reuse lessons learned in new projects. Project team members and stakeholders will find that the integrated communications features of the ER Project 1000 suite facilitate a real-time dialogue between all members and ensure no issues slip though the cracks.

Describe the ideal end-user environment for the current version of your product (size of organization, level of project management sophistication, effort and commitment required).

Size of organization: The ER Project 1000 product suite is ideal for managing projects with team sizes of ten to one thousand people per project in organizations where multiple projects are being performed at the same time. Project teams may be centralized or dispersed using client/server and Web-based communications technologies.

Level of sophistication: The tool suite is best suited for organizations that are moving beyond basic project management to a medium level of project management maturity or higher. These organizations are typically implementing tracking, costing, project management standards, risk/issue management, time tracking, centralized resource management, and possibly earned value. ER Project 1000 also supports organizations implementing a project office, best practices, process improvement, and reusable project templates. These features make ER Project 1000 an ideal platform for organizations implementing CMM level 2 or higher maturity levels.

Effort and commitment required: Successful implementation of the ER Project 1000 tool suite centers on an organization's commitment to realizing repeatable project management results from enterprisewide standardization of business processes and practices. Because of it's integrated design and simple interface, ER Project 1000 delivers numerous advantages over standard project management tool sets with less staff effort.

Future strategies for this product.

Eagle Ray's future strategies include building new modules, expanding current modules, interfacing with corporate business systems, and preparing the product suite for the global marketplace. Major planned enhancements include significant modifications to the estimation module, costing module, methodology/process management module, and the Internet/intranet/Web capabilities. In addition, we will be constructing a problem/defect-tracking module.

We will be expanding the interfaces that integrate the ER Project 1000 system with additional enterprise business systems. Such systems include costing/accounting systems, human resources (HR) systems, and additional commercial products. We also plan to complete our internationalization/localization efforts to prepare the ER Project 1000 for global distribution.

Product's target market.

ER Project 1000 is suitable for commercial and government organizations, which are managing projects that range from small workgroup-level projects to projects that span the entire enterprise. Essentially, the tool suite will support any project environment where the project team has access to or is working with computers.

What are your product's three main benefits? (How does using the product add value to the customer?)

1. Total integrated project management solution: The ER Project 1000 is an integrated, total project management solution providing complete support for the entire project management life cycle. The integrated tool suite does not require multiple add-on tools from different vendors, resulting in fewer hidden costs and less frustration. Project managers will find it easy to manage projects with a higher level of maturity by using the various features of the tool—for example, risk management, issue tracking, management by threshold, and multiproject capabilities.

2. Best practices/process improvement platform: The ER Project 1000 integrated process/ methodology management platform provides a sophisticated yet easy-to-use platform for implementing best practices, estimation metrics, organizational standards, documentation templates, and process improvement. Organizations can capture, integrate, and reuse their project knowledge and project plan templates from an enterprisewide integrated platform.

3. Enterprisewide tracking and communications: The ER Project 1000 facilitates communications between all project stakeholders. Program managers and executives can perform crossproject rollups, dynamic drill-down, and cost, schedule, and earned-value analysis for up-to-date information on all enterprise projects. The project team members can access all of project infor-

mation on the project website, and receive activity assignments and report status using Java timesheets. Automatic issue notification alerts project managers about possible deviations in cost and schedule. The built-in report writer lets you extract and summarize any data in the enterprisewide project database using customized formats.

Describe your quality management process. List any relevant certifications.

The Eagle Ray quality assurance program is a comprehensive system that employs a series of product walkthroughs, builds, quality gates, configuration management, defect tracking, and comprehensive testing. The development staff members are constantly conducting requirements, design, and code walkthroughs in coordination with weekly product builds and passing mandatory quality gates. The quality assurance program is integrated with our beta testing program to ensure that all product releases undergo rigorous real-world testing prior to release.

Comprehensive testing scenarios include unit testing, integration testing, platform testing, stress testing, concurrency testing, environment testing, security testing, usability testing, vertical testing, upgrade testing, business scenario testing, and independent qualification testing.

During the design and construction of the ER Project 1000 product, Eagle Ray brought in several project management industry experts to assist in the design of the software functionality and usability. This process will be continued to ensure that our future enhancements meet the real-world needs of project management organizations. Additionally, Eagle Ray continues to invest heavily in the training of team members in technical and project management areas.

Discuss your product pricing structure. Include volume discount levels, concurrent user options, site licenses, cost of implementation, and other issues.

Call for latest prices.

eRoom

Describe what the product is designed to do.

eRoom is a Web-based project coordination tool. It provides a persistent project space on the Web, giving all your team members access to the latest project information and status.

Team members can either create or drag in any Windows application file. They can review and revise project files, discuss issues, and take votes. eRoom notifies team members when project information arrives or changes, permitting immediate response and rapid progress.

eRooms are protected by full NT network security—only people you make eRoom members can access the project eRoom.

Top three product differentiators; describe what makes your product unique.

1. Easy to use: No adjustment or training required with familiar browser and Windows interface. No HTML experience needed—uses your Windows applications and files.
2. Administered by end users, not IT, so it works at the speed of the team.
3. Since an eRoom is on the Web, it works both within your organization and outside with partners, contractors, and customers.

To what business processes can this tool be applied?

Development projects.
Consulting projects.
Intercompany discussions and negotiations.

Describe the ideal end user environment for the current version of your product (size of organization, level of project management sophistication, effort and commitment required).

Medium to large organizations, fast-cycle, distributed project teams, team members who need to reach and work on the project from anywhere, anytime.

Future strategies for this product.

Support real-time interaction within the project team, allow members to be notified immediately when particular project information changes, and extend the API to allow even more integration and customization.

Product's target market.

Consulting companies, manufacturing/high technology companies, and professional services providers.

What are your product's three main benefits? (How does using the product add value to the customer?)

Project team can create and manage the project eRoom quickly without needing IT, using the desktop browser and applications they use today.

The project lives and grows in the eRoom, so new team members can quickly come up to speed and project files can be *harvested* and reused after the project is completed.

IT likes it because it complies with common standards, and it allows users to proceed without heavy support.

Describe your quality management process. List any relevant certifications.

No answer given.

Discuss your product pricing structure. Include volume discount levels, concurrent user options, site licenses, cost of implementation, and other issues.

eRoom server at $4,995 per server; clients start at $199 per user.

Volume discount and site license pricing available on request.

Cost of implementation: Server maintenance contract—$750/yr; client maintenance contract—$30/yr per user; consulting services and outsourcing available.

Global Project Management System (GPMS)

Describe what the product is designed to do.

The Global Project Management System (GPMS) is designed for efficient planning and control function and will organize the management of projects.

This productive, extremely flexible and fast easy-to-use system is the right tool to cover the requirements of a central project management system regarding document management, groupware aspects, database management, messaging, workflow, and project planning tools.

GPMS offers a high degree of multifunctional features, which will optimize the interactions of several project teams regarding communication and cooperation. All relevant information and documents concerning the project will be provided by the GPMS to the access of authorized team members. GPMS offers all major advantages of modern document management, workflow management, and groupware systems in the intranet and Internet.

GPMS will increase your profitability due to more efficient project work and communication. It will increase the experience of the project members (internal and external) and allow them to concentrate their efforts on core competence business.

All the relevant results could be easily identified by functions like index search, complete text search, etc.

GPMS is the right software for successful project management and communication; moreover, it enables the controlling department to access and overview received services and invoices regarding relevant projects. The team leader is able to check out with the GPMS the qualification and the special skills of each team member for the selection of required team members.

The special concept of access control provides information and documents only to entitled persons and groups dedicated to work with them (e.g., contract documents can be read, changed, and deleted only by top management). External project members and customers could have a special secure access to their project information, for example via the Internet, which permits them to have an active impact on the path forward of the project.

The feature *office automation* will give great support in easily doing the day-to-day correspondence. This includes the automatic assumption of contact names or address files for the automatic transfer into faxes, letters, or any other communication forms.

The feature *contact manager* will organize all project-relevant business contacts when no established scheduling system exists. All required time-related information, milestones, appointments, or events could be scheduled and double-checked.

The *time management* feature will give an overview or update documentation regarding the project history at any time. The *trigger* function handles all required reminders about milestones, contract expiration date, birthdays, etc.

GPMS will provide an outstanding complete collection of project-relevant data without any additional special effort or separate input of the project members. It will file and handle information into a dedicated company *intelligent brain-form*. This complex *knowledge management system* will create a great advantage that helps to process projects in a faster and more effective way and to generate more business in the market.

Top three product differentiators; describe what makes your product unique.

1. Project management and communication system for global integration of project members using functionality of standard database, document management, groupware, messaging, workflow, and project planning tools.
2. Knowledge management system for reuse of project results.
3. Productive, extremely flexible, easy-to-use system.

To what business processes can this tool be applied?

Top management, controlling, marketing, sales, human resources, and any other business units.

Describe the ideal end-user environment for the current version of your product (size of organization, level of project management sophistication, effort and commitment required).

The company should use Microsoft client and server software. Groups and organizational units from five to one thousand members, as GPMS can *only* be the document management system for the project team. For example, the project plan can be used as *only a document* (as it often is today). On the other hand, GPMS is the knowledge management system that provides *all* information about project-related topics.

Future strategies for this product.

Complete integration of all project-related data in the MS SQL server database, especially all data created by Microsoft Project 98.

Product's target market.

Consulting companies and any kinds of companies that do project-related business (internal and external).

What are your product's three main benefits? (How does using the product add value to the customer?)

1. Opportunity for highly efficient and structural project work and communication.

2. Access to a company-dedicated knowledge management system with no extra input requirements (knowledge/results are created throughout the daily working process).

3. Offering wide support in easily doing the day-to-day work.

Describe your quality management process. List any relevant certifications.

ISO 9001 ff /Microsoft Solution Provider certification /Fabasoft Partner certification.

Discuss your product pricing structure. Include volume discount levels, concurrent user options, site licenses, cost of implementation, and other issues.

GPMS is based on the Fabasoft Components. The Components Base and CIS are needed to run GPMS. Base and CIS have a retail price of DM 900 per used computer. No additional costs for servers.

GPMS is shipped at a price of DM 300, conforming to the Fabasoft Components license scheme.

The cost of implementation varies depending on the size of the installation and the company size. GPMS can be used *out of the box* with an implementation effort of about three days for user and template management.

One-day training suits most of the users because of the generic integration of standard office and project management products. Administrators should be trained three to five days.

Maintenance for an average installation is about two days per month (depending on the amount of new users and new projects).

Mesa/Vista (Mesa/Vista Systems Guild)

Describe what the product is designed to do.

Mesa/Vista helps project teams manage, monitor, and comply with quality and government regulations by providing process management capabilities and access to all legacy and current project data through a Web browser. Mesa/Vista provides process management capabilities and integrates a development team's existing product environment, including tools like Rational Rose, TD Technologies' SLATE, Cayenne Teamwork, or any tool with an MPX interface, such as Microsoft Project.

Mesa/Vista links information between stand-alone products and exposes project data to authorized project team members, empowering them to anticipate and solve problems at early stages in the project life cycle.

Mesa/Vista automates the documentation process. This shaves time from a project that must comply with government or other regulatory standards because the documentation is available as soon as the project is complete.

Top three product differentiators; describe what makes your product unique.

1. Patent-pending technology intuitively links graphical objects such as those found in developer's modeling tools, not only within the stand-alone tool but also between tools.

2. Provides support of any business process through dynamic exchange of information.

3. Connects legacy and current data between development team's business and engineering tools.

To what business processes can this tool be applied?

Software Engineering Institute (SEI) CMM levels 1–5, ISO-compliancy regulations, and FDA requirements management.

Describe the ideal end user environment for the current version of your product (size of organization, level of project management sophistication, effort and commitment required).

The ideal end-user environment for Mesa/Vista is a distributed, process-conscious product-development group needing visibility and access to legacy and current project data across multiple platforms.

An organization trying to achieve or improve upon an SEI CMM level, achieve an ISO 9000 quality standard, or comply with FDA requirements will greatly benefit from the Mesa/Vista environment.

Commitment: All project-related communications would go through the Mesa/Vista environment for it to provide complete, automated project status information.

Future strategies for this product.

Future strategy for Mesa/Vista includes integrating all engineering and business data together to be shared and accessed by the entire product development team, no matter where the data resides.

Plug-ins will include more scheduling tools, databases, business tools, document editing tools, and modeling tools—all the tools the entire team would use within a product development environment.

Mesa/Vista will create an environment of collaboration and expose information to help all members of the team work together without restraint of hardware or system requirements.

Product's target market.

Mesa/Vista is ideal for process-conscious project managers of distributed product development teams in the telecommunication, automotive, aerospace, medical, and software industries.

What are your product's three main benefits? (How does using the product add value to the customer?)

1. Provides accessibility to data from places other than the data's native machine, minimizing the number of copies of each software product that needs to be purchased.

2. Saves time by providing online access to all project data, rather than printing and faxing information in order to share it.

3. Automatic documentation mechanism for ease of tracking government regulations or quality standards control.

Describe your quality management process. List any relevant certifications.

Mesa/Vista is used to manage the development of Mesa/Vista. Also, extensive internal and external testing is done of the Mesa/Vista product line. Mesa has provided the software to Young America's design team (NYYC's challenger in the America's Cup 2K) in exchange for feedback on Mesa/Vista and suggestions for improvements based on their real-life use of the product line.

Discuss your product pricing structure. Include volume discount levels, concurrent user options, site licenses, cost of implementation, and other issues.

Contact vendor.

Microsoft Project 98 (Microsoft)

Describe what the product is designed to do.

Microsoft Project 98 is an ideal tool for planning and tracking projects of all sizes. Because it is easy to use, it is an ideal tool for all levels of project management experience from the newcomer to the experienced project manager. Microsoft Project 98 focuses on three areas:

1. Control—gives users more control over their project plans.

2. Communication—improves project communication so everyone stays informed and involved.

3. Compatibility—provides programmability features so it can serve as a stand-alone product or as part of a broader company solution.

Top three product differentiators; describe what makes your product unique.

1. Ease of use: Microsoft Project 98 requires little or no training to begin using it to manage projects, so the *startup* costs required of new customers are much lower when compared to other

project management software tools. The navigation map also helps inexperienced project managers and new Microsoft Project 98 customers to map their functional responsibilities to Microsoft Project 98's features.

2. Extensibility: Microsoft Project 98 is a pioneer in extensibility. It can store data in an open database format and supports VBA. Customers can easily integrate project management data with their existing corporate business systems, which enables Microsoft Project 98 to accommodate ever-increasing complexity as customers' project management needs change and grow throughout the organization.

3. Integration with other Microsoft applications: Microsoft Project 98 incorporates the best of Microsoft Office to make a tool that is easy to learn and use.

To what business processes can this tool be applied?

Microsoft Project 98 can be applied to any process for which the customer can identify specific tasks and their respective durations and dependencies. Customers can use Microsoft Project 98 to easily compare cost and profitability by project, balance resource requirements across projects, and track dependencies across multiple projects to assess a project's impact on the bottom line. Microsoft Project 98 can also be used to integrate project metrics with corporate accounting, human resources, timesheets, or manufacturing systems and organize project documentation so it is readily available to everyone involved in a project.

Describe the ideal end-user environment for the current version of your product (size of organization, level of project management sophistication, effort and commitment required).

Microsoft Project 98 is used in end-user environments of all sizes—from individuals planning single-resource projects to large corporations with thousands of employees. Customers with widely varying project management backgrounds can also use it. Even newcomers to project management principles can learn to use Microsoft Project 98 quickly and easily with the product's built-in help and other easy-to-use features. Microsoft Project 98 even contains features to extend a project team's communication capability over the Web or any MAPI-compliant E-mail system. And, customers won't *outgrow* Microsoft Project 98 since its programmability features allow them to tailor the program to their organization's unique and changing needs.

Future strategies for this product.

Microsoft will continue to focus on improved collaboration, performance, and ease of use in future versions of Microsoft Project. Microsoft Project has always focused on bringing project management techniques to a wider audience via improved ease of use and expanded communication capabilities for project teams and will continue to do so in the future.

Product's target market.

Anyone who deals with budgets, assignments, and deadlines can take advantage of the benefits offered by Microsoft Project 98. If you have thousands of details to manage, or even a few dozen, you're a potential Microsoft Project 98 customer.

What are your product's three main benefits? (How does using the product add value to the customer?)

1. Easy to learn and can grow with customers' projects and organization.
2. Ability to plan and track multiple projects in a consolidated manner.
3. Helps customers track and manage costs that affect the bottom line.

Describe your quality management process. List any relevant certifications.

Microsoft Project's quality management process begins with developing a product vision based on input from customers, internal and external developers, the product support team, and usability engineers. This ensures that the development process focuses on the right objectives, and that decisions regarding product quality reflect all of these perspectives.

Microsoft maintains a high developer to test ratio throughout the software development process to ensure that potential *bugs* are identified and resolved as early in the development cycle as possible. The testing process is based on five core attributes: 1) source code version control; 2) making the code testable; 3) use of automation for broader scenario testing; 4) beta testing—both internal and external; and 5) detailed bug tracking and reporting (throughout all Microsoft product groups in order to share learning).

Finally, a new product is released only when the managers from development, testing, program management, and product support agree as a team that the product is ready. No product will be released until this agreement is reached.

Discuss your product pricing structure. Include volume discount levels, concurrent user options, site licenses, cost of implementation, and other issues.

The estimated retail price of Microsoft Project 98 is $499. Microsoft also offers several multiple-license pricing agreements. Detailed information on these agreements is available at www.microsoft.com/licensing.

The cost of implementation varies based on previous experience with project management principles, experience with other project management software tools, and the size and complexity of a customer's projects. Little or no training is needed for Microsoft Project 98 due to the extensive built-in help and other user-assistance features included in the product. Many additional low-cost books, self-help tools, and other training materials for Microsoft Project 98 are widely available. Microsoft Project 98's built-in VBA programmability features also help limit the cost of additional customization.

Milestones, Etc. (Kidasa)

Describe what the product is designed to do.

Milestones, Etc. is designed to provide an easy-to-use product to produce high-quality schedules in a Gantt format.

Top three product differentiators; describe what makes your product unique.

1. Easy to learn.
2. Easy to use.
3. Easy to update schedules.

To what business processes can this tool be applied?

Scheduling of projects.

Describe the ideal end-user environment for the current version of your product (size of organization, level of project management sophistication, effort and commitment required).

Desktop Windows environment.

Future strategies for this product.

Continue to add user-requested features to make product do more, but still maintain ease of use.

Product's target market.

People who need to quickly produce schedules.

What are your product's three main benefits? (How does using the product add value to the customer?)

1. Enables customer to easily produce high-quality Gantt charts.
2. Enables customer to spend less time creating Gantt charts.
3. Enables customer to spend less time updating Gantt charts.

Describe your quality management process. List any relevant certifications.

Follow standard commercial software development guidelines.

Discuss your product pricing structure. Include volume discount levels, concurrent user options, site licenses, cost of implementation, and other issues.

Single-user licenses are $199. Workgroup pricing is also available.

Cost of implementation: Just the amount of time it takes to go over the supplied tutorials, usually no more than a few hours.

PlanView Software (PlanView Inc.)

Describe what the product is designed to do.

PlanView Software has modules that manage the flow of work (projects and nonprojects) and enhance communication among distributed staff and managers. Work is requested, scheduled, progressed, and closed using the Web.

Top three product differentiators; describe what makes your product unique.

1. All desktop interfaces are browser based.
2. Resource-centric views of work capacity.
3. *Unlimited* scalability: Four thousand plus users at some sites.

To what business processes can this tool be applied?

Multiproject management, service request management, resource management, workflow management, work and resource *portfolio* management.

Describe the ideal end user environment for the current version of your product (size of organization, level of project management sophistication, effort and commitment required).

Organization with one hundred to multiple thousands of employees (we have implementations of four thousand plus), managed by five plus managers with access to a central database; includes matrix-style organizations.

Future strategies for this product.

Further conversion to Web browser-based interfaces; even easier report generation and Web publishing; more E-mail notification and document attachment.

Product's target market.

The resource-centric approach to work management is typically most useful for organizations with a highly skilled workforce of limited availability; with twenty plus managers, and one hundred plus staff; using client/server.

What are your product's three main benefits? (How does using the product add value to the customer?)

1. Web-based interfaces since June '97.
2. All managers and contributors access the same central repository.
3. Staff reporting ETC affects project progress.

Describe your quality management process. List any relevant certifications.

PlanView follows the guidelines set out in the book *Best Practices of Rapid Development* by Steve McConnell.

Discuss your product pricing structure. Include volume discount levels, concurrent user options, site licenses, cost of implementation, and other issues.

It is different for each case, but basically the cost is $200–$400 per seat, with volume discounts. The repository products are included. Standard SQL database is extra. Implementation and training are extra.

Cost of implementation: We offer a range of implementation packages, from rapid to standard, which include training. Additional services billed at time and cost. Phone and online tech support are free. Maintenance packages offered.

Project Control 6.0

Describe what the product is designed to do.

The Project Control Software suite supports communications management across the entire organization. The system delivers information to all levels of the organization, from employees to project management, functional management, enterprise management, global management.

Project Control Software extends desktop project management software into an enterprisewide management and reporting solution, by consolidating volumes of project files from leading project management software systems such as Microsoft Project, Primavera, and others. Project Control Software supports multiple operating systems (Windows, Macintosh, Unix) and databases (Oracle, Access, Microsoft SQL, Sybase). The entire Project Control software suite runs on a Web browser or LAN. The enterprise rollup design supports the matrix organization's need to roll up projects to program or initiative, as well as the resource perspective by business unit and organizational structure.

The Project Control software suite supports the project office across all phases of the project management life cycle from standard estimating and budgeting though timesheets and status tracking and integration with any accounting system for actual costs and earned value analysis. The process manager module enables project management standards, processes, and training management through its document management and issues-tracking functionalities.

Top three product differentiators; describe what makes your product unique.

1. No technology limits: Project Control Software supports all operating systems (Windows, Macintosh, Unix), consolidates files from multiple project management software systems (Microsoft Project, Primavera, and more), using your choice of databases (Oracle, Access, Microsoft SQL, Sybase) in a LAN or Internet solution. It is designed to integrate easily with existing business systems (such as accounting software) so an organization can leverage existing systems and immediately see productivity increases without changing everything.

2. The project office: The design and integration of Project Control software modules supports the project office across all phases of the project management life cycle, from standard estimating and budgeting though timesheets and status tracking and accounting integration for actual costs and earned value analysis.

3. Enterprise project management: Project Control software offers a suite of integrated modules that can be used to deliver the big picture of project management across a distributed organization, as well as tracking the details. The Enterprise rollup design supports the matrix organization's need to roll up projects to program or initiative, as well as the need to view data from a resource perspective by business unit and organizational structure. The entire Project Control software suite (not just the time tracking) runs on a Web browser or LAN.

To what business processes can this tool be applied?

Project Control software's enterprise rollup design supports the matrix organization's need to roll up projects to program or initiative, as well as the need to view data from a resource perspective by business unit and organizational structure.

The system supports project management, ERP, project office development, ISO registration, strategic planning, process management, methodology implementation, cost/schedule management, capability maturity module (CMM) compliance, global information technology deployment, SAP, Peoplesoft, etc., implementations.

Describe the ideal end user environment for the current version of your product (size of organization, level of project management sophistication, effort and commitment required).

Any organization operating in a competitive environment that manages multiple projects and resources to meet business goals and to increase profitability and productivity. For example, a geographically distributed matrix organization with medium to high volume of project-based activities being managed in a standard desktop scheduling software. The system delivers information to all levels of the organization, from employees to project management, functional management, enterprise management, and global management.

Future strategies for this product.

Project Control, the publisher of Project Control Software, was founded in 1989, developed the first Internet project management product in 1996, and is committed to its position as a technology leader in Internet project management software. Future plans include expanding functionality to better support the project office and to continually update Project Control software features, based on ongoing client input. Contact the publisher for more details on upcoming releases.

Product's target market.

Organizations using Project Control software represent companies in a wide variety of industries, including finance, services, pharmaceutical, federal government, defense, manufacturing, automotive, software publishing, etc. The disciplines typically involved in implementation include enterprise management, information technology, new product development, the project office, and engineering.

What are your product's three main benefits? (How does using the product add value to the customer?)

Client organizations can greatly improve productivity and lower costs when Project Control system is in place. It provides the ability to view all projects in a central repository, the ability to do efficient enterprise resource and cost planning, and to fully support the needs of the project office across all phases and areas of the project management process.

Describe your quality management process. List any relevant certifications.

Project Control, publishers of Project Control Software, follows standard and accepted practices for design, development, testing, and support for computer software. Project Control has set corporate objectives to achieve Level 2 and Level 3 CMM compliance, using the CMM from the SEI.

Discuss your product pricing structure. Include volume discount levels, concurrent user options, site licenses, cost of implementation, and other issues.

Project Control Software is priced by the module, with scalable client-seat pricing based on number of users. Price quotations are available, based on the current Project Control software product and pricing schedule.

Cost of implementation: Price quotations are available and include costs of product, implementation, training, tech support, annual maintenance, etc. Quotations are based on the current Project Control software product and pricing schedule, which is available to qualified organizations.

ProjectExchange Hyperlink (Information Management Services, Inc.)

Describe what the product is designed to do.

This product was designed to help individuals across the organization manage project, task, resource, and assignment scope-related documents. Multiple hyperlinks are viewed by stakeholders across the entire enterprise.

Top three product differentiators; describe what makes your product unique.

1. Easily integrated with any document management or Web publishing solution.
2. Content access security, based on project, task, resource, and assignment.
3. Three-tier client/server-based architecture provides a system scalable across the entire enterprise.

To what business processes can this tool be applied?

Our tools are utilized across multiple business processes.

Describe the ideal end user environment for the current version of your product (size of organization, level of project management sophistication, effort and commitment required).

Our primary market includes Global 5000 organizations with objectives to increase their returns on people, time, and financial investments. We initially assist event-driven divisions within these organizations, with the ultimate goal of benefiting every user in the organization.

Future strategies for this product.

Internet communication capabilities are limitless. We will continue to provide innovative solutions via the Internet to help organizations communicate among team members.

Product's target market.

Based on our experience, clients who benefit most from our products and services include: information systems, professional services, product development, engineering, and other event-driven organizations. Among these groups, each has further defined a set of unique objectives critical to increasing their competitiveness. IMS provides the ProjectExchange Enterprise Toolkit to achieve these objectives from the departmental level to the entire enterprise.

What are your product's three main benefits? (How does using the product add value to the customer?)

1. A Web-based thin client provides easy access across the enterprise and among external business partners.
2. Links relate people, projects, and time to directory files and/or Web URLs providing clear scope definition.
3. A Web-based client application provides a lower cost of ownership.

Describe your quality management process. List any relevant certifications.

We have continually improved our system development methodology since 1991. Over time, our SDLC has incorporated the best practices learned while deploying ProjectExchange in world-class organizations across the globe. Our Research & Development division utilizes ProjectExchange, and quality measures are persistent throughout our methods and processes.

Discuss your product pricing structure. Include volume discount levels, concurrent user options, site licenses, cost of implementation, and other issues.

Please consult IMS for current pricing.

Cost of implementation: Implementation costs vary and depend upon a particular organization's business requirements and level and availability of in-house expertise. We offer the following services to help achieve organizational objectives:

- Installation
- Process, methods, and integration consulting
- Project office support
- ProjectExchange add-on solution development
- Implementation management
- Microsoft Project and ProjectExchange two-day course
- ProjectExchange for Project Managers one-day course

- ProjectExchange for Team Members one-half day course
- MS Project Introduction one-day course
- MS Project Basic two-day course
- Project Planning & Management Fundamentals three-day course
- Executive briefing on project management.

Annual maintenance is offered at 15 percent of the license costs. Maintenance includes telephone support and product upgrades.

Project Integrator (PI) 2.0 Enterprise Edition

Describe what the product is designed to do.

SSL Project Integrator (PI) is a team-oriented project and process management tool that enables you to graphically define, track, report, and communicate projects, processes, tasks, and deliverables. Additionally, PI manages and maintains resources and clients, both locally and remotely.

Top three product differentiators; describe what makes your product unique.

All project processes (external, internal, and administrative) are managed via PI's graphic and interactive RoadMap. High-level steps graphically depict process flow. Each step can be drilled-down to display task lists, task details, resource delegation, deliverables, and quality checklists.

Teams can be defined at the project level, and are pulled from the database resource pool. Assigned tasks and open issues are sent to a team member's reminder window for immediate delegation and communication. Resources drag and drop tasks to a timecard for immediate project updating, and open issues remain on the reminder window until they are closed.

A wide range of reports is available. Each report can be filtered and pull data from the database for macroanalysis or microanalysis and reporting. Users can also define their own reports, and any level of information can be exported from the database.

To what business processes can this tool be applied?

Any external, internal, or administrative business process, regardless of simplicity or complexity.

Describe the ideal end user environment for the current version of your product (size of organization, level of project management sophistication, effort and commitment required).

Project-based organizations of any size (PI allows definition of teams, departments, and business units). Organizations do not need to be well versed in project management practices and techniques. Implementation and training is simple when compared to sophisticated project management tools. A commitment to distributed project/process management (DPM) is required (the delegation of tasks and deliverables to distributed teams and team members, and distribution of the project management process).

Future strategies for this product.

Tailor versions of PI to specific industries by leveraging SME from same.

Full integration to other cost accounting applications. (Currently, PI is integrated with SBT Executive Series, although data can be exported to virtually any application.)

Product's target market.

Project Integrator was created for project-oriented organizations (engineering, marketing, advertising, accounting, consulting, design firms, etc.) that have a need to enforce consistent quality in their project process and delivery and minimize nonproductive hours.

What are your product's three main benefits? (How does using the product add value to the customer?)

Distribution of the project process (tasks, issues, deliverables, etc.) to local and remote team members via LAN, DBMS, and Internet tools.

Immediate feedback of status of all projects and tasks, allowing macro and micro views of the entire organization's performance at any given time.

All aspects of a business (external, internal, and administrative activity, including deliverables) are managed in a central DBMS and repository. Communications, projects, tasks, deliverables, issues, costs, clients; resources, etc. are all managed via one tool in one database.

Describe your quality management process. List any relevant certifications.

Our documented quality assurance (QA) process includes the use of test script software. We are currently implementing ISO 9001 and expect registry by early 1999.

Discuss your product pricing structure. Include volume discount levels, concurrent user options, site licenses, cost of implementation, and other issues.

PI's price is based on the number of users, and volume discounts are available.

Cost of implementation: Implementation lead time and required training is minimal when compared to high-end, sophisticated project management tools and suites.

Project KickStart

Describe what the product is designed to do.

Project KickStart is an easy-to-use project planning software for managers, executives, consultants, and incidental project planners. The software leads users through an eight-step process to create a work breakdown structure for projects. Project KickStart then allows the user to flesh out the task list by considering the goals and objectives of the project, identifying people involved in the effort and anticipating obstacles or risks to be encountered in performing the work. Team members can be assigned to each of the tasks. Project KickStart then produces a project summary, which is an overview of who is doing what. Reports can be generated for each of the individual project team members. Through the easy-to-use menu-based system, the project can be exported to project management software. Project KickStart includes a Gantt chart for quick scheduling and built-in *hot links* to Microsoft Project, SureTrak, Super Project, Project Scheduler 7, Time Line, Milestones Etc., Word and Excel.

Top three product differentiates; describe what makes your product unique.

1. Can be used by virtually all corporate departments for project planning. No training necessary.
2. Provides a framework for brainstorming, planning, and scheduling projects.
3. Links with project management software such as Microsoft Project, SureTrak, Project Scheduler, adding value to each program as a front-end planning wizard.

To what business processes can this tool be applied?

Large sales are often treated as projects. Project KickStart enables sales people to begin fleshing out the details of the customer requirements and the deliverables right away.

It can be used in conjunction with a training session, where users can have a successful experience planning their actual projects.

Consultants can use Project KickStart with clients to guide them through the process of planning a project.

It can be used *on the fly* for fast plans, e.g., recovering from a toxic spill.

Describe the ideal end user environment for the current version of your product (size of organization, level of project management sophistication, effort and commitment required).

Project KickStart works great with any size organization. It has been successfully deployed at Sodexo Marriott Services, Eli Lilly, and Longs Drugs, as well as for many consultants, schools, and nonprofits.

Project KickStart lets nonproject managers follow a sound planning methodology without even knowing it.

Its ease of use makes it ideal to get people to follow a project planning methodology.

Future strategies for this product.

Project KickStart is available as a stand-alone program and as a wizard in Primavera SureTrak 2. We view Project KickStart as a universal planner and look forward to it being incorporated into other programs.

We see the benefit of Web enabling Project KickStart and are looking into developing it.

Product's target market.

Users of project management software, e.g., Microsoft Project, organizations that have small to mid-sized projects and would benefit from an easy to use project planner, and SOHO and small office users.

What are your product's three main benefits? (How does using the product add value to the customer?)

1. Fast and easy project planning.
2. Improved involvement of project team.
3. Improved coordination of project approaches within an organization.

Describe your quality management process. List any relevant certifications.

In addition to internal testing, we have worked with professional testers to identify and eliminate bugs.

Our many users have also identified areas for improvement, which we are addressing.

Discuss your product pricing structure. Include volume discount levels, concurrent user options, site licenses, cost of implementation, and other issues.

First copy: $99.95; $59.95 per copy for additional copies.

Site license of 100–300 users: $6,000.

Cost of implementation: For site licenses, six-month maintenance fee is 15 percent of site license fee.

ProjectSite for the Web

Describe what the product is designed to do.

ProjectSite allows you to build a secure project website where users can log in to view and update Microsoft Project information using any Java-capable Web browser. From graphical, high-level management reports to weekly to-do lists, ProjectSite allows you to easily create any view you can imagine. A 100 percent pure Java calendar allows end users to update task progress by drag-and-drop methods.

Top three product differentiators; describe what makes your product unique.

1. Complete Web-based access to Microsoft Project schedules.
2. Open architecture allows for complete customization.
3. User- and role-based security keeps project data safe.

To what business processes can this tool be applied?

Dissemination and updating of project information, as well as team communication.

Describe the ideal end user environment for the current version of your product (size of organization, level of project management sophistication, effort and commitment required).

Companies or departments using Microsoft Project where five or more people (who are not project managers) have an interest in viewing and updating project information using a Web browser.

Future strategies for this product.

Database support with qualified updating.

Product's target market.

Users of Microsoft Project in groups of five or more, covering all industry segments.

What are your product's three main benefits? (How does using the product add value to the customer?)

1. Improves schedule quality and timeliness through improved team awareness.
2. Reduces need for project meetings.
3. No client setup required (Web-based).

Describe your quality management process. List any relevant certifications.

Internally documented.

Discuss your product pricing structure. Include volume discount levels, concurrent user options, site licenses, cost of implementation, and other issues.

Server: $1,495. Client license: $50 each.
Cost of implementation: Free E-mail and Web support.

Schedule Insight

Describe what the product is designed to do.

Schedule Insight is a read-only browser of Microsoft Project schedules and is designed for executives, managers, and staff that need quick, no-nonsense access to Microsoft Project schedule information. It automatically rolls up multiple projects by company, project, department, resource, and task. A built-in report writer allows users to create their own reports.

Top three product differentiators; describe what makes your product unique.

1. Read-only browser of Microsoft Project schedules
2. Familiar spreadsheet and folder architecture for ease of use.
3. All views and reports can be customized by the end user.

To what business processes can this tool be applied?

Dissemination of project information.

Describe the ideal end-user environment for the current version of your product (size of organization, level of project management sophistication, effort and commitment required).

Companies or departments using Microsoft Project where five or more people (who are not project managers) have an interest in viewing and printing project information for their own needs.

Future strategies for this product.

Database support with qualified updating.

Product's target market.

Users of Microsoft Project in groups of five or more covering all industry segments.

What are your product's three main benefits? (How does using the product add value to the customer?)

1. Improves schedule quality and timeliness through improved team awareness.
2. Reduces need for project meetings.
3. Empowers individuals to obtain their own project information.

Describe your quality management process. List any relevant certifications.

Internally documented.

Discuss your product pricing structure. Include volume discount levels, concurrent user options, site licenses, cost of implementation, and other issues.

Single user—$99. Network license—$995 (unlimited users).

The point-and-click interface with read-only capabilities allows users to quickly and safely learns on their own while project data always remains safe. In addition, the online tutorial and free E-mail support greatly minimize implementation costs.

WebProject

Describe what the product is designed to do.

WebProject is designed for geographically dispersed project teams. WebProject is a Java-based project management tool with powerful collaboration and communications features. WebProject incorporates unique knowledge management/best practices capability.

Top three product differentiators; describe what makes your product unique.

WebProject is the first (only) pure Java project management suite that can utilize an open architecture database backend. WebProject allows corporations to utilize Oracle, SQL Server, Informix, Sybase, or other databases in their enterprise project management.

WebProject has introduced the first knowledge management/best practices capability within a project management software suite.

WebProject enables global project communication including project issues boards, threaded task discussions, virtual project status meetings, and remote project statusing and updates.

To what business processes can this tool be applied?

Geographically dispersed project teams, projects that need to have access from remote locations, or integrating WebProject's proprietary information exchange with MS Project, Primavera, or other desktop systems.

WebProject allows the extraction of knowledge from the enterprise, such as resource capabilities or company *best practices*.

Describe the ideal end-user environment for the current version of your product (size of organization, level of project management sophistication, effort and commitment required).

WebProject is an easy-to-use Java project management tool that will enable teams to communicate and collaborate from remote locations. WebProject is designed for the enterprise and will work well with project teams as well.

Future strategies for this product.

WebProject has established many *firsts* in the project management industry. We will continue to move the industry forward with our new technologies on the Web and with Java.

Product's target market.

Geographically dispersed project teams, enterprise project management systems, integration with Primavera, MS Project, and other project management systems.

What are your product's three main benefits? (How does using the product add value to the customer?)

1. Enterprise project communication.
2. Project collaboration.
3. Geographically dispersed updates and communication.

Describe your quality management process. List any relevant certifications.

WebProject adheres to strict standards and processes for quality, both in development and customer service.

Discuss your product pricing structure. Include volume discount levels, concurrent user options, site licenses, cost of implementation, and other issues.

WebProject is priced at $790 for starter package including the WebProject server. WebProject does provide enterprise and site licensing.

Graphics Add-Ons

	AMS REALTIME Vision	Artemis GlobalView & ProjectView	Dekker TRAKKER Activity Based Cost Management and Performance System	Enterprise Project	ER Project 1000	FastTrack Schedule 5.02	GRANEDA BarKeeper	GRANEDA Personal	GRANEDA Project Showcase
Custom graphics									
Gantt charts	Y	Y	Y	Y	Y	Y	Y	Y	Y
Network logic diagrams	Y	N	Y	Y	Y	N	N	Y	Y
WBS	Y	Y	Y	Y	Y	N	N	Y	Y
Other structure drawings	N	N	Y	Y	Y	N	N	Y	Y
Gantt charts									
Text wrapping	Y	Y	Y	Y	N	Y	Y	Y	Y
Multiple rows of text per activity	Y	Y	Y	Y	Y	Y	Y	Y	Y
Zones (horizontal bands labeled based on a field value)	Y	N	Y	Y	Y	Y	N	Y	Y
Multiple milestones	Y	Y	Y	Y	Y	Y	Y	Y	Y
Highlight critical path in charts	Y	N	Y	Y	Y	N	Y	Y	Y
Variable timescale Gantt charts	Y	Y	Y	N	Y	N	Y	Y	Y
Variable timescale (timephased network logic)	Y	Y	Y	N	Y	N	Y	Y	Y
Network logic drawings									
Zones (horizontal bands labeled based on a field value)	N	N	Y	Y	Y	N	N	Y	Y
User-defined node positioning	Y	N	Y	Y	Y	N	N	N	N
Multiple milestones	Y	N	Y	Y	Y	N	N	Y	Y
Variable timescale	Y	N	Y	N	Y	N	N	Y	Y
Breakdown structures									
User-defined box styles	Y	Y	Y	N	Y	N	N	Y	Y
User-defined positioning	Y	Y	Y	N	N	N	N	N	N
Mixes connecting line styles (dotted, solid, etc)	N	N	Y	N	N	N	N	N	N
Collapse/expand to any level	Y	Y	Y	N	Y	N	N	Y	Y
Number of levels supported:	7	Unlim.	Unlim.		25	N	N	39	39
Management graphics									
Pie charts	N	Y	Y	Y	N	N	N	Y	Y
Trend charts	Y	Y	Y	Y	Y	N	N	Y	Y
Bar charts	Y	Y	Y	Y	Y	N	N	Y	Y
Scatter diagrams	N	Y	Y	Y	N	N	N	Y	Y
Histograms									
Horizontal bars	N	Y	Y	Y	Y	N	N	Y	Y
Vertical bars	Y	Y	Y	N	Y	N	N	Y	Y
3D effects	Y	Y	Y	Y	Y	N	N	N	N
Mountain charts	N	N	Y	Y	N	N	N	Y	Y

Supported data sources (list):	AMS REALTIME	SQL databases	TRAKKER	ODBC	ER Project 1000	ASCII	MPX, CSV	Most project management systems and almost all databases	Most project management systems and almost all databases
Reporting									
Report writer	Y	Y	Y	Y	Y	Y	Y	N	N
Report wizard	N	N	Y	Y	Y	Y	N	N	N
Publishes as HTML	Y	Y	Y	Y	Y	Y	Y	N	N
Number of user-defined fields	100	Unlim.	Unlim.	0	100	65,000	Unlim.	Y	Y
Drill-down/roll-up *	Y	Y	Y	Y	Y	Y	N	Y	Y
Import/export	Y	Y	Y	Y	Y	Y	Y	Y	Y
Automatic E-mail notification	N	N	Y	N	Y	Y	N	N	N
Macro recorder/batch capable	Y	Y	Y	Y	N	N	N	Y	Y
Can "canned" reports be modified?	Y	Y	Y	Y	Y	Y	Y	Y	Y
Sort, filter	Y	Y	Y	Y	Y	Y	Y	Y	Y
Architecture									
Databases supported	Oracle, any ODBC-compliant DB	Oracle	Oracle, MS SQL Server, Informix, MS Access, FoxPro	Oracle, Sybase, Informix, MS SQL Server, MS Access	Oracle, MS SQL Server, Interbase				
Supports distributed databases	Y	N	Y	Y	Y	N	N	N	N
Three-tier client/server	Y	Y	Y	Y	Y	N	Y	Y	Y
Client operating systems	Win 95/NT/3.x, Solaris, HP, RS, Mac	Win NT, HP-UX, Solaris	Win 95/98/NT	Win 95/98/NT	Win 95/98/NT 3.51/NT 4.0 (ER Project Satellite also Java and Win 3.x)	Win 95/98/NT 4.0/NT 5.0/3.x, Mac	Win	Win NT, Unix	Win NT, Unix

Graphics Add-Ons

	AMS REALTIME Vision	Artemis GlobalView & ProjectView	Dekker TRAKKER Activity Based Cost Management and Performance System	Enterprise Project	ER Project 1000	FastTrack Schedule 5.02	GRANEDA BarKeeper	GRANEDA Personal	GRANEDA Project Showcase
Server operating systems	Win 95/NT/3.x, Solaris, HP, RS, Mac	N/A	Win NT, Novell, Unix	Unix, Win NT	Win NT, Unix		Win	Most	Most
Network operating systems	TCP/IP, Banyan, Novell, IPX	IPX, Novell, Win NT	Win NT, Novell, Unix	Novell, Win NT, others	Win, NetBEU/NetBios, TCP/IP, Novell	Win NT, Novell, Banyan, AppleTalk	Win		
Minimum client configuration	8 MB RAM, 20 MB disk, 486 or better	Win 95	16 MB RAM, 1 GB HD, SVGA	486, 16 MB memory	Pentium, 16 MB memory (ER Project Satellite 8 MB)	Win: 386DX or higher, Win 3.1x or higher, 4 MB RAM, 10 MB HD. Mac: Mac Plus or higher, System 7.0 or higher, 4 MB RAM, 10 MB HD	PC w/Pentium 100+, 32 MB RAM, VGA	486,16 MB RAM,10 MB disk, Win 95/98/NT/3.x	486,16 MB RAM,10 MB disk, Win 95/98/NT/3.x
Minimum server configuration	32 MB RAM, 100 MB Disk, Pentium or better	N/A	128 MB RAM, 10 GB HD	Pentium 200 CPU, 128 MB, 1 GB	Pentium, 32 MB memory		PC w/Pentium 100+, 32 MB RAM, VGA		
Client runs under Web browser	Y	Y		Y	Y	Y	N	Y	Y
Open architecture									
Supports OLE	Y	Y	Y	Y	N	Y	Y	N	N
Documented Object Model	N	N/A	Y	Y	Y	N	N	N	N
Documented Application Programming Interface (API)	Y	Y	Y	Y	N	N	N	Y	Y
Simultaneous edit of data file	Y	N	Y	Y	Y	N	N	N	N
Does product have a programming language?	Y	Y	Y	Y	N	N	N	N	N
Are years stored as four-digit numbers?	N	Y	Y	Y	Y	Y	Y	Y	Y
Online help									
Right mouse click	N	Y	Y	N	Y	Y	Y	Y	Y
Hover buttons	Y	Y	Y	N	Y	Y	Y	Y	Y
Interactive help	Y	Y	Y	Y	Y	Y	Y	Y	Y

Help search feature	Y	Y	Y	Y	Y	Y	Y
Web access to product knowledge base *	Y	N	Y	Y	Y	N	N
Vendor information							
Training							
Computer-based training	Y	Y	Y	N	N	N	N
Training materials available	Y	Y	Y	Y	Y	Y	Y
Customized training materials	Y	Y	Y	Y	Y	Y	Y
Online tutorial	Y	Y	N	Y	Y	N	N
Consulting available from vendor	Y	Y	Y	Y	Y	Y	Y
Site license discounts	Y	Y	Y	Y	Y	Y	Y
Enhancement requests *	Y	Y	Y	Y	Y	Y	Y
Modify source code, support through upgrades *	Y	Y	Y	Y	N	Y	N
Global presence							
Global offices	Y	Y	N	Y	N	Y	Y
Multi-lingual technical support	Y	Y	Y	Y	N	Y	Y
Language versions (list):	Chin, Dutch, Eng, Fr, Ger, Jpn, Kor, Pol, Rus	Eng	Eng, Span	Eng	Eng, Ger, Swed	Eng, Ger, Fr	Ger, Eng, Fr
Audit Software Quality Assurance process? *	Y	Y	Y	Y	Y	N	Y
Security							
Configurable access priviledges *	Y	Y	Y	Y	Y	Y	N
Passwords expire (forced update)	N	Y	Y	N	N	N	N
Electronic approvals	Y	Y	Y	Y	N	Y	N
Password protect files	Y	Y	Y	Y	Y	N	N

Graphics Add-Ons

	Graphics Server	Mesa/Vista	Milestones, Etc.	Open Plan	OPX2 Pro (Schedule Management)	PERT Chart EXPERT	PlanView Software	Primavera Project Planner (P3) 2.0	ProChain	Project Control 6.0 - Report Manager Module
Custom graphics										
Gantt charts	Y	Y	Y	Y	Y	N	Y	Y	Y	Y
Network logic diagrams	Y	N	N	Y	Y	Y	N	Y	N	Y
WBS	N	N	N	Y	Y	N	Y	N	N	Y
Other structure drawings	N	Y	N	Y	Y	Y	N	N	N	Y
Gantt charts										
Text wrapping	Y	N	Y	Y	Y		Y	Y	N	Y
Multiple rows of text per activity	Y	Y	Y	Y	Y		Y	Y	Y	N
Zones (horizontal bands labeled based on a field value)	Y	Y	Y	Y	Y		Y	Y	N	Y
Multiple milestones	Y	Y	Y	Y	Y		Y	Y	Y	Y
Highlight critical path in charts	Y	Y	N	Y	Y		Y	Y	Y	Y
Variable timescale Gantt charts	Y	Y	Y	Y	Y		N	Y	Y	Y
Variable timescale (timephased network logic)	Y	N	N	Y	Y		N	Y	N	Y
Network logic drawings										
Zones (horizontal bands labeled based on a field value)	Y	N	N	Y	Y	Y	N	Y	N	N
User-defined node positioning	Y	N	N	Y	Y	Y	N	Y	N	N
Multiple milestones	Y	N	N	Y	Y	Y	N	Y	N	N
Variable timescale	Y	N	N	Y	N	Y	N	N	N	N
Breakdown structures										
User-defined box styles	N	N	N	Y	Y		N	N	N	N
User-defined positioning	N	N	N	Y	Y		N	Y	N	N
Mixes connecting line styles (dotted, solid, etc)	N	N	N	N	Y		N	Y	N	N
Collapse/expand to any level	N	N	N	Y	Y		Y	Y	N	N
Number of levels supported:	N	N	N	30	Unlim.		Unlim.	20	N	0
Management graphics										
Pie charts	N	Y	N	N	Y		Y	N	N	Y
Trend charts	Y	Y	N	N	Y		Y	Y	Y	Y
Bar charts	Y	Y	Y	Y	Y		Y	Y	Y	Y
Scatter diagrams	N	N	N	N			Y	N	N	Y
Histograms										
Horizontal bars	N	Y	N	N	N		Y	N	N	Y
Vertical bars	Y	Y	Y	Y	Y		Y	Y	Y	Y
3D effects	N	N	N	Y	N		N	N	N	N
Mountain charts	N	N	N	N	Y		Y	Y	N	Y

Supported data sources (list):	All Enterprise Controller Modules	Any MPX, MS Project 98		Oracle, MS SQL Server, Sybase, MS Access, FoxPro	OPX2 Pro, MS Project, Scitor Project Scheduler, SAP R/3, Oracle Projects, user-defined (CSV,SQL)	MPP, MPX, MPD, MDB, TXT, CSV, DBF	Planner, Excel, Milestones Etc, MS Project +	P3		Most desktop PM software such as MS project, P3, and others
Reporting										
Report writer	Y	Y	Y	Y	Y	N	Y	Y	Y	Y
Report wizard	N	N	Y	N	N	N	Y	Y	N	N
Publishes as HTML	Y	Y	Y	Y	Y	Y	Y	Y	Y	Y
Number of user-defined fields	Multiple	25	200	Unlim.	Unlim.	50	Unlim.	20	250	60
Drill-down/roll-up *	Y	Y	Y	Y	Y	Y	Y	Y	N	Y
Import/export	Y	Y	Y	Y	Y	Y	Y	Y	Y	Y
Automatic E-mail notification	N	Y	Y	N	Y	N	Y	N	N	N
Macro recorder/batch capable	N	N	Y	Y	Y	N	N	Y	Y	Y
Can "canned" reports be modified?	Y	Y	Y	Y	Y	Y	Y	Y	Y	Y
Sort, filter	Y	Y	Y	Y	Y	Y	Y	Y	Y	Y
Architecture										
Databases supported	Oracle	MS SQL Server	Any	Oracle, MS SQL Server, Sybase, MS Access, FoxPro	Oracle, MS SQL Server, Informix, Sybase, Ingres	Y	Oracle, Sybase, SQL Server, etc.	Btrieve	MS Access	Oracle, MS Access, MS SQL Server, Sybase
Supports distributed databases	Y	N	N	N	Y	Y	N	N	N	Y
Three-tier client/server	Y	N	N	N	Y	Y	Y	N	N	Y
Client operating systems	Win 95/NT/3.x	Y	Win	Win 95 or later	Win 95/98/NT/3.x, Mac, Unix	Y	Win 95/98/NT	Win 95/NT/3.x	Win 95/NT	Win 95/98/NT

Graphics Add-Ons

	Graphics Server	Mesa/Vista	Milestones, Etc.	Open Plan	OPX2 Pro (Schedule Management)	PERT Chart EXPERT	PlanView Software	Primavera Project Planner (P3) 2.0	ProChain	Project Control 6.0 - Report Manager Module
Server operating systems	Unix, Win NT	Y	Win	Specified by database vendor	Win NT, Unix	All	NT, UNIX, Novell, IIS, Netscape	Most popular operating systems (e.g., Novell)		Unix, Win NT, HP, Sybase, others
Network operating systems	Novell, Win NT	Y	Any	Win 95 or later	TCP/IP (Ethernet, Token Ring, WAN)	All	NT, UNIX, Novell, IIS, Netscape	Most popular operating systems (e.g., Novell)		Novell, IPX, XPX, Banyan, MS Network, TCP/IP
Minimum client configuration	16 MB RAM		N	Pentium or compatible, Win 95 or later; 16 MB RAM	486+ 16 MB RAM (light client), P100+ 32 MB RAM (fat client)	1	486/66, 8 MB RAM, Win3.x	486, 32 MB RAM	Same as MS Project	PC 486/66 processor or above. Win 95 or Win NT V4. 16 MB RAM
Minimum server configuration	64 MB RAM		N	Server optional	P2xx+ 128 MB RAM	1	486/66, 32 MB RAM, Novell	Not specified		Any server supporting Oracle 7 or above
Client runs under Web browser	N	Y	N	N	N	Y	Y	N	N	Y
Open architecture										
Supports OLE	Y	N	Y	Y	Y	Y	Y	Y	Y	Y
Documented Object Model	Y	Y	Y	Y	Y	Y	Y	Y	Y	N
Documented Application Programming Interface (API)	Y	Y	Y	N	N	Y	Y	Y	Y	N
Simultaneous edit of data file	Y	Y	Y	Y	Y	N	N	Y	N	Y
Does product have a programming language?	Y	N	Y	N	Y	N	Y	N	Y	N
Are years stored as four-digit numbers?	Y	Y	Y	Y	Y	Y	Y	N	N	Y
Online help										
Right mouse click	Y	N	Y	Y	Y	Y	Y	Y	Y	N
Hover buttons	Y	N	Y	Y	Y	Y	Y	Y	Y	Y
Interactive help	N	Y	Y	Y	Y	Y	Y	Y	Y	N

	1	2	3	4	5	6	7	8
Help search feature	Y	Y	Y	Y	Y	Y	Y	Y
Web access to product knowledge base *	Y	N	Y	Y	Y	N	N	Y

Vendor information

Training

	1	2	3	4	5	6	7	8
Computer-based training	N	N	Y	N	Y	Y	N	Y
Training materials available	Y	Y	Y	Y	Y	Y	Y	Y
Customized training materials	Y	Y	Y	Y	Y	Y	Y	Y
Online tutorial	N	Y	Y	N	N	Y	Y	Y
Consulting available from vendor	Y	Y	Y	Y	Y	Y	Y	Y
Site license discounts	Y	Y	Y	Y	Y	Y	Y	Y
Enhancement requests *	Y	N	Y	Y	Y	Y	Y	Y
Modify source code, support through upgrades *	Y	Y	Y	Y	Y	Y	N	Y

Global presence

	1	2	3	4	5	6	7	8
Global offices	Y	N	Y	Y	Y	Y	Y	Y
Multi-lingual technical support	N	N	Y	N	Y	Y	Y	N
Language versions (list):	Eng	Eng	Eng, Ital, Fr, Ger, Mand, Hangul, Rus	Eng, Fr	Eng	Eng, Fr, Ger	Ger	English

	1	2	3	4	5	6	7	8
Audit Software Quality Assurance process? *	Y	N	N	Y	Y	Y	N	Y

Security

	1	2	3	4	5	6	7	8
Configurable access priviledges *	Y	Y	Y	Y	N	Y	Y	Y
Passwords expire (forced update)	Y	N	N	N	N	Y	N	N
Electronic approvals	Y	Y	N	Y	N	Y	N	Y
Password protect files	Y	N	Y	Y	N	Y	N	Y

Graphics Add-Ons

	Project-r	Project Scheduler 7.6	ProjectSite for the Web	QEI Exec	SAS Software	Schedule Insight	VARCHART	WBS Chart for Project	WebProject	X-Gantt
Custom graphics										
Gantt charts	Y	Y	N	Y	Y	Y	Y	N	Y	Y
Network logic diagrams	N	Y	N	Y	Y	N	Y	N	N	N
WBS	N	Y	N	Y	Y	N	Y	Y	Y	N
Other structure drawings	N	Y	Y	Y	Y	N	Y	Y	Y	N
Gantt charts										
Text wrapping	Y	Y	N	Y	N	Y	Y		Y	Y
Multiple rows of text per activity	Y	Y	N	Y	Y	Y	Y		Y	Y
Zones (horizontal bands labeled based on a field value)	Y	Y	N	Y	Y	Y	Y		N	Y
Multiple milestones	Y	Y	N	Y	Y	Y	Y		Y	Y
Highlight critical path in charts	Y	Y	N	Y	Y	Y	Y		Y	Y
Variable timescale Gantt charts	Y	Y	N	Y	Y	Y	Y		Y	Y
Variable timescale (timephased network logic)	Y	N	N	Y	Y	N	Y		N	Y
Network logic drawings										
Zones (horizontal bands labeled based on a field value)		N	N	Y	Y	N	Y		N	N
User-defined node positioning		Y	N	Y	Y	N	Y		N	N
Multiple milestones		Y	N	Y	Y	N	Y		N	N
Variable timescale		N	N	Y	Y	N	Y		N	N
Breakdown structures										
User-defined box styles		Y	N	Y	Y	N	Y	Y	N	N
User-defined positioning		Y	N	Y	Y	N	Y	Y	N	N
Mixes connecting line styles (dotted, solid, etc)		N	N	Y	N	N	Y	Y	N	N
Collapse/expand to any level		Y	N	Y	N	N	Y	Y	N	N
Number of levels supported:		10	N	Unlim.	Unlim.	N	Unlim.	1,000,000		
Management graphics										
Pie charts	Y	N	Y	N	Y	N	N		N	N
Trend charts	Y	N	Y	N	Y	N	N		N	N
Bar charts	Y	Y	Y	N	Y	N	Y		N	Y
Scatter diagrams	Y	N	Y	N	Y	N	N		N	N
Histograms										
Horizontal bars	Y	N	Y	N	Y	N	Y		Y	N
Vertical bars	Y	Y	Y	Y	Y	N	Y		Y	N
3D effects	Y	N	Y	Y	Y	N	Y		N	N
Mountain charts	Y	N	Y	Y	Y	N	Y		Y	N

Supported data sources (list):	.MPX Files	PS7	MS Project	From within product, or can import data from other systems via fixed-length ASCII, delimited ASCII, dBASE, MPX files. Also can use DDE	Most major formats	MS Project	Any	MPP, MPX, MPD, MDB, TXT, CSV, DBF	MPX, Primavera, other ERP and project management vendors	Any
Reporting										
Report writer	Y	Y	Y	N	Y	Y	N	N	N	N
Report wizard	Y	Y	N	N	N	N	N	N	Y	N
Publishes as HTML	N	Y	Y	N	Y	N	N	Y	Y	N
Number of user-defined fields	20	Unlim.	80	Unlim.	Unlim.	40	Unlim.	50	Varies	Unlim.
Drill-down/roll-up *	Y	Y	Y	Y	N	Y	Y	Y	Y	Y
Import/export	Y	Y	Y	Y	Y	Y	Y	Y	Y	Y
Automatic E-mail notification	N	N	N	N	N	N	Y	N	Y	Y
Macro recorder/batch capable	N	Y	N	Y/N	Y	N	Y	N	Y	Y
Can "canned" reports be modified?	Y	Y	Y	Y	Y	Y	Y	Y	Y	Y
Sort, filter	Y	Y	Y	Y	Y	Y	Y	Y	Y	Y
Architecture										
Databases supported		Via ODBC: Oracle, Sybase, MS SQL Server, MS Access, et al.	MS SQL Server, MS Access, Oracle, ODBC	N/A	Most major databases		Any	Y		Any
Supports distributed databases	Y	Y	N	N	Y	Y	Y	Y	Y	Y
Three-tier client/server	Y	N	Y	N	Y	Y	Y	Y	Y	Y
Client operating systems	Win 95/98/NT	Win 95/98/NT4	Any Web browser	Win 95/NT/3.x with Win 32s, Solaris	MVS, CMS, VSE; OpenVMS for VAX and AXP; Solaris, HP-UX, AIX, Digital Unix, MIPS ABI, Intel ABI; Win 95/NT, Mac, OS/2	Win 3.x and higher	Win, Unix, Mac	All	Any Java-enabled OS	Win

Graphics Add-Ons

	Project-r	Project Scheduler 7.6	ProjectSite for the Web	QEI Exec	SAS Software	Schedule Insight	VARCHART	WBS Chart for Project	WebProject	X-Gantt
Server operating systems	Win 95/98/NT	N/A	Win NT 4.0 or higher	N/A	MVS, CMS, VSE; OpenVMS for VAX and AXP; Solaris, HP-UX, AIX, Digital Unix, MIPS ABI, Intel ABI; Win 95/NT, Mac, OS/2	Win NT 3.5 and higher	Win, Unix, Mac	All	Any Java-enabled OS	Win
Network operating systems	8 MB	Novell, Win NT	Web/http	LAN Manager, TCP/IP, Novell	Supports all major network environments, including LAN Server, TCP/IP, Warp Server, Novell	Any	Pentium 166+, 32 MB RAM, VGA	1	Any Java-enabled OS	Win
Minimum client configuration	8 MB	486 or better, 16 MB memory, 15 MB HD	Any web browser	486, 16 MB RAM, mouse, XGA graphics	Varies by platform	12 MB memory, 12 MB disk	Pentium 166+, 32 MB RAM, VGA	1	Web-enabled browser	Pentium 166+, 32 MB RAM, VGA
Minimum server configuration	8 MB		64 MB memory, 200 MB disk	N/A	Varies by platform	16 MB memory, 20 MB disk	N	All	Any Java-enabled OS	
Client runs under Web browser		N	Y	N	Y	N	Y		Y	Y
Open architecture										
Supports OLE	N	Y	Y	N	N	N	Y	Y	N	N
Documented Object Model	N	Y	Y	Y	N	N	Y	Y	N	N
Documented Application Programming Interface (API)	N	Y	Y	Y	N	N	Y	Y	N	N
Simultaneous edit of data file	N	Y	Y	N	Y	N	Y	N	Y	Y
Does product have a programming language?	N	N	Y	Y	Y	N	Y	N	N	N
Are years stored as four-digit numbers?	Y	Y	Y	Y	Y	N	Y	Y	Y	Y
Online help										
Right mouse click	Y	Y	Y	N	Y	Y	N	Y	N	Y
Hover buttons	Y	N	Y	Y	Y	Y	N	Y	Y	Y
Interactive help	Y	Y	Y	Y	Y	Y	Y	Y	Y	N

Help search feature	Y	Y	Y	Y	Y	Y	Y	Y
Web access to product knowledge base *	N	N	N	N	Y	Y	Y	Y
Vendor information								
Training								
Computer-based training	Y	N	N	N	N	Y	Y	N
Training materials available	Y	N	Y	N	Y	Y	Y	Y
Customized training materials	Y	N	Y	N	Y	Y	Y	Y
Online tutorial	Y	Y	N	Y	Y	Y	Y	N
Consulting available from vendor	Y	Y	Y	Y	Y	Y	Y	Y
Site license discounts	Y	Y	Y	Y	Y	Y	Y	Y
Enhancement requests *	Y	Y	Y	Y	Y	Y	Y	Y
Modify source code, support through upgrades *	Y	Y	N	Y	Y	Y	Y	Y
Global presence								
Global offices	N	N	Y	N	Y	Y	Y	Y
Multi-lingual technical support	N	N	Y	N	Y	N	Y	Y
Language versions (list):	Eng, Fr, Ger, Jpn	Eng	Jpn	Eng	Eng, Ger, Fr	Eng	Eng, Ger	Eng, Ger, Fr
Audit Software Quality Assurance process? *	Y	N	Y	Y	Y	Y	Y	Y
Security								
Configurable access priviledges *	N	Y	Y	N	Y	N	Y	Y
Passwords expire (forced update)	N	Y	N	N	Y	N	Y	Y
Electronic approvals	N	N	N	N	Y	N	Y	Y
Password protect files	N	Y	Y	N	Y	N	Y	N

349

VENDOR RESPONSES TO NARRATIVE QUESTIONS

Graphics Add-Ons

AMS REALTIME Vision

Describe what the product is designed to do.

Vision lets you communicate your project plan with dazzling graphic or tabular reports. Use or modify any of our standard reports, or design your own, using our cross-platform built-in drawing tools. Add custom graphics and logos, annotations, different first and last pages.

Print paper reports or graphic PDF output for Internet publishing. Tabular reports can be printed to HTML, clipboard, Windows metafile, or pict files.

Thumbnail drill-downs can be customized to include standard company reports.

Top three product differentiators; describe what makes your product unique.

Cross-platform drawing tools make this the only multiplatform tool that works across Unix, Windows, and Macintosh platforms.

Reports (and all project files) are directly binary compatible across all platforms. No conversion is required.

To what business processes can this tool be applied?

Any project, resource, or cost reporting at any level will benefit from this outstanding reporting tool.

Describe the ideal end user environment for the current version of your product (size of organization, level of project management sophistication, effort and commitment required).

AMS REALTIME is used by global companies in very large enterprise environments, all the way down to small companies with just a few people.

While AMS REALTIME is used to support extremely sophisticated project management processes, it can still be used to benefit users with little or no project management background. Users can grow into the software as their project management expertise evolves.

To make any project management implementation successful, senior management must be committed to supporting the process, and other participants must make the effort to be trained to use the tools and follow through. Working with a consultant to help adapt the software to your business practices and needs and to document these processes is the best way to ensure success.

Future strategies for this product.

Future development strategies include more active Web enablements, a more complex three-tiered server design to facilitate global replication, and more resource tools. AMS has always been on the cutting edge of technology, and we are dedicated to bringing our customers the best of this ever-changing world.

Product's target market.

Products are used across a wide variety of client bases. AMS does not target any particular market, but is widely used in manufacturing, oil and gas, nuclear power, automotive, pharmaceutical, aerospace, software development, construction, research and development, and many other industries.

AMS REALTIME software allows for a flexible implementation that integrates with customer business processes.

What are your product's three main benefits? (How does using the product add value to the customer?)

AMS REALTIME Vision gives program managers, project managers, and resource managers a clearly visible picture of the status of their project and other information. Each piece is a part of the solution that supports the whole enterprisewide management process.

AMS REALTIME gives program managers, project managers, rescue managers, and employees the tools to work within their functional areas. Each piece is a part of the solution that supports the whole enterprisewide management process.

Describe your quality management process. List any relevant certifications.

Advanced Management Solutions is fully committed to providing the highest quality software and services to all our clients. We have implemented many internal standards and processes in order to ensure that we can track and manage our software development process to the highest standard of quality possible.

Concurrent versions system has been implemented to help manage multiple programmers at multiple development sites. Peer review of source code and design strategy meetings with high-level program development leaders continue to ensure that our software remains on the leading edge of our evolving technology.

A dedicated testing department manages the initial alpha testing, which encompasses new functionality, system-process testing, and full regression testing. Beta testing is initially performed internally. After a stable point has been reached, beta testing is extended to select client users. Client beta testing not only provides clients with an edge in using new software features, but also greatly expands the test environment scope relating to different hardware environments. As AMS REALTIME is one of the most flexible and highly configurable management products on the market today, client testing adds an exceptional dimension to our testing process.

Discuss your product pricing structure. Include volume discount levels, concurrent user options, site licenses, cost of implementation, and other issues.

Product price is different for clients, based on their requirements for software and implementation. Volume discounts and site licenses are available. Please request a quote from an AMS sales representative for your specific requirements.

Cost of implementation: Annual maintenance is based on 20 percent of the current product cost, and includes all software upgrades (while support is active) and telephone hotline technical support. Training cost is based upon topics, requirements, training equipment and site, and days requested. Please request a quote from an AMS sales representative for your specific requirements.

Artemis GlobalView and ProjectView

Describe what the product is designed to do.

Views offers two reporting tools, based on user requirements. One is provided within ProjectView (project scheduling). The other is GlobalView, a unique online analytical processing tool that enables users to drill down through Views data.

These tools facilitate effective decision-making at all levels of an organization. This will be achieved by configuring the data presentations specifically to organizational roles—e.g., project manager, resource manager, financial manager, and senior manager.

Where a more consistent periodic analysis is required, the appropriate data may be presented in a *briefing book* of reports. This provides managers with all the data necessary to understand where and how project resources, deadlines, and costs are being managed.

Top three product differentiators; describe what makes your product unique.

Currently, there are no competitive products on the market. The key differentiators are as follows.

1. User requires no understanding of underlying project management software.
2. One report provides interactive *drill-through* access to all associated data.
3. Point and *Ditto*.

To what business processes can this tool be applied?

All those supported by the Views Suite.

Describe the ideal end user environment for the current version of your product (size of organization, level of project management sophistication, effort and commitment required).

Businesses that need to provide managers and executives with real-time information and reports on project, resource, and cost performance.

Future strategies for this product.

Artemis is committed to continually enhancing our products' functionality and applicability to meet or exceed the demands of project management professionals.

Product's target market.

Executives, project managers, and team leaders within organizations using Artemis Views.

What are your product's three main benefits? (How does using the product add value to the customer?)

1. Fully graphical user interface.
2. Briefing books for push-button reporting.
3. Drill-down analysis and management by exception.

Describe your quality management process. List any relevant certifications.

Internal software audits and reporting procedures. Formal Year 2000 testing and compliance process.

Discuss your product pricing structure. Include volume discount levels, concurrent user options, site licenses, cost of implementation, and other issues.

Artemis Views can be purchased and deployed as a fully integrated suite or as a series of independent applications.

Available as registered user and concurrent pricing. Volume discounts and site licenses are available.

Cost of implementation varies.

Dekker TRAKKER Activity Based Cost Management and Performance System

Describe what the product is designed to do.

The TRAKKER Report Writer and Graphics module is an integrated component of the TRAKKER suite of tools. This system feature provides the user with presentation-quality reports and graphs from the wealth of data contained in the TRAKKER database.

Through this tool, the data within TRAKKER can be sorted, filtered, summarized, and distributed to meet the unique reporting requirements of any organization.

In addition, the TRAKKER Report Writer provides business, earned value, schedule and analytical report forms, and graphics.

Top three product differentiators; describe what makes your product unique.

1. The Report Writer and Graphics module is an integrated component of the system. The same tool provided to the user is used by DTMI to develop the hundreds of formats provided with the product.

2. All standard forms delivered with the product are provided to allow the user to modify or enhance these reports.

3. The output of the TRAKKER Report Writer integrates directly with the Microsoft Office suite of tools and can publish directly to the Web.

To what business processes can this tool be applied?

Presentation development, management briefings, customer reporting, business analysis, and Web-based reporting.

Describe the ideal end user environment for the current version of your product (size of organization, level of project management sophistication, effort and commitment required).

The TRAKKER Report Writer is designed for organizations that have specific reporting requirements. Although this tool enables end users to customize the output generated by TRAKKER, the Report Writer has the capability and sophistication to meet any reporting requirement. This attribute makes the TRAKKER Report Writer a powerful tool, which IT professionals can utilize in support of their user environment.

Future strategies for this product.

The reporting capabilities of TRAKKER allow users to sort, select, summarize, and distribute data to meet any reporting requirement. In addition, a number of TRAKKER reports and graphics provide the user with the ability to drill down into the detail data.

DTMI is working to further enhance this capability of the system.

Product's target market.

R&D, government, software, medical, electronics, and aerospace.

What are your product's three main benefits? (How does using the product add value to the customer?)

1. End-user oriented tool. The report writer in TRAKKER utilizes a graphical layout tool and wizards that walk the user through the process of developing reports and graphs.

2. As an integrated feature in TRAKKER, the Report Writer has direct access to the wealth of data maintained within the system. This tool has enabled DTMI to develop business, government, and analytical reports to meet the most stringent requirements.

Any report developed using this tool has all the features and functions of a standard TRAKKER report and will function as an integrated feature of the TRAKKER system.

3. All reports delivered with the system are available for customization. This provides the user with a starting point for developing custom reports.

Describe your quality management process. List any relevant certifications.

DTMI has modeled our development process from the Microsoft model while incorporating the quality guidelines established in ISO 9000.

Discuss your product pricing structure. Include volume discount levels, concurrent user options, site licenses, cost of implementation, and other issues.

DTMI offers both single and concurrent user licenses of TRAKKER. Our flexible pricing enables both small and large organizations to cost effectively implement costing and earned value.

TRAKKER pricing includes a progressive discount for volume purchases with reasonable thresholds for single and multisite licenses.

Further, DTMI offers both public and private training courses for both new and advanced users. DTMI also offers consulting services to support the enterprise implementation of TRAKKER.

Cost of implementation: DTMI provides training for both the discipline of scheduling and attributes of TRAKKER. These workshops include Basic Project Management, TRAKKER Application Workshop, TRAKKER Intermediate Workshop, TRAKKER Report Writer Workshop, and TRAKKER MIS Integrator's Workshop.

Through these courses, an enterprise can completely implement the TRAKKER system.

In addition to our classroom training, DTMI offers consulting services to guide users though a structured approach to implementing TRAKKER.

Enterprise Project (jeTECH DATA SYSTEMS, INC)

Describe what the product is designed to do.

Enterprise Project is a powerful new client/server software application that offers project-based organizations a simple way to define and staff projects, and record project labor and expenses throughout their enterprises. Essentially a suite of robust, user-friendly applications integrated into a single desktop, this comprehensive project management system enables team members to accurately plan and track labor resources across all projects. Perfect either as a *stand-alone* solution or as the ideal complement to the jeTECH labor-management system—Enterprise Labor—it is particularly well suited for multiuser, enterprisewide installations. Together, Enterprise Labor and Enterprise Project are the only systems currently on the market with extensive capabilities and integrated products for both the salaried professional (engineers and computer programmers, for instance) and the hourly employee (from factory workers to registered nurses).

Users access all functions via a single desktop with a Microsoft Office 98 *look and feel*. The system integrates completely with Enterprise Labor and Microsoft Project, as well as most popular accounting and HR systems. In today's competitive environment, effective and efficient use of labor resources is key to completing mission-critical projects on time, on budget. Enterprise Project gives project leaders a comprehensive, potent tool with which to manage scarce technical resources.

With Enterprise Project, managers can budget and schedule projects based on staff skills and availability. Project team members can manage their own tasks, report actual labor and travel expenses, and provide status reports on these tasks. The system calculates actual project costs by automatically incorporating labor costs, material costs, and travel expenses.

Project managers can define and manage both contract and noncontract-based projects, and control work authorizations that will keep each project under control and on budget. As a project manager, you simply create activities for your projects, assign appropriate resources to these activities and define how labor will be charged to a contract. And by allowing employees to only charge preassigned tasks, Enterprise Project prevents performance of unauthorized work.

Enterprise Project enables all users to report labor charges right from their PC or workstation. Project managers need no longer compile project team information manually. Users can now report project time as well as other time, and the system automatically processes and transmits it to an interfaced time-and-attendance system for payroll use.

Enterprise Project includes a contract maintenance module. Companies with hourly employees contracted with outside firms—for instance, security guards or programmers—would benefit from using this module without the rest of the project management system. This module is primarily designed, however, to accommodate projects being managed for clients. This module allows contract managers to define contract information including budgets and rates per hour, as well as all products and services purchased by the customer. They can then use this information to evaluate projects based on user-defined deliverables. Contract maintenance is by no means static. So jeTECH has designed Enterprise Project to handle change orders, R&D projects, and discounts. A variety of unique reporting features enables contract managers to view cost overruns, variances, and milestone completions.

Top three product differentiators; describe what makes your product unique.

1. Resource scheduling from a common resource pool in a multiproject environment.
2. Integrated time collection and status reporting.
3. Sensitivity analysis (what-if scenarios).

To what business processes can this tool be applied?

Project planning/management, enterprise resource scheduling/management, time collection, performance measurement, time and expense reporting, budgeting and estimating, and project accounting.

Describe the ideal end-user environment for the current version of your product (size of organization, level of project management sophistication, effort and commitment required).

Any resource-constrained enterprise (IT, high-tech R&D, engineering) with multiple projects and multiple sites. Requires a low level of project management sophistication.

Future strategies for this product.

Maintenance and repair operations, incorporation of process ware/templates, enterprise-level project and resource integration, and full Internet capabilities.

Product's target market.

Companies with *task-oriented* professionals such as engineers, architects, IS professionals, researchers, advertising/marketing professionals, etc. See also the previous response to "ideal end-user environment."

What are your product's three main benefits? (How does using the product add value to the customer?)

1. Improved resource utilization and efficiencies.
2. Reduction in time to complete projects.
3. Cost control.

Describe your quality management process. List any relevant certifications.

Our current quality management process includes in-house testing, which incorporates both automated and manual processes and procedures.

Discuss your product pricing structure. Include volume discount levels, concurrent user options, site licenses, cost of implementation, and other issues.

Pricing is structured on a named-user basis. Pricing will also be dependent on a number of variables including the size of the enterprise, number of project managers, number of facilities, etc. Consequently, pricing is provided to each customer when we have been able to familiarize ourselves on their operations and their anticipated use of the system.

Several options are available for training, tech support, annual maintenance, etc. Costs are provided to each customer when they have been able to select the options deemed best for their operations.

ER Project 1000

Describe what the product is designed to do.

The ER Project 1000 is an integrated suite of project management tools, which provide an enterprisewide project management solution. ER Project 1000 includes schedule/time management, centralized resource management, methodology/process management, project-workgroup communications, timesheets, risk/issue management, and enterprisewide cross-project tracking. Based on a client/server architecture with a centralized relational database, the ER Project 1000 provides networked access, multiproject capability, and true multiuser concurrency. It scales easily from handling small workgroup projects to large programs at the enterprise level.

Top three product differentiators; describe what makes your product unique.

1. Addresses the total project management life-cycle solution for the enterprise: Unlike most project management tools, the ER Project 1000 provides a completely integrated and centralized project management platform to support the entire life cycle of project management. Based on a client/server relational database (Oracle/SQL Server) architecture, ER Project 1000 fully supports today's multiproject/multiuser project environment. The product suite integrates full methodology/process management capabilities, project workgroup communications, and enterprisewide project tracking capabilities.

2. Provides a completely integrated suite of project management tools: The ER Project 1000 tool suite integrates industrial-strength project management functions with rich-process improvement functionality and proactive management features. ER Project 1000 provides all the necessary industrial-strength core project management functions. Key features include support for WBS/OBS/RBS structures, cost, schedule, earned value analysis, built-in report writer, timesheet approvals, and centralized resource management. ER Project 1000 takes advantage of the Web by providing Java timesheets and extensive project website publishing capability. Best practices/process improvement is easily accomplished with the methodology manager and support for organizational standards, work products, and estimation. ER Project 1000 delivers an impressive array of proactive management features. These features include risk management, issue management, management by threshold, and full project tracking.

3. Is easy to use and implement: ER Project 1000 was designed with a simple, intuitive interface. Extensive wizards assist users for complex operations. ER Project 1000 can easily be configured to your organization by using our centralized administration functions and component architecture.

To what business processes can this tool be applied?

ER Project 1000 is a wrap-around solution for organizations that need to implement mature project management practices, proactively manage their projects, improve business processes, implement standards and documentation, and communicate at multiple levels. Eagle Ray's advanced suite of tools provides project managers with an integrated platform for project planning, time tracking, resource management, and executive oversight. With features such as risk management, issue tracking, and management by threshold, the ER Project 1000 gives project managers the ability to proactively manage complex projects and stay focused on the key issues.

Organizations that engage in process improvement/best practices will find that the ER Project 1000 methodology manager is the ideal platform for developing and delivering best practices to each new project plan. Project managers will be able to easily document and reuse lessons learned in new projects. Project team members and stakeholders will find that the integrated communications features of the ER Project 1000 suite facilitate a real-time dialogue between all members and ensure no issues slip though the cracks.

Describe the ideal end-user environment for the current version of your product (size of organization, level of project management sophistication, effort and commitment required).

Size of organization: The ER Project 1000 product suite is ideal for managing projects with team sizes of ten to one thousand people per project in organizations where multiple projects are being performed at the same time. Project teams may be centralized or dispersed using client/server and Web-based communications technologies.

Level of sophistication: The tool suite is best suited for organizations that are moving beyond basic project management to a medium level of project management maturity or higher. These organizations are typically implementing tracking, costing, project management standards, risk/issue management, time tracking, centralized resource management, and possibly earned value. ER Project 1000 also supports organizations implementing a project office, best practices, process improvement, and reusable project templates. These features make ER Project 1000 an ideal platform for organizations implementing CMM level 2 or higher maturity levels.

Effort and commitment required: Successful implementation of the ER Project 1000 tool suite centers on an organization's commitment to realizing repeatable project management results from enterprisewide standardization of business processes and practices. Because of its integrated design and simple interface, ER Project 1000 delivers numerous advantages over standard project management tool sets with less staff effort.

Future strategies for this product.

Eagle Ray's future strategies include building new modules, expanding current modules, interfacing with corporate business systems, and preparing the product suite for the global marketplace. Major planned enhancements include significant modifications to the estimation module, costing module, methodology/process management module, and the Internet/intranet/Web capabilities. In addition, we will be constructing a problem/defect-tracking module.

We will be expanding the interfaces that integrate the ER Project 1000 system with additional enterprise business systems. Such systems include costing/accounting systems, HR systems, and additional commercial products. We also plan to complete our internationalization/localization efforts to prepare the ER Project 1000 for global distribution.

Product's target market.

ER Project 1000 is suitable for commercial and government organizations, which are managing projects that range from small workgroup-level projects to projects that span the entire enterprise. Essentially, the tool suite will support any project environment where the project team has access to or is working with computers.

What are your product's three main benefits? (How does using the product add value to the customer?)

1. Total integrated project management solution: The ER Project 1000 is an integrated, total project management solution providing complete support for the entire project management life cycle. The integrated tool suite does not require multiple add-on tools from different vendors, resulting in fewer hidden costs and less frustration. Project managers will find it easy to manage projects with a higher level of maturity by using the various features of the tool—for example, risk management, issue tracking, management by threshold, and multiproject capabilities.

2. Best practices/process improvement platform: The ER Project 1000 integrated process/methodology management platform provides a sophisticated yet easy-to-use platform for implementing best practices, estimation metrics, organizational standards, documentation templates, and process improvement. Organizations can capture, integrate, and reuse their project knowledge and project plan templates from an enterprisewide integrated platform.

3. Enterprisewide tracking and communications: The ER Project 1000 facilitates communications between all project stakeholders. Program managers and executives can perform cross-project rollups, dynamic drill-down, and cost, schedule, and earned-value analysis for up-to-date information on all enterprise projects. The project team members can access all of project information on the project website, and receive activity assignments and report status using Java timesheets. Automatic issue notification alerts project managers about possible deviations in cost and schedule. The built-in report writer lets you extract and summarize any data in the enterprisewide project database using customized formats.

Describe your quality management process. List any relevant certifications.

The Eagle Ray quality assurance program is a comprehensive system that employs a series of product walkthroughs, builds, quality gates, configuration management, defect tracking, and comprehensive testing. The development staff members are constantly conducting requirements, design, and code walkthroughs in coordination with weekly product builds and passing mandatory quality gates. The quality assurance program is integrated with our beta testing program to ensure that all product releases undergo rigorous real-world testing prior to release.

Comprehensive testing scenarios include unit testing, integration testing, platform testing, stress testing, concurrency testing, environment testing, security testing, usability testing, vertical testing, upgrade testing, business scenario testing, and independent qualification testing.

During the design and construction of the ER Project 1000 product, Eagle Ray brought in several project management industry experts to assist in the design of the software functionality and usability. This process will be continued to ensure that our future enhancements meet the real-world needs of project management organizations. Additionally, Eagle Ray continues to invest heavily in the training of team members in technical and project management areas.

Discuss your product pricing structure. Include volume discount levels, concurrent user options, site licenses, cost of implementation, and other issues.

Call for latest prices.

FastTrack Schedule 5.02

Describe what the product is designed to do.

FastTrack Schedule 5.02 makes it easy to organize tasks, meet deadlines, and achieve project goals. Whether you need to schedule a day's worth of activities or plan a project into the twenty-first century, FastTrack Schedule creates presentation-quality timelines.

New collaboration and automation pro tools provide real-time scheduling across an intranet or the Internet, and customized macros through Visual Basic. Enhance your schedules with graphics, logos, floating text blocks, and titles, then export them directly.

Top three product differentiators; describe what makes your product unique.

1. Easy to use and learn.
2. Highly customizable; presentation-quality project scheduling.
3. Outstanding price/performance ratio.

To what business processes can this tool be applied?

All processes benefiting from the application of project scheduling.

Describe the ideal end user environment for the current version of your product (size of organization, level of project management sophistication, effort and commitment required).

FastTrack Schedule 5.02 is ideal for professionals and support staff who are not project managers by vocation and who seek a project scheduling application requiring little or no training.

Future strategies for this product.

Continued enhancements and new technology for professionals and support staff requiring easy-to-use, customizable, presentation-quality project-scheduling applications.

Product's target market.

AEC: architecture, engineering, contracting.
Aerospace, manufacturing, and production.
Marketing, advertising, and entertainment.

What are your product's three main benefits? (How does using the product add value to the customer?)

1. The easiest project scheduling application to learn and use.
2. Highly customizable, presentation-quality project scheduling.
3. Outstanding price/performance ratio.

Describe your quality management process. List any relevant certifications.

No answer given.

Discuss your product pricing structure. Include volume discount levels, concurrent user options, site licenses, cost of implementation, and other issues.

AEC Software offers single-user licenses, server version concurrent-usage licenses, and site licenses. Contact AEC Software at 703/450-1980 for price quotation.

Cost of implementation: Multivolume training tapes available, $49 each. Free and unlimited technical support for all registered users. One- and three-year maintenance agreements available; call for quotation.

GRANEDA BarKeeper

Describe what the product is designed to do.

Create simple Gantt charts from within any OLE client (like MS Word, PowerPoint, etc.) either on the fly or import of MS Project data. All chart information is embedded in the client object, so documents containing Gantt charts can be E-mailed/shared and posted to the Web. Recipients can export data back into MS Project, Excel, etc.

Top three product differentiators; describe what makes your product unique.

1. Complete OLE Server.
2. Extremely easy to use right from within PowerPoint.
3. Easy import/export with MS Project.

To what business processes can this tool be applied?

Project status briefings, Web posting of project information.
Sharing of project data for merge into MS Project.
Low-end tool for users that do not need full project management system.

Describe the ideal end user environment for the current version of your product (size of organization, level of project management sophistication, effort and commitment required).

Medium- to large-sized organizations where team members have job classifications other than project management, but are still required to report status of their piece of the project. Little to no project management sophistication is required. Minimal effort or commitment is required to install and use effectively.

Future strategies for this product.

Add zoning, improve scheduling, and add wizards.

Product's target market.

Low-end, multifunctional users that need to produce project-status Gantt charts quickly, and share them with higher-end planners or post on the Web.

What are your product's three main benefits? (How does using the product add value to the customer?)

Works from within already-known OLE clients (like MS PowerPoint, Excel, Word).
Eliminates the need for costly additional licenses of more sophisticated project management software for low-end users.

Facilitate communication among project management team members without the *baggage* of a full project management system.

Describe your quality management process. List any relevant certifications.

ISO 9002 certified.

Discuss your product pricing structure. Include volume discount levels, concurrent user options, site licenses, cost of implementation, and other issues.

Single copy: $99; discounts at 100, 500, 1,000, and 5,000.

Cost of implementation: Training—one-half day, up to twenty per class, $495. Tech support via phone and E-mail. Annual maintenance—15 percent of purchase price.

GRANEDA Personal

Describe what the product is designed to do.

GRANEDA Personal is an add-on graphics package for project management systems. It can take data from almost any project management system and produce clear and easy-to-read project management reports.

Top three product differentiators; describe what makes your product unique.

1. Can take data from any tool or database and produce reports that are easy to read and understand.

2. Reports can be run over and over again.

To what business processes can this tool be applied?

Not limited to a specific process.

Describe the ideal end user environment for the current version of your product (size of organization, level of project management sophistication, effort and commitment required).

GRANEDA Personal is generally intended for lower-level project management sophistication and requires a very small commitment.

Future strategies for this product.

GRANEDA will continue to evolve to follow current technology trends and ease of use.

Product's target market.

GRANEDA Personal is a *lower-end* tool, and its targeted market is those companies that require less sophisticated reporting but still need clear and easy-to-follow reports.

What are your product's three main benefits? (How does using the product add value to the customer?)

1. Clear, easy-to-read reports.

2. Since most companies have several data sources, GRANEDA can pull the data from all different sources and make all the reports look the same. This way, management always sees the same report regardless of the source.

3. Since companies are maturing in project management and its tools, your investment in GRANEDA is not lost because of a change in project management tools.

Describe your quality management process. List any relevant certifications.

No answer given.

Discuss your product pricing structure. Include volume discount levels, concurrent user options, site licenses, cost of implementation, and other issues.

$495 single-user discounts start at five users and above. Site licenses available.
One-day training course.
Telephone and E-mail support.
Annual maintenance at 15 percent.

GRANEDA Project Showcase

Describe what the product is designed to do.

GRANEDA Project Showcase is an add-on graphics package for project management systems. It can take data from almost any project management system and produce clear and easy-to-read project management reports.

Top three product differentiators; describe what makes your product unique.

1. Can take data from any tool or database and produce reports that are easy to read and understand.
2. Reports can be run over and over again.

To what business processes can this tool be applied?

Not limited to a specific process.

Describe the ideal end user environment for the current version of your product (size of organization, level of project management sophistication, effort and commitment required).

GRANEDA Project Showcase is generally intended for higher-level project management sophistication and requires a larger commitment.

Future strategies for this product.

GRANEDA will continue to evolve to follow current technology trends and ease of use.

Product's target market.

Since Project Showcase is a *higher-end* tool, its targeted market is those companies that require more sophisticated reporting.

What are your product's three main benefits? (How does using the product add value to the customer?)

1. Clear, easy-to-read reports.
2. Since most companies have several data sources, GRANEDA can pull the data from all different sources and make all the reports look the same. This way, management always sees the same report regardless of the source.
3. Since companies are maturing in project management and its tools, your investment in GRANEDA is not lost because of a change in project management tools.

Describe your quality management process. List any relevant certifications.

No answer given.

Discuss your product pricing structure. Include volume discount levels, concurrent user options, site licenses, cost of implementation, and other issues.

$2,495 single-user discounts start at five users and above. Site licenses available.
Two-day training course.
Telephone and E-mail support.
Annual maintenance at 15percent.

Graphics Server

Describe what the product is designed to do.

Graphics Server is a graphical report writing tool, which is integrated to our enterprise controller suite of project management software. The package can also access and produce reports on data held in third-party systems.

Top three product differentiators; describe what makes your product unique.

1. Integration of schedules and budgets.
2. Interface capability to corporate systems.
3. Ease of data access.

To what business processes can this tool be applied?

Graphical reporting of corporate application data.

Describe the ideal end user environment for the current version of your product (size of organization, level of project management sophistication, effort and commitment required).

Medium to large organizations.
Users would have to be reasonably computer literate to exploit the full power of this reporting tool.

Future strategies for this product.

Web enabling. Further integration to E-mail and other business systems.

Product's target market.

Organizations looking for a reporting tool to provide excellent graphical representations of their corporate data.

What are your product's three main benefits? (How does using the product add value to the customer?)

1. Developed specifically to assist the reporting requirements of project management software.
2. Reduces rekeying of data and operating costs.
3. Provides integrated management of cost, budget, and scheduling information.

Describe your quality management process. List any relevant certifications.

We have internal auditable quality procedures in place, which are equivalent to ISO 9000 standards. Accredited Investors in People.

Discuss your product pricing structure. Include volume discount levels, concurrent user options, site licenses, cost of implementation, and other issues.

Pricing based on number of concurrent users for the module.
Discounts available for volume and multisite implementations.
Full pricing available on application.

Cost of implementation: Annual maintenance 15 percent of license costs. Cost of professional services available on request.

Mesa/Vista

Describe what the product is designed to do.

Mesa/Vista helps project teams manage, monitor, and comply with quality and government regulations by providing process management capabilities and access to all legacy and current project data through a Web browser.

Mesa/Vista provides process management capabilities and integrates a development team's existing product environment, including tools like Rational Rose, TD Technologies' SLATE, Cayenne Teamwork, or any tool with an MPX interface, such as Microsoft Project.

Mesa/Vista links information between stand-alone products and exposes project data to authorized project team members, empowering them to anticipate and solve problems at early stages in the project life cycle.

Mesa/Vista automates the documentation process. This shaves time from a project that must comply with government or other regulatory standards because the documentation is available as soon as the project is complete.

Top three product differentiators; describe what makes your product unique.

1. Patent-pending technology intuitively links graphical objects such as those found in developer's modeling tools, not only within the stand-alone tool but also between tools.

2. Provides support of any business process through dynamic exchange of information.

3. Connects legacy and current data between development team's business and engineering tools.

To what business processes can this tool be applied?

SEI CMM levels 1–5, ISO-compliancy regulations, FDA requirements management.

Describe the ideal end user environment for the current version of your product (size of organization, level of project management sophistication, effort and commitment required).

The ideal end-user environment for Mesa/Vista is a distributed, process-conscious product development group needing visibility and access to legacy and current project data across multiple platforms.

An organization trying to achieve or improve upon an SEI CMM level, achieve an ISO 9000 quality standard, or comply with FDA requirements will greatly benefit from the Mesa/Vista environment.

Commitment: All project-related communications would go through the Mesa/Vista environment for it to provide complete, automated project status information.

Future strategies for this product.

Future strategies for Mesa/Vista include integrating all engineering and business data together to be shared and accessed by the entire product development team, no matter where the data resides.

Plug-ins will include more scheduling tools, databases, business tools, document-editing tools, and modeling tools—all the tools the entire team would use within a product development environment.

Mesa/Vista will create an environment of collaboration, and expose information to help all members of the team work together without restraint of hardware or system requirements.

Product's target market.

Mesa/Vista is ideal for process-conscious project managers of distributed product development teams in the telecommunication, automotive, aerospace, medical, and software industries.

What are your product's three main benefits? (How does using the product add value to the customer?)

Provides accessibility to data from places other than the data's native machine, minimizing the number of copies of each software product that needs to be purchased.

Saves time by providing online access to all project data, rather than printing and faxing information in order to share it.

Automatic documentation mechanism for ease of tracking government regulations or quality standards control.

Describe your quality management process. List any relevant certifications.

Mesa/Vista is used to manage the development of Mesa/Vista. Also, extensive internal and external testing is done of the Mesa/Vista product line.

Mesa has provided the software to Young America's design team (NYYC's challenger in the America's Cup 2K) in exchange for feedback on Mesa/Vista and suggestions for improvements based on their real-life use of the product line.

Discuss your product pricing structure. Include volume discount levels, concurrent user options, site licenses, cost of implementation, and other issues.

Contact vendor.

Milestones, Etc. (Kidasa)

Describe what the product is designed to do.

Milestones, Etc. is designed to provide an easy-to-use product to produce high-quality schedules in a Gantt format.

Top three product differentiators; describe what makes your product unique.

1. Easy to learn.
2. Easy to use.
3. Easy to update schedules.

To what business processes can this tool be applied?

Scheduling of projects.

Describe the ideal end-user environment for the current version of your product (size of organization, level of project management sophistication, effort and commitment required).

Desktop Windows environment.

Future strategies for this product.

Continue to add user-requested features to make product do more, but still maintain ease of use.

Product's target market.

People who need to quickly produce schedules.

What are your product's three main benefits? (How does using the product add value to the customer?)

1. Enables customer to easily produce high-quality Gantt charts.
2. Enables customer to spend less time creating Gantt charts.
3. Enables customer to spend less time updating Gantt charts.

Describe your quality management process. List any relevant certifications.

Follow standard commercial software development guidelines.

Discuss your product pricing structure. Include volume discount levels, concurrent user options, site licenses, cost of implementation, and other issues.

Single-user licenses are $199. Workgroup pricing is also available.

Cost of implementation: Just the amount of time it takes to go over the supplied tutorials, usually no more than a few hours.

Open Plan (Welcom)

Describe what the product is designed to do.

Welcom's Open Plan is an enterprisewide project management system that substantially improves a company's ability to manage and complete multiple projects on time and within budget with a limited workforce. Unlike less-sophisticated products, Open Plan is a highly integrated, comprehensive software system that can be customized to fit specific corporate requirements. It is the most technically advanced client/server project management system on the market, using the latest in Microsoft Windows development technology.

The three versions of Open Plan are:

Open Plan Professional: Easy to use and powerful enough to manage even the largest projects. Open Plan Professional gives professional project managers such vital tools as advanced resource management, multiproject support, support for client/server databases, and the flexibility to customize the interface to support organization and industry-specific procedures.

Open Plan Desktop: Designed for occasional access to projects and ideal for executive users and tactical team members. Open Plan Desktop has extensive ease-of-use features and an affordable price point for companywide deployment. The system is well-suited for users who usually work on individual components of a larger project. Users can roll their individual projects up to Open Plan Professional for a broader view of the overall project.

Open Plan Enterprise: Very similar to Open Plan Professional, integrates with popular ERP applications such as Baan and SAP. The resulting component-based suite automatically disseminates project data throughout an organization, giving users better control over enterprisewide multiproject planning, management, and implementation.

Top three product differentiators; describe what makes your product unique.

1. Multiproject.
2. Advanced resource modeling.
3. Open architecture.

To what business processes can this tool be applied?

Enterprise resource modeling, business process reengineering, project management, earned value analysis, risk assessment, and process modeling.

Describe the ideal end-user environment for the current version of your product (size of organization, level of project management sophistication, effort and commitment required).

Medium to large organizations for which project management is a serious business requirement. Meets the needs of users whose level of expertise varies from novice/occasional to advanced.

Future strategies for this product.

Our vision for the future is to provide a suite of component-based products that work together to provide advanced project management functionality using the very latest technology.

Welcom's development plans include extending the products' multiproject and enterprise resource modeling capabilities while moving to a distributed applications architecture with Web technology being a significant component. Plans also include leveraging existing integrations with Baan and SAP, and expanding integrations to include other ERP vendors.

Product's target market.

Fortune 1000 companies, government and multinational organizations implementing enterprisewide project management.

What are your product's three main benefits? (How does using the product add value to the customer?)

1. Increase quality of project communications.
2. Reduce cycle time through effective resource management.
3. Increase integration of project management with business systems.

Describe your quality management process. List any relevant certifications.

Adhere to standard industry processes in release and version strategies, including automated regression testing. ISO 9000 certified in the United Kingdom.

Discuss your product pricing structure. Include volume discount levels, concurrent user options, site licenses, cost of implementation, and other issues.

Please call for pricing.
Training courses and consulting: Please call for pricing.
Tech support: No charge with current maintenance.
Maintenance: First year is free with software purchase. Renewed annually.

OPX2 Pro (Planisware)

Describe what the product is designed to do.

All graphic functions quoted here are standard features of OPX2 scheduling and cost management software; no external add-on is required.

Top three product differentiators; describe what makes your product unique.

1. Ability to draw several bars on the same line of the Gantt charts.

To what business processes can this tool be applied?

Project management: R&D project management (new product development, portfolio management), matrix organizations, IS departments, and software houses.

Scheduling of small serial manufacturing, engineering projects, heavy maintenance, and integration activities.

Cost management for public contract management, defense and aerospace programs, in-house product development, and subcontracting.

Describe the ideal end-user environment for the current version of your product (size of organization, level of project management sophistication, effort and commitment required).

Organization: from one hundred to twenty thousand resources managed.

Level of project management sophistication: previous experience of other project management software implementation is profitable for implementing OPX2.

To be implemented using a methodology suited for enterprisewide consolidation: activity coding, resource identification, and ERP interfaces.

Future strategies for this product.

Development of partnerships with ERP providers.
International development (multilingual support and distributors).
Focus on decision-support functions.

Product's target market.

Manufacturing: defense and aerospace, car/truck, drug/cosmetics development.
ICT: IS departments (enterprises and administrations), software house, telecommunications, and electronics.
Engineering: construction, energy, and space.

What are your product's three main benefits? (How does using the product add value to the customer?)

1. For the organization: standardization of concepts and reporting process for project management in all departments; breaking of barriers between cost and schedule.
2. For the users: Less time spent to collect and enter data, more time available to analyze them.
3. For the management: Real visibility on activity progress for top management, and long-term historization of project data at multiproject scale.

Describe your quality management process. List any relevant certifications.

TEMPO (Thomson-CSF software development methodology). TEMPO is compliant with ISO 9001 standards.
No specific certification for Planisware.

Discuss your product pricing structure. Include volume discount levels, concurrent user options, site licenses, cost of implementation, and other issues.

OPX2 Pro (Scheduling + Cost Management + Report builder): from $12,000 (server + first concurrent user license).
Typical user configurations: $17,000 to $1,000,000. Concurrent user licenses: yes. Site licenses: yes.
Cost of implementation: Twenty-five to 80 percent of license cost for consulting and training.
Annual maintenance: Fifteen percent of license cost (including tech support and upgrade of new releases).
Training: contact OPX2 distributors in each country.

PERT Chart EXPERT

Describe what the product is designed to do.

PERT Chart EXPERT is a Windows application for planning and displaying projects using PERT charts, logic, and network diagrams. PERT Chart EXPERT can be used as an add-on to your existing project management system or as a stand-alone system.

As an add-on to Microsoft Project, PERT Chart EXPERT is installed directly into Microsoft Project and interacts seamlessly to exchange data. PERT Chart EXPERT contains extensive PERT charting capabilities unlike those found in MS Project's PERT chart.

PERT Chart EXPERT can also be used as a stand-alone to quickly and easily sketch a project plan in a PERT chart environment. In addition, PERT Chart EXPERT can create charts from Primavera Systems' P3 and SureTrak software.

Top three product differentiators; describe what makes your product unique.

1. PERT Chart EXPERT creates time-scaled and time-oriented PERT charts and Network diagrams.

2. PERT charts can be grouped or zoned in horizontal bands across the page.

3. Produces the most easy-to-understand and easy-to-follow PERT charts with minimal effort, and supports all Windows-compatible printers and plotters.

To what business processes can this tool be applied?

Presentation and communication of projects.

Project planning.

Project tracking and statusing.

Describe the ideal end user environment for the current version of your product (size of organization, level of project management sophistication, effort and commitment required).

PERT Chart EXPERT is designed for the novice project manager who wants to produce PERT charts of their projects quickly and easily, yet contains many advanced features for the expert who needs to create elaborate PERT charts.

Contains the power and flexibility to be used on any size project in any size organization.

Fits into your existing project management system to create charts of existing plans, or can be used to create projects from scratch.

Future strategies for this product.

Extensive Web-based tools will be added in future releases.

OCX and Active X controls are also being considered for future releases.

Product's target market.

PERT Chart EXPERT is for anyone who needs to create or display a PERT chart or *logic* diagram of their projects showing tasks and dependencies between tasks.

PERT Chart EXPERT is for existing Microsoft Project users who want a more comprehensive and flexible PERT chart display.

PERT Chart EXPERT is also for the P3 and SureTrak user (or any other project management software user that can generate an MPX file of their projects).

What are your product's three main benefits? (How does using the product add value to the customer?)

1. PERT Chart EXPERT makes it easy to create PERT charts from your existing project plans.

2. PERT Chart EXPERT allows you to create PERT charts quickly and easily by clicking and dragging to create tasks and dependencies.

3. PERT Chart EXPERT contains all of the necessary features to produce many different styles of PERT charts displaying all of the data that you need.

Describe your quality management process. List any relevant certifications.

No answer given.

Discuss your product pricing structure. Include volume discount levels, concurrent user options, site licenses, cost of implementation, and other issues.

Single copies are $199 each. Quantity discounts are as follows: Five to nine copies are $180 each; ten to twenty-four copies are $160 each; and twenty-five to fifty copies are $130 each. Site licenses are available; call for details.

Network licenses are priced on a per-user basis (not concurrent user) and are as follows: A five-user network license is $900; a ten-user network license is $1,600; a fifteen-user license is $2,250; and a twenty-user license is $2,800. Larger licenses are available.

Cost of implementation: PERT Chart EXPERT comes with a user's guide, tutorials, and extensive online help. Training needs are usually minimal. Technical support is free. No annual maintenance. Visit our website at www.criticaltools.com

PlanView Software

Describe what the product is designed to do.

PlanView Software has modules that manage the flow of work (projects and nonprojects) and enhance communication among distributed staff and managers. Work is requested, scheduled, progressed, and closed using the Web.

Top three product differentiators; describe what makes your product unique.

1. All desktop interfaces are browser based.
2. Resource-centric views of work capacity.
3. *Unlimited* scalability: Four thousand plus users at some sites.

To what business processes can this tool be applied?

Multiproject management, service request management, resource management, workflow management, work and resource *portfolio* management.

Describe the ideal end user environment for the current version of your product (size of organization, level of project management sophistication, effort and commitment required).

Organization with one hundred to multiple thousands of employees (we have implementations of four thousand plus), managed by five plus managers with access to a central database; includes matrix style organizations.

Future strategies for this product.

Further conversion to Web browser-based interfaces; even easier report generation and Web publishing; more E-mail notification, and document attachment.

Product's target market.

The resource-centric approach to work management is typically most useful for organizations with a highly skilled workforce of limited availability; with twenty plus managers, and one hundred plus staff; using client/server.

What are your product's three main benefits? (How does using the product add value to the customer?)

1. Web-based interfaces since June '97.
2. All managers and contributors access the same central repository.
3. Staff reporting ETC affects project progress.

Describe your quality management process. List any relevant certifications.

PlanView follows the guidelines set out in the book *Best Practices of Rapid Development* by Steve McConnell.

Discuss your product pricing structure. Include volume discount levels, concurrent user options, site licenses, cost of implementation, and other issues.

It is different for each case, but basically the cost is $200–400 per seat, with volume discounts. The repository products are included.

Standard SQL database is extra. Implementation and training are extra.

Cost of implementation: We offer a range of implementation packages, from rapid to standard, which include training. Additional services billed at time and cost. Phone and online tech support are free. Maintenance packages offered.

Project Scheduler 7 (Scitor Corp.)

Describe what the product is designed to do.

PS7 is built to take full advantage of today's technology. Whether you're performing basic task scheduling on your desktop or working on multiple megaprojects using our powerful SQL database repository, PS7 will meet your needs.

Wizards, Guides, Tip-of-the-Day suggestions, and field-level help provide an easy-to-navigate path to project management. You'll find PS7 provides extraordinary flexibility to organize, consolidate, and view project information.

For serious users, PS7 provides support for subprojects, grouped projects, accounting periods, time-phased availability, inflation factors, multiple cost tables, earned value, unlimited user fields/formulas, five baselines, custom reports and much more.

The add-on package, Project Communicator (described in the Timesheets section) permits resources to view their task assignments, and report back actual work and estimated remaining work via a powerful two-tier client/server database system.

Top three product differentiators; describe what makes your product unique.

1. Approachable Power: PS7 meets the needs of the most demanding project management professionals, without sacrificing the ease-of-use demanded in today's state-of-the-art applications.

2. Scalability: PS7 is designed and built from the ground up to scale from the single desktop user to the entire enterprise.

3. Customer Support: PS7 is in its seventh generation, and continues to be designed and built by project management professionals for project management professionals.

To what business processes can this tool be applied?

Project planning and tracking; resource management and team communications; cost estimation and control.

Describe the ideal end-user environment for the current version of your product (size of organization, level of project management sophistication, effort and commitment required).

PS7 is designed to meet the needs of all sizes of organizations, including individuals, product teams, workgroups and the enterprise. As the most configurable project management package available, PS7 meets the needs of beginning project managers on up to serious project management professionals.

Future strategies for this product.

We will continue to provide leading-edge project management products and services by listening to and working with customers to predict the future needs of a changing management environment.

Product's target market.

General business and professional project management in all major industries.

What are your product's three main benefits? (How does using the product add value to the customer?)

1. Plans and tracks project/resource costs and schedules.
2. Allows early detection and resolution of problems.
3. Facilitates communications between all stakeholders.

Describe your quality management process. List any relevant certifications.

Best commercial practices.

Discuss your product pricing structure. Include volume discount levels, concurrent user options, site licenses, cost of implementation, and other issues.

Single unit $595, discounts at ten, twenty-five and fifty-plus. $2,900 for five-pack concurrent licenses, discounts at two, five, and ten-plus. Site licenses available for 500-plus licenses. Regional and on-site training and consulting is available. Telephone tech support is free.

Project-r (PLANTRAC)

Describe what the product is designed to do.

Project-r gives project information its greatest impact. It is designed to read an MS Project mpx file and give you the ability to produce hundreds of attractive charts to make a good impression.

Top three product differentiators; describe what makes your product unique.

1. Multiple tasks per line.
2. Variable calendar.
3. Report enhancer and embellisher.

To what business processes can this tool be applied?

All projects.

Describe the ideal end-user environment for the current version of your product (size of organization, level of project management sophistication, effort and commitment required).

Project management software users capable of producing mpx files who want to improve Gantt chart reporting.

Future strategies for this product.

Improved graphics and communication.

Product's target market.

All software capable of mpx files.

What are your product's three main benefits? (How does using the product add value to the customer?)

1. Complete Gantt chart flexibility.
2. More concise charts.
3. Better project communications.

Describe your quality management process. List any relevant certifications.

Quality management is based on a mix of PRINCE and ISO 9000 methodology.

Discuss your product pricing structure. Include volume discount levels, concurrent user options, site licenses, cost of implementation, and other issues.

$199 single copy; site licenses $85 per copy.

Implementation and training is $960 per day. Technical support is provided by telephone, fax and E-mail free for the first six months and thereafter at 17.5 percent of purchase price (includes upgrades and enhancements).

ProjectSite for the Web

Describe what the product is designed to do.

ProjectSite allows you to build a secure project website where users can log in to view and update Microsoft Project information using any Java-capable Web browser. From graphical, high-level management reports to weekly to-do lists, ProjectSite allows you to easily create any view you can imagine. A 100 percent pure Java calendar allows end users to update task progress by drag-and-drop methods.

Top three product differentiators; describe what makes your product unique.

1. Complete Web-based access to Microsoft Project schedules.
2. Open architecture allows for complete customization.
3. User- and role-based security keeps project data safe.

To what business processes can this tool be applied?

Dissemination and updating of project information, as well as team communication.

Describe the ideal end user environment for the current version of your product (size of organization, level of project management sophistication, effort and commitment required).

Companies or departments using Microsoft Project where five or more people (who are not project managers) have an interest in viewing and updating project information using a Web browser.

Future strategies for this product.

Database support with qualified updating.

Product's target market.

Users of Microsoft Project in groups of five or more, covering all industry segments.

What are your product's three main benefits? (How does using the product add value to the customer?)

1. Improves schedule quality and timeliness through improved team awareness.
2. Reduces need for project meetings.
3. No client setup required (Web-based).

Describe your quality management process. List any relevant certifications.

Internally documented.

Discuss your product pricing structure. Include volume discount levels, concurrent user options, site licenses, cost of implementation, and other issues.

Server: $1,495. Client license: $50 each.

Cost of implementation: Free E-mail and Web support.

SAS Software

Describe what the product is designed to do.

The project management capabilities of SAS software are designed to help you plan, manage, and track single or multiple projects. These projects can range from the small to the very large, from the simple to the complex. Next, SAS software gives you the tools to add information on the progress that has been made in completing the tasks scheduled.

Top three product differentiators; describe what makes your product unique.

1. The most obvious differentiator for the SAS software project management tools is their ability to run on virtually every major operating system—PC, Unix, mainframe, or Macintosh.

2. Another distinct feature of SAS software project management is its integration with an unparalleled suite of operations research and management science tools.

3. Finally, SAS Institute Inc., the world's largest privately held software vendor, has a record of steady growth and commitment to its customers. We've been in business since 1976 (providing project management software since 1983).

To what business processes can this tool be applied?

The project management tools in SAS software can be applied to any business process, but you will obtain the best results when you apply them to processes for which you have at least approximate starting dates or times.

Describe the ideal end-user environment for the current version of your product (size of organization, level of project management sophistication, effort and commitment required).

SAS software's project management tools can really be applied in any user environment, but some users will get more benefit from the tools' capabilities than others. In general, an ideal user of SAS software project management tools should be well acquainted with project management processes.

Owing to its flexibility, SAS software can easily accommodate users with widely varying levels of commitment. Users less committed to the SAS system may choose to store their project data in another database format.

SAS software can also accommodate users of varying technical expertise.

Future strategies for this product.

Continued multiplatform support and the addition of features designed to increase the software's usefulness and ease of use.

Product's target market.

The target market for SAS software project management is the user who is not satisfied with a "one size fits all" solution or a strictly "off the shelf" product. We aim for users who want to take direct control of their project models.

What are your product's three main benefits? (How does using the product add value to the customer?)

Using SAS software for project management has many advantages, but the most prominent benefits come from gaining direct, detailed control over your project models and the schedules that arise from them.

Describe your quality management process. List any relevant certifications.

In software development at SAS Institute, we recognize that quality is not simply added to the software product by testing at the end of development. Developing quality SAS software requires building quality into each step of the software development process.

Discuss your product pricing structure. Include volume discount levels, concurrent user options, site licenses, cost of implementation, and other issues.

Price varies. Technical support and maintenance are included in the annual license fee.

Schedule Insight

Describe what the product is designed to do.

Schedule Insight is a read-only browser of Microsoft Project schedules and is designed for executives, managers, and staff who need quick, no-nonsense access to Microsoft Project schedule information. It automatically rolls up multiple projects by company, project, department, resource, and task. A built-in report writer allows users to create their own reports.

Top three product differentiators; describe what makes your product unique.

1. Read-only browser of Microsoft Project schedules.
2. Familiar spreadsheet and folder architecture for ease of use.
3. All views and reports can be customized by the end user.

To what business processes can this tool be applied?

Dissemination of project information.

Describe the ideal end user environment for the current version of your product (size of organization, level of project management sophistication, effort and commitment required).

Companies or departments using Microsoft Project where five or more people (who are not project managers) have an interest in viewing and printing project information for their own needs.

Future strategies for this product.

Database support with qualified updating.

Product's target market.

Users of Microsoft Project in groups of five or more, covering all industry segments.

What are your product's three main benefits? (How does using the product add value to the customer?)

1. Improves schedule quality and timeliness through improved team awareness.
2. Reduces need for project meetings.
3. Empowers individuals to obtain their own project information.

Describe your quality management process. List any relevant certifications.

Internally documented.

Discuss your product pricing structure. Include volume discount levels, concurrent user options, site licenses, cost of implementation, and other issues.

Single user—$99; network license—$995 (unlimited users).

Cost of implementation: The point-and-click interface, with read-only capabilities, allows users to quickly and safely learn on their own while your project data always remains safe. In addition, the online tutorial and free E-mail support greatly minimizes implementation costs.

Varchart

Describe what the product is designed to do.

Varchart provides software development toolkit for users to build their own PM graphics module for both interactive editing and reporting. Extremely flexible, thousands of options to get just the look and feel users want and need.

Top three product differentiators; describe what makes your product unique.

1. Unlimited number of tasks can be displayed, edited.
2. API-callable functions make it possible to write your own graphics package with VB, C++, Delphi, etc.
3. All print and Web publishing functionality included.

To what business processes can this tool be applied?

Project planning, ERP, MRP, conference room scheduling, network management, and more.

Describe the ideal end-user environment for the current version of your product (size of organization, level of project management sophistication, effort and commitment required).

Medium to large-sized organization with IS staff, programmers, and sophisticated planners. Level of effort and commitment required is high.

Future strategies for this product.

Provide libraries in the form of OCX programming tools, provide more source-code samples, create Wizards and CBT.

Product's target market.

PM, ERP, MRP, and large organizations with programming staffs.

What are your product's three main benefits? (How does using the product add value to the customer?)

1. Complete flexibility for creating interactive graphical editing and reporting functionality.
2. Simple API allows users to shave months off development times.
3. Already contains Web posting and print functionality.

Describe your quality management process. List any relevant certifications.

ISO 9002-certified.

Discuss your product pricing structure. Include volume discount levels, concurrent user options, site licenses, cost of implementation, and other issues.

Base SDK: Between $3,500 and $7,000 depending on which options are selected. Small run-time fee based upon volume. Multiuser discounts. Training available at $995/day plus T&L. Tech support via phone and E-mail. Annual maintenance is 15 percent of SDK price.

WBS Chart (Critical Tools, Inc.)

Describe what the product is designed to do.

WBS Chart is a Windows application used for planning and displaying projects using a tree-style diagram known as a work breakdown structure (WBS) chart. A WBS chart displays the structure of a project showing summary (phase) and detail levels.

WBS Chart can be used as an add-on to your existing project management system or as a stand-alone system. As an add-on to Microsoft Project, WBS Chart is installed directly into Microsoft Project and interacts seamlessly to exchange data.

WBS Chart can also be used stand-alone to quickly and easily sketch a project plan in a WBS chart environment. Plan new projects using a "top-down" approach and transfer this information to Microsoft Project or other project management application.

Top three product differentiators; describe what makes your product unique.

1. Creates work breakdown structure charts of existing projects. Automatically create WBS charts from Microsoft Project plans and other programs that can produce mpx files.

2. Create projects manually by clicking and dragging in a WBS chart environment with many custom features for planning and displaying the project data.

3. Supports all Windows compatible printers and plotters.

To what business processes can this tool be applied?

Presentation and communication of projects; project planning; project tracking and statusing.

Describe the ideal end-user environment for the current version of your product (size of organization, level of project management sophistication, effort and commitment required).

WBS Chart is designed for the novice project manager who wants to produce WBS charts of their projects quickly and easily yet contains many advanced features for the expert who needs to create elaborate WBS charts.

Contains the power and flexibility to be used on any size project in any size organization.

Fits into your existing project management system to create charts of existing plans or can be used to create projects from scratch.

Future strategies for this product.

Extensive Web-based tools will be added in future releases. OCX and Active X controls are also being considered for future releases.

Product's target market.

WBS Chart is for the project manager who needs to present the overall organization and structure of their projects to upper management, clients or the project team—anyone who needs to create or display a WBS chart of a project showing the structure of the project in a top-down view. It is also for existing Microsoft Project users who want to display and modify their projects in a WBS chart view.

What are your product's three main benefits? (How does using the product add value to the customer?)

1. Makes it easy to create WBS charts from your existing project plans.

2. Allows you to create WBS charts quickly and easily by clicking and dragging to create phases, tasks and the organization of a project.

3. Contains all of the necessary features to produce many different styles of WBS charts displaying all of the data that you need.

Describe your quality management process. List any relevant certifications.

No answer given.

Discuss your product pricing structure. Include volume discount levels, concurrent user options, site licenses, cost of implementation, and other issues.

Single copies are $199 each. Quantity discounts: five to nine copies $180 each; ten to twenty-four copies $160 each; twenty-five to fifty copies $130 each. Site licenses are available.

Network licenses are priced on a per user basis (not concurrent user) as follows: a five-user network license is $900, a ten-user network license is $1,600, a fifteen-user license is $2,250 and a twenty-user license is $2,800. Larger licenses are available.

WBS Chart comes with a user's guide, tutorials and extensive online help. Training needs are usually minimal. Technical support is free. No annual maintenance.

WebProject

Describe what the product is designed to do.

WebProject is designed for geographically dispersed project teams. WebProject is a Java-based project management tool with powerful collaboration and communications features. WebProject incorporates unique knowledge management/best practices capability.

Top three product differentiators; describe what makes your product unique.

1. WebProject is the first (only) pure Java project management suite that can utilize an open architecture database backend. WebProject allows corporations to utilize Oracle, SQL Server, Informix, Sybase, or other databases in their enterprise project management.
2. WebProject has introduced the first knowledge management/best practices capability within a project management software suite.
3. WebProject enables global project communication, including project issues boards, threaded task discussions, virtual project status meetings, and remote project statusing and updates.

To what business processes can this tool be applied?

Geographically dispersed project teams, projects that need to have access from remote locations, or integrating WebProject's proprietary information exchange with MS Project, Primavera, or other desktop systems.

WebProject allows the extraction of *knowledge* from the enterprise, such as resource capabilities or company *best practices*.

Describe the ideal end user environment for the current version of your product (size of organization, level of project management sophistication, effort and commitment required).

WebProject is an easy-to-use Java project management tool, which will enable teams to communicate and collaborate from remote locations. WebProject is designed for the enterprise and will work well with project teams as well.

Future strategies for this product.

WebProject has established many *firsts* in the project management industry. We will continue to move the industry forward with our new technologies on the Web and with JAVA.

Product's target market.

Geographically dispersed project teams, enterprise project management systems, integration with Primavera, MS Project, and other project management systems.

What are your product's three main benefits? (How does using the product add value to the customer?)

1. Enterprise project communication.
2. Project collaboration.
3. Geographically dispersed updates and communication.

Describe your quality management process. List any relevant certifications.

WebProject adheres to strict standards and processes for quality, both in development and customer service.

Discuss your product pricing structure. Include volume discount levels, concurrent user options, site licenses, cost of implementation, and other issues.

WebProject is priced at $790 for starter package, including the WebProject server. WebProject does provide enterprise and site licensing.

Xgantt

Describe what the product is designed to do.

Xgantt provides an Active-X (OCX) programming object for VB, C++, Delphi, Centura, and more to create custom interactive Gantt applications quickly and easily.

Top three product differentiators; describe what makes your product unique.

1. Active-X object.
2. Print (preview) and Web-posting functionality included.
3. Virtually plug-n-play with most programming languages.

To what business processes can this tool be applied?

Virtually any application requiring time-phased graphical editing and display via a Gantt chart.

Describe the ideal end-user environment for the current version of your product (size of organization, level of project management sophistication, effort and commitment required).

Any organization needing a RAD tool to develop Gantt applications. Effort to implement is low.

Future strategies for this product.

Add Wizards, tutorials, and CBT.

Product's target market.

Any organization needing a RAD tool to develop Gantt applications.

What are your product's three main benefits? (How does using the product add value to the customer?)

1. Rapid Application Development (RAD).
2. Works in any programming environment that accepts OCX objects.
3. Print (preview) and Web-posting functionality available.

Describe your quality management process. List any relevant certifications.

ISO 9002 certified.

Discuss your product pricing structure. Include volume discount levels, concurrent user options, site licenses, cost of implementation, and other issues.

$3,495 for single copy. Volume discounts: $875 for each additional copy. Small run-time fee per user based on volume. Training: $995/day up to twelve per class. Tech support via phone and E-mail. Annual maintenance: 15 percent of purchase (not including run-time fees).

Timesheets

	AMS ABT CONNECT & ABT TEAM	AMS REALTIME Solo	Artemis TrackView	AutoPLAN Enterprise	Cascade WEBTime	Dekker Inergy	Enterprise Project	ER Project 1000	ET Enterprise	Innate Timesheets
Timesheet features										
Support for project and non-project time	Y	Y	Y	Y	Y	Y	Y	Y	Y	Y
Timesheets generated from scheduling software	Y	Y	Y	Y	Y	Y	Y	Y	N	Y
Users can add tasks not on schedule	Y	Y	Y	Y	Y	Y	Y	N	Y	Y
Supports rate escalation	Y	Y	Y	N	N	Y	Y	Y	N	Y
Status reporting by task	Y	Y	Y	Y	Y	Y	Y	Y	Y	Y
Customizable user interface (view/suppress fields)	Y	Y	Y	Y	Y	Y	Y	Y	Y	Y
Number of user defined fields		Unlim.	Unlim.	Y	Y	Y	0	N	16	Y
Incorporates business rules and data validation criteria	Y	N	Y	Y	Y	Y	Y	Y	Y	Y
Can user retrieve approved timesheet for adjustments	Y	Y	Y	Y	N	Y	Y	Y	Y	Y
Can retrieve feature be turned off?	Y	Y	Y	Y		Y	Y	Y	Y	Y
Timecard adjustments recorded in audit trail	Y	Y	Y	Y	Y	Y	Y	N	Y	Y
ETC in effort	Y	Y	Y	Y	Y	Y	Y	Y	N	Y
ETC in duration	Y	Y	Y	Y	Y	Y	Y	Y	N	Y
Remaining duration	Y	Y	Y	Y	Y	Y	Y	Y	N	Y
Reports										
Creates a report identifying changes made to the schedule	Y	Y	Y	Y	Y	Y	Y	N	N	Y
Exception reports	Y		Y	Y	Y	Y	Y	Y	Y	Y
Summary reports	Y	Y	Y	Y	Y	Y	Y	Y	Y	Y
Web enablement										
Can timesheet be updated through a Web browser?	Y	Y	Y	Y	Y	N	Y	Y	Y	Y
Which browsers/versions are supported?	I.E. 4.0, Netscape	Netscape	Internet Explorer, Netscape Navigator	Navigator 3.0 or later, IE 3.0 or later	MS Internet Explorer 4.72 and above, Netscape 4.04 and above		Netscape 3.0 and greater	Netscape 4.x and above, Explorer 4.x and above	Internet Explorer V. 3.0 and higher, Netscape V. 3.0 and higher	Internet Explorer, Netscape
Security										
Approver security	Y	Y	Y	Y	Y	Y		Y	Y	Y
Alternate approvers	Y	Y	Y	Y	Y	Y		Y	Y	Y
Field level security: lock specific fields	Y	Y	Y	N	Y	Y		N	Y	Y
Management validation: approve/reject electronically	Y	Y	Y	Y	Y	Y		Y	Y	Y
Miscellaneous										
Runs served (doesn't have to be installed on each client)	Y	Y	Y	Y		Y	Y	Y	Y	Y
Drill-Down/roll-Up	Y	Y	Y	Y		Y	Y	Y	Y	Y

Reporting

Report writer	Y	Y	Y	N	Y	Y	Y	Y	Y	Y
Report wizard	Y	N	Y	Y	N	Y	Y	Y	Y	Y
Publishes as HTML	Y	N	Y	Y	Y	Y	Y	Y	Y	Y
Number of user-defined fields		Unlim.	Unlim.	Y	Unlim.	Y	0	100	Unlim.	Unlim.
Drill-down/roll-up *	Y	Y	Y	Y	Y	Y	Y	Y	Y	Y
Import/export	Y	Y	Y	Y	Y	Y	Y	Y	Y	Y
Automatic E-mail notification *	N	N	N	Y	Y	Y	N	N	N	Y
* Macro recorder/batch capable	Y	Y	Y	Y	Y	Y	Y	Y	N	N
Can "canned" reports be modified?	Y	Y	Y	N	Y	Y	Y	Y	N	N
Sort, filter	Y	Y	Y	Y	Y	Y	Y	Y	Y	Y

Architecture

Databases supported (list):	Oracle, MS SQL Server, Sybase, Informix	ODBC compliant, proprietary	Oracle, Sybase, MS SQL Server, SQL Base	Oracle	Oracle	Oracle, MS SQL Server, Informix, MS Access, FoxPro	Oracle, Sybase, Informix, MS SQL Server, MS Access	Oracle, MS SQL Server, Interbase	Oracle, MS SQL Server, Sybase, Centura SQL Base	MS Access, MS SQL Server, Oracle
Supports distributed databases	Y	Y	Y	Y	Y	Y	Y	Y	N	N
Three-tier client/server	Y	Y	Y	Y	Y	Y	Y	Y	Y	N
Client operating systems	Win 95/98/NT	Win 95/NT/3.x, Solaris, HP, RS, Mac	Win 95/98/NT	Win 95/NT/3.x, Solaris, HP-UX, AIX	Win 95/98/NT	Win 95/98/NT	Win 95/98/NT	Win 95/98/NT	Win 95/98/NT 3.51/NT 4.0 (ER Project Satellite also Java and Win 3.x)	Win
Server operating systems	Win NT	Win 95/NT/3.x, Solaris, HP, RS, Mac	Win 95/NT, HP-UX Unix, Solaris, VMS	Win NT, Solaris, HP-UX, AIX	Unix, Win NT	Win NT, Novell, Unix	Unix, Win NT	Win NT, Unix	Win NT	Any that support Win
Network operating systems	TCP/IP compatible	TCP/IP, Banyan, Novell, IPX	Novell, IPX, Win NT	Win NT, Novell, Unix	TCP/IP	Win NT, Novell, Unix	Novell, Win NT, others	Win, NetBEUI/NetBios, TCP/IP, Novell	Win NT, Novell, Unix	Any that support Win

Timesheets

	ABT CONNECT & ABT TEAM	AMS REALTIME Solo	Artemis TrackView	AutoPLAN Enterprise	Cascade WEBTime	Dekker Inergy	Enterprise Project	ER Project 1000	ET Enterprise	Innate Timesheets
Minimum client configuration	Pentium 133	8 MB RAM, 20 MB disk, 486 or better	32 MB RAM, 64 MB RAM recommended	P5 32 MB	PC 486/66 processor or above. Win 95 or Win NT V4. 16 MB RAM	16 MB RAM, 1 GB HD, SVGA	486, 16 MB memory	Pentium, 16 MB memory (ER Project Satellite 8 MB)	66 MHz 486 processor, 16 MB RAM	Pentium
Minimum server configuration	Pentium 266	32 MB RAM, 100 MB disk, Pentium or better	User dependent	P5 32 MB, Unix machine with 64 MB	Any server supporting Oracle 7 or above	128 MB RAM, 10 GB HD	Pentium 200 CPU, 128 MB, 1 GB	Pentium, 32 MB memory	133 MHz Pentium processor, 32 MB RAM	Capacity consideration only
Client runs under Web browser	Y	Y	Y	Y	Y	Y	Y	Y	Y	Y
Open architecture										
Supports OLE	Y	N	Y	Y	Y	Y	Y	N	Y	Y
Documented Object Model	Y	Y	Y	Y	Y	Y	Y	Y	N	Y
Documented Application Programming Interface (API)	Y	Y	Y	Y	Y	Y	Y	N	Y	Y
Simultaneous edit of data file	Y	N	Y	N	Y	Y	Y	Y		Y
Does product have a programming language?	N	N	Y	Y	Y	Y	Y	N	Y	Y
Are years stored as four-digit numbers?	Y	N	Y	Y	Y	Y	Y	Y	Y	Y
Online help										
Right mouse click	Y	N	Y	N	N	Y	N	Y	Y	Y
Hover buttons	Y	Y	Y	Y	Y	Y	N	Y	Y	Y
Interactive help	Y	Y	Y	Y	Y	Y	Y	Y	Y	Y
Help search feature	Y	Y	Y	Y	Y	Y	Y	Y	Y	Y
Web access to product knowledge base *	Y	Y	Y	Y	N	N	N	Y	Y	Y
Vendor information										
Training										
Computer-based training	Y	Y	Y	Y	Y	Y	Y	N	N	Y
Training materials available	Y	Y	Y	Y	Y	Y	Y	Y	Y	Y
Customized training materials	Y	Y	Y	Y	Y	Y	Y	Y	N	Y
Online tutorial	Y	N	Y	N	N	Y	N	Y	N	Y

	1	2	3	4	5	6	7	8	9
Consulting available from vendor	Y	Y	Y	Y	Y	Y	Y	Y	Y
Site license discounts	Y	Y	Y	Y	Y	Y	Y	Y	Y
Enhancement requests *	Y	Y	Y	Y	Y	Y	Y	Y	Y
Modify source code, support through upgrades *	Y	Y	Y	Y	Y	Y	Y	Y	Y
Global presence									
Global offices	Y	Y	Y	Y	Y	N	N	Y	Y
Multilingual technical support	Y	Y	Y	Y	Y	Y	N	N	Y
Language versions (list):	Eng, Fr, Ger, Jpn	Fr, Ital, Ger	Eng, Fr	Eng, Fr	Eng	Eng, Span	Eng	Eng	Eng, Fr, Ger
Audit Software Quality Assurance process? *	Y	Y	Y	Y	Y	Y	Y	Y	Y
Security									
Configurable access priviledges *	Y	Y	Y	Y	Y	Y	Y	Y	Y
Passwords expire (forced update)	N	N	N	N	Y	Y	N	Y	Y
Electronic approvals	Y	Y	Y	Y	Y	Y	Y	Y	Y
Password protect files	Y	Y	Y	Y	Y	Y	Y	Y	Y

Timesheets

Timesheet features	Intelligent Planner	Microsoft Project 98	Open Plan/Spider	OPX2 TimeCard	Panorama	PlanView Software	PRISM	Project Commander	Project Communicator (add-on to PS7)	Project Control 6.0 - Time Manager
Support for project and non-project time	Y	N	Y	Y	Y	Y	Y	Y	Y	Y
Timesheets generated from scheduling software	Y	Y	Y	Y	N	Y	N	Y	Y	Y
Users can add tasks not on schedule	Y	N	N	Y	Y	Y	Y	Y	Y	Y
Supports rate escalation	Y	Y	Y	Y	Y	Y	Y	Y	Y	Y
Status reporting by task	Y	Y	Y	Y	Y	Y	Y		PS7	Y
Customizable user interface (view/suppress fields)	Y	Y	Y	Y	Y	Y	N		N	Y
Number of user defined fields	Unlim.	360	Y	5	N	Unlim.	N		PS7-Unlim.	60
Incorporates business rules and data validation criteria	Y	N	N	Y	Y	Y	Y		Y	Y
Can user retrieve approved timesheet for adjustments	Y	N	N	N	Y	N	Y		Y	Y
Can retrieve feature be turned off?	Y	N	N		Y	Y	Y		Y	Y
Timecard adjustments recorded in audit trail	Y	N	Y	N	N	N	Y	Y	Y	Y
ETC in effort	N	Y	Y	Y	N	Y	Y	Y	Y	Y
ETC in duration	Y	N	Y	Y	N	Y	Y	Y	Y	N
Remaining duration	Y	N	Y	Y	N	Y	Y	Y	Y	N
Reports										
Creates a report identifying changes made to the schedule	Y	N	Y	Y	N	Y	N	Y	PS7-Y	Y
Exception reports	Y	Y	Y	Y	Y	Y	Y	Y	PS7-Y	Y
Summary reports	Y	Y	Y	Y	Y	Y	Y	Y	PS7-Y	Y
Web enablement										
Can timesheet be updated through a Web browser?	Y	Y	Y	Y	N	N	N	Y	N	Y
Which browsers/versions are supported?	Internet Explorer 4.0, Netscape Navigator 4.1	IE 3.0 or higher; Netscape Navigator 3.0 or higher	Internet Explorer 4.0, Netscape Navigator 4.0, with a Java plug-in	MS IE 3 and +, Netscape Navigator 3 and +, Opera		Netscape, Internet Explorer		IE, Netscape	N/A	Netscape, MS Internet Explorer 3.x, 4.x
Security										
Approver security	Y	Y	Y	Y	Y	Y	Y		Y	Y
Alternate approvers	Y	Y	Y	Y	Y	Y	Y		N	Y
Field level security: lock specific fields	Y	N	Y	N	Y	Y	Y		Y	Y
Management validation: approve/reject electronically	Y	Y	Y	Y	Y	Y	Y		Y	Y
Miscellaneous										
Runs served (doesn't have to be installed on each client)	Y	Y	Y	Y	Y	Y	Y		N	Y
Drill-Down/roll-Up	Y	N	Y	Y	Y	Y	Y		Y	Y

	1	2	3	4	5	6	7
Reporting							
Report writer	Y	Y	Y	Y	Y	PS7-Y	Y
Report wizard	Y	N	N	N	N	PS7-Y	N
Publishes as HTML	Y	Y	Y	Y	N	PS7-Y	Y
Number of user-defined fields	100	360	Unlim.	Unlim.	Unlim.	PS7-Y	60
Drill-down/roll-up *	Y	N	Y	Y	Y	PS7-Y	Y
Import/export	Y	Y	Y	Y	Y	PS7-Y	Y
Automatic E-mail notification *	Y	N	N	Y	Y	PS7-Y	N
* Macro recorder/batch capable	Y	Y	Y	Y	N	PS7-Y	Y
Can "canned" reports be modified?	Y	Y	Y	Y	Y	PS7-Y	Y
Sort, filter	Y	Y	Y	Y	Y	PS7-Y	Y
Architecture							
Databases supported (list):	Oracle, Sybase, MS SQL Server, Informix, Centura	MS Access, MS SQL Server, or Oracle	Oracle, MS SQL Server, MS Access, Sybase, FoxPro	Oracle, MS SQL Server, Informix, Sybase, Ingres	Proprietary	Via ODBC: Oracle, Sybase, MS SQL Server, MS Access, et al.	Oracle, MS Access, MS SQL Server, Sybase
Supports distributed databases	Y	Y	Y	Y	Y	Y	Y
Three-tier client/server	Y	N	Y	Y	N	N	Y
Client operating systems	Win 95/NT	Win 95/98/NT 3.51 with Service Pack 5 or later/NT 4.0 with Service Pack 2 or later	Any Java enabled	any Web browser : Win 95/98/NT/3.x, Mac, Unix, OS/2	Win 95/98/NT	Win 95/98/NT4/3.x w/Win 32S extension	Win 95/98/NT
Server operating systems	Win NT	Win 95/98/NT 3.51 with Service Pack 5 or later/NT 4.0 with Service Pack 2 or later	Win NT, Unix	Win NT, Unix, Novell, IIS, Netscape	Win NT, Novell	N/A	Unix, Win NT, HP, Sybase, others
Network operating systems	TCP/IP, NetBios	Any Win-supported network	TCP/IP	http + TCP/IP (Ethernet, Token Ring, WAN)	Win 95/NT, Novell	Novell, Win NT	Novell, IPX, XPX, Banyan, MS Network, TCP/IP

Timesheets

	Intelligent Planner	Microsoft Project 98	Open Plan/Spider	OPX2 TimeCard	Panorama	PlanView Software	PRISM	Project Commander	Project Communicator (add-on to PS7)	Project Control 6.0 - Time Manager
Minimum client configuration	Pentium 120, 16 MB RAM, 1 GB disk	486 or higher processor with 12 MB memory for Win 95 or 16 MB for Win 98 or NT	Pentium or compatible, Win 95 or later: 16 MB RAM, Rec. 32 MB	486 + 8 MB RAM		486/66, 8 MB RAM, Win 3.1+	80486 PC/compatible processor, 16 MB RAM, 20 MB HD, 800x600 PIXEL display, Win-compatible printer		Win 3.x	PC 486/66 processor or above. Win 95 or Win NT V4. 16 MB RAM
Minimum server configuration	Pentium 233, 128 MB RAM, 1 GB disk	Run from server is available; configuration depends on number of users connecting to server	As recommended by database vendor	P2xx + 128 MB RAM		486/66, 32 MB RAM, Novell	80489 PC/compatible processor (Pentium recommended), 24 MB RAM, 10 MB free HD space, 800x600 PIXEL display, Win-compatible printer		N/A	Any server supporting Oracle 7 or above
Client runs under Web browser	Y	Y	Y	Y		Y	N		N	Y
Open architecture										
Supports OLE	N	Y	Y	N		Y	N		PS7	Y
Documented Object Model	N	Y	Y	N		Y	N		PS7	N
Documented Application Programming Interface (API)	Y	N	N	N		Y	N		PS7	N
Simultaneous edit of data file	Y	N	Y	Y		N	Y		Y	Y
Does product have a programming language?	Y	Y	N	Y		Y	N		N	N
Are years stored as four-digit numbers?	Y	Y	Y	Y		Y	Y		Y	Y
Online help										
Right mouse click	N	Y	Y			Y	Y		Y	N
Hover buttons	N	Y	Y			Y	Y		N	Y
Interactive help	Y	Y	Y			Y	Y		Y	N
Help search feature	Y	Y	Y			Y	Y		Y	Y
Web access to product knowledge base *	Y	Y	Y			Y	N	.	N	Y
Vendor information										
Training										
Computer-based training	N	N	Y			Y	N		N	Y
Training materials available	Y	Y	Y			Y	Y		Y	Y
Customized training materials	Y	N	Y			Y	Y		Y	Y
Online tutorial	Y	Y	Y			N	Y		Y	Y

Consulting available from vendor	Y	Y	Y	Y	Y	Y	Y
Site license discounts	Y	Y	Y	Y	Y	Y	Y
Enhancement requests *	Y	Y	Y	Y	Y	Y	Y
Modify source code, support through upgrades *	Y	N	Y	Y	Y	Y	Y
Global presence							
Global offices	Y	Y	Y	Y	Y	N	Y
Multilingual technical support	Y	Y	Y	Y	N	N	N
Language versions (list):	Eng, Fr, Ger, Dutch	Ger, Fr, Swed, Ital, Span, Dan, Nor, Jpn, Traditional Chin, Simplified Chin, Kor, Heb, Brzl. Port	Eng, Ital, Fr, Ger, Mand, Rus, Hangul	Eng, Fr	Eng	Eng, Fr, Ger	Eng
Audit Software Quality Assurance process? *	Y	N	N	Y	N	N	Y
Security							
Configurable access priviledges *	Y	N	Y	Y	Y	Y	Y
Passwords expire (forced update)	N	N	Y	N	Y	N	N
Electronic approvals	Y	Y	N	Y	Y	N	Y
Password protect files	Y	Y	Y	Y	Y	Y	Y

Timesheets

	Project Integrator 2.0 Enterprise Edition	time controller	TimeControl	TimeScope	TimeWizard	WebProject	Webster 2.1 for Primavera	WebTime & TimeReview	WorkLink Progress Sheet
Timesheet features									
Support for project and non-project time	Y	Y	Y	Y	Y	Y	Y	Y	Y
Timesheets generated from scheduling software	Y	N	Y	Y	Y	Y	Y	Y	N
Users can add tasks not on schedule	Y	Y	Y	Y	Y	Y	Y	Y	Y
Supports rate escalation	Y	Y	N	Y	Y	N	N	Y	Y
Status reporting by task	Y	Y	Y	Y	Y	Y	Y	Y	Y
Customizable user interface (view/suppress fields)	Y	N	Y	Y	Y	Y	N	Y	Y
Number of user defined fields	1	None	Unlim.	32	30	Y	N	Y	0
Incorporates business rules and data validation criteria	Y	Y	Y	Y	Y	Y	N	Y	Y
Can user retrieve approved timesheet for adjustments	Y	Y	Y	Y	Y	Y	N	Y	Y
Can retrieve feature be turned off?	Y	Y	Y	Y	Y	Y	N	Y	Y
Timecard adjustments recorded in audit trail	Y	Y	Y	Y	Y	Y	Y	Y	Y
ETC in effort	Y	Y	Y	Y	Y	Y	Y	Y	Y
ETC in duration	Y	N	Y	Y	N	Y	Y	Y	Y
Remaining duration	Y	N	Y	Y	N	Y	Y	Y	Y
Reports									
Creates a report identifying changes made to the schedule	Y	Y	Y	Y	Y	Y	Y	Y	Y
Exception reports	Y	Y	Y	Y	Y	Y	Y	Y	Y
Summary reports	Y	Y	Y	Y	Y	Y	Y	Y	Y
Web enablement									
Can timesheet be updated through a Web browser?	Y	Y	Y	Y	Y	Y	Y	Y	Y
Which browsers/versions are supported?	Netscape 3.0/up, Explorer 4.0/up	Explorer 4.0, Netscape	All Java enabled	All	IE, Netscape	Netscape Navigator, MS Internet Explorer, any Java-enabled browser	All 3.0+	Browser independent	Explorer 4.0 or later
Security									
Approver security	Y	Y	Y	Y	Y	Y	Y	Y	Y
Alternate approvers	Y	Y	Y	Y	Y	Y	N	Y	Y
Field level security: lock specific fields	N	Y	Y	Y	Y	Y	Y	Y	Y
Management validation: approve/reject electronically	Y	Y	Y	Y	Y	Y	Y	Y	Y
Miscellaneous									
Runs served (doesn't have to be installed on each client)	N	N	Y	Y	Y	Y	Y	Y	N
Drill-Down/roll-Up	Y	Y	Y	Y	Y	Y	Y	Y	Y

Reporting

Report writer	Y	N	Y	N	Y	Y	Y	Y	Y
Report wizard	N	N	N	Y	Y	N	Y	N	Y
Publishes as HTML	Y	N	Y	Y	Y	N	Y	Y	Y
Number of user-defined fields	0	N	N	Varies	Y	32	Unlim.	Multiple	Unlim.
Drill-down/roll-up *	Y	N	Y	Y	Y	Y	Y	Y	Y
Import/export	Y	N	N	Y	Y	Y	Y	Y	Y
Automatic E-mail notification *	N	N	N	Y	Y	N	Y	N	Y
* Macro recorder/batch capable	N	N	N	Y	Y	N	Y	Y	Y
Can "canned" reports be modified?	Y	N	Y	Y	Y	Y	Y	Y	Y
Sort, filter	Y	N	Y	Y	Y	Y	Y	Y	Y

Architecture

Databases supported (list):	MS Access, Oracle, MS SQL Server	Oracle, MS SQL Server, Sybase	Btrieve	Oracle, MS SQL Server, Sybase, Informix any JDBC-enabled database	MS SQL Server, Sybase, Oracle	All ODBC	Oracle, Sybase, MS SQL Server, FoxPro, MS Access	Oracle, MS Access	MS SQL Server, Oracle, Sybase, SQL Anywhere
Supports distributed databases	Y	Y	Y	Y	Y	Y	Y	Y	N
Three-tier client/server	Y	Y	Y	Y	Y	Y	Y	Y	Y
Client operating systems	Win 95/98/NT	Browser	Win 95/98/NT	Win 95/NT, Unix, Linux, any Java-enabled OS	Win 95/98/NT	Win 95/NT/3.x, Unix	Win 95/98/NT, Java	Win 95/NT/3.x	Win 95/NT
Server operating systems	Win, Unix	Unix, Win NT	Win NT	Win 95/NT, Unix, Linux, any Java-enabled OS	Win NT	Win 95/NT/3.x, Unix	Any	Unix, Win NT	Win NT
Network operating systems	Win, Novell	Multiple	Any TCP/IP	Win 95/NT, Unix, Linux, any Java-enabled OS		Win, Novell	Any	Novell, Win NT	Novell, Win NT, Banyan

Timesheets

Feature	Project Integrator 2.0 Enterprise Edition	time controller	TimeControl	TimeScope	TimeWizard	WebProject	Webster 2.1 for Primavera	WebTime & TimeReview	WorkLink Progress Sheet
Minimum client configuration	P166 MHz, 16 MB RAM, 30 MB HD	16 MB RAM	Win: 16 MB RAM, 12 MB disk. Java: Any Java-enabled browser including Win, Unix, etc.	1.5 MB RAM, 2 MB disk	Pentium, 16 MB memory	Web-enabled browser	8 MB RAM 2.5 HD, Win 95	Browser dependent	Pentium, 24 MB
Minimum server configuration	P166 MHz, 16 MB RAM, 30 MB HD	64 MB RAM	Dependent on database	5 MB RAM, 5 MB disk	Varies	Win 95/NT, Unix, Linux, any Java-enabled OS	32 RAM, 10 HD, Win NT 4.0 SP3, TCP/IP	Pentium w/128 MB	Pentium, 32 MB
Client runs under Web browser	Y	Y	Y	Y	Y	Y	Y	Y	N
Open architecture									
Supports OLE	Y	Y	Y	Y	N	N	N	N	Y
Documented Object Model	N	Y	N	Y/N	N	N	Y	N	N
Documented Application Programming Interface (API)	N	Y	N	Y/N	N	N	Y	N	N
Simultaneous edit of data file	Y	Y	Y	Y	Y	Y	Y	Y	Y
Does product have a programming language?	N	Y	N	Y/N	N	N	N	N	N
Are years stored as four-digit numbers?	Y	Y	Y	Y	Y	Y	Y	Y	Y
Online help									
Right mouse click	N	Y	Y	N	N	N	Y	N	Y
Hover buttons	Y	Y	Y	N	N	Y	Y	N	Y
Interactive help	N	N	Y	Y	Y	Y	Y	N	Y
Help search feature	Y	Y	Y	Y	Y	Y	Y	Y	Y
Web access to product knowledge base *	Y	Y	Y	Y	N		N	N	Y
Vendor information									
Training									
Computer-based training	N	N	N	Y	N	N	N	N	N
Training materials available	Y	Y	Y	Y	Y	Y	N	Y	Y
Customized training materials	Y	Y	Y	Y	Y	Y	N	Y	Y
Online tutorial	N	N	N	N	N	Y	Y	N	N

Consulting available from vendor	Y	Y	Y	Y	Y	Y	Y	Y
Site license discounts	Y	Y	Y	Y	Y	N	N	Y
Enhancement requests *	Y	Y	Y	Y	Y	Y	Y	Y
Modify source code, support through upgrades *	Y	N	Y	Y	Y	Y	Y	Y
Global presence								
Global offices	N	Y	Y	Y	Y	N	N	Y
Multilingual technical support	N	Y	N	Y	Y	Y	N	Y
Language versions (list):	Eng	Eng, but the interface is modifiable by end users into other languages	Eng	Fr, Ger	Eng, Ger	Eng, Ger, Fr, Span, Port, Ital	Eng	Eng, Fr, Ital
Audit Software Quality Assurance process? *	Y	Y	N	Y	Y	N	Y	Y
Security								
Configurable access priviledges *	Y	Y	Y	Y	Y	Y	Y	Y
Passwords expire (forced update)	Y	N	N	N	Y	N	N	Y
Electronic approvals	Y	Y	Y	Y	Y	Y	Y	Y
Password protect files	DBMS	Y	Y	N	Y	Y	Y	Y

Vendor Responses to Narrative Questions

Timesheets

ABT Connect and ABT Team (ABT Corporation)

Describe what the product is designed to do.

ABT Connect and ABT Team provide two implementation approaches for secure time capture/ team update. ABT Connect provides a Web-based option, and ABT Team provides a client/server option.

Top three product differentiators; describe what makes your product unique.

1. Robust project management repository.
2. Highly integrated tool set.
3. Flexible time capture/team communciations functionality.

To what business processes can this tool be applied?

Program and project management processes; resource management processes; process management processes.

Describe the ideal end user environment for the current version of your product (size of organization, level of project management sophistication, effort and commitment required).

ABT Connect and ABT Team can benefit organizations of fifty to fifty thousand project-related resources, whatever the level of project management maturity.

Future strategies for this product.

Extend functionality and enhance scalability.

Product's target market.

Enterprise project management.

What are your product's three main benefits? (How does using the product add value to the customer?)

1. Improved executive decision-making.
2. The discipline of 100 percent time capture is extended to the organization.
3. Improved resource utilization.

Describe your quality management process. List any relevant certifications.

ABT's test enginering organization provides extensive in-house product quality testing, using a series of proprietary testing methodologies supplemented by external resources, to perform activities such as high-volume benchmarking. ABT's test group has also been instrumental in contributing to the definition of IEEE Year 2000 testing standards.

Discuss your product pricing structure. Include volume discount levels, concurrent user options, site licenses, cost of implementation, and other issues.

Pricing is on a named-user basis. List prices: ABT Connect/ABT Team—$100. Volume discounts apply.

Cost of implementation: Rapid implementation—six-week process enablement around RM tool set = $75k. Additional services include project management maturity evaluation, tool training, project management concepts training, process customization and implementation, and systems integration/custom programming work.

Annual maintenance (client support program) = 15 percent of purchase price.

AMS REALTIME Solo

Describe what the product is designed to do.

Employee timecards provide a graphic list of all assigned tasks. Employees can choose from assigned tasks and post actual hours by task, hours, and minutes or by percentage of a working day. Employees can be given access rights to use drill-down menus to report unplanned work. Nonproject tasks, such as sick and vacation time, are also tracked.

Employees can enter estimates-to-complete by task to communicate early or late expected completions. Employees can see the impact of their own level-of-effort changes on the complete dates for their parts of the work for each task.

Organization hierarchy and access controls provide a security layer to ensure data integrity and protection. Management approval of actuals and estimates provide data verification.

Top three product differentiators; describe what makes your product unique.

1. Remote timesheets can be customized by any company to maintain a corporate image. Project and resource management modules interact in a way that mirrors real workflow processes, giving real-time visibility of accurate status information. Fully integrated schedule, resource, and cost give you an accurate look at one or more projects from any perspective.

2. AMS REALTIME Resources has a fast and powerful database that is both efficient and fully extendable, allowing unprecedented customization. Linked tables allow for efficient and powerful data access and control. ODBC drivers allow external access to the data, including calculated reports.

3. All software runs native on Windows (95, NT, 3.x), Macintosh, Sun, Solaris, HP, and RS with identical look and feel and direct data access from any platform.

To what business processes can this tool be applied?

AMS REALTIME time-reporting tools are generally used in operational work, or any kind of process where communication is critical to measure progress and changes. AMS REALTIME is designed to allow automated project statusing that automatically feeds earned value performance measurements. Communication between employees doing the work and managers tracking the work is automated, providing everyone with a clear picture of the work needs.

Describe the ideal end user environment for the current version of your product (size of organization, level of project management sophistication, effort and commitment required).

AMS REALTIME is used by global companies in very large enterprise environments, all the way down to small companies with just a few people. While AMS REALTIME is used to support extremely sophisticated project management processes, it can still be used to benefit users with little or no project management background. Users can grow into the software as their project management expertise evolves. To make any project management implementation successful, senior management must be committed to supporting the process, and other participants must make the effort to be trained to use the tools and follow through. Working with a consultant to help adapt the software to your business practices and needs and to document these processes is the best way to ensure success.

Future strategies for this product.

Future development strategies include more active Web enablements, a more complex three-tiered server design to facilitate global replication, and more resource tools. AMS has always been on the cutting edge of technology, and we are dedicated to bringing our customers the best of this ever-changing world.

Product's target market.

Products are used across a wide variety of client bases. AMS does not target any particular market, but is widely used in manufacturing, oil and gas, nuclear power, automotive, pharmaceutical, aerospace, software development, construction, research and development, and many other industries. AMS REALTIME software allows for a flexible implementation that integrates with customer business processes and organization structure.

What are your product's three main benefits? (How does using the product add value to the customer?)

1. Remote access allows users who are off-site to report their time and see plan changes. Resources can be effectively utilized by providing managers with visibility and control over planned, unplanned, and nonproject work.

2. All work assignments are instantly communicated to employees, who also have a medium to effectively communicate work performed, status, and other issues. Organizational hierarchy and access control protects data access and viability.

3. Selective automation allows managers to eliminate drudgery and inaccuracy, while still maintaining control over critical project and resource decisions.

Describe your quality management process. List any relevant certifications.

Advanced Management Solutions is fully committed to providing the highest quality software and services to all our clients. We have implemented many internal standards and processes in order to ensure that we can track and manage our software development process to the highest standard of quality possible. Concurrent versions system has been implemented to help manage multiple programmers at multiple development sites. Peer review of source code and design strategy meetings with high-level program development leaders continue to ensure that our software remains on the leading edge of our evolving technology.

A dedicated testing department manages the initial alpha testing, which encompasses new functionality, system process testing, and full regression testing. Beta testing is initially performed internally. After a stable point has been reached, beta testing is extended to select client users. Client beta testing not only provides clients with an edge in using new software features, but also greatly expands the test environment scope relating to different hardware environments. As AMS REALTIME is one of the most flexible and highly configurable management products on the market today, client testing adds an exceptional dimension to our testing process.

Discuss your product pricing structure. Include volume discount levels, concurrent user options, site licenses, cost of implementation, and other issues.

Product price is different for clients, based on their requirements for software and implementation. Volume discounts and site licenses are available. Please request a quote from an AMS sales representative for your specific requirements.

Cost of implementation: Annual maintenance is based on 20 percent of the current product cost, and includes all software upgrades (while support is active) and telephone hotline technical support. Training cost is based upon topics, requirements, training equipment and site, and days requested. Please request a quote from an AMS sales representative for your specific requirements.

Artemis TrackView

Describe what the product is designed to do.

Artemis TrackView is a simple, effective time-tracking system designed to give organizations visibility and understanding of staff activities around the world. It is designed for project staff, resource managers and project managers. It provides clear, detailed effort tracking through a LAN-based or Windows application.

Top three product differentiators; describe what makes your product unique.

1. Timesheet tool for both local and remote users.
2. Scalable up to thousands of users.
3. Integrated with other Views applications such that its data is used to update plans held in ProjectView, or used as input for existing billing and financial systems.

To what business processes can this tool be applied?

TrackView enables managers to assign, approve and track staff activity around the world, and consolidate and report on this information in a way that is meaningful to an organization. It enables project managers and resource managers to monitor and approve work against assigned and unassigned work.

Describe the ideal end-user environment for the current version of your product (size of organization, level of project management sophistication, effort and commitment required).

For organizations where people are the critical resource, tracking time and effort is essential.

Both the ad-hoc and the most sophisticated organization, in terms of project management, as well and the large or small organization make for ideal user environment.

Future strategies for this product.

Artemis is committed to continually enhancing our product's functionality and applicability to meet or exceed the demands of project management professionals.

Product's target market.

Artemis products are used in over twenty-five industry sectors from banking and finance to aerospace and defense. Any organization that wants to improve their results using a project-centric management technique can benefit from using the Views suite of products.

What are your product's three main benefits? (How does using the product add value to the customer?)

1. Track View helps organizations identify key resources and activities, update project performance, and gain an accurate view of staff progress and performance.
2. In turn, this enables managers to prevent redundant effort, set and update realistic project goals, and make better business decisions.

Describe your quality management process. List any relevant certifications.

Internal software audits and reporting procedures. Formal Year 2000 testing and compliance process.

Discuss your product pricing structure. Include volume discount levels, concurrent user options, site licenses, cost of implementation, and other issues.

Artemis Views can be purchased and deployed as a fully integrated suite or as a series of independent applications. Available as registered user and concurrent pricing. Volume discounts and site licenses are available. Implementation costs vary.

AutoPLAN Enterprise (Digital Tools)

Describe what the product is designed to do.

AutoPLAN Enterprise Release 4 is a Web-based software and process solution to help high-tech, engineering, and telecommunications companies predict, control, and improve cycle time of critical program development and deployment. The solution set provides deep functionality across the entire spectrum of product life-cycle elements including pipeline management, project management, resource alignment, process effectiveness, and document support and team collaboration. AutoPLAN Enterprise integrates realistic planning, resource-centric management, status and forecast tracking, team collaboration, process support, escalation management, and program execution across globally distributed organizations.

Organizations are evolving from functional teams to matrix or program teams, and this is creating cross-functional or multidisciplinary project teams. AutoPLAN Enterprise recognizes three different organizational patterns that coexist: dynamic peer-to-peer, functional, and program management. AutoPLAN Enterprise offers these organizations both project-centric and resource-centric management. AutoPLAN Enterprise addresses everyone involved in product development and deployment including executives; program, product, resource, and project managers; and team leaders and team members, as well as teams from marketing, operations, service, and quality.

As a result of extensive process and product consulting with clients engaged in new product development and deployment, DTI has distilled four key reasons why products are late and descoped:

1. Product development pipeline and deployment structures that are not aligned with the company's time-to-market goals.

2. Unrealistic plans, overcommitted resources, and unmanaged cross-functional dependencies.

3. Status and forecast decisions that are based on hearsay, rather than on facts or experience.

4. A lack of consistent processes that fit the company culture and practice, which is further exacerbated by distributed cross-functional teams.

Avoiding late and descoped products requires an overall view of product and project status, the involvement of cross-functional teams, and decision evaluation tools. Increasingly accelerated product development cycles and shorter product life cycles require organizations to disseminate information quickly to remain competitive. To support today's geographically dispersed product development environments, organizations require a common platform that enables effective cross-functional collaboration and communication on product development issues. It is also imperative that the introduction of new product information can be easily accessible by each stakeholder. Common platforms and accessible information by each stakeholder will result in accelerated organizational learning and decision-making within the organization.

DTI has created a cycle time management (CTM) framework comprising both application and process support. This framework emphasizes the critical components involved in introducing and deploying the right products and services to the market at the right time. Introducing and deploying these products and services requires companies to institute well-defined new product planning and execution processes, complemented with customer management and performance measurement processes. The new planning processes should consist of product portfolio, technology portfolio, product planning, and resource planning. The execution processes must consist of advanced technology development, platform development, product development, market introduction and deployment.

CTM enables companies to strike a balance between flexibility and discipline that is tailored to their organization and culture. The CTM framework supports a flexible *shrink-to-fit* process, which is adaptable to an organization's process maturity. This process will provide a road map for decision-making and progress tracking within a new product introduction and deployment pipeline.

CTM consists of six fundamental elements: 1) processes, 2) projects, 3) resources, 4) documents, 5) deliverables, and 6) analysis. These six elements form the foundation objectives that drive AutoPLAN Enterprise. Organizations require a well-defined and structured process to accomplish their goals. Projects make up the mechanisms through which detailed plans and schedules are generated, executed, and tracked. Every organization faces resource constraints; thus, resource management is a critical component of CTM. All projects have deliverables associated with them either in the form of documents or the product itself. And, all projects must be managed to ensure quality deliverables. Analysis tools enable various levels of stakeholders to evaluate and ensure proper support of all elements necessary to meet CTM objectives.

Top three product differentiators; describe what makes your product unique.

1. AutoPLAN Enterprise enables organizations to manage their pipeline of resources across programs and across the phase gates of each project. It assures an escalation process for critical issues, such as overallocations, by monitoring boundary conditions and alerting appropriate people to the issues. Project managers are interested in the completion of tasks or milestones, while resource managers need to know all of the work planned for their resources. Both project and resource managers must collaborate to create realistic plans for meeting project objectives, as well as juggle those resources and plans on a day-to-day basis as changes occur. The nature of this work requires a resource-centric view of the plan, not just an activity-centric view. A resource-centric view will allow resource managers to view and allocate activities to their scarce resources, rather than allocating resources to their activities. AutoPLAN Enterprise enables resource management by providing a resource-centric Gantt bar that displays overallocated resources. Managing overallocations can be as easy as reassigning activities to another resource.

Program management is a collaborative effort. Success depends upon identifying and communicating critical issues. Such identification and communication must be inherent in the system. AutoPLAN Enterprise is designed with a communications backbone. A mechanism of triggers identifies critical issues (e.g., when milestone or cost exceeds a threshold boundary) and automatically alerts and draws attention to these critical issues. Project bulletin boards within AutoPLAN Enterprise also enhance communication by providing a context-sensitive vehicle for communicating information across the project team. In addition, AutoPLAN Enterprise supports electronic mail systems, enabling triggers and bulletin board messages to be communicated to the various levels of stakeholders.

2. AutoPLAN Enterprise supports the distributed nature of project teams by matching real-world strategy with key scalable technologies. Enterprise customers need distributed project management capabilities that cater to multisite resource management, work distribution, progress tracking, global scheduling, consolidation, reporting, integration, and collaboration. DTI has met this challenge by investing over one hundred man-years in an enterprise-level, three-tier, distributed client/server architecture that leverages both Java and Internet technologies. AutoPLAN Enterprise provides full support for multiple internal operating divisions and external suppliers. AutoPLAN Enterprise leverages many platforms—Internet, Windows, NT, and Unix—providing reliable access across the organization. Additionally, AutoPLAN Enterprise enables common project data to be shared by different projects at different locations while being maintained in a central data center that is managed by pool server software. Project data is maintained at each geographic location on either individual or multiple servers, depending on the number of internal operating divisions and projects. A divisional pool server can also be implemented to share the project data within divisional projects. AutoPLAN Enterprise application servers are capable of scalable distributed processing, and only the server needs the capacity for large multiproject operations. AutoPLAN Enterprise has multiserver cross-project dependency links. For example, the owner of a schedule that depends on the completion of activities in another project can create cross-project links that automatically update his schedule when changes occur in the other project, even if that project resides on a different server.

3. AutoPLAN Enterprise leverages client/server/Web technologies. The promise of Java, which AutoPLAN Enterprise supports, is that enterprise deployments, including organizations with heterogeneous environments, can be cost-effectively supported. DTI Web products are easier to use than Microsoft Project and are cheaper to deploy. The rapid spread of Internet protocols and Web servers into corporate infrastructure make the Internet an ideal vehicle to support both enterprise computing and mobile employees. In addition, systems administration is simplified since no maintenance is required on the client side.

A very practical use of AutoPLAN Enterprise Web clients is that they can run in a disconnected mode on the Internet. With AutoPLAN Enterprise, the user can simply log on and save activities and other information to a local file. She can then continue to work while disconnected. At any time, the connection can be reestablished, either remotely or locally, and the data is resynchronized. This may be useful for dial-up connections when working remotely. The Web server handles all communications with the Web clients, whether they are communicating via the Internet, dial-up, LAN, or WAN. The AutoPLAN Enterprise Web clients can be run from any browser that supports Java 1.1, and the Web server will dynamically download the Java code to run the application on the client. DTI's Web strategy supports *thin* client computing. In this case, database-oriented servers are serving lightweight clients through Web servers and standard protocols. The AutoPLAN Enterprise Web clients are ideally suited for running on a Java-based network computer.

To what business processes can this tool be applied?

From business analysis and redesign to system implementation and training, DTI has established its own process to support the customer through all phases of CTM system implementation. However, as to applying AutoPLAN Enterprise to the customer's business processes, DTI takes a very pragmatic approach. DTI has established processes to help customers with the following seven business pains:

1. Managing the development and deployment pipeline in detail.

2. Top-down and bottom-up planning that enables managers to use team members' knowledge during up-front planning.

3. Juggling resources realistically, so that resources are not overcommitted and parochial allocations are not made, but rather a mechanism for cooperation on resource tradeoffs is created.

4. Creating an organizational memory that captures organizational experience for reuse the next time.

5. Obtaining weekly integrated tracking information on how programs are progressing against their plans. This can be achieved by capturing actual time spent, estimates-to-complete, percent complete, and actual start and finish.

6. Problem identification, escalation, and collaboration that allows management and the team to receive adequate notice of impending issues.

7. Interactive decision evaluation to understand the domino effect of a problem in one project and its possible cross-program impact, and obtain a swift resolution between participants.

Any combination of these processes will help organizations better understand and make use of critical path methodology, work breakdown structures, resource management, cost and earned value techniques, multiproject resource scheduling, resource allocation, status tracking, report generation, matrix management solutions, integration with other systems, middleware design, project management process design, project rollups, report generation, database design, customized product training courses, generic project management training, and more.

Describe the ideal end-user environment for the current version of your product (size of organization, level of project management sophistication, effort and commitment required).

AutoPLAN Enterprise is ideal for high-tech, engineering, and telecommunications organizations engaged in distributed product development and deployments. Its usage also extends to these organizations' distributors and partners. The role-based nature of AutoPLAN Enterprise spans all people involved, from executive management to the entire cross-functional product team. This includes experienced project and program managers, resource and development managers, and the team members creating or deploying the product. The AutoPLAN Enterprise Web client is specifically designed for those team leaders who are not full-time, experienced project managers. In fact, DTI has designed the AutoPLAN Enterprise Web client to be easier to use and more functional than Microsoft Project.

Organizations can start at either the program level right away and manage the overall pipeline of projects and resources at the business unit level, or at the individual project level. The Auto-PLAN Enterprise Web client is not only easier to use than Microsoft Project, but is also capable of managing cross-functional dependencies and resources and offering enterprise scalability when the organization is ready to expand.

Coordinating distributed projects is a difficult task. It involves resources not only from multiple projects, but also from multiple functions within those projects. The program manager responsible must understand all of the interactions and milestones required to complete the project, but he cannot and should not develop and manage the entire plan himself. Instead, he should rely on the distributed functional leaders who are responsible for their piece of the project to plan and execute that piece. As a program manager, he needs to be able to integrate the individual team plans into a single comprehensive project plan. In many organizations, this integration of people and data is difficult; AutoPLAN Enterprise is designed to help with this. Having processes in place, underpinned by enterprise software, is key to predicting, controlling, and improving product/project cycle times.

Future strategies for this product.

AutoPLAN Enterprise has been designed with an integrated product management platform for all information related to meeting CTM objectives. DTI will continue to support features needed for CTM, including pipeline and portfolio management. Future strategies will enhance the ability of customers to make informed decisions based on a comprehensive presentation of relevant data with powerful drill-down capabilities, further collaborative features that utilize the intranet and Internet, and continuing support for the free-flowing nature of the engineering culture. Application wizards will help first-time users, accelerate deployment, and reduce training cost. Process support is key to productivity improvements and to adhering to organizationwide standards. Existing process-support capabilities will be enhanced using the capabilities of Web technology and with more exchange of information across subsystems. Large organizations are geographically distributed to take advantage of global efficiencies. Local and global workgroups must collaborate and respond quickly to changing environment and work content. Both executive management and front-line team members must have access anytime, anywhere, and in any manner to enterprisewide product/project information located on geographically distributed servers. Existing multiserver capabilities of AutoPLAN Enterprise are being enhanced using Oracle.

AutoPLAN Enterprise will support key technologies including Oracle, NT 5.0, middleware, and Java. Distributed objects capability using industry-standard specifications such as CORBA will be incorporated. In addition, the AutoPLAN Enterprise application-programming interface will provide CORBA-compliant objects for seamless integration with other applications. The collaboration capabilities of AutoPLAN Enterprise will be enhanced by incorporating a workflow server. This workflow server will be based on industry-standard specifications and will incorporate process modeling and messaging components to enable customers to configure the collaboration features based upon their business needs. The security system will have additional features to address the security risks associated with the Internet. Directory servers conforming to LDAP standards will be incorporated for seamless integration with the underlying operating environment. This in turn will provide responsive security, configurability, and flexibility features.

Product's target market.

AutoPLAN Enterprise is specifically designed to support high-tech, engineering, and telecommunications organizations in predicting, controlling, and improving cycle time of critical program development and deployment.

What are your product's three main benefits? (How does using the product add value to the customer?)

1. AutoPLAN Enterprise provides at least a 10 percent improvement in enterprise time-to-market of product development and deployment. Viewing the value of CTM from an annual R&D cost perspective: consider a product development group of one thousand people, with an annual R&D expenditure of $100M. A modest 10 percent improvement would represent a cost savings value of $10M, with a revenue enhancement value of three to five times this.

2. AutoPLAN Enterprise facilitates an organization's transformation from functional project teams to matrix, or program-organized high-performance project teams. It also supports distributed teams resulting from acquisitions. It does both of these by providing built-in communication and rollup features from distributed multiserver projects. This support enables teamwide problem identification, escalation, collaboration, and resolution. AutoPLAN Enterprise recognizes that three

different organizational patterns coexist: 1) dynamic peer-to-peer, 2) functional, and 3) program management. AutoPLAN Enterprise offers these organizations both project-centric and resource-centric management.

3. AutoPLAN Enterprise accommodates joint ventures, subcontracting, mergers and acquisitions, and reorganizations by leveraging the Web to minimize deployment and support costs. The creation of plans, assignment of work, and integration of activities across multiple functions and distributed work teams is critically important. However, that is only part of the story. With the Internet, AutoPLAN Enterprise can also efficiently equip thousands of personnel involved in the product-development process with the information they need to do the best possible job. Demand for skilled workers has been great, and turnover has risen as employees move from one company or job to another. The best practices in the world are of no value to a company if those who know those practices move on without first passing along the knowledge. Best practices developed at one site need to be shared with other sites, and a process for doing that is required. AutoPLAN Enterprise solves these problems through URL references and retrieval capability. With URL features, AutoPLAN Enterprise can help preserve best practices and other information and disseminate them geographically and functionally to team members currently doing the job. AutoPLAN Enterprise can also have associated URL references that point to mission-critical information/documentation that will enable product/project teams to achieve the activity. These references can also be attached to the top-level program schedule for project leader use, or at specific functional schedules (e.g., to provide sourcing with specific third-party vendor requirements). URLs can enable:

■ Sharing best practice information from one team to another
■ Referencing documentation with checklists
■ Sharing engineering notes on installation processes.

Also, with the speed of organizational changes, a mix of project-scheduling system usage is expected. As most people are educated on Microsoft Project, AutoPLAN Enterprise can coexist with its projects and data. AutoPLAN Enterprise's GUIs are not only familiar to Microsoft Project users, the Web version is easier and thus leverages simplicity and ease of use with enterprise functionality.

Describe your quality management process. List any relevant certifications.

DTI achieves excellence in product quality and customer satisfaction through its quality management process. DTI's quality objective is to build quality into its products and services at all stages of product life cycle from requirement collection to customer usage. DTI's dedication to quality is reflected in its quality mission: "Doing things right the first time."

DTI's quality management group performs the functions of the software engineering process group as defined by the industry-standard CMM. The quality management group plans and implements DTI's quality system, which consists of processes and guidelines. The processes detail out *what* is required for converting a set of inputs to outputs in the form of activities and tasks, primary and cooperative responsibilities, deliverables, and entry and exit criteria. The guidelines detail *how* to carry out the identified activities to ensure quality and consistency. The involvement of DTI personnel at all levels is fundamental to the implementation of the quality process. DTI personnel are drawn from various groups in the organization to author processes and guidelines, and all undergo training programs on the quality system.

DTI follows processes within Level 2 and Level 3 of the CMM. Some of the key processes within these levels include market requirement analysis, functional specification, high- and low-level design, coding, testing, release management, customer support, training, and maintenance. In addition, in-depth reviews are built into each of these processes.

DTI recognizes that enterprise growth and profitability are significantly impacted by time-to-market of new products in globally competitive high-tech markets. With this in mind, DTI's product development and quality processes are focused on meeting customer needs and requirements. Therefore, DTI collaborates with its customers both in product definition and in assuring that the product functions are implemented as intended. To facilitate the fast-track delivery of innovative products and services, DTI has created process initiatives for increased test automation, usage of tools that will enable teams to better assess the quality of their work products, management of development tools, reuse of objects across products, and tightly controlled configuration management.

DTI's quality management process focuses on periodic reviews and feedback, which are a means of monitoring the adherence of organizational activities to the process. Corrective and preventive actions play an important role in continuous improvement of the quality system and thereby the organizational activities.

DTI has a well-qualified team for quality management. DTI's teams, besides having the appropriate educational qualifications, have quality management-related certifications; some are certified quality analysts, and some hold certificates related to the CMM and its use. Many also have extensive internal audit experience.

The quality management group interacts periodically with key personnel of different functions within the organization and identifies new processes, guidelines, and improvements within the existing framework. The general approach to new process/guideline introduction is to discuss with representative users, define the process, pilot the process after review, evaluate the pilot implementation, revise the process based on feedback, plan organizationwide implementation, implement, measure, and maintain.

DTI is planning to get CMM certification at the appropriate level. The approach that would be followed for securing the certification includes mapping key process areas of the CMM to existing processes, identifying the *gaps*, preparing the implementation plan that describes how these gaps will be addressed, and executing the plan.

Discuss your product pricing structure. Include volume discount levels, concurrent user options, site licenses, cost of implementation, and other issues.

DTI's objective is to offer an integrated solution with a pricing structure that is based on enterprise requirements reflecting enterprise needs and individual needs. AutoPLAN Enterprise supports a floating license configuration, which allows any user to log into the system and consume one license. When the user has finished with the application, that license will be released for other users. Each floating license provides one concurrent use of the product. AutoPLAN Enterprise also supports a personal license configuration. Typical installations will use both personal and concurrent licensing.

Annual product maintenance is 15 percent of the list cost. Product maintenance entitles customers to engineering patches, updates, and upgrades, and phone, fax, and E-mail response to issues. Professional services are separate from DTI product maintenance. As part of the business relationship with customers, DTI takes part in joint planning to identify the customer's business needs and services sought from DTI. Professional services are charged separately on an as-needed basis. These services are performed either at the customer site, online, or at DTI's headquarters in Cupertino, California. Professional services typically fall into two categories: 1) product consulting/implementation design review and 2) implementation support. Product consulting/implementation design review discusses areas such as, "How do I apply the software with a suitable process to solve a business need?" and, "Which processes will we implement, how, and when to meet organizational objectives?" Implementation support consists of product training, project office services, upgrade migration services, systems administration services, and integration services.

Cascade WEBTime (Mantix)

Describe what the product is designed to do.

Cascade WEBTime captures vital data from across the enterprise to provide you with the most accurate picture of how staff time is being used, future resource requirements, and project progress. Accessed via a standard browser and the intranet/Internet, WEBTime allows all of the team members to report directly into the program database with timesheets, forecasts, and commentary on progress and issues. This input is via a simple form, without the need to access project/program management systems.

Project and line managers review and approve the bookings of each of their staff, and at the same time are alerted to any new issues or changes in the plan. The system provides comprehensive tabular and graphical reporting as standard. The intuitive end-user reporting tool also provides the ability to create ad-hoc reports and additional analysis. WEBTime includes a standard interface with Cascade PgM and Cascade Version 4 program management systems to enable automatic updating of progress, cost, and forecast across all of your projects.

Top three product differentiators; describe what makes your product unique.

Access is via the intranet or the World Wide Web; the only software required on the client machine is a standard browser. This allows for easy global communication and simple system maintenance.

Information entered through WEBTime is stored directly in an Oracle database, thereby ensuring complete data integrity. Partially completed timesheets can be saved for later submission, and all bookings are validated by the assigned manager. The timesheets are prefilled with tasks that have been assigned to the individual in the planning system. Unplanned task information can be entered and passed back.

To what business processes can this tool be applied?

Cascade WEBTime can be applied to any business process that requires people to work on projects. The information it provides is essential for project performance monitoring and control.

Describe the ideal end user environment for the current version of your product (size of organization, level of project management sophistication, effort and commitment required).

The concepts behind Cascade WEBTime and the software architecture are completely scaleable. Any size of organization, from local operations up to global enterprises of many thousands of users, would benefit from Cascade WEBTime, irrespective of the level of project management sophistication. The effort and commitment required to implement Cascade WEBTime depends on the customer's requirements for the system and the existing business processes. The ease of use and simplicity of the forms typically allows WEBTime to be quickly implemented.

Future strategies for this product.

Mantix Systems will continue to develop Cascade WEBTime to ensure that it remains a world-leading program management solution.

Product's target market.

As a leading program management solution's provider, Mantix Systems has a proven track record with some of the world's leading organizations in fifteen countries. This is in markets that include telecommunications, IT, utilities, government, pharmaceuticals, aerospace, and defense.

What are your product's three main benefits? (How does using the product add value to the customer?)

Implementing WEBTime along with Cascade PgM allows the project team members to better communicate and collaborate with project and resource managers. Keeping track of individuals' time helps organizations manage to their most valuable and scarce resource—people. Finally, WEBTime allows organizations to get valuable R&D tax credits.

Describe your quality management process. List any relevant certifications.

The quality management process within Mantix Systems is accredited by and conforms to ISO 9000.

Discuss your product pricing structure. Include volume discount levels, concurrent user options, site licenses, cost of implementation, and other issues.

The price of Cascade WEBTime depends on the type of functionality required and the number of users. Please contact Mantix Systems for details that are specific to your requirements.

Dekker Inergy (DTMI)

Describe what the product is designed to do.

The electronic timecard (ETC) provides a timely labor reporting and billing system to meet the requirements of project-oriented companies. The system provides an in-depth solution for both managers (in charge of projects within a matrix organization) and accountants (responsible for collecting billing and payroll information). In environments where a time collection system is already established, Inergy's ETC module can be used to accumulate timecard information from a job cost system to help managers determine time-charging trends on either a project or an enterprisewide basis. The system provides complete human resource management functionality and employee credential history for companies that need to keep in compliance with various government regulations and ISO 9000.

Top three product differentiators; describe what makes your product unique.

1. Integrates directly with all TRAKKER modules.
2. Extensive direct/indirect rate management features.
3. Integrates with Microsoft Office and Back Office tools.

To what business processes can this tool be applied?

Time collection, payroll backup, billing, human resource management, and employee credential management.

Describe the ideal end user environment for the current version of your product (size of organization, level of project management sophistication, effort and commitment required).

Dekker Inergy is targeted for organizations of one thousand or more employees with an enterprise requirement for time collection. Inergy is designed to simplify the time-collection process while improving the accuracy and timeliness of data.

Future strategies for this product.

To further enhance the integration of Inergy with Microsoft Office and Microsoft Back Office tools. In addition, DTMI is planning Web-based implementations of Inergy.

Product's target market.

R&D, government, software, medical, electronics, and aerospace.

What are your product's three main benefits? (How does using the product add value to the customer?)

1. Integration with activity-based costing and project accounting—TRAKKER.
2. Integration with MS Office and MS Back Office.
3. Simplicity of use for the timecard user.

Describe your quality management process. List any relevant certifications.

DTMI has modeled our development process from the Microsoft model while incorporating the quality guidelines established in ISO 9000.

Discuss your product pricing structure. Include volume discount levels, concurrent user options, site licenses, cost of implementation, and other issues.

DTMI offers both single and concurrent user licenses of TRAKKER. Our flexible pricing enables both small and large organizations to cost effectively implement costing and earned value. TRAKKER pricing includes a progressive discount for volume purchases with reasonable thresholds for single and multisite licenses.

Further, DTMI offers both public and private training courses for both new and advanced users. DTMI also offers consulting services to support the enterprise implementation of TRAKKER.

Cost of implementation: DTMI provides training for both the discipline of scheduling and attributes of TRAKKER. These workshops include Basic Project Management, TRAKKER Application Workshop, TRAKKER Intermediate Workshop, TRAKKER Report Writer Workshop, and TRAKKER MIS Integrator's Workshop. Through these courses, an enterprise can completely implement the TRAKKER system.

In addition to our classroom training, DTMI offers consulting services to guide users though a structured approach to implementing TRAKKER.

Enterprise Project (jeTECH DATA SYSTEMS, INC.)

Describe what the product is designed to do.

Enterprise Project is a powerful new client/server software application that offers project-based organizations a simple way to define and staff projects, and record project labor and expenses throughout their enterprise. Essentially a suite of robust, user-friendly applications integrated into a single desktop, this comprehensive project management system enables team members to accurately plan and track labor resources across all projects. Perfect either as a *stand-alone* solution or as the ideal complement to the jeTECH labor-management system-Enterprise Labor, it is particularly well suited for multiuser, enterprisewide installations. Together, Enterprise Labor and Enterprise Project are the only systems currently on the market with extensive capabilities and integrated products for both the salaried professional (engineers and computer programmers, for instance) and the hourly employee (from factory workers to registered nurses).

Users access all functions via a single desktop with a Microsoft Office 98 *look and feel*. The system integrates completely with Enterprise Labor and Microsoft Project, as well as with most popular accounting and HR systems. In today's competitive environment, effective and efficient use of labor resources is key to completing mission-critical projects on time, on budget. Enterprise Project gives project leaders a comprehensive, potent tool with which to manage scarce technical resources.

With Enterprise Project, managers can budget and schedule projects based on staff skills and availability. Project team members can manage their own tasks, report actual labor and travel expenses, and provide status reports on these tasks. The system calculates actual project costs by automatically incorporating labor costs, material costs, and travel expenses.

Project managers can define and manage both contract and noncontract-based projects, and control work authorizations that will keep each project under control and on budget. As a project manager, you simply create activities for your projects, assign appropriate resources to these activities and define how labor will be charged to a contract. And by allowing employees to only charge preassigned tasks, Enterprise Project prevents performance of unauthorized work.

Enterprise Project enables all users to report labor charges right from their PC or workstation. Project managers need no longer compile project team information manually. Users can now report project time, as well as other time, and the system automatically processes and transmits it to an interfaced time-and-attendance system for payroll use.

Enterprise Project includes a contract maintenance module. Companies with hourly employees contracted with outside firms—for instance, security guards or programmers—would benefit from using this module without the rest of the project management system. This module is primarily designed, however, to accommodate projects being managed for clients. This module allows contract managers to define contract information including budgets and rates per hour, as well as all products and services purchased by the customer. They can then use this information to evaluate projects based on user-defined deliverables. Contract maintenance is by no means static; so, jeTECH has designed Enterprise Project to handle change orders, R&D projects, and discounts. A variety of unique reporting features enables contract managers to view cost overruns, variances, and milestone completions.

Top three product differentiators; describe what makes your product unique.

1. Resource scheduling from a common resource pool in a multiproject environment.
2. Integrated time collection and status reporting.
3. Sensitivity analysis (what-if scenarios).

To what business processes can this tool be applied?

Project planning/management, enterprise resource scheduling/management, time collection, performance measurement, time and expense reporting, budgeting and estimating, and project accounting.

Describe the ideal end user environment for the current version of your product (size of organization, level of project management sophistication, effort and commitment required).

Any resource-constrained enterprise (e.g., IT, high-tech R&D, engineering) with multiple projects and multiple sites. Requires a low level of project management sophistication.

Future strategies for this product.

Maintenance and repair operations, incorporation of process ware/templates, enterprise-level project and resource integration, and full Internet capabilities.

Product's target market.

Companies with *task-oriented* professionals such as engineers, architects, IS professionals, researchers, advertising/marketing professionals, etc. See also the previous response to "ideal end user environment."

What are your product's three main benefits? (How does using the product add value to the customer?)

1. Improved resource utilization and efficiencies.
2. Reduction in time to complete projects.
3. Cost control.

Describe your quality management process. List any relevant certifications.

Our current quality management process includes in-house testing, which incorporates both automated and manual processes and procedures.

Discuss your product pricing structure. Include volume discount levels, concurrent user options, site licenses, cost of implementation, and other issues.

Pricing is structured on a named-user basis. Pricing will also be dependent on a number of variables including the size of the enterprise, number of project managers, number of facilities, etc. Consequently, pricing is provided to each customer when we have been able to familiarize ourselves on their operations and their anticipated use of the system.

Cost of implementation: Several options are available for training, tech support, annual maintenance, etc. Costs are provided to each customer when they have been able to select the options deemed best for their operations.

ER Project 1000 (Eagle Ray Software Systems)

Describe what the product is designed to do.

The ER Project 1000 is an integrated suite of project management tools, which provide an enterprisewide project management solution. ER Project 1000 includes schedule/time management, centralized resource management, methodology/process management, project-workgroup communications, timesheets, risk/issue management, and enterprisewide cross-project tracking. Based on a client/server architecture with a centralized relational database, the ER Project 1000 provides networked access, multiproject capability, and true multiuser concurrency. It scales easily from handling small workgroup projects to large programs at the enterprise level.

Top three product differentiators; describe what makes your product unique.

1. Addresses the total project management life-cycle solution for the enterprise: Unlike most project management tools, the ER Project 1000 provides a completely integrated and centralized project management platform to support the entire life cycle of project management. Based on a client/server relational database (Oracle/SQL Server) architecture, ER Project 1000 fully supports today's multiproject/multiuser project environment. The product suite integrates full methodology/process management capabilities, project workgroup communications, and enterprisewide project tracking capabilities.

2. Provides a completely integrated suite of project management tools: The ER Project 1000 tool suite integrates industrial-strength project management functions with rich-process improvement functionality and proactive management features. ER Project 1000 provides all the necessary industrial-strength core project management functions. Key features include support for WBS/organizational breakdown structure/RBS structures, cost, schedule, earned value analysis, built-in report writer, timesheet approvals, and centralized resource management. ER Project 1000 takes advantage of the Web by providing Java timesheets and extensive project website publishing capability. Best practices/process improvement is easily accomplished with the methodology manager and support for organizational standards, work products, and estimation. ER Project 1000 delivers an impressive array of proactive management features. These features include risk management, issue management, management by threshold, and full project tracking.

3. Is easy to use and implement: ER Project 1000 was designed with a simple, intuitive interface. Extensive wizards assist users for complex operations. ER Project 1000 can easily be configured to your organization by using our centralized administration functions and component architecture.

To what business processes can this tool be applied?

ER Project 1000 is a wrap-around solution for organizations that need to implement mature project management practices, proactively manage their projects, improve business processes, implement standards and documentation, and communicate at multiple levels. Eagle Ray's advanced suite of tools provides project managers with an integrated platform for project planning, time tracking, resource management, and executive oversight. With features such as risk management, issue tracking, and management by threshold, the ER Project 1000 gives project managers the ability to proactively manage complex projects and stay focused on the key issues.

Organizations that engage in process improvement/best practices will find that the ER Project 1000 methodology manager is the ideal platform for developing and delivering best practices to each new project plan. Project managers will be able to easily document and reuse lessons learned in new projects. Project team members and stakeholders will find that the integrated communications features of the ER Project 1000 suite facilitate a real-time dialogue between all members and ensure no issues slip though the cracks.

Describe the ideal end-user environment for the current version of your product (size of organization, level of project management sophistication, effort and commitment required).

Size of organization: The ER Project 1000 product suite is ideal for managing projects with team sizes of ten to one thousand people per project in organizations where multiple projects are being performed at the same time. Project teams may be centralized or dispersed using client/server and Web-based communications technologies.

Level of sophistication: The tool suite is best suited for organizations that are moving beyond basic project management to a medium level of project management maturity or higher. These organizations are typically implementing tracking, costing, project management standards, risk/issue management, time tracking, centralized resource management, and possibly earned value. ER Project 1000 also supports organizations implementing a project office, best practices, process improvement, and reusable project templates. These features make ER Project 1000 an ideal platform for organizations implementing CMM level 2 or higher maturity levels.

Effort and commitment required: Successful implementation of the ER Project 1000 tool suite centers on an organization's commitment to realizing repeatable project management results from enterprisewide standardization of business processes and practices. Because of its integrated design and simple interface, ER Project 1000 delivers numerous advantages over standard project management tool sets with less staff effort.

Future strategies for this product.

Eagle Ray's future strategies include building new modules, expanding current modules, interfacing with corporate business systems, and preparing the product suite for the global marketplace. Major planned enhancements include significant modifications to the estimation module, costing module, methodology/process management module, and the Internet/intranet/Web capabilities. In addition, we will be constructing a problem/defect-tracking module.

We will be expanding the interfaces that integrate the ER Project 1000 system with additional enterprise business systems. Such systems include costing/accounting systems, HR systems, and additional commercial products. We also plan to complete our internationalization/localization efforts to prepare the ER Project 1000 for global distribution.

Product's target market.

ER Project 1000 is suitable for commercial and government organizations, which are managing projects that range from small workgroup-level projects to projects that span the entire enterprise. Essentially, the tool suite will support any project environment where the project team has access to or is working with computers.

What are your product's three main benefits? (How does using the product add value to the customer?)

1. Total integrated project management solution: The ER Project 1000 is an integrated, total project management solution providing complete support for the entire project management life cycle. The integrated tool suite does not require multiple add-on tools from different vendors, resulting in fewer hidden costs and less frustration. Project managers will find it easy to manage projects with a higher level of maturity by using the various features of the tool—for example, risk management, issue tracking, management by threshold, and multiproject capabilities.

2. Best practices/process improvement platform: The ER Project 1000 integrated process/methodology management platform provides a sophisticated yet easy-to-use platform for implementing best practices, estimation metrics, organizational standards, documentation templates, and process improvement. Organizations can capture, integrate, and reuse their project knowledge and project plan templates from an enterprisewide integrated platform.

3. Enterprisewide tracking and communications: The ER Project 1000 facilitates communications between all project stakeholders. Program managers and executives can perform cross-project rollups, dynamic drill-down, and cost, schedule, and earned-value analysis for up-to-date information on all enterprise projects. The project team members can access all of project information on the project website, and receive activity assignments and report status using Java timesheets. Automatic issue notification alerts project managers about possible deviations in cost and schedule. The built-in report writer lets you extract and summarize any data in the enterprisewide project database using customized formats.

Describe your quality management process. List any relevant certifications.

The Eagle Ray quality assurance program is a comprehensive system that employs a series of product walkthroughs, builds, quality gates, configuration management, defect tracking, and comprehensive testing. The development staff members are constantly conducting requirements, design, and code walkthroughs in coordination with weekly product builds and passing mandatory quality gates. The quality assurance program is integrated with our beta testing program to ensure that all product releases undergo rigorous real-world testing prior to release.

Comprehensive testing scenarios include unit testing, integration testing, platform testing, stress testing, concurrency testing, environment testing, security testing, usability testing, vertical testing, upgrade testing, business scenario testing, and independent qualification testing.

During the design and construction of the ER Project 1000 product, Eagle Ray brought in several project management industry experts to assist in the design of the software functionality and usability. This process will be continued to ensure that our future enhancements meet the real-world needs of project management organizations. Additionally, Eagle Ray continues to invest heavily in the training of team members in technical and project management areas.

Discuss your product pricing structure. Include volume discount levels, concurrent user options, site licenses, cost of implementation, and other issues.

Call for latest prices.

ET Enterprise

Describe what the product is designed to do.

ET Enterprise, an advanced time collection and reporting system, enables project-oriented businesses to track, manage and account for time, by employee and by project across the enterprise. It also enables supervisors to do online approvals and reviews of the their employees.

Top three product differentiators; describe what makes your product unique.

1. Flexible, easy to use.
2. Three-tier client/server application with Web access.
3. Project-oriented time tracking system with audit trail.

To what business processes can this tool be applied?

Time collection, labor management, and payroll.

Describe the ideal end-user environment for the current version of your product (size of organization, level of project management sophistication, effort and commitment required).

ET is scalable for organizations from 50–10,000-plus employees. ET is user-friendly and does not require much training for the end user or supervisor.

Future strategies for this product.

ET Enterprise has recently released an Expense Report application, to add to the Web Timesheet application. In the future, Expense Reports will also be Web-enabled.

Product's target market.

Aerospace and defense, architecture and design, biotechnology, computer technology and services, consulting, engineering and environmental, government, government contractors, insurance, not-for-profits, pharmaceuticals, public relations and marketing, research and development, software development, systems integration, telecommunications companies, R&D firms, government contractors, not-for-profit organizations, insurance companies.

What are your product's three main benefits? (How does using the product add value to the customer?)

1. Reduces timesheet errors, which results in accurate and timely billing.
2. Delivers timely information to project managers who need to track the status of their projects (Report Writer).
3. Gathers employee time from every corner of the company, via LANs, WANs, intranets or the Internet.

Describe your quality management process. List any relevant certifications.

ET Enterprise goes through an extensive QC process and is then tested in Deltek labs and pilot programs.

Discuss your product pricing structure. Include volume discount levels, concurrent user options, site licenses, cost of implementation, and other issues.

There is a $7,500, 100-user minimum (not including cost of Web Timesheets or Expense Reports) sold as on named-user basis in fifty-user increments. Volume discounts are available as user count increases.

Additional applications (WebET and Expense Reports) range from 15 percent to 25 percent of base price. Cost of implementation is typically less than 1:1 ratio of the cost of software.

Ongoing phone support is unlimited with a quarterly fee ranging from 15 percent to 20 percent of software cost. Includes all fixes, enhancements and new product versions.

Training prices are typically $340/day.

Innate Timesheets

Describe what the product is designed to do.

See who's doing what across the multiproject workload.

Top three product differentiators; describe what makes your product unique.

1. Two-way interfaces with Microsoft Project and Project Workbench.
2. Highly customizable in data fields and layout.
3. Very simple timesheet entry.

To what business processes can this tool be applied?

The process of capturing effort spent and estimates to completion in a multiproject or departmental environment.

Describe the ideal end user environment for the current version of your product (size of organization, level of project management sophistication, effort and commitment required).

Working successfully in environments of three thousand timesheet users per database.

Future strategies for this product.

Off-the-shelf interfaces with finance systems.

Product's target market.

Organizations that need to analyze how their staff spend their time, bill clients, and measure performance.

What are your product's three main benefits? (How does using the product add value to the customer?)

1. Client billing based on effort expended.
2. Staff utilization analysis and reporting.
3. Update estimating metrics by comparing actual effort with that budgeted.

Describe your quality management process. List any relevant certifications.

Best practice software product development, based on twenty years of industry experience.

Discuss your product pricing structure. Include volume discount levels, concurrent user options, site licenses, cost of implementation, and other issues.

Based on the number of timesheet users and administrators.

Cost of implementation: Simple software modules support evolutionary change. Costs of implementation well below industry average.

Intelligent Planner (Augeo Software)

Describe what the product is designed to do.

Optimize the allocation of resources across multiple projects, determine costs, and provide metrics for continuous process improvement.

Top three product differentiators; describe what makes your product unique.

1. Global repository for data and business rules.
2. Closed-loop system, from project proposal to time/expenses tracking.
3. Simulation and opimization based on skills and availability of resources.

To what business processes can this tool be applied?

Business processes involving the allocation of human resources, such as professional services and information services.

Describe the ideal end user environment for the current version of your product (size of organization, level of project management sophistication, effort and commitment required).

Mid-sized to large-scale professional-services organizations sharing pool of scarce resources. Large IT departments managing budgets and resources on strategic projects. Consulting companies managing portfolio of intellectual activities.

Future strategies for this product.

One hundred percent Web-based management of project portfolio. Knowledge management integration. Advanced data-mining features.

Product's target market.

Professional services organization. Large-scale IT departments with cost-controlled project management. Consulting companies.

What are your product's three main benefits? (How does using the product add value to the customer?)

1. Optimize scarce resource predictability.
2. Increase speed, throughput, and responsiveness.
3. Executive visibility.

Describe your quality management process. List any relevant certifications.

Source control. Usability verification process. Worldwide beta program.

Discuss your product pricing structure. Include volume discount levels, concurrent user options, site licenses, cost of implementation, and other issues.

Concurrent-user pricing for client-server modules, named-user pricing for Web modules. Volume discount, site license. Implementation requires ten to twenty days of consulting

Cost of implementation: Training—project managers (two days); administrator (three days); Web users (half day).

Annual maintenance (includes new releases and online assistance): Fifteen percent license fee.

Microsoft Project 98 (Microsoft)

Describe what the product is designed to do.

Microsoft Project 98 is an ideal tool for planning and tracking projects of all sizes. Because it is easy to use, it is an ideal tool for all levels of project management experience from the newcomer to the experienced project manager. Microsoft Project 98 focuses on three areas:

1. Control—gives users more control over their project plans.

2. Communication—improves project communication so everyone stays informed and involved.

3. Compatibility—provides programmability features so it can serve as a stand-alone product or as part of a broader company solution.

Top three product differentiators; describe what makes your product unique.

1. Ease of use: Microsoft Project 98 requires little or no training to begin using it to manage projects, so the *startup* costs required of new customers are much lower when compared to other project management software tools. The navigation map also helps inexperienced project managers and new Microsoft Project 98 customers to map their functional responsibilities to Microsoft Project 98's features.

2. Extensibility: Microsoft Project 98 is a pioneer in extensibility. It can store data in an open database format and supports VBA. Customers can easily integrate project management data with their existing corporate business systems, which enables Microsoft Project 98 to accommodate ever-increasing complexity as customers' project management needs change and grow throughout the organization.

3. Integration with other Microsoft applications: Microsoft Project 98 incorporates the best of Microsoft Office to make a tool that is easy to learn and use.

To what business processes can this tool be applied?

Microsoft Project 98 can be applied to any process for which the customer can identify specific tasks and their respective durations and dependencies. Customers can use Microsoft Project 98 to easily compare cost and profitability by project, balance resource requirements across projects, and track dependencies across multiple projects to assess a project's impact on the bottom line. Microsoft Project 98 can also be used to integrate project metrics with corporate accounting, human resources, timesheet, or manufacturing systems and organize project documentation so it is readily available to everyone involved in a project.

Describe the ideal end-user environment for the current version of your product (size of organization, level of project management sophistication, effort and commitment required).

Microsoft Project 98 is used in end-user environments of all sizes—from individuals planning single-resource projects to large corporations with thousands of employees. Customers with widely varying project management backgrounds can also use it. Even newcomers to project management principles can learn to use Microsoft Project 98 quickly and easily with the product's built-in help and other easy-to-use features. Microsoft Project 98 even contains features to extend a project team's communication capability over the Web or any MAPI-compliant E-mail system. And, customers won't *outgrow* Microsoft Project 98 since its programmability features allow them to tailor the program to their organization's unique and changing needs.

Future strategies for this product.

Microsoft will continue to focus on improved collaboration, performance, and ease of use in future versions of Microsoft Project. Microsoft Project has always focused on bringing project management techniques to a wider audience via improved ease of use and expanded communication capabilities for project teams and will continue to do so in the future.

Product's target market.

Anyone who deals with budgets, assignments, and deadlines can take advantage of the benefits offered by Microsoft Project 98. If you have thousands of details to manage, or even a few dozen, you're a potential Microsoft Project 98 customer.

What are your product's three main benefits? (How does using the product add value to the customer?)

1. Easy to learn and can grow with customers' projects and organization.
2. Ability to plan and track multiple projects in a consolidated manner.
3. Helps customers track and manage costs that affect the bottom line.

Describe your quality management process. List any relevant certifications.

Microsoft Project's quality management process begins with developing a product vision based on input from customers, internal and external developers, the product support team, and usability engineers. This ensures that the development process focuses on the right objectives, and that decisions regarding product quality reflect all of these perspectives.

Microsoft maintains a high developer to test ratio throughout the software development process to ensure that potential *bugs* are identified and resolved as early in the development cycle as possible. The testing process is based on five core attributes: 1) source code version control; 2) making the code testable; 3) use of automation for broader scenario testing; 4) beta testing—both internal and external; and 5) detailed bug tracking and reporting (throughout all Microsoft product groups in order to share learning).

Finally, a new product is released only when the managers from development, testing, program management, and product support agree as a team that the product is ready. No product will be released until this agreement is reached.

Discuss your product pricing structure. Include volume discount levels, concurrent user options, site licenses, cost of implementation, and other issues.

The estimated retail price of Microsoft Project 98 is $499. Microsoft also offers several multiple-license pricing agreements. Detailed information on these agreements is available at www.microsoft.com/licensing.

The cost of implementation varies based on previous experience with project management principles, experience with other project management software tools, and the size and complexity of a customer's projects. Little or no training is needed for Microsoft Project 98 due to the extensive built-in help and other user-assistance features included in the product. Many additional low-cost books, self-help tools, and other training materials for Microsoft Project 98 are widely available. Microsoft Project 98's built-in VBA programmability features also help limit the cost of additional customization.

Open Plan/Spider (Welcom)

Describe what the product is designed to do.

Realizing that different users require varying levels of access, Welcom, developer of the advanced project management software system, Open Plan, introduces Spider. Spider is a Web-based tool that provides team members a way to remotely progress and review Open Plan data—all without users ever needing a copy of Open Plan on their computers. Spider is a convenient and versatile Web-enabled statusing tool capable of meeting your unique needs, as well as those of your clients. Clients can also access project status information in a read-only format. With Spider, you can effectively manage business anywhere, anytime. Managers can assign, approve, and track staff activity worldwide. All views are password protected.

Top three product differentiators; describe what makes your product unique.

1. Platform independent.
2. Do not need Open Plan on the client server to status resources and activities.
3. Can status/progress resources and activities separately or together.

To what business processes can this tool be applied?

Project control, earned value management, resource management, project management, enterprise resource management, business process reengineering, and risk assessment.

Describe the ideal end user environment for the current version of your product (size of organization, level of project management sophistication, effort and commitment required).

Medium to large organizations for whom enterprisewide project management is a serious business requirement. Meets the needs of user expertise whose level of users varies from novice/occasional to advanced.

Future strategies for this product.

Our vision for the future is to provide a suite of component-based products that work together to provide advanced project management functionality using the very latest technology. Development plans also include extending multiproject and resources-modeling capabilities.

Product's target market.

Fortune 1000 companies, government and multinational organizations implementing enterprisewide project management.

What are your product's three main benefits? (How does using the product add value to the customer?)

1. Reduces time spent progressing work.
2. Can be used without Open Plan.
3. Remote user capabilities.

Describe your quality management process. List any relevant certifications.

Adhere to standard industry processes in release and version strategies, including automated regression testing. ISO 9000 certified in the United Kingdom.

Discuss your product pricing structure. Include volume discount levels, concurrent user options, site licenses, cost of implementation, and other issues.

Please call for pricing

Cost of implementation: Training course and consulting—please call for pricing. Tech support—no charge with current maintenance. Maintenance—first year is free with software purchase. Renewed annually.

OPX2 Timecard (Planisware)

Describe what the product is designed to do.

OPX2 Timecard is the complementary timesheet for OPX2 Pro scheduling and cost management software.

Top three product differentiators; describe what makes your product unique.

1. One hundred percent compliance with HTML 3.
2. Can be used with Netscape and Microsoft browsers.

To what business processes can this tool be applied?

Project management: R&D project management (new product development, portfolio management), matrix organizations, IS departments, and software houses.

Scheduling of: small serial manufacturing, engineering projects, heavy maintenance, and integration activities.

Cost management for: public contract management, defense and aerospace programs, in-house product development, and subcontracting.

Describe the ideal end user environment for the current version of your product (size of organization, level of project management sophistication, effort and commitment required).

Organization: From one hundred to twenty thousand resources managed.

Level of project management sophistication: Previous experience of other project management software implementation is profitable for implementing OPX2.

To be implemented using a methodology suited for enterprisewide consolidation: activity coding, resource identification, and ERP interfaces.

Future strategies for this product.

Development of partnerships with ERP providers, international development (multilingual support and distributors), focus on decision-support functions.

Product's target market.

Manufacturing: Defense and aerospace, car/truck, drug/cosmetics development.

ICT: IS departments (enterprises and administrations), software house, telecommunications, and electronics.

Engineering: construction, energy, and space.

What are your product's three main benefits? (How does using the product add value to the customer?)

1. For the organization: standardization of concepts and reporting process for project management in all departments; breaking of barriers between cost and schedule.

2. For the users: Less time spent to collect and enter data, more time available to analyze them.

3. For the management: Real visibility on activity progress for top management and long-term historization of project data at multiproject scale.

Describe your quality management process. List any relevant certifications.

TEMPO (Thomson-CSF software development methodology), which is compliant with ISO 9001 standards. No specific certification for Planisware.

Discuss your product pricing structure. Include volume discount levels, concurrent user options, site licenses, cost of implementation, and other issues.

OPX2 Pro (scheduling + cost management + report builder): From $12,000 (server + first concurrent user license).

Typical user configurations: $17,000 to $1,000,000. Concurrent user licenses: yes. Site licenses: yes.

Cost of implementation: Twenty-five to 80 percent of license cost (consulting, training). Annual maintenance—15 percent of license cost (including tech support and upgrade of new releases). Training—contact OPX2 distributors in each country.

Panorama Program Manager

Describe what the product is designed to do.

Panorama Program Manager comprises five modules, which together form a fully integrated application but which can, if required, be used independently or can be integrated with preferred third party applications. Interfaces can also be provided to other applications.

Financial Control & Performance Measurement: Consolidates financial and performance information for any number of projects and provides multilevel views of all data. Departmental managers and team leaders can be provided with short-term tactical perspective.

Time Recording: This module is the collection point for all time expended by project staff. Timesheets may be entered by individual members of staff, or as a batch process. Extensive online validation ensures that mispostings are kept to a minimum.

Top three product differentiators; describe what makes your product unique.

1. *Scope:* Addresses in a single integrated application the major application areas required for comprehensive program management.

2. *Flexibility:* Inherent flexibility means that the system can be implemented to suit most companies' requirements without the need for bespoke development.

3. *Customization:* Ability to incorporate bespoke features to client's specification and willingness to provide support to customized elements.

To what business processes can this tool be applied?

Estimation, bid management, and project control.

Describe the ideal end-user environment for the current version of your product (size of organization, level of project management sophistication, effort and commitment required).

Typical users will have in excess of two hundred employees and be managing either large, complex projects or a large number (>150) of small/medium-size projects.

They will usually have experience of project management and already be users of project management tools.

A typical implementation will be six to twelve months and require the involvement of an implementation team that at any one time might include five to ten client staff.

Future strategies for this product.

Web-based operation; Integration of work flow management and document storage and retrieval.

Product's target market.

Cross-industry.

What are your product's three main benefits? (How does using the product add value to the customer?)

1. Consolidation of all project data to provide a corporate view of performance.
2. Standardization of project control methodology through use of a single corporatewide system.
3. Easy access at all levels in the organization of all aspects of project performance.

Describe your quality management process. List any relevant certifications.

In-house change control and configuration management software and control systems.

Discuss your product pricing structure. Include volume discount levels, concurrent user options, site licenses, cost of implementation, and other issues.

On application.

PlanView Software (PlanView, Inc.)

Describe what the product is designed to do.

PlanView's time accounting modules let all users launch a browser to report all their time worked. Then, managers approve the data before it is released for general use.

Top three product differentiators; describe what makes your product unique.

1. Tracks and manages service requests as well as projects.
2. Integrates with financial and HR systems to drive chargebacks, etc.
3. Projects are progressed by the staff reporting their time.

To what business processes can this tool be applied?

Multiproject management, service request management, resource management, workflow management, work and resource *portfolio* management.

Describe the ideal end user environment for the current version of your product (size of organization, level of project management sophistication, effort and commitment required).

Organization with one hundred to multiple thousands of employees. (we have implementations of four thousand plus), managed by five plus managers with access to a central database; includes matrix-style organizations.

Future strategies for this product.

Further conversion to Web browser-based interfaces; even easier report generation and Web publishing; more E-mail notification and document attachment.

Product's target market.

The resource-centric approach to work management is typically most useful for organizations with a highly skilled workforce of limited availability; with twenty plus managers, and one hundred plus staff; using client/server.

What are your product's three main benefits? (How does using the product add value to the customer?)

1. Replaces legacy time reporting while it integrates with work management.
2. Projects are progressed by the staff reporting their work.
3. All work of the organization is tracked and managed.

Describe your quality management process. List any relevant certifications.

PlanView follows the guidelines set out in the book *Best Practices of Rapid Development* by Steve McConnell.

Discuss your product pricing structure. Include volume discount levels, concurrent user options, site licenses, cost of implementation, and other issues.

It is different for each case, but basically the cost is $200–400 per seat, with volume discounts. The repository products are included. Standard SQL database is extra. Implementation and training are extra.

Cost of implementation: We offer a range of implementation packages, from rapid to standard, which include training. Additional services billed at time and cost. Phone and online tech support are free. Maintenance packages offered.

PRISM (SofTech Inc.)

Describe what the product is designed to do.

PRISM allows for the tracking and invoicing of employee time, expenses, equipment, and materials within a project-based environment. This flexible/scaleable Windows has several security/permission levels to ensure that program access is controlled.

PRISM allows for detailed budgeting against projects, while fast drilldown into budgeted, submitted, approved, and billed figures provides users with valuable cost data. Scheduling needs are fulfilled by PRISM's tie-in to MS Project. Procuring of materials is handled through PRISM's purchasing module, which tracks purchases from RFQ to receipt of vendor invoices. Business development and client and vendor-tracking efforts are maintained through PRISM's sophisticated contact-manager tool that incorporates import and export functionality, as well as several sort, filter, and classification features.

Top three product differentiators; describe what makes your product unique.

PRISM provides users with access to real-time project information with a project, rather than accounting orientation. PRISM is truly project-oriented and provides organizations with a wide range of project accounting information.

The development efforts of PRISM are very customer driven, and the off-the-shelf pricing structure, flexibility, and scalability of the program make it an affordable tool for any size organization.

To what business processes can this tool be applied?

PRISM can be used to fulfill project accounting requirements and can also be used as a purchasing and business development tool.

Describe the ideal end user environment for the current version of your product (size of organization, level of project management sophistication, effort and commitment required).

The ideal user environment for the current release version of PRISM is a small to mid-sized (less than 250 employees) firm, typically in an engineering or related industry. The firm will have a need for a project management system that addresses generation and reporting of real-time project information and costs, the procuring of materials, and client, prospect, and vendor management. Users require a broad range of information that will allow them to track and report overall project performance. However, the firm does not require, or cannot justify, the cost of a specialized program that calculates statistical risk and performance analysis. The off-the-shelf nature of PRISM makes training and implementation time requirements relatively minimal.

Future strategies for this product.

PRISM is in a high development phase with plans to continually enhance and add to the functionality of the program. Increased program functionality is both a function of customer demand and request, as well as one of technology advancement. Some of the features that will be added to the program over the next twelve months include: remote time and expense sheet entry, two-way transfer, and update of schedule information between PRISM and Microsoft Project, manpower loading, multiple currency handling, and a detailed quote and estimate component.

Product's target market.

PRISM's target market includes small to mid-sized (less than 250 employees) Canadian and United States engineering and related industry firms that require a project management tool that allows for budgeting, time management, expense and materials tracking, and real-time project reporting with a focus on a low cost or off-the-shelf solution.

What are your product's three main benefits? (How does using the product add value to the customer?)

1. PRISM's entry, submission, and approval methodologies both reduce the potential for errors (in charging to the wrong project) and increase efficiency of these processes.

2. PRISM provides timely project-costing information that allows management to make informed project-based decisions while projects can still be affected, leading to improved overall project performance.

3. Because project information generated in PRISM is real time, lags between approval and invoicing of the client are reduced, resulting in increased cash flow.

Describe your quality management process. List any relevant certifications.

SofTech has a detailed internal quality management process that systematically outlines and handles release, testing, and documentation procedures.

Discuss your product pricing structure. Include volume discount levels, concurrent user options, site licenses, cost of implementation, and other issues.

The base installation price of PRISM is $4,000, giving clients a network-ready version of the program and one concurrent license, or a single fixed license, for non-networked environments. The second concurrent license is $2,000; the third is $1,000; the fourth and fifth are $500 each. Beyond five, concurrent licenses are sold in packs of five for $1,500. Base installation price includes software, one day of training (exclusive of travel-related expenses), ninety days of free upgrades, and twenty hours or twenty calls of phone support. PRISM Light is also available for organizations with five or fewer employees for $1,500. Multisite installation pricing is negotiable.

Cost of implementation: Included in the base installation price of PRISM is one day of training (exclusive of travel-related expenses), ninety days of free upgrades (past installation date), and twenty hours or twenty calls of phone support. Annual maintenance agreements can be purchased for a cost of $1,000 per year, plus $100 per concurrent user license. This maintenance package entitles users to an unlimited amount of phone support, any upgrades or new releases for the year, and any minor custom work required.

Additional custom work on related or unrelated products is available, and fees will be determined on a per-contract or work-required basis.

Project Communicator (Scitor Corporation)

Describe what the product is designed to do.

Project Communicator is an enterprisewide project communications system built on top of a powerful database. Seamlessly integrated with Project Scheduler 7, it enables project team members to communicate schedule status to the project manager.

By electronically collecting actual hours worked and remaining estimates from team members, the project manager can evaluate, approve (or question), track, and reallocate work faster and more accurately—all before updating the project database.

Team members use the component called Project Communicator-Team (PC-Team) to display their assigned tasks and enter progress and other information. Project Communicator can be installed on most ODBC-compatible databases including Access, Oracle, and SQL Server. The team clients can be run on Windows 95, NT, or Windows 3.1. The manager client requires Windows 95 or NT.

Top three product differentiators; describe what makes your product unique.

1. Ease of use.
2. Scalability: Project Communicator is designed and built from the ground up to scale from the single desktop user to the entire enterprise.
3. Customer support: Project Communicator is not just another software product. Project Communicator has been designed and built by project management professionals as an easy-to-use product for nonproject management professionals.

To what business processes can this tool be applied?

Project planning and tracking, resource management and team communications, cost estimation and control.

Describe the ideal end user environment for the current version of your product (size of organization, level of project management sophistication, effort and commitment required).

Project Communicator is designed to meet the needs of all sizes of organizations, including: individuals, product teams, workgroups, and the enterprise.

Future strategies for this product.

We will continue to provide leading edge project management products and services by listening to and working with customers to predict the future needs of a changing management environment.

Product's target market.

General business and professional project management; all major industries.

What are your product's three main benefits? (How does using the product add value to the customer?)

1. Tracks project/resource costs and schedules.
2. Allows *early* detection and resolution of problems.
3. Facilitates communications between all stakeholders.

Describe your quality management process. List any relevant certifications.

Best commercial practices.

Discuss your product pricing structure. Include volume discount levels, concurrent user options, site licenses, cost of implementation, and other issues.

$2,000 per ten-user pack. Volume discounts available.

Cost of implementation: Training—regional and on-site training and consulting is available. Telephone tech support—no charge. Annual maintenance—not applicable.

Project Control Software, Version 6.0 - Time Manager (Project Control)

Describe what the product is designed to do.

Timesheets integrated with your project management files on LAN or Web. Timesheets can be edited, approved, and frozen. Handles nonproject time, generic roles, and time charged to nonassigned projects. Supports task assignment distribution and task status updating, based on individual user profiles. Print or E-mail timesheets and task assignments. The time manager module is part of the Project Control Software suite.

Project Control Software extends desktop project management software into an enterprisewide management and reporting solution, by consolidating volumes of project files from leading project management software systems such as Microsoft Project, Primavera, and others. Project Control Software supports multiple operating systems (Windows, Macintosh, Unix), and databases (Oracle, Access, Microsoft SQL, Sybase). The entire Project Control Software suite runs on a Web browser or LAN. The enterprise rollup design supports the matrix organization's need to roll up projects to program or initiative, as well as the resource perspective by business unit and organizational structure.

The Project Control Software suite supports the project office across all phases of the project management life cycle, from standard estimating and budgeting though timesheets and status tracking and integration with any accounting system for actual costs and earned value analysis.

Top three product differentiators; describe what makes your product unique.

1. No technology limits: Project Control Software supports all operating systems (Windows, Macintosh, Unix), consolidates files from multiple project management software systems (Microsoft Project, Primavera, and more), using your choice of databases (Oracle, Access, Microsoft SQL, Sybase) in a LAN or Internet solution. It is designed to integrate easily with existing business systems (such as accounting software), so an organization can leverage existing systems and immediately see productivity increases without changing everything.

2. The project office: The design and integration of Project Control Software modules supports the project office across all phases of the project management life cycle, from standard estimating and budgeting though timesheets and status tracking and accounting integration for actual costs and earned value analysis.

3. Enterprise project management: Project Control Software offers a suite of integrated modules that can be used to deliver the big picture of project management across a distributed organization, as well as tracking the details. The enterprise rollup design supports the matrix organization's need to roll up projects to program or initiative, as well as the need to view data from a resource perspective by business unit and organizational structure. The entire Project Control Software suite (not just the time tracking) runs on a Web browser or LAN.

To what business processes can this tool be applied?

Project Control Software's enterprise rollup design supports the matrix organization's need to roll up projects to program or initiative, as well as the need to view data from a resource perspective by business unit and organizational structure.

The system supports project management, ERP, project office development, ISO registration, strategic planning, process management, methodology implementation, cost/schedule management, CMM compliance, global information technology deployment, SAP, Peoplesoft, etc. implementations.

Describe the ideal end user environment for the current version of your product (size of organization, level of project management sophistication, effort and commitment required).

Any organization operating in a competitive environment that manages multiple projects and resources to meet business goals, and to increase profitability and productivity—for example, a geographically distributed matrix organization with medium to high volume of project-based activities being managed in a standard desktop scheduling software. The system delivers information to all levels of the organization, from employees to project management, functional management, enterprise management, and global management.

Future strategies for this product.

Project Control, the publisher of Project Control Software, founded in 1989, developed the first Internet project management product in 1996, and is committed to its position as a technology leader in Internet project management software. Future plans include expanding functionality to better support the project office and to continually update Project Control Software features based on ongoing client input. Contact the publisher for more details on upcoming releases.

Product's target market.

Organizations using Project Control Software represent companies in a wide variety of industries, including finance, services, pharmaceutical, federal government, defense, manufacturing, automotive, software publishing, etc. The disciplines typically involved in implementation include enterprise management, information technology, new product development, the project office, and engineering.

What are your product's three main benefits? (How does using the product add value to the customer?)

Client organizations can greatly improve productivity and lower costs when Project Control system is in place. It provides the ability to:
1. View all projects in a central repository.
2. Do efficient enterprise resource and cost planning, and to fully support the needs of the project office across all phases and areas of the project management process.

Describe your quality management process. List any relevant certifications.

Project Control, publishers of Project Control Software, follows standard and accepted practices for design, development, testing, and support for computer software. Project Control has set corporate objectives to achieve Level 2 and Level 3 CMM compliance, using the CMM from the Software Engineering Institute.

Discuss your product pricing structure. Include volume discount levels, concurrent user options, site licenses, cost of implementation, and other issues.

Project Control Software is priced by the module, with scalable client-seat pricing based on number of users. Price quotations are available and are based on the current project control software product and pricing schedule.

Cost of implementation: Price quotations are available and include costs of product, implementation, training, tech support, annual maintenance, etc. Quotations are based on the current project control software product and pricing schedule, which is available to qualified organizations.

Project Integrator (PI) 2.0 Enterprise Edition (System Solvers, Ltd.)

Describe what the product is designed to do.

SSL Project Integrator (PI) is a team-oriented project and process management tool that enables you to graphically define, track, report, and communicate projects, processes, tasks, and deliverables. Additionally, PI manages and maintains resources and clients, both locally and remotely.

Top three product differentiators; describe what makes your product unique.

All project processes (external, internal, and administrative) are managed via PI's graphic and interactive RoadMap. High-level steps graphically depict process flow. Each step can be drilled down to display task lists, task details, resource delegation, deliverables, and quality checklists.

Teams can be defined at the project level and are pulled from the database resource pool. Assigned tasks and open issues are sent to a team member's reminder window for immediate delegation and communication. Resources drag and drop tasks to a timecard for immediate project updating, and open issues remain on the reminder window until they are closed.

A wide range of reports is available. Each report can be filtered and pull data from the database for macroanalysis or microanalysis and reporting. Users can also define their own reports, and any level of information can be exported from the database.

To what business processes can this tool be applied?

Any external, internal, or administrative business process, regardless of simplicity or complexity.

Describe the ideal end user environment for the current version of your product (size of organization, level of project management sophistication, effort and commitment required).

Project-based organizations of any size (PI allows definition of teams, departments, and business units). Organizations do not need to be well versed in project management practices and techniques. Implementation and training is simple when compared to sophisticated project management tools. A commitment to DPM is required (the delegation of tasks and deliverables to distributed teams and team members, and distribution of the project management process).

Future strategies for this product.

Tailor versions of PI to specific industries by leveraging SME from same.

Full integration to other cost-accounting applications (currently, PI is integrated with SBT Executive Series, although data can be exported to virtually any application).

Product's target market.

Project Integrator was created for project-oriented organizations (engineering, marketing, advertising, accounting, consulting, design firms, etc.) that have a need to enforce consistent quality in their project process and delivery, and minimize nonproductive hours.

What are your product's three main benefits? (How does using the product add value to the customer?)

1. Distribution of the project process (tasks, issues, deliverables, etc.) to local and remote team members via LAN, DBMS, and Internet tools.

2. Immediate feedback of status of all projects and tasks, allowing macroviews and microviews of the entire organization's performance at any given time.

3. All aspects of a business (external, internal, and administrative activity, including deliverables) are managed in a central DBMS and repository. Communications, projects, tasks, deliverables, issues, costs, clients' resources, etc. are all managed via one tool in one database.

Describe your quality management process. List any relevant certifications.

Our documented QA process includes the use of test-script software. We are currently implementing ISO 9001 and expect registry by early 1999.

Discuss your product pricing structure. Include volume discount levels, concurrent user options, site licenses, cost of implementation, and other issues.

PI's price is based on the number of users, and volume discounts are available.

Cost of implementation: Implementation lead time and required training is minimal when compared to high-end, sophisticated project management tools and suites.

time controller

Describe what the product is designed to do.

Details of timesheet information to be recorded against each project are processed by time controller. The module includes a sophisticated Human Resource Register, which supports a wide range of options for recording and costing labor-hours.

Top three product differentiators; describe what makes your product unique.

1. Functional Human Resource Register.
2. Single entry point for daily, weekly and monthly timesheets.
3. Forms Integrated Work Management System when used with other modules in the controller suite.

To what business processes can this tool be applied?

Timesheet entry; labor costing; Human Resource Management.

Describe the ideal end-user environment for the current version of your product (size of organization, level of project management sophistication, effort and commitment required).

Medium to large multisite organizations. Provides for the vagaries of offshore work. Usually involves a degree of change management during the move from existing processes

Future strategies for this product.

Web interface; increased facility to E-mail reports.

Product's target market.

Offshore oil and gas, utilities, service organizations, any companies looking to record their employees time to back-charge to clients.

What are your product's three main benefits? (How does using the product add value to the customer?)

1. Integrates to billing system to provide invoicing details.
2. Single data entry system for daily, weekly and monthly timesheets.
3. Multiple costing scenarios for employee, employer and customer rates.

Describe your quality management process. List any relevant certifications.

We have internal auditable quality procedures in place equivalent to ISO 9000 standards. Accredited Investors in People.

Discuss your product pricing structure. Include volume discount levels, concurrent user options, site licenses, cost of implementation, and other issues.

System is priced per number of concurrent users for each module. Discounts available for volume and multisite implementations. Annual maintenance: 15 percent of license costs.

TimeControl (HMS)

Describe what the product is designed to do.

TimeControl is a project-oriented timesheet system. It is a full client-server application supporting Oracle, Sybase, SQL Server, FoxPro, and MS Access databases. TimeControl is preconfigured to link directly to MS Project, Primavera's P3, and Welcom's Open Plan and Cobra. Its Link Wizard allows interfaces to be defined for virtually any finance system. TimeControl is designed to support the needs of both the financial department and the project management structure, simultaneously replacing in some cases multiple timesheet systems.

Top three product differentiators; describe what makes your product unique.

1. TimeControl's matrix approval process allows actuals to be authorized for financial department use and project use simultaneously.

2. TimeControl's validation rules allow business rules and approval rules to be automated, and thus to distribute the validation process to every user.

3. TimeControl can store its data in numerous databases including FoxPro, MS Access, Oracle, Sybase, and SQL Server

To what business processes can this tool be applied?

TimeControl is ideally suited to provide labor-actual information for both the financial department and the project management group simultaneously. It can be used to provide auditable, validated data for payroll, billing, budget versus actual variance, time and attendance, and activity-based costing. TimeControl also allows project progress data to be collected, such as task-remaining duration, percent complete, or resource-remaining duration, and then to automatically transfer this data along with labor hours to project management systems.

Describe the ideal end user environment for the current version of your product (size of organization, level of project management sophistication, effort and commitment required).

TimeControl is designed to be completely scalable. It is in use by organizations as small as a dozen people and in organizations who have thousands of users. End users of the product require no training or additional assistance. TimeControl administrators must dedicate some portion of their time to maintaining the TimeControl database.

Future strategies for this product.

HMS has just released a Java interface for TimeControl, and future releases will expand the connectivity and communications aspect of the product. Future releases and add-on modules will allow more functionality for expense and cost management, additional automated processes for system maintenance, and more external links to other systems. Already, links are being established to tie TimeControl to Baan and SAP's ERP environments.

Product's target market.

TimeControl is already in use in a wide range of industries. The target for the product is any organization that has a labor-intensive project environment. TimeControl is used extensively in the I/S, banking, defense, aerospace, and engineering industries.

What are your product's three main benefits? (How does using the product add value to the customer?)

1. One of TimeControl's most immediate benefits is to provide an auditable, trackable collection of labor actuals. Its full-audit trail and extensive validation functionality make it ideally suited for organizations where this is essential.

2. Another benefit of using TimeControl is the enormous savings in time in collecting labor actuals. This is made possible by insulating the end user from most of the functionality, making it very simple to use.

3. Finally, TimeControl's ability to link directly to project management products such as MS Project, Primavera's P3, and Welcom's Open Plan and Cobra make it possible to collect grassroots actuals, and transfer them automatically to the scheduling system.

Describe your quality management process. List any relevant certifications.

TimeControl undergoes extensive internal testing and then a beta program, which covers all databases supported and as many platforms as possible before release. Iterative versions are tested in the field before any upgrades are released. Finally, HMS's Quality Assurance department signs off on the status of the product before release, after having run a series of scripts to ensure that the new version is behaving as it should.

Discuss your product pricing structure. Include volume discount levels, concurrent user options, site licenses, cost of implementation, and other issues.

TimeControl pricing starts at $175 per license with discounts for volume, which bring the per-license price as low as $50. Everything required is contained in the TimeControl package. There are no additional perserver licenses or module licenses. Licenses are based on an *active* user basis, with entries in the TimeControl user table flagged as active or inactive. There are no mandatory installation or assistance charges.

Cost of implementation: There are no obligatory additional costs to implement TimeControl. Consulting prices from HMS Software for implementation assistance start at $1,200 per day. Technical support for TimeControl is included for one year with the price of the package. This includes unlimited access to our Tech Support hotline and any upgrades released during the year. Support contracts can be purchased annually after the first year at a price based on 20 percent of the current package price.

TimeScope TimeSheet

Describe what the product is designed to do.

Track personnel and project costs, time, expenses, budgets, and billables.

Top three product differentiators; describe what makes your product unique.

1. Multilevel organization support with rollup.
2. Complete project tracking and accounting software fully integrated.
3. Extensive time-phased budgeting features.

To what business processes can this tool be applied?

Information technology, engineering, consulting, R&D, and auditing.

Describe the ideal end user environment for the current version of your product (size of organization, level of project management sophistication, effort and commitment required).

Information services, information technology, engineering, consulting, auditing, R&D, from small groups to large multilevel organizations, and novice or advanced users.

Future strategies for this product.

No answer given.

Product's target market.

Information technology, engineering, consulting, R&D, auditing, and professional services.

What are your product's three main benefits? (How does using the product add value to the customer?)

1. Includes everything needed for project tracking and project accounting.
2. Highly flexible, yet easy to use.
3. Built-in multilevel organizational support.

Describe your quality management process. List any relevant certifications.

No answer given.

Discuss your product pricing structure. Include volume discount levels, concurrent user options, site licenses, cost of implementation, and other issues.

Time Sheet: $175 per user. Executive Toolkit: $375 per user.
Extensive quantity discounts and site licenses.
Cost of implementation: Training—$1,500.00 per day; support—15 percent of purchase per year.

TimeWizard (AC Software, Inc.)

Describe what the product is designed to do.

TimeWizard enables you to integrate all aspects of your company's time-accounting requirements. You can create activities and assignments for employees, and enforce business rules at timesheet entry.

Top three product differentiators; describe what makes your product unique.

1. The interface controller allows TimeWizard and other corporate systems to communicate with one another. ProjectLink allows two-way transfer of data between TimeWizard and project management systems. Databridge Toolkit provides the capability for you to create automated links to other systems, e.g., in Payroll, HR, etc.
2. TimeWizard is completely customizable with fourteen custom activity fields, ten custom detail codes, and thirteen custom employee fields.
3. TimeWizard provides multiple methods for remote time capture, including remote access via WAN or RAS, polling processor, and intranet/Internet solutions.

To what business processes can this tool be applied?

Current customers include financial, technology, manufacturing, communications, and medical.

Describe the ideal end user environment for the current version of your product (size of organization, level of project management sophistication, effort and commitment required).

Application can be used across the enterprise of organizations with one hundred to ten thousand plus users.

Future strategies for this product.

TimeWizard Enterprise will offer Java applet and HTML timesheets, so that users can enter the system on the Internet. This product utilizes the NetDynamics enterprise network application platform.

Product's target market.

Product's flexibility makes it a true horizontal application.

What are your product's three main benefits? (How does using the product add value to the customer?)

1. Increase timesheet accuracy and reduce operating costs.
2. Share your time-accounting data across the enterprise.
3. Produce quality reports using the embedded Crystal Reports software.

Describe your quality management process. List any relevant certifications.

Working toward SEI software CMM level 3.

Discuss your product pricing structure. Include volume discount levels, concurrent user options, site licenses, cost of implementation, and other issues.

Product is priced per seat, and volume discounts are associated via tier level.

Cost of implementation: Training—provide three levels of general and customized training: user, manager, and administrator. Consulting—installation averages one week to two weeks, with additional system integration available. Maintenance (includes tech support)—20% of purchase price.

WebProject

Describe what the product is designed to do.

WebProject is designed for geographically dispersed project teams. WebProject is a Java-based project management tool with powerful collaboration and communications features. WebProject incorporates unique knowledge management/best practices capability.

Top three product differentiators; describe what makes your product unique.

WebProject is the first (only) pure Java project management suite that can utilize an open architecture database backend. WebProject allows corporations to utilize Oracle, SQL Server, Informix, Sybase, or other databases in their enterprise project management.

WebProject has introduced the first knowledge management/best practices capability within a project management software suite.

WebProject enables global project communication including project issues boards, threaded task discussions, virtual project status meetings, and remote project statusing and updates.

To what business processes can this tool be applied?

Geographically dispersed project teams, projects that need to have access from remote locations, or integrating WebProject's proprietary information exchange with MS Project, Primavera, or other desktop systems.

WebProject allows the extraction of knowledge from the enterprise, such as resource capabilities or company *best practices*.

Describe the ideal end-user environment for the current version of your product (size of organization, level of project management sophistication, effort and commitment required).

WebProject is an easy-to-use Java project management tool that will enable teams to communicate and collaborate from remote locations. WebProject is designed for the enterprise and will work well with project teams as well.

Future strategies for this product.

WebProject has established many *firsts* in the project management industry. We will continue to move the industry forward with our new technologies on the Web and with Java.

Product's target market.

Geographically dispersed project teams, enterprise project management systems, integration with Primavera, MS Project, and other project management systems.

What are your product's three main benefits? (How does using the product add value to the customer?)

1. Enterprise project communication.
2. Project collaboration.
3. Geographically dispersed updates and communication.

Describe your quality management process. List any relevant certifications.

WebProject adheres to strict standards and processes for quality, both in development and customer service.

Discuss your product pricing structure. Include volume discount levels, concurrent user options, site licenses, cost of implementation, and other issues.

WebProject is priced at $790 for starter package including the WebProject server. WebProject does provide enterprise and site licensing.

WebTime & TimeReview (IMS Information Management Services, Inc.)

Describe what the product is designed to do.

WebTime is a browser-based interactive timesheet, providing the flexibility to report actual progress against Microsoft Project assignments and nonscheduled activities in a single timesheet interface at any time via the World Wide Web. TimeReview utilizes a three-tier client/server architecture, providing organizations with the ability to verify team-member compliance with organizational time reporting standards.

TimeReview logic is stored in the middle-tier application server and is easily modified to handle various compliance business rules. Organizations can establish different compliance methods for different team members. Employees may have time automatically validated, upon reaching a definable threshold, while contractors may require a manager to manually verify reported time. Optionally, team members and/or managers are notified when status updating is delinquent. Verification rules are resource dependent and organizationally defined. Validated time is stored in a transaction table, with a time interval that is flexibly defined, allowing for integration with various accounting systems. In addition to defining approval time intervals, TimeReview also provides organizations with the ability to establish archival time intervals. Archiving enterprise information can provide multiple historical baselines.

TimeReview ensures that you receive a maximum return on your enterprise work management solution by enforcing organizational time-reporting compliance guidelines. ProjectExplorer (sold separately) provides communication of assignments from Microsoft Project. Assignments are added to WebTime, and actual progress committed by team members automatically updates the manager of the project. Team members utilize WebTime to record project and nonproject actual progress, and to provide schedule feedback. This Web-based timesheet works independent of ProjectExplorer, giving users a choice of either interface to manage activities from various managers, all in a consistent manner.

By closing the loop between project managers, team members, and other project stakeholders, managers are freed from the tedious task of disseminating information and gathering progress and estimates, while team members obtain task ownership and are provided a mechanism to provide schedule feedback. This ensures that all team members are tied into the planning process with minimum effort expended.

Top three product differentiators; describe what makes your product unique.

1. Functionally complete and easy to use.
2. Developed by a market leader that introduced the first timesheet for Microsoft Project in 1994.
3. Lower cost of ownership.

To what business processes can this tool be applied?

Our tools are utilized across multiple business processes.

Describe the ideal end user environment for the current version of your product (size of organization, level of project management sophistication, effort and commitment required).

Our primary market includes Global 5000 organizations with objectives to increase returns on people, time, and financial investments. We initially assist event-driven divisions within these organizations, with the ultimate goal of benefiting every user in the organization.

Future strategies for this product.

We believe the project management industry of yesterday is transforming, and will become the work management industry of tomorrow. With the increase in use from large projects to both small and medium-sized projects, the opportunity to provide a complete enterprise work management solution has surfaced. Project management traditionally does not include accounting for activities not scheduled nor part of a project. In every organization, a portion of activities is not planned using critical path techniques. Due to the demand that nonproject activities place on an organization team, the growth in work management software will continue. The integration of both project and nonproject activities is essential to successfully balance the demands placed upon the organization. We will continue to be a timesheet market leader.

Product's target market.

Based on our experience, clients who benefit most from our products and services include information systems, professional services, product development, engineering, and other event-driven organizations. Among these groups, each has further defined a set of unique objectives critical to increasing their competitiveness. IMS provides the ProjectExchange Enterprise Toolkit to achieve these objectives from the departmental level to the entire enterprise.

What are your product's three main benefits? (How does using the product add value to the customer?)

1. An easy-to-use Web-based thin client provides a lower cost of ownership.
2. A single timesheet for project and nonproject activities improves efficiency and helps balance demands placed on the organization.
3. Three-tier client/server-based architecture provides a system scalable across the entire enterprise.

Describe your quality management process. List any relevant certifications.

We have continually improved our system development methodology since 1991. Over time, our SDLC has incorporated the best practices learned while deploying ProjectExchange in world-class organizations across the globe. Our Research & Development division utilizes ProjectExchange, and quality measures are persistent throughout our methods and processes.

Discuss your product pricing structure. Include volume discount levels, concurrent user options, site licenses, cost of implementation, and other issues.

Please consult IMS for current pricing.

Cost of implementation: Implementation costs vary and depend upon a particular organization's business requirements and level and availability of in-house expertise. We offer the following services to help achieve organizational objectives:

- Installation
- Process, methods, and integration consulting
- Project office support
- ProjectExchange add-on solution development
- Implementation management
- Microsoft Project and ProjectExchange two-day course
- ProjectExchange for Project Managers one-day course
- ProjectExchange for Team Members one-half-day course
- MS Project Introduction one-day course
- MS Project Basic two-day course
- Project Planning & Management Fundamentals three-day course
- Executive briefing on project management.

Annual maintenance is offered at 15 percent of the license costs. Maintenance includes telephone support and product upgrades.

WorkLink

Describe what the product is designed to do.

The WorkLink Progress Sheet is designed for daily capture of actual hours and progress against an individual's work assignments.

Top three product differentiators; describe what makes your product unique.

1. Combined time capture and work progressing functionality.
2. Supports work reforecasting, without changing the budget.
3. Coding structures can be drawn from common corporate systems including Oracle, P3 and Indus EMPAC.

To what business processes can this tool be applied?

Time reporting and approval; progress reporting.

Describe the ideal end-user environment for the current version of your product (size of organization, level of project management sophistication, effort and commitment required).

The user environment typically consists of owner organizations that manage their own projects. These organizations often have their own technical staff of engineers and designers. Their projects usually involve a mix of external procurement and internal design costs. They usually have extensive project management expertise.

Future strategies for this product.

Application functionalities: integrated workflow management and support for evolving international project management standards.

System architecture: move toward DCOM model.

Product's target market.

Medium to large public or private organizations that manage their own projects. Many are in the power generation and distribution business. Others are in the transportation, construction or related sectors.

What are your product's three main benefits? (How does using the product add value to the customer?)

1. Reduce omissions by applying a proven project cost management methodology.
2. Reduce dependency on disparate systems and improve reporting consistency due to a centralized data repository.
3. Eliminate duplicate data entry through direct integration with scheduling and ERP systems.

Describe your quality management process. List any relevant certifications.

Multiphased methodology based on Optiplan's fourteen-year software development experience. Software quality is monitored through a combination of automated tools and external usability testing. Optiplan participates in national and international software quality associations.

Discuss your product pricing structure. Include volume discount levels, concurrent user options, site licenses, cost of implementation, and other issues.

WorkLink licensing is based on a concurrent usage model. Volume discounts and site licenses are available. The cost of implementation includes onsite user training, support hotline and possible application enhancements. Software subscription and support services range from 20 percent to 25 percent of the license costs.

Web Publishers

	ABT Publisher	AutoPLAN Enterprise	Enterprise Project	ER Project 1000	eRoom	Mesa/Vista	Milestones, Etc.	Open Plan/Web Publisher
Builds websites								
Creates and publishes the web site	Y	N	N	Y	Y	N	Y	N
Drag-and-drop website editing	Y	N	N	N	Y	N	N	N
Generates website from Windows subdirectory structure	Y	N	N	N	N	N	Y	N
Server operating systems supported	Y	N	N	NT, Unix	NT/IIS	N	All	Any
Publishes to website:								
Drawings (CAD, etc)	Y	N	N	N	Y	Y	Y	N
Database queries	Y	N	N	Y	N	Y	Y	N
Links to other websites	Y	Y	N	Y	Y	Y	Y	N
Office automation documents	Y	N	N	Y	Y	Y	Y	N
Can link from different source servers	Y	N	N	N	Y	Y	Y	N
Communications features								
Team "push" communication channels	Y	N	Y	N	Y	Y	N	N
Threaded discussion	Y	N	N	Y	Y	Y	N	N
Bulletin board	Y	N	Y	N	Y	N	N	N
Newsgroups	Y	N	N	N	N	N	N	N
Team management								
Creates and delivers action items	Y	N	Y	N	Y	Y	N	N
Creates and delivers task lists	Y	N	Y	Y	Y	Y	N	Y
Delegates work requests to team	Y	N	Y	N	N	N	N	N
Document management								
Version control	N	N	Y	N	Y	Y	N	N
Document collaboration	N	N	Y	Y	Y	Y	Y	N
Online project management methodology	Y	N	Y	Y	N	Y	N	N
Online templates	Y	N	Y	Y	Y	Y	Y	N
Features								
Action items	Y	N	Y	N	Y	Y	Y	Y
Risk documentation	Y	N	Y	Y	N	Y	N	N
Issues management	Y	N	Y	Y	Y	Y	N	N
Meeting minutes	Y	N	Y	Y	Y	Y	N	N
Agendas	Y	N	Y	Y	N	Y	N	N
Project templates	Y	N	Y	Y	Y	Y	N	Y
HTML generation								
Generates HTML pages with links to supporting documents *	Y	N	Y	Y	N	Y	Y	Y
Publishes reports readable in a "generic" format (e.g., Adobe Acrobat) *	Y	Y	Y	N	Y	Y	Y	Y

PM tools supported	ABT Workbench, MS Project			MS Project, Primavera		Milestones, Etc.	Open Plan
Generic reader formats supported					Adobe Acrobat Reader	PDF	HTML, PDF
Online help							
Right mouse click	Y	N	N	Y	N	Y	N
Hover buttons	Y	N	N	Y	N	Y	Y
Interactive help	Y	N	Y	Y	Y	Y	N
Help search feature	Y	N	Y	Y	Y	Y	Y
Web access to product knowledge base	Y	N	N	Y	N	Y	Y

Web Publishers

	OPX2 Intranet Server	PlanView Software	Prolog Website	Project Commander	Project Control 6.0	ProjectSite for the Web	WebProject	Webster 2.1 for Primavera/Web Publishing Wizard in P3 and SureTrak
Builds websites								
Creates and publishes the web site	Y	Y	Y	Y	Y	N	Y	Y
Drag-and-drop website editing	N	N	N		N	Y	Y	N
Generates website from Windows subdirectory structure	N	N	Y		Y	Y	Y	N
Server operating systems supported	Win NT, Unix	Y	Y			Win NT 4.0 or higher	Win 95/NT, Unix, Linux, any Java-enabled OS	NT
Publishes to website:								
Drawings (CAD, etc)	N	Y	Y		Y	Y	N	Y
Database queries	Y	N	Y		Y	Y	Y	N
Links to other websites	Y	Y	Y		Y	Y	Y	Y
Office automation documents	N	Y	Y		Y	Y	Y	N
Can link from different source servers	Y	Y	Y		Y	Y	Y	Y
Communications features								
Team "push" communication channels	N	Y	N		Y	Y	Y	N
Threaded discussion	N	Y	N		Y	N	Y	N
Bulletin board	N	Y	N		Y	N	Y	N
Newsgroups	N	N	N		Y	N	Y	N
Team management								
Creates and delivers action items	Y	Y	Y	Y	Y	N	Y	Y
Creates and delivers task lists	Y	Y	Y		Y	N	Y	Y
Delegates work requests to team	Y	Y	Y		N	N	Y	Y
Document management								
Version control	N	N	Y		Y	N	Y	N
Document collaboration	N	Y	Y		N	N	Y	N
Online project management methodology	N	Y	Y		Y	N	N	N
Online templates	N	Y	Y		Y	N	Y	N
Features								
Action items	N	Y	Y	Y	Y	N	Y	Y
Risk documentation	N	Y	Y		N	N	Y	N
Issues management	N	Y	Y	Y	Y	N	Y	N
Meeting minutes	N	Y	Y		Y	N	Y	N
Agendas	N	Y	Y		Y	N	Y	N
Project templates	N	Y	Y		Y	N	Y	N
HTML generation								
Generates HTML pages with links to supporting documents *	Y	Y	Y		Y	Y	Y	Y
Publishes reports readable in a "generic" format (e.g., Adobe Acrobat) *	Y	N	Y		Y	Y	Y	Y

PM tools supported	OPX2 (direct), MS Project, Scitor Project Scheduler (indirect)		MS Project, Primavera, and others	MS Project 98	WebProject has a proprietary technology for sharing information with MS Project, Primavera, and other PM and ERP systems	Primavera
Generic reader formats supported	PDF (Acrobat)		Adobe Acrobat		MPX	HTML, Acrobat
Online help						
Right mouse click	Y	Y	N	Y	N	Y
Hover buttons	Y	Y	Y	Y	Y	N
Interactive help	Y	Y	N	Y	Y	N
Help search feature	Y	Y	Y	Y	Y	Y
Web access to product knowledge base	Y	Y	Y	Y	Y	N

VENDOR RESPONSES TO NARRATIVE QUESTIONS

Web Publishers

ABT Publisher

Describe what the product is designed to do.

A Web-based program and project communication tool, ABT Publisher addresses the need that faces all enterprise program and project management environments: effectively communicating the status of the programs and projects that comprise the enterprise portfolio. ABT Publisher delivers comprehensive information to those who need it, when they need it.

Top three product differentiators; describe what makes your product unique.

1. ABT Publisher offers knowledge-centric reporting with refreshed information from the ABT Repository, reflecting the latest project status.
2. ABT Publisher offers safe and secure information access.
3. Acts as a virtual project notebook—connecting your project home page to a URL address, a related project site, doc files, spreadsheets, or other applications.

To what business processes can this tool be applied?

Communications management, program and project management, and process management.

Describe the ideal end user environment for the current version of your product (size of organization, level of project management sophistication, effort and commitment required).

ABT Publisher can benefit organizations of fifty to fifty thousand project-related resources, with every constituency benefiting from the information that ABT Publisher distributes across the enterprise.

Future strategies for this product.

Extend functionality, and enhance scalability.

Product's target market.

Enterprise project management.

What are your product's three main benefits? (How does using the product add value to the customer?)

1. Improved communications management.
2. Integrated project stakeholder information base.
3. Improved data integrity (from repository-refreshed information).

Describe your quality management process. List any relevant certifications.

ABT's test enginering organization provides extensive in-house product quality testing using a series of proprietary testing methodologies, supplemented by external resources to perform activities such as high-volume benchmarking. ABT's test group has also been instrumental in contributing to the definition of IEEE Year 2000 testing standards.

Discuss your product pricing structure. Include volume discount levels, concurrent user options, site licenses, cost of implementation, and other issues.

Pricing is on a named-user basis. List prices: ABT Publisher—$75. Volume discounts apply.

Cost of implementation: Rapid implementation—six-week process enablement around RM tool set = $75k. Additional services include project management maturity evaluation, tool training, project management concepts training, process customization and implementation, and systems integration/custom programming work.

Annual maintenance (client support program) = 15 percent of purchase price.

AutoPLAN Enterprise (Digital Tools)

Describe what the product is designed to do.

AutoPLAN Enterprise Release 4 is a Web-based software and process solution to help high-tech, engineering, and telecommunications companies predict, control, and improve cycle time of critical program development and deployment. The solution set provides deep functionality across the entire spectrum of product life-cycle elements including pipeline management, project management, resource alignment, process effectiveness, and document support and team collaboration. AutoPLAN Enterprise integrates realistic planning, resource-centric management, status and forecast tracking, team collaboration, process support, escalation management, and program execution across globally distributed organizations.

Organizations are evolving from functional teams to matrix or program teams, and this is creating cross-functional or multidisciplinary project teams. AutoPLAN Enterprise recognizes three different organizational patterns that coexist: dynamic peer-to-peer, functional, and program management. AutoPLAN Enterprise offers these organizations both project-centric and resource-centric management. AutoPLAN Enterprise addresses everyone involved in product development and deployment including executives; program, product, resource, and project managers; and team leaders and team members, as well as teams from marketing, operations, service, and quality.

As a result of extensive process and product consulting with clients engaged in new product development and deployment, DTI has distilled four key reasons why products are late and descoped:

1. Product development pipeline and deployment structures that are not aligned with the company's time-to-market goals.

2. Unrealistic plans, overcommitted resources, and unmanaged cross-functional dependencies.

3. Status and forecast decisions that are based on hearsay, rather than on facts or experience.

4. A lack of consistent processes that fit the company culture and practice, which is further exacerbated by distributed cross-functional teams.

Avoiding late and descoped products requires an overall view of product and project status, the involvement of cross-functional teams, and decision evaluation tools. Increasingly accelerated product development cycles and shorter product life cycles require organizations to disseminate information quickly to remain competitive. To support today's geographically dispersed product development environments, organizations require a common platform that enables effective cross-functional collaboration and communication on product development issues. It is also imperative that the introduction of new product information can be easily accessible by each stakeholder. Common platforms and accessible information by each stakeholder will result in accelerated organizational learning and decision-making within the organization.

DTI has created a cycle time management (CTM) framework comprising both application and process support. This framework emphasizes the critical components involved in introducing and deploying the right products and services to the market at the right time. Introducing and deploying these products and services requires companies to institute well-defined new product planning and execution processes, complemented with customer management and performance measurement processes. The new planning processes should consist of product portfolio, technology portfolio, product planning, and resource planning. The execution processes must consist of advanced technology development, platform development, product development, market introduction and deployment.

CTM enables companies to strike a balance between flexibility and discipline that is tailored to their organization and culture. The CTM framework supports a flexible *shrink-to-fit* process, which is adaptable to an organization's process maturity. This process will provide a road map for decision-making and progress tracking within a new product introduction and deployment pipeline.

CTM consists of six fundamental elements: 1) processes, 2) projects, 3) resources, 4) documents, 5) deliverables, and 6) analysis. These six elements form the foundation objectives that drive AutoPLAN Enterprise. Organizations require a well-defined and structured process to accomplish their goals. Projects make up the mechanisms through which detailed plans and schedules are generated, executed, and tracked. Every organization faces resource constraints; thus, resource management is a critical component of CTM. All projects have deliverables associated with them either in the form of documents or the product itself. And, all projects must be managed to ensure quality deliverables. Analysis tools enable various levels of stakeholders to evaluate and ensure proper support of all elements necessary to meet CTM objectives.

Top three product differentiators; describe what makes your product unique.

1. AutoPLAN Enterprise enables organizations to manage their pipeline of resources across programs and across the phase gates of each project. It assures an escalation process for critical issues, such as overallocations, by monitoring boundary conditions and alerting appropriate people to the issues. Project managers are interested in the completion of tasks or milestones, while resource managers need to know all of the work planned for their resources. Both project and resource managers must collaborate to create realistic plans for meeting project objectives, as well as juggle those resources and plans on a day-to-day basis as changes occur. The nature of this work requires a resource-centric view of the plan, not just an activity-centric view. A resource-centric view will allow resource managers to view and allocate activities to their scarce resources, rather than allocating resources to their activities. AutoPLAN Enterprise enables resource management by providing a resource-centric Gantt bar that displays overallocated resources. Managing overallocations can be as easy as reassigning activities to another resource.

Program management is a collaborative effort. Success depends upon identifying and communicating critical issues. Such identification and communication must be inherent in the system. AutoPLAN Enterprise is designed with a communications backbone. A mechanism of triggers identifies critical issues (e.g., when milestone or cost exceeds a threshold boundary) and automatically alerts and draws attention to these critical issues. Project bulletin boards within AutoPLAN Enterprise also enhance communication by providing a context-sensitive vehicle for communicating information across the project team. In addition, AutoPLAN Enterprise supports electronic mail systems, enabling triggers and bulletin board messages to be communicated to the various levels of stakeholders.

2. AutoPLAN Enterprise supports the distributed nature of project teams by matching real-world strategy with key scalable technologies. Enterprise customers need distributed project management capabilities that cater to multisite resource management, work distribution, progress tracking, global scheduling, consolidation, reporting, integration, and collaboration. DTI has met this challenge by investing over one hundred man-years in an enterprise-level, three-tier, distributed client/server architecture that leverages both Java and Internet technologies. AutoPLAN Enterprise provides full support for multiple internal operating divisions and external suppliers. AutoPLAN Enterprise leverages many platforms—Internet, Windows, NT, and Unix—providing reliable access across the organization. Additionally, AutoPLAN Enterprise enables common project data to be shared by different projects at different locations while being maintained in a central data center that is managed by pool server software. Project data is maintained at each geographic location on either individual or multiple servers, depending on the number of internal operating divisions and projects. A divisional pool server can also be implemented to share the project data within divisional projects. AutoPLAN Enterprise application servers are capable of scalable distributed processing, and only the server needs the capacity for large multiproject operations. AutoPLAN Enterprise has multiserver cross-project dependency links. For example, the owner of a schedule that depends on the completion of activities in another project can create cross-project links that automatically update his schedule when changes occur in the other project, even if that project resides on a different server.

3. AutoPLAN Enterprise leverages client/server/Web technologies. The promise of Java, which AutoPLAN Enterprise supports, is that enterprise deployments, including organizations with heterogeneous environments, can be cost-effectively supported. DTI Web products are easier to use than Microsoft Project and are cheaper to deploy. The rapid spread of Internet protocols and Web servers into corporate infrastructure make the Internet an ideal vehicle to support both enterprise computing and mobile employees. In addition, systems administration is simplified since no maintenance is required on the client side.

A very practical use of AutoPLAN Enterprise Web clients is that they can run in a disconnected mode on the Internet. With AutoPLAN Enterprise, the user can simply log on and save activities and other information to a local file. She can then continue to work while disconnected. At any time, the connection can be reestablished, either remotely or locally, and the data is resynchronized. This may be useful for dial-up connections when working remotely. The Web server handles all communications with the Web clients, whether they are communicating via the Internet, dial-up, LAN, or WAN. The AutoPLAN Enterprise Web clients can be run from any browser that supports Java 1.1, and the Web server will dynamically download the Java code to run the application on the client. DTI's Web strategy supports *thin* client computing. In this case, database-oriented servers are serving lightweight clients through Web servers and standard protocols. The AutoPLAN Enterprise Web clients are ideally suited for running on a Java-based network computer.

To what business processes can this tool be applied?

From business analysis and redesign to system implementation and training, DTI has established its own process to support the customer through all phases of CTM system implementation. However, as to applying AutoPLAN Enterprise to the customer's business processes, DTI takes a very pragmatic approach. DTI has established processes to help customers with the following seven business pains:

1. Managing the development and deployment pipeline in detail.

2. Top-down and bottom-up planning that enables managers to use team members' knowledge during up-front planning.

3. Juggling resources realistically, so that resources are not overcommitted and parochial allocations are not made, but rather a mechanism for cooperation on resource tradeoffs is created.

4. Creating an organizational memory that captures organizational experience for reuse the next time.

5. Obtaining weekly integrated tracking information on how programs are progressing against their plans. This can be achieved by capturing actual time spent, estimates-to-complete, percent complete, and actual start and finish.

6. Problem identification, escalation, and collaboration that allows management and the team to receive adequate notice of impending issues.

7. Interactive decision evaluation to understand the domino effect of a problem in one project and its possible cross-program impact, and obtain a swift resolution between participants.

Any combination of these processes will help organizations better understand and make use of critical path methodology, work breakdown structures, resource management, cost and earned value techniques, multiproject resource scheduling, resource allocation, status tracking, report generation, matrix management solutions, integration with other systems, middleware design, project management process design, project rollups, report generation, database design, customized product training courses, generic project management training, and more.

Describe the ideal end-user environment for the current version of your product (size of organization, level of project management sophistication, effort and commitment required).

AutoPLAN Enterprise is ideal for high-tech, engineering, and telecommunications organizations engaged in distributed product development and deployments. Its usage also extends to these organizations' distributors and partners. The role-based nature of AutoPLAN Enterprise spans all people involved, from executive management to the entire cross-functional product team. This includes experienced project and program managers, resource and development managers, and the team members creating or deploying the product. The AutoPLAN Enterprise Web client is specifically designed for those team leaders who are not full-time, experienced project managers. In fact, DTI has designed the AutoPLAN Enterprise Web client to be easier to use and more functional than Microsoft Project.

Organizations can start at either the program level right away and manage the overall pipeline of projects and resources at the business unit level, or at the individual project level. The Auto-PLAN Enterprise Web client is not only easier to use than Microsoft Project, but is also capable of managing cross-functional dependencies and resources and offering enterprise scalability when the organization is ready to expand.

Coordinating distributed projects is a difficult task. It involves resources not only from multiple projects, but also from multiple functions within those projects. The program manager responsible must understand all of the interactions and milestones required to complete the project, but he cannot and should not develop and manage the entire plan himself. Instead, he should rely on the distributed functional leaders who are responsible for their piece of the project to plan and execute that piece. As a program manager, he needs to be able to integrate the individual team plans into a single comprehensive project plan. In many organizations, this integration of people and data is difficult; AutoPLAN Enterprise is designed to help with this. Having processes in place, underpinned by enterprise software, is key to predicting, controlling, and improving product/project cycle times.

Future strategies for this product.

AutoPLAN Enterprise has been designed with an integrated product management platform for all information related to meeting CTM objectives. DTI will continue to support features needed for CTM, including pipeline and portfolio management. Future strategies will enhance the ability of customers to make informed decisions based on a comprehensive presentation of relevant data with powerful drill-down capabilities, further collaborative features that utilize the intranet and Internet, and continuing support for the free-flowing nature of the engineering culture. Application wizards will help first-time users, accelerate deployment, and reduce training cost. Process support is key to productivity improvements and to adhering to organizationwide standards. Existing process-support capabilities will be enhanced using the capabilities of Web technology and with more exchange of information across subsystems. Large organizations are geographically distributed to take advantage of global efficiencies. Local and global workgroups must collaborate and respond quickly to changing environment and work content. Both executive management and front-line team members must have access anytime, anywhere, and in any manner to enterprisewide product/project information located on geographically distributed servers. Existing multiserver capabilities of AutoPLAN Enterprise are being enhanced using Oracle.

AutoPLAN Enterprise will support key technologies including Oracle, NT 5.0, middleware, and Java. Distributed objects capability using industry-standard specifications such as CORBA will be incorporated. In addition, the AutoPLAN Enterprise application-programming interface will provide CORBA-compliant objects for seamless integration with other applications. The collaboration capabilities of AutoPLAN Enterprise will be enhanced by incorporating a workflow server. This workflow server will be based on industry-standard specifications and will incorporate process modeling and messaging components to enable customers to configure the collaboration features based upon their business needs. The security system will have additional features to address the security risks associated with the Internet. Directory servers conforming to LDAP standards will be incorporated for seamless integration with the underlying operating environment. This in turn will provide responsive security, configurability, and flexibility features.

Product's target market.

AutoPLAN Enterprise is specifically designed to support high-tech, engineering, and telecommunications organizations in predicting, controlling, and improving cycle time of critical program development and deployment.

What are your product's three main benefits? (How does using the product add value to the customer?)

1. AutoPLAN Enterprise provides at least a 10 percent improvement in enterprise time-to-market of product development and deployment. Viewing the value of CTM from an annual R&D cost perspective: consider a product development group of one thousand people, with an annual R&D expenditure of $100M. A modest 10 percent improvement would represent a cost savings value of $10M, with a revenue enhancement value of three to five times this.

2. AutoPLAN Enterprise facilitates an organization's transformation from functional project teams to matrix, or program-organized high-performance project teams. It also supports distributed teams resulting from acquisitions. It does both of these by providing built-in communication and rollup features from distributed multiserver projects. This support enables teamwide problem identification, escalation, collaboration, and resolution. AutoPLAN Enterprise recognizes that three different organizational patterns coexist: 1) dynamic peer-to-peer, 2) functional, and 3) program management. Auto-PLAN Enterprise offers these organizations both project-centric and resource-centric management.

3. AutoPLAN Enterprise accommodates joint ventures, subcontracting, mergers and acquisitions, and reorganizations by leveraging the Web to minimize deployment and support costs. The creation of plans, assignment of work, and integration of activities across multiple functions and distributed work teams is critically important. However, that is only part of the story. With the Internet, AutoPLAN Enterprise can also efficiently equip thousands of personnel involved in the product-development process with the information they need to do the best possible job. Demand for skilled workers has been great, and turnover has risen as employees move from one company or job to another. The best practices in the world are of no value to a company if those who know those practices move on without first passing along the knowledge. Best practices developed at one site need to be shared with other sites, and a process for doing that is required. AutoPLAN Enterprise solves these problems through URL references and retrieval capability. With URL features, AutoPLAN Enterprise can help preserve best practices and other information and disseminate them geographically and functionally to team members currently doing the job. AutoPLAN Enterprise can also have associated URL references that point to mission-critical information/documentation that will enable product/project teams to achieve the activity. These references can also be attached to the top-level program schedule for project leader use, or at specific functional schedules (e.g., to provide sourcing with specific third-party vendor requirements). URLs can enable:

- Sharing best practice information from one team to another
- Referencing documentation with checklists
- Sharing engineering notes on installation processes.

Also, with the speed of organizational changes, a mix of project-scheduling system usage is expected. As most people are educated on Microsoft Project, AutoPLAN Enterprise can coexist with its projects and data. AutoPLAN Enterprise's GUIs are not only familiar to Microsoft Project users, the Web version is easier and thus leverages simplicity and ease of use with enterprise functionality.

Describe your quality management process. List any relevant certifications.

DTI achieves excellence in product quality and customer satisfaction through its quality management process. DTI's quality objective is to build quality into its products and services at all stages of product life cycle from requirement collection to customer usage. DTI's dedication to quality is reflected in its quality mission: "Doing things right the first time."

DTI's quality management group performs the functions of the software engineering process group as defined by the industry-standard CMM. The quality management group plans and implements DTI's quality system, which consists of processes and guidelines. The processes detail out *what* is required for converting a set of inputs to outputs in the form of activities and tasks, primary and cooperative responsibilities, deliverables, and entry and exit criteria. The guidelines detail *how* to carry out the identified activities to ensure quality and consistency. The involvement of DTI personnel at all levels is fundamental to the implementation of the quality process. DTI personnel are drawn from various groups in the organization to author processes and guidelines, and all undergo training programs on the quality system.

DTI follows processes within Level 2 and Level 3 of the CMM. Some of the key processes within these levels include market requirement analysis, functional specification, high- and low-level design, coding, testing, release management, customer support, training, and maintenance. In addition, in-depth reviews are built into each of these processes.

DTI recognizes that enterprise growth and profitability are significantly impacted by time-to-market of new products in globally competitive high-tech markets. With this in mind, DTI's product development and quality processes are focused on meeting customer needs and requirements. Therefore, DTI collaborates with its customers both in product definition and in assuring that the product functions are implemented as intended. To facilitate the fast-track delivery of innovative products and services, DTI has created process initiatives for increased test automation, usage of tools that will enable teams to better assess the quality of their work products, management of development tools, reuse of objects across products, and tightly controlled configuration management.

DTI's quality management process focuses on periodic reviews and feedback, which are a means of monitoring the adherence of organizational activities to the process. Corrective and preventive actions play an important role in continuous improvement of the quality system and thereby the organizational activities.

DTI has a well-qualified team for quality management. DTI's teams, besides having the appropriate educational qualifications, have quality management-related certifications; some are certified quality analysts, and some hold certificates related to the CMM and its use. Many also have extensive internal audit experience.

The quality management group interacts periodically with key personnel of different functions within the organization and identifies new processes, guidelines, and improvements within the existing framework. The general approach to new process/guideline introduction is to discuss with representative users, define the process, pilot the process after review, evaluate the pilot implementation, revise the process based on feedback, plan organizationwide implementation, implement, measure, and maintain.

DTI is planning to get CMM certification at the appropriate level. The approach that would be followed for securing the certification includes mapping key process areas of the CMM to existing processes, identifying the *gaps*, preparing the implementation plan that describes how these gaps will be addressed, and executing the plan.

Discuss your product pricing structure. Include volume discount levels, concurrent user options, site licenses, cost of implementation, and other issues.

DTI's objective is to offer an integrated solution with a pricing structure that is based on enterprise requirements reflecting enterprise needs and individual needs. AutoPLAN Enterprise supports a floating license configuration, which allows any user to log into the system and consume one license. When the user has finished with the application, that license will be released for other users. Each floating license provides one concurrent use of the product. AutoPLAN Enterprise also supports a personal license configuration. Typical installations will use both personal and concurrent licensing.

Annual product maintenance is 15 percent of the list cost. Product maintenance entitles customers to engineering patches, updates, and upgrades, and phone, fax, and E-mail response to issues. Professional services are separate from DTI product maintenance. As part of the business relationship with customers, DTI takes part in joint planning to identify the customer's business needs and services sought from DTI. Professional services are charged separately on an as-needed basis. These services are performed either at the customer site, online, or at DTI's headquarters in Cupertino, California. Professional services typically fall into two categories: 1) product consulting/implementation design review and 2) implementation support. Product consulting/implementation design review discusses areas such as, "How do I apply the software with a suitable process to solve a business need?" and, "Which processes will we implement, how, and when to meet organizational objectives?" Implementation support consists of product training, project office services, upgrade migration services, systems administration services, and integration services.

Enterprise Project (jeTECH DATA SYSTEMS, INC.)

Describe what the product is designed to do.

Enterprise Project is a completely integrated solution (all applications share a common database and operate on the same hardware platform). Consequently, our response to the narrative questions here repeats what we supplied for the Suites chapter, as those responses apply to all our applications.

Enterprise Project is a powerful new client/server software application that offers project-based organizations a simple way to define and staff projects, and record project labor and expenses throughout their enterprise. Essentially a suite of robust, user-friendly applications integrated into a single desktop, this comprehensive project management system enables team members to accurately plan and track labor resources across all projects. Perfect either as a *stand-alone* solution or as the ideal complement to the jeTECH labor-management system—Enterprise Labor—it is particularly well-suited for multiuser, enterprisewide installations. Together, Enterprise Labor and Enterprise Project are the only systems currently on the market with extensive capabilities and integrated products for both the salaried professional (engineers and computer programmers, for instance) and the hourly employee (from factory workers to registered nurses).

Users access all functions via a single desktop with a Microsoft Office 98 *look and feel*. The system integrates completely with Enterprise Labor and Microsoft Project, as well as with most popular accounting and human resource (HR) systems. In today's competitive environment, effective and efficient use of labor resources is key to completing mission-critical projects on time, on budget. Enterprise Project gives project leaders a comprehensive, potent tool with which to manage scarce technical resources.

With Enterprise Project, managers can budget and schedule projects based on staff skills and availability. Project team members can manage their own tasks, report actual labor and travel expenses, and provide status reports on these tasks. The system calculates actual project costs by automatically incorporating labor costs, material costs, and travel expenses.

Project managers can define and manage both contract and noncontract-based projects, and control work authorizations that will keep each project under control and on budget. As a project manager, you simply create activities for your projects, assign appropriate resources to these activities, and define how labor will be charged to a contract. And by allowing employees to only charge preassigned tasks, Enterprise Project prevents performance of unauthorized work.

Enterprise Project enables all users to report labor charges right from their PC or workstation. Project managers need no longer compile project team information manually. Users can now report project time, as well as other time, and the system automatically processes and transmits it to an interfaced time-and-attendance system for payroll use.

Enterprise Project includes a contract maintenance module. Companies with hourly employees contracted with outside firms—for instance, security guards or programmers—would benefit from using this module without the rest of the project management system. This module is primarily designed, however, to accommodate projects being managed for clients. This module allows contract managers to define contract information including budgets and rates per hour, as well as all products and services purchased by the customer. They can then use this information to evaluate projects based on user-defined deliverables. Contract maintenance is by no means static. So jeTECH has designed Enterprise Project to handle change orders, R&D projects, and discounts. A variety of unique reporting features enables contract managers to view cost overruns, variances, and milestone completions.

Top three product differentiators; describe what makes your product unique.

1. Resource scheduling from a common resource pool in a multiproject environment.
2. Integrated time collection and status reporting.
3. Sensitivity analysis (what-if scenarios).

To what business processes can this tool be applied?

Project planning/management, enterprise resource scheduling/management, time collection, performance measurement, time and expense reporting, budgeting and estimating, and project accounting.

Describe the ideal end-user environment for the current version of your product (size of organization, level of project management sophistication, effort and commitment required).

Any resource-constrained enterprise (IT, high-tech R&D, engineering) with multiple projects and multiple sites. Requires a low level of project management sophistication.

Future strategies for this product.

Maintenance and repair operations, incorporation of process ware/templates, enterprise-level project and resource integration, and full Internet capabilities.

Product's target market.

Companies with *task-oriented* professionals such as engineers, architects, IS professionals, researchers, advertising/marketing professionals, etc. See also the previous response to "ideal end-user environment."

What are your product's three main benefits? (How does using the product add value to the customer?)

1. Improved resource utilization and efficiencies.
2. Reduction in time to complete projects.
3. Cost control.

Describe your quality management process. List any relevant certifications.

Our current quality management process includes in-house testing, which incorporates both automated and manual processes and procedures.

Discuss your product pricing structure. Include volume discount levels, concurrent user options, site licenses, cost of implementation, and other issues.

Pricing is structured on a named-user basis. Pricing will also be dependent on a number of variables including the size of the enterprise, number of project managers, number of facilities, etc. Consequently, pricing is provided to each customer when we have been able to familiarize ourselves on their operations and their anticipated use of the system.

Several options are available for training, tech support, annual maintenance, etc. Costs are provided to each customer when they have been able to select the options deemed best for their operations.

ER Project 1000 (Eagle Ray Software Systems)

Describe what the product is designed to do.

The ER Project 1000 is an integrated suite of project management tools, which provide an enterprisewide project management solution. ER Project 1000 includes schedule/time management, centralized resource management, methodology/process management, project-workgroup communications, timesheets, risk/issue management, and enterprisewide cross-project tracking. Based on a client/server architecture with a centralized relational database, the ER Project 1000 provides networked access, multiproject capability, and true multiuser concurrency. It scales easily from handling small workgroup projects to large programs at the enterprise level.

444

Top three product differentiators; describe what makes your product unique.

1. Addresses the total project management life-cycle solution for the enterprise: Unlike most project management tools, the ER Project 1000 provides a completely integrated and centralized project management platform to support the entire life cycle of project management. Based on a client/server relational database (Oracle/SQL Server) architecture, ER Project 1000 fully supports today's multiproject/multiuser project environment. The product suite integrates full methodology/process management capabilities, project workgroup communications, and enterprisewide project tracking capabilities.

2. Provides a completely integrated suite of project management tools: The ER Project 1000 tool suite integrates industrial-strength project management functions with rich-process improvement functionality and proactive management features. ER Project 1000 provides all the necessary industrial-strength core project management functions. Key features include support for WBS/organizational breakdown structure/RBS structures, cost, schedule, earned value analysis, built-in report writer, timesheet approvals, and centralized resource management. ER Project 1000 takes advantage of the Web by providing Java timesheets and extensive project website publishing capability. Best practices/process improvement is easily accomplished with the methodology manager and support for organizational standards, work products, and estimation. ER Project 1000 delivers an impressive array of proactive management features. These features include risk management, issue management, management by threshold, and full project tracking.

3. Is easy to use and implement: ER Project 1000 was designed with a simple, intuitive interface. Extensive wizards assist users for complex operations. ER Project 1000 can easily be configured to your organization by using our centralized administration functions and component architecture.

To what business processes can this tool be applied?

ER Project 1000 is a wrap-around solution for organizations that need to implement mature project management practices, proactively manage their projects, improve business processes, implement standards and documentation, and communicate at multiple levels. Eagle Ray's advanced suite of tools provides project managers with an integrated platform for project planning, time tracking, resource management, and executive oversight. With features such as risk management, issue tracking, and management by threshold, the ER Project 1000 gives project managers the ability to proactively manage complex projects and stay focused on the key issues.

Organizations that engage in process improvement/best practices will find that the ER Project 1000 methodology manager is the ideal platform for developing and delivering best practices to each new project plan. Project managers will be able to easily document and reuse lessons learned in new projects. Project team members and stakeholders will find that the integrated communications features of the ER Project 1000 suite facilitate a real-time dialogue between all members and ensure no issues slip though the cracks.

Describe the ideal end-user environment for the current version of your product (size of organization, level of project management sophistication, effort and commitment required).

Size of organization: The ER Project 1000 product suite is ideal for managing projects with team sizes of ten to one thousand people per project in organizations where multiple projects are being performed at the same time. Project teams may be centralized or dispersed using client/server and Web-based communications technologies.

Level of sophistication: The tool suite is best suited for organizations that are moving beyond basic project management to a medium level of project management maturity or higher. These organizations are typically implementing tracking, costing, project management standards, risk/issue management, time tracking, centralized resource management, and possibly earned value. ER Project 1000 also supports organizations implementing a project office, best practices, process improvement, and reusable project templates. These features make ER Project 1000 an ideal platform for organizations implementing CMM level 2 or higher maturity levels.

Effort and commitment required: Successful implementation of the ER Project 1000 tool suite centers on an organization's commitment to realizing repeatable project management results from enterprisewide standardization of business processes and practices. Because of it's integrated design and simple interface, ER Project 1000 delivers numerous advantages over standard project management tool sets with less staff effort.

Future strategies for this product.

Eagle Ray's future strategies include building new modules, expanding current modules, interfacing with corporate business systems, and preparing the product suite for the global marketplace. Major planned enhancements include significant modifications to the estimation module, costing module, methodology/process management module, and the Internet/intranet/Web capabilities. In addition, we will be constructing a problem/defect-tracking module.

We will be expanding the interfaces that integrate the ER Project 1000 system with additional enterprise business systems. Such systems include costing/accounting systems, HR systems, and additional commercial products. We also plan to complete our internationalization/localization efforts to prepare the ER Project 1000 for global distribution.

Product's target market.

ER Project 1000 is suitable for commercial and government organizations, which are managing projects that range from small workgroup-level projects to projects that span the entire enterprise. Essentially, the tool suite will support any project environment where the project team has access to or is working with computers.

What are your product's three main benefits? (How does using the product add value to the customer?)

1. Total integrated project management solution: The ER Project 1000 is an integrated, total project management solution providing complete support for the entire project management life cycle. The integrated tool suite does not require multiple add-on tools from different vendors, resulting in fewer hidden costs and less frustration. Project managers will find it easy to manage projects with a higher level of maturity by using the various features of the tool—for example, risk management, issue tracking, management by threshold, and multiproject capabilities.

2. Best practices/process improvement platform: The ER Project 1000 integrated process/methodology management platform provides a sophisticated yet easy-to-use platform for implementing best practices, estimation metrics, organizational standards, documentation templates, and process improvement. Organizations can capture, integrate, and reuse their project knowledge and project plan templates from an enterprisewide integrated platform.

3. Enterprisewide tracking and communications: The ER Project 1000 facilitates communications between all project stakeholders. Program managers and executives can perform cross-project rollups, dynamic drill-down, and cost, schedule, and earned-value analysis for up-to-date information on all enterprise projects. The project team members can access all of project information on the project website, and receive activity assignments and report status using Java timesheets. Automatic issue notification alerts project managers about possible deviations in cost and schedule. The built-in report writer lets you extract and summarize any data in the enterprisewide project database using customized formats.

Describe your quality management process. List any relevant certifications.

The Eagle Ray quality assurance program is a comprehensive system that employs a series of product walkthroughs, builds, quality gates, configuration management, defect tracking, and comprehensive testing. The development staff members are constantly conducting requirements, design, and code walkthroughs in coordination with weekly product builds and passing mandatory quality gates. The quality assurance program is integrated with our beta testing program to ensure that all product releases undergo rigorous real-world testing prior to release.

Comprehensive testing scenarios include unit testing, integration testing, platform testing, stress testing, concurrency testing, environment testing, security testing, usability testing, vertical testing, upgrade testing, business scenario testing, and independent qualification testing.

During the design and construction of the ER Project 1000 product, Eagle Ray brought in several project management industry experts to assist in the design of the software functionality and usability. This process will be continued to ensure that our future enhancements meet the real-world needs of project management organizations. Additionally, Eagle Ray continues to invest heavily in the training of team members in technical and project management areas.

Discuss your product pricing structure. Include volume discount levels, concurrent user options, site licenses, cost of implementation, and other issues.

Call for latest prices.

Mesa/Vista (Mesa/Vista Systems Guild)

Describe what the product is designed to do.

Mesa/Vista helps project teams manage, monitor, and comply with quality and government regulations by providing process management capabilities and access to all legacy and current project data through a Web browser. Mesa/Vista provides process management capabilities and integrates a development team's existing product environment, including tools like Rational Rose, TD Technologies' SLATE, Cayenne Teamwork, or any tool with an MPX interface, such as Microsoft Project.

Mesa/Vista links information between stand-alone products and exposes project data to authorized project team members, empowering them to anticipate and solve problems at early stages in the project life cycle.

Mesa/Vista automates the documentation process. This shaves time from a project that must comply with government or other regulatory standards because the documentation is available as soon as the project is complete.

Top three product differentiators; describe what makes your product unique.

1. Patent-pending technology intuitively links graphical objects, such as those found in developer's modeling tools, not only within the stand-alone tool but also between tools.
2. Provides support of any business process through dynamic exchange of information.
3. Connects legacy and current data between development team's business and engineering tools.

To what business processes can this tool be applied?

SEI CMM levels 1–5, ISO compliancy regulations, FDA requirements management.

Describe the ideal end user environment for the current version of your product (size of organization, level of project management sophistication, effort and commitment required).

The ideal end-user environment for Mesa/Vista is a distributed, process-conscious product development group needing visibility and access to legacy and current project data across multiple platforms.

An organization trying to achieve or improve upon an SEI CMM level, achieves an ISO 9000 quality standard, or complies with FDA requirements will greatly benefit from the Mesa/Vista environment.

Commitment: All project-related communications would go through the Mesa/Vista environment for it to provide complete, automated project status information.

Future strategies for this product.

Future strategies for Mesa/Vista include integrating all engineering and business data together to be shared and accessed by the entire product development team, no matter where the data resides.

Plug-ins will include more scheduling tools, databases, business tools, document-editing tools, and modeling tools—all the tools the entire team would use within a product development environment.

Mesa/Vista will create an environment of collaboration and expose information, to help all members of the team work together without restraint of hardware or system requirements.

Product's target market.

Mesa/Vista is ideal for process-conscious project managers of distributed product development teams in the telecommunication, automotive, aerospace, medical, and software industries.

What are your product's three main benefits? (How does using the product add value to the customer?)

1. Provides accessibility to data from places other than the data's native machine, minimizing the number of copies of each software product that needs to be purchased.
2. Saves time by providing online access to all project data, rather than printing and faxing information in order to share it.
3. Automatic documentation mechanism for ease of tracking government regulations or quality standards control.

Describe your quality management process. List any relevant certifications.

Mesa/Vista is used to manage the development of Mesa/Vista. Also, extensive internal and external testing is done of the Mesa/Vista product line. Mesa has provided the software to Young America's design team (NYYC's challenger in the America's Cup 2K) in exchange for feedback on Mesa/Vista and suggestions for improvements based on their real-life use of the product line.

Discuss your product pricing structure. Include volume discount levels, concurrent user options, site licenses, cost of implementation, and other issues.

Contact vendor.

Open Plan/Web Publisher

Describe what the product is designed to do.

Provides Web access to project-related information within Open Plan. Welcom's Open Plan is an enterprisewide project management system that substantially improves a company's ability to manage and complete multiple projects on time and within budget with a limited workforce. Unlike less sophisticated products, Open Plan is a highly integrated, comprehensive software system that can be customized to fit specific corporate requirements. It is the most technically advanced client/server project management system on the market, using the latest in Microsoft Windows development technology.

Top three product differentiators; describe what makes your product unique.

1. Provides up-to-the-minute project information.
2. Part of Open Plan's project management solution.
3. Batch reporting capabilities make it easy to support multiproject implementations.

To what business processes can this tool be applied?

Enterprise resource modeling, business process reengineering, project management, earned value analysis, risk assessment, and process modeling.

Describe the ideal end user environment for the current version of your product (size of organization, level of project management sophistication, effort and commitment required).

Medium to large organizations for which project management is a serious business requirement. Meets the needs of users whose level of expertise varies from novice/occasional to advanced.

Future strategies for this product.

Continue to enhance Web capabilities. Our vision for the future is to provide a suite of component-based products that work together to provide advanced project management functionality using the very latest technology.

Product's target market.

Fortune 1000 companies, government, and multinational organizations implementing enterprisewide project management.

What are your product's three main benefits? (How does using the product add value to the customer?)

1. Provides easy access to current project information.
2. Adds batch-reporting capabilities to Open Plan.
3. Provided as a standard component with Open Plan.

Describe your quality management process. List any relevant certifications.

Adhere to standard industry processes in release and version strategies, including automated regression testing. ISO 9000 certified in the United Kingdom.

Discuss your product pricing structure. Include volume discount levels, concurrent user options, site licenses, cost of implementation, and other issues.

Please call for pricing information. Included in price of Open Plan.

Cost of implementation: Training courses and consulting—please call for pricing information. Tech support—no charge with current maintenance. Maintenance—first year is free with software purchase. Renewed annually.

OPX2 Intranet Server

Describe what the product is designed to do.

OPX2 Intranet Server provides a simple and secure access to OPX2 project charts, forms, and tables on an intranet.

Top three product differentiators; describe what makes your product unique.

1. High-quality graphics integration in intranet pages.
2. Customization of forms and reports without programming.
3. Full dynamic access to data, in read and update modes.

To what business processes can this tool be applied?

No answer given.

Describe the ideal end user environment for the current version of your product (size of organization, level of project management sophistication, effort and commitment required).

No answer given.

Future strategies for this product.

No answer given.

Product's target market.

No answer given.

What are your product's three main benefits? (How does using the product add value to the customer?)

No answer given.

Describe your quality management process. List any relevant certifications.

No answer given.

Discuss your product pricing structure. Include volume discount levels, concurrent user options, site licenses, cost of implementation, and other issues.

No answer given.

PlanView Software (PlanView, Inc.)

Describe what the product is designed to do.

PlanView Sotware has modules that manage the flow of work (projects and nonprojects), and enhance communication among distributed staff and managers. Work is requested, scheduled, progressed, and closed using the Web.

Top three product differentiators; describe what makes your product unique.

1. All desktop interfaces are browser based.
2. Drag and drop with all Microsoft Office applications.
3. Easy three-step process to Web publish PlanView reports.

To what business processes can this tool be applied?

Multiproject management, service request management, resource management, workflow management, work and resource *portfolio* management.

Describe the ideal end user environment for the current version of your product (size of organization, level of project management sophistication, effort and commitment required).

Organizations with one hundred to multiple thousands of employees (we have implementations of four thousand plus), managed by five plus managers with access to a central database; includes matrix-style organizations.

Future strategies for this product.

Further conversion to Web browser-based interfaces, even easier report generation, and Web publishing; more E-mail notification and document attachment.

Product's target market.

The resource-centric approach to work management is typically most useful for organizations with a highly skilled workforce of limited availability; with twenty plus managers, and one hundred plus staff; using client/server.

What are your product's three main benefits? (How does using the product add value to the customer?)

1. Easy three-step process to turn PlanView reports to Web reports.

2. Report views support needs of multiple levels of management.
3. All user interfaces available as Web browsers.

Describe your quality management process. List any relevant certifications.

PlanView follows the guidelines set out in the book *Best Practices of Rapid Development* by Steve McConnell.

Discuss your product pricing structure. Include volume discount levels, concurrent user options, site licenses, cost of implementation, and other issues.

It is different for each case, but basically the cost is $200–$400 per seat, with volume discounts. The repository products are included. Standard SQL database is extra. Implementation and training are extra.

We offer a range of implementation packages, from rapid to standard, which include training. Additional services billed at time and cost. Phone and online tech support are free. Maintenance packages offered.

Prolog WebSite

Describe what the product is designed to do.

Prolog WebSite is an Internet window through which users can see and use Prolog Manager. Subcontractors, architects, engineers, and even owners can use the browser-based interface provided by Prolog WebSite to collaborate on a project with the general contractor.

Top three product differentiators; describe what makes your product unique.

1. Real-time data access with extended security, not simply posted static information.
2. The ability to write directly to the project database.

To what business processes can this tool be applied?

Any perspective of the A/E/C environment.

Describe the ideal end-user environment for the current version of your product (size of organization, level of project management sophistication, effort and commitment required).

Designed to meet needs of a broad spectrum of organizations, from major government agencies, to smaller organizations. Interface and software process aptitude is minimal; information storage and manipulation abilities of Prolog WebSite are vast.

Future strategies for this product.

Continued enhancement of the data collaboration model. Integration of more data entry points.

Product's target market.

A/E/C; public and private owners and agencies; subcontractors.

What are your product's three main benefits? (How does using the product add value to the customer?)

1. Real-time access to project information.
2. The ability to route important correspondences to key players while writing directly to the project database.
3. Viewing and printing live reports via Web browser.

Describe your quality management process. List any relevant certifications.

Extensive Quality Assurance testing, client-based Product Development Advisory Council.

Discuss your product pricing structure. Include volume discount levels, concurrent user options, site licenses, cost of implementation, and other issues.

$1,500 server license, $350 concurrent access licenses. Fifteen percent annual maintenance contract.

WebProject

Describe what the product is designed to do.

WebProject is designed for geographically dispersed project teams. WebProject is a Java-based project management tool with powerful collaboration and communications features. WebProject incorporates unique knowledge management/best practices capability.

Top three product differentiators; describe what makes your product unique.

WebProject is the first (only) pure Java project management suite that can utilize an open architecture database backend. WebProject allows corporations to utilize Oracle, SQL Server, Informix, Sybase, or other databases in their enterprise project management.

WebProject has introduced the first knowledge management/best practices capability within a project management software suite.

WebProject enables global project communication including project issues boards, threaded task discussions, virtual project status meetings, and remote project statusing and updates.

To what business processes can this tool be applied?

Geographically dispersed project teams, projects that need to have access from remote locations, or integrating WebProject's proprietary information exchange with MS Project, Primavera, or other desktop systems.

WebProject allows the extraction of knowledge from the enterprise, such as resource capabilities or company *best practices*.

Describe the ideal end-user environment for the current version of your product (size of organization, level of project management sophistication, effort and commitment required).

WebProject is an easy-to-use Java project management tool that will enable teams to communicate and collaborate from remote locations. WebProject is designed for the enterprise and will work well with project teams as well.

Future strategies for this product.

WebProject has established many *firsts* in the project management industry. We will continue to move the industry forward with our new technologies on the Web and with Java.

Product's target market.

Geographically dispersed project teams, enterprise project management systems, integration with Primavera, MS Project, and other project management systems.

What are your product's three main benefits? (How does using the product add value to the customer?)

1. Enterprise project communication.
2. Project collaboration.
3. Geographically dispersed updates and communication.

Describe your quality management process. List any relevant certifications.

WebProject adheres to strict standards and processes for quality, both in development and customer service.

Discuss your product pricing structure. Include volume discount levels, concurrent user options, site licenses, cost of implementation, and other issues.

WebProject is priced at $790 for starter package including the WebProject server. WebProject does provide enterprise and site licensing.

Chapter 7

Risk Management Software

In today's business environment, change is inevitable. Change creates uncertainty, and uncertainty creates risk. Whether a project is complex or small, schedule risks (such as zero float), cost risks (such as poor estimates), and/or technical risks (such as design errors) occur. The challenge resides with the project manager to control risk.

The risk management techniques that exist today range widely from simple range estimating to complex simulations (Monte Carlo). The software packages that fall under this category materialize several of these risk management techniques.

Within the software packages, we find the following techniques: three-point estimating with weighting factors, *what-if* analysis, probability analysis with multiple distribution scenarios, graphical representations, and, ultimately, expert systems that provide information based on professional experience.

The products that are available target a wide range of industries and processes—research and development (R&D), government, software, medical, electronics, aerospace, professional services, consulting companies, large-scale IT departments, telecommunications, engineering companies—as well as a range of product sophistication that is dependent on the complexity of the project.

Most of these products are applicable to general project management needs; many of them are also applicable to a subset, such as small or enterprisewide projects.

In summary, your overall approach must be not to select the most sophisticated project management software there is, but to select the one that will provide project managers with enough data, early warning, and ability to perform adequate risk analysis to reduce uncertainty over time.

Risk management is detailed in Chapter 11 of *A Guide to the Project Management Body of Knowledge (PMBOK™ Guide)*.

What to Expect:

Risk management software provides features like:
- Documentation of project risks
- Mathematical schedule simulation
- Risk mitigation planning.

What the Data Reveals

Many products had complementary features. Selection will depend on the user's project management maturity, the understanding of statistical techniques, and the need for informational output.

What the Majority of Vendors Offer

Ease of use (tutorials, minimal statistical knowledge, understandable graphical and tabular reports, and executive visibility) enables estimators to quickly get a *feel* for high-risk areas. The majority of products are Windows compatible.

All have interactive help and help-search capabilities.

All offer site license discounts and product enhancements per customer request.

What a Minority of Vendors Offer

Vendors are yet not making multilingual technical support available (although one, Open Plan, is available in seven languages—English, Italian, French, Mandarin, Russian, Hangul, German).

Few products indicate that the client runs on a Web browser.

Few products suggest and document mitigation strategies based on a knowledge database.

In spite of the call for *open architecture* products, five vendors out of the thirteen respondents have proprietary databases.

Very few vendors show, in their future strategies, integration with enterprise business systems (i.e., accounting, human resource (HR) systems).

Unique Features That Surfaced in Vendor Responses to the Narrative Questions

The risk management module from Dekker TRAKKER assigns a consequence and an outcome to each risk parameter. As the project progresses, these parameters are updated with a probability of occurrence, resulting in a status. The status provides information that allows the identification of exceptions and areas that require attention. In this same product, the drill-down capabilities allow the user to reach into the detail elements that contributed to the specific condition, which may produce a more real-time approach to corrective actions.

ER Project 1000 includes features to execute *issues management* and *management by threshold*.

What's New and Exciting

Seven vendors recorded that they can perform Monte Carlo simulation (including cost, schedule, and resource simulation).

ER Project 1000 offers automatic issue notification, which alerts project managers about possible deviations in cost and schedule.

Mesa/Vista Risk Manager offers an automatic documentation mechanism for ease of tracking government regulations and quality standards control.

Future strategies noted by other vendors include continued development; additional features per user requests; new modules, interfacing with corporate business systems; methodology/process management module, Internet/Web capabilities; advance data-mining features, knowledge management integration; computer based training; and intelligent solution generator.

A reminder: The data in the matrix and in the narrative responses were supplied by the vendors and have not been independently verified.

Risk Management

	@RISK Professional for Project	Dekker TRAKKER Risk Management Module	Enterprise Project	ER Project 1000	Intelligent Planner	Mesa/Vista Risk Manager	Monte Carlo (in combination with Primavera Project Planner)	Open Plan	PLANTRAC-MARSHAL
Simulations									
Monte Carlo Simulation?	Y	Y	N	N	N	N	Y	Y	Y
Custom sample size ?	Y	Y	N	N	N	N	Y	Y	Y
Performs schedule simulation	Y	Y	Y	Y	Y	N	Y	Y	Y
Performs cost simulation	Y	Y	Y	Y	Y	N	Y	N	Y
Performs resource simulation	Y	Y	Y	Y	Y	N	Y	N	Y
Analysis									
Analyzes schedule risk									
Standard deviation & variance	Y	Y	Y	N	Y	N	Y	Y	Y
Other statistical coefficients (e.g., mean to complete, confidence interval, median, mode, mean)	Y	Y	N	Y	N	N	Y	Y	
Based on project data (e.g., determine overloaded resources, dependencies at risk)	N	Y	Y	Y	Y	N	Y	Y	Y
By experiment, comparing runs	Y	Y	Y	Y	Y	N	Y	Y	Y
Analyze cost risk									
Standard deviation & variance	Y	Y	Y	N	Y	N	Y	N	Y
Other statistical coefficients (e.g., mean to complete, % confidence level, median, mode, mean)	Y	Y	Y	Y	N	N	Y	N	Y
Graphical representations									
Histograms	Y	Y	Y	Y	Y	Y	Y	Y	Y
Gantt chart	Y	Y	Y	Y	Y	N	Y	Y	Y
Comprehensive reports (i.e., tabular)	Y	Y	Y	Y	Y	N	Y	Y	Y
Features									
Calculation of expected monetary value (risk event probability x risk event value)	Y	Y	Y	Y	Y	Y	N	N	Y
Track criticality index	Y	Y	N	Y	Y	Y	N	Y	Y
Suggest and document mitigation strategies based on knowledge database	N	Y	Y	N	N	Y	N	N	N
Ability to enter assumptions and analysis defaults (example: time or resource constraints)	Y	Y	Y	N	Y	Y	Y	Y	Y
Capability to import and export from/to other standard office automation tools.	Y	Y	Y	N	Y	Y	Y	Y	Y
Risk identification (e.g., checklist)	N	Y	N	Y	Y	Y		Y	Y
Identification of "hangers," sources of risk	N	Y	N	Y	Y	Y	N	Y	Y
Tracks historic risk data (i.e., to be used as a baseline) in order to enable comparisons with ongoing changes.	Y	Y	N	N	Y	Y	Y	Y	N
Support of probability distribution curves									
Uniform	Y	Y	Y	N	N	N	Y	Y	Y

Risk Management

	@RISK Professional for Project	Dekker TRAKKER Risk Management Module	Enterprise Project	ER Project 1000	Intelligent Planner	Mesa/Vista Risk Manager	Monte Carlo (in combination with Primavera Project Planner)	Open Plan	PLANTRAC-MARSHAL
Simulations									
Monte Carlo Simulation?	Y	Y	N	N	N	N	Y	Y	Y
Custom sample size ?	Y	Y	N	N	N	N	Y	Y	Y
Performs schedule simulation	Y	Y	Y	Y	Y	N	Y	Y	Y
Performs cost simulation	Y	Y	Y	Y	Y	N	Y	N	Y
Performs resource simulation	Y	Y	Y	Y	Y	N	Y	N	Y
Analysis									
Analyzes schedule risk									
Standard deviation & variance	Y	Y	Y	N	Y	N	Y	Y	Y
Other statistical coefficients (e.g., mean to complete, confidence interval, median, mode, mean)	Y	Y	N	Y	N	N	Y	Y	Y
Based on project data (e.g., determine overloaded resources, dependencies at risk)	N	Y	Y	Y	Y	N	Y	Y	Y
By experiment, comparing runs	Y	Y	Y	Y	Y	N	Y	Y	Y
Analyze cost risk									
Standard deviation & variance	Y	Y	Y	N	Y	N	Y	N	Y
Other statistical coefficients (e.g., mean to complete, % confidence level, median, mode, mean)	Y	Y	Y	Y	N	N	Y	N	Y
Graphical representations									
Histograms	Y	Y	Y	Y	Y	Y	Y	Y	Y
Gantt chart	Y	Y	Y	Y	Y	N	Y	Y	Y
Comprehensive reports (i.e., tabular)	Y	Y	Y	Y	Y	N	Y	Y	Y
Features									
Calculation of expected monetary value (risk event probability x risk event value)	Y	Y	Y	Y	Y	Y	N	N	Y
Track criticality index	Y	Y	N	Y	Y	Y	N	Y	Y
Suggest and document mitigation strategies based on knowledge database	N	Y	Y	N	N	Y	N	N	N
Ability to enter assumptions and analysis defaults (example: time or resource constraints)	Y	Y	Y	N	Y	Y	Y	Y	Y
Capability to import and export from/to other standard office automation tools.	Y	Y	Y	N	Y	Y	Y	Y	Y
Risk identification (e.g., checklist)	N	Y	N	Y	Y	Y	Y	Y	Y
Identification of "hangers," sources of risk	N	Y	N	Y	Y	Y	N	Y	Y
Tracks historic risk data (i.e., to be used as a baseline) in order to enable comparisons with ongoing changes.	Y	Y	N	N	Y	Y	Y	Y	N
Support of probability distribution curves									
Uniform	Y	Y	Y	N	N	N	Y	Y	Y

Comparison table (rotated on page). Columns 1–9 correspond to the nine products; row labels at left.

Feature	1	2	3	4	5	6	7	8	9
Triangular	Y	Y	Y	N	N	N	Y	Y	Y
Normal	Y	Y	Y	N	N	N	Y	Y	Y
Beta	Y	Y	Y	N	N	N	Y	Y	Y
Maximum and minimum duration	Y	Y	Y	N	N	N	Y	Y	Y
Program Evaluation and Review technique (PERT)	Y	N	N	N	N	N	N	N	Y
Input of low, most likely, and high duration	Y	Y	Y	N	N	N	N	Y	Y
Reporting									
Report writer	Y	Y	Y	Y	Y	Y	N	Y	Y
Report wizard	Y	N	N	N	Y	Y	N	Y	Y
Publishes as HTML	N	Y	N	Y	Y	Y	N	Y	N
Number of user defined fields	20	Unlim.	20	25	100	100	0	Unlim.	Unlim.
Drill-down/roll-up *	Y	Y	N	Y	Y	Y	Y	Y	N
Import/export	Y	Y	N	Y	Y	Y	Y	Y	Y
Automatic E-mail notification *	N	N	N	Y	Y	Y	N	N	N
Macro recorder/batch capable *A76	Y	Y	N	N	Y	N	Y	Y	N
Can "canned" reports be modified?	Y	Y	N	Y	Y	Y	Y	Y	Y
Sort, filter	Y	Y	Y	Y	Y	Y	Y	Y	Y
Architecture									
Databases supported (list)	ODBC	Oracle, MS SQL Server, Sybase, MS Access, FoxPro	Btrieve	MS SQL Server	Oracle, Sybase, MS SQL Server, Informix, Centura	Oracle, MS SQL Server, Interbase	Oracle, Sybase, Informix, MS SQL Server, MS Access	Oracle, MS SQL Server, Informix, MS Access, FoxPro	N/A
Supports distributed databases	N	Y	N	N	N	Y	Y	Y	N
Three-tier client/server	N	Y	N	N	Y	Y	Y	Y	N
Client operating systems	Win 95/98/NT	Win 95 or later	Win 95/NT/3.x	Win 95/NT	Win 95/98/NT 3.51/NT 4.0 (ER Project Satellite also Java and Win 3.x)	Win 95/98/NT	Win 95/98/NT	Win 95/98/NT	N/A
Server operating systems	Win 95/98/NT	Specified by database vendor		Win NT	Win NT	Win NT, Unix	Unix, Win NT	Win NT, Unix	N/A
Network operating systems	Win 95/98/NT	Any that support Win	Most popular operating systems	TCP/IP, NetBios	Win, NetBEUI/NetBios, TCP/IP, Novell	Win, NetBEUI/NetBios, TCP/IP, Novell	Novell, Win NT, others	Win NT, Novell, NFS	N/A
Minimum client configuration	8 MB	Pentium or compatible, Win 95 or later: 16 MB RAM, Rec. 32 MB	486, 8 MB RAM	Pentium 120, 16 MB RAM, 1 GB disk	Pentium, 16 MB memory (ER Project Satellite 8 MB)	486 and 16 MB memory	Pentium 200 CPU, 128 MB, 1 GB	32 MB RAM, 1 GB disk drive, SVGA	N/A
Minimum server configuration	8 MB	Server optional	Not specified	Pentium 233, 128 MB RAM, 1 GB disk	Pentium, 32 MB memory	Pentium 233, 128 MB RAM, 1 GB disk	Pentium 233, 128 MB RAM, 1 GB disk	128 MB RAM, 10 GB HD	N/A
Client runs under Web browser	N	N	N	Y	Y	Y	Y	N	N

Risk Management

	@RISK Professional for Project	Dekker TRAKKER Risk Management Module	Enterprise Project	ER Project 1000	Intelligent Planner	Mesa/Vista Risk Manager	Monte Carlo (in combination with Primavera Project Planner)	Open Plan	PLANTRAC-MARSHAL
Open architecture									
Supports OLE	Y	Y	Y	N	N	N	N	Y	N
Documented Object Model	N	Y	Y	Y	N	Y	N	Y	N
Documented Application Programming Interface (API)	N	Y	Y	N	Y	Y	N	N	N
Simultaneous edit of data file	N	Y	Y	Y	Y	Y	Y	Y	N
Does product have a programming language?	N	Y	Y	N	Y	N	N	N	N
Are years stored as four-digit numbers?	Y	Y	Y	Y	Y	Y	N	Y	Y
Online help									
Right mouse click	Y	Y	N	Y	N	N	N	Y	Y
Hover buttons	Y	Y	N	Y	N	N	N	Y	Y
Interactive help	Y	Y	Y	Y	Y	Y	N	Y	Y
Help search feature	Y	Y	Y	Y	Y	Y	Y	Y	Y
Web access to product knowledge base *	Y	N	N	Y	Y	N	N	Y	N
Vendor information									
Training									
Computer-based training	Y	Y	Y	N	N	N	N	Y	Y
Training materials available	N	Y	Y	Y	Y	Y	Y	Y	Y
Customized training materials	N	Y	Y	Y	Y	Y	Y	Y	Y
Online tutorial	Y	Y	N	Y	Y	Y	N	Y	Y
Consulting available from vendor	N	Y	Y	Y	Y	Y	Y	Y	Y
Site license discounts	Y	Y	Y	Y	Y	Y	Y	Y	Y
Enhancement requests *	N	Y	Y	Y	Y	N	Y	Y	Y
Modify source code, support through upgrades *	N	Y	Y	Y	Y	Y	N	Y	Y
Global presence									
Global offices	Y	Y	N	N	Y	N	Y	Y	N
Multilingual technical support	Y	Y	Y	N	Y	N	Y	Y	N
Language versions (list):	Fr, Ger, Span	Eng	Eng, Span	Eng	Eng, Fr, Ger, Dutch	Eng		Eng, Ital, Fr, Mand, Rus, Hangul, Ger	Eng
Audit Software Quality Assurance process? *	N	Y	Y	Y	Y	Y	N	N	Y
Security									
Configurable access privileges *	N	Y	Y	Y	Y	Y	Y	Y	N
Passwords expire (forced update)	N	Y	Y	N	N	Y	N	N	N
Electronic approvals	N	Y	Y	Y	Y	Y	N	N	N
Password protect files	N	Y	Y	Y	Y	N	Y	Y	N

Risk Management

	Project Risk Analysis	Project Self-Assessment Kit	Risk+	RiskTrak	SLIM / SLIM-Control	WebProject
Simulations						
Monte Carlo Simulation?	Y	N	Y	N	Y	N
Custom sample size ?	Y	N	Y	Y	Y	N
Performs schedule simulation	N	N	Y	Y	Y	Y
Performs cost simulation	Y	N	Y	Y	Y	Y
Performs resource simulation	N	N	Y	Y	Y	Y
Analysis						
Analyzes schedule risk						
Standard deviation & variance	N	Y	Y	N	Y	N
Other statistical coefficients (e.g., mean to complete, confidence interval, median, mode, mean)	N	Y	Y	N	Y	N
Based on project data (e.g., determine overloaded resources, dependencies at risk)	N	Y	Y	N	Y	N
By experiment, comparing runs	N	N	Y	N	Y	N
Analyze cost risk						
Standard deviation & variance	Y	N	Y	Y	Y	N
Other statistical coefficients (e.g., mean to complete, % confidence level, median, mode, mean)	Y	Y	Y	Y	Y	N
Graphical representations						
Histograms	Y	Y	Y	N	Y	Y
Gantt chart	N	N	Y	N	Y	Y
Comprehensive reports (i.e., tabular)	Y	Y	Y	Y	Y	Y
Features						
Calculation of expected monetary value (risk event probability x risk event value)	Y	N	N	Y	Y	N
Track criticality index	N	N	Y	Y	Y	N
Suggest and document mitigation strategies based on knowledge database	N	Y	N	Y	Y	Y
Ability to enter assumptions and analysis defaults (example: time or resource constraints)	N	N	Y	Y	Y	Y
Capability to import and export from/to other standard office automation tools.	Y	Y	Y	Y	Y	Y
Risk identification (e.g., checklist)	N	Y	N	Y	Y	Y
Identification of "hangers," sources of risk	N	Y	N	Y	Y	Y
Tracks historic risk data (i.e., to be used as a baseline) in order to enable comparisons with ongoing changes.	N	Y	N	Y	Y	Y
Support of probability distribution curves						
Uniform	N	N	Y	N		N
Triangular	Y	N	Y	Y		N
Normal	Y	Y	Y	Y	Y	N
Beta	N	N	Y	N		N

Risk Management

	Project Risk Analysis	Project Self-Assessment Kit	Risk+	RiskTrak	SLIM / SLIM-Control	WebProject
Maximum and minimum duration	N	Y	N	Y	Y	N
Program Evaluation and Review technique (PERT)	N	N	Y	N	N	N
Input of low, most likely, and high duration	N	N	Y	Y	Y	N
Reporting						
Report writer	N	Y	Y	Y	Y	N
Report wizard	N	N	Y	Y	N	Y
Publishes as HTML	N	Y	Y	N	N	Y
Number of user defined fields	0	0	MS Project	0	0	Variable
Drill-down/roll-up *	N	N	Y	Y	Y	Y
Import/export	N	N	Y	Y	Y	Y
Automatic E-mail notification *	N	N	Y	Y	N	Y
Macro recorder/batch capable *A76	N	N	Y	Y	Y	Y
Can "canned" reports be modified?	N	Y	Y	Y	Y	Y
Sort, filter	N	N	Y	Y	Y	Y
Architecture						
Databases supported (list)		N/A	Same as MS Project	All ODBC	N/A	Oracle, MS SQL Server, Informix, Sybase, any JDBC-enabled database
Supports distributed databases	N	N	N	Y	N/A	Y
Three-tier client/server	N	N	N	Y	N/A	Y
Client operating systems	Win 95/98/3.x	Win 95/98	Win 95/98/NT/3.x	Win	Win 95/3.x	Win 95/NT, Unix, Linux, any Java-enabled OS
Server operating systems	N/A	N/A	Any that support Win clients	Win, Unix	All	Win 95/NT, Unix, Linux, any Java-enabled OS
Network operating systems	N/A	N/A	Any that support Win clients	Any Win	MS, NW	Win 95/NT, Unix, Linux, any Java-enabled OS
Minimum client configuration	16 MB RAM, 2 MB HD space	MS-Excel	486 with 16 MB RAM	Win 95, Pentium II	486	Java-enabled Browser
Minimum server configuration	N/A	N/A	N/A	Win 95, Pentium II, 16 MB	All	Win 95/NT, Unix, Linux, any Java-enabled OS
Client runs under Web browser	N	N	N	N	N	Y

Open architecture					
Supports OLE	N	Y	N	Y	N
Documented Object Model	N	N	N	N	N
Documented Application Programming Interface (API)	N	N	N	N	N
Simultaneous edit of data file	N	N	N	N	Y
Does product have a programming language?	N	N	N	N	N
Are years stored as four-digit numbers?	Y	Y	Y	Y	Y
Online help					
Right mouse click	N	Y	N	Y	N
Hover buttons	N	Y	N	N	Y
Interactive help	Y	Y	Y	Y	Y
Help search feature	Y	Y	Y	Y	Y
Web access to product knowledge base *	N	N	N	Y	Y
Vendor information					
Training					
Computer-based training	N	Y	N	N	Y
Training materials available	Y	Y	Y	Y	Y
Customized training materials	N	Y	Y	Y	Y
Online tutorial	N	N	Y	Y	Y
Consulting available from vendor	N	Y	Y	Y	Y
Site license discounts	Y	Y	Y	Y	Y
Enhancement requests *	Y	Y	Y	Y	Y
Modify source code, support through upgrades *	N	Y	N	Y	Y
Global presence					
Global offices	N	N	Y	Y	Y
Multilingual technical support	N	N	N	Y	Y
Language versions (list):	Eng	Eng	Eng	Eng	Eng, Ger
Audit Software Quality Assurance process? *	N	Y	Y	Y	Y
Security					
Configurable access privileges *	N	N	N	N	Y
Passwords expire (forced update)	N	N	N	N	Y
Electronic approvals	N	N	Y	N	Y
Password protect files	N	Y	Y	N	Y

463

Vendor Responses to Narrative Questions

@RISK Professional for Project (Palisade Corporation)

Describe what the product is designed to do.

Add risk analysis to Microsoft Project via Monte Carlo simulation. Allows uncertainty to be defined in any numeric field. Results include graphs and detailed statistics.

Top three product differentiators; describe what makes your product unique.

1. Links directly to Microsoft Project 4.x and higher.
2. Large number of distributions supported.
3. Advanced modeling techniques: probabilistic branching and if/then conditional modeling.

To what business processes can this tool be applied?

Any process that can be modeled in Microsoft Project can be simulated using @RISK.

Describe the ideal end-user environment for the current version of your product (size of organization, level of project management sophistication, effort and commitment required).

Any size organization; familiarity with MS Project; familiarity with basic statistics; easy-to-implement basic simulation; models become more detailed the more it is used.

Future strategies for this product.

Continued development; additional features per user requests.

Product's target market.

Project managers, planners, anyone who uses MS Project on a day-to-day basis.

What are your product's three main benefits? (How does using the product add value to the customer?)

1. Account for risks in any project.
2. Determine which projects are going to come in on time and under budget.
3. Identify critical tasks not listed by project.

Describe your quality management process. List any relevant certifications.

Extensive in-house testing and closed beta testing.

Discuss your product pricing structure. Include volume discount levels, concurrent user options, site licenses, cost of implementation, and other issues.

@RISK for Project: $695.
@RISK Professional for Project: $995.
Volume discounts and site licenses available.
Free, unlimited tech support.
Maintenance contracts available.

Dekker TRAKKER Risk Management Module (DTMI)

Describe what the product is designed to do.

The risk management system in TRAKKER goes well beyond heuristic modeling by providing a system that enables the tracking and statusing of the model to continually provide feedback on cost, schedule, and technical risk parameters as the project progresses to completion. Within the TRAKKER system, each risk parameter is assigned a consequence and an outcome. As the project progresses, these elements are updated with a probability of occurrence that results in a status. This information can then be reduced to identify the exceptions and areas requiring attention. The drill-down capability allows the user to identify the status of a risk parameter and drill down into the detail elements contributing to the specific condition and review the status brief. With this approach, analysts, management, and technical supervisors have more time to review corrective actions and evaluate the outcome, based on real-time feedback from the project and technical leads.

Top three product differentiators; describe what makes your product unique.

1. Continual update of the risk parameters from real-time project data rather than a periodic heuristic model.
2. Integration with the cost, schedule, and technical performance modules within TRAKKER.
3. Integration with Microsoft Office and Microsoft Back Office.

To what business processes can this tool be applied?

Risk management, schedule analysis, cost analysis and technical performance measurement.

Describe the ideal end-user environment for the current version of your product (size of organization, level of project management sophistication, effort and commitment required).

One of the key attributes of the TRAKKER system is scalability. TRAKKER has been designed to integrate into a business environment by establishing an organization's business rules within the system. This architecture enables TRAKKER to fit the needs and sophistication of any implementation. This flexibility enables TRAKKER to support a variety of implementation approaches. TRAKKER installations typically provide access to a range of users including cost account managers, cost/schedule analysts, and financial managers to meet the unique requirements of each for information and output. Typical TRAKKER clients range from companies of one thousand employees to Fortune 500 corporations.

Future strategies for this product.

Dekker, Ltd. will continue to enhance the integration of TRAKKER with MS Office and MS Back Office suite of tools. The design of the TRAKKER architecture will continue to focus on making data more visual and accessible to the complete range of system users.

Product's target market.

R&D, government, software, medical, electronics, and aerospace.

What are your product's three main benefits? (How does using the product add value to the customer?)

1. Integration with the TRAKKER ABC/ABM system.
2. Real-time drill down into the detail of a risk condition.
3. Integration with Microsoft Office and Microsoft Back Office tools.

Describe your quality management process. List any relevant certifications.

DMTI has modeled our development process from the Microsoft model while incorporating the quality guidelines established in ISO 9000.

Discuss your product pricing structure. Include volume discount levels, concurrent user options, site licenses, cost of implementation, and other issues.

DMTI offers both single and concurrent user licenses of TRAKKER. Our flexible pricing enables both small and large organizations to cost effectively implement costing and earned value management systems. TRAKKER pricing includes a progressive discount for volume purchases with reasonable thresholds for single and multisite licenses. Further, DMTI offers both public and private training courses for both new and advanced users. DMTI also offers consulting services to support the enterprise implementation of TRAKKER.

DMTI provides training for both the application of risk management and TRAKKER risk module. Through these courses, an enterprise can completely implement Dekker risk management system. In addition to our classroom training, DMTI offers consulting services to guide users though a structured approach to implementing TRAKKER.

Enterprise Project (jeTECH DATA SYSTEMS, INC.)

Describe what the product is designed to do.

Enterprise Project is a completely integrated solution (all applications share a common database and operate on the same hardware platform). Consequently, our responses to the narrative questions here repeats what we supplied for the "Suites" chapter, as those responses apply to all of our applications.

Enterprise Project is a powerful new client/server software application that offers project-based organizations a simple way to define and staff projects, and record project labor and expenses throughout their enterprise. Essentially a suite of robust, user-friendly applications integrated into a single desktop, this comprehensive project management system enables team members to accurately plan and track labor resources across all projects. Perfect either as a *stand-alone* solution or as the ideal complement to the jeTECH labor-management system—Enterprise Labor—it is particularly well suited for multiuser, enterprisewide installations. Together, Enterprise Labor and Enterprise Project are the only systems currently on the market with extensive capabilities and integrated products for both the salaried professional (engineers and computer programmers, for instance) and the hourly employee (from factory workers to registered nurses).

Users access all functions via a single desktop with a Microsoft Office 98 *look and feel*. The system integrates completely with Enterprise Labor and Microsoft Project, as well as with most popular accounting and HR systems. In today's competitive environment, effective and efficient use of labor resources is key to completing mission-critical projects on time, on budget. Enterprise Project gives project leaders a comprehensive, potent tool with which to manage scarce technical resources.

With Enterprise Project, managers can budget and schedule projects based on staff skills and availability. Project team members can manage their own tasks, report actual labor and travel expenses, and provide status reports on these tasks. The system calculates actual project costs by automatically incorporating labor costs, material costs, and travel expenses.

Project managers can define and manage both contract and noncontract-based projects, and control work authorizations that will keep each project under control and on budget. As a project manager, you simply create activities for your projects, assign appropriate resources to these activities and define how labor will be charged to a contract. And by allowing employees to only charge preassigned tasks, Enterprise Project prevents performance of unauthorized work.

Enterprise Project enables all users to report labor charges right from their PC or workstation. Project managers need no longer compile project team information manually. Users can now report project time, as well as other time, and the system automatically processes and transmits it to an interfaced time-and-attendance system for payroll use.

Enterprise Project includes a contract maintenance module. Companies with hourly employees contracted with outside firms—for instance, security guards or programmers—would benefit from using this module without the rest of the project management system. This module is primarily designed, however, to accommodate projects being managed for clients. This module allows contract managers to define contract information including budgets and rates per hour, as well as all products and services purchased by the customer. They can then use this information to evaluate projects based on user-defined deliverables. Contract maintenance is by no means static. So, jeTECH has designed Enterprise Project to handle change orders, R&D projects, and discounts. A variety of unique reporting features enables contract managers to view cost overruns, variances, and milestone completions.

Top three product differentiators; describe what makes your product unique.

1. Resource scheduling from a common resource pool in a multiproject environment.
2. Integrated time collection and status reporting.
3. Sensitivity analysis (what-if scenarios).

To what business processes can this tool be applied?

Project planning/management, enterprise resource scheduling/management, time collection, performance measurement, time and expense reporting, budgeting and estimating, and project accounting.

Describe the ideal end-user environment for the current version of your product (size of organization, level of project management sophistication, effort and commitment required).

Any resource-constrained enterprise (IT, high-tech R&D, engineering) with multiple projects and multiple sites. Requires a low level of project management sophistication.

Future strategies for this product.

Maintenance and repair operations, incorporation of process ware/templates, enterprise-level project and resource integration, and full Internet capabilities.

Product's target market.

Companies with *task-oriented* professionals such as engineers, architects, IS professionals, researchers, advertising/marketing professionals, etc. See also the previous response to "ideal end-user environment."

What are your product's three main benefits? (How does using the product add value to the customer?)

1. Improved resource utilization and efficiencies.
2. Reduction in time to complete projects.
3. Cost control.

Describe your quality management process. List any relevant certifications.

Our current quality management process includes in-house testing, which incorporates both automated and manual processes and procedures.

Discuss your product pricing structure. Include volume discount levels, concurrent user options, site licenses, cost of implementation, and other issues.

Pricing is structured on a named-user basis. Pricing will also be dependent on a number of variables including the size of the enterprise, number of project managers, number of facilities, etc. Consequently, pricing is provided to each customer when we have been able to familiarize ourselves with their operations and their anticipated use of the system.

Several options are available for training, tech support, annual maintenance, etc. Costs are provided to each customer when he has been able to select the options deemed best for his operations.

ER Project 1000 (Eagle Ray Software Systems)

Describe what the product is designed to do.

The ER Project 1000 is an integrated suite of project management tools, which provide an enterprisewide project management solution. ER Project 1000 includes schedule/time management, centralized resource management, methodology/process management, project-workgroup communications, timesheets, risk/issue management, and enterprisewide cross-project tracking. Based on a client/server architecture with a centralized relational database, the ER Project 1000 provides networked access, multiproject capability and true multiserver concurrency. It scales easily from handling small workgroup projects to large programs at the enterprise level.

Top three product differentiators; describe what makes your product unique.

1. Addresses the total project management life-cycle solution for the enterprise: Unlike most project management tools, the ER Project 1000 provides a completely integrated and centralized project management platform to support the entire life cycle of project management. Based on a client/server relational database (Oracle/SQL Server) architecture, ER Project 1000 fully supports today's multiproject/multiserver project environment. The product suite integrates full methodology/process management capabilities, project workgroup communications, and enterprisewide project tracking capabilities.

2. Provides a completely integrated suite of project management tools: The ER Project 1000 tool suite integrates industrial-strength project management functions with rich process improvement functionality and proactive management features. ER Project 1000 provides all the necessary industrial-strength core project management functions. Key features include support for WBS/organizational breakdown structure/ RBS structures, cost, schedule, earned value analysis, built-in report writer, timesheet approvals, and centralized resource management. ER Project 1000 takes advantage of the Web by providing Java timesheets and extensive project website publishing capability. Best practices/process improvement is easily accomplished with the methodology manager and support for organizational standards, work products, and estimation. ER Project 1000 delivers an impressive array of proactive management features. These features include risk management, issue management, management by threshold, and full project tracking.

3. Is easy to use and implement: ER Project 1000 was designed with a simple, intuitive interface. Extensive wizards assist users for complex operations. ER Project 1000 can easily be configured to your organization by using our centralized administration functions and component architecture.

To what business processes can this tool be applied?

ER Project 1000 is a wrap-around solution for organizations that need to implement mature project management practices, proactively manage their projects, improve business processes, implement standards and documentation, and communicate at multiple levels. Eagle Ray's advanced suite of tools provides project managers with an integrated platform for project planning, time tracking, resource management, and executive oversight. With features such as risk management, issue tracking, and management by threshold, the ER Project 1000 gives project managers the ability to proactively manage complex projects and stay focused on the key issues.

Organizations who engage in process improvement/best practices will find that the ER Project 1000 methodology manager is the ideal platform for developing and delivering best practices to each new project plan. Project managers will be able to easily document and reuse lessons learned in new projects. Project team members and stakeholders will find that the integrated communications features of the ER Project 1000 suite facilitate a real-time dialogue between all members and ensures that no issues slip though the cracks.

Describe the ideal end-user environment for the current version of your product (size of organization, level of project management sophistication, effort and commitment required).

Size of organization: The ER Project 1000 product suite is ideal for managing projects with team sizes of ten to one thousand people per project, in organizations where multiple projects are being performed at the same time. Project teams may be centralized or dispersed using client/server and Web-based communications technologies.

Level of sophistication: The tool suite is best suited for organizations that are moving beyond basic project management to a medium level of project management maturity or higher. These organizations are typically implementing tracking, costing, project management standards, risk/issue management, time tracking, centralized resource management, and possibly earned value. ER Project 1000 also supports organizations implementing a project office, best practices, process improvement, and reusable project templates. These features make ER Project 1000 an ideal platform for organizations implementing capability maturity model (CMM) level 2 or higher maturity levels.

Effort and commitment required: Successful implementation of the ER Project 1000 tool suite centers on an organization's commitment to realizing repeatable project management results from enterprisewide standardization of business processes and practices. Because of its integrated design and simple interface, ER Project 1000 delivers numerous advantages over standard project management tool sets with less staff effort.

Future strategies for this product.

Eagle Ray's future strategies include building new modules, expanding current modules, interfacing with corporate business systems, and preparing the product suite for the global marketplace. Major planned enhancements include significant modifications to the estimation module, costing module, methodology/process management module, and the Internet/intranet/Web capabilities. In addition, we will be constructing a problem/defect-tracking module.

We will be expanding the interfaces that integrate the ER Project 1000 system with additional enterprise business systems. Such systems include costing/accounting systems, HR systems, and additional commercial products. We also plan to complete our internationalization/localization efforts to prepare the ER Project 1000 for global distribution.

Product's target market.

ER Project 1000 is suitable for commercial and government organizations, which are managing projects that range from small workgroup-level projects to projects that span the entire enterprise. Essentially, the tool suite will support any project environment where the project team has access to or is working with computers.

What are your product's three main benefits? (How does using the product add value to the customer?)

1. Total integrated project management solution: The ER Project 1000 is an integrated, total project management solution providing complete support for the entire project management life cycle. The integrated tool suite does not require multiple add-on tools from different vendors, resulting in fewer hidden costs and less frustration. Project managers will find it easy to manage projects with a higher level of maturity by using the various features of the tool—for example, risk management, issue tracking, management by threshold, and multiproject capabilities.

2. Best practices/process improvement platform: The ER Project 1000 integrated process/methodology management platform provides a sophisticated, yet easy-to-use platform for implementing best practices, estimation metrics, organizational standards, documentation templates, and process improvement. Organizations can capture, integrate, and reuse their project knowledge and project plan templates from an enterprisewide integrated platform.

3. Enterprisewide tracking and communications: The ER Project 1000 facilitates communications between all project stakeholders. Program managers and executives can perform cross-project rollups, dynamic drilldown, and cost, schedule, and earned-value analysis for up-to-date information on all enterprise projects. The project team members can access all project information on the project website, and receive activity assignments and report status using Java timesheets. Automatic issue notification alerts project managers about possible deviations in cost and schedule. The built-in report writer lets you extract and summarize any data in the enterprisewide project database using customized formats.

Describe your quality management process. List any relevant certifications.

The Eagle Ray quality assurance (QA) program is a comprehensive system that employs a series of product walkthroughs, builds, quality gates, configuration management, defect tracking, and comprehensive testing. The development staff members are constantly conducting requirements, design, and code walkthroughs in coordination with weekly product builds and passing mandatory quality gates. The QA program is integrated with our beta testing program to ensure that all product releases undergo rigorous real-world testing prior to release.

Comprehensive testing scenarios include unit testing, integration testing, platform testing, stress testing, concurrency testing, environment testing, security testing, usability testing, vertical testing, upgrade testing, business scenario testing, and independent qualification testing.

During the design and construction of the ER Project 1000 product, Eagle Ray brought in several project management industry experts to assist in the design of the software functionality and usability. This process will be continued to ensure that our future enhancements meet the real-world needs of project management organizations. Additionally, Eagle Ray continues to invest heavily in the training of team members in technical and project management areas.

Discuss your product pricing structure. Include volume discount levels, concurrent user options, site licenses, cost of implementation, and other issues.

Call for latest prices.

Intelligent Planner (Augeo Software)

Describe what the product is designed to do.

Optimize the allocation of resources across multiple projects, determine costs, and provide metrics for continuous process improvement.

Top three product differentiators; describe what makes your product unique.

1. Global repository for data and business rules.
2. Closed-loop system, from project proposal to time/expenses tracking.
3. Simulation and optimization based on skills and availability of resources.

To what business processes can this tool be applied?

Business processes involving the allocation of human resources, such as professional services and information services.

Describe the ideal end-user environment for the current version of your product (size of organization, level of project management sophistication, effort and commitment required).

Mid-sized to large-scale professional services organizations sharing pool of scarce resources; large IT departments managing budgets and resources on strategic projects; or consulting companies managing a portfolio of intellectual activities.

Future strategies for this product.

Knowledge management integration; 100 percent Web-based management of project portfolio; and advanced data-mining features.

Product's target market.

Professional services organizations; large-scale IT departments with cost-controlled project management consulting companies.

What are your product's three main benefits? (How does using the product add value to the customer?)

1. Optimize scare resource predictability.
2. Increase speed, throughput, and responsiveness.
3. Executive visibility.

Describe your quality management process. List any relevant certifications.

Source control. Usability verification process. Worldwide beta program.

Discuss your product pricing structure. Include volume discount levels, concurrent user options, site licenses, cost of implementation, and other issues.

Concurrent user pricing for client-server modules, named-user pricing for Web modules. Volume discount, site license. Implementation requires ten to twenty days of consulting.

Training: Project managers (two days), administrators (three days), Web users (half-day).

Annual maintenance (includes new releases and online assistance): Fifteen percent of license fee.

Mesa/Vista Risk Manager (Mesa/Vista Systems Guild)

Describe what the product is designed to do.

Mesa/Vista Risk Manager helps project teams manage, monitor, and comply with quality and government regulations by providing access to all legacy and current project data through a Web browser. Mesa/Vista provides process management capabilities and integrates a development team's existing product environment, including tools like Rational Rose, TD Technologies' SLATE, Cayenne Teamwork, or any tool with an MPX interface, such as Microsoft Project.

Mesa/Vista links information between stand-alone products and exposes project data to authorized project team members, empowering them to anticipate and solve problems at early stages in the project life cycle.

Mesa/Vista Risk Manager will assess risk at any point of the project, to allow project team members to make necessary changes early in the life cycle to save time.

Top three product differentiators; describe what makes your product unique.

1. Patent-pending technology intuitively links graphical objects such as those found in developer's modeling tools, not only within the stand-alone tool but also between tools.
2. Provides support of any business process through dynamic exchange of information.
3. Connects legacy and current data between development team's business and engineering tools.

To what business processes can this tool be applied?

SEI CMM levels 1–5, ISO-compliancy regulations, FDA requirements management.

Describe the ideal end-user environment for the current version of your product (size of organization, level of project management sophistication, effort and commitment required).

The ideal end-user environment for Mesa/Vista is a distributed, process-conscious product development group needing visibility and access to legacy and current project data across multiple platforms.

An organization trying to achieve or improve upon an SEI CMM level, achieve an ISO 9000 quality standard, or comply with FDA requirements will greatly benefit from the Mesa/Vista environment.

Commitment: All project-related communications would go through the Mesa/Vista environment for it to provide complete, automated project status information.

Future strategies for this product.

Future strategies for Mesa/Vista Risk Manager include providing more templates for standardized risk management control.

Plug-ins will include more scheduling tools, databases, business tools, document-editing tools, and modeling tools—all the tools an engineer would ideally use within a product development environment.

Computer-based training will be available for Mesa/Vista Risk Manager.

Product's target market.

Mesa/Vista Risk Manager is ideal for process-conscious project managers of distributed product development teams in the telecommunication, medical, and software industries, who need to monitor and assess the state of risk throughout the life cycle of the project.

What are your product's three main benefits? (How does using the product add value to the customer?)

1. Provides automated analysis of current status of the project and how it compares to the anticipated schedule.

2. A project manager can propose changes, and Mesa/Vista Risk Manager will anticipate the impact that those changes will have on the timeline and resource allocations of the project.

3. Automatic documentation mechanism for ease of tracking government regulations or quality standards control.

Describe your quality management process. List any relevant certifications.

Mesa/Vista is used to manage the development of Mesa/Vista. Also, extensive internal and external testing is done of the Mesa/Vista product line.

Mesa has provided the software to Young America's design team (New York Yacht Club's challenger in the America's Cup 2000) in exchange for feedback on Mesa/Vista and suggestions for improvements based on its real-life use of the product line.

Discuss your product pricing structure. Include volume discount levels, concurrent user options, site licenses, cost of implementation, and other issues.

Contact vendor.

Monte Carlo (in conjunction with Primavera Project Planner)

Describe what the product is designed to do.

Monte Carlo helps project managers create more realistic schedules and resource plans. They can simulate the performance of a project and evaluate the likelihood of finishing on time or within budget. They have information to make mid-project corrections. Project managers can quantify the risk for all or part of projects, helping them reduce the risk of delivering late or running over budget by choosing among alternative approaches and strategies.

Monte Carlo assesses the impact of actual progress and resource availability changes on the remainder of the schedule. It allows project managers to assess the risk of a single phase, a group of resources, or a set of activities. Perform what-if analysis with the risk adjusted to an acceptable level, and see the effect of that change on the entire project. Monte Carlo makes it easy to examine the likelihood that an activity will become critical.

No other answers given.

Open Plan (Welcom)

Describe what the product is designed to do.

Welcom's Open Plan is an enterprisewide project management system that substantially improves a company's ability to manage and complete multiple projects on time and within budget with a limited workforce. Unlike less sophisticated products, Open Plan is a highly integrated, comprehensive software system that can be customized to fit specific corporate requirements. It is the most technically advanced client/server project management system on the market, using the latest in Microsoft Windows development technology. The three versions of Open Plan are:

Open Plan Professional: Easy to use and powerful enough to manage even the largest projects, Open Plan Professional gives professional project managers such vital tools as advanced resource management, multiproject support, support for client/server databases, and the flexibility to customize the interface to support organization and industry-specific procedures.

Open Plan Desktop: Designed for occasional access to projects and ideal for executive users and tactical team members, Open Plan Desktop has extensive ease-of-use features and an affordable price point for companywide deployment. The system is well suited for users who usually work on individual components of a larger project. Users can roll their individual projects up to Open Plan Professional for a broader view of the overall project.

Open Plan Enterprise: Very similar to Open Plan Professional, Open Plan Enterprise integrates with popular enterprise resource planning (ERP) applications such as Baan and SAP. The resulting component-based suite automatically disseminates project data throughout an organization, giving users better control over enterprisewide multiproject planning, management, and implementation.

Top three product differentiators; describe what makes your product unique.

1. Multiproject.
2. Advanced resource modeling.
3. Open architecture.

To what business processes can this tool be applied?

ERP, business process reengineering, project management, earned value analysis, risk assessment, and process modeling.

Describe the ideal end-user environment for the current version of your product (size of organization, level of project management sophistication, effort and commitment required).

Medium to large organizations for which project management is a serious business requirement. Meets the needs of users whose level of expertise varies from novice/occasional to advanced.

Future strategies for this product.

Our vision for the future is to provide a suite of component-based products that work together to provide advanced project management functionality using the very latest technology.

Welcom's development plans include extending the products' multiproject and enterprise resource modeling capabilities while moving to a distributed applications architecture with Web technology being a significant component. Plans also include leveraging existing integrations with Baan and SAP, and expanding integrations to include other ERP vendors.

Product's target market.

Fortune 1000 companies, government and multinational organizations implementing enterprisewide project management.

What are your product's three main benefits? (How does using the product add value to the customer?)

1. Increase quality of project communications.
2. Reduce cycle time through effective resource management.
3. Increase integration of project management with business systems.

Describe your quality management process. List any relevant certifications.

Adhere to standard-industry processes in release and version strategies, including automated regression testing. ISO 9000 certified in the United Kingdom

Discuss your product pricing structure. Include volume discount levels, concurrent user options, site licenses, cost of implementation, and other issues.

Please call for pricing.

Cost of implementation: Training courses and consulting: Please call for pricing. Tech support: No charge with current maintenance. Maintenance: First year is free with software purchase; renewed annually.

PLANTRAC-MARSHAL (Computerline)

Describe what the product is designed to do.

PLANTRAC-MARSHAL provides an effective system for simulating project risks and for calculating and forecasting the effects. Unlike other risk systems, PLANTRAC-MARSHAL does not provide information for the mathematician or statistician. The information is provided in a very understandable form for project personnel, which allows risks to be forecast and properly managed.

Top three product differentiators; describe what makes your product unique.

1. Really easy to use.
2. Powerful risk simulation.
3. Understandable graphical and tabular reports.

To what business processes can this tool be applied?

All projects requiring risk assessment and management.

Describe the ideal end-user environment for the current version of your product (size of organization, level of project management sophistication, effort and commitment required).

Both small and large organizations benefit. It can be used as a casual planner, by a professional project manager, and for corporate risk assessment and management.

Future strategies for this product.

Knowledge base.

Product's target market.

All projects.

What are your product's three main benefits? (How does using the product add value to the customer?)

1. Better understanding of risks.
2. Improved project performance.
3. Profitable projects.

Describe your quality management process. List any relevant certifications.

Quality management is based on a mix of PRINCE and ISO 9000 methodology.

Discuss your product pricing structure. Include volume discount levels, concurrent user options, site licenses, cost of implementation, and other issues.

$450 single copy; $275 per user site license.

Implementation and training is $960 per day. Technical support is provided by telephone, fax, and E-mail. Free for first six months. Thereafter 17.5 percent of purchase price (includes upgrades and enhancements).

Project Risk Analysis (Katmar Software)

Describe what the product is designed to do.

Project Risk Analysis uses Monte Carlo simulation to calculate the overall capital risk on projects, and to calculate the financial contingency required to limit the risk to any desired level. The cost range for each element of the estimate is entered using built-in statistical distributions, and the program will display the overall risk in various graphical and tabular reports. Estimates that have been built up in spreadsheets can be imported for risk analysis.

Top three product differentiators; describe what makes your product unique.

1. Very easy to use because it is specifically set up for contingency analysis.
2. Users require minimal statistical knowledge.
3. Detailed tutorials and examples included in manual.

To what business processes can this tool be applied?

Capital project cost finalization.

Describe the ideal end-user environment for the current version of your product (size of organization, level of project management sophistication, effort and commitment required).

Project Risk Analysis can be used by organizations of all sizes. Assumes estimating techniques are well established but requires no prior risk analysis experience. Models can be set up with minimal effort, as Project Risk Analysis is specifically geared to contingency analysis.

Future strategies for this product.

Our aim is to add flexibility while maintaining the simple and easy-to-use structure.

Product's target market.

Project Risk Analysis is for project management and cost-engineering professionals who are more at home with estimating and costing than with statistics, but still need the power and accuracy of rigorous statistical techniques like Monte Carlo analysis.

What are your product's three main benefits? (How does using the product add value to the customer?)

1. Gives confidence to investment decisions.
2. Enables estimators to quickly get a *feel* for high-risk areas.
3. Reports generated are ideal for back-up justification in requests to top management for contingency funds.

Describe your quality management process. List any relevant certifications.

In-house, plus volunteer beta testers.

Discuss your product pricing structure. Include volume discount levels, concurrent user options, site licenses, cost of implementation, and other issues.

Single-user license $80; site license $250. Evaluation copy free from: http://users.lia.net/katmar Free E-mail support and free upgrades within twelve months of purchase.

Project Self-Assessment Kit

Describe what the product is designed to do.

Designed to prevent surprises in software projects by quickly measuring twenty-two project-level metrics, measuring overall project risk, and identifying specific strengths and risks.

Top three product differentiators; describe what makes your product unique.

1. Focused on the key factors that make software projects successful.
2. Uses the strength of project teams to manage risk.
3. Tactical, project orientation to optimize schedule and cost for a specific project.

To what business processes can this tool be applied?

Software projects. Best applied at the conclusion of planning or up to 50 percent through implementation.

Describe the ideal end-user environment for the current version of your product (size of organization, level of project management sophistication, effort and commitment required).

Software groups with seven- to seventy-person project teams. Typically takes one-half day to perform a self-assessment, for individuals with any level of PM sophistication.

Future strategies for this product.

Project-class specific versions.

Product's target market.

Software development organizations and MIS/IT shops who do not have enough time or resources for "manual" risk management methods.

Project Management Offices responsible for multiple software projects.

Software QA organizations responsible for ensuring the quality of processes used by projects.

What are your product's three main benefits? (How does using the product add value to the customer?)

1. Provides early warning of "surprises."
2. By preventing surprises, can prevent schedule and cost overruns.
3. Can be used to measure and compare multiple projects.

Describe your quality management process. List any relevant certifications.

In-house testing, followed by beta test cycle. Product has been available since July 1997.

Discuss your product pricing structure. Include volume discount levels, concurrent user options, site licenses, cost of implementation, and other issues.

$795 for a single-user license, unlimited projects.

Telephone and E-mail technical support included. No maintenance fees. Training materials included.

Risk+

Describe what the product is designed to do.

Risk+ is a comprehensive risk analysis tool that integrates seamlessly with Microsoft Project 4.0/4.1/98 to quantify the cost and schedule uncertainty associated with projects. Since Risk+ is an add-on to MS Project, all of the features of MS Project are available to Risk+.

Top three product differentiators; describe what makes your product unique.

1. Completely integrated with MS Project.
2. Exceptional ease of use.
3. High-quality output.

To what business processes can this tool be applied?

Proposal development, vendor selection, project scheduling, and resource planning.

Describe the ideal end-user environment for the current version of your product (size of organization, level of project management sophistication, effort and commitment required).

Project management professional familiar with critical path scheduling and MS Project.

Future strategies for this product.

Integration with other scheduling tools.

Product's target market.

Anyone that conducts critical path scheduling.

What are your product's three main benefits? (How does using the product add value to the customer?)

No answer provided.

Describe your quality management process. List any relevant certifications.

No answer provided.

Discuss your product pricing structure. Include volume discount levels, concurrent user options, site licenses, cost of implementation, and other issues.

No answer given.

RiskTrak

Describe what the product is designed to do.

Real-time information: Whether you want to connect people in different parts of a building or around the world, RiskTrak's networking capability allows your organization to view, track, analyze, communicate, and report on risks throughout the duration of a program or project on 24/7/365 basis. RiskTrak imposes no restrictions on the type of network or its support, and performs on any network software and hardware combination.

Twenty-four-hour team involvement: RiskTrak's risk editor and mitigation editor allow your team members to update risk information and test multiple mitigation strategies twenty-four hours a day in real time, increasing organizational involvement and awareness of risk.

Ultimate reporting capability: RiskTrak's SQL engine enables you to query, sift, sort, extract, and report data from your projects. Up-to-the-minute detailed risk management plans, top-level graphical charts, and risk assessment reports can be generated at will.

Fully compatible: RiskTrak's polymorphic database allows you to exchange data with Microsoft Access or any ODBC-relational database. Import your current WBS or an entire project. RiskTrak accepts Microsoft Project Exchange Files (*.MPX) or any other database files in *.CSV format. The import engine feature for *.CSV files allows you to visually map fields from Microsoft Excel or other spreadsheets into RiskTrak fields.

Standardize your process: RiskTrak's system of *interview experts* are electronic questionnaires that take your qualitative questions and generate quantitative data that is used to create and update projects. The interviews are nondestructive, enabling multiple input at any stage of the program.

Control and security: RiskTrak allows you to set specific user permissions and E-mail notifications, enabling full control over your project. RiskTrak also provides an unalterable audit trail.

Customizable to your needs: As a standard feature, RiskTrak ships with experts based on the SEI taxonomy-based questionnaire and the GAO's Y2K program assessment checklist. Customized experts can be configured for any industry, business process, WBS, earned value management system, program plan, audit questionnaire, or Y2K program.

User friendly: RiskTrak is Windows-based software with a *point and click, drag and drop* interface, allowing for a quick learning curve. RiskTrak is a stand-alone product that works on Win 98, Win 95, Windows NT.

Top three product differentiators; describe what makes your product unique.

1. Network software for true enterprisewide risk management.
2. Fully customizable for any industry, WBS, business process.
3. Interview expert system creates and updates projects.

To what business processes can this tool be applied?

RiskTrak can be used as is for any business process or customized for specific requirements.

Describe the ideal end-user environment for the current version of your product (size of organization, level of project management sophistication, effort and commitment required).

Medium to large businesses and agencies would be best served due to RiskTrak's networking capability. RiskTrak is designed for a quick learning curve but is a very powerful tool, useful at the highest levels of project/program management.

Future strategies for this product.

Year 2000 program risk management; EMU/Euro program risk management; enterprisewide risk management.

Product's target market.

Private and public sector Year 2000 programs.
Medium to large private sector businesses.
Government agencies and programs.

What are your product's three main benefits? (How does using the product add value to the customer?)

1. Help assure risks are not overlooked.
2. Builds an awareness of risk throughout the organization.
3. Coordinates resources and ideas to deal with risks.

Describe your quality management process. List any relevant certifications.

No answer given.

Discuss your product pricing structure. Include volume discount levels, concurrent user options, site licenses, cost of implementation, and other issues.

Multiple levels of discounts available. Call for pricing, based on your needs assessment. Negotiation on a per-seat basis. Maintenance is a percentage of seat cost.

Tech support is available by phone or E-mail.

SLIM/SLIM-Control

Describe what the product is designed to do.

Macro software estimation and forecasting tools that enable managers to control project schedule, cost, and quality. Includes extensive *what-if* capabilities and industry reference benchmarks.

Top three product differentiators; describe what makes your product unique.

1. Dynamic what-if analysis for estimates and forecasts.
2. Industry reference trends for size, time, effort, staffing, and quality.
3. Reliability modeling and graphical risk analysis.

To what business processes can this tool be applied?

Feasibility analysis, bidding, estimation, project planning, statements of work, project control, outsourcing, risk management, and change management.

Describe the ideal end-user environment for the current version of your product (size of organization, level of project management sophistication, effort and commitment required).

All software development organizations with at least twenty-five people in development concerned with the accuracy of software planning and management.

Future strategies for this product.

Open architecture on MS ACCESS database; automated aggregation of subsystem estimates; intelligent solution generator.

Product's target market.

Horizontal market: All software development organizations and IT organizations.

What are your product's three main benefits? (How does using the product add value to the customer?)

1. Proactive what-if analysis for schedule, cost, and quality.
2. Data collection and calibration mechanism.
3. Industry reference data.

Describe your quality management process. List any relevant certifications.

Author of seventy-five plus papers and books on managing software development and quality. See the publications list on www.qsma.com.

Discuss your product pricing structure. Include volume discount levels, concurrent user options, site licenses, cost of implementation, and other issues.

Range from single-user licensing to site licensing. Stand-alone or server based.

All technical support, upgrades, and enhancements are included in the license fee.

Training is included for one person per product. Additional training is available on-site or at QSM facilities.

WebProject

Describe what the product is designed to do.

WebProject is designed for geographically dispersed project teams. WebProject is a Java-based project management tool with powerful collaboration and communications features. WebProject incorporates unique knowledge management/best practices capability.

Top three product differentiators; describe what makes your product unique.

WebProject is the first (only) pure Java project management suite that can utilize an open architecture database backend. WebProject allows corporations to utilize Oracle, SQL Server, Informix, Sybase, or other databases in their enterprise project management.

WebProject has introduced the first knowledge management/best practices capability within a project management software suite.

WebProject enables global project communication including project issues boards, threaded task discussions, virtual project status meetings, and remote project statusing and updates.

To what business processes can this tool be applied?

Geographically dispersed project teams, projects that need to have access from remote locations, or integrating WebProject's proprietary information exchange with MS Project, Primavera, or other desktop systems.

WebProject allows the extraction of knowledge from the enterprise, such as resource capabilities or company *best practices*.

Describe the ideal end-user environment for the current version of your product (size of organization, level of project management sophistication, effort and commitment required).

WebProject is an easy-to-use Java project management tool that will enable teams to communicate and collaborate from remote locations. WebProject is designed for the enterprise and will work well with project teams as well.

Future strategies for this product.

WebProject has established many *firsts* in the project management industry. We will continue to move the industry forward with our new technologies on the Web and with Java.

Product's target market.

Geographically dispersed project teams, enterprise project management systems, integration with Primavera, MS Project, and other project management systems.

What are your product's three main benefits? (How does using the product add value to the customer?)

1. Enterprise project communication.
2. Project collaboration.
3. Geographically dispersed updates and communication.

Describe your quality management process. List any relevant certifications.

WebProject adheres to strict standards and processes for quality, both in development and customer service.

Discuss your product pricing structure. Include volume discount levels, concurrent user options, site licenses, cost of implementation, and other issues.

WebProject is priced at $790 for starter package including the WebProject server. WebProject does provide enterprise and site licensing.

Appendix A

Survey Respondents by Product Name

Note: Not all survey respondents provided contact information on questionnaires.

@RISK Professional for Project
Palisade Corporation
Vera Gilliland
Phone: 607/277-8000
veramg@palisade.com

ABT Connect & ABT Team
ABT Planner
ABT Publisher
ABT Repository
ABT Resource
ABT Workbench (repository-based)
ABT Corporation
Ed Farrelly
Phone: 707/793-8300 ext. 3102
edf@abtcorp.com

ADEPT Production Module
Decision Dynamics Technologies, Inc. (DDTI)
Coleen Pilliod
Phone: 301/657-8500 ext. 105
cpilliod@decisiondynamics.com

Allegro
Deltek Systems, Inc.
Cristina Sirtori
Phone: 703/734-8606 ext. 4451
csirtori@deltek.com

AMS REALTIME Projects
AMS REALTIME Solo
AMS REALTIME Vision
Advanced Management Solutions
Richard Hayden
Phone: 703/968-8073
haydenr@amsusa.com

Artemis CostView
Artemis GlobalView & Project View
Artemis ProjectView
Artemis TrackView
ArtemisViews
Artemis Management Solutions
Phone: 800/477-6648
Patrick Perugini
pperugini@artemispm.com

AutoPlan Enterprise
Digital Tools
Jeff Mills
Phone: 408/366-6250
jeffm@digit.com

Cascade PgM
Cadcade WEB Time
Mantix
Tom Issac
Phone: 703/834-3940 ext. 208
tisaac@mantix.com

CA-SuperProject 4.0 and
CA SuperProject\Net 1.0
Computer Associates
David Thompson
Phone: 703/708-3142
thoda09@cai.com

Changepoint Corporation
Chuck Tatham
Phone: 905/886-7000
marketing@changepoint.com

Cobra 3.2 Cost Management System
Welcom
Steve Cook
Phone: 800/324-6337
info@welcom.com

DecisionTools Suite
Palisade Corporation
Vera Gilliland
Phone: 607/277-8000
veramg@palisade.com

Dekker Inergy
Dekker TRAKKER Activity Based Cost Management and Performance System
Dekker TRAKKER Advanced Cost
Dekker TRAKKER Risk Management Module
DTMI
Ron Barry
Phone: 909/384-9000
r.barry@dtrakker.com

Enterprise Controller
Enterprise Project
jeTECH DATA SYSTEMS, INC.
Phil Goodge, Product Marketing Manager
Phone: 805/383-8500 ext. 1123
pgoodge@jetechdata.com

ER Project 1000
Eagle Ray Software Systems, Inc.
Brad Roberts
Phone: 800/650-7510
brad@eagleray.com

ERoom
Instinctive Technology, Inc.
Francois Gossieaux
Phone: 617/497-6300 ext. 151
fgossieaux@instinctive.com

FastTrack Schedule 5.02
AEC Software, Inc.
Ryan Kish, MarCom Manager
Phone: 703/450-1980
rkish@aecsoft.com

Global Project Management System (GPMS)
2S Smart Solutions GmbH
Christian Uhrig
Phone: +49-6103-75075-0
info@smart-solutions.de

**GRANEDA BarKeeper
GRANEDA·Personal
GRANEDA Project Showcase**
American Netronic
Gary Jones
Phone: 562/795-0147
garyj@netronic-us.com

GroupProject
Corporate Project Solutions Ltd.
Ivan Lloyd
Phone: +16-28-482854
ivan_lloyd@cps.co.uk

How's it going
LogicAbility, Inc
Adrienne Scott
Phone: 416/823-4347
logic@hows-it-going.com

**Innate Multi-Project & Timesheets,
Innate Multi-Project (with Microsoft
Project), Innate Resource Manager,
Innate Timesheets**
Innate
Barry Muir
Phone: 312/781-9674
sales@innate.co.uk

Intelligent Planner
Augeo Software
Mike Sayer
Phone: 408/271-0422
mike.sayer@augeo.com

JobPROMS
Kildrummy Technologies Ltd.
Simon Nuttal-Smith
Phone: +44-181-870-3213
ops@kildrummy.co.uk

KIDASA Software, Inc.
Sue Butler
Phone: 512/328-0167
sbutler@kidasa.com

Mesa/Vista
Mesa/Vista Systems Guild
Maribeth McNair
Phone: 401/828-8500
mbm@mesasys.com

Micro Planner X-Pert
Micro Planning International
Brad Pirrung
Phone: 800/852-7526
sales@microplanning.com

MicroFusion Millennium
Integrated Management Concepts
Richard Haskins
Phone: 805/376-3306
rhaskins@intgconcepts.com

Microsoft Project 98
Microsoft Corporation
Kris Tibbetts
Phone: 425/936-8337
kristibb@microsoft.com

**MinuteMan Project Management
Software**
MinuteMan Systems
Bob Kochem
Phone: 617-489-5639
bck@minuteman-systems.com

**MonteCarlo (in combination with
Primavera Project Planner)**
Primavera
C. Kelly
Phone: 610/667-8600
sales@primavera.com

Netmosphere
Scott Hetherington
Phone: 650/655-4815
scott@netmosphere.com

**Open Plan, Open Plan Web Publisher,
Open Plan/Project Management
Director, Open Plan/Spider**
Welcom
Heather Howard
Phone: 281-558-0514
hhoward@welcom.com

OPP, P3 Connect
C/S Solutions
Gary Troop
Phone: 310/798-6396
gtroop@cs-solutions.com

**OPX2, OPX2 Intranet Server,
OPX2 Pro, OPX2 Timecard**
Planisware
Francois Pelissolo
Phone: +33-1-41-4800-55
francois.pelissolo@planisware.fr

Panorama
Panorama Software Corporation Ltd.
Cliff Sutton
Phone: +44-1932-252226
info@panorama.com

PERT Chart EXPERT
Critical Tools
Jim Spiller
Phone: 512/342-2232
jspiller@criticaltools.com

**PLANTRAC-APROPOS
PLANTRAC-CORoNET
PLANTRAC-MARSHAL
PLANTRAC-OUTLOOK Level 4**
Computerline, Inc.
Walford Pears
Phone: +44-1483-768095
computerline@compuserve.com

PlanView Software
PlanView Inc.
Wendy Wheeler
Phone: 512-346-8600
wwheeler@planview.com

PPS Corporate v4.0
PPS-Project Planning Systems
Christer Kallstrom
Phone: +46-8-6547060
christer.kallstrom@pps.se

**Primavera Project Planner (P3) 2.0,
Primavera Prospective**
Primavera
C. Kelley
Phone: 610/667-8600
sales@primavera.com

PRISM
SofTech Inc.
Michelle Deacon
Phone: 403/273-1275 ext. 404
info@softechine.com

ProChain
Creative Technology Labs, LLC
Bill Lynch
Phone: 703/490-8821
blynch@ProChain.com

ProjectCommander
Project Assistants, Inc.
Gus Cicala
Phone: 302/529-7075
gcicala@projectassistants.com

Project Connect for wInsight
C/S Solutions
Gary Troop
Phone: 310/798-6396
gtroup@cs-solutions.com

**Project Control Software-V 6.0,
Report Manager Module,
Project Office Manager,
Resource Manager,
Time Manager**
Project Control
Amy Duckett
Phone: 410/897-1091
aduckett@projectcontrol.com

**ProjectExchange
ProjectExchange Hyperlink
ProjectExchange Portfolio Wizard
ProjectExplorer for Microsoft Project**
Information Management Services Inc.
Jeff Nummelin
Phone: 781/340-4400
info@imscorp.com

**Project Integrator (PI) 2.0 Enterprise
Ed.**
System Solvers, Ltd.
Jim Jablonski
Phone: 248/588-7400 ext. 244
jaj@sslinfo.com

Project KickStart
Experience in Software, Inc.
Carolyn Burd
Phone: 510/644-0694
cb@projectkickstart.com

Project Risk Analysis
Katmar Software
Harvey Wilson
Phone: +27-31-822-351
katmar@dbn.lia.net

Project Scheduler 7.6
Scitor Corporation
Mark Stout
Phone: 800/533-9876
mstout@scitor.com

Project Self-Assessment Kit
KLCI, Inc.
Peter Kulik
Phone: 888/664-0484
pkulik@klci.com

Project-r
Computerline
Walford Pears
Phone: + 44-1483-768095
computerline@compuserve.com

ProjectSite for the Web
Kalyn Corporation
Tim Johnson
Phone: 800/595-2596
info@kalyn.com

Prolog Manager V 5.0, Prolog Executive Version 1.0
Prolog Website
Meridian Project Systems.
sales@mps-inc.com

QEI Exec
PCF Limited
Richard Jebb
Phone: +44-1494 775322
rwj@pcfltd.demon.co.uk

QuickGantt for Windows
Ballentine & Company, Inc.
Ann Ballentine
Phone: 800/536-6677
qgantt@ballantine-inc.com

Rational Concepts, Inc.
Dan Cornell
Phone: 760/632-0444
sales@rationalconcepts.com

Resource Manager
Kalyn Corporation
Tim Johnson
Phone: 800/595-2596
info@kalyn.com

ResourceXchange for Microsoft Project
Information Management Services
Jeff Nummelin
Phone: 781-340-4400
Info@imscorp.com

Results Management 5.0
ABT Corporation
Ed Farrelly
Phone: 707/793-8300 ext. 3102
edf@abtcorp.com

Risk+
ProjectGear, Inc.
Paige Price
Phone: 253/761-9091
pprice@cs-solutions.com

RiskTrak
Risk Services & Technology
Toby J. Trudel
Phone: 603/673-9907
trudel@risktrak.com

SAS Software
SAS Institute
Edward P. Hughes
Phone: 919/677-8000 ext. 6916
saseph@wnt.sas.com

Schedule Insight
Kalyn Corporation
Tim Johnson
Phone: 800/595-2596
info@kalyn.com

SLIM/SLIM-Control
QSM Associates, Inc.
Carl B. Foote
Phone: 413/499-0988
carlf@qsma.com

Spreadsheet Scheduler
User Solutions, Inc.
Jim Convis
Phone: 248-496-1934
jc@usersol.com

Superbudget
Ramdor
Erik Mikisch
Phone: 617/753-7383
ramdor@world.std.com

Sure Track Project Management
Primavera
C. Kelly
Phone: 610/667-8600
sales@primavera.com

TeamWork
Project Assistants, Inc.
Gus Cicala
Phone: 302/539-7075
gcicala@projectassistants.com

TimeControl
HMS
Ermy Valenti
Phone: 514/695-8122
info@hmssoftware.ca

TimeScope Timesheet
TimeScope
sales@timescope.com

TimeWizard
AC Software, Inc.
Bruce Gibson
Phone: 888/463-9973
bruce.gibson@timewzrd.com

TurboProject Professional 3.0
International Microcomputer Software, Inc.
Alex Taylor
Phone: 415/257-3000 ext. 379
ataylor@imsisoft.com

Varchart
American Netronic
Gary Jones
Phone: 562-795-0147
garyj@netronic-us.com

WBS Chart
Critical Tools
Jim Spiller
Phone: 512/342-2232
jspiller@criticaltools.com

Web Publishing Wizard in P3
Primavera
C. Kelly
Phone:
sales@primavera.com

WebProject
CRIS
Marc O Brien
Phone: 650/574-0578
mobrien@wproj.com

Webster for Primavera
Primavera
C. Kelly
Phone:
ckelly@primavera.com

WebTime & TimeReview
Information Management Services Inc.
Jeff Nummelin
Phone: 781-340-4400
info@inscorp.com

X-Gantt
Ballentine & Company, Inc.
Ann Ballentine
Phone: 800/536-6677
qgantt@ballantine-inc.com

Appendix B

Survey Respondents by Product Category

Note: Not all survey respondents provided contact information on questionnaires.

Suites

2S Smart Solutions, GmbH
Christian Uhrig
Phone: +49-6103-750750
info@smart-solutions.de

ABT Corporation
Ed Farrelly
Phone: 707/793-8300 ext. 3102
edf@abtcorp.com

AEC Software, Inc.
Ryan Kish
Phone: 703/450-1980
rkish@aecsoft.com

Advanced Management Solutions Inc.
Richard Hayden
Phone: 703/968-8073
hayden@amsusa.com

Artemis Management Solutions
Patrick Perugini
Phone: 800/477-6648
pperugini@artemispm.com

Augeo Software
Mike Sayer
Phone: 408/271-0422
mike.sayer@augeo.com

Ballantine & Company Inc.
Ann Ballantine
Phone: 800/536-6677
ggantt@ballantine-inc.com

ChangePoint Corporation
Chuck Tatham
Phone: 905/886-7000
marketing@changepoint.com

Computerline Ltd.
Walford Pears
Phone: +44-1483-768095
computerline@compuserve.com

Corporate Project Solutions, Ltd.
Ivan Lloyd
Phone: +16-28-482854
ivan_lloyd@cps.co.uk

Critical Tools
Jim Spiller
Phone: 512/342-2232
jspiller@criticaltools.com

Decision Dynamics Technologies Inc.
Coleen Pilliod
Phone: 301/657-8500 ext. 105
cpilliod@decisiondynamics.com

Dekker
Ron Barry
Phone: 909/384-9000
r.barry@dtrakker.com

Digital Tools
Jeff Mills
Phone: 408/366-6250
jeffm@digit.com

Eagle Ray Software Systems Inc.
Brad Roberts
Phone: 800/650-7510
brad@eagleray.com

Information Management Services Inc.
Jeff Nummelin
Phone: 781/340-4400
info@imscorp.com

Innate
Barry Muir
Phone: 312/781-9674
sales@innate.co.uk

Instinctive Technology, Inc.
Francois Gossieaux
Phone: 617/497-6300 ext. 151
fgossieaux@instinctive.com

Integrated Management Concepts
Richard Haskins
Phone: 805/376-3306
rhaskins@intgconcept.com

jeTECH Data Systems Inc.
Phil Goodge
Phone: 805/383-8500 ext. 1123
pgoodge@jetechdata.com

LogicAbility, Inc.
logic@how's-it-going.com

Mantix Systems Inc.
Tom Isaac
Phone: 703/834-3940 ext. 208
tisaac@mantix.com

Mesa Systems Guild Inc.
Maribeth McNair
Phone: 401/828-8500
mbm@mesasys.com

Microsoft Corporation
Kris Tibbetts
Phone: 425/936-8337
ktibbetts@microsoft.com

Palisade
Vera Gilliland
Phone: 607/277-8000
veramg@pallisade.com

Panorama Software Corp., Ltd.
Cliff Sutton
Phone: +44-1932-252226
info@panorama.com

PFC Ltd.
Richard Jebb
Phone: +44-1494-775322
rwj@pfcltd.demon.co.uk

Planisware
Francois Pelissolo
Phone: +33-1-41-4800-55
francois.pelissolo@planisware.fr

PlanView, Inc.
Wendy Wheeler
Phone: 512/346-8600
wwheller@planview.com

PPS-Project Planning Systems
Christer Kallstrom
Phone: +46-8-6547060
christer.kallstrom@pps.se

Project Control
Amy Duckett
Phone: 253/761-9091
aduckett@projcontrol.com

Rational Concepts Inc.
Dan Cornell
Phone: 760/632-0444
sales@rationalconcepts.com

SAS Institute
Edward P. Hughes
Phone: 919/677-8000 ext. 6916
saseph@wnt.sas.com

System Solvers, Ltd.
Jim Jablonski
Phone: 248/588-7400 ext. 244
jaj@sslinfo.com

Web Project Inc.
Marc O'Brien
Phone: 650-574-0578
mobrien@wproj.com

Welcom
Heather Howard
Phone: 281/558-0514
hhoward@welcom.com

Process Management

ABT Corporation
Ed Farrelly
Phone: 707/793-8300 ext. 3102
edf@abtcorp.com

Advanced Management Solutions Inc.
Richard Hayden
Phone: 703/968-8073
hayden@amsusa.com

Computerline, Ltd.
Walford Pears
Phone: +44-1483-768095
computerline@compuserve.com

Dekker Technologies Management, Ltd. (DTMI)
Ron Barry
Phone: 909/384-9000
r.barry@dtrakker.com

Digital Tools
Jeff Mills
Phone: 408:366-6250
jeffm@digit.com

Eagle Ray Software Systems, Inc.
Brad Roberts
Phone: 800/650-7510
brad@eagleray.com

Experience in Software, Inc.
Carolyn Burd
Phone: 510/644-0694
cb@projectkickstart.com

Information Management Services Inc.
Jeff Nummelin
Phone: 781/340-4400
info@imscorp.com

jeTECH Data Systems Inc.
Phil Goodge
Phone: 805/383-8500 ext. 1123
pgoodge@jetechdata.com

Kidasa Software Inc.
Sue Butler
Phone: 512/328-0167
sbutler@kidasa.com

Mantix Systems Inc.
Tom Isaac
Phone: 703/834-3940 ext. 208
tisaac@mantix.com

Mesa Systems Guild Inc.
Maribeth McNair
Phone: 401/828-8500
mbm@mesasys.com

PlanView, Inc.
Wendy Wheeler
Phone: 512/346-8600
wwheeler@planview.com

Project Assistants Inc.
Gus Cicala
Phone: 302/529-7075
gcicala@projectassistants.com

Project Control
Amy Duckett
Phone: 410/897-1091
aduckett@projcontrol.com

Mesa/Visa Systems Guild
Maribeth McNair
Phone: 401/828-8500
mbm@mesasys.com

System Solvers, Ltd.
Jim Jablonski
Phone: 248/588-7400 Ext. 244
jaj@sslinfo.com

Welcom
Heather Howard
Phone: 281/558-0514
hhoward@welcom.com

Web Project Inc.
Marc O'Brien
Phone: 650/574-0578
mobrien@wproj.com

Schedule Management

2S Smart Solutions, GmbH
Christian Uhrig
Phone: +49-6103-750750
info@smart-solutions.de

ABT Corporation
Ed Farrelly
Phone: 707/793-8300 ext. 3102
edf@abtcorp.com

Advanced Management Solutions, Inc.
Richard Hayden
Phone: 703/968-8073
haydenr@amsusa.com

AEC Software Inc.
Ryan Kish
Phone: 703/450-1980
rkish@aecsoft.com

Artemis Management Solutions
Patrick Perugini
Phone: 800/477-6648
pperugini@artemispm.com

Augeo Software
Mike Sayer
Phone: 408/271-0422
mike.sayer@augeo.com

Ballentine & Company, Inc.
Ann Ballentine
Phone: 800/536-6677
qgantt@ballentine-inc.com

Computerline Ltd.
Walford Pears
Phone: +44-1483-768095
computerline@compuserve.com

Computer Associates
David Thompson
Phone: 703/708-3142
toda09@cai.com

Creative Technology Labs, LLC
Bill Lynch
Phone: 703/490-8821
blynch@prochain.com

Dekker Technology Mgt. Inc. (DTMI)
Ron Barry
Phone: 909/384-9000
r.barry@dtrakker.com

Deltek Systems Inc.
Cristina Sirtori
Phone: 703/734-8606 ext. 4451
csirtori@deltek.com

Digital Tools
Jeff Mills
Phone: 703/734-8606 ext. 4451
jeffm@digit.com

Eagle Ray Software Systems, Inc.
Brad Roberts
Phone: 800/650-7510
brad@eagleray.com

Experience in Software, Inc.
Carolyn Burd
Phone: 510-644-0694
cb@projectkickstart.com

HMS Software Inc.
Ermy Valenti
Phone: 514/695-8122
info@hmssoftware.com

IMSI
Alex Taylor
Phone:415/257-3000 ext. 379
ataylor@imsisoft.com

Information Management Services. Inc.
Jeff Nummelin
Phone: 781/340-4400
info@inscorp.com

Innate, Inc.
Barry Muir
Phone: 312/781-9674
sales@innate.co.uk

Instinctive Technology, Inc.
Francois Gossieaux
Phone: 617-497-6300 ext. 151
fgossieaux@instinctive.com

Integrated Management Concepts
Richard Haskins
Phone: 805/376-3306
rhaskins@intgconcept.com

jeTECH Data Systems Inc.
Phil Goodge
Phone: 805/383-8500 ext. 1123
pgoodge@jetechdata.com

Kalyn Corporaton
Tim Johnson
Phone: 800/595-2596
info@kalyn.com

KIDASA Software, Inc.
Sue Butler
Phone: 512/328-0167
sbutler@kidasa.com

Mantix Systems Inc.
Tom Issac
Phone: 703/834-3940 ext. 208
tissac@mantix.com

Mesa Systems Guild Inc.
Maribeth McNair
Phone: 401/828-8500
mbm@mesasys.com

Micro Planning International
Brad Pirrung
Phone: 800/852-7526
sales@microplanning.com

Microsoft Corporation
Kris Tibbetts
Phone: 425/936-8337
kristibb@microsoft.com

Minute Man Systems
Bob Kochem
Phone: 617/489-5639
bck@minuteman-systems.com

Netmosphere
Scott Hetherington
Phone: 650/655-4815
scott@netmosphere.com

Panorama Software Corp., Ltd.
Cliff Sutton
Phone: +44-1932-252226
info@panorama.com

PFC Ltd.
Richard Jebb
Phone: +44-1494-775322
rwj@pfcltd.demon.co.uk

Planisware
Francois Pelissolo
Phone: +33-1-41-4800-55
francois.pelissolo@planisware.fr

PlanView, Inc.
Wendy Wheeler
Phone: 512/346-8600
wwheeler@planview.com

Primavera
C. Kelly
Phone: 610/667-8600
sales@primavera.com

Project Assistants Inc.
Gus Cicala
Phone: 302/529-7075
gcicala@projectassistants.com

Project Control
Amy Duckett
Phone: 410/897-1091
aduckett@projcontrol.com

PPS – Project Planning Systems
Christer Kallstrom
Phone: +46-8-6547060
christer.kallstrom@pps.se

SAS Institute
Edward P. Hughes
Phone: 919/677-8000 ext. 6916
saseph@wnt.sas.com

Scitor Corporation
Mark Stout
Phone: 800/533-9876
mstout@scitor.com

SofTech Inc.
Michelle Deacon
Phone: 403/273-1275 ext. 404
info@softechinc.com

Welcom
Steve Cook
Phone: 800/324-6337
info@welcom.com

Web Project Inc.
Marc O'Brien
Phone: 650/574-0578
mobrien@wproj.com

Cost Management

2S Smart Solutions, GmbH
Christian Uhrig
Phone: +49-6103-750750
info@smart-solutions.de

Advanced Management Soutions, Inc.
Richard Hayden
Phone: 703/968-8073
hayden@amsusa.com

Artemis Management Solutions
Patrick Perugini
Phone: 800/477-6648
pperugini@artemispm.com

Ballantine & Company, Inc.
Ann Ballantine
Phone: 800/536-6677
ggantt@ballantine-inc.com

Computerline Ltd.
Walford Pears
Phone: +44-1483-768095
computerline@compuserve.com

C/S Solutions
Gary Troop
Phone: 310-798-6396
gtroop@cs-solutions.com

Dekker Technology Mgt. Inc. (DTMI)
Ron Barry
Phone: 909/384-9000
r.barry@dtrakker.com

Digital Tools
Jeff Mills
Phone: 408/366-6250
jeffm@digit.com

Eagle Ray Software Systems, Inc.
Brad Roberts
Phone: 800/650-7510
brad@eagleray.com

Integrated Management Concepts
Richard Haskins
Phone: 805/376-3306
rhaskins@intgconcept.com

Integrated Management Concepts
Richard Haskins
Phone: 805-736-3306
rhaskins@intgconcepts.com

jeTECH Data Systems, Inc.
Phil Goodge
Phone: 805/383-8500 ext. 1123
pgoodge@jetechdata.com

Kildrummy Technologies Ltd.
Simon Nuttal-Smith
Phone: +44-181-870-3213
ops@kildrummy.co.uk

Mantix
Tom Issac
Phone: 703/834-3940 ext. 208
tissac@mantix.com

Mico Planning International
Brad Pirrung
Phone: 800/852-7526
sales@microplanning.com

Optiplan Systems, Inc.
Michael Follinsbee
Phone: 514/935-3808
optiplan@costlink.com

Panorama Software Corp., Ltd.
Cliff sutton
Phone: +44-1932-252226
info@panorama.com

PFC Ltd.
Richard Jebb
Phone: +44-1494 775322
rwj@pfcltd.demon.co.uk

Planisware
Francois Pelissolo
Phone: +33-1-41-4800-55
francois.pelissolo@planisware.fr

PlanView Inc.
Wendy Wheeler
Phone: 512/346-8600
wwheeler@planview.com

Primavera
C. Kelly
Phone: 610/667-8600
sales@primavera.com

Project Control
Amy Duckett
Phone: 410/897-1091
aduckett@projcontrol.com

QSM Associates, Inc.
Carl B. Foote
Phone: 413/499-0988
carlf@qsma.com

Ramdor
Erik Mikisch
Phone: 617/753-7383
ramdor@world.std.com

Scitor Corporation
Mark Stout
Phone: 800/533-9876
mstout@scitor.com

Web Project Inc.
Marc O'Brien
Phone: 650/574-0578
mobrien@wproj.com

Welcom
Steve Cook
Phone: 800-324-6337
info@welcom.com

Resource Management

ABT Corporation
Ed Farrelly
Phone: 707/793-8300 ext. 3102
edf@abtcorp.com

Advanced Management Solutions, Inc.
Richard Hayden
Phone: 703/968-8073
haydenr@amsusa.com

Augeo Software
Mike Sayer
Phone: 408/271-0422
mike.sayer@augeo.com

Computerline Ltd.
Walford Pears
Phone: +44-1483-768095
computerline@compuserve.com

Creative Technology Labs. LLC
Bill Lynch
Phone: 703/490-8821
blynch@prochain.com

Deltek Systems Inc.
Cristina Sirtori
Phone: 703/734-8606 ext. 4451
scirtori@deltek.com

Dekker Technologies Management Institute, Ltd.
Ron Barry
Project Control
Phone: 909/384-9000
r.barry@dtrakker.com

Digital Tools
Jeff Mills
Phone: 408/366-6250
jeffm@digit.com

Eagle Ray Software Systems Inc.
Brad Roberts
Phone: 800/650-7510
brad@eagleray.com
Information Management Services Inc.
Jeff Nummelin
Phone: 781/340-4400
info@imscorp.com

IMSI
Alex Taylor
Phone: 415/257-3000 ext. 379
ataylor@imsisoft.com

Innate Inc.
Barry Muir
Phone: 312/781-9674
sales@innate.co.uk

JeTECH Data Systems Inc.
Phil Goodge
Phone: 805/383-8500 ext. 1123
pgoodge@jetechdata.com

Kidasa Software Inc.
Sue Butler
Phone: 512/328-0167
sbutler@kidasa.com

Mantix Systems, Inc.
Tom Isaac
Phone: 708/834-3940 ext. 208
tisaac@mantix.com

Micro Planning International
Brad Pirrung
Phone: 800/852-7526
sales@microplanning.com

Microsoft Corporation
Kris Tibbetts
Phone: 425/936-8337
ktibbets@microsoft.com

Netmosphere
Scott Hetherington
Phone: 650/655-4815
scott@netmosphere.com

Optiplan Systems Inc.
Michael Follinsbee
Phone: 514/935-3808
optiplan@costlink.com

Panorama Software Corp., Ltd.
Cliff Sutton
Phone: +44-1932-252226
info@panorama.com

PFC Ltd.
Richard Jebb
Phone: +44-1494-775322
rwj@pfcltd.com

PlanView, Inc.
Wendy Wheeler
Phone: 512/346-8600
wwheeler@planview.com

Project Control
Amy Duckett
Phone: 253/761-9091
pprice@cs-solutions.com

SAS Institute
Edward P. Hughes
Phone: 919/677-8000 ext. 6916
saseph@wnt.sas.com

Scitor Corporation
Mark Stout
Phone: 800/533-9876
mstout@scitor.com

System Solvers, Ltd.
Jim Jablonski
Phone: 248/588-7400 ext. 244
jaj@sslinfo.com

Web Project Inc.
Marc O'Brien
Phone: 650/574-0578
mobrien@wproj.com

Welcom
Heather Howard
Phone: 281/558-0514
hhoward@welcom.com

Risk Assessment and Management

Computerline Ltd.
Walford Pears
Phone: +44-1483-768095
computerline@compuserve.com

Dekker
Ron Barry
Phone: 909/384-9000
r.barry@dtrakker.com

Eagle Ray Software Systems Inc.
Brad Roberts
Phone: 800/650-7510
brad@eagleray.com

jeTECH Data Systems Inc.
Phil Goodge
Phone: 805/383-8500 ext. 1123
pgoodge@jetechdata.com

Katmar Software
Harvey Wilson
Phone: +27-31-822-351
katmar@dbn.lia.net

KLCI Inc.
Peter Kulik
Phone: 888/664-0484
pkulik@klci.com

Mesa Systems Guild Inc.
Maribeth McNair
401/828-8500
mbm@mesasys.com

Palisade Corporation
Vera Gilliland
Phone: 607/277-8000
veramg@palisade.com

PlanView, Inc.
Wendy Wheeler
Phone: 512/346-8600
wwheeler@planview.com

Primavera
C. Kelly
Phone: 302/529-7075
sales@primavera.com

ProjectGear Inc.
Paige Price
Phone: 410/897-1091
price@cs-solutions.com

QSM Associates, Inc.
Carl B. Foote
Phone: 413/499-0988
carlf@qsma.com

Risk Services & Technology
Toby J. Trudel
Phone: 603/673-9907
trudel@risktrak.com

Web Project Inc.
Marc O'Brien
Phone: 650/574-0578
mobrien@wproj.com

Welcom
Steve Cook
Phone: 800/324-6337
info@welcom.com

Communications Management

ABT Corporation
Ed Farrelly
Phone: 707/793-8300 ext. 3102
edf@abtcorp.com

American Netronic
Gary Jones
Phone: 562/795-0147
garyj@netronic-us.com

Critical Tools
Jim Spiller
Phone: 512/342-2232
jspiller@criticaltools.com

Digital Tools
Jeff Mills
Phone: 408/366-6250
jeffm@digit.com

Eagle Ray Software Systems, Inc.
Brad Roberts
Phone: 800/650-7510
brad@eagleray.com

Experience in Software, Inc.
Carolyn Burd
Phone: 510/644-0694
info@projectkickstart.com

Information Management Services Inc.
Jeff Nummelin
Phone: 781/340-4400
info@imscorp.com

Instinctive Technology, Inc.
Francois Gossieaux
Phone: 617/497-6300 ext. 151
fgossieaux@instinctive.com

Kalyn Corporation
Tim Johnson
Phone: 800/595-2596
info@kalyn.com

Kidasa Software Inc.
Sue Butler
Phone: 512/328-0167
sbutler@kidasa.com

Mantix Systems Inc.
Tom Isaac
Phone: 703/834-3940 ext. 208
tisaac@mantix.com

Mesa Systems Guild Inc.
Maribeth McNair
Phone: 401/828-8500
mbm@mesasys.com

Microsoft Corporation
Kris Tibbetts
Phone: 425/936-8337
ktibbetts@microsoft.com

Netmosphere
Scott Hetherington
Phone: 650/655-4815
scott@netmosphere.com

Project Control
Amy Duckett
Phone: 410/897-1091
aduckett@projcontrol.com

System Solvers, Ltd.
Jim Jablonski
Phone: 248-588-7400 ext. 244
jaj@sslinfo.com

Web Project Inc.
Marc O'Brien
Phone: 650/574-0578
mobrien@wproj.com

Communications Subcategory: Graphics Add-Ons

AEC Software, Inc.
Ryan Kish
Phone: 703/450-1980
rkish@aecsoft.com

Advanced Management Solutions
Richard Hayden
Phone: 703/968-8073
hayden@amsusa.com

American Netronic
Gary Jones
Phone: 562/795-0147
garyj@netronic-us.com

Artemis Management Solutions
Patrick Perugini
Phone: 800/477-6648
pperugini@artemispm.com

Computerline Ltd.
Walford Pears
Phone: +44-1483-76095
computerline@compuserve.com

Creative Technology Labs, LLC
Bill Lynch
Phone: 730/490-8821
blynch@prochain.com

Critical Tools
Jim Spiller
Phone: 512/342-2232
jspiller@criticaltools.com

Dekker
Ron Barry
Phone: 909/384-9000
r.barry@dtrakker.com

Eagle Ray Software Systems, Inc.
Brad Roberts
Phone: 800/650-7510
brad@eagleray.com

jeTECH Data Systems Inc.
Phil Goodge
Phone: 805/383-8500 ext. 11230
pgoodge@jetechdata.com

Kalyn Corporation
Tim Johnson
Phone: 800/595-2596
info@kalyn.com

Kidasa Software Inc.
Sue Butler
Phone: 512/328-0167
sbutler@kidasa.com

Mesa Systems Guild Inc.
Maribeth McNair
Phone: 401/828-8500
mbm@mesasys.com

PFC Ltd.
Richard Jebb
Phone: +44-1494-775322
rwj@pfcltd.demon.co.uk

Planisware
Francois Pelissolo
Phone: +33-1-41-4800-55
francois.pelissolo@planisware.fr

PlanView, Inc.
Wendy Wheeler
Phone: 512/346-8600
wwheeler@planview.com

Project Control
Amy Duckett
Phone: 410/897-1091
aduckett@projcontrol.com

SAS Institute
Edward P. Hughes
Phone: 919/677-8000 ext. 6916
saseph@wnt.sas.com

Scitor Corporation
Mark Stout
Phone: 800/533-9876
mstout@scitor.com

Web Project Inc.
Mark O'Brien
Phone: 650-574-0578
mobrien@wproj.com

Welcom
Heather Howard
Phone: 281-558-0514
hhoward@welcom.com

Communications Subcategory: Timesheets

ABT Corporation
Ed Farrelly
Phone: 707/793-8300 ext. 3102
ddf@abtcorp.com

AC Software, Inc.
Bruce Gibson
Phone: 888/463-9973
bruce.gibson@timewzrd.com

Advanced Management Solutions Inc.
Richard Hayden
Phone: 703/968-8073
hayden@amsusa.com

Artemis Management Solutions
Patrick Perugini
Phone: 800/477-6648
pperugini@artemispm.com

Dekker Technologies Management Inc. (DTMI)
Ron Barry
Phone: 909/384-9000
r.barry@dtrakker.com

Deltek Systems, Inc.
Cristina Sirtori
Phone: 703/734-8606 ext. 4451
csirtori@deltek.com

Eagle Ray Software Systems, Inc.
Brad Roberts
Phone: 800/650-7510
brad@eagleray.com

HMS
Ermy Valenti
Phone: 514/695-8122
info@hmnssoftware.ca

Information Management Services Inc.
Jeff Nummelin
Phone: 781/340-4400
info@imscorp.com

Innate
Barry Muir
Phone: 312/781-9674
sales@innate.co.uk

jeTECH Data Systems Inc.
Phil Goodge
Phone: 805/383-8500 ext. 1123
pgoodge@jetechdata.com

Mantix Systems Inc.
Tom Isaac
Phone: 703/834-3940 ext. 208
tisaac@mantix.com

Microsoft Corporation
Kris Tibbetts
Phone: 425/936-8337
ktibbetts@microsoft.com

Optiplan Systems, Inc.
Michael Follinsbee
Phone: 514/935-3808
optiplan@costlink.com

Planisware
Francois Pelissolo
Phone: +33-1-41-4800-55
francois.pelissolo@planisware.fr

PlanView, Inc.
Wendy Wheeler
Phone: 512/346-8600
wwheeler@planview.com

Project Assistants Inc.
Gus Cicala
Phone: 302/529-7075
gcicala@projectassistants.com

Project Control Inc.
Amy Duckett
Phone: 410-897-1091
aduckett@projcontrol.com

PPS-Project Planning Systems
Christer Kallstrom
Phone: +46-8-6547060
christer.kallstrom@pps.se

Scitor Corporation
Mark Stout
Phone: 800/533-9876
mstout@scitor.com

SofTech Inc.
Michelle Deacon
Phone: 403/273-1275 ext. 404
info@softechinc.com

System Solvers, Ltd.
Jim Jablonski
Phone: 248/588-7400 Ext. 244
jaj@sslinfo.com

Time Scope
Phil Jacobsen
Phone: 760/632-8888
sales@timescope.com

Web Project Inc.
Marc O'Brien
Phone: 650-574-0578
mobrien@wproj.com

Welcom
Heather Howard
Phone: 281/558-0514
hhoward@welcom.com

Communications Subcategory: Web Publishers

ABT Corporation
Ed Farrelly
Phone: 707/793-8300 ext. 3102
edf@abtcorp.com

American Netronic
Gary Jones
Phone: 562-795-0147
garyj@netronic-us.com

Digital Tools
Jeff Mills
Phone: 408/366-6250
jeffm@digit.com

Eagle Ray Software Systems Inc.
Brad Roberts
Phone: 800/650-7510
brad@eagleray.com

Information Management Services
Jeff Nummelin
Phone: 781/340-4400
info@inscorp.com

Instinctive Technology Inc.
Francois Gossieaux
Phone: +617/497-6300 ext. 151
f.gossieaux@instinctive.com

jeTECH Data Systems Inc.
Phil Goodge
Phone: 805/383-8500 ext. 1123
pgoodge@jetechdata.com

Kalyn Corporaton
Tim Johnson
Phone: 800/595-2596
info@kalyn.com

Kidasa Software Inc.
Sue Butler
Phone: 512/328-0167
sbutler@kidasa.com

Mesa Systems Guild Inc.
Maribeth McNair
Phone: 401-828-8500
mbm@mesasys.com

Planisware
Francois Pelissolo
Phone: +33-1-41-4800-55
francois.pelissolo@planisware.fr

PlanView, Inc.
Wendy Wheeler
Phone: 512/346-8600
wwheeler@planview.com

Project Control
Amy Duckett
Phone: 410/897-1091
aduckett@projcontrol.com

SAS Institute
Edward P. Hughes
Phone: 919/677-8000 ext. 6916
saseph@wnt.sas.com

Welcom
Heather Howard
Phone: 281-558-0514
hhoward@welcom.com

UPGRADE YOUR PROJECT MANAGEMENT KNOWLEDGE WITH FIRST-CLASS PUBLICATIONS FROM PMI

Successful Information System Implementation, Second Edition
Successful implementation of information systems technology lies in managing the behavioral and organizational components of the process. Past data on this subject has involved mostly case studies, but this book provides practical information those implementing information systems can use now. Pinto and Millet offer practical information on "approaching the subject from a managerial, rather than a technical, perspective." The second edition of this work covers such topics as implementation theory, prioritizing projects, implementation success and failure, critical success factors, and more!
ISBN: 1-880410-66-4

Recipes for Project Success
This book is destined to become "the" reference book for beginning project managers, particularly those who like to cook! Practical, logically developed project management concepts are offered in easily understood terms in a lighthearted manner. They are applied to the everyday task of cooking-from simple, single dishes, such as homemade tomato sauce for pasta, made from the bottom up, to increasingly complex dishes or meals for groups that in turn require an understanding of more complex project management terms and techniques. The transistion between cooking and project management discussions is smooth, and tidbits of information provided with the receipes are interesting and humorous.
ISBN: 1-880410-58-3 (paperback)

Tools and Tips for Today's Project Manager
This guide book is valuable for understanding project management and performing to quality standards. Includes project management concepts and terms—old and new—that are not only defined but also are expalined in much greater detail than you would find in a typical glossary. Also included are tips on handling such seemingly simple everyday tasks as how to say "No" and how to avoid telephone tag. It's a reference you'll want to keep close at hand.
ISBN: 1-880410-61-3 (paperback)

The Juggler's Guide to Managing Multiple Projects
This comprehensive book introduces and explains task-oriented, independent, and interdependent levels of project portfolios. It says that you must first have a strong foundation in time management and priority setting, then introduces the concept of Portfolio Management to timeline multiple projects, determine their resource requirements, and handle emergencies, putting you in charge for possibly the first time in your life!
ISBN: 1-880410-65-6 (paperback)

New Resources for PMP Candidates
The following publications are resources that certification candidates can use to gain information on project management theory, principles, techniques, and procedures.